W9-CHO-782

CONTEMPORARY MUSICIANS

ISSN 1044-2197

CONTEMPORARY MUSICIANS

PROFILES OF THE PEOPLE IN MUSIC

LEIGH ANN DeREMER, Editor

VOLUME 34
Includes Cumulative Indexes

GALE GROUP

THOMSON LEARNING

Detroit • New York • San Diego • San Francisco
Boston • New Haven, Conn. • Waterville, Maine
London • Munich

While every effort has been made to ensure the reliability of the information presented in this publication, the Gale Group does not guarantee the accuracy of the data contained herein. Gale accepts no payment for listing; and inclusion in the publication of any organization, agency, institution, publication, service, or individual does not imply endorsement of the editors or publisher. Errors brought to the attention of the publisher and verified to the satisfaction of the publisher will be corrected in future editions.

Contents

Introduction ix

Cumulative Subject Index 237

Cumulative Musicians Index 265

Alkaline Trio 1
Hard-driving punk

Jessica Andrews 4
Country singer with voice beyond her years

Christine Anu 7
One of Australia's brightest musical stars

Aqua 9
Danish pop outfit

Ash 12
Popular 1990s British pop group

Aswad 14
One of reggae's institutions

Sherrié Austin 18
Traditional country influences

David Axelrod 20
Composer/producer covered mix of genres

Samuel Barber 23
Distinguished composer

Tracy Bonham 26
Groundbreaking rock singer/violinist

Bon Jovi 29
Boys from New Jersey continue success

Buckethead 34
Experimental guitarist shrouded in mystery

Buckwheat Zydeco 37
Eclecticism important to Zydeco master

R.L. Burnside 40
1990s popularity after 40 years in blues

José Carreras 43
Tenor an opera legend

John Carter 47
Leading jazz clarinetist

Martin Carthy 50
Renowned British folk musician

Ceili Rain 53
Intriguing mix of rock and Celtic sounds

The Chordettes 55
Sweethearts of 1950s pop

Kyung Wha Chung 58
Korean violinist a national icon

Cold 61
Hard-core rock

Cold Chisel 63
Enduring Australian rock group

John Corigliano 66
Pulitzer Prize-winning composer

David Coverdale 69
Solo success beyond Whitesnake

The Damned 73
Classic British punk

David Darling 77
A "maverick cellist"

Wild Bill Davison 79
Legendary jazz cornetist

Down By Law 82
Kept punk rock vision alive

Eve 84
Rapper competes on own terms

Lara Fabian 87
Canadian chanteuse

Neil Finn 90
Left his Crowded House behind

Jeffrey Gaines 93
Cover song meant big break

Vince Gill 96
Country superstar

Billy Gilman 99
Young country star makes Grammy history

Ginuwine 102
Smooth R&B sounds

Julius Hemphill 105
Visionary jazz composer and saxophonist

Al Hibbler 108
Captivating jazz vocalist

Alan Hovhaness 111
Trailblazing interest in world music

K-Ci & JoJo 114
Jodeci alumni find success

Ali Akbar Khan 117
"Giant of Indian classical music"

The Kingsmen 120
"Louie Louie" a pop classic

Moe Koffman 123
Celebrated Canadian jazz multi-instrumentalist

Lorie Line 126
Liberace-style New Age pianist

Israel "Cachao" López 129
Embodies twentieth-century Latin music

Love 132
1960s psychedelic rock

Matthew Good Band 135
Canadian Juno Award winners

Joey McIntyre 138
Former New Kid launches solo career

Sarah McLachlan 141
Ethereal pop still earning accolades

Men at Work 144
Rock from the Land Down Under

Luis Miguel 147
Grammy Award-winning Latin star

moe. 150
Jam-oriented rock group

Montgomery Gentry 152
"Redneck country rock"

James Moody 155
Famed jazz saxophonist

M.O.P. 159
Growling East Coast rap duo

Ultra Naté 162
Dance music diva

The Presidents of the United States of America .. 164
Light-hearted, fun-filled rock

Kelly Price 167
Called Aretha Franklin of her generation

Rockapella 170
Successful a cappella group

The Romantics 173
Enduring 1980s rock

Shihad 176
Internationally recognized New Zealand act

Jessica Simpson 179
Teen pop superstar

Sisqó 182
Caused sensation with "Thong Song"

Sister Hazel 185
   Acoustic rock with crossover appeal

Solas 188
   Traditional, yet innovative Celtic folk

The Spongetones 190
   Beatlesque rock

Spoon 192
   Texas indie rock

Spyro Gyra 195
   Developed own jazz hybrid

Stereo MC's 198
   British hip-hop pioneers

The String Cheese Incident 201
   Popular jam band

Tamia 203
   Tenacious R&B vocalist

Third Day 206
   Southern-influenced Christian rock

George Thorogood 209
   Proved he was "Bad to the Bone"

Tyrese 212
   Singing important to multitalented performer

U2 215
   Rock icons with a conscience

VAST 220
   Unique alternative rock mix

George Walker 222
   Prolific classical composer

The Warren Brothers 226
   Sibling duo turned country music stars

Bill Wells 229
   Jazz without rules

Iannis Xenakis 231
   Genius of mathematically derived music

Hans Zimmer 234
   Composer for popular films

Introduction

Fills in the Information Gap on Today's Musicians

Contemporary Musicians profiles the colorful personalities in the music industry who create or influence the music we hear today. Prior to *Contemporary Musicians,* no quality reference series provided comprehensive information on such a wide range of artists despite keen and ongoing public interest. To find biographical and critical coverage, an information seeker had little choice but to wade through the offerings of the popular press, scan television "infotainment" programs, and search for the occasional published biography or expose. *Contemporary Musicians* is designed to serve that information seeker, providing in one ongoing source in-depth coverage of the important names on the modern music scene in a format that is both informative and entertaining. Students, researchers, and casual browsers alike can use *Contemporary Musicians* to meet their needs for personal information about music figures; find a selected discography of a musician's recordings; and uncover an insightful essay offering biographical and critical information.

Provides Broad Coverage

Single-volume biographical sources on musicians are limited in scope, often focusing on a handful of performers from a specific musical genre or era. In contrast, *Contemporary Musicians* offers researchers and music devotees a comprehensive, informative, and entertaining alternative. *Contemporary Musicians* is published four times per year, with each volume providing information on about 80 musical artists and record-industry luminaries from all the genres that form the broad spectrum of contemporary music—pop, rock, jazz, blues, country, New Age, folk, rhythm and blues, gospel, bluegrass, rap, and reggae, to name a few—as well as selected classical artists who have achieved "crossover" success with the general public. *Contemporary Musicians* will also occasionally include profiles of influential nonperforming members of the music community, including producers, promoters, and record company executives. Additionally, beginning with *Contemporary Musicians 11,* each volume features new profiles of a selection of previous *Contemporary Musicians* listees who remain of interest to today's readers and who have been active enough to require completely revised entries.

Includes Popular Features

In *Contemporary Musicians* you'll find popular features that users value:

- **Easy-to-locate data sections:** Vital personal statistics, chronological career summaries, listings of major awards, and mailing addresses, when available, are prominently displayed in a clearly marked box on the second page of each entry.

- **Biographical/critical essays:** Colorful and informative essays trace each subject's personal and professional life, offer representative examples of critical response to the artist's work, and provide entertaining personal sidelights.

- **Selected discographies:** Each entry provides a comprehensive listing of the artist's major recorded works.

- **Photographs:** Most entries include portraits of the subject profiled.

- **Sources for additional information:** This invaluable feature directs the user to selected books, magazines, newspapers, and online sources where more information can be obtained.

Helpful Indexes Make It Easy to Find the Information You Need

Each volume of *Contemporary Musicians* features a cumulative Musicians Index, listing names of individual performers and musical groups, and a cumulative Subject Index, which provides the user with a breakdown by primary musical instruments played and by musical genre.

Available in Electronic Formats

Diskette/Magnetic Tape. *Contemporary Musicians* is available for licensing on magnetic tape or diskette in a fielded format. The database is available for internal data processing and nonpublishing purposes only. For more information, call (800) 877-GALE.

Online. *Contemporary Musicians* is available online as part of the Gale Biographies (GALBIO) database accessible through LEXIS-NEXIS, P.O. Box 933, Dayton, OH 45401-0933; phone: (937) 865-6800, toll-free: (800) 543-6862.

We Welcome Your Suggestions

The editors welcome your comments and suggestions for enhancing and improving *Contemporary Musicians*. If you would like to suggest subjects for inclusion, please submit these names to the editor. Mail comments or suggestions to:

The Editor
Contemporary Musicians
Gale Group, Inc.
27500 Drake Rd.
Farmington Hills, MI 48334-3535

Or call toll free: (800) 347-GALE

Alkaline Trio

Punk group

Originating in Chicago's vibrant punk scene during late 1996, Alkaline Trio developed a fervent fan base throughout the Midwest while releasing several full-length and extended-play albums of hard-driving music with emotionally direct lyrics. Building their following through extensive touring, the band's members were finally able to give up their day jobs as bike messengers and record store clerks after the release of *Godd**mit!,* the group's first full-length album, in 1998. While a deal with Vagrant kept them with an independent label, Alkaline Trio nonetheless confronted the dilemma that countless punk bands had faced before it: in the face of greater acclaim, could it remain devoted to its own artistic vision and retain its integrity with a fan base skeptical of mainstream success? While the 2001 release of *From Here to Infirmary* confirmed the band's commitment to maintaining its artistic ideals, some fans questioned the group's decision to tour as the opening act with crossover success Blink 182.

The members of Alkaline Trio played with a number of Chicago-area bands while they were in their teens and early twenties. As founder Matt Skiba recalled in a 1998 interview with radio show *All Ages* available on the group's website, "We all knew each other from doing shows with other bands and we became friends years ago and it turned out that we all wanted to do the same thing." Skiba, a singer and guitarist, had once played drums for Jerkwater and the Blunts, while Glenn Porter had been a member of 88 Finger Louie. Together with bassist Rob Doran, a longtime friend of

Skiba's, the three came together in late 1996 to form Alkaline Trio. The original lineup did not last long, however, and by the end of 1997, Doran had left the group. He was replaced by Dan Andriano, who had also played with a number of Chicago punk bands, including Slapstick and Tuesday. The membership of Alkaline Trio changed again in 2000 when Glenn Porter departed; Mike Felumlee, once the drummer for the Smoking Popes, took his place.

Despite the almost constant changes in personnel, Alkaline Trio released several full-length and extended-play albums during its first four years together. With the original three members, the band released the EP *For Your Lungs Only* in 1997 on Asian Man Records. Unfortunately, the band's commitment to touring in support of the release caused its first personnel change when Doran decided to devote his time to finishing college instead of going on the road. Quickly recruiting Andriano as his replacement on bass, Alkaline Trio started to build its audience through word-of-mouth and constant touring. However, its members still struggled to make ends meet. Both Skiba and Porter worked in Chicago as bike messengers, while Andriano worked in a record store. It was only after the release of the band's first full-length album in 1998, *Godd**nit!,* that its members could concentrate solely on music. For Skiba, the opportunity came not a moment too soon; as he commented in an interview with Jeremy Estes of Line and Ink online in September of 2000, "I had to take more and more time off from the company I was working for because of the band. Eventually, they were like, 'You can't keep disappearing,' so I was like, 'Fine, I quit.'"

With the band's members free to tour and record full-time, they soon gained a following as one of the leading punk bands in the Midwest, a reputation that grew with the release of *Godd**nit!.* The album featured song lyrics that touched on a number of harrowing topics, such as suicide on "Trouble Breathing," emotional breakdowns on "My Little Needle," and police brutality on "Cop." Considering the subject matter on *Godd**nit!,* Alkaline Trio's music was often referred to as "emo-core," or "emotional hardcore," a label the band acknowledged, yet resisted. "I guess the kind of music we play someone might consider emo-influenced punk," Skiba explained in the *All Ages* interview. "It's probably a pretty close description, but emo has become kind of a catch phrase. I think people hear the word emo and automatically assume certain things. We play rock n' roll that comes natural to us."

The group's next full-length release, 1999's *Maybe I'll Catch Fire,* further developed the band's repertoire of emotionally scathing songs, most of them penned by Skiba. In "Radio," the song's alcoholic protagonist wished a suicidal demise for his lover, while "Maybe I'll Catch Fire" surveyed a mindset of alienation and depression. Like many songs on the first album, both

For the Record . . .

Members include **Dan Andriano** (born c. 1979), bass guitar, vocals; **Rob Doran** (left group, 1997), bass guitar, vocals; **Mike Felumlee**, drums, vocals; **Glenn Porter** (left group, 2000), drums; **Matt Skiba** (born c. 1977), guitar, vocals.

Formed group in Chicago, IL, 1996; released first full-length album, *Godd**nit!,* 1998; released *Maybe I'll Catch Fire*, 2000; released third album, *From Here to Infirmary,* 2001.

Addresses: *Record company*—Vagrant Records, 2118 Wilshire Boulevard #361, Santa Monica, CA 90403, website: http://www.vagrant.com; Asian Man Records, P.O. Box 35585, Monte Sereno, CA 95030-5585, website: http://www.asianmanrecords.com. *Website*—Alkaline Trio Official Website: http://www.alkalinetrio.com.

tracks made references to suicide and self-mutilation, although the band insisted that airing such feelings was therapeutic for themselves and their audience. "We definitely like to write songs about darker things, but we like to think of it as a celebration of the evil ideas that run through everybody's head," Skiba explained to Allison Stewart in the *Chicago Tribune*. In another profile with the Punk Interviews website, Skiba further defined his commitment to emo-core and its importance to the audience: "It's punk music, but with the same purpose like blues. You sing about it, so you don't have to think about it anymore." Fans agreed that the band produced music with powerful emotional content; a review of *Maybe I'll Catch Fire* on the HARS online magazine website warned, "If you are broken-hearted then please listen to this album with caution because you may feel an urge to stab yourself with the nearest sharp object."

With two full-length albums and a compilation of singles releases, *The Alkaline Trio*, issued on Asian Man Records in 2000, the band seemed poised to join the crossover success of emo-influenced punk bands such as Blink 182, Green Day, and Offspring. The band even toured as the opening act for Blink 182 on its 2001 tour, a decision that worried some of its fans who equated mainstream success with selling out. When the group announced it had signed a new deal with independent label Vagrant Records, its members had to go on the defensive regarding their decision to leave Asian Man Records. Respected for its integrity of

pricing its products almost at-cost, Asian Man was a small, do-it-yourself-run label operating out of its founder's garage. While the setup was fitting for groups in the garage-band league, by 2001 Alkaline Trio had grown too popular to remain with the label. According to all involved, the departure for Vagrant was an amicable one, and the band looked forward to a wider distribution network for its releases. Skiba told Line and Ink, "Our main complaint about our last couple of records is that people can't find them…. I'm sure that there'll be a pretty good push behind our stuff [by Vagrant] to make it available to as many people as we can without sacrificing any of our artistic freedom or any of the other anti-perks that major labels have."

Although the Alkaline Trio's first Vagrant release, 2001's *From Here to Infirmary,* contained some brighter melodies, it retained the dark lyrics that had become the band's trademark. Typical subject matter included the anxiety of a trip to a psychiatrist in "Take Lots with Alcohol" and the alienation of "Crawl," which included the decidedly anti-romantic lines, "Got a taste of you, threw up all night/I got more sick with every sour, second-rate kiss." For all the nihilism, however, *From Here to Infirmary* was the group's most successful outing yet. Mainstream publications now took notice, with *Rolling Stone* hailing the album's "effortless hooks and Skiba's hysterical lyrics." A *Los Angeles Times* concert review welcomed the band's latest offering as a necessary jolt to pop-punk music. With "a depth of feeling and musical ideas that could propel a stagnant genre forward," the review also compared the band to the Clash and Skiba's stage and song writing presence to the Replacements' Paul Westerberg. While these were heady tributes to a band whose remaining founding member had yet to turn 25 years old, the Alkaline Trio's devoted fan base would doubtless agree.

In 2001, Alkaline Trio completed its duties as an opening act for Blink 182 and continued on the road for a series of concerts with other Vagrant Records bands, including Saves the Day, Dashboard Confessional, and No Motiv. The group also considered its future as an increasingly MTV-friendly act and the impact of widespread success on its music. "But the way I look at it," Skiba told Line and Ink, "we're doing it independently and more importantly by our standards. We want as many people to get our music as possible, and I would be lying if I said that we didn't want to be a huge band."

Selected discography

For Your Lungs Only (EP), Asian Man, 1998.
Godd**nit!, Asian Man, 1998.
I Lied My Face Off (EP), Asian Man, 1999.
Maybe I'll Catch Fire, Asian Man, 1999.

The Alkaline Trio, Asian Man, 2000.
(Contributor) *Living Tomorrow Today: A Benefit for Ty Cambra,* Asian Man, 2001.
From Here to Infirmary, Vagrant, 2001.

Sources

Periodicals

Billboard, May 26, 2001, p. 53.
Chicago Tribune, November 10, 2000.
Los Angeles Times, June 5, 2001.
Rolling Stone, June 7, 2001.

Online

Alkaline Trio Official Website, http://www.alkalinetrio.com (June 25, 2001).
Asian Man Records, http://www.asianmanrecords.com (June 26, 2001).
HARS, http://www.happyasrawsewage.com/detailreview.asp?Id=164 (June 26, 2001).
Line and Ink, http://www.lineandink.indiegroup.com/AK3.html (June 25, 2001).
Punk International, http://www.punkinternational.com/alkalinetrio1.html (June 26, 2001).
Punk Interviews, http://www.acornweb.com/punk/interviews/alkalinetrio3.html (June 26, 2001).
Vagrant Records, http://www.vagrant.com (June 25, 2001).

—Timothy Borden

Jessica Andrews

Singer, songwriter

Photograph by Kevork Djansezian. AP/World Wide Photos. Reproduced by permission.

Since first hitting the country music charts before she could drive, Jessica Andrews has been compared to other teen singers including LeAnn Rimes, Britney Spears, and Christina Aguilera. Country music has turned to the pop-inflected songs of its teen stars to rejuvenate the genre, but with the release of her second album *Who I Am* in 2001, Andrews has proven her commitment to country music and received critical attention for a style and voice mature beyond her years. Chuck Taylor noted in *Billboard,* "There's a depth and vulnerability about her vocal prowess that seem to convey experience, rooted pain, and the wisdom of many more years than she has endured."

Andrews was raised in Huntingdon, Tennessee, just a few hours drive from Nashville. She was brought up in a musical family and singing was a big part of her childhood. All of that singing at home paid off early for Andrews. When she was in fourth grade, her older sister heard her singing Dolly Parton's "I Will Always Love You" and encouraged Andrews to enter the school talent show. Andrews took first prize with Whitney Houston's version of the song, and her singing career was launched. Andrews put together a band and started performing locally at fairs and even some bars; by the time she was 12 years old, Andrews had gained a local reputation as a singer.

Family friends raved about the young singer to music producer Byron Gallimore, who had worked with country superstars Tim McGraw and JoDee Messina. Gallimore agreed to hear Andrews sing and was immediately convinced of her talent. Andrews notes in her website biography, "I started snapping my fingers, and I went right into my lower register and sang that Shania [Twain] song 'If You're Not In It For Love.' He stopped me right away. I don't know what he heard in my voice, but he called everyone into his office and had me start again. When I finished the song, he asked if it was okay to put this thing into high gear." Gallimore arranged for a showcase in Paris, Tennessee, not long after first meeting Andrews. James Stroud of DreamWorks Nashville signed the young singer immediately.

Before Andrews even had time to release her first album, she was invited to record a song for the 1998 album *The Prince of Egypt—Nashville,* which was certified gold. The only artist to debut on that recording, Andrews was in the company of such musicians as Alison Krauss, Vince Gill, and Clint Black. The song, "I Will Be There For You," was also released on Andrews' debut album *Heart Shaped World* in 1999. Other songs from the album include "Riverside," about an innocent night spent with a young lover by the river, and "You Go First," about first kisses. "Unbreakable Heart," written by Benmont Tench, went to number 24 on *Billboard*'s Hot Country Singles and Tracks chart. That song illustrates that, while much of her material reflects Andrews' youth, she is also able to take on deeper topics; it is about loss and the only thing that God didn't

For the Record . . .

Born c. 1985; daughter of Vicki (a school bus driver) and Jessie Andrews (a factory worker).

Released single "I Will Be There For You," 1998; signed with DreamWorks Nashville, released debut album *Heart Shaped World,* 1999; toured with Faith Hill and Trisha Yearwood, performed at Fan Fair music festival; released *Who I Am,* 2001.

Awards: Academy of Country Music Award, Best New Female Vocalist, 2000.

Addresses: *Record company*—DreamWorks Records, 1516 16th Avenue South, Nashville, TN, (615) 463-4600, website: http://www.dreamworksrec.com. *Website*—Jessica Andrews Official Website: http://www.jessicaandrews.com.

make—an unbreakable heart. Chuck Taylor described the recording in *Billboard* as "one of country radio's most beautiful songs " of 1999.

Andrews' first album received generally positive reviews, even in a field packed with other very young female singers. Bill Friskics-Warren, writing for the *Washington Post,* found that "Andrews already exhibits the pluck and mastery of country's platinum-selling female vocalists," but he also noted that "refreshingly, she never forgets that she's just out of junior high school." Alex Henderson of *All Music Guide* also found Andrews' freshman work to be promising: "Andrews specializes in a sleek, commercial blend of pop, country and rock. But as much sweetness as she projects, Andrews isn't bubble gum.... [I]t's clear that [she] is capable of depth."

The album attracted the attention of the Academy of Country Music, as well, and Andrews was named Best New Female Vocalist in May of 2000. Andrews performed at the country music festival Fan Fair in Nashville, and she also began touring with established country stars like Faith Hill and Trisha Yearwood. Reflecting on the experience, Andrews said in her website biography, "I know how serious these women are about music and their performances. So I took the offers to tour with Faith, and then Trisha, not only as a huge honor but as an opportunity to learn from the best."

The lessons the young singer received from these established musicians went into creating her next album, *Who I Am,* and her first attempts at songwriting. Andrews worked with songwriters Bekka Bramlett and Annie Roboff to write "Good Friend to Me," based on the recent breakup of her first love relationship. While the song was not one of the hits from the album, Andrews did have success with several other tracks, including "Karma" and "Never Had It So Good." The title song from the album went to number one on the country charts. "Who I Am" marks Andrews' growth as a musician and also reflects the rootedness and innocence that characterize her: "I am Rosemary's granddaughter/The spitting image of my father/And when the day is done, my mama's still my biggest fan."

The strong pop influences on the album turned some reviewers off, even as Andrews experienced the greatest commercial success of her young career. Alanna Nash of *Entertainment* considered Andrews' sophomore work proof that she is on her way to becoming a "bombastic pop diva," and called Nashville producer Gallimore the "new king of schlock." Most critics, though, considered the album a milestone for the singer, marking a passage to a more mature performing style. Maria Konicki Dinoia applauded the album in *All Music Guide,* remarking that it showed Andrews' "appealing new confidence." She wrote that Andrews' vocals "are strong and convincing," and called the songs on the album "snappy and infectious." Michael Paoletta of *Billboard* also considered the album a success. He noted that Andrews' singing was marked by its "power, range, and intuition." Paoletta also made the prediction that "this could be the artist's breakthrough project."

Selected discography

(Contributor) *The Prince of Egypt—Nashville,* DreamWorks Nashville, 1998.
Heart Shaped World, DreamWorks Nashville, 1999.
Who I Am, DreamWorks Nashville, 2001.

Sources

Periodicals

Billboard, March 11, 2000, p. 78; June 10, 2000, p. 32; February 24, 2001, p. 23; March 17, 2001, p. 39; April 21, 2001, p. 25.
Entertainment Weekly, March 2, 2001, p. 71.
People, May 8, 2000; April 2, 2001, p. 39.
Washington Post, April 18, 1999, p. G5.

Online

"Jessica Andrews," *All Music Guide,* http://www.allmusic.com (July 1, 2001).
"Jessica Andrews," DreamWorks Records, http://www.dreamworksrec.com (July 1, 2001).

Jessica Andrews Official Website, http://www.jessicaandrews
.com (July 1, 2001).

—*Christine Kelley*

Christine Anu

Singer, songwriter

The world watched as the Olympic Games were held in Sydney in 2000 and as one of Australia's brightest musical stars, Christine Anu, dazzled her fellow Aussies and new fans worldwide. It had been five years since the release of her platinum debut album *Stylin' Up,* but the high-energy singer exploded back onto the Australian music scene in 2000. Anu's single "Sunshine on a Rainy Day" spent weeks on the Top 40 chart, and her second album, *Come My Way,* was well received by critics and fans alike. Anu shone at the closing ceremony of the Olympic Games in Sydney as she performed the song "Island Home," an anthem for aboriginal and islander Australians, for an audience of millions.

Born in 1970 in Cairns, Queensland, Australia, Anu is the daughter of Torres Straight Islanders. The Torres Straight divides the Cape York Peninsula in northern Australia and Papua New Guinea. Torres Straight Islanders are indigenous Australians. Anu lived on the islands for part of her childhood, and her father taught her the island songs that continue to influence her work. Anu draws deeply on her Aboriginal roots to inspire her music, seamlessly incorporating traditional indigenous rhythms with modern dance beats, reflecting her own experience as a Torres Straight Islander in twenty-first century Australia.

Before Anu began her recording career, she was trained as a dancer by the National Aboriginal and Islander Skills Development Association (NAISDA). She received her associate's degree in dance in 1992, and toured North America, Europe, and Australia with the respected Bangarra Dance Company. As early as 1993, though, Anu had turned to singing. She spent some time as a backup singer for the band Rainmakers, and her first recorded release was a collaboration with prominent Australian songwriter Paul Kelly on a dance mix titled "Last Train." Anu professed a deep respect for Kelly, telling Kathy McCabe of the *Sunday Telegraph*, "I'm in reverence just being in the presence of this man, knowing so many songs that have touched my heart have come from him." Anu would collaborate with Kelly again on both of her full-length albums.

Anu signed with the Mushroom label and had her first real hit with her version of "My Island Home," a song borrowed from the Warumpi Band, an Aboriginal group. The song appeared on Anu's 1995 debut album, *Stylin' Up*. Anu worked with Kelly on many of the songs, and she also collaborated with David Bridie of the band Not Drowning Waving. While these two men contributed to the album, Anu notes that she really became a songwriter while working on the album. She told Michael Smith of *Drum Media*, "I discovered my writing talents through making it…. I didn't realize until I'd finished it that I'd written nine songs and discovered I was a songwriter!" Reflecting Anu's own eclectic influences, the album draws from a range of pop styles as well as Aboriginal music. Glenn Baker of *Billboard* noted that the recording is a "blend of indigenous Australian funk, soul, hip-hop, rap, and reggae," and quoted a *Juice* magazine rave that called the album "one of the most sublime and stylish reflections of Australia's cultural melting pot ever to be recorded."

Stylin' Up proved as popular with fans as with critics. The album quickly went platinum in Australia, and Anu's freshman effort was named Best Aboriginal Album of 1995 by the Australian Record Industry Association (ARIA). She enjoyed several top 40 hits from the album, including "Party" and "Island Home," and in 1996 Anu won another ARIA Award, this time for Best Female Artist. That same year, Anu was honored by the Deadly Sounds National Aboriginal and Islander Music Awards by being named Best Female Artist.

Following the tremendous success of her first album, Anu contributed two songs—"Nutbod" and "Now Until the Break of Day," both from *Midsummer Night's Dream*—to director, writer, and producer Baz Luhrmann's compilation, *Something for Everybody*. In 1997 the musician and dancer also tried her hand at acting, landing a spot in *Little Shop of Horrors* and the role of Mimi in the Australian version of *Rent*. After a successful two-year run in Australia, Anu was offered a chance to play Mimi on Broadway, but she turned the role down in order to pursue another acting job, this time in film. Anu portrayed Arabia in Luhrmann's film *Moulin Rouge*. The character was an exotic dancer, and the musical allowed Anu to show off her talent for dancing. The multitalented performer also guest-starred on *Wildside,* a drama series produced by ABC, and was

For the Record . . .

Born in 1970 in Cairns, Queensland, Australia; children: Kuiam. *Education*: Associate's degree in dance from the National Aboriginal and Islander Skills Development Association (NAISDA), 1992.

Toured with Bangarra Dance Company, 1992-93; released single "Last Train" with Paul Kelly, 1993; signed with the Mushroom label, released debut album *Stylin' Up*, 1995; starred in Australian production of *Rent*, 1998-99; acted in Baz Luhrmann's film *Moulin Rouge*, 2000; performed in the closing ceremony of the Sydney Olympic Games, 2000; released *Come My Way*, 2001.

Awards: Australian Record Industry Association (ARIA) Award, Best Aboriginal Album for *Stylin' Up*, 1995; ARIA Award, Best Female Artist, 1996; Deadly Sounds National Aboriginal and Islander Music Award, Best Female Artist, 1996.

Addresses: *Record company*—Festival Mushroom Group, 27 Dudley St., West Melbourne VIC, Australia 3003, website: http://www.mushroom.com.au. *Website*—Christine Anu Official Website: http://www.christineanu.com.au.

scheduled to star in the musical *Hair* on tour in Australia in the fall of 2001.

After a very busy five years between her acting career and raising her child, Kuiam, Anu jumped back onto Australia's Top 40 chart in 2000 with "Sunshine on a Rainy Day." The song later appeared on her second full-length recording, *Come My Way*, released by Festival Mushroom Records. The album was written in London and recorded in Sydney with the help of United Kingdom producer Stuart Crichton. Anu once again collaborated with Kelly; the album includes Anu's version of his "Beat of Your Heart."

Another song on the album, "Coz I'm Free," was written as a tribute to Cathy Freeman, the Australian track star who shares Anu's Aboriginal roots. Anu spoke about her motivation for writing the song in a Mushroom press release: "I met Cathy at the ARIA Awards a couple of years ago but it wasn't until I saw her in

Seville last year that 'Coz I'm Free' came together. I watched her win at Seville [the World Championships] and then we caught up in London not long afterwards.... She's so inspiring—her focus, how hard she trains, all that she's achieved. When I watched the race in Seville, the camera zoomed in on her tattoo and I got the idea then for a song." With Freeman's gold-medal winning performance in the 2000 Sydney Olympics, and Anu's own stellar appearance at the closing ceremony of the games, the two women became heroes of Aboriginal Australia.

Come My Way, like *Stylin' Up*, received warm reviews from critics. Anu's second release showed a greater pop influence, and the rapping that made an appearance on the first album was replaced with more dance songs. But Anu continues to embrace her Islander heritage, and she includes sounds of indigenous music in the mix. Steve Rendle of the *Evening Post* called *Come My Way* "a great pop record" and "magic." He also noted that "Anu's voice is a sparkling joy." Anu's enthusiastic fans seem to agree and are eager to see what the dancer, singer, songwriter, and actress will try her hand at next.

Selected discography

Stylin' Up, Mushroom, 1995.
(Contributor) *Something for Everybody*, EMD/Capitol, 1998.
Come My Way, Festival Mushroom, 2001.

Sources

Periodicals

Billboard, July 8, 1995, p. 55; September 23, 2000, pp. 58-59; September 30, 2000, p. 50.
Courier-Mail, June 13, 2001, p. 2.
Drum Media, December 3, 1996.
Evening Post (Wellington, New Zealand), April 12, 2001.
New Straits Times (Malaysia), October 8, 1995, p. 14.
Sunday Telegraph (Sydney, Australia), June 4, 2000.
USA Today, September 29, 2000, p. 7F.

Online

"Christine Anu," *All Music Guide*, http://www.allmusic.com (June 20, 2001).
"Christine Anu," Mushroom Records, http://www.mushroom.com.au (June 20, 2001).
Christine Anu Official Website, http://www.christineanu.com.au (June 20, 2001).

—*Christine Kelley*

Aqua

Pop group

Until August of 1997, Denmark was not known for its contribution to international pop music. Although a few bands from that country had scored hit singles in the modern era, Denmark was a musical nonentity compared to its Nordic counterparts, Sweden and Norway. With the single "Barbie Girl," however, Copenhagen's Aqua firmly established a Danish presence on charts around the world. The single, already a number one hit in its native land, soon climbed into the top ten in England and the United States. While some reviewers questioned the staying power of a band that became renown for an homage to the Barbie doll, several other strong tracks from Aqua's debut album soon put such criticisms to rest.

The future members of Aqua took divergent paths to international acclaim. Two of the group's members, Claus Norreen and Søren Rasted, worked together in 1989 on the soundtrack for the Danish film *Freaky Friday*, but subsequently took day jobs at a gas station. The two continued to write music together while experimenting with keyboards, drum machines, and other electronic instruments. René Dif, who became one of the group's vocalists, had also achieved some success in the music world as one of Scandinavia's best-known deejays. Joining forces with Norreen and Rasted in

Photograph by Kristian Linnemann. Hulton/Archive. Reproduced by permission.

For the Record . . .

Members include **René Dif** (born on October 17, 1967, in Copenhagen, Denmark), vocals; **Claus Norreen** (born on June 5, 1970, in Copenhagen, Denmark), keyboards, electronic instruments; **Lene Grawford Nystrøm** (born on October 2, 1973, in Tonsberg, Norway), vocals; **Søren Rasted** (born on June 13, 1969, in Copenhagen, Denmark), keyboards, electronic instruments.

Formed group in Copenhagen, Denmark, as Joyspeed, early 1990s; released first album, *Aquarium,* as Aqua, 1997; single "Barbie Girl" became breakthrough international hit, released second album, *Aquarius,* 2000.

Awards: Dansk Grammy Awards, Best New Danish Act, Best Danish Band, Best Pop Album, Best Single, and Best Video, 1997.

Addresses: *Record company*—MCA Universal Records, 1755 Broadway, 8th Floor, New York, NY 10019, website: http://www.mcarecords.com. *Website*—Aqua Official Website: http://www.aqua.dk.

1995, Dif invited television presenter Lene Grawford Nystrøm, who was presenting and occasionally singing on a Norwegian variety game show, to join them in a new musical endeavor. The first partnership, under the name Joyspeed, was only marginally successful. The band secured a record contract and released the single "Itzy Bitzy Spider," which spent one week on the Swedish charts, before asking to be released from the contract.

The band regrouped under the name Aqua and gained a new recording contract with the Danish division of Universal Records in 1996. The second incarnation of the group proved to be immediately successful. Its initial offering, the dance track "Roses Are Red," gained club play throughout Denmark and remained in the top ten on the pop charts from October of 1996 until April of the following year, an astounding chart run. "My Oh My," another dance-oriented track with simple lyrics, joined "Roses Are Red" in the top ten after its release in February of 1997, granting Aqua the rare feat of having two hit songs on the charts simultaneously. Both tracks also logged time at the top of the pop chart. When the band's first album, *Aquarium,* was released in March of 1997, it debuted at number one

and reached double-platinum status in Denmark in two weeks with sales of more than 100,000 copies.

The group's playful image greatly aided its initial popularity with the public. "The band wanted to project a comic-book image through hair and clothing stylings and colors used in graphics," reported the managing director of its record company in a *Billboard* profile in September of 1997. "The effect shows on the records, posters, and all point-of-sale material, all of which match perfectly to the animated music and lyrics." In fact, the band's third single release in Denmark, "Barbie Girl," would emphasize each of these factors and bring the band international success far surpassing any other Danish band.

Inspired by viewing a children's exhibit on Mattel's Barbie doll, a popular toy with generations of girls around the world, Rasted came up with the lyric "Life in plastic, it's fantastic," which served as the basis for a tongue-in-cheek homage to the figure. With Nystrøm singing in a squeaky falsetto voice as Barbie and Dif rapping as her boyfriend, Ken, the song presented various scenes in the typical day of the "blonde bimbo doll in a fantasy world." Although some of the lyrics were mildly suggestive, Rasted insisted in an August 1997 *Billboard* interview that "The spirit [of the song] is fun. We didn't make the song to hurt the doll, the girls, or the men and women" who were Barbie doll fans.

Unfortunately, the maker of the Barbie doll took another view. Once the song hit number one throughout Scandinavia and raced up the charts in the United States, Mattel sued MCA Universal Records, claiming trademark infringement on its creation and asking for an injunction against further distribution of Aqua's single and album. Although *Aquarium* contained a disclaimer that stated "The song 'Barbie Girl' is a social comment and was not created or approved by the makers of the doll," Mattel insisted in a September 27, 1997 *Billboard* review of the lawsuit that "This is a business issue, not a freedom of speech issue. This is a two-billion dollar company, and we don't want it messed around with, and situations like this gradually lead to brand erosion." Eventually, however, Mattel saw the promotional value in the song and ceased its legal efforts.

For its part, Aqua viewed the lawsuit as only a minor interruption in its pursuit of international success. The group made extensive promotional appearances in Europe, the Far East, and America, which it saw as its biggest challenge. As Rasted told *Billboard* in August of 1997 just after the release of "Barbie Girl": "America has always been the biggest dream, because a Danish band has never had a song on the American charts." (Strictly speaking, Rasted's comment was not quite correct: the Danish band Laid Back had scored a hit with the track "White Horse" during the 1980s, although it quickly assumed one-hit wonder status.) With a marketing strategy designed to sell its album instead of the band's single releases, however, MCA Universal fought to prevent Aqua from sharing a similar fate. In its effort to get the public to buy *Aquarium* instead of just purchasing "Barbie Girl," the record company distributed only a limited number of the single track. Although this scarcity prevented the song from hitting the top of the charts in the United States, it increased sales of the album. As of late 2001, *Aquarium* had sold more than 2.7 million copies in the United States of its total sales of 14 million around the world. It was helped by the inclusion of the album's mid-tempo ballad, "Turn Back Time," on the soundtrack of the Gwyneth Paltrow film, *Sliding Doors.* The song was also used in the film's television advertisements in the United States and soared to number one on the British pop charts.

Aqua capped the success of its first album with a string of Dansk Grammy Awards. In February of 1998, the band received honors for Best Single and Best Video for "Barbie Girl," Best Pop Album for *Aquarium,* and Best New Danish Act and Best Danish Band. Dif was astounded by the reception: "This tops anything we have ever accomplished. We had never anticipated what would happen to us," he told *Billboard.* "We've been around the world two or three times, but it's a fantastic sign of recognition to be accepted in our home country." Nystrøm agreed, accepting one award in tears, saying, "We've received awards from a lot of countries, but this is something that we can really put into perspective." By now staples of the music press, Aqua was Denmark's best-known cultural export since actress and one-time Sylvester Stallone spouse, Brigitte Nielsen.

Released in February of 2000, Aqua's second album, *Aquarius,* featured a moodier set of songs than its predecessor, although the band's sense of irony was still in place. Rasted told *Billboard* in January of 2000, "It's still the kind of pop songs that we do, but with more substance to it." Nystrøm countered, "It's still cheesy, though." The leadoff single from the collection, "Cartoon Heroes," captured this spirit, invoking the band's own image as the basis for another dance-oriented track that hit the top of the charts in Denmark, Norway, and Italy and the top ten throughout Europe. Norreen explained the band's wide-ranging appeal on its sec-

ond album: "There are two sides to Aqua: the immediate meaning of the lyrics and the deeper point shrouded in irony. A lot of kids will relate to the 'Cartoon Heroes' idea, while older people will see the humor." With the single "Around the World" following "Cartoon Heroes" up the international charts in 2000, Aqua had assured its position as one of the most successful Scandinavian groups since Abba and Ace of Base. "A lot of people thought we were a one-hit and one-album wonder," Nystrøm told *Billboard.* "But we will show we're here to stay."

By the fall of 2001, though, Aqua stated on their official website that they did not intend to immediately make a third album. The group instead decided to take a break but insisted that they remain best friends. Lack of direction was cited as the reason for the breakup. The members of Aqua planned to pursue individual careers in music using their own London recording studio as a starting point.

Selected discography

Aquarium, MCA Universal, 1997.
(Contributor) *Sliding Doors* (soundtrack), MCA Universal, 1998.
Aquarius, MCA Universal, 2000.

Sources

Periodicals

Billboard, August 30, 1997, p. 92; September 6, 1997, p. 7; September 27, 1997, p. 106; February 21, 1998, p. 49; September 11, 1999, p. D-3; January 15, 2000; p. 15; February 26, 2000, p. 53.
Q, April 2000, p. 87.
Top of the Pops (England), April 2000, p. 7; May 2000, pp. 8, 64-65.

Online

Aqua Official Website, http://www.aqua.dk (June 16, 2001).

—Timothy Borden

Ash

Rock group

Among the most popular pop groups in the United Kingdom during the 1990s, Ireland's Ash scored hits with the singles "Oh Yeah," "Girl from Mars," and "Kung Fu." Bass guitarist Mark Hamilton, drummer Rick McMurray, and guitarist/lead vocalist Tim Wheeler differed college plans to pursue the success the young group experienced after the release of their debut album, *1977*, in 1996. An edgier version of the bubblegum pop of American musical contemporaries Hanson, Ash took "cherry-syrup melodies and summer-lovin' couplets of adolescent pop and dunked them in a tart coating of punkish clangor" on the album, according to Jeff Gordinier of *Fortune* magazine. The group continued their success with the release of *Nu-Clear Sounds* in 1998 and *Free All Angels* in 2001.

Twelve-year-olds Wheeler and Hamilton formed the metal act Vietnam in 1989 after receiving guitars as gifts for Christmas. The duo quickly changed its sound, however, after seeing a neighborhood punk band cover The Stooges' "I Wanna Be Your Dog." In June of 1992, schoolmate Rick McMurray joined the band as a drummer. With the addition of McMurray, the group soon produced their first demo tape at Cosmic Rayz Studio. The following September, Ash recorded its first single, "Jack Names the Planets," which was released on the indie label La La Land Records in February of 1994. *New Musical Express* (*NME*) praised the "teen punkers from Belfast with swell, bitty lead breaks like The Undertones and odd American accents like they've been hanging out with Evan Dando (formerly of the Lemonheads) and Pavement." To promote the single, Ash headed to England to perform a series of shows during their Easter high school break. The tour led to a deal with Infectious Records, which released the group's *Trailer* EP the following November. Ash's popularity grew, and in January of 1995 the band was nominated for Best New Band in *NME*'s Brat Awards.

To keep its success growing, Ash released the single "Kung Fu" in March of 1995. It reached number 57 on the singles charts, the first chart placement for the group. Deciding to make a career of music, the trio dropped out of high school in August of 1995. Two days after leaving school, Ash played the prestigious Glastonbury Festival. Several singles followed, including "Girl from Mars," which hit number eleven on the charts, "Angel Interceptor," which moved into the number 14 spot in October of 1995, a cover of Smokey Robinson and the Miracles' "Get Ready" in 1995, and "Goldfinger," a number five hit in April of 1996. Fame at an early age took its toll on Ash. Wheeler endured a drug-induced nervous breakdown, and Hamilton suffered from several bouts of alcohol poisoning.

In May of 1996, Ash released its debut full-length album, *1977*, which topped the United Kingdom charts. Of the group and the album, *NME* said that "Ash's heads have been turned far more by an American alternative tradition than British indie of late." The English music magazine predicted that the band would overcome "the brief shelf-life and potential stigma of being an ooh-aren't-they-so-young teen phenomenon." Unlike Ash's previous releases, *1977*—named for Wheeler and Hamilton's birth year and the year in which their favorite movie, *Star Wars*, was released—touched on the trio's debaucherous ways. Drug and alcohol abuse did not hinder Ash's success, however. The album reached number one on the United Kingdom album charts and spawned five hit singles including "Oh Yeah," "Girl from Mars," and "Kung Fu."

Instead of returning to the studio, Ash released the live record *Live at the Wireless* in March of 1997 on its own Death Star Records. According to Ash's official website, the band needed a woman's touch and hired second guitarist Charlotte Hatherley. Following Hatherley's addition to the group, Ash scored the number ten hit "A Life Less Ordinary" from the Ewan McGregor and Cameron Diaz film of the same name. Comparing Ash to the Beach Boys' Brian Wilson, Bono, the lead singer of fellow Irish rockers U2, invited the band to perform as part of a free peace rally in Belfast in May of 1998. More than 2,000 Catholic and Protestant school children attended the event designed to endorse a "Yes" vote for the Belfast Peace Agreement.

In October of 1998, Ash sent its second studio album, *Nu-Clear Sounds*, to stores. The album peaked at number seven on the charts. Despite the album's popular success, *NME* panned the single "Numbskull": "This is the sound of teeth-grinding, gray-misted pre-

For the Record . . .

Members include **Mark Hamilton** (born on March 21, 1977), bass; **Charlotte Hatherley** (born on June 20, 1977; joined group, 1997), guitars, vocals; **Rick McMurray** (born on July 11, 1975), drums; **Tim Wheeler** (born on January 4, 1977), guitars, vocals.

Formed group in Downpatrick, Northern Ireland, 1992; signed with La La Land Records, 1994; released single "Jack Names the Planets," 1994; signed with Infectious Records, released *Trailer* EP, 1994; released *1977*, 1996; released *Live at the Wireless* on own Death Star Records, 1997; released *Nu-Clear Sounds,* 1998; released *Free All Angels*, 2001.

Addresses: *Record company*—Infectious Records, London, England, website: http://www.mushroomuk.com/maininfectious.htm. *Website*—Ash Official Website: http://www.ash-official.com.

menstrual tension." The video, however, fueled the single's success. The controversial piece featured group sex, drug abuse, self-mutilation, and a naked Wheeler. Hatherley explained to the British Broadcasting Corporation (BBC) online that Wheeler chose to do the video in part to contradict his image. "I think it goes against Tim's usual image in the press—getting away from that babyface indie kid," Hatherley said. "It starts off pretty tame and then it escalates, but I think they'll be able to show some clips somewhere."

In 1999, Ash shied away from the stage for the most part. Though the group wasn't playing regular shows, Ash stayed in the press. Hatherley and Wheeler were hired as models for designer Calvin Klein's Spring 2000 advertising campaign. *Star Wars* fans, Ash was thrilled when actor McGregor asked the group to entertain during a premiere party for *Episode One: The Phantom Menace*. To further promote its 2001 album, *Free All Angels*, Ash headlined the *NME* Brat Awards. In an interview with the music magazine, McMurray stated that Hatherley had written songs for the album, but he wasn't sure of the record's direction and seemed jaded by the commercial disappointment of *Nu-Clear Sounds*. "We're almost not mainstream anymore, rather strangely," McMurray said.

For Wheeler, the process of recording *Free All Angels* was much more "natural" than *Nu-Clear Sounds,* he told the BBC. "I think the last album, we were reacting to what people expected of us, so we did somethin completely different. With this album, we just didn't care and just wrote whatever came out. It was a much more natural process."

Reclaiming its penchant for controversy, Ash purchased 300 copies of a single by pop group Westlife and burned them in a city park during an autograph session in Leeds, England. "We were doing an in-store appearance and the manager gave them to us. Westlife epitomize everything that's mind-numbing and contrived about the music industry," Hatherley told Teletext about the incident.

Upon its release, *Free All Angels* debuted at number one. "Never underestimate the power of a great record. It got us back on the radio and seemed to be used as a backing track for a few sporting events. That certainly helped relaunch us as a band," Wheeler told the *Glasgow Evening Times*.

Selected discography

Trailer (EP; includes "Jack Names the Planets"), Infectious, 1994.
1977 (includes "Oh Yeah," "Kung Fu," "Girl from Mars"), Infectious, 1996.
Live at the Wireless, Death Star, 1997.
Nu-Clear Sounds (includes "Numbskull"), Infectious, 1998; DreamWorks (U.S.), 1999.
Free All Angels, Infectious, 2001.

Sources

Periodicals

Birmingham Post (England), May 12, 2001.
Fortune, October 11, 1999.
Glasgow Evening Times (Scotland), May 21, 2001.
The People (London, England), April 18, 2001.

Online

"Ash," *New Musical Express*, http://www.nme.com/NME/External/Artists/Artist_Biog/0,1231,art4111,00.html (July 25, 2001).
"Ash Get Their Kit Off," BBC Online, http://www.bbc.co.uk/radio1/artist_area/ash/122.shtml (September 22, 2001).
"Ash: Still Shining," BBC Online, http://www.bbc.co.uk/worldservice/arts/highlights/010212_ash.shtml (September 23, 2001).
"People Vs Ash," BBC Online, http://www.bbc.co.uk/radio1/alt/alt_features/feature_people_vs_ash.shtml (September 23, 2001).
Teletext, http://www.geocities.com/alternator_team/tel07apr01.html (July 25, 2001).

—Christina Fuoco

Aswad

Reggae group

After 25 years and two dozen albums, Britain-based Aswad has become of one reggae's institutions. Not only has the band outlasted almost every other band to emerge from the vibrant London reggae scene of the 1970s, it has also survived numerous personnel changes over the years. The group even avoided the pitfalls of succumbing to its own success; after securing a number one single, Aswad continued to develop its style regardless of its presence on the charts. Known for its energetic live shows, the band has also sustained its popularity with an extensive tour schedule in Europe, Japan, and the Americas. For its longevity alone, Aswad ranks among the most notable reggae bands, as well as one of the most commercially successful.

Developed in Jamaica from the 1960s onward, reggae mixed traditional Caribbean rhythms, a prominent bass line, and often socially profound lyrics with elements of American jazz and R&B. In Britain, where many of the island's immigrants had settled after World War II, independent record companies brought the latest reggae releases to Jamaican expatriates. By the mid 1960s homegrown British reggae bands, such as the Cimarons, had sprung up among the immigrants and their children. Largely ignored by commercial radio and

Photograph by Jack Barron. ©S.I.N./Corbis. Reproduced by permission.

For the Record . . .

Members include **Brinsley "Dan" Forde** (born in 1952 in Guyana), vocals, guitar; **Angus "Drummie Zeb" Gaye** (born in 1959 in London, England), vocals, drums; **Donald "Benjamin" Griffiths** (born in 1954 in Jamaica); **Courtney Hemmings**; **George "Ras Levi" Oban** (left group, 1980), bass; **Tony "Gad" Robinson** (replaced Oban), bass.

Formed group in London, England, c. 1974; released first, self-titled album, 1976; scored number one single "Don't Turn Around," released *Distant Thunder*, 1988; released *Rise and Shine*, 1994; released *Big Up*, 1997; released *Roots Revival*, 1999; released twenty-fifth anniversary concert album, 2001.

Addresses: *Record company*—Ark 21 Records, 14724 Ventura Blvd., Penthouse Suite, Sherman Oaks, CA 91403, website: http://www.ark21.com. *Website—* Aswad at Ark 21 Records: http://www.ark21.com/ aswad/indexold.htm.

the major records labels, it was not until the mid 1970s that reggae began to be heard on a significant scale outside of the Anglo-Jamaican community in Britain.

Emerged on 1970s British Reggae Scene

Formed around 1974 in London, the group Aswad was one of many bands that emerged during the fertile period in British reggae music. Deriving its name from the Arabic word for "black," the group initially performed with five members. In addition to mainstay Angus "Drummie Zeb" Gaye on drums and vocals, the band included George "Ras Levi" Oban, Courtney Hemmings, Donald "Benjamin" Griffiths, and Brinsley "Dan" Forde on lead vocals. Forde was perhaps the best-known of the members at the time of the band's formation. As a child actor, he had appeared in several British Broadcasting Corporation (BBC) programs. Over the years, the group's lineup would change several times. By the 1990s, Aswad was a trio consisting of Gaye and Forde, joined by Tony Gad after 1980 on bass. In the late 1990s, however, Forde also left the band, and Aswad carried on as a duo.

In its first incarnation, Aswad reflected the multicultural, immigrant environment that made British reggae somewhat distinct from its island counterpart. After all, most of its members came from different countries: Gaye was born in London, Forde in Guyana, and Griffiths in Jamaica. Reflecting this diversity, the members found influences in Jamaican styles such as ska and rocksteady, precursors to reggae, as well as American jazz. Like many reggae artists, however, the band's lyrical output often focused on themes of struggle and survival in the midst of racial hostility. The band's first single, 1976's "Back to Africa," referred to a longing for an idyllic mother land, while the follow-up single, "Three Babylon," was a statement against police brutality.

With its signing to Mango Records in 1975, a division of Chris Blackwell's Island Records, Aswad became the first reggae group from outside Jamaica signed to the renown label. A pioneer in his own right, Blackwell had facilitated the development of reggae in Britain in the early 1960s by producing some of the leading reggae artists in Jamaica and importing their records to the émigré Jamaican community in Britain and around the world. By the 1970s, Island Records was recognized as the premier international reggae label, a fact that established Aswad's credibility with reggae audiences from the start.

With "Back to Africa," Aswad found immediate success as the single hit number one on the British reggae charts. The band was also in demand as a backing group for visiting Jamaican reggae stars, including Black Uhuru and Bob Marley. Aswad also took part in the creative alliance between reggae and punk rock at the end of the 1970s, performing with New Wave acts such as the Police and Elvis Costello. With reggae's popularity at an ebb in Britain after 1980, however, one of the group's outstanding releases, 1981's *New Chapter,* sold poorly despite the critical approval. Searching for direction, the band went back to its roots, recording some old Jamaican dancehall standards before pushing on with more mainstream pop efforts.

Hit Number One with "Don't Turn Around"

Aswad's previous experimentation with jazz fusion, R&B, and various Jamaican styles had led some critics to question their commitment as bona-fide reggae artists. The band's breakthrough success in 1988 seemed to confirm this skepticism. Taking a tune co-written by prolific American songwriter Diane Warren—best known at the time for penning hits by DeBarge, Laura Branigan, and Michael Bolton—Aswad's version of "Don't Turn Around" hit number one on the singles chart in Britain in early 1988. The group followed the chart-topper with another hit co-authored by Warren, the top 20 single "Give a Little Love." In similar fashion, Aswad's 1988 album *Distant Thunder* hit the top ten on the album charts in Britain.

Firmly established with mainstream audiences in Britain, Aswad continued to score on the charts with hits such as "On and On" in 1989 and "Next to You" in 1990, yet reggae purists continued to criticize the band for becoming too pop-oriented. In a 1994 *Billboard* interview to promote the release of *Rise and Shine*, Gaye acknowledged that some Aswad fans had not approved of the band's crossover appeal. "They were saying those albums were OK, but that our older projects had more true flavor.... For the last few albums, we had been recording at the most expensive places in London. For *Rise and Shine,* we decided to record in a place that had a certain atmosphere that we were looking for." The change in venue helped *Rise and Shine* recover some of the band's old fan base while maintaining its mainstream popularity as the single "Shine" hit the top 30 in Britain. *Rise and Shine* also proved extremely popular in Japan where Aswad became one of the most popular international artists of the 1990s. *Rise and Shine* was one of the biggest-selling albums in Japan in 1994, in part because Aswad allowed Sony Records to press a domestic release of the album for the Japanese market, a rarity for an international artist in the country.

Changes in Reggae Music

The changes in Aswad's musical direction were reflected in the reggae world itself. As Gaye commented in a 1994 *Billboard* interview, "Music used to have a real message. It's still youthdriven music, but a lot of the newer forms—hip-hop and house and dub—changed reggae." In particular, according to Gaye, the use of new technologies in the studio took the feel of modern reggae far away from its roots: "A lot of kids out there today can't play the [reggae] beat, so they use computers to create them." For all its mainstream success, Aswad remained firmly identified as one of the great British reggae groups, along with Steel Pulse.

Summarizing the band's accomplishment upon the release of its *Reggae Greats* album in 1998, a *Q* magazine reviewer noted its "rightful place in the history books as one of the few reggae bands to make a lasting impact on a mainstream (i.e. white) audience," while reviving the old criticism of Aswad as lacking in authenticity. The fact that Swedish pop group Ace of Base had an international number one hit with a remake of "Don't Turn Around" in 1994 had done little to restore the band's reputation. Still, after more than 20 years of varying degrees of success, the members of Aswad had outlasted most of their original colleagues and many of their critics. With Brinsley Forde's departure from the group, Gaye and Gad continued with the 1999 release *Roots Revival,* which included cover versions of the Bob Marley songs "Caution" and "Thank You Lord," in addition to a contribution from Sting on the group's rendition of the Police song "Invisible Sun."

On August 22, 2000, Aswad performed a concert in London that marked the band's twenty-fifth anniver-

sary, a tribute that was recorded and released the following year as *25 Live: 25th Anniversary.* Although it had not achieved commercial success in the United States, where urban and mainstream radio programmers typically ignored reggae releases, Aswad remained a popular concert draw in Britain, the Caribbean, and Japan. Despite a lack of recognition after its initial period of critical acclaim, the group also maintained an eager fan base willing to stick with the band throughout its musical and personnel changes. As a *Q* reviewer commented in October of 1999, "The future for Aswad's breezy, lightweight reggae looks fairly bright."

Selected discography

Aswad, Mango, 1976.
Hulet, Mango, 1978.
New Chapter, Columbia, 1981.
Showcase, Mango, 1981.
Not Satisfied, CBS, 1982.
A New Chapter of Dub, Mango, 1982.
Live and Direct, Mango, 1983.
Rebel Souls, Mango, 1984.
To the Top, Mango, 1986.
Renaissance, Stylus, 1988.
Distant Thunder, Mango, 1988.
Crucial Tracks: The Best of Aswad, Mango, 1989.
Next to You, Alex, 1990.
Too Wicked, Mango, 1990.
Firesticks, Alex, 1993.
Rise and Shine, Rhino, 1994.
Rise and Shine Again, Mesa, 1995.
Dub: The Next Frontier, Mesa, 1995.
Greatest Hits, Alex, 1995.
Big Up, Atlantic, 1997.
Roots Rocking: The Island Anthology, Island, 1997.
Roots Revival, Ark 21, 1999.
Millennium Edition, Universal, 2000.
25 Live: 25th Anniversary, Paras, 2001.

Sources

Books

Broughton, Simon, et al., editors, *World Music: The Rough Guide Volume 2,* The Rough Guides Ltd., 1999.
McAleer, Dave, *The All Music Book of Hit Singles,* Carlton Books, Ltd., 1994.

Periodicals

Billboard, July 2, 1994, p. 22; January 28, 1995, p. 57; August 5, 1995, p. 57; July 17, 1999, p.37; August 19, 2000, p. 73.
Q, October 1995; September 1998; October 1999.

Online

"Aswad," Ark 21 Records, http://www.ark21.com/aswad/indexold.htm (June 23, 2001).

Blackworld, http://www.blackworld.com/proffs/artistes/aswad.htm (June 23, 2001).

Reggae Train, http://www.reggaetrain.com/bioaswad.html (June 23, 2001).

—*Timothy Borden*

Sherrié Austin

Singer, songwriter

Australian singer and songwriter Sherrié Austin broke new ground with her 2001 release, *Followin' a Feelin'*. While she had several hits with her first two pop-infused albums and sales close to half a million records, Austin chose to leave Arista, an established label, and sign with the independent Wrensong. The singer took a year off from touring and recording to focus on songwriting, and the result was an album that returns to traditional country music and reflects early influences such as Dolly Parton and Loretta Lynn.

Born in Sydney, Australia, Austin was exposed to country music at an early age. Her mother loved the genre and played Parton and Johnny Cash records at home; Austin started singing by the age of 13. She told Chet Flippo of *Billboard* about her early influences: "I loved Dolly. She was my absolute favorite. I loved the songs she was writing, as well as Linda Ronstadt and Olivia Newton-John. I was also a '70s baby and love that music, like Elton John and Simon & Garfunkel and Bread." Austin's parents began traveling with her around Australia to sing at country music festivals with a tent packed in the back of their van. Her big break came when she was just 14 year old—she opened for Cash during his 1985 tour of Australia. Although Austin was building a reputation as a singer, she declined an invitation from the Australian Country Music Association to move to Nashville when she was 15 years old because she felt she was just too young.

Two years later, though, Austin and her family moved to Los Angeles, California, so she could pursue her singing career. Once in Los Angeles, Austin landed a role as Pippa McKenna on the popular NBC sitcom *Facts of Life*. An actress at age 17, Austin remained committed to music and took voice and keyboard lessons with Robert Edwards, vocal coach to Linda Ronstadt. While in Los Angeles, Austin worked with Colourhaus, a pop band led by Phil Radford. The singer was still drawn to country, though, and moved to Nashville when she was 22 years old.

When Austin got to the country music capital, she arranged a meeting with Will Rambeaux, who would be a co-producer on three albums and collaborator on many songs. In 1995, Austin signed with Arista Nashville. Then president of the division, Tim DuBois saw potential in Austin, and the label allowed her two years to develop her debut album. *Words* appeared in 1997, drawing critical attention and popular response. Four songs from the album—"Innocent Man," "One Solitary Tear," "Put Your Heart in It," and "Lucky In Love"—made it onto the country charts, and Country Music Television (CMT) named Austin its Rising Star. Video play boosted the sales of all of Austin's albums, showcasing her sparkling good looks. But the singer does not rely on her looks alone, and critics have commended her both for her vocal talent and her interesting musical arrangements. The album combines country and pop sounds, producing what Chet Flippo of *Billboard* called "a mature mix of earthy love songs and uptempo numbers." Maria Konicki of *All Music Guide* called *Words* a "spectacular debut," and identified Austin as one of the genre's "fresh sounding female vocalists."

Austin's second album was even more commercially successful than her debut. *Love in the Real World,* released in 1999, included "Never Been Kissed," which went to number one on the *Billboard* Hot Country Singles and Tracks charts for sales, video, and dance. The label, while continuing to rely on traditional marketing, introduced some high-tech distribution techniques: Austin's website gave fans another way of connecting with the singer, and "Never Been Kissed" was delivered to radio by email through Liquid Audio, making her one of the first artists to utilize that technology.

The success of the single "Never Been Kissed" and the album *Love in the Real World* was fueled by Austin's personality and big voice; Chaz Malibu of KRST radio in Albuquerque, New Mexico, told *Billboard,* "[Austin] has so much spunk....When she sings, you can just hear the attitude, and it's great." The sophomore album retained the pop feel of *Words,* but some reviewers found the fusion uncomfortable. Maria Konicki noted in *All Music Guide* that she felt the record was "a bit of a disappointment," since it wasn't really pop nor was it truly country. *Billboard*'s Paul Verna, though, called the singer "effervescent," and thought Austin showed "a marked progression and maturity" on *Love in the Real World.* Ralph Novak of *People* also praised the album, calling the songs "thoughtful, melodious compositions" and noting that Austin displays "an unusually mature mind and voice."

True success did not come easily to Austin, though, even after the release of her second album. Arista was subsumed by RCA Label Group, and Austin had to decide whether to stay with the new Arista or move on. She chose to join Wrensong, an independent label for which she had already been writing. Austin also took a year off from touring and recording to focus on her songwriting; she told Ray Waddell of *Billboard* that the year was spent "detoxing my soul." The resulting album, *Followin' a Feelin',* was released in 2001. The title sums up Austin's process: she focused not on what would sell on the radio, but returned to the inspiration that led her to country music in the first place. *Followin' a Feelin'* is a collection of nine original songs—many collaborations with Rambeaux—and one cover, of Dolly Parton's 1974 hit "Jolene." Austin's songs also reflect her return to traditional country music, and Konicki found the result "virtually flawless." She also

wrote that "Austin sounds liberated, confident, and energized" on the album.

Partnered with Wrensong, Austin was poised to take a more active role in the marketing and promotion of her third album. She continued to tour and remained a presence on the Internet, and the label used targeted marketing as a way of reaching her fans. Austin commented on the new arrangement in *Billboard,* saying, "This is very exciting and fulfilling, because I was always interested in both sides of the business. I get to contribute not only as an artist, singer, and songwriter but also in making marketing, A&R, and promotional decisions." The shift in focus seems to have reinvigorated Austin, and the positive critical response to *Followin' a Feelin'* indicates that there is a market for her new music.

Selected discography

Words, Arista, 1997.
Love in the Real World, Arista, 1999.
Followin' a Feelin', Wrensong, 2001.

Sources

Periodicals

Billboard, June 14, 1997, p. 26; May 15, 1999, p. 21; July 3, 1999, p. 32; August 7, 1999, p. 19; August 14, 1999, p. 30; February 17, 2001, p. 33.
Entertainment Weekly, August 13, 1999, p. 76.
People, September 27, 1999, p. 45.

Online

"Sherrié Austin," *All Music Guide,* http://www.allmusic.com, (July 1, 2001).
"Sherrié Austin," Listen.com, http://www.listen.com, (July 1, 2001).
"Sherrié Austin," Wrensong, http://www.wrensong.com, (July 1, 2001).
Sherrié Austin Official Website, http://www.sherrieaustin.com, (July 1, 2001).

—Christine Kelley

David Axelrod

The long and varied career of David Axelrod has spanned six decades and covered musical trends from cool jazz during the 1950s to hip-hop at the millennium. In between, Axelrod produced several successful artists, including a series of hits for Lou Rawls in the mid 1960s, as well as several of his own albums as a composer, arranger, and songwriter. Largely relegated to the status of a trivia note during the 1980s, Axelrod's reputation was resurrected by hip-hop deejays and artists during the 1990s, who found in his jazz-fusion experiments excellent backing samples for their contemporary works. Now elevated to iconic status, Axelrod has pushed for the re-release of his lesser-known works while serving as a musical inspiration for a new generation of musicians.

Born on April 17, 1936, in the Crenshaw district of Los Angeles, California, Axelrod's future musical direction was influenced by the multicultural environment of the mostly African American neighborhood. At the time Axelrod's parents moved into the area, it was changing from a working-class white district south of downtown Los Angeles into an area of predominantly African American stores, businesses, and homes. Even today, Crenshaw remains one of the most notable African American communities in Los Angeles, with a cultural scene that includes museums devoted to black history and an active political life strengthened by some of the city's most ardent African American activists. During Axelrod's youth, the Crenshaw district included the main thoroughfare of African American cultural life in Los Angeles: Central Avenue—a street filled with music clubs, barbershops, beauty parlors, and other institutions of the African American community. The fact that Axelrod was white did not prevent him from absorbing many of these influences.

Axelrod was also influenced by the rough-and-tumble atmosphere of his family life. His father worked as a union organizer for the Industrial Workers of the World (IWW), a sometimes radical organization under constant attack by businesses and the government for its militant stance on workers' rights. Eventually, Axelrod's father toiled as a garment worker, a low-paying occupation often accompanied by sweatshop working conditions. At home, however, Axelrod remembered that weekend jitterbug parties were the highlight of the week, with his parents clearing their living room to make room for dancing. As a teenager at Los Angeles' Dorsey High School, Axelrod did not stay off the streets for long. Frequenting some of the clubs along Central Avenue, the young man soon earned a reputation as a brawler. "The thing was, at that time, the cops were so crooked," he recalled of his early clubbing days to *Los Angeles Magazine.* "I think if you were in diapers and you could pay cash, nobody bothered you, long as you could pay for the drinks." Before long, Axelrod was left with a long scar on his stomach from a street fight and a damaged eye from a boxing match.

With unspecified troubles, possibly both legal and extralegal, Axelrod left Los Angeles in the early 1950s and spent a year exploring the jazz clubs in New York City. Upon returning to his native city, the burgeoning hipster dabbled in heroin as part of Los Angeles' beatnik scene. After meeting jazz pianist Gerald Wiggins, however, Axelrod was inspired to study music composition. Before long, Axelrod's love of music and familiarity with the Los Angeles jazz community led him to work as both a talent scout and record producer. Riding the crest of the city's reputation as the center of the 1950s "cool jazz" movement—at its best, a mixture of precise musicianship with complex arrangements demanding a listener's total attention—Axelrod established a reputation as a producer with excellent live recording skills.

Although Axelrod's most significant productions involved saxophonist Cannonball Adderley, his work with R&B singer Lou Rawls on Capitol Records in the mid 1960s was his most commercial success. Indeed, with Rawls' string of hits on the R&B and pop charts, Axelrod was one of the most sought-after producers at Capitol. With its signature headquarters—a building shaped like a stack of records on Hollywood and Vine in Los Angeles—and acts such as the Beach Boys and the Beatles on its roster, Capitol Records was the center of the pop music industry during the 1960s. In addition to his work with Rawls, Axelrod also produced such avant-garde efforts as the *Mass in F Minor* by the Electric Prunes in 1967. A psychedelic rock album with religious themes, the *Mass* foreshadowed Axelrod's

For the Record . . .

Born on April 17, 1936, in Los Angeles, CA.

Jazz musician in Los Angeles, CA, late 1950s; produced albums for Lou Rawls, mid 1960s; released debut album as composer, 1968; works sampled by hip-hop artists, 1990s; compilation albums released, 1999-2000.

Addresses: *Record company*—Fantasy Records, Tenth and Parker, Berkeley, CA 94710, website: http://www.fantasyjazz.com.

own musical direction. That same year, one of Axelrod's productions, *Mercy, Mercy, Mercy,* won a Grammy Award for Best Instrumental Jazz Performance for the Cannonball Adderley Quintet.

With a string of commercial and artistic successes behind him, Axelrod also found an opportunity to realize his own musical vision and recorded *Songs of Innocence,* released in 1968 on Capitol Records. Like the album *Mass in F Minor, Songs of Innocence* offered an eclectic, and often psychedelic array of songs, in this case based on the poetry of William Blake. Blake's work also inspired Axelrod's second album, *Songs of Experience,* released in 1969. Like many musicians from the jazz world, Axelrod's albums followed the trend toward jazz fusion, expanding the boundaries of the genre to include elements of funk, R&B, rock, and even classical music. In Axelrod's case, the emphasis on jazz-funk fusion predominated, although he made occasional ventures into easy listening territory, such as his version of the Carly Simon hit "You're So Vain" on his 1974 album *Heavy Axe.* Upon the album's reissue as part of *The Axelrod Chronicles* in 2000, *Rolling Stone* online commented, "It would be eminently suitable for background soundtrack music for 1970s films and made-for-TV movies," adding that its tracks "sound more like quickly assembled, made-to-order filler music for video productions, the horns sometimes sounding like those of school marching bands, with touches of early-'70s-style electric keyboards and wah-wahing funk-rock guitars."

Axelrod continued to serve as a producer for Cannonball Adderley and other jazz artists during the 1970s while composing his own original works. His 1980 release, *Marchin',* however, would mark the end of his most active phase as a recording artist. As music trends shifted away from experimental fusion artists like Axelrod, the decade was dominated by highly stylized, mainstream R&B-pop productions by Michael Jackson and Madonna as well as the enduring popularity of heavy metal artists. There seemed to be little room for an iconoclastic figure like Axelrod, and even less interest in his laid-back, jazz-funk music. By 1988, the producer and composer was living with his fourth wife in a dismal apartment in Tarzana, California. He continued to study music composition and expand his musical vision with two releases, 1993's *Requiem: The Holocaust* and 1995's *The Big Country,* but his works were largely ignored. Especially troubling to Axelrod was the reception for the *Requiem* album, inspired by the Nazi death camps of the Holocaust. In later years, Axelrod would lobby strenuously for its re-release, arguing that its brief release in 1993 prevented it from becoming his most enduring work.

After the disappointing reception of *Requiem: The Holocaust,* it seemed that Axelrod's presence in the music industry was all but over. In 1996, however, Josh Davis—a California turntable artist performing under the name DJ Shadow—sampled some of Axelrod's work on his debut album, *Endtroducing....* Like Axelrod's best work during the late 1960s, *Endtroducing ...* expanded the boundaries of its genre with its eclectic influences; in this case, DJ Shadow had taken hip-hop and fashioned it into "trip-hop," a label that referred to its ethereal and sometimes psychedelic feel. Soon, Axelrod's music was fashionable again. Working again with DJ Shadow and his U.N.K.L.E. collaboration with other hip-hop deejays, Axelrod was asked to remix a track on the 1998 *Psyence Fiction* album. That same year, another Axelrod sample appeared on Lauryn Hill's acclaimed *The Miseducation of Lauryn Hill,* further enhancing Axelrod's trendy status. In 1999, rapper Dr. Dre sampled Axelrod for his work *Chronic 2001.*

In light of his unexpected popularity, Axelrod released two compilation albums of his earlier works. *1968 to 1970: An Axelrod Anthology* was reissued in 1999 and *The Axelrod Chronicles* followed the next year; riding the wave of interest in Axelrod, some of his earlier albums were also reissued. Once again an active producer in demand for hip-hop remixes, Axelrod enjoyed his renewed success. "Maybe I haven't left big footsteps, but I've left something," he told *Los Angeles Magazine.* "People all over the world seem to be listening to my music. So, what the hell?"

Selected discography

Songs of Innocence, Capitol, 1968.
Songs of Experience, Capitol, 1969.
Earth Rot, Capitol, 1970.
Rock Messiah, RCA, 1972.
The Auction, Decca, 1974.
Heavy Axe, Fantasy, 1974.
Seriously Deep, Polydor, 1975.
Strange Ladies, MCA, 1978.
Marchin', MCA, 1980.

Requiem The Holocaust, Liberty, 1993.
The Big Country, Liberty, 1995.
1968 to 1970: An Axelrod Anthology, Stateside, 1999.
The Axelrod Chronicles, Fantasy, 2000.

Sources

Books

Carr, Ian, et al., editors, *Jazz: The Rough Guide,* The Rough Guides, 1995.
Gioia, Ted, *The History of Jazz,* Oxford University Press, 1997.

Periodicals

Los Angeles Magazine, March 2001, p. 136.
Q, March 1999.

Online

All About Jazz, http://www.allaboutjazz.com/bios/cabio.htm (June 27, 2001).
Fantasy Records, http://www.fantasyjazz.com/catalog/axelrod_d_cat.html (June 26, 2001).
Recording Academy, http://www.grammy.com (June 27, 2001).
Rolling Stone.com, http://www.rollingstone.com/recordins/review.asp?aid=R+++484623&cf=1357746 (June 26, 2001).

—*Timothy Borden*

Samuel Barber

Composer

Samuel Barber is regarded as one of the most distinguished composers to emerge in twentieth-century America. His talent was recognized early, and he proved to be a precocious student during his years at the Curtis Institute during the mid 1920s. Later, during the course of his lengthy career, he composed 48 opus-length works. Barber, who is generally regarded as a neo-Romantic composer, is admired for an extremely lyrical quality that permeates his compositions, works that are also characterized by a high degree of tonality. Barber wrote 103 songs in addition to his major compositions and received recognition repeatedly during a career that produced two Pulitzer Prize-winning works. Composed in 1936, *Adagio for Strings* is among Barber's best-known compositions. He was a member of both the National Institute of Arts and Letters and the American Academy of Arts and Letters.

Samuel Osborne Barber II was born on March 9, 1910, to a well-educated, middle-class family in West Chester, Pennsylvania. He was the elder of two children and the only son of Marguerite McLeod Beatty and her physician husband, Samuel Leroy Barber. Barber, who was named for his paternal grandfather, came by his musical talent from his mother's family. From an early age, Barber was exposed to the culture of professional musicians. Most notably, his composer uncle Sidney Homer, and Homer's wife, Louise, who was a performer with the Metropolitan Opera, served as mentors.

Barber began his musical studies with piano lessons at age six and composed his first piece of music one year later. His mother, who was a pianist, took it upon herself to record her young son's compositions in manuscript format. By the age of ten, Barber had undertaken the daunting task of composing an opera. The work, called the *Rose Tree,* was based on a libretto which was supplied by the family's cook. Although Barber never completed the work, the score remains a testament to his prodigy.

Completed First Orchestral Composition

As a teenager, Barber attended at the prestigious Curtis Institute of Music in Philadelphia, Pennsylvania, where he studied piano, voice, and composition beginning in 1924. Prior to his enrollment at Curtis, Barber had studied organ from age eleven and played for services at the Westminster Presbyterian Church in his hometown. In addition to his bent for piano and organ, Barber was a talented baritone. During his years at Curtis, he distinguished himself most notably as a student of composition under Rosario Scalero. Scalero, who recognized Barber's genius very quickly, worked with Barber for nine years. By 1931 Barber had completed his first orchestral composition, *Overture to the School for Scandal.* The following year he left the

Professional Prominence

Barber's first major orchestral work, *Overture to the School for Scandal*, received its world premiere with the Philadelphia Orchestra under conductor Alexander Smallens in 1933. In 1935-36 Barber received an extended Pulitzer traveling scholarship and thereafter supported himself largely by means of fellowship grants and by composing works on commission. Also in 1935 Barber won the Prix de Rome and spent some years at the American Academy in Rome in fulfillment of the prize. Barber was commissioned to write his Symphony No. 2 by the Army Air Forces while serving as a corporal during World War II. He taught briefly at the Curtis Institute, collected royalties for his works, and received Guggenheim Fellowships in 1945, 1947, and again in 1949. In 1946 he accepted a commission to compose a ballet score for Martha Graham's planned presentation of *Medea*. After completing that project, entitled *Cave of the Heart*, Barber subsequently expanded the original ballet music into seven movements for full orchestra in 1947. He reworked the score a second time in 1955, resulting in a single full-length movement called *Medea's Dance of Vengeance*. In 1949 Barber accepted a commission to compose a work for piano to be performed by Vladimir Horowitz in celebration of the twenty-fifth anniversary of the League of Composers.

Barber's work, which is most memorable for its extremely lyrical quality, includes 103 solo songs. In many instances, the composer took his inspiration from literary illusion, turning to the celebrated Anglo-Saxon poets—James Agee, William Butler Yeats, James Joyce, and others—for text and inspiration in composing his songs. Among his more popular lyrical works, Barber's *Hermit Songs* were taken from works of Irish poetry which he adapted to music for the American soprano Leontyne Price. *Hermit Songs* marked the first in an ongoing series of collaborations between Barber and Price that began with Price's *Hermit Songs* concert in 1953 and endured for two decades. In 1966, on commission for the opening of the new Metropolitan Opera House at the Lincoln Center in New York City, Barber wrote the opera *Antony and Cleopatra* with Price earmarked for the starring role of Cleopatra. That work featured an original libretto by Franco Zeffirelli, although much of the premiere production was flawed. Barber later rewrote the work in collaboration with Menotti.

Pulitzer Prize Winner

In 1958 the Metropolitan Opera produced Barber's opera, *Vanessa,* a highly successful work featuring Menotti's libretto. That work won the first of two Pulitzer Prizes for Barber. He won a second Pulitzer along with a Music Critics Circle Award in 1962 for Piano Concerto No. 1, which had its premiere at the Avery Fisher

institute to work as a composer, subsidizing his early career through singing and teaching. Additionally, he completed his studies and graduated in 1934 with a bachelor's degree in music.

Throughout his professional career, Barber's private life sometimes caused scandal because of an intimate living relationship he maintained with fellow musician Gian Carlo Menotti. The close personal friendship between the two men began when they were students at the Curtis Institute. Menotti lived for a time at the Barber household, and Barber traveled with Menotti on numerous occasions to Milan, Italy, to visit with Menotti's family. Furthermore, Barber lived much of his adult life in New York City, sharing living quarters with Menotti. Likewise, Barber spent 12 years in the close companionship of Valentin Herranz, which gave further credence to already existing notions of Barber's rumored homosexuality and caused continual dismay among the less politically correct art patrons of Barber's era.

Music Hall (then Philharmonic Hall) at the Lincoln Center.

Barber's most celebrated work is the *Adagio for Strings*, which he composed when he was newly out of the Curtis Institute. The composition was performed along with Barber's *Essay for Orchestra* in a world premiere by the NBC Symphony Orchestra in 1938 under conductor Arturo Toscanini. The *Adagio* was heard prominently once again in 1945 at the funeral of President Franklin D. Roosevelt and was heard thereafter on many momentous and somber occasions, including the funerals of physicist Albert Einstein in 1955 and Princess Grace of Monaco in 1982.

Although the *Adagio* was not included among the selections at Barber's own funeral, he was nonetheless serenaded with his own music for several months by a stream of his friends and colleagues as he lay on his deathbed, terminally ill from cancer. He died on January 23, 1981, in New York City.

Selected compositions

Overture to the School for Scandal, G. Schirmer, 1931.
First Essay for Orchestra, G. Schirmer, 1937.

Adagio for Strings, G. Schirmer, 1938.
Concerto for Violin and Orchestra, G. Schirmer, 1939.
Symphony No. 2, G. Schirmer, 1942.
Medea—Cave of the Heart, G. Schirmer, 1947.
Medea—Ballet Suite, G. Schirmer, 1947.
Medea's Dance of Vengeance, G. Schirmer, 1955.
Vanessa, G. Schirmer, 1957.
Piano Concerto No. 1, G. Schirmer, 1962.
Antony and Cleopatra, G. Schirmer, 1966.
Third Essay for Orchestra, G. Schirmer, 1978.

Sources

Books

Encyclopedia of World Biography, second edition, Gale Research, 1998.
Scribner Encyclopedia of American Lives, Volume 1: 1981-1985, Charles Scribner's Sons, 1998.

Online

"Samuel Barber—Biography," G. Schirmer Inc., http://www.schirmer.com/composers/barberworks.html (June 26, 2001).

—*Gloria Cooksey*

Tracy Bonham

Singer, songwriter, violinist

Tracy Bonham has been compared to other groundbreaking female musicians of her generation, namely Alanis Morissette and Liz Phair, but she has retained her own sound. Bonham's music, while hard rocking and sometimes characterized as angry, has been influenced by her classical training in violin and voice. On her 2000 release, *Down Here,* her skill as a violinist is showcased and the lyrics reflect a more contemplative talent. The album also marks a moment of passage in Bonham's life: she has matured into her own voice, blending the frustration of youth with the lessons of life as a full-fledged musician.

Bonham was born on March 16, 1967, in Eugene, Oregon, where she was raised. Her father died when she was just two years old, and her mother remarried a loan officer, Edward Robertson. Bonham was the youngest of nine half- and step-siblings. Because her mother was a music teacher, Bonham was encouraged early on to develop her talents. She began playing violin when she was just nine years old and attended the respected Interlochen Arts Camp in Michigan at age 16 but was expelled for smoking. After high school, Bonham received a scholarship to the University of Southern California to study classical violin. She soon became disillusioned, though, and dropped out. Bonham moved to Boston, Massachusetts, and in 1987, enrolled at the Berklee School of Music where she focused on jazz and the study of voice.

While living in Boston, Bonham waitressed and recorded jingles for advertisements. She also developed a taste for rock and began experimenting with music outside the scope of her classical training. She told *Billboard* magazine, "Gradually, my tastes changed to the Pixies and the Buzzcocks. I took up rock 'n' roll around '92 and was inspired by woman singers like Sam Phillips and Jennifer Trynin. I got in touch with my feelings in a way I never could have with classical music, where you can bury things for the sake of discipline." That effort to branch out paid off in 1994 with Bonham's first hit, "The One," released by Curve of the Earth on the *Girl* compilation. The song, a caustic lyric about an ex-lover, led to some critical attention for the singer. The Boston Music Awards named her Best New Artist, Best Female Vocalist, and "The One" was named Best Indie Single in 1995.

Even with a popular single and the well-received EP *The Liverpool Sessions* under her belt, Bonham faced the formidable challenge of making a living in rock music as a female artist. When she signed with Island and recorded her first full-length album, Bonham filled the recording with songs that reflected the desire and struggle that fueled her during the early 1990s. As Tim White noted in *Billboard*, *The Burdens of Being Upright* is "the keen accrual of a lifetime of musical seasoning and six years of occupational struggle." The first hit from the album, "Mother, Mother," sums up the experience of the struggling musician as she calls home.

For the Record . . .

Born Tracy Kristin Bonham on March 16, 1967, in Eugene, OR; daughter of Donald Lewis Bonham (an editor) and Lee Anne Leach (a music teacher); married Steve Slingeneyer, 1998. *Education:* Studied violin at the University of Southern California; studied voice and violin at the Berklee School of Music, Boston, MA.

Released single "The One," 1994; released EP *The Liverpool Sessions,* 1995; signed with Island Records, released debut LP *The Burdens of Being Upright,* 1996; performed with two consecutive Lilith Fair tours; released *Down Here,* 2000.

Awards: Boston Music Awards, Best New Artist, Best Female Vocalist, and Best Indie Single for "The One," 1995.

Addresses: *Record company*—Island Records, 825 8th Avenue, 24th Floor, New York, NY 10019, website: http://www.islandrecords.com. *Website*—Tracy Bonham Official Website: http://www.tracybonham.com.

Even as she tells her mother that things are going well, Bonham screams about how it really is: "I'm hungry/ I'm dirty/ I'm losing my mind/Everything's fine."

Bonham's willingness to tell the unflinching truth and to reveal her feelings in her music puts her in the company of other hard-rocking women, including Courtney Love, Aimee Mann, and Liz Phair. Although she has often been compared to Alanis Morissette in the press, Bonham's passions are channeled differently. As Sean Slade, co-producer of *The Burdens of Being Upright,* told *Entertainment Weekly,* "You don't get the me-against-the-world feeling from her that you get from Alanis Morissette. She's so not showbiz; she doesn't have that phony melodramatic quality." Bonham's straightforward style and evocative songs about life as a woman landed her a spot in Lilith Fair—a megatour showcasing women musicians that traveled throughout the United States and Canada—for two consecutive years.

Bonham writes, sings, and plays guitar on *The Burdens of Being Upright,* which has been praised for its accessible pop feel. Peter Castro reviewed the album for *People,* noting, "Bonham has an uncommon knack for embroidering her rage with catchy melodies." Bon-ham's official website biography calls her guitar playing "untrained but inspired," and Bonham herself notes, "I'm not a good guitar player, but I've got a style that works for me. There's a stupidity in my playing that makes it fresh, and I want to keep that ignorance." The combination of heavy guitar and searing lyrics worked for Bonham. *The Burdens of Being Upright* went gold and was nominated for two Grammy Awards in 1996.

It took four years after *The Burdens of Being Upright* for Bonham to release another album, mostly because of the turmoil and uncertainty at Island during those years. *Down Here* took the singer two years to write and had to be recorded intermittently because of corporate changes at the label. Musicians backing Bonham on her second album include Pete Thomas, Steve Slingeneyer, and Sebastian Steinberg. She worked with producers Mitchell Froom and Tchad Blake on most of the songs, but Mark Endert produced three cuts. The album was finally released in the spring of 2000.

The break between albums seems to have allowed Bonham's music a chance to mature as *Down Here* shows a development both in style and in content. Bonham reflected in her official website biography, "While making the first record, I rebelled against my classical training…. With this record I've embraced my classical background and coupled that with the heavy guitar sounds that I love. Now I'm making music that sounds like me, past and present." Bonham's lyrics also reflect a change. While her early recordings have a definite angry edge, the material on *Down Here* has a different tone. Bonham commented to Chuck Taylor in *Billboard,* "I've grown up a lot and become more confident without the growing pains that come in the early 20s. These new songs dig deep and help me accept myself for who I am." By maintaining a strong female voice in her music, Bonham hopes to redirect the attention of those who may feel that appearance is everything. "I hope my message is that you can embrace your imperfections and not be swayed by TV…. There's more out there," she told *Billboard.*

Selected discography

(Contributor) *Girl,* Curve of the Earth, 1994.
The Liverpool Sessions (EP), CherryDisc, 1995.
The Burdens of Being Upright, Island/Def Jam, 1996.
Down Here, Island/Def Jam, 2000.

Sources

Periodicals

Billboard, January 20, 1996, p. 3; March 4, 2000, p. 1.
Cosmopolitan, December 1996, p. 186-190.

Detroit Free Press, July 12, 1996.
Entertainment Weekly, March 15, 1996, p. 64; June 21, 1996,
    p. 21-22; April 21, 2000, p. 78.
People, March 25, 1996, p. 24.

Online

"Tracy Bonham," *All Music Guide,* http://www.allmusic.com
    (June 25, 2001).
"Tracy Bonham," sing365.com, http://www.sing365.com
    (September 5, 2001).
Tracy Bonham Official Website, http://www.tracybonham.
    com (June 25, 2001).

—*Christine Kelley*

Bon Jovi

Rock group

"Bon Jovi was responsible for the most organic-sounding technopop-metal hybrids of the '80s," wrote *Spin's* Chuck Eddy in 1993 of the megapopular five-member band named after its lead singer, Jon Bon Jovi. Credited as one of the creators of "metal lite" or "pop metal"—heavy metal rock softened by top 40 lyrics—the band rose to prominence with the help of millions of MTV-watching teenage listeners during a decade dominated by pop giants Madonna and Michael Jackson. Eddy characterized Bon Jovi's sound as "dirty-white-boy guitars, a pinch of rockabilly twang, and maybe a couple of classically orchestrated disco strings" in his critique of the band's chartbusting 1986 album *Slippery When Wet.* Indeed, the New Jersey rockers who are the state's second-most-famous musical export (after working-class hero Bruce Springsteen), have not only survived but thrived in an ever-changing, intensely competitive industry. Thanks to their music skills, carefully polished image, loyalty to fans, and collective good looks, Bon Jovi has sold more than 90 million records globally. "We just want kids to have fun, nothing more—and nothing less," [Jon Bon Jovi] stated in a 1986 interview in *Rolling Stone.* "We aren't U2, we aren't gonna change the

Photograph by Martin Meissner. AP/World Wide Photos. Reproduced by permission.

world.... We're a rock band, and that's all we're supposed to be."

Born on March 2, 1962, in Sayreville, New Jersey, Jon Bon Jovi is the oldest son of Italian-Americans John and Carol Bongiovi. John Sr., a hairdresser, was notorious for closely cropping his three young sons' hair. Mrs. Bongiovi, a gift-shop owner and former Playboy bunny, planted the seed of her son's love of music when she brought home a guitar for seven-year-old Jon. "I was very much the average American kid," he told Jill Selsman in *Interview*. "I wanted to be an astronaut, a cop, or a baseball player. I remember my first experience with a guitar very well.... I flung it down the steps and heard it going *oing, oing, oing*. I remember hearing that and thinking, that's pretty cool. It took another seven years for me to want to get into it, though."

As a teenager Jon was influenced by the music of folk rocker Bob Dylan, Irish mystic-soulman Van Morrison, and fellow New-Jerseyites Springsteen and South Side Johnny and the Asbury Jukes. He played in several bands, including the Atlantic City Expressway (his first), the Rest, and the Raze. A highlight of his early career came when Springsteen joined the Atlantic City Expressway onstage for an impromptu jam session in an Asbury Park nightclub, a "near religious" experience for Jon.

Following high school graduation, the already ambitious singer and musician was ready to leave Sayreville, an industrial town he considered a dead end. Jon's cousin, Tony Bongiovi, part-owner of the Power Station, a well-known New York City recording studio, gave him a job sweeping floors. The perks of the position included rubbing elbows with Rolling Stone Mick Jagger and pop star David Bowie and recording demo tapes with professional back-up bands during non-peak hours. During this period, Jon attempted to interest record companies in his music, with little success.

"Runaway" Kicked off Career

In 1982 one of Jon's demo songs, "Runaway," became a surprise hit following local radio airplay of a compilation album featuring amateur groups. Soon thereafter, the budding rock star was signed by Mercury Records, a division of PolyGram, and suddenly found himself in need of a permanent band. He assembled some of his early Jersey Shore mates—Tico Torres, Dave Bryan, Alec John Such, and Dave Sabo, who was eventually replaced by Richie Sambora—as The Wild Ones and watched Mercury turn "Runaway" into a national hit. Properly marketing the band, which had since become simply Bongiovi, was critical to Mercury executives, who insisted on a spelling change to minimize what they apparently deemed the too-Italian character of Jon Bon Jovi's surname. Thus was born the phoneticized Bon Jovi; the singer took this opportunity to change his name as well. Though the band would develop a strong group identity, Mercury did not offer Torres, Bryan, Such, and Sambora a contract, effectively making them Jon's employees.

In 1984 the group released its first album, *Bon Jovi*, and began touring as the opening act for established acts such as .38 Special, Ted Nugent, Eddie Money, Judas Priest, and ZZ Top. As his ensemble began to enjoy coast-to-coast attention, Jon Bon Jovi landed in the middle of lawsuit brought by his cousin Tony, who claimed to have advanced Jon's career and now wanted payment for his efforts. The suit was settled out of court, with Tony Bongiovi winning a producer's credit, cash award, and royalties on the group's first release—as well as a one percent royalty on the next two albums. This infuriated Jon, who considered

Tony's influence minimal at best. Despite the legal wrangling, the first album sold well and laid the groundwork for the band's basic sound: a big beat with catchy lyrics.

Bon Jovi was quickly followed in 1985 by *7800 Fahrenheit*—the melting point of rock—which achieved platinum sales in 1987. Though critics were generally unimpressed with the band and considered them more "fluff" than "stuff," the teenage crowd couldn't get enough of them. "The whole younger rock movement was in dire need of someone to come along and be a superstar," national radio programmer Fred Jacobs explained to the *Detroit Free Press,* elaborating, "The pop ranks have had so many people in the past few years … but the young rockers really haven't had anybody to get them into the arenas and throw their fists in the air and get nuts about."

Slippery **Breakthrough**

In 1986, *Slippery When Wet,* Bon Jovi's third and best-selling album to date was released to largely positive reviews. Audiences savored the combination of heavy metal guitar crunch and upbeat lyrics. With singles like "You Give Love a Bad Name," "Living on a Prayer," and "Wanted Dead or Alive," the band had reached a new plateau of success. This was due, in part, to the increasing prominence of music videos, which allowed for superior marketing of the "videogenic" quintet. "Nobody knew what Bon Jovi was," guitarist Richie Sambora later told the *Detroit Free Press.* "It could've been a spaghetti or a jeans company for all they knew. We said, 'No actors, no actresses, no concept. We're going for simplicity. Just come and film us live, at a show.' All of a sudden, Bon Jovi became Bon Jovi. It was clearly defined. What's Bon Jovi? It's a rock 'n' roll band."

Sambora also attributed the album's success to the group's ability to fill a niche in the music business. "There was a need by the people for a Bon Jovi," he said in a 1989 *Rolling Stone* interview, echoing radio programmer Jacobs. "Just a good-time entertainment band, you know? A bridge between [pop crooner] Phil Collins and [hard rock outfit] Whitesnake." Despite this confidence, the group was ill prepared for their emerging superstar status and experienced some growing pains. "With the first two albums, we were happy to have enough money to go to McDonald's," Jon Bon Jovi told Edna Gundersen of *USA Today.* "We went through the phase of buy, buy, buy!," he continued. "It's hard to grow up when that kind of success is thrust upon you."

But grow up they did. The band embarked on a grueling world tour to promote *Slippery When Wet,* which had reached number one on the album charts, then immediately launched into writing and recording

its follow-up, *New Jersey,* released in 1988. That album generated more hits, including "Lay Your Hands on Me," "Bad Medicine," "I'll Be There for You," and "Blood on Blood," ultimately reaching number one. *High Fidelity's* Ken Richardson wrote of the album, "The first ten minutes are absolutely thrilling: 'Lay Your Hands on Me' proves the band *can* play undiluted metal, and 'Bad Medicine' proves it can add some of that mean streak to its pop sense."

New Jersey was the first American album released on the former-U.S.S.R.'s state-owned record company Melodiya, a move that prompted Bon Jovi to visit the Soviet Union during the its 16-month tour. Though completely unintentional, Jon Bon Jovi took some flak on the home front for naming the album after his home state as it was perceived as a jab at Bruce Springsteen. "I went to hell for calling the album *New Jersey,*" he groused in the *Chicago Tribune.* "Springsteen owns the state. Somewhere along the line, when nobody was looking, he bought it."

The band would not release another album for four years—an eternity in pop music; rumors abounded that the group was on the verge of splitting. The band members were, in fact, suffering from severe burnout, the result of virtually non-stop recording and touring. "For years we spent every waking moment together, even vacations," said Sambora in a 1992 article in *USA Today.* "People thought we were crazy to live, eat and breathe this band. We needed to get away from each other."

During the self-imposed hiatus from 1989 to 1991, both Sambora and Jon Bon Jovi released solo albums. Jon's *Blaze of Glory* (1990), a collection of songs written for or inspired by the western *Young Guns II,* delivered tumbleweed authenticity but didn't overwhelm critics. The title track was "a slow, dusty clone of 'Wanted Dead or Alive,'" according to *People's* Craig Tomashoff. Greg Sandow of *Entertainment Weekly* called it "thin if you don't share his cowboy thang" and rated it a C+. Sambora's solo album, *Stranger in This Town* (1991), fared only marginally better with Sandow, who awarded it a B-, remarking, "Gotta love Richie Sambora's solo meditations for their brooding mood. But only a few of the songs stand out."

New Maturity

Several significant events in Jon Bon Jovi's life occurred during the break from the band: In 1989 he married his girlfriend of ten years, Dorothea Hurley; two years later he started his own label, Jambco Records, and produced albums for Aldo Nova and Billy Falcon, as well as producing and co-writing songs for Cher, Stevie Nicks, and Hall & Oates. He and Sambora also set off on a two-week cross-country motorcycle trip that would significantly affect their creative juices;

formerly apolitical, the two observed some of the country's social ailments first-hand and decided to incorporate awareness-raising messages into their next album, thereby displaying a new maturity. On the image front, Jon Bon Jovi revamped his style by cutting his trademark dirty-blond tangle of hair; the result was a more contemporary look for the matinee-idol-handsome heartthrob.

Although 1992's much-anticipated *Keep the Faith* debuted at number five on the *Billboard* charts, the fully rested Bon Jovi were concerned about the album's long-term prospects. Much had changed on the hard rock scene since the success of *New Jersey,* with Seattle's so-called "grunge" bands Soundgarden, Pearl Jam, and Nirvana riding an unprecedented alternative-rock wave of popularity. Undeterred, Jon Bon Jovi faced this challenge head-on, dismissing long-time manager Doc McGhee and undertaking management of the band himself.

"Success is a funny thing," he told Roy Trakin in a 1993 *Music Express* interview. "I enjoyed it, but no one seemed to care for the five of us the way they cared about keeping the machine running. By the time the *New Jersey* tour was over, nobody even said goodbye to one another." "We're on our own now," he continued. "It's five grown-up guys who are supporting ourselves with no one to congratulate or blame but ourselves.... This is our turn on the firing line, and we'll see what comes of it."

Critical reaction to *Keep the Faith* was lukewarm despite a major publicity effort by Mercury. *Spin*'s Eddy called "Dry County," inspired by Jon's motorcycle trek to California, "[an] interminable opus about economic depression in a hamlet where booze is illegal." Of "Bed of Roses"—which nonetheless became a hit—Eddy wrote, "Sounds like Billy Joel—a vodka-soaked holy-ghost piano waltz." Yet *Rolling Stone* praised "I'll Sleep When I'm Dead," assessing, "This booming combination of hammerhead vocal hooks and weekend-warrior hedonism is classic Bon Jovi. If Jon and the boys didn't invent this sure-shot formula, they certainly own the patent."

Though not the smash of their former efforts, *Keep the Faith* seemed to satisfy fans, and Jon Bon Jovi was confident that the band's core group of admirers would truly "keep the faith." Criticism in some circles that he had "sold out" to commercial interests led the rock veteran to respond in *USA Today:* "For the first time I'm not impressed with money or numbers. I got wiser and I learned to deal with success.... I can take valid criticism very easily, but not from a gunslinger out to beat me up before he even listens to the album. There are certain critics in the world who aren't ever going to like me no matter what. What can I do? I'm not out to make them happy."

Continued Success

Hoping to capitalize on the release of their multiplatinum-selling greatest hits collection entitled *Cross Road*, Bon Jovi released *These Days* in 1995. The album featured the lead single "This Ain't A Love Song," "Diamond Ring, " an acoustic ballad, and "Something for the Pain," a true rock song. "I think it's the most introspective record we've done," Jon Bon Jovi told *Billboard* in 1995. The group toured widely in support of the album, including three sold-out shows at Wembley Stadium in London, England. The year 2000 saw the release of *Crush*, the group's first album for Island/Def Jam Music Group after the label subsumed Mercury Records in a merger between Universal/PolyGram. David E. Thigpen of *Time* called the album "a piece of vintage '90s pop-metal, as straightforward as a stretch of the New Jersey Turnpike." Though not the blockbuster success of *Slippery When Wet,* the album was certified multiplatinum in 2001.

Jon Bon Jovi has enjoyed a budding career as an actor, appearing in such films as *Moonlight and Valentino* in 1995, *Destination Anywhere* in 1997, *Homegrown* in 1998, *U-571* in 2000, and *Pay It Forward* in 2001. He and Sambora continue to build successful solo careers, and Torres has looked beyond the stage to find success as an artist and as the creator of a baby clothing line called Rock Star Baby.

Selected discography

Bon Jovi, Mercury, 1984.
7800 Fahrenheit, Mercury, 1985.
Slippery When Wet, Mercury, 1986.
New Jersey, Mercury, 1988.
Keep the Faith, Mercury, 1992.
Cross Road, Mercury, 1994.
These Days, Mercury, 1995.
Crush, Island/Mercury, 2000.
One Wild Night: Live 1985-2001, Universal, 2001.

Sources

Periodicals

Billboard, June 12, 1993; May 20, 1995; May 13, 2000.
Chicago Tribune, March 19, 1989.
Detroit Free Press, March 8, 1987; May 25, 1987.
Entertainment Weekly, December 11, 1992.
High Fidelity, January 1989.
Interview, December 1990.
Music Express, January 1993.
People, October 1, 1990; November 30, 1998.
Rolling Stone, November 20, 1986; February 9, 1989, December 10, 1992.
Spin, January 1993.

Time, June 26, 2000, p. 74.
USA Today, November 9, 1992.

Online

"Bon Jovi," *RollingStone.com,* http://www.rollingstone.com (August 13, 2001).

Bon Jovi Official Website, http://www.bonjovi.com (August 13, 2001).

Internet Movie Database, http://www.imdb.com (August 30, 2001).

Recording Industry of America, http://www.riaa.com (August 13, 2001).

Additional information for this profile was obtained from Jambco/PolyGram Records, 1992.

—Mary Scott Dye

Buckethead

Guitarist

The experimental guitarist known as Buckethead is shrouded in such a self-perpetuated mystery that no publicist or record label truly knows the musician. Also known as Brian Carroll, the guitar guru even speaks about Buckethead in the third person. Buckethead's own website offers no more of a clue to the identity of the "masked, inverted KFC-bucket wearing 'mutant guitar virtuoso.'" Carroll has turned his obsession with horror films, martial arts, and robots into a stage persona that gives him the freedom to play the high-speed, highly technical guitar music he loves. As the masked Buckethead, he creates an "alternative mental universe" onstage, according to Joel Selvin of the *San Francisco Chronicle*.

Buckethead's website states that he was "raised in a chicken coop by chickens," but suburban Los Angeles, California, is closer to the truth. As a child, Carroll grew up fascinated with horror films, martial arts, classical music theory, heavy metal music, and Disneyland—which he claims to have visited over 500 times. He took karate lessons from the age of ten, and the walls of his childhood bedroom were plastered with posters of Bruce Lee, Michael Jackson, and *The Texas Chainsaw Massacre*'s Leatherface. His bookshelf was loaded with books on Niccolo Paganini, Nicolas Slonimsky, Glenn Gould, and magic. He also collected robot toys. James Rotondi noted in *Guitar Player* that it seemed Buckethead's visual obsessions and collecting have as much to do with his playing style as any musical influence or his study of classical theory. Buckethead picked up the guitar by the time he was 13 years old,

inspired by AC/DC's Angus Young and Black Sabbath's Randy Rhoads. Though he liked playing sports, he was drawn to guitar "because it was something you could do all by yourself," he told Rotondi.

Watching Buckethead play in his highly technical style at a breakneck pace "is humbling," Rotondi wrote. "But he makes it look incredibly easy, as if technical wizardry were second nature." It may be second nature to him, but Buckethead developed his own talent by keenly observing the intricate details of guitar masters' playing styles and then mimicking them. He also studied a great range of highly technical classical texts, including Slonimsky's *Thesaurus of Scales and Melodic Patterns,* as well as country music instructional books and videos. In addition to reading, listening, and watching, Buckethead took lessons with guitar virtuoso Paul Gilbert of Mr. Bigs. He honed his technique, right-hand/left-hand independence and theory, with classical guitar studies. Ultimately, Buckethead turned away from the study of guitar to his own experimentation with it. "Taking people away in their imaginations is a lot more important to Buckethead than freaking people out with the guitar.... He never thinks about scales or techniques," he told Joe Gore in *Guitar Player*.

Buckethead's sound may be just as difficult to categorize. Heavy metal and funk play heavily in Buckethead's work, but as his website biography states, he is as comfortable "chicken country pickin'" as he is "recreating the sound of a roller coaster with his guitar." He claims many of his songs are conceived as soundtracks for thrill rides at his imaginary amusement park, Bucketheadland. He has cited his influences as varied—from Paul Gilbert, fusion guitarist Shawn Lane, and Swedish technical guitar whiz Yngwie Malmsteen, to Angus Young from AC/DC, 1970s funk guitarist Bootsy Collins, and Michael Jackson, an influence on Buckethead's stage moves.

In 1989, after watching the horror film *Halloween IV,* the young guitarist sought out a mask like the one worn in the movie by the character Michael Myers. The local store he went to had a similar white mask, which Carroll liked just as much. Also that same evening, his father brought a bucket of fried chicken home for dinner. In a moment of inspiration, Carroll donned the mask and turned the bucket upside down on his head, looked in the mirror, and Buckethead was born. "It was just one of those things" he told Rotondi. "After that, I wanted to be that thing all the time." The Buckethead guise seemed like a perfect fit for Carroll's unique playing style and allowed him to play more freely. "I thought it made sense with the way I play" he continued. "I play all this weird stuff, but if I just look like me, it just isn't going to work. But if I'm, like, this weird freak.... It opened the door to endless possibilities."

The alter ego is a source of tremendous freedom for Carroll and another way to keep his childhood loves

For the Record . . .

Born Brian Carroll c. 1969.

Created Buckethead persona, 1989; introduced Buckethead with the Deli Creeps, early 1990s; recorded *Transmutation (Mutatis Mutandis)* with Praxis, 1992; recorded solo debut, *Bucketheadland,* produced by Bootsy Collins, 1992; released *Dreamatorium* as Death Cube K, and *Sacrifist* with Praxis, 1994; released *Metatron* with Praxis, 1995; released *Day of the Robot,* 1996; released *Disembodied* as Death Cube K and *Plays Disney,* 1997; released *Colma,* 1998; released *Monsters & Robots,* 1999; played on Guns n' Roses reunion tour, 2000; released *Somewhere Over the Slaughterhouse,* 2001.

Addresses: *Record company*—Stray Records, 4430 Telegraph Ave., PMB 72, Oakland CA 94609. *Website*—Buckethead Official Website: http://www.bucket headland.com.

In 1994 Buckethead released *Dreamatorium* under the moniker Death Cube K, which is an anagram for Buckethead, with Bill Laswell. "The album was a dark, quasi-ambient duet with Laswell that highlighted his cinematic flair, clean-toned melancholy and improvisational sensitivity," Rotondi wrote. Buckethead told Gore that the album was full of "weird ambient stuff, real stark and scary." For the guitarist, the improvisational freedom he has while recording is the result of lots of practice. He likened it to shooting so many baskets in basketball practice that at game time, the player has the control to shoot without much thought.

In addition to his solo work, Buckethead's involvement with countless projects and other musicians has been another form of study for him. He has recorded with Giant Robot, Cobra Strike, Arcana, and El Stew, and formed his own group, GR2. In 2000, he played guitar on the Guns n' Roses reunion tour. Just a few of his guest appearances include 1993's *Octave of the Holy* with jazz bassist Jonas Hellborg and drummer Michael Shrieve, Henry Kaiser's *Hope You Like Our New Direction,* Anton Fier's *Dreamspeed,* Bootsy Collins' *Zillatron,* Will Ackerman's *The Opening of Doors,* Derek Bailey and John Zorn's *Company 91,* the Axiom *Funkcronomicon* collection, and Jon Hassell's *Dressing for Pleasure.* He has also contributed to various movie soundtracks and scores, including *The Last Action Hero, Mighty Morphin' Power Rangers: The Movie, Beverly Hills Ninja,* and both *Mortal Kombat* films.

Selected discography

As Buckethead

Bucketheadland, Avant, 1992.
Giant Robot, Sony Japan, 1994.
Day of the Robot, Subharmonic, 1996.
Plays Disney, Avant, 1997.
Colma, CyberOctave, 1998.
Monsters & Robots, EMI, 1999.
Somewhere Over the Slaughterhouse, Stray, 2001.

As Death Cube K

Dreamatorium, Strata, 1994.
Disembodied, Ion, 1997.
Tunnel, TDRSmusic, 1999.

As Giant Robot

Giant Robot, NTT Records, 1996.

With Praxis

Transmutation (Mutatis Mutandis), Axiom, 1992.
Sacrifist, Subharmonic, 1994.
Metatron, Subharmonic, 1995.
Transmutation Live, Douglas, 1998.

alive in his music. "I can work anything into that character and make it totally work: all the things I love in my life, like Disney, Giant Robot, Texas Chainsaw," he told Rotondi. "Even though I'm wearing a mask and have a character, it's more real, more about what I'm really like, because I'm too shy to let a lot of things out. Every reason I became Buckethead and am Buckethead has to do with the way I live. It's not because I thought it'd be successful. I never use anything that isn't part of what I really loved as a child or love right now."

It was with the band the Deli Creeps that Carroll introduced Buckethead. It was his first band to gain notoriety in the San Francisco Bay Area. The group disbanded soon after forming, though the members re-formed briefly in 1996. Buckethead made his major label debut in 1992 as a member of the band Praxis. After getting a copy of one of Buckethead's homemade videos, legendary Parliament/Funkadelic (P-funk) guitarist Bootsy Collins, with fellow P-Funk member Bernie Worrell on keyboards, became part of the first Praxis ensemble. The group debuted in 1992 with the Bill Laswell-produced release, *Transmutation.* Praxis would release five more albums, including *Sacrifist* in 1994, *Metatron* in 1995, and three live and collection albums. Collins became a frequent collaborator and produced Buckethead's first solo album, *Bucketheadland.*

Collection, Douglas, 1998.
Warszawa, InnerRhythmic, 1999.

Sources

Periodicals

Guitar Player, June 1994, p. 45; November 1996, p. 92.
Los Angeles Times, April 24, 2000, p. F-5.
San Francisco Chronicle, April 13, 1997, p. 52.
Washington Post, November 12, 1999, p. N07.

Online

"Buckethead," *All Music Guide,* http://www.allmusic.com (May 31, 2001).
Buckethead Official Website, http://www.bucketheadland.com (May 31, 2001).

—*Brenna Sanchez*

Buckwheat Zydeco

Instrumentalist, singer

The renewed interest in zydeco music owes much to Stanley "Buckwheat Zydeco" Dural, who worked with one of the genre's masters before forming his own group, Buckwheat Zydeco and the Ils Sont Partis Band, in 1979. Within a few years, Dural had become the first zydeco artist to be signed by a major label, Island Records, and during the 1990s, he played at major events including the closing ceremonies of the 1996 Summer Olympics in Atlanta, Georgia, and both of President Bill Clinton's inaugural celebrations. Despite the mainstream acceptance of zydeco music, however, Dural has continued to insist on preserving its cultural integrity as a distinct, although eclectic, genre. "If you're calling it a Cajun band, or you're calling it a jazz band, then you have the wrong people performing for you," Dural told Michael Tisserand in his book, *The Kingdom of Zydeco.* "You see, I didn't come this far saying that I'm somebody I'm not. And if you don't have that identity, man, you're just lost."

Born on November 14, 1947, Stanley Joseph Dural, Jr. was the fourth of thirteen children in the Dural family. His parents farmed around the Lafayette, Louisiana area, and young Dural had numerous jobs before he reached his teens. In addition to working as a delivery boy, catching crawfish, and raising chickens, he also

For the Record . . .

Born Stanley Joseph Dural, Jr. on November 14, 1947, in Lafayette, LA.

Played the piano professionally as a teenager; led Buckwheat and the Hitchhikers band, 1971-76; switched to the accordion, formed Buckwheat Zydeco and the Ils Sont Partis Band, 1979; released several albums of zydeco music, 1980s–1990s; established Tomorrow Recordings, 1999.

Addresses: *Record company*—Tomorrow Recordings, P.O. Box 561, Rhinebeck, NY 12572. *Website*—Buckwheat Zydeco Official Website: http://www.buckwheat zydeco.com.

picked cotton with his family in the fields where he picked up some of the traditional songs of his French-speaking Creole elders. Although the term Creole had first been applied to the descendants of European immigrants to southern Louisiana during the eighteenth century, over time it came to denote inhabitants with predominantly African and French origins. In contrast, Cajun inhabitants traced their ancestry to the Acadians expelled from Nova Scotia, Canada, by British authorities in 1755 who were furious over the Acadians' refusal to ally with them in their colonial wars with the French and local indigenous tribes. Many of the exiled Acadians eventually settled in Louisiana where they became known as "Cajuns." Like the Creoles, Cajuns were primarily working-class people who preserved their French heritage, particularly the French language, over succeeding generations. Although the two groups shared many cultural traits in their southern Louisiana home, however, differences of race often kept them apart.

For Creoles and Cajuns alike, the urban center of the region was not New Orleans, but the smaller city of Lafayette, about 80 miles to the west. There were a large number of music clubs around the city and its outlying districts, and Dural, having earned the nickname "Buckwheat" for his hair, which resembled that of the *Little Rascals* serial character, soon came to play in a number of them as a pianist. In fact, Dural was a professional piano player by the time he was ten years old, and in his teens played for his idol, Fats Domino, as well as for Little Richard and Ray Charles. Dural disappointed his father, however, by refusing to play the accordion, a traditional instrument in zydeco music and one that the elder Dural often played at home. "Me and my dad, we had a big problem," Dural told Tisser-

and. "He'd never been out to see me perform from the age of nine until 1979, because he didn't want me to play R&B…. And I was one of the biggest critics about accordion music, but I wouldn't tell that to him. In my generation, you don't tell that to your dad, man."

One of the chief reasons that Dural was so opposed to zydeco music was that he, like many other young Creoles, considered it a distinctly old-fashioned kind of music. Indeed, zydeco seemed to be losing ground in the era after World War II. For many, its traditional mix of African rhythms and simple instruments such as the accordion, fiddle, and washboard (or *frottoir*) played with spoons could not match the appeal of contemporary R&B and rock 'n' roll. One of the few musicians to forge ahead during the era was one of Dural's eventual mentors, Clifton Chenier, who happened to be a friend of Dural's father. Chenier was acknowledged as the "King of Zydeco" from the 1960s onward. He even claimed to have invented the term zydeco, a word derived from the traditional Creole song, "*Les haricots sont pas sales*" ("The snap-beans aren't salted"), that referred to the poverty that Creoles often endured. Whatever the true origins of the term, Chenier was its undisputed master, and when Dural agreed to play at a Chenier concert in 1976, it was a revelation to the young musician.

Dural had just dissolved his own 15-member funk band, Buckwheat and the Hitchhikers, and joined Chenier as a keyboardist for two years before taking up the accordion. In 1979, he felt that he had mastered the instrument and formed another band, Buckwheat Zydeco and the Ils Sont Partis Band, a term that loosely translates as "And they're off!," a typical comment from an announcer at the beginning of a horse race. Dural's timing was fortunate, as zydeco was just beginning to find an audience outside of its traditional home in Louisiana. "In October of seventy-nine I built the band, and between eighty and eighty-one I was touring Europe," he told Tisserand. The band quickly released two albums on small labels before joining Rounder Records in 1983. As one of the leading labels for roots, bluegrass, and folk-oriented music, Rounder helped familiarize the public with zydeco, and Dural gained two Grammy Award nominations for 1983's *Turning Point* and 1986's *Waitin' for My Ya-Ya*.

Zydeco became even trendier with the release of *The Big Easy* in 1987. The movie, starring Dennis Quaid as a Cajun detective, featured Dural and his band on its soundtrack and gave a huge boost to the interest in all things Cajun and Creole. Like many Creoles, however, Dural saw the rise in popularity of zydeco music as a mixed blessing as many of those who enjoyed the music assumed it was a Cajun tradition. Although the two musical types shared many common traits, they had grown increasingly distinct after World War II when Cajuns tended to listen to country-and-western music and Creoles tuned into R&B stations. As a result of these influences, zydeco bands emphasized the accordion while Cajun music favored the fiddle; while Cajuns sang more song lyrics in French, zydeco bands usually sang in English. Larger zydeco ensembles also added horn sections, electric guitars, and drums in addition to the accordion, washboard, and fiddle. Although his own music incorporated a range of contemporary influences, Dural nonetheless tried to raise awareness of the importance of these differences in order to preserve Creole culture. As he reflected to Tisserand after playing at the Atlanta Olympic Games, "I think our people here should put full force behind the artists and the culture, because that's what we live by. If it's bad, try to help it. If it's good, continue to push it. That's what I'm about."

Dural's status as a leading zydeco musician was confirmed with his signing to Island Records in 1986, the first such contract between a major label and a zydeco artist. His major-label debut, *On a Night Like This* in 1987, featured some traditional zydeco tunes in addition to covers of rock songs, including the title track by Bob Dylan. "This album is different than anything else I ever did before," Dural told Ben Sandmel for his book *Zydeco!* "This one has more of a mixture, mixing in some pop and R&B, more of a 'now generation' thing, but there's traditional zydeco, too." Dural also changed his recording habits for the album, taking a week to rehearse the material with his band before entering the studio; in the past, they had simply shown up and began recording. "You can hear the difference. They took time with the setup and the recording too," he told Sandmel. "The sound quality is a lot better, and I like that."

Buckwheat Zydeco continued to release albums throughout the 1990s on several different labels, often suffering from record company mergers and buyouts. In 1998, frustrated at the constant turnover in the music industry, Dural formed his own label, Tomorrow Recordings, and immediately reissued the band's 1997 album *Trouble* as its first release. With "ten tracks of propulsive, rollicking dance party music," *People* welcomed the album as a "swamp-boogie joy ride," a sentiment that was common among reviewers of the band's work. In 1999, Tomorrow Recordings released *The Buckwheat Zydeco Story: A 20-Year Party* in honor of the band's two decades of music. The band also remained a favorite on the concert circuit, playing with everyone from Eric Clapton to U2.

Selected discography

One for the Road, Paula/Flyright, 1979.
100% Fortified Zydeco, Black Top, 1983.
Turning Point, Rounder, 1983.
Waitin' for My Ya-Ya, Rounder, 1986.
Buckwheat Zydeco Party, Rounder, 1987.
On a Night Like This, Island, 1987.
Ils Sont Partis, Blues, 1988.
Taking It Home, PolyGram, 1988.
Zydeco Party, Rounder, 1988.
Where There's Smoke There's Fire, Island, 1990.
On Track, Charisma, 1992.
Five Card Stud, PolyGram, 1994.
Trouble, Atlantic, 1997.
The Buckwheat Zydeco Story: A 20-Year Party, Tomorrow, 1999.
Down Home Live, Tomorrow, 2001.

Sources

Books

Broughton, Simon, et al., editors, *World Music: The Rough Guide Volume 2,* The Rough Guides Ltd., 1999.
Morton, Desmond, *A Short History of Canada: Fifth Edition,* McClelland and Stewart, Ltd., 2000.
Sandmel, Ben, with Rick Olivier, *Zydeco!,* University Press of Mississippi, 1999.
Tisserand, Michael, *The Kingdom of Zydeco,* Arcade Publishing, 1998.

Periodicals

Billboard, November 28, 1998, p. 55.
Kansas City Star, February 26, 2001.
New Orleans Magazine, October 1998, p. 42; January 2000, p. 32.
People, January 25, 1999, p. 39.
Rolling Stone, March 19, 1992, p. 92.

Online

Buckwheat Zydeco Official Website, http://www.buckwheat zydeco.com (July 4, 2001).

—Timothy Borden

R. L. Burnside

Guitarist

Guitarist R.L. Burnside became a pivotal figure on the contemporary blues scene during the early 1990s after more than 40 years as a musician. His albums on the Fat Possum label, including *Bad Luck City* in 1991 and *Too Bad Jim* in 1994, created a raw, edgy blues that purists loved. "Both recordings also adequately capture the feeling of what it must be like to be in Junior Kimbrough's juke joint," wrote Richard Skelly of *All Music Guide,* "where both men have been playing this kind of raw, unadulterated blues for over 30 years." By the mid 1990s, however, Burnside also showed himself willing to experiment. He recorded and toured with the Jon Spencer Blues Explosion, generating the blues-meets-industrial rock of *A Ass Pocket of Whiskey* in 1996. The album, along with the techno-tinged release *Come on In* in 1998, had the effect of alienating older fans while attracting younger ones. Through it all, Burnside stayed above the fray by sticking to what he does best: writing songs, singing, and playing the guitar.

It took more than 40 years for Burnside's musical career to start in earnest. Born on November 23, 1926, in Mississippi, Burnside worked as a sharecropper on a small farm as a young man. He attempted to play the harmonica but never quite mastered it. At the age of 16

Born Robert Lee Burnside on November 23, 1926, in Mississippi; married Alice Mae Taylor, 1949; children: eight sons, four daughters.

Began playing guitar, age 16; started performing publicly, age 21; left Mississippi, traveling to Chicago and Memphis, mid 1940s; returned to Mississippi to work as a sharecropper and commercial fisherman, playing music on weekends, 1950s; recorded by George Mitchell of Arhoolie Records, 1967; toured Canada, 1969; performed with Sound Machine, 1970s-1980s; signed to Fat Possum Records, recorded *Bad Luck City*, 1991; released *Too Bad Jim*, 1994; recorded *A Ass Pocket of Whiskey* with the Jon Spencer Blues Explosion, 1996; worked with producer Tom Rothrock on *Come on In*, 1998; released *Wish I Was in Heaven Sitting Down*, 2000; released *Well Well Well* and *Burnside on Burnside*, 2001.

Addresses: *Record company*—Fat Possum Records, P.O. Box 1923, Oxford, MS 38655-1923, (662) 473-9994, website: http://www.fatpossum.com.

he began playing guitar, and by 21, he began performing in public. Burnside's father played guitar, but his biggest influences came from local players like Rainie Burnette and Jesse Vortis. His principal influence, however, was Fred McDowell. "He [McDowell] was a big influence on me," Burnside told Ed Mabe of Perfect Sound Forever online. "He started me. I watched him and he was the first guy I saw play the blues."

Despite Burnside's love of music, there were few opportunities to turn music into a paying occupation. Discouraged with his life as a sharecropper, Burnside moved to Chicago in the mid 1940s. There he lived with his father who had also moved to the city. Though he had put his guitar aside at the time, Burnside nonetheless absorbed the intoxicating sounds of his new environment. He also met Muddy Waters, who had married his first cousin. "I was working during the day at the foundry," he recalled to Kenny Brown of Blues on Stage online, "and every night I'd go over to Muddy's. We only lived a couple of blocks apart." He also caught Waters' Friday night show at the Zanzibar and frequented Mackerel Street on Sundays to hear players like Little Walter, Jimmy Rogers, and Chuck Berry. Tragically, within a year of each other, Burnside's father, uncle, and two brothers were murdered in

the late 1940s. Burnside chronicles the losses on *Wish I Was in Heaven Sitting Down*. Burnside married Alice Mae Taylor in 1949; the couple had 12 children.

After returning to Mississippi in 1959, Burnside began performing at house parties and juke joints, building a local reputation. "They pay about $15 or $10 for you to play all night," Burnside told Marian Montgomery of *Rolling Stone*. "Course you get all the whiskey you want!" He usually played electric guitar because of the excessive noise in the juke joints, but when George Mitchell of Arhoolie Records recorded him in 1967, Burnside's regular guitar was broken and he played an acoustic model. Because of this, Burnside would be incorrectly categorized as a solo country blues player for a number of years. The recording, however, did give the bluesman much needed exposure outside of Mississippi. In 1969, Burnside embarked on his first tour in Montreal, Canada.

During the 1970s and 1980s, Burnside played with Sound Machine, a band consisting of two of his sons, Joseph and Daniel, and then son-in-law Calvin Jackson. His real break would have to wait until the early 1990s, though, when he was featured in former *New York Times* critic Robert Palmer's documentary, *Deep Blues*. Tony Nassar of the Manhattan Blues Alliance online recalled seeing the film: "They find him [Burnside] living in the kind of poverty most people can only imagine. He brings his old St. Louis Music electric guitar onto the porch of his shack (there is no other word) and launches into the hypnotic, droning "Jumper on the Line." Instantly, everyone in the movie theater must have begun tapping his or her foot."

On Palmer's advice, Matthew Johnson of the fledgling Fat Possum Records sought Burnside out and signed him. In 1991, with Palmer onboard as producer, *Bad Luck City* was released. Critics warmly embraced *Bad Luck City* and its follow-up, *Too Bad Jim*, in 1994. This was down and dirty jukebox blues, deeply felt, and music a listener could dance to. "R.L. Burnside lays down some of the most funky, low down blues coming out of the Delta these days," wrote the Delta Boogie online. *Too Bad Jim* became one of the most influential blues albums of the 1990s. The music was raw and at times unrehearsed, giving it an immediacy lacking on heavily polished blues albums. "This is unfussy music, hell, it's sloppy in the best way," Nassar noted. Along with artists like Junior Kimbrough, Burnside proved that 1940s and 1950s juke joint blues still had the power to speak to contemporary listeners.

Too Bad Jim also brought Burnside to the attention of Jon Spencer of the Jon Spencer Blues Explosion. These seemingly incongruous players, a bluesman born in the 1920s and a post-punk indie band, joined forces in 1996 to make a record. *A Ass Pocket of Whiskey* retained the raw, edginess of the earlier Burnside recordings while adding a heavy dose of industrial rock. Some critics loved it. "This is the real stuff—raw, urgent, humorous and spiritual...," wrote George H. Lewis of Popular Music and Society online. Others disliked the change, believing that Jon Spencer's brashness mocked the blues form. The release of *Come on In* in 1998, complete with trip-hop rhythms provided by producer Tom Rothrock (who also produced Beck's first album), only furthered the controversy for purists. These albums and the video for "Let My Baby Ride," however, also introduced Burnside to a younger audience.

While his latest releases have been more traditional and are less likely to end up on MTV, Burnside continues to receive exposure from "It's Bad You Know," featured on the television series *The Sopranos*. Burnside doesn't seem to worry about these controversies but keeps to what he does best: playing the blues. His no nonsense approach, coupled with his willingness to experiment, has offered a road map for revitalizing the blues for the next generation. Burnside also continues influencing the next generation by touring and releasing a steady stream of new albums, spreading the gospel of the blues and certifying himself as its emissary. "I listen to a lot of ... music but I always just stay with the blues," he told Mabe. "It's all the roots of music. That's where all the music started from, the blues. And we got to try to keep 'em alive."

Selected discography

Bad Luck City, Fat Possum, 1991.
Deep Blues (soundtrack), Atlantic, 1992.
Too Bad Jim, Fat Possum, 1994.
A Ass Pocket of Whiskey, Matador, 1996.
Mr. Wizard, Fat Possum, 1997.
Come on In, Epitaph, 1998.
Wish I Was in Heaven Sitting Down, Fat Possum, 2000.
Well Well Well, M.C., 2001.
Burnside on Burnside, Fat Possum, 2001.

Sources

Books

Rucker, Leland, editor, *MusicHound Blues: The Essential Album Guide,* Visible Ink Press, 1998.

Periodicals

Austin American-Statesman, November 30, 2000.
Dallas Morning News, December 1, 2000.
Interview, December 2000.
Los Angeles Times, October 21, 2000.
Seattle Post-Intelligencer, January 19, 2001.

Online

"A Ass Pocket of Whiskey," Popular Music and Society, http://www.findarticles.com (June 27, 2001).
"R.L. Burnside," *All Music Guide,* http://www.allmusic.com (June 6, 2001).
"R.L. Burnside," Manhattan Blues Alliance, http://www.frontiernet.net/~nycblues/reviewsnf.html#burn (June 25, 2001).
"R.L. Burnside & Kenny Brown at The Minnesota Zoo, August 1, 1998," Blues on Stage, http://www.geocities.com/BourbonStreet/Delta/1915/burnside-intv.html (June 25, 2001).
"R.L. Burnside Not Ready for Heaven Yet," *Rolling Stone.com,* http://www.rollingstone.com (June 25, 2001).
"RL Burnside: One Bad-Ass Bluesman," Perfect Sound Forever, http://www.furious.com/perfect/rlburnside.html (June 6, 2001).
"R.L. Burnside—Too Bad Jim," Delta Boogie, http://www.deltaboogie.com (June 27, 2001).

—*Ronnie D. Lankford, Jr.*

José Carreras

Opera singer

The tenor voice "has always electrified operagoers more than any other kind of voice, male or female," José Carreras asserted, as quoted by Helena Matheopoulos in *Divo: Great Tenors, Baritones, and Basses Discuss Their Roles.* "Something about the physical qualities of this sound and of its vibrations, to say nothing of those high notes at the top of the register, seem to arouse an instant, visceral excitement in the audience." Judging from critical and popular reactions, since early in his career Carreras has easily validated this belief. In a 1978 article for the *New York Times,* John Gruen attested to Carreras' "aura of immediacy and theatrical credibility," a product of his "superior voice of lyric, verging on dramatic, quality [and] romantic good looks which invariably enhance any role he undertakes." But as Carreras' career and life progressed, his dominant human spirit, exemplified in his life story of triumph followed by tragedy followed by triumph again, informed his various stage personas and was communicated to his receptive audiences. After more than 60 operatic roles and 150 recordings, Carreras remains one of opera's brightest stars.

Carreras was born in on December 5, 1946, in Barcelona, Spain, then a country ravaged by World War II and oppressed by the fascist Francisco Franco government. Carreras' family was poverty-stricken—his father had been a teacher before the Spanish Civil War but lost his position due to his Republican loyalties. When Carreras was seven years old, he saw a film about the great Italian operatic tenor Enrico Caruso that made a lasting impression on him. After listening to their son's constant imitation of Caruso, Carreras' non-musical parents realized the young boy's potential and enrolled him in the Barcelona Conservatory where, for eight years, he studied music in addition to a traditional curriculum. Afterward, Carreras entered the University of Barcelona to pursue a career in chemistry, concurrently beginning voice lessons with a non-professional, Jaime Francisco Puig. Carreras left the university after only two years, however, deciding to return to the Barcelona Conservatory to continue musical studies. Puig remained his only vocal instructor.

Luck and Hard Work

These dramatic career moves might have proven unsuccessful for an average individual, but given Carreras' "talent, drive, ambition, and ... professionalism," according to Gruen, he was able to attain his goal of becoming a professional opera singer. Gruen also commented on the way luck and the friendship of the Caballes—the famous soprano Montserrat and her manager/brother Carlos—provided the young Carreras with opportunities to prove his talent. Montserrat Caballe was so impressed by Carreras' debut opposite her in the 1970 Barcelona production of Gaetano Donizetti's *Lucrezia Borgia,* that she and her brother helped guide the young tenor's budding career.

Born José Maria Carreras Coll on December 5, 1946, in Barcelona, Spain; son of José Maria (a teacher and traffic policeman) and Maria Antonia (a hairdresser; maiden name, Coll) Carreras; married Mercedes, 1971; divorced, c. 1990; children: Alberto, Julia. *Education*: Attended Barcelona Conservatory, 1954-62; attended the University of Barcelona, c. 1963-64; studied voice with Jaime Francisco Puig, beginning c. 1963.

Professional operatic debut at the Liceo Opera House, Barcelona, Spain, as Gennaro in *Lucrezia Borgia*, 1970-71; made Italian debut at Parma as Rodolfo in *La Boheme*, 1971; American debut with the New York City Opera as Pinkerton in *Madama Butterfly*, 1972; London debut at Covent Garden as Alfredo in *La Traviata*, 1974; New York Metropolitan Opera debut as Cavaradossi in *Tosca*, 1974; La Scala, Milan, debut as Riccardo in *Un Ballo in Maschera*, 1975; other performances include Rodolfo in *Luisa Miller*, the Duke in *Rigoletto*, Edgardo in *Lucia di Lammermoor*, Romeo in *Romeo et Juliette*, Radames in *Aida*, Don José in *Carmen*, and roles in *Don Carlos* and *Andrea Chenier*; founded the International José Carreras Leukemia Foundation, 1988; first performance with Three Tenors, 1990; embarked on concert tour, served as musical director for Summer Olympics in Barcelona, Spain, 1992.

Awards: First place, Giuseppe Verdi Competition, Parma, Italy, 1971; Grammy Award, Best Classical Vocal Performance for *Carreras, Domingo, Pavarotti*, 1990; Prince of Asturias Award, 1991; Albert Schweitzer Music Award, 1996; other awards include Grand Prix du Disque, Academy of Paris; Luigi Illica Prize; Sir Lawrence Olivier Award; gold medal, New York Spanish Institute; gold medal, City Vienna; gold medal, His Majesty the King of Spain, City of Barcelona; International Emmy Award for video of *A Life Story*.

Addresses: *Record company*—Warner Classics/Atlantic Records, 1290 Avenue of the Americas, 27th Floor, New York, NY 10104, phone: (212) 707-2892, fax: (212) 405-5470.

In 1971 Carreras made his Italian debut singing the role of Rodolfo in composer Puccini's opera *La Boheme*; he also won the Giuseppe Verdi Competition held in Parma, Italy. The following year he made his American debut at the New York City Opera as Pinkerton in Puccini's *Madama Butterfly*. "Rodolfo, Cavaradossi, Alfredo, Edgardo, and the Duke in [Giuseppe Verdi's] *Rigoletto* followed. He then bowed at Covent Garden, Buenos Aires, and Vienna—all between 1973 and 1974. Over the next two years came the Met [New York Metropolitan Opera] and La Scala [Milan], and his fortune was made," Nancy Malitz recounted in *Ovation*. "His singing was natural, unaffected, disarmingly lyrical," wrote *New York Times* critic Theodore W. Libbey, Jr., explaining Carreras' sudden rise. "His voice had a lustrous sheen in the upper register, with flashes of fire that set it somehow, indefinably, apart." From recital recordings to operatic performances, Carreras continued his ascent.

More Dramatic Roles

Despite winning these accolades, however, Carreras explained to Matheopoulos in *Divo* that he "couldn't bear a boring career consisting of going around the world year after year with a repertoire of half a dozen roles even if I were to sing them near-perfectly." This desire for variety, coupled with a deepening change in voice that most tenors experience in their thirties, moved Carreras in the early 1980s into more dramatic roles. But a more important force that pushed him away from romantic hero parts to those in revolutionary, political settings, like Umberto Giordano's *Andrea Chenier*, was his father's political legacy. "Anything against justice—social justice, it is against myself. Anything against freedom or democracy, it is against myself, it's against society. So this is inside myself, this character," Carreras explained in *José Carreras: A Life Story*, a television biography produced for London Weekend Television.

Beginning in the mid 1980s, Carreras explored the repertoire of popular music, and it marked the first time he received widespread negative criticism. Although a commercial success, the 1985 recording of Leonard Bernstein's *West Side Story*, with its casting of operatic stars Kiri Te Kanawa and Carreras in the lead roles, was faulted by critics. The *New Republic*'s Edward Rothstein dismissed Carreras' venture, saying Carreras "lets nothing come through his singing other than the fact of his studied singing." While subsequent recordings by Carreras in the popular genre received mixed reactions as well, his operatic performances continued to earn almost unanimous support.

Diagnosed with Leukemia

On July 15, 1987, when "he was at the height of his career, possessed of an instantly recognizable, warm and lustrous voice that he commanded with ravishing delicacy and musical intelligence," as Malitz noted in *Ovation,* Carreras stopped singing. He was diagnosed with acute lymphocytic leukemia. For almost a year, Carreras underwent chemotherapy and bone marrow manipulation in an attempt to stop the disease. The treatment was ultimately successful, but many in the opera community worried that the effects of the disease might prevent him from fulfilling his destiny as one of the world's great tenors. Carreras, quoted in his television biography, dismissed concerns about such issues: "You see the other dimension in life. And then you have time to think much more about your spirit, about the spiritual side of your life, about God, about religion, about faith. And you can arrive to certain conclusions."

After his return to the stage in July of 1988, Carreras' voice displayed few scars. Instead, it carried a greater, deeper weight. Hilary Finch, writing for *Opera,* described a recital soon after his return: "The first sound of the raw, resurrected human voice leaping joyfully, two stairs at a time, up the rising lines of [Alessandro] Scarlatti's 'Gia il sole dal Gange' immediately cut through the cant. This was the *same* voice: highly strung in its inflection, lithe of movement, dusky in undertone, brilliant, if still driven, to the top. What had changed was the intensity of delivery and the urgency of communication."

In January of 1992 it was announced that Carreras would not only be embarking on his first major concert tour in the United States since his recovery, but that he would also serve as the music director of the 1992 Summer Olympics to take place in his hometown of Barcelona. His responsibilities included arranging the music played at the opening and closing ceremonies.

Success with the Three Tenors

Carreras joined with Luciano Pavarotti and Placido Domingo to form the Three Tenors in 1990. With a mix of opera classics and show tunes, concerts by the Three Tenors helped to make opera accessible to a wider audience and create musical events of unprecedented popularity. The trio's first performance took place at the Baths of Caracalla in Rome, Italy, in July of 1990 to mark the end of the World Cup soccer tournament. More than one billion people saw the television broadcast of the performance, and the CD, entitled *Carreras, Domingo, Pavarotti: The Three Tenors In Concert,* became the top-selling classical release of all time. Subsequent concerts took place at Dodger Stadium in Los Angeles, California, in 1994 before a crowd of more than 50,000 people and a television audience of again more than one billion, and in Paris, France, in 1998. The three opera superstars, with conductors Zubin Mehta and James Levine, continued infrequent performances together in such locations as Atlanta,

Georgia; Las Vegas, Nevada; Vancouver and Toronto, Canada; and Seoul, Korea, during the 1990s and early 2000s.

Selected discography

Ave Maria, Philips, 1984.
Love Is Jose Carreras, Philips, 1984.
You Belong to My Heart, Philips, 1984.
(With Kiri Te Kanawa and others) *West Side Story,* Deutsche Grammophon, 1985.
(With Placido Domingo and Luciano Pavarotti) *Carreras, Domingo, Pavarotti: The Three Tenors In Concert,* London, 1990.
(With Montserrat Caballe and Placido Domingo) *From the Official Barcelona Olympic Games Ceremony,* RCA Victor Red Seal, 1992.
Zarzuelas, Erato, 1993.
José Carreras in Concert, Legacy, 1995.
Merry Christmas, CBS, 1995.
Celebration of Christmas, Elektra/Asylum, 1996.
Passion, Elektra/Asylum, 1996.
My Romance, Elektra/Asylum, 1997.
Caresses, B.C.I., 1998.
The Best of José Carreras, Erato, 1998.
A Tribute to Operetta: A Franz Lehar Gala, Polygram, 1999.
Pure Passion, Erato, 1999.
Love Songs from Spain, E2, 2000.

Selected writings

Singing from the Soul: An Autobiography, Y.C.P. Publications, 1991.

Sources

Books

Carreras, José, *Singing from the Soul: An Autobiography,* Y.C.P., 1991.
Matheopoulos, Helena, *Divo: Great Tenors, Baritones, and Basses Discuss Their Roles,* Harper & Row, 1986.

Periodicals

Detroit Free Press, December 5, 1991.
Gramophone, January 1977.
Maclean's, January 11, 1999.
New Republic, July 15, 1985; July 22, 1985.
Newsweek, June 10, 1985; July 22, 1991.
New York, November 2, 1987.
New York Times, February 26, 1978; November 22, 1981.
Opera, April 1983; May 1987; June 1989.
Ovation, August 1989.
Publishers Weekly, April 5, 1991.
Time, April 1, 1985.
Variety, May 1, 2000.

Online

"Jose Carreras," *All Music Guide,* http://www.allmusic.com (September 12, 2001).

"Jose Carreras," http://www.jcarreras.com (September 4, 2001).

Tibor Rudas Presents—The Three Tenors, http://www.three tenors.com (September 4, 2001).

Additional information for this profile was obtained from the television biography *José Carreras: A Life Story,* London Weekend Television, 1991.

—Rob Nagel

John Carter

Clarinetist, composer

John Carter was a leading jazz clarinetist for more than 40 years. The fusion of Carter's interest in African American history and jazz composition led to one of his greatest professional accomplishments, the five-album series *Roots and Folklore: Episodes in the Development of American Folk Music*, during the 1980s. The work "traces in musical form the intersection of preslavery African civilizations and Western cultures and their ensuing entwined history," according to the *Nation*. Carter worked with jazz luminaries including Ornette Coleman, Dewey Redman, James Newton, Bobby Bradford, Red Callender, and Alvin Batiste.

From childhood in Fort Worth, Texas, where Carter was born on September 24, 1928, he shared a love of jazz with three contemporaries: saxophonist and jazz composer Ornette Coleman, drummer Charles Moffett, and saxophonist Dewey Redman. Carter absorbed the pulsing gospel hymns at the local Baptist church and the classic pieces of Duke Ellington, Count Basie, and Cab Calloway, which his parents played on their home phonograph. He studied alto saxophone but had an immediate affinity for the clarinet when he started playing the instrument at age 12. He first performed Texas blues in Woodman's Hall in Anacostia, a jazz center in Washington, D.C. Carter teamed with Coleman in the 1940s.

Following graduation with a Bachelor of Arts degree in music education from Lincoln University at the age of 19 and completion of a Master of Arts degree in music education from the University of Colorado, Carter was ready for a career in jazz performance. After marrying wife Gloria and beginning a family, a desire for security compelled him to teach music in the Fort Worth public school system, a position he held from 1949-61. Paralleling his classroom work, Carter experimented with the clarinet and found that it was the instrument he was best able to express himself on.

Resettled at an elementary school in Los Angeles, California, Carter taught music for 21 years in that city's public school system. In 1964, he joined with musical pal Bobby Bradford, six years his junior, who joined him for clarinet-trumpet duos and a tour of the northeastern United States with their unique brand of Texas jazz. Simultaneously, Carter nurtured local progressive jazz artists at his own club, Rudolph's. Driven by intellectual curiosity, he performed on flute and saxophone while refining a mastery of the clarinet, breaching customary artistic boundaries and matching up against Bradford's solid musicality.

By 1965, Carter and Bradford established a quartet with bassist Tom Williamson and Bruz Freeman on drums, which they maintained until Carter's death in 1991. Until 1970, the combo traveled as the New Arts Jazz Ensemble. As part of the Hat Art jazz series, they recorded five of Carter's original works on *Seeking*, released in 1991, including "Karen on Monday," "Sticks and Stones," and "In the Vineyard." During the late 1970s, Carter and Bradford toured Europe and joined pianist Horace Tapscott in recordings. The two played a concert at the University of California-Los Angeles (UCLA) featuring the Art Ensemble of Chicago, an alliance recorded as *Tandem 1*, a musical version of call-and-response sermon style, in 1979. Carter broke free for a virtuoso rendition of "Les Masses Jigaboo," an arcing harmonic riff with improvisations and abrupt transitions that challenged his horn. He joined the James Newton woodwind quintet in 1980, and a year later, Carter began performing with Alvin Batiste, Jimmy Hamilton, and David Murray in the Clarinet Summit quartet, a multi-generational, multi-sytlistic foursome recording on the Black Saint and India Navigation labels.

When Carter's daughter and three sons reached maturity in the early 1980s, he gave up the classroom for full-time jazz clarinet, establishing the Wind College in Los Angeles. On his own record label, he recorded with Bradford and Newton such classics as *Night Fire*, comprised of "Morning Bell," "Juba Stomp," and "Buckin.'" For *Dance of the Love Ghosts*, Carter teamed brass, synthesizer, kete drum, and dawuro drum to perform "The Captain's Dilemma," "Moon Waltz," and the title song, all original works. Carter summarized his vision of jazz in a five-part suite recorded as *Roots and Folklore: Episodes in the Development of American Folk Music,* consisting of five individual discs released in installments during the

For the Record . . .

Born John Wallace Carter on September 24, 1928, in Fort Worth, TX; died on March 31, 1991. *Education*: Bachelor of Arts degree in music education, Lincoln University, Jefferson, MO, 1949; Master of Arts degree in music education, University of Colorado, 1956.

Played with Ornette Coleman, 1940s; taught music in the Fort Wort, TX, public school system, 1949-61, and the Los Angeles, CA, public school system, 1961-82; established a traveling combo later known as the New Arts Jazz Ensemble with partner Bobby Bradford, 1965; opened Rudolph's, a jazz club nurturing new talent, in Los Angeles, 1960s; headlined recordings on Flying Dutchman, Moers Music, and Revelations labels, 1960s-1970s; formed Clarinet Summit, 1981; left teaching for full-time jazz composition and performance, founded the Wind College, 1980s; completed five-part jazz master-work, *Roots and Folklore: Episodes in the Development of American Folk Music*, 1989; work reprised by Francois Houle's album, *In the Vernacular—Music of John Carter*, 1998.

Awards: *Down Beat* magazine's Hall of Fame, 1991.

1980s—*Dauwhe, Castles of Ghana, Dance of the Love Ghosts, Fields,* and *Shadows on a Wall.*

Critical response to Carter's work focused on his lyricism, rich texture, fluidity, and free melodic expression. Comparisons to jazz master Wynton Marsalis placed Carter above the jazz talent in beauty, spontaneity, and range. Jazz tuba player Red Callender, who joined Carter, Bradford, and Newton to record *Dauwhe,* praised Carter's command of his instrument in *Rough Guides,* "I had never heard anybody with such control on the clarinet.... His complete mastery of the instrument is astounding." His virtuoso vocal and horn work in *Castles of Ghana* brought favorable comparisons to Marsalis. Individual pieces blending clarinet, trumpet, violin, cornet, trombone, drums, and acoustic bass carried evocative titles: "Evening Prayer," "Conversations," "The Fallen Prince," and "Theme of Desperation." In 1996, for "Sippi Strut," "Spats," "Hymn to Freedom," and "And I Saw Them" in *Shadows on a Wall,* Carter earned four stars from *Q* magazine and five from the *NAPRA Trade Journal.* Of the final recording, David Grogan, reviewing for *People* maga-

zine, called Carter an "avant-garde composer with a passion for history" and dubbed him "the Alex Haley of the Jazz world."

Carter influenced the styles of his pupils Julius Hemphill and Peter Epstein, as well as contemporaries Newton, Murray, and Bradford. His work inspired numerous tributes, including a ferocious, yet lyric recording of "Sticks and Stones" and "Karen on Monday" by jazz clarinetist Francois Houle on the album *In the Vernacular—Music of John Carter,* released in 1998.

One of the first clarinetists to express a humanistic Pan-African vision in jazz, Carter improvised at the extremes of personal emotion, yet controlled his probes through precise, impressionistic melody. His tonal research led him through the enslavement of African Americans and their resulting poverty in the plantation South to their flight to the North in search of independence through factory labor. Passionate, intellectual, and focused on his music, Carter influenced an era of clarinet players. Carter died suddenly of complications from the removal of a non-malignant lung tumor on March 31, 1991.

Selected discography

Flight For Four, Flying Dutchman, 1969.
Seeking, Hat Art, 1969; reissued, 1991.
John Carter, Flying Dutchman, 1969.
Self-Determination Music, Flying Dutchman, 1970.
Secrets, Revelation, 1972.
Echoes From Rudolph's, Ibedon, 1977.
Suite of Early American Folkpieces for Solo Clarinet, Black Saint, 1979.
Night Fire, Black Saint, 1979.
Dauwhe, Black Saint, 1982.
Castles of Ghana, Gramavision, 1985.
Dance of the Love Ghosts, Gramavision, 1986.
Fields, Gramavision, 1988.
Comin' On, Hat Art, 1988.
Shadows on a Wall, Gramavision, 1989.
West Coast Hot, Novus, 1991.
Suite of Early American Folkpieces (re-release), Moers Music, 1994.
Variations, Moers Music, 1994.
Tandem 1, Emanem, 1996.
Message to Venus, Orchard, 1999.
Downtown Blues, Breeze, 1999.
USA Concerts West, Robidrol/Newtone, 2000.

Sources

Books

Cook, Richard, and Brian Morton, editors, *The Penguin Guide to Jazz on CD,* Penguin Books, 1998.
Kernfeld, Barry, editor, *The New Grove Dictionary of Jazz,* Macmillan, 1988.
Unterberger, Richie, *The Rough Guide to Music USA,* Rough Guides Ltd., 1999.

Periodicals

Audio, March 1990.

Austin Chronicle, April 12, 1991.

Christian Science Monitor, October 5, 1983.

Down Beat, November 1982; April 1985; August 1985; March 1990; June 1991; September 1991; November 1982.

High Fidelity, July 1986.

Jazz Times, May 2000.

Los Angeles Times, September 5, 1990, April 14, 1991.

NAPRA Trade Journal, Spring 1996.

Nation, October 21, 1991.

New York Times, January 3, 1988; February 5, 1988; April 2, 1991.

People, April 9, 1990.

Wire, October 1990.

Online

"In the Vernacular—The Music of John Carter," http://www. allaboutjazz. com/REVIEWS/R1198_11.HTM (September 26, 2001).

"John Carter," http://www.agoron.com/˜msnyder/clarinet/ carter.htm (September 26, 2001).

"John Carter" *Rough Guides* biography at Amazon.com, http://www.amazon.com (September 26, 2001).

—*Mary Ellen Snodgrass*

Martin Carthy

Singer, songwriter, composer

On October 25, 2000, a long-running feud between two of contemporary music's legends finally came to an end when Paul Simon invited British folk singer Martin Carthy onstage in London, England, to join him in performing "Scarborough Fair." In the mid 1960s, when Simon took a sabbatical to London to reconsider his future in music, he had learned the traditional folk ballad from Carthy, who was the leader of England's folk revival. Using Carthy's arrangement of the song in a subsequent recording, Simon enjoyed a hit song with "Scarborough Fair/Canticle" in 1968 as part of the duo Simon and Garfunkel. In Carthy's opinion, however, Simon failed to give him proper credit for arranging the song, a grievance that remained a point of contention between the musicians for decades. Thus, the audience at Simon's London concert was surprised to hear him introduce Carthy for a performance of the song. As Carthy told Paul Castle in an interview on the About Folk Music website, however, "[I]t was time to let go…. In fact, in an interview ten years ago or so, Paul thanked publicly all the musicians and others he had known in England in the sixties, and this gave a shove to that train of thought in me." The "Scarborough Fair" controversy behind him, Carthy could now properly enjoy the accolades as Britain's leading folk musician without the distractions of long-ago feuds.

Martin Dominic Forbes Carthy was born on May 20, 1941, in Hatfield, England, a town just north of London. Coming of age in Britain's postwar era of the late 1950s—when a new wave of plays, movies, and music reshaped the country's cultural landscape—Carthy was profoundly influenced by singer Lonnie Donegan, who popularized skiffle music with a string of hits including "Rock Island Line," "Cumberland Gap," and "Tom Dooley." In its most basic form, skiffle was an improvised fusion of folk and jazz elements that sometimes used objects such as washboards and jugs as instruments. In this do-it-yourself spirit, the skiffle craze in Britain gave rise to hundreds of amateur bands attempting to emulate Donegan's international success. Although he first worked as an assistant stage manager for several theater companies, Carthy's love of skiffle found him playing the coffeehouse circuit around London. Joining the Thameside Four as a singer and guitarist, Carthy appeared on the group's 1963 release, *The Thamesiders and Davy Graham.* However, Carthy soon became a featured solo performer at the center of the folk revival movement of the late 1950s and early 1960s at London's Troubadour Folk Club.

Revived Old Folk Tunes

Abandoning his studies with the trombone, Carthy's talent with the guitar and mandolin served as fitting accompaniments to his direct and unpretentious style of singing. Carthy's most outstanding contribution to the folk music revival, however, was his ability to unearth folk songs and melodies that were in danger of disappearing from Britain's musical heritage. Going back to early twentieth-century recordings and even older transcriptions of folk songs, Carthy resurrected the tunes, sometimes coming up with new arrangements or adapting the basic material into almost-new songs. A sort of musical anthropologist, Carthy was perhaps the best-known folk music figure in England by the time he recorded his first album in 1965, the self-titled *Martin Carthy.* The release cemented his reputation as a singer and musician. As *Q* magazine summarized the album's importance upon its reissue in 1993, "Martin Carthy's debut album set new standards for the British folk revival…. [W]ith this album he was on his way to becoming one of the folk scene's foremost attractions."

As a mentor to many folk musicians in London, Carthy also befriended Bob Dylan during his stay in the city in 1965. While appearing in a television play there, Dylan heard Carthy's rendition of "Lord Franklin." Inspired by its melody, Dylan reworked it into his own song, "Bob Dylan's Dream," which subsequently appeared on his album *Freewheelin'* along with a note of recognition to Carthy for his contribution to the song. More controversial was Simon's adaptation of Carthy's arrangement of the traditional song "Scarborough Fair," which Carthy had included on his own 1965 album. After Simon heard Carthy perform the song in concert, he discussed it in depth with the folk singer, who gave Simon a copy of its arrangement, including its chords and words. After the song was included as the opening

For the Record . . .

Born Martin Dominic Forbes Carthy on May 20, 1941, in Hatfield, Hertfordshire, England.

Played professionally at Troubadour Folk Club in London, England, early 1960s; has played with groups Steeleye Span, Albion Country Band, and Waterson: Carthy; released solo albums, 1960s–; released compilation *The Carthy Chronicles: Rare, Live and Classic Carthy*, 2001.

Awards: Member of the British Empire (MBE), 1998.

Addresses: *Record company*—Free Reed Records, The Cedars, Belper, Derbyshire, DE56 IDD, United Kingdom, website: http://www.free-reed.co.uk; Topic Records, c/o Glass Ceiling PR, 50 Stroud Green Road, Finsbury Park, London N4 3ES, United Kingdom, website: http://www.topicrecords.co.uk. *Management*—Moneypenny Agency and Management, The Stables, Westwood House, Main Street, North Dalton, Driffield, East Yorkshire, YO25 9XA, United Kingdom.

track on the 1966 Simon and Garfunkel album *Parsley, Sage, Rosemary & Thyme* without giving credit to Carthy, a minor feud was started between the two men. For several years, Simon stubbornly refused to acknowledge Carthy's contribution, and Carthy continued to question Simon's integrity. The spat was settled publicly during the October of 2000 concert when Simon called Carthy to invite him to perform onstage.

Musical Collaborations

Fortunately, most of Carthy's musical collaborations were much more amicable and productive. During the rest of the 1960s, he released an album each year, featuring original material as well as new arrangements of traditional songs. Carthy also collaborated extensively with fiddler Dave Swarbrick, who worked with Carthy as a musician, arranger, and performer. The duo also released six albums between 1966 and 1969 when Swarbrick joined the folk-rock group Fairport Convention. Carthy himself would join another folk-rock band, Steeleye Span, in 1970. He remained with the group only a short time. In 1972, after marrying folk singer Norma Waterson, Carthy devoted most of his collaborative energies to performing with his wife and her family, although he performed with the Albion Country Band for a brief period as well.

One of the highlights of Carthy's solo work was the 1976 release *Crown of Horn*. After its reissue in 1995, *Q* paid tribute by saying, "At times he's given the impression of keeping traditional English folk music alive almost on his own." The 1999 album *Signs of Life,* featuring a rendition of the Bee Gees hit "New York Mining Disaster 1941," also won him praise as "the best of his class" from the magazine, which welcomed his first solo album in over ten years. Among his collaborations was the 2000 album *Broken Ground,* recorded under the Waterson: Carthy name with his wife. The album received standout praise for its presentation of traditional gypsy music. "This music is not, in their hands, anything other than living material," wrote a *New Internationalist* reviewer.

The Next Generation

After 40 years of performing, Carthy was known not only for his own work, but as the husband and father of important folk music musicians in their own right. Waterson received a prestigious Mercury Prize nomination in 1996 for her self-titled album, a feat that daughter Eliza Carthy duplicated in 1998 with her acclaimed solo album *Red Rice*. Although Eliza Carthy continued to appear as a singer and violinist with her parents as part of Waterson: Carthy, her own musical directions took her into techno, reggae, and dance music territory as well, a trend that continued with her 2000 release *Angels & Cigarettes*. The first folk musician signed to a major label in Britain in more than 20 years, Eliza Carthy nevertheless insisted on remaining true to her less commercial roots. As she told the *Los Angeles Times,* "Waterson: Carthy is sacrosanct. I'll be doing this as long as my parents want."

Carthy was not short of honors of his own, however. In 1998, he was named a Member of the British Empire (MBE), an honor that caused him to reflect once again on his place in the folk music community. Hesitant to accept the award at first for its connotations to British imperialism, Carthy decided that it was offered to highlight the continued importance of folk music in modern Britain. "A bit of profile isn't gonna hurt us," he told the *Dirty Linen* newsletter in explaining his decision, adding with characteristic modesty, "And I say 'us,' the plural, for the folk scene—isn't gonna hurt us at all." Carthy's own profile was helped with the 2001 release of the *Carthy Chronicles* compilation, a capstone to a recording career that spanned five decades, as well as a sixtieth-birthday concert that celebrated his life and work with a host of musical colleagues where he was acknowledged as a musician, scholar, and mentor.

Selected discography

Martin Carthy, Topic, 1965.
Second Album, Topic, 1966.

Byker Hill, Topic, 1967.
But Two Came By, Topic, 1968.
Prince Heathen, Topic, 1969.
Because It's There, Topic, 1971.
Crown of Horn, Topic, 1971.
Out of the Cut, Topic, 1971.
Sweet Wivelsfield, Topic, 1971.
Selections, Pegasus, 1971.
Shearwater, Mooncrest, 1972.
Landfall, Topic, 1977.
Right of Passage, Topic, 1988.
Life and Limb (live), Green Linnet, 1991.
Skin & Bone, Green Linnet, 1992.
Kershaw Sessions, Strange Fruit, 1995.
Signs of Life, Topic, 1999.
Collection, Topic, 1999.
The Carthy Chronicles: Rare, Live and Classic Carthy, Free Reed, 2001.

Sources

Books

Broughton, Simon, et al., editors, *World Music: The Rough Guide Volume 1,* The Rough Guides Ltd., 1999.

Hanif Kureishi and Jon Savage, editors, *The Faber Book of Pop,* Faber and Faber, 1995.

Periodicals

Billboard, October 3, 1998, p. 1; November 11, 2000, p. 73.
Los Angeles Times, March 11, 2001.
New Internationalist, January/February 2000, p. 47.
New Statesman, November 27, 1998, p. 42.
Q, May 1993; March 1996; June 1996; January 1999; September 1999; June 2001.
Toronto Star, March 22, 2001.

Online

About Folk Music, http://folkmusic.about.com/musicperform/folkmusic (June 22, 2001).
Dirty Linen, http://www.dirtynelson.com/linen/84/marty.html (June 22, 2001).
Topic Records, http://www.topicrecords.co.uk/martin_carthy_topic_records.html (June 20, 2001).
Waterson: Carthy Official Website, http://www.folkicons.co.uk/wcart.html (June 20, 2001).

—*Timothy Borden*

Ceili Rain

Folk rock group

Ceili Rain has achieved critical acclaim for its spiritually influenced pop/rock music with a Celtic flair. A group that "weaves pop, rock, and Celtic sounds into an intriguing musical tapestry," according to Paul Verna of *Billboard*, the musicians take their name from the Gaelic word *ceili,* which refers to "a party with live music and dancing." This Nashville-based team of instrumentalists and vocalists, led by veteran songwriter Bob Halligan, Jr., has earned a large following among Christian youth. The Ceili Rain message nonetheless is about life, not specifically about Christianity. According to Halligan, Ceili Rain is spiritual but is not affiliated with a specific religious group. The band's goal is to inspire its listeners regardless of religious preference or tradition.

Founder, songwriter, lead singer, and Ceili Rain spokesperson Bob Halligan is himself the son of a professional concert violinist, his birth father. At the age of two months, Halligan went to live with his adoptive parents who raised him in Syracuse, New York. He wrote his first song at age 15, and after high school, he majored in music at Hamilton College in Clinton, New York. Interestingly, he began his professional career as an electrician, although a job as a skilled laborer lasted for just two days for Halligan. After that he abandoned the work-a-day world, realizing very quickly that his real niche in life was centered squarely on songwriting and performance.

Halligan first signed a music-publishing contract in 1982. Subsequently, the heavy metal ensemble Judas Priest made a hit of his song "(Take These) Chains," which earned royalties for Halligan for many years afterward. The group later turned to Halligan when compiling its 1984 album, *Defenders of the Faith,* for which Halligan churned out another classic hit song, "Some Heads Are Gonna Roll." Thus, even before he conceived of Ceili Rain, Halligan was well-established as a songwriter in his own right, having also collaborated on a series of songs with Michael Bolton. In addition to Bolton and Judas Priest, other top industry artists recorded Halligan's tunes, including Cher, Joan Jett, Kathy Mattea, and Kiss. In 1985 alone, as a growing number of recording stars incorporated Halligan's songs into their respective repertoires, Halligan saw more than two dozen of his songs put to disc by pop and rock bands and by soloists. With Halligan's songwriting experience, it is of little surprise that Ceili Rain displays a natural bent for flavoring its songs with rock music, although the group avoids hard, heavy metal sounds.

Halligan signed a recording contract with ATCO Records in 1991 and released a solo debut of his own music that year, even while formulating the concept of Ceili Rain. Performing as a soloist he developed an aversion to presenting himself as a simple one-man acoustic act on the coffeehouse circuit and set out to establish instead a full band with a bigger sound and greater energy. He moved to Nashville in 1995 and re-invented himself by assembling his new group and creating a trademark fusion sound of rock and Celtic influences in the process. When Ceili Rain released its self-titled album on Punch Records in 1998, Verna called it a "stunning debut" in *Billboard*. That year the band toured Europe, including a stop in Rome for the World Youth Day celebration. The group then moved to an independent label and released a self-produced live album, *We're Making a Party,* in 1999.

From the beginning, Ceili Rain featured the unique sounds of tin whistles, exotic percussion, and bagpipes, along with more traditional instruments, including violin, accordion, and drums. The original clan consisted of Chris Carmichael on strings (violin and cello), Rick Cua on bass, and Tony Hooper on electric guitar. Also heard were violinist Michael MacCaniess, along with drummer Cactus Moses, and percussionist Lang Bliss. Multifaceted musician Hunter Lee added the tin whistle, uilleann pipes, Irish flute, highland pipes, and didgeridoo. Ceili Rain included a range of songs on their debut album, yet each was basically a lighthearted ditty about love, life, or eternity. The musicians revealed themselves to be equally comfortable with performing love songs, such as "I Don't Need a Picture," as they were with dispensing tunes suggestive of spirituality and the afterlife. The album offers a whimsical allegory in a ballad about St. Peter at heaven's gates entitled "All the Lumber You Sent." Also featured on the album is Halligan's musical musing about hell in the form of a song called "666 Degrees." For listeners with a more cynical bent, the album offers

For the Record . . .

Members include **Raymond Arias**, lead guitar; **Lang Bliss**, percussion; **Chris Charmichael**, violin, cello; **Buddy Connolly**, button accordion; **Rick Cua**, bass; **Chris Eddy**, drums; **Bob Halligan, Jr.** (founding member), lead vocals, acoustic guitar, piano, harmonica; **Bob "Buff" Harmon**, bass; **Tony Hooper**, electric guitar; **Hunter Lee**, tin whistle, uilleann pipes, Irish flute, highland pipes, didgeridoo; **Michael MacCaniess**, violin; **Burt Mitchell**, bagpipes, tin whistle, violin; **Cactus Moses**, drums; **Gretchen Priest**, fiddle.

Formed by singer/songwriter Bob Halligan, Jr., 1995; signed with Punch Records, 1997; released debut album, *Ceili Rain (Say Kay-lee),* 1997; released *Erasers on Pencils* on own Mima Rekidz label, 2000.

Addresses: *Business*—Ceili Rain, 629 Wason Branch Dr., Franklin, TN 37064, (615) 791-9986. *Website*—Ceili Rain Official Website: http://www.ceilirain.com. *E-mail*—ceilimail@mindspring.com.

songs like "Long Black Cadillac," an upbeat tune that conjures the illusion not of a limousine, but rather of a hearse.

By 2000 Ceili Rain had settled comfortably into a septet lineup, including Halligan on vocals, with Raymond Arias on lead guitar and Gretchen Priest on violin, and featuring award-winning accordion player Buddy Connolly. Burt Mitchell added Celtic vigor to the tone of the ensemble by means of his performances on bagpipes and tin whistle, while Bob "Buff" Harmon fills out the Ceili Rain sound on bass. For diversion there is drummer Lang Bliss who is an original member of the band. He proves himself to be not only long on tenacity but also long on ingenuity as he is capable of turning an object like a venetian blind into a percussion tool. Bliss also contributes to the visual appeal of the group, wearing his hair in an easily identifiable, stark white shade of blond.

Ceili Rain is the realization of Halligan's lifelong dream. He collaborates in songwriting for the septet along with his wife, Linda, and with his longtime friend, Cua, a former bassist for the band. For Halligan, the music elicits a distinctly aesthetic vein that was by definition conspicuously missing from the indelicate compositions and lyrics that he once offered to Kiss, Judas Priest and others in the heavy metal arena. Although he continues to sell songs on occasion to other artists, he reserves his greatest effort nonetheless for Ceili Rain, which forms the central focus of his career.

In 2000 Ceili Rain returned to Europe to participate in the celebration of the Millennium World Youth Day Jubilee. Later that year the septet released an independent third album, *Erasers on Pencils,* on its own Mima Rekidz label.

Selected discography

Ceili Rain (Say Kay-lee), Punch, 1997.
We're Makin' a Party (live), Ceili Rain, 2000.
Erasers on Pencils, Mima Rekidz, 2000.

Sources

Periodicals

Billboard, March 7, 1998; April 25, 1998; November 11, 2000.
Record (Bergen County, NJ), August 9, 1991.
Tennessean, January 4, 1998.

Online

"Bob Halligan," *All Music Guide,* http://www.allmusic.com/cg/amg.dll (June 25, 2001).
"Ceili Rain," *All Music Guide,* http://www.allmusic.com/cg/amg.dll (June 25, 2001).
Ceili Rain Official Website, http://www.ceilirain.com/intro.html (June 25, 2001).
"Entertainment Guide," *Washington Post,* http://yp.washingtonpost.com/E/E/WASDC/0001/32/27/cs1.html (June 25, 2001).
"Erasers on Pencils," *All Music Guide,* http://www.all music.com/cg/amg.dll (June 25, 2001).
ESP Magazine, http://www.espmagazine.com/2001/1324/ceilirain.html (June 25, 2001).

—*Gloria Cooksey*

The Chordettes

Vocal group

Hulton/Archive. Reproduced by permission.

No study of the popular music of the 1950s would be complete without including a female singing group called the Chordettes. Their harmonies on such memorable recordings as "Lollipop" and "Mr. Sandman" were indeed sounds of the times, a period of transition from simple-minded, romantic popular music to the driving beat of rock 'n' roll. In total, the group placed 13 songs in the top 100 during the 1950s and early 1960s. Most of the Chordettes' recordings fall into the pop category, although a few, particularly in the later years, carry at least a hint of the revolutionary changes that were coming in American music.

Founding Chordettes member Jinny Osborn listened to the dulcet harmonies of barbershop singing as a young girl in Sheboygan, Wisconsin. She came by her exposure to this uniquely American musical form through her father's association with the Society for the Preservation and Encouragement of Barbershop Quartet Singing in America, Inc., a group formed during the late 1930s. It was Osborn who in 1946 got together with three college friends in Sheboygan to form the Chordettes. The original group consisted of Janet Ertel, Carol Bushman, Dorothy Schwartz, and Osborn. The most significant of their influences was barbershop quartet singing, but the group was also inspired by the success of a popular folk-singing troupe called the Weavers. The group's earliest appearances were in and around Sheboygan, and during its early years, the quartet sang a cappella. Some of the group's earliest songs were adaptations for women of classic barbershop arrangements.

The group's big break came in 1949 with an appearance on Arthur Godfrey's immensely popular talent show. Shortly after they won the on-air talent contest, they were persuaded to sign on as regulars on the Godfrey show. The group was also signed to a recording contract with Columbia Records. For Columbia, the Chordettes recorded a number of 10-inch EPs (extended-play 45 rpm records), none of which was particularly memorable. During the four years they appeared as regulars on the Godfrey television show, they became closely acquainted with Archie Bleyer, who served as musical director for Godfrey from 1949 until 1954. Their relationship with Bleyer was to play an important role in the group's development. The early 1950s saw changes in the makeup of the group. In 1952, Schwartz left and was replaced by Lynn Evans; the following year, Margie Needham replaced Osborn.

In December of 1952, Bleyer formed his own record label called Cadence Records. The first artist he signed was Julius LaRosa, a singer who also appeared as a regular on the Godfrey show. For the first ten months of Cadence's existence, LaRosa was its only recording artist. Bleyer began signing other artists to the Cadence label in October of 1953. These included the Chordettes, who gave Cadence its first number one record in 1954 with "Mr. Sandman," a song which more

For the Record . . .

Members include **Carol Buschman**, baritone vocals; **Janet Ertel** (died in 1988), bass vocals; **Lynn Evans** (joined group, 1952), lead vocals; **Margie Needham** (joined group, 1953), tenor vocals; **Jinny Osborn** (left group, 1953), tenor vocals; **Nancy Overton**, bass vocals; **Dorothy Schwartz** (left group, 1952), lead vocals.

Formed as an a cappella, folk-oriented vocal group in Sheboygan, WI, 1946; appeared as contestants on the CBS television show *Arthur Godfrey's Talent Scouts* and won, 1949; became regulars on the show, 1949-53; scored hits with "Mr. Sandman," "Lollipop," and "Born to Be with You," 1950s; disbanded, 1961; reformed, 1988.

than any of the group's other hits reflected the influence of barbershop quartet singing on their sound. The song, in fact, uses the bell chord—one of barbershop singing's favorite embellishments—as its central motif. Although the relationship between Bleyer and the Chordettes began as professional, it became personal before long. Bleyer and singer Janet Ertel were married in 1954. (In an interesting footnote, the Bleyers' daughter Janet later married another successful Cadence recording artist, Phil Everly, half of the Everly Brothers.)

Although the group would release a number of hit songs in the years to come, none matched the success of "Mr. Sandman." The song not only rocketed to number one on *Your Hit Parade* but managed to stay there for seven weeks. Interestingly, the male voice (representing Mr. Sandman) heard on the record was none other than Bleyer. The next big hit for the Chordettes came in 1956 with their recording of "Eddie My Love," which made it into the top 20. Recordings of the same song by the Teen Queens and Fontane Sisters also managed to work their way up the charts to the top 20 in 1956.

In the wake of the sensation they had created with "Mr. Sandman," the Chordettes found themselves in demand throughout the show business world. They performed for President Dwight Eisenhower and entertained on countless radio programs, including disc jockey Alan Freed's popular show. Booking agencies for the nation's top nightclubs were eager to sign the group, and they made innumerable appearances on television variety shows, including those hosted by Ed Sullivan, Gary Moore, and Robert Q. Lewis. They later became regulars on the Lewis show.

After the success of "Eddie My Love" earlier in 1956, the Chordettes enjoyed a major hit later that year with "Born to Be with You," which made it into the top ten. This was followed late in 1956 with "Lay Down Your Arms." The following year they hit the charts again with the playful ballad "Just Between You and Me." Perhaps the most memorable of all of the Chordettes' hits was "Lollipop," released in 1958. Although it never achieved the success the group had enjoyed with "Mr. Sandman," the unforgettable song climbed to number two on the popular music charts. It represented Bleyer's attempt to give the group the rock 'n' roll sound they had not previously had. The bubblegum lyrics of the song have lived on long beyond the life of the group itself: "Lollipop, lollipop, oooh lolli, lolli, lolli...." The Chordettes also enjoyed hits with two theme songs from other media. "Zorro," which climbed to number 17 in 1958, was a vocal version of the instrumental theme for the hit television show of the same name. In 1961, the group released "Never on Sunday," the title song of the hit movie starring Melina Mercouri. "Never on Sunday" made it to number 13 on the pop charts. Shortly after the release of "Never on Sunday" in 1961, the group disbanded. Original member Janet Ertel died of cancer in 1988, the same year the group re-formed and performed on the *Royal New York Doo-Wop Show*.

Although the songs of this immensely popular girl group may seem simple and even sappy to contemporary pop music fans, the Chordettes' sound was very much a part of the era in which the group lived and performed. It is impossible to imagine American music of the 1950s without the unique sounds of the Chordettes.

Selected discography

Singles

"Mr. Sandman," Cadence, 1954.
"The Wedding," Cadence, 1956.
"Eddie My Love," Cadence, 1956.
"Born to Be with You," Cadence, 1956.
"Lay Down Your Arms," Cadence, 1956.
"Just Between You and Me," Cadence, 1957.
"Lollipop," Cadence, 1958.
"Zorro," Cadence, 1958.
"Never on Sunday," Cadence, 1961.

Compilations

The Best of the Chordettes, Rhino, 1989.
The Chordettes' Greatest Hits, Curb, 1996.
Golden Classics, Collectables, 1997.

Sources

Books

Graff, Gary, and Daniel Durchholz, *MusicHound Rock: The Essential Album Guide*, Visible Ink Press, 1999.

Online

"Archie and the Metronome: The Cadence Records Story," BSNPubs.com, http://www.bsnpubs.com/cadencestory.html (June 25, 2001).

"Chordettes," http://www.geocities.com/sunsetstrip/alley/4795/facts111.htm (June 25, 2001).

"The Chordettes," Euronet, http://www.euronet.nl/users/wvbrecht/chordett.htm (June 19, 2001).

"The Chordettes," http://www.tsimon.com/chardett.htm (June 19, 2001).

"The Chordettes," Primarily A Cappella, http://www.singers.com/jazz/vintage/chordettes.html (June 19, 2001).

"The Chordettes—Biography," Yahoo! Music, http://musicfinder.yahoo.com/ (June 19, 2001).

—Don Amerman

Kyung Wha Chung

Violinist

Photograph by Graham Wood. Hulton/Archive. Reproduced by permission.

Fluid, elegant, and lyric, violinist Kyung Wha Chung was the first Western-style classical virtuoso to emerge from Korea. An engaging performer who challenges listeners to share her perceptive interpretations, she has performed under the leading conductors of the era. Publication of her work creates excitement among collectors, especially Koreans, who look on Chung as a national icon.

Born Chung Kyung Wha on March 26, 1948, in Seoul, Korea, Chung is the daughter of music lovers Won Sook Lee and Chun Chai. Through exposure to a variety of songs, concerts, and symphonies at home, she shared a love of music with her brothers and sisters. Her younger sister Myung Wha took up the cello; brother Myung Whun studied piano and became a world-class conductor. At her mother's urging, Chung chose the violin and observed that its tonal range and timbre resembled the human voice. By 1952, she was performing with orchestras and made her first national tour at the age of 12.

In the early 1960s, to gain more opportunities in music education for their children, the family moved to the United States. At age 13, Chung received a seven-year scholarship. She began studying privately with Ivan Galamian at the Juilliard School of Music where her sister Myung Wha also enrolled. The school surprised Chung. Later, she remarked, "I was shocked by the high standard of the music there, and my only goal was to reach that high level," she told *Asia Week*. She adored Galamian but realized his bias toward female artists. She commented to *American Record Guide* after his death, "[He] loved me deeply, but that did not change how he felt about female students. He had already been let down by a number of girl prodigies who abandoned their professional goals in their teens, or who had run off and got married."

At the age of 19, Chung won first prize in the Leventritt Competition, an honor she shared with Itzhak Perlman. Chung made her European debut in 1970 at London's Royal Festival Hall playing the Tchaikovsky Concerto with conductor André Previn and the London Symphony. Her intensity, delicacy, and dramatic stage presence brought invitations for three more London concerts and a televised performance. Of the mounting list of successes, she confided modestly to Thor Eckert, Jr. of the *Christian Science Monitor*, "My career was one miracle after another."

Concertgoers recognized Chung's ability to sink into a performance, drawing out a spirit and fire with deft strokes of the bow. Absorbed in hypnotic phrasing, she ranged from gentle to tempestuous. After her impeccable rendering of Bartok's Second Violin Concerto at the Champs Elysee Theater in Paris for the seventieth birthday of composer Pierre Boulez, listeners demanded eight curtain calls. Kyung Soo Won, conductor of the Seoul Philharmonic Orchestra, marveled at the

For the Record . . .

Born Chung Kyung Wha on March 26, 1948, in Seoul, Korea. *Education*: Studied with Ivan Galamian at the Juilliard School of Music.

Debuted in London, England, with André Previn and the London Symphony, 1970; recorded best-selling album *Con Amore*, 1987; recorded Bartók's Violin Concerto No. 2 with Simon Rattle and the City of Birmingham Symphony Orchestra, 1988; named honorary ambassador of the United Nations Drug Control Program, 1992; recorded Brahms' violin sonatas with pianist Peter Frankl, 1997; recorded *Souvenirs*, 1999; recorded *Celibidache Conducts Strauss and Respighi Violin Sonatas*, 2000.

Awards: First Prize, Leventritt Competition, 1967; Medal of Civil Merit from the South Korean government, 1972; *Gramophone* Award for Bartók's Violin Concerto No. 2, 1988; *Gramophone* Award for *Celibidache Conducts Strauss and Respighi Violin Sonatas*, 2000.

Addresses: *Record company*—Angel/EMI Records, 304 Park Avenue South, New York, NY 10010, phone: (212) 253-3200, fax: (212) 253-3011, website: http://www.emiclassics.com.

uniqueness of her tone and technique in *Asia Week*: "These days, young musicians all play the same, but she is markedly different from all the others."

Chung's mastery of the Western classical canon quickly brought invitations from symphonies in Chicago, Boston, Cleveland, Philadelphia, Los Angeles, New York, Anchorage, Vancouver, Berlin, Vienna, Israel, Helsinki, Munich, Hong Kong, and Paris. She also toured the United States, Europe, and Japan. For Angel/EMI, London/Decca, RCA, and Deutsche Grammophon, has she recorded a broad span of violin solos, including Bartok, Mendelssohn, Bruch, Vivaldi, and Tchaikovsky. In 1972, a proud homeland awarded her the Medal of Civil Merit from the South Korean government.

Chung let music dominate her life until age 36, when she disobeyed the injunctions of Galamian, her first mentor. After she married a British businessman in 1984 and bore two sons, Frederick and Eugene, she pared her performance schedule by 50 percent. With the firstborn, she snuggled him into a basket and placed it close to the recital podium. Staying close to family enabled her to develop bilingualism in her sons and take them on tour and on visits to Korea. Of the change in her life, she affirmed her duties to home: "As a mother, your priorities change. The children come first." The reward for her fans was a new-found soulfulness, a product of judgment and maturity that rid her of attempts to please everyone but herself.

In 1988, domestication did not inhibit Chung from recording Bartók's Violin Concerto No. 2 with Simon Rattle and the City of Birmingham Symphony Orchestra, the first album to win her an award from *Gramophone* magazine. In 1997, she recorded Brahms' violin sonatas with pianist Peter Frankl and followed in 1999 with the crowd-pleasing *Souvenirs*, an anthology of short pieces performed with Lithuanian pianist Itamar Golan. She patterned the serene program after her best-selling album *Con Amore*, which sold over 100,000 after its release in 1987, making it a Korean classic. In 2000, she received a second *Gramophone* Award for *Celibidache Conducts Strauss and Respighi Violin Sonatas*, performed with Krystian Zimerman.

Categorized with string masters Midori and Yo-Yo Ma, Chung has helped bridge the chasm that once isolated the Asian arts from the West. To maintain ties with her siblings and homeland, she has performed for Korean audiences with the Chung Trio, comprised of herself, London-based Myung Wha, cello instructor at Korea's National School of Music, and pianist Myung Whun, the artistic director of the Paris Bastille Opera House. The chamber ensemble recorded a critically acclaimed performance of Beethoven's Piano Trios Op. 11 and 97 and, in 1997, toured Seoul, Kwangju, Inchon, Taegu, Chinju, and Pusan. To rapt audiences, she and her sister paired violin with cello for Mendelssohn's Violin Sonata in F major and Schumann's Violin Sonata No. 1 in A major. The trio wowed listeners with a grand finale, the Brahms Piano Trio No. 2 in C major.

In March of 2001, *Los Angeles Times* arts critic Daniel Cariaga summed up the quintessence of Chung's technique and musicality in one word—satisfying. Her intent is to nurture artistic development in Korea's young musicians. In limited spare time, Chung gardens and gives violin lessons. Since June of 1992, she and her musical brother and sister have served as honorary ambassadors of the United Nations Drug Control Program. To raise money for the cause, they have performed recitals in Chicago, New York, Rome, and Seoul. Chung currently lives in Manhattan, New York, and southern England, but was quoted by *Asia Week* as saying, "I'm Korean, and there's nothing that will change that."

Selected discography

Con Amore, EMI, 1987.
Bartók's Violin Concerto No. 2 and Rhapsodies 1 and 2, EMI, 1988.
Franck: Sonata for Violin and Piano/ Debussy: Sonatas/ Ravel: Introduction and Allegro, UNI/London Classics, 1988.
Camille Saint-Saëns: Introduction and Rondo capriccioso in A, Polygram, 1992.
Beethoven/Bruch, EMI, 1992.
Tchaikovsky: Piano Concerto Nos.1-3/Violin Concerto, UNI/ Phillips, 1997.
Beethoven Triple Concerto, Deutsche Grammophon, 1997.
Bruch: Violin Concerto/Scottish Fantasia, Polygram, 1997.
Brahms' Violin Sonatas 1-3, EMI, 1998.
Souvenirs: A Collection of Favourite Violin Pieces, EMI, 1999.
Kyung Wha Chung Performs Bruch: Concerto for violin in G, UNI/Penguin Classics, 1999.
Celibidache Conducts Strauss and Respighi Violin Sonatas, Deutsche Grammophon, 2000.

Sources

Books

The Complete Marquis Who's Who, Marquis Who's Who, 2001.

Periodicals

American Record Guide, October 1982; January-February 1999; March 1, 2000.
Audio, April 1985.
Chicago Tribune, July 6, 1989; December 1, 1992; March 20, 2001.
Christian Science Monitor, May 4, 1989.
Consumers' Research, June 1982.
Korea Herald, August 16, 1999.
Los Angeles Times, March 10, 2001.
Musical America, November 1990.
New West, March 24, 1980.
New York Times, November 4, 1988; November 24, 1998.
People, November 8, 1982.
Seattle Times, November 11, 1997.
Stereo Review, April 1985.

Online

Biography Resource Center, http://galenet.galegroup.com/ servlet/BioRC (June 28, 2001).
"Chung Kyung Wha," *Asia Week*, http://168.131.50.85/class/ col_eng/young/chung.html (June 28, 2001).
"Chung Kyung Wha," Korean Overseas Information Service, http://www.natural.cau.ac.kr/PChem/JOO/chungkw.html (June 28, 2001).
"Chung Kyung Wha," Melting Pot, http://meltingpot.fortun ecity.com/slovakia/583/mus3.htm (June 28, 2001).
"Kyung-Wha Chung," EMI Classics, http://www.emiclas sics.com/artists/biogs/chung.html (June 28, 2001).

—*Mary Ellen Snodgrass*

Cold

Rock group

The 1998 self-titled debut album for the hard-core rock group Cold was only in stores for two months before Universal Music Group subsumed A&M Records, the label to which Cold was signed. With its sophomore album, *13 Ways to Bleed on Stage*, the group received a second opportunity to warm up to rock fans. "I'm glad we got to make another record. It's kind of a bummer that it took so long and we had to do it again. At least, out of all the bands on A&M, we lasted. At least we were privileged enough to get another deal," lead vocalist Scooter Ward told *Contemporary Musicians*.

An early incarnation of Cold formed during the mid 1980s when Ward and drummer Sam McCandless met at a Jacksonville, Florida-area high school. They performed with several garage bands before being introduced to bassist Jeremy Marshall and guitarist Matt Laughren. When they were in their early twenties, the quartet, dubbed Grundig, moved to Atlanta, Georgia, where there were more clubs in which to play. Ward told *Rolling Stone* magazine that Grundig didn't further its career in Atlanta as it had hoped. "Atlanta was into R.E.M.-ish stuff. We'd play on the outskirts of town, sometimes for two people." Laughren eventually left Grundig and was replaced by Kelley Hayes, who answered a "guitarist wanted" ad in a newspaper. Hayes did not audition for the part. Instead, he took the group to a nightclub. Grundig was impressed by the fact that Hayes knew the majority of the people in the club, and he was hired. Frustrated with the musical orientation of Atlanta, Ward quit the group. His discontent would help to drive the songs on Cold's debut album.

After reconciling with the group, Ward and the band returned to Jacksonville in 1996 and soon thereafter met fellow local musician Fred Durst of the rock group Limp Bizkit, who was interested in covering a Grundig song. Ward visited Durst's home to perform a series of songs on an acoustic guitar. Impressed with Ward's abilities, Durst signed him and Grundig to his Flip label and recruited Ross Robinson to produce the record. Robinson's credits include Korn, Slipknot, and Limp Bizkit. "Ross is, to me, the best metal producer you can get. He just drags the heaviness out of everything, like with Slipknot. It's amazing what he does. When you record with Ross one time, you gotta give it your all. You have to go off like you would onstage," Ward told *Contemporary Musicians*. During the recording process, Ward learned that German stereo manufacturer Grundig was trying to sue him and the band for $300,000 over use of its name. "I thought, what are you talking about? We don't have any money. Everybody was throwing names around. Wes (Borland), the Limp Bizkit guitarist, said he had a great idea: Cold. It was the perfect name. It fits the music," Ward told *Contemporary Musicians*.

The eponymous debut album, filled with references to drug addiction and aliens, was released on June 2, 1998, on A&M Records. In a review for MTV Online, Bryan Reesman wrote that the album's "strong nod to the Seattle sound of the early '90s is quite prominent—there's plenty of detuned guitars, throbbing bass, and an overall dominating dissonance." European media raved about the record. According to Cold's official A&M Records biography, the German magazine *Kerrang* notes, "There's nothing better than slapping a debut album on the deck and finding yourself swamped by an excitingly alien new sound.... Cold songs are evil. They crawl under your scalp and build a nest." Doug Reese of *Billboard* noted that "the gritty yowl of Ward's vocals, in addition to some full-of-pain lyrics, complement Cold's sludgy instrumentation."

To push the record, Cold toured with Soulfly, The Urge, and Gravity Kills throughout the United States. Two months after the release of *Cold*, A&M stopped promoting the album after Universal Music Group took over A&M Records and Flip. In 1999, Cold re-signed with Interscope and the affiliate label Flip. Later that year, Cold returned to the studio with producer Adam Kasper in Seattle, Washington, to work on what was to become *13 Ways to Bleed on Stage*. The songs were written in Los Angeles and Jacksonville, however Ward was influenced by his surroundings in Seattle, namely the World Trade Organization riots. "It was on the same street as the studio. Everyday, we would go into the studio and right outside the window was the police riot bus. There were smoke bombs going off. We would just stand at the door all day and watch," Ward told *Contemporary Musicians*.

For *13 Ways to Bleed on Stage*, Cold called in former Limp Bizkit member Terry Balsamo to play guitar in mid 1999. On *Cold* and onstage, Ward had played guitar parts, but with *13 Ways to Bleed on Stage,* he wanted to concentrate solely on vocals. "With a guitar around, I wasn't as personal with the crowd as I wanted to be. I wanted more energy and intimacy. I can concentrate more on vocals and performance now," Ward explained in his record company biography.

Besides Kasper, who had worked in the studio with the Foo Fighters and Nirvana, Cold asked Durst and Chris Vrenna, formerly of Nine Inch Nails, to produce as well. "We wanted programming, but not too computer sounding because we're an organic band," Marshall said in the group's A&M biography. Vrenna agreed, adding subtle electronic touches to *13 Ways to Bleed on Stage* which contradict heavy guitars and angst-ridden lyrics with piano and melodies. Fellow Flip artist Aaron Lewis, lead singer for the band Staind, made vocal appearances on the songs "Send in the Clowns" and "Bleed." Cold previewed the new songs while on the road with the Tattoo the Earth tour and Limp Bizkit in the summer of 2000.

Selected discography

Cold (includes "Around the World"), A&M, 1996; Geffen/Flip/Interscope, 2001.
13 Ways to Bleed on Stage (includes "Send in the Clowns" and "Bleed"), Geffen/Flip/Interscope, 2000.

Sources

Periodicals

Billboard, November 1, 1997, p. 12.
Rolling Stone, July 19, 2001, p. 26.

Online

MTV Online, http://www.mtv.com/bands/cold/263791/album.j html (July 25, 2001).

Additional information was provided by A&M publicity materials, 1998, Interscope publicity materials, 2000, and an interview with Scooter Ward on June 29, 2001.

—*Christina Fuoco*

Cold Chisel

Rock group

With the October 1998 release of *The Last Wave of Summer,* rock group Cold Chisel hit the top of the Australian charts, a stunning feat for a band that had formed 25 years earlier. More impressive was the fact that the band dominated the music scene after a hiatus of 15 years. After breaking up in 1983, most of the band's members were not talking to one another. Adding to the tension, competition among the former bandmates' solo projects seemed to confirm that Cold Chisel would never be revived. Given the band's enduring popularity even after its dissolution, however, the media hype around a Cold Chisel reunion never dwindled. With a persistent former manager and eager record company behind them, Cold Chisel alumni regrouped for a series of rehearsals that eventually led them into the recording studio and out on the road for one of the most successful tours in Australian concert history.

Cold Chisel came together in the southern Australian city of Adelaide, best known for the imposing architecture of its buildings and the rock-solid reputation of its residents, who founded the city as free immigrants, not as convict transportees. In the decades after World War II, Adelaide was once again the destination for thousands of European immigrants; among the new

Photograph by Laurent Rebours. AP/World Wide Photos. Reproduced by permission.

settlers was the Swan family of Glasgow, Scotland, who moved to the city in 1961. As teenagers in Adelaide, two of the Swan sons developed a serious interest in music, and in 1973, John Swan helped found a band with guitarist Ian Moss under the name Orange. A native of Alice Springs, one of Australia's most remote cities, Moss had performed with a number of bands before moving to Adelaide. Joined by keyboardist Don Walker, bassist Les Kaczmarek, and drummer Steven Prestwich, who had immigrated to Australia from Liverpool, England, in 1971, the band soon faced its first personnel change: John Swan was replaced as lead vocalist by his younger brother, James, who adopted the name Jimmy Barnes. The group changed its name to Cold Chisel in 1974, taking its inspiration from the title of a song written by Walker.

For the first four years of its existence, Cold Chisel played a series of small venues across Australia while developing a repertoire of original songs and gaining experience as live performers. Increasingly, the intense stage presence of Jimmy Barnes became the band's focal point, although Walker's songwriting also put the band a notch above its hard-rocking competitors on the music scene. In 1977, the band relocated to Sydney and redoubled its efforts to get a contract with a record label, an effort that included a number of demo sessions. Finally, in September of 1977, Cold Chisel signed with the Australian division of WEA/

Elektra Records. By the time it entered the studio to record its debut, however, Kaczmarek had left the band and was replaced by Phil Small.

Cold Chisel, released in 1978, reached the top 40 on the Australian album chart, but it was the single "Khe Sanh" that gained more attention. A blistering song written by Walker about a Vietnam veteran's disillusionment and despair, "Khe Sanh" was banned by Australian radio for its lyrics. Although the song contained no direct profanities, its subject matter was controversial enough, and it missed making the national top 40. Later in 1978, the band released a live EP, *You're 13, You're Beautiful, and Your Mine,* which did somewhat better. The band also gained valuable exposure as the opening act for some of the day's most popular international acts, including Foreigner and Peter Frampton in 1978, and Rod Stewart the following year.

Cold Chisel's status as an opening act changed with the release of its second full-length album in 1979, *Breakfast at Sweethearts*, which earned platinum sales in the first year of its release. The band also conducted a three-month tour of Australia that continued to enhance its reputation for enthusiastic crowds and pointed controversies. The use of a picture of a burning monk on its concert posters earned Cold Chisel criticism from many in the music press, although the band defended its decision. When a riot broke out in Newcastle, Australia, while the band was in town for a concert, some linked the violence with the group. At the end of the year, Cold Chisel faced another challenge when its arena tour with other Australian acts—a first in the local music industry—was beset by weather, health, and equipment problems. By the end of 1980, however, Cold Chisel was beyond doubt the biggest band in the country.

The 1980 release of *East* confirmed Cold Chisel's status as Australia's hottest band. The group regularly broke concert attendance and sales records throughout the country, and its albums occupied long runs in the top ten. The band was unable, however, to find a significant audience outside of its home territory. *East* barely made the *Billboard* album chart, despite American tours with Heart, Joe Walsh, Ted Nugent, Loverboy, and Cheap Trick. The lack of an international breakthrough, combined with some tensions among individual band members, gradually sapped the band's strength. "By 1983 the band I knew and loved had been killed anyway," recalled Walker in an interview posted on the band's website. "And by late 1983 I wasn't much interested in the work involved in keeping what was left alive." The other members of Cold Chisel shared the sentiment, and after a farewell concert tour and album, the band split up at the end of 1983.

For the most part, the individual members of Cold Chisel enjoyed great success on their own. Prestwich became a member of the Little River Band, which achieved much greater international record sales than Cold Chisel ever enjoyed, and Walker worked on a number of solo and collaborative efforts with Australian musicians. Moss scored a number one album in Australia with his 1989 release *Matchbook,* which contained the chart-topping single "Tucker's Daughter." Moss won five awards from the Australian Record Industry Association (ARIA) for *Matchbook* and "Tucker's Daughter," although his subsequent projects were somewhat less successful. Of all the former Cold Chisel bandmates, the career of Jimmy Barnes was the most notable. Releasing a series of hit albums in the decade after Cold Chisel's demise, Barnes became "the nation's best-known working-class man, affectionately known to most Australians as 'Barnesy,'" according to the *Sydney Morning Herald.* Like Cold Chisel, however, Barnes never achieved a sizable audience in North America or Europe, and in the mid 1990s he faced significant financial problems despite his success on the charts. As Barnes admitted in a 1998 *Cyber Times* online interview, "I did the classic rock star mistake. I made huge amounts of money but managed to spend even more."

Gradually, the members of Cold Chisel came to terms with their past differences. In 1993, Moss and Walker worked with Barnes on a track for his album *Soul Deep,* an experience that showed them that they could work together amicably. "It did take us some time to get over some niggly things, and there had been some sour grapes, so it was the first time that any of us had worked together since the split. It was a real milestone," Barnes told *Billboard* in 1995. Still, progress toward a full-fledged Cold Chisel production moved along slowly. "Any time there was a mention of the band getting back together, it was very quickly squashed," Small explained to *Australian Musician* magazine online. "There just was not the vibe at any of those times. There was never any question around it, it was just always passed up." The incentive to re-form was immense, however, given the band's enduring popularity. A release of archived tracks in 1994, *Teenage Love,* proved that the band was still among Australia's most popular acts. In fact, Cold Chisel had sold more records after it broke up than during its active recording career, a rare achievement in the recording industry.

Gathering for a series of rehearsals in Sydney, Australia, in May of 1997, the band's members quickly set their sights on producing an album that would live up to the band's past glories. "It's got to be the best we can possibly be otherwise there's no point in doing it," Small told *Australian Musician.* "What we've built up after fifteen years without even being together could so easily be destroyed by doing a rat s**t gig and putting out a second-rate album." The release of Cold Chisel's *The Last Wave of Summer* in 1998 did not disappoint

its fans. When the first single from the album, "Yakuza Girls," was made available on the Internet, it received almost a quarter-million hits within 12 hours, and the album's release was a major event, debuting at number one on the charts. Cold Chisel's tour was equally successful, with sold-out dates across Australia.

Although the band still hungered for success in America and Europe, Cold Chisel's reunion was a validation for its members. And while solo projects still occupied some of their time—notably, Jimmy Barnes' starring role as a tough guy in the Australian film *Foolproof*—the newfound joy that the bandmates found in playing together meant that Cold Chisel would remain a force on the contemporary Australian music scene.

Selected discography

Cold Chisel, Elektra, 1978.
You're 13, You're Beautiful, and You're Mine (EP), Elektra, 1978.
Breakfast at Sweethearts, Elektra, 1979.
East, Elektra, 1980.
Swingshift, Elektra, 1981.
Circus Animals, Polydor, 1982.
Northbound: The Best of Cold Chisel, Teldec, 1983.
Twentieth Century, WEA, 1984.
Teenage Love, Alex, 1995.
Razor Songs, WEA, 1996.
Once Around the Sun, Mushroom, 1998.
The Last Wave of Summer, Mushroom, 1998.
The Best of Cold Chisel, WEA, 1998.
Last Stand, Import, 1999.

Sources

Periodicals

Billboard, January 14, 1995, p. 37; September 27, 1997, p. 67; October 24, 1998, p. 57; January 13, 2001, p. 51.

Online

Australian Musician, http://www.australianmusic.asn.au/mag/summer98/chisel.html (June 28, 2001).
Australian Record Industry Association, http://www.aria.com.au (June 28, 2001).
Cold Chisel Official Website, http://www.coldchisel.com.au (June 28, 2001).
Cyber Times, http://www.cyber-times.org/people/p250698.html (June 28, 2001).
Mushroom Records, http://www.mushroom.com (June 28, 2001).
Sydney Morning Herald, http://www.smh.com.au/entertainment/cannes33.html (June 28, 2001).

—Timothy Borden

John Corigliano

Composer

Since the mid 1960s, when he won an award for his professional debut, Sonata for Violin and Piano, composer John Corigliano has worked in a diverse number of classical music forms, including oratorios for large-scale stage productions, orchestral works for symphonies and smaller ensembles, movie soundtracks, and even a full-scale opera. Long respected by critics and audiences in the classical music community, Corigliano earned wider public recognition in 2000-01, some 40 years into his career as a composer, when he won an Academy Award for the soundtrack to *The Red Violin* and a Pulitzer Prize for his Symphony No. 2. Corigliano also embraced the chance to lead public discussions of classical music, often appearing for question-and-answer sessions before his works were performed. "It makes a very big difference when the audience actually sees a human being talk about his piece and then hears it.... They open up their ears and they finally say, 'This guy has something to say to us.'" Basking in critical acclaim and public attention, Corigliano became a rarity among contemporary classical composers: he actually verged on becoming a household name.

John Corigliano, Jr. was born on February 16, 1938, in New York, New York, to a family surrounded by music. His father was an established figure in the classical music world in his own right, holding the first violinist, or concertmaster, position with the New York City Philharmonic from 1943 to 1966; his mother was a pianist. With such a pedigree, it was no surprise that the younger Corigliano studied music at Columbia University, where he completed his Bachelor of Arts degree while studying under composer, conductor, and electronic music pioneer Otto Luening. After finishing his studies at Columbia, Corigliano complemented his musical training at the Manhattan School of Music with composer Vittorio Giannini. Corigliano also studied with composer Paul Creston before making his first professional mark with the Sonata for Violin and Piano at the Festival dei Due Mondi at Spoleto, Italy, in 1964. Commonly known as the Spoleto Festival, the annual artistic gathering was a forum for modern dance, theater, music, and visual arts pieces. Corigliano's award for his chamber music piece earned him a reputation as one of the brightest young American composers of the day.

Made Mark as Experimental Composer

Corigliano gained additional experience while working with legendary New York Philharmonic conductor and composer Leonard Bernstein on his Young People's Concerts series, which ran for 14 seasons beginning in 1958. Corigliano also made his mark as an experimental composer with his 1970 work *The Naked Carmen,* described as an electric rock opera inspired by Bizet's classic work. During the 1970s the composer also presented works such as *Etude Fantasy,* a work for the solo piano, Oboe Concerto, and Clarinet Concerto, the last of which was recognized as a breakthrough work for Corigliano at the time of its debut at the New York Philharmonic under Bernstein's direction in 1977.

Corigliano's next major achievement, composing the score for the 1981 science fiction film *Altered States,* brought him his widest audience yet. The William Hurt movie was a box office hit and Corigliano shared in its critical praise, earning his first Academy Award nomination. Although he did not win the award, Corigliano welcomed the opportunity to expand his musical horizons on the film. "I pulled out all the stops of my experimental side because it was a wild film," he recalled in a 2000 profile in *Advocate.* The film score also became one of the "stepping stones" in Corigliano's career, as he related in an interview with the *Twentieth Century Ltd.* classical music program, as after its success he received a number of prestigious commissions from symphony orchestras. One of these works, commissioned by the Chicago Symphony Orchestra during his residency there, resulted in Corigliano's Symphony No. 1, written in response to the AIDS crisis.

Symphony No. 1 and *The Ghosts of Versailles*

Although Symphony No. 1 was composed as a personal remembrance to friends lost to AIDS, Corigliano's work was embraced on a wider level by orchestras and audiences around the world immediately after its debut in 1991. One of his most enduring and universal works, Corigliano described it as "a tragic symphony" with several possible meanings depending on its interpretation. "But the wonderful thing about music," he told *Twentieth Century Ltd.,* "is there are no words, and that gives you the freedom to get what you want out of it, to hear it the way you want to hear it." The Chicago Symphony's recording of Symphony No. 1 won two Grammy Awards, for Best New Composition and Best Orchestral Performance, but these were not the only awards that Corigliano won for his work that year. In addition to being inducted into the American Academy and Institute of Arts and Letters for his body of work, Corigliano also received the Grawemeyer Award, perhaps the most prestigious award for composition, for Symphony No. 1.

Corigliano received recognition as Composer of the Year from both the International Classical Music Awards and Musical America for his other outstanding work of 1991, the opera *The Ghosts of Versailles.* Written in collaboration with librettist William M. Hoffman, the work was Corigliano's first venture into opera, but one that met with immediate critical success. As its title reflected, the production presented the ghosts of several eighteenth-century French aristocrats, including Marie Antoinette, who gathered at Versailles to hear a new opera. Although the format was a novel one for the composer, he brought the eclectic elements that he used in other works to produce "an atmospheric mix of serialism, romanticism, neoclassicism, Turkish pastiche and electronics," as a *Newsweek* reviewer noted. Despite the complexity of the opera's score, however, Corigliano succeeded in making *The Ghosts of Versailles* an accessible work. As he told *Newsweek,* "Music is very often a foreign language, even to music lovers. That's one reason I vote for clarity at all times."

Making musical sense from a variety of sources had become the composer's trademark and the basis for his critical and commercial success. "We are exposed all the time, barraged really, with a variety of worlds of music," he told *Twentieth Century Ltd.* "So the idea of shutting that out of my vocabulary seemed ridiculous." During the 1990s, Corigliano continued to branch out into pieces that included another Grammy Award-winning composition, 1996's *String Quartet,* as well as the cantata *Of Rage and Remembrance,* inspired by his own earlier Symphony No. 1. Corigliano also reworked selections from *The Ghosts of Versailles* into a piece for cello and piano called *Phantasmagoria.*

Although Corigliano had enjoyed his past work on movie soundtracks—which included the 1985 film

Revolution in addition to *Altered States*—he was reluctant to take on another film project because of the loss of control a composer suffers during the film's production and editing. The proposal for *The Red Violin*, however, intrigued Corigliano as a unique opportunity. The story of a violin with tragic origins that travels from owner to owner over the course of 300 years, the film featured the violin's music as a central element of the plot. In fact, Corigliano's score helped to construct the film's plot. Because of production delays with the film, he had completed the score before much of the film had been shot. To some, the film was almost irrelevant to enjoying Corigliano's work. "The score is filled with fire and blood," as the *National Review* noted. "It can be savored all on its own, celluloid aside."

Debuting in 1997 as *The Red Violin Chaconne for Violin and Orchestra* with the San Francisco Symphony, the work was another stunning success. After the film was released in 1999, Corigliano won the Academy Award for Best Original Film Score. In 2001, Corigliano learned that he had received the Pulitzer Prize for his composition Symphony No. 2, a string orchestra piece commissioned by the Boston Symphony Orchestra. Corigliano also looked forward to reworking *The Dylan Thomas Trilogy,* his 1999 oratorio performed by a chorus using the poet's work as a reference point, into a unified piece. In addition, the composer continued his ventures into combining the human voice and electronic instruments, a direction that had already resulted in the 1998 work *Vocalise* with the New York Philharmonic. One of the few remaining challenges for Corigliano was to conduct a performance of one of his compositions. "I did conduct once or twice," he told *Twentieth Century Ltd.* with characteristic self-effacement. "It made me too nervous."

Selected discography

Altered States (soundtrack), BMG-RCA, 1981.
Phantasmagoria: Music of John Corigliano, Sony Classics, 1990.
Poem in October/Oboe Concerto/3 Irish Folk Song Settings, BMG-RCA, 1990.
Corigliano: Concerto for Clarinet and Orchestra/Barber: Op. 47, New World, 1992.
John Corigliano: Of Rage and Remembrance/Symphony No. 1, BMG-RCA , 1996.
Five American Clarinet Quintets, Delos, 1998.
The Red Violin (soundtrack), Sony Classics, 1999.

Sources

Periodicals

Advocate, May 9, 2000, p. 59.
Christian Science Monitor, June 25, 1999, p. 15; May 4, 2001, p. 18.
National Review, July 12, 1999, p. 57.
Newsweek, December 30, 1991, p. 58.

Online

About Classical Music, http://www.classicalmusic.about.com/musicperform/classicalmusic/library/weekly/aa032700a.htm (June 18, 2001).
Fine Arts Management, http://www.fineartsmanagement.com/artists/bio.asp?artistid=9 (June 18, 2000).
Sony Classical Music, http://www.sonyclassical.com/artists/corigliano/bio.html (June 18, 2001).
Twentieth Century Ltd.—Simon Fraser University, http://www.sfu.ca/twentieth-century-ltd/corigliano1/html (June 19, 2001).

—Timothy Borden

David Coverdale

Singer, songwriter

David Coverdale is a successful singer and songwriter who has sold more than 40 million albums over the course of his career. The bluesy rock vocalist has been a fixture in the recording industry since the early 1970s, first as a member of the supergroup Deep Purple, and later as the founder of Whitesnake. Performing with legendary musicians such as Ritchie Blackmore, Jimmy Page, Tommy Aldridge, and Jon Lord, and raising his infant blues-rock band to heavy-metal stardom, Coverdale has firmly established himself as a notable force in the world of hard rock.

Coverdale was born on September 22, 1951, in Saltburn-by-the-Sea, Cleveland, England. His love for music developed early. Even as a toddler, he was singing along to records. Around the age of 14, the aspiring singer began performing professionally and developing the voice which made him famous. "I don't think my voice had broken," he explained to *Sounds* magazine in 1974. "And that's when I first learnt how to sing with my stomach, which sounds silly, but it's totally different from a normal voice." Coverdale continued to work on his craft until he witnessed legendary soul musician Ray Charles perform "Yesterday" one afternoon while watching Alan Freeman's *Pick of the Pops*. The experience moved him to tears. "I'd heard the Beatles version but this had the hairs standing on my neck. I thought it must be good to have a voice like that and that sort of feel. I started thinking 'I'm a person, I can feel … why can't I emphasize it in what I'm doing.' That's when I started borrowing records and started listening to more than The Pretty Things … going beyond the R&B thing," Coverdale told *Sounds*. He continued to develop his talent as well as his interest in soul, playing mainly with local bands such as The Fabuloso Brothers.

At the age of 22, while working at a local boutique, Coverdale spotted an article in British music publication *Melody Maker*. There was a picture of keyboardist Jon Lord accompanied by a significant line in the text: "Deep Purple still looking for vocalist—considering unknown." Coverdale wanted the opportunity to audition. He contacted several influential people from the local music scene in an attempt to try to reach Deep Purple. Unfortunately, his efforts proved fruitless. Still determined, he proceeded to ask friend Roger Barker, manager of the Redcar jazz club, to intervene. Barker, as with many of Coverdale's friends, had confidence in the singer's ability, but initially felt that he was setting his sights too high. Regardless, the club owner pulled the right strings, and after sending in a tape, Coverdale landed the audition and ultimately got the position as new lead singer for one of the world's biggest rock bands.

Comprised of a powerhouse of accomplished musicians, Deep Purple enjoyed a soaring wave of success with their early 1970s albums and hit singles, including the classic "Smoke on the Water," from the record

Machine Head. Despite their rising popularity, tension was apparent between Ritchie Blackmore and Ian Gillian, two of the group's principal members. In 1973, Gillian left the group and Coverdale became the new lead singer for Deep Purple. The ambitious vocalist proved to be a worthy successor, collectively moving the band in a different direction. Though, as Coverdale pointed out in *Sounds*, "I never considered myself to be a replacement, it was a new thing. As far as they were concerned it was a new band. They just had a reputation to live up to and an excellent one at that." The group's next record, *Burn*, became a top ten hit. Coverdale stayed with Deep Purple for the next three years and released two additional albums, *Storm-*

bringer and *Come Taste the Band*. In 1976, after a particularly disastrous tour, Coverdale left the group because he was unhappy with personal conflicts and musical direction within Deep Purple. Shortly thereafter, the group broke up.

Following his departure, Coverdale relocated himself and his family to West Germany where he began writing music for his first solo effort entitled *Whitesnake*. The record was issued in a reptile sleeve and contained a strong collection of rock ballads. However, London was in the midst of a punk explosion and the album failed to break any ground. In 1978 Coverdale returned to the United Kingdom and assembled a band to support his second record, *Northwinds*, recruiting the same session players he used to record his debut solo album. The group, which included Mickey Moody, Bernie Marsden, Brian Johnston and Dick Dowles, debuted in February of 1978 as David Coverdale's Whitesnake. A blues-based EP, *Snakebite*, followed several months later, ambitiously highlighting the Bobby Bland soul classic, "Ain't No Love in the Heart of the City." The song soon became a constant in the band's repertoire.

Whitesnake was a soulful hard rock group that had slightly provocative lyrical content laid over heavy-handed rock tracks and ballads. The band was a source of amusement and controversy for the British press. While journalists were often impressed with the group's obvious talents, many had a problem with Coverdale's racy lyrics, though, as writer Carol Clerk explained in a 1984 issue of *Melody Maker*. "There's a humor about Whitesnake, a tendency to take an idea, an element of truth or a simple observation and exaggerate it to such over-the-top proportions that it's pointless, really, to take offense."

The *Snakebite* EP proceeded to make the United Kingdom top 100 and the band went though various lineup changes. Several moderately successful albums followed, including *Trouble, Live at Hammersmith* and *Lovehunter*. The band had its first legitimate hit with "Fool for Your Loving" from the 1980 release, *Ready an' Willing*. The song climbed gingerly up the American charts, reaching number 53 and finally initiated American interest. Thereafter, Whitesnake crossed the Atlantic and served as an opening act for megagroups AC/DC and Jethro Tull. As legitimate stars in Europe, this was a large departure from their normal concert experience. The group was accustomed to taking American celebrities such as Ozzy Osbourne, Billy Squier, and ZZ Top as openers for their shows. Whitesnake's next three records, *Live in the Heart of the City, Come An' Get It* and *Saints & Sinners* all made the British top ten (*Come An' Get It* made the American top 200). In 1982 and 1983, the group cemented their hard rock star position as headliners for the infamous Monsters of Rock festival at Castle Donnington in England.

Despite the fact that Whitesnake was a force to reckon with in Europe, they had hardly made a dent in the United States music market. This changed in 1984, though, when the band released *Slide It In,* a record which helped put them on the American map. The platinum album was a certified hit in the United Kingdom. A revamped and different version of *Slide It In* made the top 50 in the United States as well. The record featured a diminished presence of the band's customary blues-infused sound with a harder edge. Even record mogul David Geffen took notice, suggesting to Coverdale that he "start taking America seriously."

The recording of the group's subsequent album, 1987's *Whitesnake,* was strewn with problems. Coverdale suffered from a deviated septum, which delayed the recording process. Additionally, serious internal conflicts within the band saw the departure of all of the musicians that worked on the record, including Coverdale's main writing partner, former Thin Lizzy axe grinder John Sykes. Coverdale replaced his band yet again, adopting, with the record label's help, a slew of heavy metal/hard rock veterans. When the singer was asked by *Billboard* in 1988 about working with musicians who didn't play on the album, he explained, "My prime concern when I was putting this lineup together was who could play the music, who could take it further and who could look good doing it." In 1987, Whitesnake shed its skin and adopted a glossier heavy metal image, one which helped make the group more alluring to a video-friendly, music-buying public.

Whitesnake was a harder, more deliberately polished album. With a new look and contemporary sound, the band catapulted up the American charts on not only the strength of their music but their videos as well. The group had three frequently played videos on MTV, all featuring Coverdale cavorting with then-girlfriend Tawny Kittaen. *Whitesnake* also contained two top ten singles, "Is this Love" and the band's first number one song, "Here I Go Again," which originally appeared on *Saints & Sinners* in 1982. The record, *Whitesnake,* went on to sell more than ten million copies and made the group valid stars worldwide. Oddly, many of the band's new fans were completely unaware that Whitesnake had existed for more than ten years in different incarnations.

In 1989, the group released *Slip of the Tongue,* which while not as successful as *Whitesnake*, did sell well over three million albums. The group, now certified headliners, toured yet again with more lineup changes, including the addition of renowned guitarist Steve Vai. A year later, Coverdale's divorce from Kittaen and unhappiness with the band's direction (most notably its glossed up image) put Whitesnake on hold.

In 1992, the prolific singer linked with superstar Led Zeppelin guitarist Jimmy Page to form a unique and critically acclaimed outfit called Coverdale/Page. The group released a successful album and toured Japan. However, Coverdale/Page was unable to sell out large concert venues in the United States, which ultimately terminated any further plans.

One last version of Whitesnake, called David Coverdale and Whitesnake, surfaced in 1994. The group released a new album, *Restless Heart,* solely in Europe in 1997 and subsequently went on its final tour. Thereafter Coverdale temporarily dropped off the musical radar. In 2000, the star vocalist released his first new solo album in over 20 years called *Into the Light.*

Selected discography

Solo

Whitesnake, EMI, 1977; reissued, Spitfire, 1999.
Northwinds, EMI, 1978.
(With Jimmy Page) *Coverdale/Page*, Geffen, 1993.
Into the Light, Dragonshead (North America), EMI (International), 2000.

With Whitesnake

Snakebite (EP), Geffen (North America), EMI (International), 1978.
Trouble, Geffen (North America), EMI (International), 1978.
Live at Hammersmith, Geffen (North America), EMI (International), 1978.
Lovehunter, Geffen, (EMI, International), 1979.
Ready an' Willing, Geffen, (North America), EMI, (International), 1980.
Live In the Heart of the City (double record UK) EMI (International), (single album US), Geffen (North America), 1980.
Come An' Get It, Geffen (North America), EMI (International), 1981.
Saints & Sinners, Geffen (North America), EMI, (International), 1982.
Slide It In, Geffen (North America), EMI (International), 1984.
Whitesnake, Geffen (North America), EMI (International), 1987.
Slip of the Tongue, Geffen (North America), EMI (International), 1989.
Greatest Hits, EMI, 1994.
Restless Heart, EMI, 1997.

With Deep Purple

Burn, Warner Bros., 1974.
Stormbringer, Warner Bros, 1974.
Come Taste the Band, Warner Bros., 1975.

Sources

Books

Larkin, Colin, editor, *The Guinness Who's Who of Heavy Metal,* Guinness Publishing Ltd., 1992.

Lazell, Barry, editor, *Rock Movers and Shakers*, Billboard Publications, 1989.

Strong, M.C., *The Great Rock Discography*, Canongate, 1998.

Periodicals

Billboard, February 13, 1988; February 20, 1988; February 3, 1990.

Creem, March 1985.

Melody Maker, December 20, 1980; April 11, 1981; June 20, 1981; January 4, 1984; March 3, 1984.

Spin, February 1990.

Sounds, November 2, 1974.

Online

David Coverdale Official Website, http://www.davidcoverdale .com (June 19, 2001).

—*Nicole Elyse*

The
Damned

Following both social and economic upheaval in England during the 1970s, disenfranchised youth responded by initiating chaos on the concert stage. The result was the beginning of the infamous British punk movement. One of the most significant groups to evolve from this genre was undoubtedly theatrical rabble-rousers the Damned. Birthed from the same notorious scene as the Sex Pistols and the Clash, the Damned stood their ground by presenting a mesh of music with dynamic performances topped with an intriguing gothic flair. They were the first British punk group to release a single and the first ambitious enough to perform in America. Most notably, however, the Damned has managed to maintain the attitude and spontaneity of punk rock without being limited by its combustible tag. The group's ability to sustain an audience for over two decades is a feat few groups have been able to accomplish.

The Damned was formed in London, England, in 1976. The group's members found each other while performing in an assortment of short-lived outfits during punk's initial days. Drummer Rat Scabies met bassist Captain Sensible in 1974 while they were both employed at Croydon Fairfield Halls cleaning toilets and working at the shows held there. Two years later Brian James and

For the Record . . .

Members include **Garrie Dreadful** (born Garrie Priest; group member, 1996-99), drums; **Brian James** (born Brian Robertson on February 18, 1955; left group, 1978), guitar; **Roman Jugg** (born on July 25, 1957; group member, 1981-89), keyboards, guitar; **Patricia Morrison** (born Patricia Rainone; joined group, 1996), bass; **Monty Oxy Moron** (joined group, 1996), keyboards; **Pinch** (born Andrew Pinching; joined group, 1999), drums; **Rat Scabies** (born Chris Millar on July 30, 1955; left group, 1977; rejoined group, 1978; left group, 1996), drums; **Captain Sensible** (born Raymond Ian Burns on April 24, 1954; left group, 1984; rejoined group, 1988; left group, 1992; rejoined group, 1996), guitar; **Spike Smith** (group member, 1999), drums; **David Vanian** (born David Letts on October 12, 1956), vocals; **Algy Ward** (born Alistair Ward on July 7, 1959; group member, 1978-80), bass; others.

Formed in London, England, 1976; played first show at London's 100 Club with the Sex Pistols, released debut single "New Rose," 1976; released *Damned, Damned, Damned*, played with the Deadboys at New York's CBGB club, released *Music for Pleasure*, 1977; disbanded and re-formed (without Brian James), 1978; signed with Chiswick Records, released *Machine Gun Etiquette*, 1979; released *The Black Album*, 1980; left Chiswick, 1981; signed with Bronze Records, released *Strawberries*, 1982; dropped from Bronze, 1983; Captain Sensible leaves, group is signed to MCA, 1984; released *Phantasmagoria*, 1985; released *Anything*, 1986; embarked on We Really Must Be Going tour, then disbands, 1989; Vanian and Sensible rejoin and put together new Damned, 1995-96; signed with Nitro Records, 2000; released *Grave Disorder*, 2001.

Addresses: *Record company*—Nitro Records, 7071 Warner Avenue, Suite F736, Huntington Beach, CA 92647. *Management*—Atrophy Pop Management, 621 Molino Avenue, Long Beach, CA 90814. *Website*—The Damned Official Website: http://www.officialdamned.com.

Scabies were playing in London S.S., a group that included future members of the Clash. Singer Dave Vanian had been previously acquainted with Scabies through another band they had played in together. The aspiring musicians finally merged to form an unnamed group, a precursor to the Damned. The lineup included future Pretender Chrissie Hynde on guitar, Sensible on bass, and Scabies on drums. Vanian, then employed as a gravedigger, was auditioned by the group to become one of their new singers. He nabbed the position mainly because he looked the part but also because Sex Pistol Sid Vicious, who was also set to audition, never showed up. The group never quite made it past the rehearsal stage, but it was obvious to most of the members that they had something special together. Hynde left the group, and Brian James was added on guitar. James christened the group the Damned after a 1969 movie of the same name. It was also a name said to be descriptive of the band's hapless state of affairs at the time.

Built Reputation on Energy and High Jinks

The group rehearsed for six weeks before playing their first show on July 6, 1976, as an opening act for the Sex Pistols at London's 100 club. The Damned quickly earned a reputation as a viable act on the circuit. Unlike many of their contemporaries, the group's songs were not fixed on politics. Instead, the Damned relied on their high-octane tunes and energetic performances to capture the audience. The group's shows were enhanced by the over-the-top high jinks of Sensible and the dynamic presence of Vanian on vocals. However, like most performances of the punk era, the Damned shows were reputed to be a violent and messy affair. The group earned this notoriety when a glass thrown at a show knocked out the eye of a patron. Years later, Sex Pistols singer Johnny Rotten claimed it was Vicious who was the perpetrator. Additionally, gobbing (or spitting at the group, a frequent occurrence at punk shows) was reported to be practiced frequently at the Damned's concerts. Fortunately, the group's reputation only added to their allure.

The Damned proceeded to play around England and at various punk festivals, one of which included the Mont de Marsan in France. This performance in particular caught the eye of producer Nick Lowe, who in turn helped the group garner the interest of fledgling punk label Stiff Records. Ultimately, the Damned landed a record deal with the label. In October of 1976, the group's first single "New Rose" beat the release of the Sex Pistols' "Anarchy in the UK," thus earning the Damned its spot in history as the first punk group to release a single. "New Rose" never charted (perhaps due to Stiff's haphazard distribution), but it did cement the Damned's position as a punk music leader. Shortly thereafter, the Damned joined the Sex Pistols, the Heartbreakers, and the Clash for the controversial

Anarchy tour, which was often cancelled and plagued with problems. The band's frustration with the cancellations as well as turmoil between management companies caused the Damned's departure from the tour shortly after it started.

In 1977 the group released their first full-length album, *Damned, Damned, Damned*, which garnered positive reviews and anchored a steady fan base for the band. The fast-footed record eventually reached number 34 on the United Kingdom charts. The group proceeded to perform its first opening shows for glam rocker Marc Bolin, but the Damned eventually graduated to headlining status themselves. In April of 1977 the Damned reached yet another milestone when they played with The Deadboys at New York's CBGB club, becoming the first British punk band to play in America.

Tensions Grew Within Group

Despite their initial good fortune, the Damned soon started to show some of the self-destructive traits of punk in late 1977. James had expressed interest in adding a second guitarist because he wanted to free himself up for more sophisticated material, although the band was mostly opposed to this decision. They eventually relented, adding Robert Edmunds (better known as Lu) to the lineup. Tensions soon started to grow. Songs by James, the group's main songwriter, were slow in coming, and it was thought that he might be trying to discourage Sensible and Scabies from contributing material of their own. After completion of the group's second album, disgruntled Scabies left the band.

The Damned's *Music for Pleasure*, produced by Pink Floyd's Nick Mason, was largely considered a disappointment as it lacked the energy of its predecessor. As one critic described in a 1977 issue of the *Record Mirror*, "It's not that it's bad. It's just that it's relentlessly mediocre." The band moved through a succession of drummers (including Jon Moss, later of Culture Club) until February of 1978 when James decided to leave the group as well. Several weeks later, the remaining members officially brought an end to the Damned. In August, the group reassembled at the Rainbow in London, smashing their instruments as a grand finale.

The individual members of the Damned all embarked on various musical endeavors, none of which was particularly successful. They found themselves performing together again (without James) by September of 1978. Vanian, Sensible, and Scabies rejoined forces, and Sensible was moved to guitar. The group also sifted through a series of bassists before settling on Algy Ward, formerly of Australian punk band the Saints. The group performed a series of secret shows first under the alias Les Punks and later as The Doomed. James had apparently registered the

Damned's name and officially held the rights to its usage. The group settled with their former guitarist, regained use of their name, and shortly thereafter was back to performing as the Damned.

In 1979, the band signed a new deal with Stiff competitor Chiswick Records and released *Machine Gun Etiquette*. As Steve Keaton explained in *Sounds* magazine, "the ridiculously fine *Machine Gun Etiquette* album … reaffirmed their position in the premiere punk league … establishing once and for all that they are a breath of fresh air … in a consistently convoluted musical arena." The album included three chart-climbing singles, including "Love Song," the Damned classic "Smash It Up," and "I Just Can't be Happy Today." The group seemed to be riding a wave of success with eventful live shows and even more acclaim upon the release of their subsequent record, *The Black Album*. However, 1982's *Strawberries* (released on the Bronze label after the group left Chiswick in 1981), though a strong record, found itself competing for attention with Sensible's solo work, namely his version of "Happy Feet" from South Pacific, a surprise number one hit in Britain. The group again faced internal turmoil, which resulted in Sensible's departure from the group in September of 1984. Longtime keyboardist Roman Jugg then stepped up to handle guitar responsibilities.

Reveled in Success

Surprisingly, Sensible's departure did not dismantle the group. Instead, the Damned reveled in one of their most successful periods. After signing with major label MCA, the group released *Phantasmagoria* in 1985. It contained the Damned's biggest hit, a cover of Barry Ryan's 1960s smash "Eloise." Unfortunately, with the exception of a few tracks (notably the Love cover "Alone Again Or"), the group's next release, titled *Anything*, was widely considered uninspired. In the late 1980s, the Damned found themselves again with a fractured lineup and no record label. The group decided to disband and proceeded to launch a series of farewell tours, the last being the We Really Must Be Going tour in Britain in 1989.

The Damned reunited in splintered lineups and performed sporadically throughout the early 1990s. In 1995 Vanian and Sensible finally rejoined, shortly thereafter putting together a new and relatively stable lineup for the Damned. Joining the group were musicians Patricia Morrison (formerly of Sisters of Mercy/Gun Club) on bass, Monty Oxy Moron on keyboards, and Garrie Dreadful on drums. Dreadful was replaced by a drummer named Spike Smith in 1998, then again in 1999 by Pinch.

The following year the Damned inked a record deal with Nitro Records, a label owned by second-generation punk musician and longtime the Damned fan, Offspring vocalist Bryan Holland. The Damned released their first studio album in 15 years entitled *Grave Disorder* in August of 2001. Twenty-five years after their inception, the Damned remains one of the most inspired groups in punk rock.

Selected discography

Damned, Damned, Damned, Stiff, 1977.
Music for Pleasure, Stiff, 1977.
Machine Gun Etiquette, Chiswick, 1979.
The Black Album, Chiswick, 1980.
Strawberries, Bronze, 1982.
Phantasmagoria, MCA, 1985.
Anything, MCA, 1986.
Grave Disorder, Nitro, 2001.

Sources

Books

Gimarc, George, *Punk Diary 1970-1979*, St. Martin's Press, 1994.
Lazell, Barry, *Punk An A-Z*, Hamlyn, 1995.
Savage, Jon, *England's Dreaming: Anarchy, Sex Pistols, Punk Rock and Beyond*, St. Martin's Press, 1993.

Periodicals

Los Angeles Times, June 28, 2000; July 3, 2000; October 29, 2000.
Melody Maker, August 13, 1977; November 5, 1977; November 26, 1977; December 24, 1977.
New Musical Express, August 10, 1977; August 13, 1977; August 24, 1977; August 27, 1977; September 17, 1977; November 5, 1977; November 26, 1977; December, 24, 1977; December 25, 1977; March 25, 1978; November 24, 1979.
Orange County Calendar, June 28, 2000.
Orange County Register, July 29, 1989; June 30, 2000.
Record Mirror, August 27, 1977; September 24, 1977; November 20, 1977; November 26, 1977; April 15, 1978.
San Francisco Weekly, July 5-11, 2000.
Sounds, October 15, 1977; November 5 ,1977; November 26, 1977; December 8, 1979.

Online

Another Great Website from The Damned, http://homepages.nildram.co.uk/~culttv/dam1.html (June 16, 2001).
Damned Official Website, http://www.officialdamned.com (June 21, 2001).
RollingStone.com, http://www.rollingstone.com (June 21, 2001).
Totally Damned, http://www.thedamned.da.ru (June 21, 2001).
Ultimate Band List, http://www.ubl.com (June 25, 2001).

—*Nicole Elyse*

David Darling

Composer, cellist

Described as a "maverick cellist" by his grass-roots music expression organization, Music for People, David Darling's music has mixed genres—including jazz, pop, rock, country, and New Age—with intellectual curiosity, playful innovation, experimentation, and creative improvisation. His evocative, breakthrough compositions for cello have earned him international respect from experimental and jazz musicians, and teachers revere him for his delightful, transformative workshops in musical expression.

Born on March 1, 1941, in Elkhart, Indiana, Darling's interest in music appeared early. At age four he began playing the piano, and by ten years of age, he began studying the cello. As a teenager, Darling took up the piano, bass, cello, and saxophone and became a bandleader for a dance band. At Indiana University, he focused on the cello and music education. Graduating in 1965, he continued in academia for four years, serving as a faculty cellist and conductor at Western Kentucky University.

In 1969, Darling's career turned from education to performance. Striking out in a new direction, Darling went to Nashville and worked with many country musicians, most notably Johnny Cash. He has also worked with other such notables as Bobby McFerrin, Spyro Gyra, Arlo Guthrie, Peter Kater, and R. Carlos Nakai. Darling also became involved with the influential group the Paul Winter Consort, an ensemble he worked with from 1969-78. The Consort included Ralph Towner and Glen Moore, with whom he would also perform as part of the chamber jazz group Gallery.

The Paul Winter Consort was groundbreaking in many ways. It was one of the first proponents of world music—African, Asian, Brazilian, and Indian—and incorporated these foreign melodies, rhythms, and sounds into jazz. This 'adventure through music' explored a wealth of sound textures. From this point on, many North American and European artists began incorporating world music into their work. Learning ethnic music with the Consort and playing it on the cello was what Darling called "mind-blowing." Prior to Darling, no one had taken the cello out of its classical context. After spending nearly a decade playing and experimenting with the Consort, Darling began his solo career.

Darling continued to experiment not only with new melodies and rhythms but also with electronic effects on the cello. His innovations with the cello changed the understanding of the instrument's capacities. Reviews of his solo efforts have been positive and even swooning. Kris Larson from *Egg* magazine, in comments at the ECM Records website, said, "His music is emerald fire on a midnight sea, an arctic exhalation amidst stifling summer heat, a northwest wind driving out a confusion of fog. It is archaic, intense and yet almost always calming." *Down Beat* magazine, in a review cited by ECM, said, "Darling's range of stylistic evocations moves from early music to ethereal, from swarthy impressionism to folk sonorities…. All is dark and wintry but somehow transcendent." A *Jazziz* magazine review, also available on the ECM website, stated, "No one has improvised on the cello with greater imagination and attention to texture, color, and tonality than Darling." The purity of his sound and the rigorousness of his experimentation have caused artists from other disciplines to approach him for collaboration.

Writer Barry Lopez was so inspired by Darling's solo work, *Dark Wood,* released in 1993, that he wrote a story to accompany it. "Disturbing the Night" was written to "create an emotional and narrative parallel to the music—a kind of literary counterpoint—with a story written under its influence…," Lopez is quoted at the ECM Records website. It is "a recapitulation of the same emotional truth from a different perspective." The wildly innovative dance ensemble Pilobolus, known to general audiences from commercials showing the company flying through the air in impossible, angular combinations, approached Darling to collaborate with them. European film director Wim Wenders has also used Darling's music for his films *Until the End of the Earth* and *Far Away, So Close*, and the legendary French film director Jean-Luc Godard felt that Darling's music would act as a suitable aural counterpart to his images in the film *Nouvelle Vague*.

Despite the profound effect of Darling's compositions on listeners and artists, they are not his only passion. Darling co-founded Music for People in 1986. The nonprofit organization offers workshops to bring the

For the Record . . .

Born on March 1, 1941, in Elkhart, IN. *Education*: Studied cello and music education at Indiana University; graduated, 1965.

Faculty cellist and conductor at Western Kentucky University, 1965-69; member of the Paul Winter Consort, 1969-78; began solo recording career with ECM Records, 1979; played with Spyro Gyra, 1980; formed chamber jazz group Gallery, 1981; co-founded Music for People, a nonprofit organization that encourages musical expression, 1986; contributed to film soundtrack for *Until the End of the World,* 1991; began recording meditative music for the Relaxation Company, 2000.

Addresses: *Business*—Music for People, P.O. Box 61, Watertown, CN 06795, (860) 274-1912, website: http://www.musicforpeople.org, e-mail: mfp@musicforpeople.org.

creative, improvisational power of music into everyone's life. The project perhaps best illustrates Darling's deeply held beliefs about the social and spiritual power of musical expression. The workshops are designed to set even the "non-musical" at ease and allow them to play with musical expression. The program's manifesto, "A Bill of Musical Rights," states that "human beings need to express themselves daily in a way that invites physical and emotional release…. Sincerely expressed emotion is at the root of meaningful musical expression…. In improvisation as in life, we must be responsible for the vibrations we send one another." In effect, it explains the belief that music is an essential creative expression for everyone. Darling's extensive work with Music for People has brought the joys of creative expression to thousands of people from all walks of life.

Darling has also dedicated over a decade of his life to the Young Audiences Art Program. The award-winning program's mission is to "instill in young people from pre-kindergarten to high school an appreciation, knowledge and understanding of the performing, visual and literary arts." Artists bring students educational, creative experiences designed especially for children.

Darling's programs show how music can stimulate learning, imagination, awareness, and balance. The intention of his creative improvisation workshops is to enhance personal growth through music.

Selected discography

Solo

Journal October, ECM, 1979.
Cycles, ECM, 1981.
(Contributor) *Nouvelle Vague* (soundtrack), ECM, 1990.
(Contributor) *Until the End of the World* (soundtrack), Warner Bros., 1991.
Cello, ECM, 1991.
Dark Wood, ECM, 1993.
Eight String Religion, Hearts of Space, 1993.
The Tao of Cello, Relaxation Company, 1993.
Musical Massage: Balance, Relaxation Company, 2000.
Musical Massage: In Tune, Relaxation Company, 2001.
Cello Blue, Hearts of Space, 2001.

With others

(With Paul Winter, Ralph Towner, Paul McCandless, Glen Moore, and Colin Walcott) *Winter Consort's Road,* A&M, 1969-70.
(With Ketil Bjornstad) *The River,* ECM, 1994.
(With Ketil Bjornstad, Terje Rypdal, Jon Christensen) *The Sea,* ECM, 1997.
(With Ketil Bjornstad, Terje Rypdal, Jon Christensen) *The Sea II,* ECM, 1998.

Sources

Periodicals

Down Beat, September 1996, p. 58.
Forbes, March 18, 1991, p. S27.

Online

"David Darling," *All Music Guide*, http://www.allmusic.com (September 24, 2001).
"David Darling," 800.com, http://www.800.com/mz/ArtistInfo.asp?A=6418 (September 24, 2001).
"David Darling," Musicolog, http://www.musicolog.com (July 16, 2001).
ECM Records, http://www.ecmrecords.com (July 16, 2001).
Music for People, http://www.musicforpeople.org (July 16, 2001).

—*Madeline Crowley*

Wild
Bill
Davison

Cornetist

Like a select group of other jazz instrumentalists, cornetist Wild Bill Davison had a talent that lives on long after his death. More than a decade after Davison died at the age of 83, record companies continue to reissue some of the more than 800 songs he recorded during his 70-year career. Jazz aficionados never tire of talking about some of the more memorable engagements played by the colorful Davison around the world.

Davison did not come by his lifelong nickname accidentally. He was a heavy drinker beginning in his teens and was known as a womanizer. Davison went through four wives before he finally got the knack of married life, settling down to a relatively monogamous relationship with his fifth wife—and love of his life—Anne Stewart. Heavy drinking and womanizing were the two most obvious characteristics that made Davison truly wild. He also enjoyed a reputation for playful antics and kleptomania as well.

In fact, given his wild streak, it's particularly amazing that Davison was a musician of such memorable ability. Beginning in childhood, he had displayed an unfailing ability to commit to memory every song he heard, and his natural ear for pitch amazed even his fellow musicians. It's equally amazing that even with a life of such excesses, Davison retained his musical abilities until the very end of his life. He practiced daily into his 80s and spent the final two decades of his life playing concert dates in Europe, where his music was extraordinarily popular.

William Edward Davison was born on January 5, 1906, in the northwest Ohio town of Defiance. The son of Edward Davison, an itinerant worker, and Anna Kreps Davison, a homemaker, he was raised by his maternal grandparents from the age of seven on. Davison displayed a love for music, as well as a natural ability to master musical instruments, at an early age. He first learned to play the mandolin, guitar, and banjo. He joined the Boy Scouts mostly because it provided an opportunity for him to learn the bugle. At age 12 he graduated from the bugle to the cornet. The sharper tones of the trumpet never really appealed to Davison, and he stayed with the cornet for the entirety of his musical career. His ear for music was so keen that after hearing a song only once he could reproduce its melody perfectly and elaborate on it with perfect chord progressions and harmonic improvisation. His ability to read music was limited, but it was a skill that he really did not need for the style of music that most interested him.

From his very early teens through the age of 17, Davison played with the Ohio Lucky Seven, an experience that helped to strengthen his musical skills. But, more importantly, he spent much of his spare time studying the playing styles of other horn players he admired. Among his early musical influences were Louis Panico, a trumpet soloist with the Isham Jones

Born William Edward Davison on January 5, 1906, in Defiance, OH; died on November 14, 1989, in Santa Barbara, CA; son of Edward and Anna (Kreps) Davison; married Anne Stewart (stage name of Anne Hendlin McLaughlin), 1954.

Started playing in obscure Midwestern dance bands; graduated to big-name clubs in Chicago and Milwaukee, 1930s; played with Eddie Condon's band in New York City, 1940s; released cornet solos on Commodore label; opened a 12-year run at Condon's Dixieland club in Greenwich Village, 1945; played with local bands rather than leading his own, late 1950s-60s; made numerous recordings and toured Europe.

Orchestra, Bix Beiderbecke, and Louis Armstrong. From 1923 to 1925, Davison was the featured soloist with the Chubb-Steinberg Orchestra of Cincinnati, moving in 1926 to the Detroit-based Seattle Harmony Kings, with which he played until 1928. When not playing gigs with these groups, he led smaller jazz bands that he put together with musicians who enjoyed the same type of music as he did.

Davison earned an enviable reputation in Midwest jazz circles, eventually winning a featured solo position with Chicago's Benny Meroff Orchestra in 1928. The four-beat, swinging jazz that Davison and other white jazz musicians of the era were playing fell more into the category of swing than the two-beat Dixieland—or New Orleans style—jazz. It came to be known as "Chicago-style" jazz, mostly because it was a sound associated with jazz musicians in the Windy City. In the early 1930s, a number of Chicago area musicians—most notably jazz guitarist Eddie Condon—left the Midwest for New York City, taking with them the label of "Chicago-style" jazz.

Despite his obvious talent and formidable reputation as a jazz stylist, Davison stayed behind in the Midwest when many of his contemporaries from the region migrated to the big time in New York. Whether it was a lack of self-confidence or ambition that held him back is unclear, but for most of the 1930s he played clubs in Chicago and Milwaukee, rarely venturing outside the region. Leaving the Meroff Orchestra in 1931, Davison formed a 12-piece band of his own, building the ensemble around his cornet and the woodwind brilliance of Frank Teschemacher, who played both the clarinet and the alto saxophone. Based in Chicago, Davison's band quickly earned the admiration of fellow

musicians, both white and black. Davison's moniker of "Wild Bill," which accurately described the musician's lifestyle off the bandstand, was first used by a Chicago-area promoter who billed him as "Wild Bill Davison, the White Louis Armstrong."

A tragic accident and labor troubles soon spelled disaster for the Chicago-based band that Davison had assembled and led. In March of 1932, a car he was driving was hit broadside, killing Davison's star wood-wind soloist, Frank Teschemacher, who was a passenger in the vehicle. Not long thereafter troubles with the local union finished off Davison's band. He moved to Milwaukee and found work with a number of bands over the next several years. Davison earned a lasting memory of Milwaukee's reputation as the country's beer capital when he was hit in the mouth by a flying beer mug in 1939. Although Davison's wild side persisted in Milwaukee, his professional billing in the Wisconsin city touted him as "Trumpet King." Perhaps he needed this period to build his self-confidence, but in 1941 he finally decided to head for New York, a destination that had lured many of the Midwest's best jazz musicians a decade earlier.

New York took Davison to its heart. He reestablished his relationship with Eddie Condon, whom he had met when both played with Benny Meroff in Chicago, and began playing dates at the city's hottest jazz clubs. From 1941 to 1942, he led the band at Nick's nightclub in Greenwich Village, and in 1943 took over the band at Jimmy Ryan's club on New York's famed "Swing Street"—52nd Street. He also collaborated in a Katherine Dunham production, recreating an original Dixieland jazz band.

Davison's first recordings of any note were made in the fall of 1943. Working with Condon's musicians but under his own name, he recorded 12 sides for Commodore Records. It was wartime and in December of 1943, Davison was drafted into the United States Army. Most of his time in the military was spent leading the band at the Grove Park Inn in the mountains of western North Carolina, a convalescent resort for injured soldiers. He remained active on the New York music scene, though, using weekend liberties to return to the city for occasional shows and recording sessions. In September of 1945, Davison was discharged from the military.

From the fall of 1945, when Eddie Condon's New York City jazz club opened, until the club was relocated in 1957, Davison led the house band and became the club's star attraction. The cornetist was at the peak of his musical powers in 1954 when he performed at the very first Newport Jazz Festival. Three years later, in 1957, Davison made his first two concert tours of Europe, earning a warm reception from European fans who seemed particularly appreciative of his style. The mid 1950s proved a particularly positive period for

Davison—both professionally and personally. In 1954 he married his fifth and final wife, actress Anne Stewart, a pairing that finally gave him a degree of stability he had not known earlier. His previous four marriages had all ended in divorce or annulment.

Davison continued to play professionally throughout the remainder of his life but played mostly with other bands instead of leading his own. Two exceptions came in 1968 and 1969 when he led his Giants of Jazz on concert tours. In the last two decades of his life there was a sharp increase in Davison's touring outside the United States, particularly in Japan and Europe, where audiences were particularly receptive to his jazz style and sound. His death in 1989 at the age of 83 came after surgery for an abdominal aneurysm, performed shortly after his return from a concert tour to Japan. Davis was cremated, and his ashes were buried in his hometown of Defiance.

Davison's distinctive rasping, driving, forceful sound—not unlike his reputation as a wild man—was only one side of this jazz great. He was capable of great sensitivity and sensuousness when playing ballads and madcap mischief and vulgarity with numbers of a humorous nature.

Selected discography

Jazz A-Plenty, Commodore, 1943; reissued, 1989.
That's A Plenty, Commodore, 1943.
Dixieland Jazz Jamboree, Commodore, 1943.
Mild and Wild, Commodore, 1943.
And His Jazz Band, Jazzology, 1944.
This Is Jazz, Vol. 1, Storyville, 1947.
Sweet and Hot, Riverside, 1947.
Showcase, Jazzology, 1947.
Individualism of..., Savoy, 1951.
Dixieland, Savoy, 1951.
Ringside at Condon's, Savoy, 1951.
Wild Bill Davison with Helen Ward, Paradox, 1952.
Wild Bill Davison, Pax, 1954.
Wild Bill Davison's Jazzologists, Jazzology, 1954.
Live! Miami Beach (1955), Pumpkin, 1955.
Pretty Wild/With Strings Attached, Arbors, 1956.
Plays the Greatest of the Greats, Dixieland, 1958.
Eddie Condon's All Stars/Wild Bill Davison's All Stars, Storyville, 1961.

'S Wonderful, Jazzology, 1962.
Rompin' 'n' Stompin', Jazzology, 1964.
Blowin' Wild, Jazzology, 1965.
With Freddy Randall and His Band, Jazzology, 1965.
Surfside Jazz, Jazzology, 1965.
After Hours, Jazzology, 1966.
Wild Bill at Bull Run, Jazzology, 1966.
Memories, Jazzology, 1966.
I'll Be a Friend with Pleasure, Fat Cat Jazz, 1968.
Lady of the Evening, Jazzology, 1968.
The Jazz Giants, Sackville, 1968.
Jazz on a Saturday Afternoon, Vol. 1 (live), Jazzology, 1970.
Jazz on a Saturday Afternoon, Vol. 2 (live), Jazzology, 1970.
Big Horn Jazz Fest '72, Big Horn, 1972.
Just a Gig, Jazzology, 1973.
Wild Bill Davison's 75th Anniversary Jazz Band, Jazzology, 1981.
Running Wild, JSP, 1981.
Sweet and Lovely, Storyville, 1988.
The Commodore Master Takes, Commodore, 1997.
Wild Bill Tapes, Munich, 1997.
Struttin' with Some Barbeque, Jazz Colours, 1998.
Wild Bill Davison With Freddie Randall & His Band, Jazzology, 1999.
Davison & Hodes Coalition, Jazzology, 1999.
Swinging Wild, Jazzology, 1999.
In New Orleans, Jazzology, 1999.

Sources

Books

The Scribner Encyclopedia of American Lives, Volume 2: 1986-1990, Charles Scribner's Sons, 1999.

Online

"The Wildest One: The Life of Wild Bill Davison," Jazzhouse, http://www.jazzhouse.org/files/sohmer1.php.3 (June 15, 2001).
"Wild Bill Davison," *All Music Guide,* http://www.allmusic.com (September 19, 2001).
"Wild Bill Davison," Excite Music, http://music.excite.com/artist/biography/-9849 (June 15, 2001).
"Wild Bill Davison," JazzCanadiana, http://www.jazzcanadiana.on.ca/_DAVIDS.htm (June 18, 2001).
"Wild Bill Davison," Sonicnet, http://www.sonicnet.com/artists/biography/504979.jhtml (June 16, 2001).

—Don Amerman

Down By Law

Punk rock group

Just as grunge was taking over popular music in the early 1990s, Down By Law sought to keep the punk-rock vision alive. "When punk rock broke and bands cashed in on fashion trends, Down By Law stayed true to its ideals," wrote Scott Puckett, publisher of the Sick to Move fanzine. From the trenches of punk-rock history, singer/songwriter Dave Smalley rose to form Down By Law as a project band—just for fun and with no commitments. A decade later, Down By Law turned out to be Smalley's longest-running band. After releasing its self-titled debut on punk's seminal Epitaph record label, the band produced *Blue, Punkrockacademyfightsong, All Scratched Up!,* and others. Joined on more than a half-dozen releases by an ever-evolving lineup of bandmates, Smalley embodied the punk-rock energy, aesthetic, and sound, but was seen as a standout by a legion of dedicated fans. Down By Law suffered whichever title a particular critic labeled them with, whether it was "hardcore," "pop-punk," or something in between. The name-game annoyed Smalley, who told the University of Delaware *Review,* "We're just a classic punk-rock band."

Smalley is a punk rock icon. He had been a pioneer of the hard-core punk movement playing in such seminal bands as Boston's DYS and Dag Nasty in Washington, D.C. Later, as the dynamic frontman to the band All, Smalley gained an even greater legion of fans after two albums and relentless touring. Smalley started Down By Law in 1991 as a project band—a group of revolving musicians to get together to record or tour, but nothing permanent. "It was the kind of deal where I would call up my friends and say, 'Hey I wrote some songs—do you want to jam?'" he said in an interview with the *Review.* "Then, all of a sudden, we were making albums and touring and visiting Europe. We never planned for it to be that way."

Smalley, the band's singer, songwriter, and cornerstone, remained at the front while the lineup changed around him. His voice clearly reflected its pure punk upbringing but stood out from that of punk's other frontmen. Smalley's voice "stands apart from others in his category based on its high-pitched, almost snotty style," wrote one critic in the independent publication *SLUG.* Also the songwriter, Smalley's songs and lyrics drove Down By Law. Fans related to his simple, heartfelt lyrics. In turn, his bandmates were proficient musicians who matched the singer's high-energy pace with their own musical dexterity.

Smalley first teamed up with ex-Clawhammer guitarist Chris Bagarozzi, drummer Dave Nazworthy, and Ed Urlik, the latter two former members of the group the Chemical People. The quartet found its home on the Epitaph record label, where it would remain until the late 1990s. The group released *Down By Law* in 1991 and *Blue* in 1992. By 1994, Down By Law had a new lineup, with "Angry" John DiMambro on bass, Hunter Oswald on drums, Sam Williams III on guitar, and Smalley up front to record 1994's *Punkrockacademyfightsong.*

While the lineup was ever-changing, Down By Law kept to a constant release and touring schedule with Epitaph, releasing *All Scratched Up!* in 1996 and *Last of the Sharpshooters* in 1997. The band toured relentlessly and fans responded. Down By Law also rewarded buyers who continued to purchase vinyl with a bonus—the vinyl release of *All Scratched Up!* contained a full side of tracks unavailable on the CD. *Last of the Sharpshooters* was Down By Law's last release on the Epitaph label.

"Down By Law deserves a place in the annals of rock 'n' roll," wrote one critic on alt.culture.guide online. Despite the band's punk packaging, the reviewer continued, Down By Law is a "good, old-fashioned rock band" creating "high-amperage rockola" that draws its sound as much from "roots rock aesthetics" and "new-wave melody" as it does "hardcore energy" and "punkish attitude." Most critics agreed that *Fly the Flag,* on the Go-Kart record label, was a more mature release, with something of a folk feel underlying Smalley's brash punk politics and delivery. The lineup on *Fly the Flag* was Smalley, Williams, Milo Todesco on drums, and Keith Davies on bass.

Fly the Flag had an obvious political message, much more so than any previous Down By Law release. The booklet to the CD contained an essay, a call for support for independence movements around the globe. The

Melkonian in *Alternative Press* went so far as to call the release a "blemish" on the band's history. "The lyrical intentions are grand," he wrote, "however, the message is blatant and sophomoric."

In 1999, Go-Kart Records put together Go-Kart Across America, a tour of the United States featuring the pioneering British punk band the Buzzcocks, the performance-art group/punk band Lunachicks, and Down By Law. The tour was arranged to support each band's new release. The tour was well received by fans in the cities it visited as it moved across the United States. The bands had a good time as well, according to Smalley, who is a stay-at-home dad when not recording or touring. A longtime fan of the Buzzcocks, he admitted in the *Review* that if someone had told him as a teen that he would one day be hanging out backstage with the band, he probably would have "had a heart attack." Down By Law released *Split* on Theologian in 2000.

Selected discography

Down By Law, Epitaph, 1991.
Blue, Epitaph, 1992.
Punkrockacademyfightsong, Epitaph, 1994.
Down By Law & Gigantor, Lost & Found, 1995.
All Scratched Up!, Epitaph, 1996.
Last of the Sharpshooters, Epitaph, 1997.
Fly the Flag, Go-Kart, 1999.
Split, Theologian, 2000.

Sources

Books

Larkin, Colin, *Encyclopedia of Popular Music,* Muze UK Ltd., 1998.

Periodicals

Free Lance-Star (Fredericksburg, VA), September 16, 1999.
Review (University of Delaware), October 19, 1999.
Rockpile (Jenkintown, PA), October 1999.

Online

"Down By Law," *All Music Guide,* http://www.allmusic.com (May 30, 2001).

Additional materials, including press clips from alt.culture.guide online, *Alternative Press,* CDNow, and *CMJ,* were provided by Go-Kart Records, 2001.

—*Brenna Sanchez*

title, *Fly the Flag,* could have had as much to do with flying one's own flag of individualism as it did with the awareness of worldwide struggles for independence. Songs about love, personal independence, and the sorry state of popular radio had always been Down By Law's strong suit, embodied on *Fly the Flag* in "Promises," "Sorry Sometimes," "Nothing Good on the Radio," and the title track. But Smalley went acutely political on this album. He related personal struggles for independence with those going on in Ireland, Bosnia, Iraq, and Tibet. "I think it's a very noble cause to fight for your own land, for a place to call your own," he said in the *Review.* "I'm a sucker for every lost cause there ever was," he told *CMJ.* It was questionable whether Down By Law's fans could relate to a track like "This is the New Breed," which laments the Republican Party's failure to remove President Bill Clinton from office. Smalley thought *Fly the Flag* may have been Down By Law's best album to date. Critics didn't whole-heartedly agree. While Jo-Ann Greene in a CDNow review online declared, "Down By Law has arrived with flying colors, and now is the perfect time to hoist its flag high," other critics were lukewarm. Dave

Eve

Rap musician

Photograph by Tina Fineberg. AP/World Wide Photos. Reproduced by permission.

While many women in the male dominated world of rap and hip-hop often opt to sell records by using blatant sexuality, rapper Eve has chosen to compete on her own terms. Female hip-hop artists who could equal the record sales and street credibility of male rappers are rare, but Eve has joined that exclusive group, which also includes Missy "Misdemeanor" Elliot and Da Brat. The self-proclaimed "pit bull in a skirt" got her start as the sole female with the hip-hop label Ruff Ryders. Her debut solo release, 1999's *Let There Be Eve: Ruff Ryders' First Lady*, debuted at number one on *Billboard*'s Top 200 and reached platinum sales that same year. Eve escaped one-hit wonder status when she released her sophomore effort, *Scorpion*, in 2001, prompting *Newsweek* to call her "hip-hop's most respected female presence."

Eve Jihan Jeffers was born in Philadelphia, Pennsylvania, c. 1979, and raised by her mother, Julie Wilcher. They lived in the Mill Creek housing projects until Eve was 14 years old, then moved to a better neighborhood. Eve regularly saw her father when she was younger, but he eventually drifted out of her life. She performed in Philadelphia talent shows with an all-girl singing group called D.G.P., or Dope Girl Posse, as a teenager. She noticed she got more attention as a rapper than she did as a singer, so she switched to rapping at the age of 13. During high school, she rapped under the nickname Eve of Destruction, but she later decided to simply use the name Eve.

Before she was 18 years old, Eve got an incredible break. Some friends arranged an impromptu audition for Eve with high-profile hip-hop artist and producer Dr. Dre. Her friends didn't tell Dre she was coming, and he was taken aback when a tape was played and Eve, out of nowhere, rapped for him. Dre saw she had talent and immediately signed her to his fledgling Aftermath record label. Eve moved to Los Angeles a week later to begin work with Dre. Though her start was promising, Eve slipped through the cracks at Aftermath, as Dre was preoccupied with the business of running a new label. After a year passed and Dre still had not done anything with Eve, her contract lapsed and she was back in Philadelphia.

In 1997, on a recommendation from Dre's parent label, Interscope, New York's Ruff Ryders record label picked Eve's career up where it had left off with Dre. Ruff Ryders subjected Eve to writing and reciting drills to polish her raw talent. She likened the experience to boot camp, but felt she had to prove herself to them. "That's what made me a better MC," she told *Newsweek*. Her skills refined, Eve appeared on the Ruff Ryders *Ryde or Die* album. In 1999, she released her first solo album, *Let There Be Eve: Ruff Ryders' First Lady*. Although *Entertainment Weekly* critic David Browne found that *Let There Be Eve* "wasn't the knockout it was supposed to be," he wrote, he admitted that "unlike most of her peers, ... [Eve] radiated power."

For the Record . . .

Born Eve Jihan Jeffers c. 1979, in Philadelphia, PA.

Rapped under the name Eve of Destruction as a teenager; signed with Dr. Dre's Aftermath record label, 1996; signed to Ruff Ryders record label, 1997; released *Let There Be Eve: Ruff Ryders' First Lady*, 1999; appeared on Ruff Ryders/Cash Money tour, 2000; released *Scorpion*, 2001.

Addresses: *Record company*—Interscope Records, 2220 Colorado Ave., 3rd Floor, Santa Monica, CA 90404, website: http://www.interscoperecords.com.

The record-buying public agreed that Eve was at least a powerful record-selling force; *Let There Be Eve* had sold more than two million copies as of 2001. Hip-hop fans adored Eve's throaty voice, tough persona, and empowered lyrics. "I just want women to know how strong they are," she told *Time.*

Another of Eve's strengths was that where other female rappers were using blatant sexuality as a tool to compete with the men of hip-hop, Eve refrained, relying solely on her skills. Though she did work a brief, difficult stint as a stripper, "Eve plans not to seduce Adam but to beguile him," wrote Marie Elsie St. Leger in *People. Time* writer Christopher John Farley noted that hard-core rappers Foxy Brown and Lil' Kim "compete with male rappers by using sex as a weapon. Eve has found a balance: she's tough enough to run with the big dogs and sensitive enough to hug a small one." *Let There Be Eve,* he continued, "established her persona—sexy but not pornographic, in your face but somewhat introspective."

The release launched the meteoric rise of Eve. Suddenly a double-platinum-selling recording artist, her life changed virtually overnight. She underestimated the drain that touring, publicity, and her other professional responsibilities would have on herself and her personal relationships. On the Ruff Ryder/Cash Money three-month, 30-city tour in 2000, Eve thought it would be fun to take along a few girlfriends. Little did she know that when she stepped offstage exhausted every night, her friends would be ready to party. Her friendships suffered. Though she made a strong showing on the tour and audiences loved her, the offstage pressures proved too much. Eve left the tour prematurely and later admitted the period after the release of *Let There Be Eve* took a toll on her. The trials of success she faced over the next two years even resulted in a mild depression. "Anybody who tells you that they haven't been depressed their first time out is lying," she told *Billboard.*

In preparation for her second release, Eve underwent a subtle makeover. Irritated by criticism of her weight, she lost about ten pounds. Stylist Kithe Brewster became her constant companion, overseeing the artist's fashion choices, which became all top-designer. Leading designers like Chanel and Gucci welcomed Eve to choose freely from their lines of high-priced, high-fashion clothing, relishing the media coverage they would receive when the star wore their fashions to high-profile events.

Many artists don't live up to the hype of their first release and Eve clearly felt the pressure was on for her critical follow-up album. "It was harder," Eve admitted in *Vibe.* "But I try not to think about the pressure." The young artist's personal changes affected the process as well. "It's all about growing up," Ruff Ryders' co-CEO Chivon Dean pointed out in *Vibe.* "Eve's a young woman, and young women go through changes. She was only 20 when she came to us. There's more maturity now."

Critics agreed that *Scorpion,* released in 2001, showcased a broader range of musical styles and was a strong second release. Browne cited the record's roots in "hard-core stomp, rhymes, boasts, and slams." But *Scorpion* also incorporated Latin horns, reggae sounds on a cover of "No, No, No," co-produced with legendary reggae artist Bob Marley's son Stephen, and gospel, heard on the duet with 1980s R&B diva Teena Marie called "Life is So Hard." In addition to cameos by Da Brat and fellow Ruff Ryder labelmate DMX, rock band No Doubt's Gwen Stefani made an appearance on "Let Me Blow Ya Mind." Former mentor Dr. Dre reappeared as producer on two of the record's tracks. When *Scorpion* was released, Browne called it "more than just a dramatic improvement over its predecessor…. *Scorpion* pumps up the volume, the rhythms, everything." One of the record's strengths cited in several reviews was Eve's exploration of her singing voice in addition to her rapping skills. It was a risk for her to sing, wrote critic Dmitri Ehrlich in *Interview,* but one from which Eve emerged as "tentative but credible." *Scorpion* has been proven both a critical and popular success; the album was certified platinum in May of 2001.

Eve's second release reflected more of her own creative vision than her first. Songs like "Love is Blind" and "Heaven Only Knows" on *Let There Be Eve* led *Entertainment Weekly* writer Barry Walters to criticize Eve as an artist "struggling to shake a gang mentality." It was clearly a criticism Eve heard, because on *Scorpion,* she demanded more creative control. "Before, the lyrics were mine, but the vision was pretty much theirs

[Ruff Ryders]," she told *Newsweek*. "After that, I promised myself I would never make a song about shooting, robbing, anything like that, 'cause it's not me." Ehrlich wrote that on *Scorpion*, Eve demonstrated that hip-hop has a "human, vulnerable side." "I just do what I feel," Eve said in an interview with *Jet*. "I do exactly what comes from my mind and from my heart. I would say it's more reality than a lot of rap that's out." *Scorpion* was proof that Eve's vision was right on. "Her intensity never flags," wrote St. Leger, and declared the release "a hip-hop tour de force."

Selected discography

(Contributor) *Bulworth* (soundtrack), Interscope, 1998.
(Contributor) *Ryde or Die Vol. 1*, Ruff Ryders/Interscope, 1999.
Let There Be Eve: Ruff Ryders' First Lady, Ruff Ryders/Interscope, 1999.
Scorpion, Ruff Ryders/Interscope, 2001.

Sources

Periodicals

Billboard, February 10, 2001.
Entertainment Weekly, October 8, 1999, p. 72; March 9, 2001, p. 78.
Interview, November 2000, p. 155; April 2001, p. 80.
Jet, April 9, 2001, p. 58.
Newsweek, March 12, 2001, p. 70.
People, March 19, 2001, p. 41.
Time, March 19, 2001, p. 74.
USA Today, March 6, 2001.
Vibe, March 2001.

Online

"Eve," *All Music Guide,* http://www.allmusic.com (May 31, 2001).
Record Industry Association of America, http://www.riaa.com (August 30, 2001).
Ruff Ryders Records, http://www.ruffryders2000.com (May 31, 2001).

—*Brenna Sanchez*

Lara Fabian

Singer, songwriter

Photograph by Andrew Wallace. Hulton/Archive. Reproduced by permission.

The comparisons between Lara Fabian and fellow Canadian chanteuse Celine Dion are almost unavoidable: both got their start as singers in the French-speaking world; both make their home in Canada's predominantly French province of Quebec (although Fabian came to Canada during the 1990s from her native Belgium); both have done soundtrack work for Disney; and both eventually began recording in English to enter the very lucrative English-speaking music market. Being compared to Dion, Fabian told *Interview,* has not discouraged her. "I've been compared to so many people—Streisand, Celine—it doesn't bother me. Why worry about being compared to the best?" Dion, of course, has already become a highly successful musical star in English, but Fabian, whose English-language album debuted in 2000, is on the verge of breakthrough success.

Born in January 1970 in the Belgian town of Etterbeek, Fabian is the daughter of a Flemish father and a Sicilian mother. It was music that gave Fabian her first name. Both parents so enjoyed the love theme from the film *Dr. Zhivago* that they named their daughter Lara. Given Fabian's family background, her multilingualism is hardly surprising. She grew up speaking Italian as her first language (her mother's native tongue), but she was also comfortable speaking in French and Flemish, the two official languages of Belgium, as well as Spanish and English, both of which she learned in school. Although the family spent most of the time in Belgium, Fabian visited her mother's Sicilian homeland frequently as a child.

Fabian inherited her passion for music from both parents. Her father is a musician who plays guitar and once sang backup vocals for Petula Clark, while her mother is musical as well and introduced Fabian to classical music. For Fabian, there has really never been any question about what she would do with her life. "I've always wanted to be a singer, ever since I was a child," she told *Canadian Musician*. "I remember driving with my father as a five-year-old girl, and I turned to him, very serious, and said, 'I am a singer.' I knew back then that I wanted to be a singer and a songwriter, and I have always been dedicated to that dream, but it has been hard work along the way."

Fabian's parents recognized the singer's talents early on and enrolled her in the Royal Conservatory of Music in Brussels when she was eight. She was single-minded in her pursuit of musical training, she told *Canadian Musician*. "Nothing else really interested me; it was always singing, playing piano, writing songs and poems, learning, being taught everything I wanted to know. It was all music, and it never stopped. I had 10 years of lessons at the conservatory in Belgium, studying classical music. I learned how to sing, play the piano, and all the theory that I needed. By the time I left, I had confidence in my skills, and I knew that the

Born in January 1970 in Etterbeek, Belgium. *Education*: Studied at the Royal Conservatory in Brussels, c. 1978-88.

Launched professional career in Belgium, c. 1984; moved to Montreal, Canada, and formed own recording label and production company, Productions Clandestines, early 1990s; released French-language album debut, *Lara Fabian*, 1991; released *Carpe Diem,* 1994; released *Pure,* 1997; released debut English-language album, self-titled, 2000.

Awards: Fourth Prize, Eurovision Song Contest, 1988; Felix Awards, Best Female Vocalist and Best Live Performance, 1995; Felix Award, Pop Album of the Year, 1997; Felix Award, Quebec Artist Having Had the Most Impact outside Quebec, 1998; Victoire de la Musique Award, New Artist of the Year, 1998; World Music Award, Best Benelux Recording Artist, 1999; Felix Award, Quebec Artist Having Had the Most Impact in a Language Other Than French, 2000; World Music Award, Best Benelux Artist, 2001.

Addresses: *Record company*—Sony Music Canada, 1121 Leslie Street, Toronto, Canada ON M3C2J9. *Management*—Productions Clandestines, Montreal, Quebec, Canada. *Website*—Lara Fabian Official Website: http://www.larafabian.com.

experience had prepared me to become a real professional."

Even before leaving the conservatory and while still in her early teens, Fabian began performing in competitions in local and regional talent shows and appearing in clubs in Brussels. Her father, who had played guitar for her since she was a little girl, continued to provide her accompaniment on some of Fabian's early performances. In 1988 at the age of 18, she entered the Eurovision Song Contest, a competition created by the state-run television stations of Europe to find the best new popular songs, and won fourth prize for her rendition of "Croire."

Fabian's first single, "L'aziza est en pleurs," released in Belgium but marketed throughout the French-speaking world, enjoyed modest success, but it was followed up by "Croire" and "Je sais," which sold 500,000 and 300,000 copies, respectively. Her first visit to Quebec came on a tour to promote her single "Je sais." This crucial visit came at a time when Fabian was feeling frustrated at the lack of opportunities in Europe. "It is a very beautiful place but very conservative, and I was young and headstrong," she told *Canadian Musician.* "I was 18 years old, and I knew what I wanted to do with my life. I wanted to explore my potential and express myself, and I was feeling stifled. People kept telling me what I should be doing and how I should conduct myself, but I didn't want to compromise, so I left and found a place where I could be myself."

When Fabian decided to move to Montreal, she brought along with her producer-arranger Rick Allison, a longtime friend and collaborator. Between them, they had two suitcases and about $1,000 in cash. Together they established an independent recording label and production company called Productions Clandestines. In August of 1991, Fabian released her first album, self-titled, in her newly adopted homeland. She had recorded the songs on the album earlier in Belgium. Her sound quickly won the hearts of listeners in Quebec. Among the more successful singles from the album were "Le jour où tu partiras," "Qui pense à l'amour?" and "Les murs." Another song, "Je m'arrêterai pas de t'aimer," offered convincing proof that Fabian was not only a compelling vocalist but a talented songwriter as well. By 1993, her first album went gold and the following year was certified platinum.

Carpe Diem, Fabian's second French-language album, was released in 1994 and quickly proved that the singer-songwriter was no one-hit wonder. In less than a month, the album had gone gold and by 1995 was certified triple platinum. Three of the singles from the album—"Tu t'en vas," "Leila," and "Si tu m'amies"—remained in the top 50 for months. To promote her second album, Fabian went on tour, appearing before more than 150,000 fans around the French-speaking world. ADISQ, Quebec's association of recording artists, rewarded Fabian's hard work with two Felix Awards in 1995: Best Female Vocalist and Best Live Performance. One of the highlights of 1995 for Fabian was an appearance she made at Paris' famed Palais des Congres with legendary Serge Lama. Together the two sang "Je suis malade," a song that Fabian had included on *Carpe Diem.*

In 1996, Walt Disney Studios tapped Fabian to supply the voice of Esmeralda in the French-language version of its animated feature, *The Hunchback of Notre Dame,* as well as the song "Que dieu aide les exclus" ("God Help the Outcasts") for the French-language soundtrack. Disney was so impressed by Fabian's rendition of the song that it was included on the English-language soundtrack as well.

As impressive as sales of *Carpe Diem* had been, Fabian's third album, *Pure,* did it one better, soaring to gold in less than two weeks. Released in June of 1997, *Pure* produced three singles—"Tout," "Je t'aime," and "Humana"—that each sold more than one million copies. While touring in France in January of 1998, Fabian got an opportunity to appear onstage with another legendary French singer. At a benefit concert for Restos du Cur, she sang a duet with Johnny Hallyday. Thousands of French fans also got to see Fabian on tour, which included two sold-out shows at the famed Olympia Theatre in Paris. Only a month later the Montreal-based singer was honored with France's Victoire de la Musique Award, the French Grammy Award equivalent, as New Artist of the Year.

It was clear that France had taken Fabian to its heart. In April of 1998, she sold out a two-night stint at the mammoth Palais des Sports in Paris. Hallyday again invited her to join him onstage, this time during a number of concerts at the Stade de France before an estimated 240,000 fans. In the fall of 1998, Fabian was back on tour in Europe, appearing before audiences that totaled more than 150,000. Back in her adopted home of Quebec in November of 1998, she received ADISQ's Felix Award for the Quebec Artist Having Had the Most Impact outside Quebec. As if to confirm ADISQ's choice, France's *Paris Match* magazine put Fabian on its cover in December to showcase her as its Revelation of the Year. Six months later, at the World Music Awards in Monaco, Fabian received the award for Best Benelux Recording Artist. So eager was Europe's French-language market for more of Fabian that in July of 1999 Polydor released a slightly modified version of her 1991 self-titled debut album. The changes included a new album cover and the addition of the song "Croire."

In the summer of 1999, Fabian traveled to New York and San Francisco to record songs for her first English-language album, also self-titled. Released on the Sony label, the album was an important venture for Fabian, who told *Interview* magazine she wanted to reach the English-speaking world "because English is the universal language. No matter where you come from, if you sing in English, you can cross over to the world."

Fabian enlisted the help of some high-powered producers to help ensure the success of her debut English-language recording. Such hit-makers as Walter Afanasieff, Patrick Leonard, and Brian Rawling each produced tracks. As for the songs on the album, Fabian wrote or co-wrote about 90 percent.

Selected discography

Lara Fabian, Productions Clandestines, 1991.
Carpe Diem, Polydor, 1994.
(Contributor) *The Hunchback of Notre Dame* (soundtrack), Disney, 1996.
Pure, Polydor, 1997.
Lara Fabian, Columbia/Sony, 2000.
(Contributor) *A.I. Artificial Intelligence* (soundtrack), Warner Bros., 2001.

Sources

Periodicals

Canadian Musician, October 1, 2000.
Interview, November 2000, p. 44.

Online

"Artist: Lara Fabian," Sing365, http://www.sing365.com (June 14, 2001).
"Lara Fabian," Sony Music, http://www.sonymusic.com/artists/LaraFabianUS/English/bio.html (June 14, 2001).
"Lara Fabian: Biography," Sonicnet.com, http://www.sonicnet.com/artists/biography/910688.jhtml (June 14, 2001).
"Lara Fabian-Biography," Yahoo! Music, http://musicfinder.yahoo.com (June 14, 2001).

—Don Amerman

Neil Finn

Singer, songwriter

Photograph by Megan Lewis. Hulton/Archive. Reproduced by permission.

On November 24, 1996, the decade-long career of the group Crowded House was celebrated with a final concert before an estimated 150,000 fans on the steps of the Sydney Opera House in Australia. Although the group's greatest hits package had just hit number one in Australia and Britain and the band remained popular in the United States, Canada, and Europe, Crowded House founder Neil Finn felt the time was right to move on. "I crave a new context to draw something special out of me as a songwriter," Finn had commented in *Billboard* when the band's demise was announced during a British concert tour in June, although he gave no details about his future plans out of respect to his bandmates. After the dramatic final appearance with the stunning view of Sydney Harbor as a backdrop, Finn retreated to his native New Zealand and took up painting, a pastime that removed him from the hype of the music world. Within two years, however, Finn made a return to the recording studio and began another chapter in his already celebrated musical career.

Neil Mullane Finn was born on May 27, 1958, in Te Awamutu, New Zealand. Known as the "Rose Town of New Zealand," Te Awamutu was a small community on the country's North Island, about 90 miles (140 kilometers) south of the major city of Auckland. Finn's parents ran an orchard together with their four children: Neil, Tim, Carolyn, and Judy. The Finns enjoyed performing music at informal family gatherings. Neil was also a devoted pop music fan, citing Donovan and the Beatles as profound influences on his development as a musician and songwriter.

Tim, six years Neil's senior, was the first Finn sibling to pursue a musical career. Performing with bands during his stint at Auckland University, Tim formed Split Enz in 1972 with some college friends. The band enjoyed limited success from its new base in Melbourne, Australia, but verged on breaking up. When one of the band's founding members left the group in 1977, Tim asked Neil to join the band. The younger Finn's first notable contribution to Split Enz, the international hit single "I Got You," brought the group to a new level of success. Several more hits followed, including "Message to My Girl," but by 1984, Split Enz had broken up.

Neil Finn paused momentarily before assembling a new set of musicians under the name Crowded House in 1984. For the next ten years, he enjoyed even greater success with hit singles such as "Don't Dream It's Over" and "Something So Strong." Tim Finn joined Crowded House for its 1991 album *Woodface,* but later decided to pursue a solo career. The brothers remained close, however, and collaborated again on the 1996 song "Mary of the South Seas," a tribute to their mother who had emigrated as a child to New Zealand from Ireland. The brothers also released the collaborative work *Finn* in 1996, an album that *Q* magazine summarized as "Some lovely songs ..., a few rather

For the Record . . .

Born Neil Mullane Finn on May 27, 1958, in Te Awamutu, New Zealand.

Joined Split Enz, 1977; formed Crowded House, 1984; dissolved band, 1996; released debut solo album, *Try Whistling This,* 1998; released *One Nil,* 2001.

Addresses: *Record company*—Parlophone/EMI, Manchester Square, London W1A 1ES, England, website: http://www.parlophone.co.uk; EMI Music New Zealand, Limited, P.O. Box 864 Auckland, New Zealand, website: http:www.emimusic.co.nz. *Website*—Neil Finn Official Website: http://www.nilfun.net.

ordinary ones and a lot of fun, particularly for the Finns. Fortunately, the fun and the spirit of the whole affair is mostly infectious."

As the brothers' collaborative efforts took precedence over Crowded House, Neil Finn realized a greater need to work as a solo artist. Announcing the end of Crowded House in June of 1996 during a British tour to support the group's greatest hits collection, *Recurring Dream,* Finn and his bandmates capped the band's success with the farewell concert at the Sydney Opera House in November of 1996. Crowded House had sold over six million albums during its career, and although some critics bemoaned the fact that Finn was quitting a band that had yet to peak in terms of its artistic accomplishment, the disappointment was matched by anticipation over what his solo career would produce.

"There's nothing that gets you more than a skillfully crafted melody and beautifully supporting chords," Finn told CNN.com upon the release of his first solo album in 1998, *Try Whistling This.* "So I'll be addicted to that for the rest of my days." Indeed, the album enhanced Finn's reputation as a wordsmith and melodic craftsman, albeit with more sparse, more somber arrangements than featured on Crowded House and Split Enz songs. *Time* South Pacific welcomed *Try Whistling This* as evidence of "an evolving New Zealand sound—one that combines darkly gothic lyrics with Polynesian sway." Finn—by now living with his wife and two sons in Auckland—agreed, telling the magazine that "it's in the end to do with something which seeps in from the land and the light and the indigenous cultures here."

Although *Try Whistling This* sold well enough in New Zealand, Australia, and England to secure the release of a follow-up album, it was decidedly less successful than his past efforts. Yet Finn refused to be compromised by his past triumphs. As he commented in a press release on his own website, "I haven't discovered fully what the Neil Finn sound is, but I'm enjoying the exploration." This exploration included writing the score for the New Zealand film *Rain,* expected to be released in 2001, and collaborating with the Australian Chamber Orchestra on musical pieces inspired by the poems of cartoonist Michael Leunig. The songwriter also prepared to publish a book focusing on his song's lyrics. Most of all, Finn retained his sense of fun on the concert stage. A tour of New Zealand in early 2001 featured amateur musicians who auditioned by sending tapes of their performances to Finn. He also enjoyed having his son, Liam, join the tour as a drummer and bassist. In all, Finn wears his reputation as a pop star lightly. As he told the *Australian* in February of 2001, "I like being in the music industry, but I don't like being immersed in it all the time."

Finn's second solo album, *One Nil,* went to the top of New Zealand's charts immediately after its March of 2001 release, although it received a critically cooler reception than his past efforts. A British Skipmusic.com reviewer was disappointed with Finn's increasingly introspective direction, claiming that *One Nil* "has seen him plumb the depths of mediocrity and climbed [sic] the stunted peaks of averageness" with the album's muted passions. Yet Finn was pleased with his second solo album, telling the *Australian* before its release, "I think it's a romantic record. It's more consistent than the first solo record. It's got a more consistent groove running through it."

Despite the album's mixed reception, Finn conducted a well received series of concerts in New Zealand to support its release. Assembling a stellar cast of musicians that included Pearl Jam lead singer Eddie Vedder; former Smiths and Electronic guitarist Johnny Marr; Ed O'Brien and Phil Selway of Radiohead; celebrated violinist and keyboardist Lisa Germano; and Finn's son, Liam, Finn and company held a five-day, sold-out concert series in Auckland that became a celebration of his entire career. Vedder had been a fan since Finn's Split Enz days, and the other musicians were longtime friends of the performer; Germano had also been a guest musician on *One Nil.* Onstage, the chemistry among the musicians and their love of performing together showed. The *Guardian* called one concert "three-and-a-half hours of the stuff that makes you fall in love with your record collection all over again."

In addition to his book publishing, orchestral work, and score writing in 2001, Finn scouted for a record deal to release *One Nil* in America where he had released *Try Whistling This* through an independent label. Finn also prepared to tour Europe before returning for another tour of Australia where he maintained his reputation as one of the region's most notable songwriters and performers. In his home country, of course, he was known simply as "New Zealand's King of Pop," an epithet bestowed upon him by the New Zealand Music website. Despite Finn's self-effacing character, it is a label that he had earned with over 20 years of outstanding contributions to popular music.

Selected discography

Solo

(Contributor) *Common Ground: Voices of Modern Irish Music*, EMI Premier, 1996.
Try Whistling This, Sony, 1998.
One Nil, EMI Parlophone, 2001.

With Crowded House

Crowded House, Capitol, 1986.
Temple of Low Men, Capitol, 1988.
Woodface, Capitol, 1991.
Together Alone, Capitol, 1994.
Recurring Dream: The Very Best of Crowded House, Capitol, 1996.
Afterglow, Capitol, 2000.

With Split Enz

True Colors, Mushroom, 1979.
Time & Tide, Mushroom, 1982.
History Never Repeats Itself: The Best of Split Enz, Universal/A&M, 1987.

With Finn Brothers

Finn, EMI/Discovery, 1996.

Sources

Periodicals

Australian, February 23, 2001; May 26, 2001.
Billboard, June 15, 1996, p. 6; December 14, 1996, p. 37; April 28, 2001, p. 62.
Observer, April 15, 2001.
Q, November 1995.
Time South Pacific, June 15, 1998, p. 76.
Times, April 7, 2001.

Online

"Neil Finn," New Zealand Music, http://www.nzmusic.com (June 18, 2001).
"Neil Finn goes solo for a melodic 'Try Whistling This,'" CNN.com, http://www.cnn.com/SHOWBIZ/Music/9808/19/neil.finn/ (June 20, 2001).
Neil Finn Official Website, http://www.nilfun.net (June 20, 2001).
"Neil Finn-One Nil," Skip Music, http://www.cyberbritain.co/uk/mp3/reveiws/98729357.html (June 20, 2001).

—Timothy Borden

Jeffrey Gaines

Singer, songwriter

Singer-songwriter Jeffrey Gaines has gone against the grain since releasing his first folk-oriented album during the grunge rage of the early 1990s. Causing difficulties for radio programmers with his boundary-crossing music, however, Gaines spent a decade trying for a commercial breakthrough. Nevertheless, Gaines built a loyal following through passionate concert performances and a series of intensely personal albums, each based on his singular voice and distinctive song narratives. Given the acclaim for his songwriting, the success of his breakthrough hit in 2001, a cover version of Peter Gabriel's "In Your Eyes," was somewhat ironic.

Gaines was born around 1966 in Harrisburg, Pennsylvania, where his father owned a carpet business. Although Harrisburg is the state's capital, it has generally been regarded as a cultural backwater in contrast to Pennsylvania's major cities, Philadelphia and Pittsburgh. Nevertheless, young Gaines pursued a number of artistic programs while he was growing up, taking up painting and drawing before devoting most of his time to singing. Although his parents were not in the music business, Gaines recalled in a *Rolling Stone* profile that music, especially R&B, was always around the house: "Soul is easy—I've heard people singing that way all my life, hangin' around under mom's ironing board, hearing Aretha Franklin and Otis Redding." In addition to R&B, Gaines was also influenced by the New Wave of the 1970s, particularly in his own songwriting. He later cited the Jam's Paul Weller, Elvis Costello, David Bowie, as well as John Lennon among his influences.

Gaines' love of music led him to test out his performing skills, and he sang with a number of Harrisburg bands in his teens and early twenties. Most of their repertoire was cover songs, although Gaines had already started writing his own material. An early professional breakthrough came at an unlikely time for the aspiring singer, who was working for his father's carpeting business while he performed with cover bands. One job had Gaines and his co-workers installing carpet in a new Harrisburg recording studio. While on the job, Gaines was asked to test out the microphones in the studio. Following an enthusiastic response to his singing, Gaines began to record some demos, which led to an offer in 1989 to join the up-and-coming band Maggie's Farm. Preferring to work as a solo artist, Gaines declined the opportunity. He moved to Philadelphia, and in 1990 his persistence paid off when he signed a contract with Chrysalis Records.

Debut Tackled Tough Subjects

Released in 1992, *Jeffrey Gaines* was "an impressive calling card," according to a *Q* magazine review: "Gaines's songs are engagingly effective in their directness, tackling subjects such as failed romance, internal

For the Record . . .

Born c. 1966 in Harrisburg, PA.

Signed recording contract with Chrysalis Records, 1990; released first album, *Jeffrey Gaines*, 1992; released *Somewhat Slightly Dazed*, 1994; released *Galore*, 1998; released *Always Be*, 2001.

Addresses: *Record company*—Artemis Records, 130 5th Avenue, 7th Floor, New York, NY 10011, website: http://www.artemisrecords.com; Rykodisc Records, P.O. Box 141, Gloucester, MA 01931-0141, website: http://www.rykodisc.com. *Website*—Jeffrey Gaines Official Website: http://www.jeffreygaines.com.

conflict, the guilt of unwanted fatherhood ("Didn't Wanna Be Daddy") and parental alcoholism ("Sorry the Very Next Day") with a lyrical style which is often uncomfortably honest." *Stereo Review* agreed, noting that "Gaines is intensely sensitive but in a completely disingenuous, unaffected way, and his grasp of the gulf between inner dreams and street realities makes these twelve unvarnished narratives completely believable." This honesty carried through into Gaines' live performances. Taking on about 200 tour dates as an opening act for Melissa Etheridge and Tom Petty, Gaines also made a number of appearances at smaller venues that highlighted the intimate nature of his self-penned songs. Gaines also started to make a name for himself on the international concert stage, which led him to add the 1986 Peter Gabriel hit "In Your Eyes" to his concerts. "Playing in places like Frankfurt, Munich, and Paris, there was often a language barrier between the people, so I tried to think of a song that was internationally known like that," he explained to *Billboard* in April of 2001. "They've enjoyed listening to my eight songs, so I like to say good night with a song where I can get the entire audience singing along."

Although his second album was "more richly textured, more righteously rocking," according to a *Billboard* review, the focus remained on Gaines' singing and songwriting. Like his debut, *Somewhat Slightly Dazed,* released in 1994, featured a collection of emotionally poignant songs. One track, "Safety in Self," was a tribute to Gaines' mother, who had died in 1993. "It's about those of us on the surviving side. She was a strong individual. Everyone lived their lives seeking her approval," Gaines told *Billboard.* "When someone like that goes away, you're out of gas—but you need to get on with it." *Somewhat Slightly Dazed* also contained

the single "I Like You," a harder rocking, rave-inspired song about friendship and romance, and "In Her Mind," a psychological portrait of a troubled woman.

Unfortunately, Gaines' work emerged at a time when the prevailing music trends were not so accommodating to a singer-songwriter who was hard to categorize as "rock," "easy listening," or "alternative." Although the subject matter of his lyrics fit in with the emotionally devastating territory shared by grunge and emo-core artists popular in the mid 1990s, Gaines' sound was decidedly more acoustic and laid back. On the other hand, his typically spare arrangements, which kept the focus of his music on his words and voice, left Gaines off the play lists of most adult contemporary stations. Caught in between radio formats, Gaines' first record company tried to gain him airplay on alternative, adult, and college radio with little success. Without radio-friendly hit songs, the commercial success of Gaines' first two albums did not come close to matching their critical acclaim.

Galore a Hit with Critics

Four years passed before Gaines released his third album, *Galore,* on independent label Rykodisc in 1998. Containing "the best songs of his career," in the opinion of the *Washington Post,* the album confirmed Gaines' status as a leading singer-songwriter. As on his first albums, *Galore*'s lyrical matter included psychological studies of beautiful women (as on "Belle du Jour") and troubled young men ("First Chapter's Last Page") and the tensions of romantic relationships. *Galore* also included more existential explorations of self-identity as well as the social commentary of "Praise or Blame," about the history of Native Americans. While it was a hit with the critics, however, *Galore* did not significantly expand Gaines' sales. Once again, radio programmers found it difficult to fit Gaines' work into a specific genre.

While *Galore* missed the mark in terms of sales, it did contain the seed of Gaines' eventual commercial breakthrough. In a special, limited edition of *Galore,* Gaines included a bonus CD of live recordings of songs from his concert performances. In addition to covering tracks by his longtime inspirations David Bowie and Elvis Costello, Gaines added the Peter Gabriel song "In Your Eyes," which he had used on his set list for several years. To some critics, the bonus live CD contained the best tracks on *Galore,* and they served as the inspiration for Gaines' fourth album, *Always Be.*

Radio Success with "In Your Eyes"

Released in 2001 by independent label Artemis Records, *Always Be* was recorded in the space of only two weeks, live in the studio. "The ink's still wet on some of the songs," Gaines commented in the record company press release for the album. "They were just solo acoustic songs that I had not even had the chance to play for the audience yet, while some of the other songs are nods to the past in that I've been playing them for a while and people who have seen me live have heard them before." Chief among the live cover versions was his concert favorite "In Your Eyes," which was released as the first single from *Always Be.* Unlike Gaines' previous efforts to break through on radio play lists, "In Your Eyes" was quickly picked up by adult contemporary stations across the United States, in part based on the familiarity of the track as a previous hit by Gabriel. Some listeners even assumed that the song was a concert track by Gabriel, given that the two artists shared somewhat similar voices.

After years of building his reputation as a singer-songwriter in his own right, Gaines now had a hit song with a cover version; however, the success of "In Your Eyes" promised to introduce a wider audience to the rest of Gaines' work. In 2001, he continued to tour extensively as the opening act for Stevie Nicks on her North American tour, while performing his own dates in front of fans who were long acquainted with his outstanding live shows. "I just stand there happy as hell to be up there," Gaines said on his record company's website. "I want people to come because the music gives them something they need."

Selected discography

Jeffrey Gaines, Chrysalis, 1992.
Somewhat Slightly Dazed, Chrysalis, 1994.
Galore, Rykodisc, 1998.
Always Be, Artemis, 2001.

Sources

Periodicals

Billboard, June 18, 1994, p. 12; August 20, 1994, p. 78; April 28, 2001, p. 47; May 5, 2001, p. 21.
Q, July 1992.
Rolling Stone, April 30, 1992, p. 31.
Stereo Review, November 1992, p. 130.
Washington Post, January 29, 1999, p. N16.

Online

Artemis Records, http://www.artemisrecords.com (June 22, 2001).
Celebrity Cafe, http://www.thecelebritycafe.com/interviews/jeffrey_gaines.html (June 28, 2001).
Night Owl, http://www.thenightowl.com/reviews/gaines.htm (June 29, 2001).
Rykodisc Records, http://www.rykodisc.com/RykoInternal/Features/344/bio.htm (June 28, 2001).

—*Timothy Borden*

Vince Gill

Singer, songwriter, guitarist

Vince Gill worked at the very edges of success for more than a decade before breaking through to country music superstardom in 1990. For many years Gill's vocal and instrumental talents were put to use in the studio by a wide spectrum of country artists. Finally, after struggling to launch his solo career for years, he found his way to fame with a haunting neo-traditional country single, "When I Call Your Name." *Chicago Tribune* music critic Jack Hurst wrote of Gill: "After six years in Nashville, a man who has sung backup on the records of more than 100 other artists finally has a megahit of his own to his credit."

Many country music enthusiasts had long felt that the talented Gill was a candidate for top success in the industry from his earliest professional efforts. In *Who's Who in New Country Music,* for instance, Andrew Vaughan noted that Gill "has for years been touted as the man most likely to become a star." With many friends in Nashville and a long string of credits for session work, songwriting, and vocals, Gill needed only to find the style that would best showcase his assets. He succeeded after years of lackluster work for RCA Records with his first MCA Nashville release, a project he called "the right record at the right time."

Vince Gill was born on April 12, 1957, in Norman, Oklahoma, where he was also raised. Fascinated by country, western, and bluegrass music from childhood, he was playing guitar and singing with a local bluegrass band while still in his teens. Gill's high, expressive tenor was ideally suited for bluegrass and in his early years he worked with such groups as the Bluegrass Alliance and a West Coast band, Sundance. Like many of the other musicians he knew, Gill was strongly influenced by rock as well as country and bluegrass. Playing with such avant-garde artists as the Bluegrass Alliances's Sam Bush and Sundance's Byron Berline, he developed a rock-flavored picking style that proved quite popular in California. He also learned to play banjo, dobro, and mandolin—ideal preparation for the studio work that would sustain him down the road.

In the mid 1970s Gill joined Pure Prairie League, a soft-rock band based in California; he was featured on three late-seventies Pure Prairie League albums, though the group's heyday preceded Gill's arrival. In 1979, during his stay in California, Gill married Janis Oliver, herself a would-be singer-songwriter. For several years Gill and his wife were content to live and work on the West Coast. Then Gill made a controversial career decision, one that absolutely confounded his California friends.

Gill had known singer Rodney Crowell since the days when the latter sang backup for country star Emmylou Harris. When Crowell decided to go solo and form his own band, he asked Gill to back him up. It was a demotion, in effect, since Gill had been singing lead with Pure Prairie League. "People were telling me,

Born Vincent Grant Gill on April 12, 1957, in Norman, OK; son of Stan (a judge) and Jerene Gill; married Janis Oliver (a singer-songwriter), April 12, 1979; divorced, 1999; married Amy Grant (a singer), 2000; children: Jenny (with Oliver), Corrina (with Grant).

Singer and guitar player with Pure Prairie League, c. 1975-80; backup singer and guitar player with Rodney Crowell, c. 1980-84; signed as solo artist with RCA Records, released first hit, "Turn Me Loose," 1984; moved to MCA Records, released first number one hit, "When I Call Your Name," 1990; released *Pocket Full of Gold*, 1991; released Grammy-winning *I Still Believe in You*, 1992; *When Love Finds You* finds crossover success, 1994; released *High Lonesome Sound*, 1996; released *The Key*, 1998; released *Let's Make Sure We Kiss Goodbye*, 2000.

Awards: Academy of Country Music (ACM) Award, New Male Vocalist of the Year, 1984; Country Music Association (CMA) Award, Single of the Year, 1990; Grammy Award, Best Male Country Vocal, 1990; CMA Awards, Vocal Event of the Year, Song of the Year, Male Vocalist of the Year, 1991; Grammy Award, Best Country Vocal Collaboration (with Steve Wariner and Ricky Skaggs), 1991; ACM Awards, Top Male Vocalist of the Year, Song of the Year, 1992; CMA Awards, Male Vocalist of the Year, Song of the Year, 1992; Grammy Awards, Best Country Song, Best Male Country Performance, 1992; CMA Awards, Vocal Event of the Year, Male Vocalist of the Year, Song of the Year, Album of the Year, Entertainer of the Year, 1993; Grammy Award, Best Country Instrumental Performance (with Asleep at the Wheel), 1993; CMA Awards, Album of the Year, Male Vocalist of the Year, Entertainer of the Year, 1994; Grammy Award, Best Male Country Vocal Performance, 1994; Grammy Awards, Best Male Country Vocal Performance, Best Country Instrumental Performance (with Randy Scruggs), 1999; Grammy Award, Best Country Instrumental Performance (with Asleep at the Wheel), 2000.

Addresses: *Record company*—MCA Nashville, 1514 South St., Nashville, TN 37212. *Website*—Vince Gill Official Website: http://www.vincegill.com.

'Man, how could you make that step backward?,'" Gill recalled in the *Lexington Herald-Leader*. "Musically, that was a giant step [forward] for me." As the 1980s began Gill moved with more focus into purely country music, forging lasting relationships with Crowell, Harris, and the man who would become his producer, Tony Brown.

Nashville proved a congenial environment for both Gill and his wife, Janis. The up-and-coming singer found as much work as he could handle as a session vocalist and musician; he worked with Crowell, Harris, Bonnie Raitt, Rosanne Cash, and Patty Loveless, to name a few. About that time Janis persuaded her sister to move east as well and the two began recording as Sweethearts of the Rodeo. In 1984 Gill signed a contract for solo work with RCA Records. His first RCA release, a mini-album called *Turn Me Loose,* yielded a top 20 hit and earned Gill the Academy of Country Music's top New Male Vocalist Award.

The sailing was not smooth thereafter, however; Gill had grand ambitions for his music, ambitions that ran counter to the prevailing winds in Nashville. "I felt I was going to be the one who could really bridge the gap between pop and country and get rock fans interested in country music," he told the *Chicago Tribune*. Through three RCA releases Gill explored his personal vision, bringing all his acoustic and vocal talents to bear. He achieved modest success and even cracked the country top ten with a duet—"If It Weren't for Him"—recorded with Rosanne Cash. Still, as Vaughan pointed out in *Who's Who in New Country Music,* Gill "wasn't the star the pundits had predicted."

In 1990 Gill severed his relationship with RCA and moved down the street to MCA Nashville, where his friend Tony Brown was working as a producer. Gill's first MCA recording, *When I Call Your Name,* was far more traditional than his previous work; it featured an Oklahoma swing number and several compelling country ballads. The album became Gill's biggest, selling four or five times more units than any of his previous releases. "It's the first real country record I've ever made, and I'm extremely proud of it," he told the *Chicago Tribune.*

Gill's pride was justifiable in light of the awards he garnered for the album's title song. "When I Call Your Name" was judged the Best Single of the Year by the Country Music Association and was awarded a Grammy as Best Country song of 1990. The album yielded other hits as well, including the Reba McEntire duet "Oklahoma Swing" and the bluegrass-styled "Never Knew Lonely." At long last Gill had stepped out of the shadows of the Nashville recording studios and into the spotlight many felt he richly deserved. His tenor vocals and chilling harmonies may not have closed the gap between country and pop, but they had enriched and enlarged the scope of bluegrass in a country format.

Gill followed up *When I Call Your Name* with *Pocket Full of Gold,* an effort replete with no-nonsense shuffles, love ballads, and a rocking version of an old traditional song. *Country Music* reviewer Rich Kienzle opened his critique of *Pocket* by stating unequivocally that the record deserved the acclaim it had garnered and allowing that it "nearly" equaled the "special" nature of *When I Call Your Name.* Citing what he felt were a few clunkers, but mostly praising the album's stand-outs, the writer applauded: "Gill's talent for uncanny twists in his songs," and in one instance, his "anguished delivery." Kienzle finished his appraisal by declaring: "Gill deserves credit for maintaining his original direction. With tight production ... combined with his clear, beautifully focused voice, he's moving in a direction that is right for him. Others should be so lucky."

Gill's star shone brighter still in 1992 when *Pocket Full of Gold* went platinum as did his 1992 release, *I Still Believe in You.* Also that year he received the honor of membership in the Grand Ole Opry. Gill went on to release three major hits in 1993, including "One More Chance." He released a true crossover album, *When Love Finds You,* in 1994. He rounded out the decade with *High Lonesome Sound* in 1996 and *The Key* and *Christmas Collection* in 1998. Gill released *Let's Make Sure We Kiss Goodbye* as well as a children's album, *The Emperor's New Clothes* in 2000.

Although Gill's marriage to Oliver ended in divorce in 1999, the couple has one daughter, Jenny, born in the early 1980s. Her voice can be heard on supporting vocals with her father on *Let's Make Sure We Kiss Goodbye.* Gill married singer Amy Grant on March 10, 2000, and one year later on March 12, 2001, the couple's daughter, Corrina Grant Gill, was born.

Considering his wide instrumental experience and proficiency in many styles, it is no surprise that Gill offers a variety of work on each album. He told the *Chicago Tribune* that he consciously tries to put "different things" on his releases so that he does not become associated with one particular sound. His biggest chal-

lenge, he said, is to find "something to home in on, something folks [are] going to react to."

Selected discography

Turn Me Loose, RCA, 1984.
The Things That Matter, RCA, 1985.
The Way Back Home, RCA, 1987.
The Best of Vince Gill, RCA, 1989.
When I Call Your Name, MCA Nashville, 1989.
Pocket Full of Gold, MCA Nashville, 1991.
I Never Knew Lonely (compilation), RCA, 1992.
I Still Believe in You, MCA, 1992.
Let There Be Peace on Earth, MCA, 1993.
When Love Finds You, MCA, 1994.
Souvenirs, MCA, 1995.
High Lonesome Sound, MCA, 1996.
The Key, MCA, 1998.
Breath of Heaven: A Christmas Collection, MCA, 1998.
Let's Make Sure We Kiss Goodbye, MCA, 2000.

Sources

Books

Vaughan, Andrew, *Who's Who in New Country Music,* St. Martin's, 1989.

Periodicals

Chicago Tribune, September 13, 1990.
Country Music, March/April 1991; November/December 1991.
Lexington Herald-Leader (KY), July 29, 1990.
People, June 10, 1991.
Stereo Review, April 1991.
Variety, December 23, 1991.

Online

"Vince Gill," *All Music Guide,* http://www.allmusic.com (September 26, 2001).
Vince Gill Official Website, http://www.vincegill.com (September 26, 2001).

—Anne Janette Johnson

Billy Gilman

Singer

Country music prodigy Billy Gilman was the youngest solo artist to be nominated for a Best Country Performance Grammy Award and the youngest artist to have a song on *Billboard*'s Country Singles chart, all unprecedented accomplishments for a singer just entering his teenage years. Gilman's debut album, *One Voice,* climbed the *Billboard* country music charts, eventually reaching platinum sales and making Gilman the top-selling debut country artist in 2000.

Born William Wendell Gilman on May 24, 1988, in Westerly, Rhode Island, Gilman is the son of Bill, an oil company technician, and Fran, a homemaker and former secretary. Raised in the Providence suburb of Hope Valley, Gilman's musical talents became apparent while he was still a toddler. His mother told of hearing three-year-old Billy singing along with Pam Tillis on "Cleopatra, Queen of Denial" from a television special the family had taped: "He watched it twice and knew the words to the whole song," his mother told *People.* "I thought, 'Oh, wow, what is this?'" She said it was clear to her that her son, even at that early age, had a musical talent that was truly unusual.

Gilman's grandmother, for whom Billy often performed at home, was the first to decide that the family needed to take steps to help develop the boy's obvious singing talent. When Gilman was eight years old, she took him to see vocal coach Angela Bacari (who was later to become his co-manager as well). Impressed with Gilman's singing voice, Bacari worked with him to improve his vocal skills as well as his stage presence. Not long after she began working with Gilman, she began arranging occasional professional engagements for him around New England. He opened for Sara Evans and Jo Dee Messina on a couple of their New England dates, and in 1998 shared the stage at the Springfield Fair in Massachusetts with Martina McBride. He and McBride teamed up on "A Broken Wing." Greg Piccolo, former saxophone player for Roomful of Blues, caught Gilman's act in Connecticut. Stunned by Gilman's talent, he sent a tape of the singer's karaoke rendition of "A Broken Wing" to Ray Benson of Asleep at the Wheel. Benson knew immediately that he was listening to something special. He was so impressed that he flew Gilman down to Austin, Texas, to cut demos of "Till I Can Make It on My Own" and "Little Bitty Pretty One." While Billy was in Austin, he came onstage with Asleep at the Wheel a couple of times and met a number of players on the Austin music scene. Benson was impressed by the youngster's knowledge of country music history. "He likes Patsy Cline, Hank (Williams) Sr., western swing—he does 'Boogie Back to Texas,' one of my songs, in his show. He's an encyclopedia of country music," he told *Billboard*.

Gilman's career began to take off when Benson sent a demo to veteran Nashville manager Scott Siman. Siman, who also manages Tim McGraw, played the tape for McGraw, George Strait, and the Dixie Chicks.

Born William Wendell Gilman on May 24, 1988, in Westerly, RI; son of Bill (an oil company technician) and Fran (a homemaker and former secretary).

Made first public appearance, age eight; signed contract with Sony Music Nashville, 1999; "One Voice," the title single from his debut album of the same name held number one spot on the *Billboard* charts for four weeks, 2000; released *Classic Christmas,* 2000; released *Dare to Dream,* 2001.

Addresses: *Record company*—Sony Nashville, 34 Music Square East, Nashville, TN 37203. *Management*—RPM Management, 209 10th Avenue South, Suite 229, Nashville, TN 37203. *Website*—Billy Gilman Official Website: http://www.billygilman.com.

"[T]hey all went wild," Siman told *Billboard.* "Tim said, 'Put a gag on that kid until my career's over.' He's just one of those kids who comes along once in a long while, nine out of 10 of whom go to Broadway, but he loves country music." With Siman as co-manager, Billy signed a contract with Sony Music Nashville in 1999.

In Gilman's official website biography, Blake Chancey, senior vice president of A&R for Sony Music Nashville, recalled the first time he saw Gilman perform: "I went to see Billy open for Alabama at the Warwick Theatre in Rhode Island. He got three standing ovations in a 30-minute set and totally blew me away." Chancey's production credits include albums by Mary Chapin Carpenter and the Dixie Chicks. He knew it would be difficult to find the right songs for Gilman, but he was determined to see if he could find the right combination. He brought in Don Cook and David Malloy as co-producers. "My hope was that David and Don could write as well as produce." As it turned out, the songwriting/production team Chancey had put together managed to produce the perfect vehicle for Gilman's debut. Among the several songs the team wrote for Billy's first album was "One Voice," a song of hope against a backdrop of troubling contemporary realities. "That song was the vehicle to introduce the world to Billy," Chancey is quoted in Gilman's official website biography. "That song needed the innocence of Billy, and Billy needed the message of the song. It was the perfect fit." The single "One Voice," released in advance of Gilman's debut album of the same name, topped the *Billboard* charts for four consecutive weeks. When the album itself was released in June of 2000,

sales exploded. Less than three months after the album's release, *One Voice* was certified platinum.

Billy had managed to stir up a good deal of attention even before the single "One Voice" was released. Appearing with Asleep at the Wheel at the Academy of Country Music Awards Show in April of 2000, Gilman sang "Roly Poly," the Bob Wells classic, and brought down the house, earning for himself the award show's first standing ovation. Before long, Gilman was booked on a number of national television shows, including *Rosie O'Donnell, Oprah, Today,* and *The Tonight Show.*

For fans or critics who suspect that Gilman is in the limelight thanks to the unceasing efforts of one or more stage parents, the singer himself will be the first to disabuse them of this mistaken notion. When he signed his contract in the fall of 1999 with Sony Music Nashville at the age of eleven, Gilman was ready, but his parents were not. "They're not pushy parents at all," he told DotMusic online. "I pushed them into the music business because I wanted it so much." Fran Gilman makes sure to keep her son grounded by asking him to help around the house—including caring for pets—when he is not on the road.

The spotlight was definitely on Gilman during 2000. In addition to appearances on television shows around the country—both local and national spots—the young star made the rounds of the country music award shows and performed at venues across the country. Topping off his whirlwind year in late November of 2000, Gilman swept the *Billboard* Video Music Awards when he walked away with prizes in all four categories for which he was nominated: Best Country New Artist clip, Best Contemporary Christian clip, Best Contemporary Christian New Artist clip, and Best Jazz/AC New Artist clip. After the show, he told *Billboard*: "I'm so happy right now I couldn't ask for more." Gilman's Christmas album, *Classic Christmas,* was certified gold before the end of 2000, having sold more than half a million copies. Sales of his third CD, *Dare to Dream,* were doing well in mid 2001 despite mixed reviews. *Billboard* conceded that the young singer's "big-time pipes and personality can't help but impress, and producers (Don) Cook and (Blake) Chancey make it all sound just great," but said that over-all, *Dare to Dream* had "pep, pop, sugar, and very little spice."

Still, despite the lukewarm reviews for his latest offering, it seems certain that Gilman will be around for some time on the American music scene. The power of his voice is undeniable. Obviously, there is some concern—particularly in the executive suites of Sony Nashville—about how well Gilman will weather the inevitable change in voice, but there is little doubt that the young singer will make the adjustment and keep on making music America wants to hear.

Selected discography

One Voice (includes "One Voice" and "I Think She Likes
  Me"), Sony Nashville, 2000.
Classic Christmas, Sony Nashville, 2000.
Dare to Dream (includes "She's My Girl" and "She's Every-
  thing I Want"), Sony Nashville, 2001.

Sources

Periodicals

Billboard, April 1, 2000; November 25, 2000; May 19, 2001.
Dallas Morning News, May 4, 2001, p. 28.
People, August 14, 2000; May 10, 2001.

Online

"Artist: Billy Gilman," Sing365.com, http://www.sing365.com
  (June 15, 2001).
"Billy Gilman Biography," BillyHeads.com, http://www.billy
  heads.com/bio.shtml (June 15, 2001).
"Billy Gilman: Biography," Sonicnet.com, http://www.sonic
  net.com/artists/biography/760719.jhtml (June 15, 2001).
Billy Gilman Official Website, http://www.billygilman.com
  (June 15, 2001).
DotMusic.com, http://www.dotmusic.com/interviews/Novem
  ber2000/interviews16548.asp (September 20, 2001).

—Don Amerman

Ginuwine

Singer

Photograph by Jim Cooper. AP/World Wide Photos. Reproduced by permission.

He chose the stage name Ginuwine for its sincerity, and what the R&B singer was sincere about was success. His first two albums, *Ginuwine...The Bachelor* and *100% Ginuwine,* both went multiplatinum as fans were drawn to his trademark smooth, seductive voice and sexy delivery, as well as his lady-killing stage presence. After the crushing loss of both of his parents, Ginuwine returned with a third, more personal release in 2001 entitled *The Life.*

Born Elgin Baylor Lumpkin to Sandra and James Lumpkin, Ginuwine was raised in Washington, D.C. He grew up listening to Michael Jackson and watching his mother's videotapes of Fred Astaire and Charlie Chaplin. "I studied showstoppers," he told the *Washington Post.* "Didn't matter who they were." Both his talent and his ambition were obvious from a young age. He began performing with a breakdancing group called Finesse Five at age 12. When his group took second place at a talent show at Suitland High School, he was less than pleased. "I was mad," he recalled in the *Washington Post.* "I was like, 'There's no room for second place, we've got to be number one. Second is second.'"

"Even before he recorded a single song," wrote David Segal in the *Washington Post,* "he considered fame something you hunt, day and night." And that is what the ambitious teen did. He first let his fingers do the walking—he found the New York offices of Sony and Atlantic in the Yellow Pages, then showed up for unsolicited auditions. Armed with a tape and a self-portrait, Ginuwine, who did not settle on his stage name until 1995, would walk in and start singing. The approach did not work. He continued performing, and in 1990, came up with the idea of meeting an influential performer in person and winning his way in. His target was the then-popular MC Hammer, who was on tour in Washington, D.C. with R&B group Jodeci. At their hotel after the show, Ginuwine found Devante Swing, Jodeci's lead singer, in the lobby playing the piano. Ginuwine was unable to introduce himself, but Swing noticed him and asked for an impromptu performance. The girls in the lobby began to scream, and Ginuwine was on his way.

Ginuwine signed a deal with Swing's label, Swing Mob, already home to then-unknowns Tim "Timbaland" Mosley and Missy "Misdemeanor" Elliot. For a time, the three shared a house in New Jersey. Ginuwine didn't get anywhere with Swing Mob, so he cut his losses and left the label. The bond with Timbaland and Elliot remained, though, as the three rose to stardom. They each appeared on the others' albums, Timbaland figuring most prominently in Ginuwine's career as the producer of his first two releases.

Ginuwine...The Bachelor was released in 1996 on Sony's 550 Music label. The debut sold more than one million copies, fueled by the sexy single, "Pony," which reached number four on *Billboard*'s Hot R&B Airplay

For the Record . . .

Born Elgin Baylor Lumpkin, c. 1971, in Washington, D.C.; son of James and Sandra Lumpkin; children: Elgin Jr., Story.

Began performing with breakdancing crew Finesse Five, age 12; signed with and eventually left Swing Mob label; signed with Sony 550 Music, 1991; released *Ginuwine...The Bachelor,* 1996; released *100% Ginuwine,* 1999; released *The Life,* 2001.

Addresses: *Record company*—Epic Records, 550 Madison Ave., New York, NY 10022. *Website*—Ginuwine Official Website: http://www.ginuwine.com.

Chart. His cover of Prince's 1980s hit "When Doves Cry" and a national tour with labelmate Aaliyah garnered fans and media attention. *100% Ginuwine* came out in 1999, achieving success comparable to the singer's debut by selling more than one million copies. Every track on the release, wrote critic Barry Walters in *Rolling Stone,* is an "often hilarious drama with libidinous lyrics, slow-burning hooks, cinematic sound effects and ... crafty, rhythmic maneuvers...."

After the release of his first two records, Ginuwine was a bona fide sex symbol. His handsome face and chiseled abdominal muscles—the product of 500 sit-ups and 500 push-ups before every stage performance—made women swoon. "His name is Ginuwine, but we like to call him Ginufine!" one female fan told *Jet.* The artist claimed that he did not see a sex symbol when he looked in the mirror: "I don't wake up in the morning, like 'Yeah, I'm a sex symbol.' I don't do that," he told *Jet.* Instead, he accepts the label as a necessary part of the job. "Whatever is positive that helps my career move forward, I'm willing to take that," he said. Another facet of the job, he admitted, was gifts from fans. Fans regularly pelt him with jewelry, cards, panties, and bras—all of which he keeps as mementos. "I take them home, wash them, and keep them," he said in *Jet.* The sex symbol also is a family man; he and fiancée Sole, a fellow soul singer, reside in Washington with their daughter Story. Ginuwine also has a son, Elgin Jr., from a previous relationship.

As diversity is integral to achieving success in the music business, Ginuwine does not simply cut records and give concerts anymore. He appeared on the *Jenny Jones* television show to unveil his own fragrance lines, G Spot for women and 100% Ginuwine for men. He made a cameo appearance in an episode of television's *Martial Law,* and co-starred in the film *Juwanna Man* with Miguel A. Nunez, Vivica A. Fox, Tommy Davidson, and rapper Lil' Kim.

Just as Ginuwine was riding high on the success he had dreamed of, his personal life was in turmoil. In 1999, his father committed suicide. The following year, cancer killed his mother. After their deaths, he was depressed, drank heavily, considered giving up performing, and even considered suicide. He abandoned work on his new record. Gradually, he recovered from his depression and resumed work on the new project. "I know that they'd want me to continue to work and that's what I always wanted to do," he told the *Washington Post.* "You can't go under too far, and I caught myself. It was about being a man and realizing that I've got people that depend on me. That made me get back in the studio." Ginuwine claimed that the record, his 2001 release *The Life,* was his most personal project to date. He dedicated it to his parents. He wrote the song "Two Reasons I Cry" for them and believed it helped him recover. "There's nothing in your life that you can't write about," he said in an interview with *Jet.* "I believed that it helped me, aided me to be able to talk to my mom and dad in song. I know they are looking down on me and smiling."

Compared to his first two multiplatinum albums, wrote critic Amy Linden in *People, The Life* was lacking. Despite glimpses of his trademark "sass and sexiness," on tracks like "There It Is" and "That's How I Get Down," something was missing. She suggested that something may have been producer Timbaland. *The Life* was Ginuwine's first release without production by Timbaland. The artist instead used the producers behind smash pop hits from Marc Anthony and Jennifer Lopez. On the previous two albums, Linden wrote, Ginuwine's "silky, seductive vocals purred beside Timbaland's jagged, hyperkinetic beats to create a uniquely edgy R&B sound." Without Timbaland, she concluded, *The Life* sounded like an empty attempt at commercial success. *Billboard* critic Rashaun Hall disagreed, declaring that "*The Life* is good," as the song "There It Is"—an anthem for hard-working men who are sick of unappreciative women—made its way up *Billboard's* Hot R&B/Hip-Hop Singles & Tracks chart. *Rolling Stone* critic Arion Berger acknowledged Ginuwine's strength as a "ladykilling crooner" with the passionate "delivery of an old-school love man," but admitted *The Life* was loaded with "trendy touches." Despite Ginuwine's genuine talents as a performer and showman, Berger wrote, "*The Life* is all naughty, disposable high points." "That's How I Get Down," the one Timbaland-produced track on the release, became a party song at clubs across the United States. In its first week on the *Billboard* album chart, *The Life* jumped to number three.

Selected discography

Ginuwine…The Bachelor, 550 Music, 1996.
100% Ginuwine, 550 Music, 1999.
(Contributor) *Romeo Must Die* (soundtrack), Virgin, 2000.
The Life, Epic, 2001.

Sources

Billboard, March 24, 2001, p. 25; April 14, 2001, p. 29.
Entertainment Weekly, November 8, 1996, p. 68.
Jet, May 7, 2001, p. 54.
People, April 23, 2001, p. 44.
Rolling Stone, April 1, 1999, p. 97; May 10, 2001, p. 88.
Washington Post, April 14, 2001, p. C1.

—Brenna Sanchez

Julius Hemphill

Composer, saxophonist

At the time of his death in 1995, saxophonist and composer Julius Hemphill was acknowledged as a prolific and visionary composer, mentor, and performer. In addition to his position as a founder and member of the World Saxophone Quartet from 1977 to 1990 and the Julius Hemphill Sextet from 1991 until his death, his composed works included pieces for duos, quartets, and big bands. Hemphill was also instrumental in the work of the Black Artists Group in St. Louis, a group of activists, artists, and musicians who attempted to bring a social message through their art to a broad audience of African Americans in the 1970s. Hemphill even founded his own record company, Mbari Records, in the attempt to retain control over his artistic vision.

Hemphill was born on January 24, 1938, in Fort Worth, Texas. The Hemphill family included a number of ministers, a fact that Hemphill later drew upon in explaining the inspiration for his career as a musician. As he told David Jackson of *Down Beat* magazine in 1975, music was "an act of giving, coming out of an intensely religious tradition." Hemphill studied music while in high school, focusing on the baritone saxophone, and later trained with jazz musician John Carter. Hemphill subsequently attended North Texas State University in Denton and Lincoln University in St. Louis, Missouri, although he did not take a degree at either institution. As he was later quoted in a *Nation* magazine profile, "It was an academic pursuit, largely hypothetical, since there were so few African Americans in the classical world." In addition to his formal

training, he gained professional experience playing with a number of R&B bands in Fort Worth.

Founded Black Artists Group

In 1964, Hemphill entered the United States Army. After his stint in the armed forces, he returned to playing as a professional musician, this time with Ike Turner. In 1967-68, he moved to St. Louis, his wife's hometown; the Hemphills would eventually have two sons. In St. Louis, Hemphill helped to revitalize one of the most active and innovative jazz scenes in the country through his participation in the Black Artists Group (BAG). While St. Louis had been the center of a vibrant jazz community in the late 1950s and early 1960s, much of the homegrown talent had left for New York City, Los Angeles, and Chicago. Consequently, the number of performance spaces for jazz artists had almost disappeared in the city, and those who remained were reduced to playing in public parks. Together with musicians Hamiet Bluiett and Oliver Lake and a host of other musicians, writers, poets, actors, painters, and dancers, Hemphill founded the BAG to refocus and revitalize the African American artistic community. In 1968, BAG successfully lobbied the state's Arts Council for a grant and soon opened the doors to a community center that provided musical training for children as well as performing space for BAG productions.

With the goal of retaining artistic control of his work, Hemphill also founded Mbari Records to record and distribute his work. One of his compositions from this period, *Dogon A.D.,* was later reissued by Freedom Records. A quartet piece, the work called for a cello in place of the traditional bass. Equally innovative was Hemphill's contribution to the 1972 multimedia production of *Kawaida,* which incorporated music and dance as well as his own concert appearances on the college circuit, often in exuberant ethnic costumes. By the mid 1970s, Hemphill had a strong enough reputation as an avant-garde composer and live performer that he appeared in such international locales as Stockholm and Paris.

World Saxophone Quartet

In 1972, the BAG disbanded and Hemphill relocated to Brooklyn, New York, with his wife and two sons. He continued his eclectic output as a musician during this period, adapting some of his work for the film *The Orientation of Sweet Willie Rollbar*, headlining African American cultural performances in New York City, and even contributing as a guest musician to the Kool and the Gang track "Hustler's Convention." Hemphill also recorded two albums of his performances as an alterego persona, Roi Boyé, for the 1977 releases *Blue Boyé* and *Roi Boyé and the Gotham Minstrels.*

For the Record . . .

Born on January 24, 1938, in Fort Worth, TX; died on April 2, 1995, in New York, NY. *Education:* Attended North Texas State University and Lincoln University.

Studied saxophone in Fort Worth, TX; moved to St. Louis after stint in U.S. Army, 1968; helped to found the Black Artists Group; established own Mbari Records; relocated to New York City, 1970s; contributed to the multimedia production of *Kawaida,* 1972; released albums and made festival appearances as the founding member of the World Saxophone Quartet, 1977-90; created Julius Hemphill Sextet, 1991.

In 1977, Hemphill rejoined with BAG partners Bluiett and Lake. Together with David Murray, they formed the World Saxophone Quartet (WSQ), which Hemphill would play with until 1990. As the primary composer of the WSQ, Hemphill's works enjoyed their greatest exposure. One work, called "Steppin,'" was even added to the Smithsonian Collection of Classic Jazz, one of the few works of the modern jazz era to receive that distinction. Although he continued to push the artistic boundaries of jazz, Hemphill did not give in to the artistic excesses that sometimes plagued other composers. As Gene Santoro wrote in *Nation,* "[H]e's never surrendered to the sheer energy of note cascades for their own virtuosic sake…. Instead, he uses his marvelous gift for lyricism to leaven even his earthiest or most avant-garde, noise-perforated outings. That thoughtful and balanced approach, that distinctive sense of control over texture and space, shows clearly in his composing as well as his approach to his horns." Gary Giddins echoed this sentiment in a *Village Voice* tribute, singling out Hemphill's "special brilliance—a clarity of purpose that made every piece singular, vividly indicative of a specific mood or idea" as the hallmark of his WSQ work.

Later Works

Although a 1982 car accident somewhat impaired Hemphill's mobility, he remained a prolific composer. In 1990, Hemphill left the WSQ and formed the Julius Hemphill Sextet. Increasingly, he composed commissioned, multimedia collaborations, including *Long Tongues: A Saxophone Opera,* which had its premiere in Washington, D.C. in 1989. Through spoken words, dance pieces, photo montages, and music, the piece told the story of the Bohemian Caverns Jazz Club over

four decades. Hemphill also worked on *The Last Supper at Uncle Tom's Cabin: The Promised Land,* which toured the United States and Europe in 1990 and 1991. Other commissioned works led Hemphill to work with groups as diverse as the Arditti String Quartet on "One Atmosphere (For Ursula)" in 1992, the Richmond Symphony on "Plan B" in 1993, and "A Bitter Glory" with the Walker Art Center and the American Music Theater Festival in 1994. Jim Macnie of *Billboard* quoted Hemphill explaining his ability to take on such a range of projects: "I don't have many particular preconceptions about anything, and that kind of makes me eligible to do something a little different, a little more personalized."

In 1991, Hemphill returned to recording, releasing *Fat Man and the Hard Blues* with his sextet on Italian label Black Saint Records. He also released a live album of his performance with cellist Abdul Wadud in 1992, *Oakland Duets.* The final album released by the Julius Hemphill Sextet during Hemphill's life, *Five Chord Stud,* was released on Black Saint Records in 1993. Hemphill made one of his last public performances at the New York Jazz Festival in 1994. Recovering from a bout with cancer and facing increasing problems with diabetes, Hemphill died on April 2, 1995.

Posthumous Tributes

Hemphill's achievements had guaranteed him an esteemed place in the pantheon of great jazz composers and musicians of the twentieth century. As one of his students, Marty Ehrlich, remarked to the *Village Voice,* "He got lumped in with the avant-garde, but he was really his own academy. One mark of his genius is that he found his musical language at a really young age—it's pretty much all there in *Dogon A.D.*"

Hemphill's reputation continued to grow after his death. In 1998, Black Saint Records released *Chile/New York: Sound Environment,* a duet that Hemphill recorded with percussionist Warren Smith in 1980. "Smith's multiple instruments paint a spacious soundscape, adding a level of depth not often present on duets," a *Texas Monthly* reviewer noted, "while Hemphill's spirited blowing skirmishes the craggy scenery with stark originality." Hemphill has also received numerous posthumous tributes from musicians who trained with him, including performances of his works by his former students.

Selected discography

Dogon A.D., Freedom, 1972.
Coon Bid'ness, Black Lion, 1975.
Live in New York, Red, 1976.
Blue Boyé, Screwgun, 1977.
Roi Boyé and the Gotham Minstrels, Sackville, 1977.

Raw Materials and Residuals, Black Saint, 1977.
Buster Bee, Sackville, 1978.
Flat-Out Jump Suite, Black Saint, 1980.
Georgia Blue, Minor Music, 1984.
Big Band, Elektra, 1988.
Fat Man and the Hard Blues, Black Saint, 1991.
Live from the New Music Cafe, Music & Arts, 1991.
Oakland Duets (live), Music & Arts, 1992.
Five Chord Stud, Black Saint, 1993.
Reflections, Freedom, 1995.
At Dr. King's Table, New World, 1997.
Chile/New York: Sound Environment, Black Saint, 1998.

Sources

Periodicals

Billboard, April 15, 1995.
Down Beat, June 1975.
Nation, March 7, 1994.
Texas Monthly, October 1998.
Village Voice, April 25, 1995; December 8, 1998.

Online

Excite Music, http://music.excite.com/artist/biography/136
453 (September 16, 2001).
KWMU (St. Louis) Jazz Unlimited Home Page, http://walden.
mo.net/~dcowsley/index.htm (September 16, 2001).
Subito Music, http://www.subitomusic.com/hemphill_bio.htm
(September 16, 2001).

—Timothy Borden

Al Hibbler

Singer

© Jack Vartoogian. Reproduced by permission.

Al Hibbler, a blind jazz vocalist who captivated generations of music lovers with his unique vocal style, died on April 24, 2001, at the age of 85. Inactive professionally for almost three decades, he is remembered best by millions of American baby boomers for his memorable rendition of "Unchained Melody," a million-selling pop hit in the mid 1950s. A versatile vocal stylist, Hibbler sang with a number of America's best-known musical artists, including Billy Taylor, Count Basie, Gerald Wilson, and Roland Kirk, but is probably best remembered for his relationship with the Duke Ellington band. While singing for Ellington, Hibbler introduced the hits "I'm Just a Lucky So-and-So" and "Do Nothin' Till You Hear from Me."

Hibbler was born blind on August 16, 1915, in Tyro, Mississippi. Because of his disability, he did not attend school until he was 15 years old. He moved with his family to Little Rock, Arkansas, at the age of 12, and three years later, enrolled in the Arkansas Conservatory for the Blind where he studied voice. He had shown an early interest in music and loved singing, a pastime that was put to good use in the conservatory's choir. He sang soprano in the choir, but before long his voice changed, and he began earning extra money by singing the blues in local bars and clubs.

Hibbler's professional career was launched in the early 1940s. Shortly after winning a talent contest in Memphis, Tennessee, he joined Jay McShann's orchestra as a vocalist in early 1942, but a past encounter with Duke Ellington soon changed the direction of Hibbler's career. Hoping to join Ellington's group as a vocalist, he had tried out with Ellington and company during a show they were playing in Little Rock in the mid 1930s. Excited by the audience's positive response to his performance, Hibbler celebrated by getting drunk. The next day, Ellington informed Hibbler that he didn't want him in the organization, saying, "I can handle a blind man but not a blind drunk," according to the *New York Times*. Fortunately, after about 16 months singing for McShann, Hibbler got another chance to show Ellington what he could do. This time he made the cut, replacing Herb Jeffries in Ellington's orchestra as its sole male vocalist (there were four female vocalists) in May of 1943. To showcase Hibbler's unique vocal style, labeled "tonal pantomime" by Ellington, the bandleader wrote lyrics for one of his popular instrumental pieces, creating the famous "Do Nothin' Till You Hear from Me." Other highlights of Hibbler's years with Ellington include his recordings of "Don't You Know I Care," "I'm Just a Lucky So-and-So," "Don't Get Around Much Any More," and "I Ain't Got Nothin' But the Blues." Another of Hibbler's most successful recordings came in 1947 when he sang the opening part of Ellington's *Liberian Suite*, entitled "I Like the Sunrise."

In many respects the marriage of Hibbler's vocal style, which lent itself most successfully to ballads, and

Ellington's big band jazz sound was an odd match. But it was a match that lasted nearly eight years despite periodic bickering between the pair over some of Hibbler's work with other bands. During his years with Ellington, Hibbler also recorded with Billy Kyle, Billy Taylor, Harry Carney, and Mercer Ellington, Duke Ellington's son. Looking back on Hibbler's years with his band, Ellington said of the blind singer: "He has ears that see." According to the *Independent*, he also said that his association with Hibbler had taught him a great deal. "I learned about senses neither he nor I ever thought we had. He had so many sounds that even without words he could tell of fantasy beyond fantasy." Of Hibbler's years with Ellington, musical arranger/producer Quincy Jones told London's *Independent*: "I liked Hibbler with Duke. He had the same sound as Harry Carney's baritone sax in the band—that coarseness, the deep-rooted earthiness and warmth."

For his part, Hibbler considered his years with Ellington an invaluable learning experience. In an interview with the *Independent*, he recalled: "Duke's tenor player taught me a lot about singing. I would sit beside him, and he'd take that horn and blow low notes right in my ear. 'Get down there, way down,' he'd say." Hibbler also recalled how he used Ellington's voice as a guide to get to the microphone. "I'd walk straight to his voice…. When it was time for me to come off, Duke would talk from the wings, and I'd follow his voice again. When we walked in the street, he'd put his shoulder to mine every so often, and I'd follow again. That way a lot of people never knew that I was blind." Although Ellington did his best to keep an eye out for the welfare of his blind singer, he was not always able to do so. During an appearance by the Ellington orchestra at the San Francisco Opera House, Hibbler stepped out the stage door to grab a breath of fresh air

while the band was playing onstage. Moments later, responding to Hibbler's screams, band members rushed outside to find that someone had crept up on the singer and ground out a lit cigarette on his face before running off.

The real reasons for Hibbler's final break with Ellington in September of 1951 are unclear, although there are some reports that blame it on differences over salary, while others trace the breakup to artistic differences. During the final years of Hibbler's eight-year run with Ellington, the singer was becoming best known for his treatment of slow-tempo numbers like "Danny Boy" and "Trees," hardly the type of music for which Ellington is remembered. Still others say Hibbler and Ellington decided to go their separate ways after one final blowup over Hibbler's work with other bands. According to one report, a solo performance by Hibbler at Boston's Hurricane Club so infuriated Ellington that he is reported to have said, according to the *Independent*: "How dare you sing without me. Who do you think you are? Billy Eckstine? Frank Sinatra?" Hibbler's reply was unprintable, irrevocably severing his relationship with Ellington.

Shortly after leaving Ellington's orchestra, Hibbler signed a recording contract with Verve Records. He recorded with a number of the era's best musicians, including Count Basie and Gerald Wilson, and in 1954 released an album *entitled Al Hibbler Sings Duke Ellington*. The following year, the singer signed a heavyweight contract with Decca Records and moved into pop music in a big way. Two singles—"Unchained Melody" and "He"—that were released on Decca Records in 1955, each sold more than one million copies and climbed into the top ten on pop music charts. In 1956, he returned to the top ten once again with his recording of "After the Lights Go Down Low." It proved to be his last big hit, however.

By the late 1950s and early 1960s, Hibbler had become active in the civil rights movement, contributing not just financial support but participating in a number of demonstrations during this volatile period in American history. On at least two occasions, he was arrested with other civil rights demonstrators—once in New Jersey in 1959 and again four years later in Alabama. Record companies, worried that Hibbler's involvement in civil rights could cost them business, generally shied away from him during this period. One exception was Frank Sinatra, who signed Hibbler to a contract with his Reprise Records shortly after the label's debut. In 1961, Hibbler released an album entitled *Monday Every Day* for Reprise. Eleven years later, in 1972, he collaborated with instrumentalist Rahsaan Roland Kirk on an album called *A Meeting of the Times*. Although he surfaced occasionally for special performances, this marked the end of Hibbler's career.

Selected discography

Al Hibbler Sings Love Songs, Verve, 1952.
Al Hibbler Sings Duke Ellington, Norgran, 1954.
After the Lights Go Down Low (includes "Autumn Winds," "Danny Boy," and "Dedicated to You"), WEA/Atlantic, 1956.
Starring Al Hibbler (includes "Stella by Starlight," "You'll Never Know," and "Do Nothin' Till You Hear from Me"), Decca, 1956.
Here's Hibbler, Decca, 1957.
Torchy and Blue, Decca, 1958.
Monday Every Day, Reprise, 1961.
A Meeting of the Times, Atlantic, 1972.
Best of Al Hibbler (includes "He," "Unchained Melody," and "Honeysuckle Rose"), Uni/Varese Sarabande, 1998.

Sources

Books

Almanac of Famous People, sixth edition, Gale Research, 1998.

Periodicals

Associated Press, April 27, 2001.
Independent (London, England), April 30, 2001, p. 6.
New York Times, April 25, 2001.

Online

"Al Hibbler," *All Music Guide*, http://www.allmusic.com (September 21, 2001).
"Al Hibbler," CDNOW, http://cdnow.com (June 18, 2001).
"Al Hibbler-Biography," Yahoo! Music, http://musicfinder.yahoo.com (June 15, 2001).
"Al Hibbler Dies," Jazzplus, http://jazzplus.com/news (June 15, 2001).
"Artist Biography: Al Hibbler," Musicplex, http://www.musicplex.com/c_lister_artistbio.cfm?aid=204 (June 15, 2001).

—Don Amerman

Alan Hovhaness

Composer

When classical composer Alan Hovhaness died in 2000, he left a legacy that reflected both his prodigious composing abilities as well as his trailblazing interest in music from around the world. Having written as many as 400 works that included operas, symphonies, concertos, oratorios, chamber works, and orchestral pieces, Hovhaness incorporated Indian, Korean, Japanese, and Armenian influences into his repertoire, forming a canon that is best described as world classical music. Considering his ability to shape the forms of classical music to his diverse inspirations, Hovhaness was not taken seriously by many in the classical world. However, his insistence on writing music that was accessible to both performers and listeners has ensured that his works—many of which have never been performed in public—will continue to influence future generations of classical musicians.

Alan Vaness Chakmakjian was born on March 8, 1911, in Somerville, Massachusetts, a nearby suburb of Boston and the home of Tufts University, where his father taught chemistry. While the elder Chakmakjian was proud of his Armenian heritage, the future composer's mother, who was of Scottish descent, discouraged him from taking an active role in Armenian ethnic and religious life during his childhood. Later, however, Hovhaness would turn to his Middle Eastern ethnic identity as a source of inspiration in his music, beginning with his Symphony No. 1, the "Exile" symphony, in 1936-37.

Hovhaness' musical aptitude was evident from a strikingly early age. By the time he was five, he had made up his own system of musical notation; essentially, he had learned music composition on his own before undertaking any formal training. He soon began to study music in earnest, however, adopting the pseudonym "Hovhaness" at the suggestion of one of his teachers. Hovhaness was also drawn as a teenager to the Armenian community in Boston and gained experience with improvising on traditional Armenian music as the organist in a local Armenian church.

Acknowledged as a prodigy during his childhood for his obvious talent, Hovhaness was accepted for study at the New England Conservatory of Music (NEC) on a scholarship in 1932. Founded in Boston in 1867, NEC ranked as one of the leading music schools in the country. During his two years there, Hovhaness studied with prolific composer Frederick Converse (1871-1940). Hovhaness supplemented this formal training with another prestigious appointment in 1942 at the Berkshire Music Center, known simply as "Tanglewood." Established in 1936 as the summer home of the Boston Symphony Orchestra, Tanglewood brought together some of the best classical musicians of the day for seminars and performances. While at Tanglewood, Hovhaness studied primarily with Czech composer Bohuslav Martinu (1890-1959), who came to the United States as an exile from Nazi Europe.

First Success with *Lousadzak*

In the 1940s, Hovhaness worked as an organist and teacher in addition to beginning his prolific career as a composer. In his first phase as a composer, Hovhaness wrote in the Baroque and Romantic styles that continued to dominate classical music. As he matured as a composer, however, he increasingly turned to more experimental composition techniques, including senza misura in his piece *Lousadzak (Dawn of Light)* for piano and string orchestra in 1944. In the work, Hovhaness repeated melodies at different tempos with various parts of the orchestra, creating a layer of sound that was both mysterious and mystical. Despite the seeming complexity of the work, however, Hovhaness more often composed pieces that were deliberately easy to play, a result of his insistence on making music that was accessible to musicians and listeners alike.

In June of 1945, the New York premier of *Lousadzak* marked Hovhaness' breakthrough with critics and the public. As reviewer and composer Lou Harrison told the *New York Times* more than 50 years after attending the event, "It was ravishing.... He deserves major status, because he wrote some of the best music around. When he first came along, there were the 12-toners, and there were the Americanists, and neither camp knew what to make of him." As Hovhaness himself recalled in a National Public Radio profile, "I believe very much in melody, but melody as far as the usual Western scales, I felt, was exhausted. All good melodies have been written by Schubert and Mozart and the old composers. So I thought I'll try using different scales."

As Harrison acknowledged, some were put off by Hovhaness' style in the 1940s as it went against the grain of contemporary classical music. One frequently repeated comment about his Symphony No. 1 had New York Philharmonic conductor Leonard Bernstein dismissing it as "filthy ghetto music." Apparently, Hovhaness took such criticisms to heart. At some point during the mid 1940s, he burned most of his compositions, an act that he undertook as a catharsis and rebirth. Indeed, the composer increasingly incorporated new musical styles from around the world into his works during the 1940s, an era that became known as Hovhaness' "Armenian Period." Drawing inspiration from Armenian folk music and traditional musical themes, Hovhaness wrote works for trumpet and strings (*Khrimian Hairig* in 1944), symphonies (Symphony No. 8, "Arjuna" in 1947), and other miscellaneous ensemble pieces (*Kohar* in 1946).

World Classical Music

Hovhaness benefited from a number of important grants during the 1950s. As a Fulbright and Rockefeller Foundation scholar, he traveled throughout Asia, including South Korea, Japan, and India. The results of these travels were immediately apparent in his music, as Hovhaness began to write in the style of Indian ragas—ancient music with traditional melodies—and gugaku—the traditional music of the Japanese court—as well as other works for Korean percussion and strings. His best known work, Symphony No. 2

("Mysterious Mountain") also dates from this period. Written in 1955, it demonstrates the other dominant interest in Hovhaness's life: a concern with spirituality. While some earlier works carried explicitly religious themes, Hovhaness increasingly explored the connection between the environment and the human spirit. Later works included *And God Created the Great Whales* in 1970, a sort of New Age orchestral piece with prerecorded humpback whale sounds intended for the popular audience, and Symphony No. 50 ("Mount St. Helens"). As his *Los Angeles Times* obituary recounted, Hovhaness once remarked, "I love mountains. They're symbolic of the meeting of Earth and heaven, man and God. They're also symbolic of the mountains you seek within yourself."

Hovhaness received a drubbing from the classical world for *And God Created the Great Whales.* Out of step with most critics, Hovhaness was accused of being too eager for a popular audience and not concerned enough with writing serious classical music. Yet the composer grew less concerned with critical attention as his career progressed. "My purpose is to create music, not for snobs but for all people—music which is beautiful and healing, to attempt what old Chinese painters called spirit resonance in melody and sound," he was quoted in the *Los Angeles Times.* In fact, Hovhaness deliberately removed himself from the center of the classical music world to avoid the distractions and pretensions that it often entailed. Although he lived in New York City for much of the 1950s, Hovhaness moved to Seattle, Washington, in 1966, where he became a composer-in-residence with the Seattle Symphony Orchestra.

Called "Major Pioneer"

Hovhaness' output remained impressive even in his final decades. The total number of works he composed is estimated to include more than 400 pieces, with more than 60 symphonies, nine operas, two ballets, 100 chamber pieces, and 23 concertos. Even a year after the composer's death in Seattle on June 21, 2000, his wife, Hinako Fujihara Hovhaness, continued to find original compositions in the piles of papers left behind.

Although Hovhaness' output was impressive, his place in the modern classical music canon has yet to be determined. As David Raymond pointed out in a 1998 *American Record Guide* review of a Hovhaness release, "This composer's music can be bland and endless, but when he's good, he's exquisite." Mark Swed of the *Los Angeles Times* admitted, "In most histories of American music, Hovhaness is a minor character," but he nevertheless predicted that "Hovhaness was a crucial figure in the whole development of the world and spiritual traditions now so much a part of the musical mainstream. The twenty-first century may well count him as a major pioneer."

Selected discography

As composer

Shalimar, Fortuna, 1987.
And God Created the Great Whales (reissue), Crystal, 1989.
Music of Alan Hovhaness, Crystal, 1989.
Lousadzak, Op. 48, Music Masters, 1990.
Lady of Light, Op. 227, Crystal, 1991.
Piano Music of Alan Hovhaness, Crystal, 1992.
Mount St. Helen's Symphony, Delos, 1993.
Symphony 46: To the Green Mountain, Delos, 1994.
Visions of a Starry Night, Koch, 1994.
Magnificat, Delos, 1995.
Songs by Hovhaness, Crystal, 2001.
Wind Music of Alan Hovhaness, Koch, 2001.
Armenian Rhapsodies, Mace, 2001.
Requiem and Resurrection, Op. 221, Crystal, 2001.

Sources

Periodicals

American Record Guide, May/June 1996, p. 128; January/February 1997, p. 122; March/April 1998, p. 143.
Los Angeles Times, June 23, 2000; June 24, 2000.
New York Times, May 20, 2001.

Online

Classical Music on the Web, http://www.musicweb.force9.co.uk/music/classrev/2000/feb00/hovanessworks.htm (July 4, 2001).
Classical Net, http://www.classical.net.music/comp.1st/hovhaness.html (July 5, 2001).

Other

All Things Considered, National Public Radio, June 22, 2000.

—Timothy Borden

K-Ci
& JoJo

R&B group

Considering that R&B duo K-Ci & JoJo has sold millions of records, it is hard to believe that there was a time when Joel "JoJo" Hailey wasn't sure if he could write a good song. It wasn't until seven years into his career that he was convinced of his talent. "I always thought I had (a talent), and after I wrote 'All My Life' and it was that big, then I realized it," Hailey told *Contemporary Musicians* about the song from the duo's multiplatinum 1997 debut album *Love Always*. "You just never know no matter what you do. You never know if it's going to be a hit or not. You can never predict that."

Brothers K-Ci & JoJo—Cedric and Joel Hailey, respectively—began their careers in music during childhood as members of their father's gospel group, Little Cedric and The Hailey Singers, in North Carolina. In the late 1980s, they met another pair of brothers, Donald "DeVante Swing" DeGrate and Dalvin DeGrate, who, like the Haileys, performed with their dad in the De-Grate Delegation. In 1990, the quartet formed Jodeci, a group that blended the vocal histrionics of gospel with R&B sounds. The quartet shopped its demo tape to several record label executives in New York City. One of the first stops was Andre Harrell's Uptown Entertainment, for whom Jodeci performed a cappella. Harrell offered them a deal that subsequently led to three platinum albums, *Forever My Lady, Diary of a Mad Band* and *The Show, The After Party, The Hotel*. In 1996, when the promotion of the latter album slowed, K-Ci & JoJo decided to temporarily split from Jodeci to record on their own. As with Jodeci, K-Ci & JoJo's success came swiftly. The Haileys collaborated with 2Pac (Tupac Shakur) on the song "How Do U Want It"/"California Love," which was later nominated for a Grammy Award. K-Ci & JoJo, along with Babyface and two of his brothers from the R&B act After 7, recorded "I Care 'Bout You" for the *Soul Food* soundtrack in 1997.

K-Ci & JoJo released their debut, *Love Always*, in 1997. The ballad-heavy record was a stark contrast to the sex-fueled work of Jodeci. K-Ci told *Billboard*'s Shawnee Smith in June of 1997 that he attributed the stylistic change to maturity. "With Jodeci, we might sing 'Freek'n You,' and with K-Ci & JoJo, we don't use the word 'sex' one time on the (whole album). Jodeci also did love songs like 'Forever My Lady,' 'Love U 4 Life,' and 'Do You Believe In Love.' So we haven't changed, we just calmed it down a little bit."

In terms of singles, *Love Always* proved fruitful. Planned Parenthood backed the single "Don't Rush (Take Love Slowly)," while "All My Life" gave the Hailey brothers their first number one hit. "All My Life" almost didn't make it on K-Ci & JoJo's album. JoJo told MTV that he penned the song about his daughter but offered it to an unnamed artist. "The song was originally supposed to be used for ... another artist, a female artist on A&M Records. But we listened to it after we got out of the studio and it was like, 'I'm keeping this, this is too hot.'" Fans felt the same way, helping boost sales of the album past the double-platinum mark, or more than two million copies.

After various award nominations, K-Ci & JoJo returned to the studio to begin work on *It's Real*, the 1999 follow-up to *Love Always*. Musicians were clamoring to work with K-Ci & JoJo, but the duo decided to keep production of the album a family affair. They paired with close confidants, including Babyface, instead of big-name knob-turners. One exception was R&B singer R. Kelly, who wrote, arranged, and produced the song "Life," which also appeared on the soundtrack for the Eddie Murphy and Martin Lawrence movie of the same name. JoJo told Aliya S. King of *Billboard* that *It's Real* as a whole mirrors the musical career plans for which he and his brother had wished. "The type of music we're doing now is what we've always felt," he said. "I think we're bringing every dimension to this album, from pop to hardcore R&B and ballads. Our music is a little different than Jodeci's, but it's still us. We wanted to make sure lots of different flavors came through. So we used a variety of producers and co-writers."

Fans responded favorably to the mix, helping to push sales of *It's Real* past the platinum mark six weeks after its release. Adding to their marketability, K-Ci & JoJo embarked on an acting career between the release of *It's Real* and the beginning of production for the duo's third album, the ballad-heavy *X*. The brothers made their television debut alongside fellow R&B stars

Chante Moore, Rahsaan Patterson, and Jesse Powell in the CBS miniseries *Shake Rattle and Roll.*

In September of 2000, the duo lent the single "Crazy" to the soundtrack for the film *Save the Last Dance,* starring relative newcomers Julia Stiles and Sean Patrick Thomas. Initially, JoJo told *Contemporary Musicians,* that MCA was skeptical about offering the song to the film: "Everybody … thought we were crazy. Nobody thought that movie was going to have that type of appeal…. The director [Thomas Carter] said ["Crazy"] would fit perfect in this particular part of the movie. He just felt the song [and put it] right where he wanted it." The film topped the box office two weeks in a row after its release on January 19, 2001.

K-Ci & JoJo entered the studio to begin work on their third album, *X,* named in celebration of the duo's ten years in music. Babyface, as well as noted hit makers Timbaland and Teddy Riley, who is synonymous with the "new jack" sound of the 1990s, penned songs for the record. 2Pac makes a posthumous appearance on *X* by way of a vocal sample on "Thug N U Thug N Me." It is noteworthy in that it is considered a throwback to Shakur's 1996 single "How Do U Want It," the first project on which K-Ci & JoJo appeared outside of Jodeci. "*X* has a very special meaning," K-Ci said in an interview on MTV. "That [refers] to the Roman numeral X, the number 10, and we're just celebrating. We're just so happy and blessed that we've been around for 10 years." The album debuted at number 21 after its release on December 5, 2000, making it K-Ci & JoJo's third straight album to enter the charts in the top 25.

A legal suit against K-Ci & JoJo tainted the celebration surrounding the release of *X.* The duo was slapped with negative publicity as well as a civil suit after K-Ci allegedly exposed himself while performing in front of a mostly female audience as part of the KIIS-FM Jingle Ball 2000 in December at the Shrine Auditorium in Los Angeles, California. He was charged with 23 counts of indecent exposure and one count of lewd conduct for the incident. In May of 2001, he pled no contest to four charges. In July he was sentenced to two years probation and $910 in fines. Several families at the event also filed a civil suit based on charges of nuisance, infliction of emotional distress, and negligence.

Now that K-Ci & JoJo have cemented their place in music, the duo spent 2001 in the studio with the DeGrates working on a new Jodeci record. The follow-up to 1995's *The Show, The After Party, The Hotel* was expected to hit stores in late 2001. JoJo explained to *Contemporary Musicians* that bringing Jodeci back into the fold was simply a matter of timing. "It was that point in our career: 'Are we going to do it?' We're not getting any younger, you know. We might as well do it while K-Ci & JoJo's name still means something and people still remember Jodeci."

Selected discography

Solo

Love Always (includes "All My Life"), MCA, 1997.
(Contributor) *Soul Food* (soundtrack), LaFace, 1997.
It's Real (includes "Tell Me It's Real"), MCA, 1999.
(Contributor) *Life* (soundtrack), Interscope, 1999.
X (includes "Crazy"), MCA, 2000.
(Contributor) *Save the Last Dance* (soundtrack), Hollywood, 2001.

With Jodeci

Forever My Lady, Uptown/MCA, 1991.
Diary of a Mad Band, Uptown/MCA, 1993.
The Show, The After Party, The Hotel, Uptown/MCA, 1995.

Sources

Periodicals

Billboard, June 7, 1997; June 5, 1999; December 2, 2000; March 23, 2001.

Online

CDNow.com News, http://www.cdnow.com (July 25, 2001).
MTV News Online, http://www.mtv.com (July 25, 2001).

Additional information was provided by MCA Records publicity materials and an interview with Joel "JoJo" Hailey on
April 12, 2001.

—*Christina Fuoco*

Ali Akbar Khan

Instrumentalist

Ali Akbar Khan may be the "giant of Indian classical music," as the *New York Times* called him, but the five-time Grammy Award nominee has brought that music to a worldwide audience. The "undisputed master" of the sarod—a 25-stringed large plucked lute on which Indian songs known as ragas are played—Khan has been named by the Indian government as a National Living Treasure. Khan is a wildly prolific musician, performer, and teacher. With more than 95 albums to his credit, he maintains an extensive touring schedule and teaches at the three Ali Akbar Colleges of Music in California, India, and Switzerland. Recognized as "one of the greatest musicians of our time," according to the *Washington Post,* Khan has been awarded the highest arts honors in India and the United States and was the first Indian musician to receive the MacArthur Foundation's genius grant. "More than anything else," Robert Browning, executive director of the World Music Institute, told the *New York Times,* "he has built a knowledge of Indian music."

Ali Akbar Khansahib was born on April 14, 1922, in Shivpur, East Bengal (Bangladesh) to the Hindustani musician Allauddin Khan. Musical talent can be traced far back in Khan's family tree to Mian Tansen, a sixteenth-century musician in the court of North India Moghul Emperor Akbar. Khan began studying voice with his father and drums with his uncle at the age of three. His father trained him on many instruments but decided that he must concentrate on voice and on the sarod. Khan practiced the complex instrument 18 hours a day for the next 20 years. "I started to learn this music at the same time I began to talk," Khan told the *Los Angeles Times.* "So it is as natural to me as speaking. It's not something I have to think about any more than I have to think about the words I'm saying." The young musician made his first public performance at the age of 13. Khan continued his studies with his father until his father was over 100 years old, though the elder Khan often beat his son for what he saw as lack of dedication.

Khan was in his early twenties when he made his first recording and soon thereafter became the court musician to the Maharaja of Jodhpur, a post he held until the Maharaja's death seven years later. The state of Jodhpur gave Khan his first title as a young man, that of Ustad, or Master Musician. When Khan received the title, his father was humored. Khan's father's pride for his son was revealed much later. Late in his life, Allauddin Khan gave his son a title of his own, that of Swara Samrat, or Emperor of Melody. Khan understood his father's delayed praise for his skill on the sarod. "If you practice for ten years," he wrote in a concert program, as quoted in the *Washington Post*, "you may be begin to please yourself, after 20 years you may become a performer and please the audience, after 30 years you may please even your guru, but you must practice for many more years before you become a true artist—then you may even please God."

Born Ali Akbar Khansahib on April 14, 1922, in East Bengal (Bangladesh); married Mary; children: Alam, Manik, Madina, and eight other living children by two previous wives.

Began musical studies with his father and uncle at age three; began performing publicly, c. 1935; held the position of court musician to the Maharaja of Jodhpur, c. late 1940s; made his first visit to the United States, made the first recording of Indian classical music on a Western record label, and was the first Indian musician to perform on American television, 1955; founded Ali Akbar College of Music in Calcutta, India, 1956; founded Ali Akbar College of Music in Marin County, CA, 1967; played with Ravi Shankar at George Harrison's Concert for Bangladesh at Madison Square Garden, 1971; performed at the United Nations in New York and at Kennedy Center in Washington, D.C. at celebrations for India's fiftieth year of independence, 1997; adjunct professor to the Department of Music at the University of California at Santa Cruz, 1999–.

Awards: Best Musician of the Year Award for *Hungry Stones* film soundtrack, 1960; President of India Award (India's highest award for the arts), 1963; President of India Award, 1966; The Grand Prix du Disque, 1968; Gold Disc Award for *Concert for Bangladesh,* 1971; Padma Bhusan Award from the Government of India, 1971; Padma Vibhusan Award (highest honor presented to a civilian in India), 1988; Kalidas Sanman Award, Madya Pradesh Academy of Music and Fine Arts, 1991; first Indian musician to receive MacArthur Foundation Fellowship, 1991; Mahatma Gandhi Cultural Award, 1992; The Bill Graham Lifetime Achievement Award, Bay Area Music Awards Foundation (BAMMIES), 1993; Governor's Award for Outstanding Achievement, The Recording Academy, 1998; Indira Gandhi Gold Plaque, Asiatic Society of Calcutta, 1998.

Addresses: *Record company*—AMMP, Alam Madina Music Productions, 74 Broadmoor Ave., San Anselmo, CA 94960. *Website*—Ali Akbar Khan/AMMP Official Website: http://www.ammp.com.

In addition to a prolific career as a recording artist and concert musician, Khan has composed and recorded music for films. His career as a composer began in India in 1953 with *Aandhiyan* by Chetan Anand. He went on to compose for *House Holder,* the first James Ivory and Ismail Merchant film, and *Little Buddha* by Bernardo Bertolucci.

Khan made his first visit to the United States in 1955 at the invitation of violinist Yehudi Menuhin, and he performed a concert at the Museum of Modern Art in New York. He also made the first recording of Indian classical music on a Western record label and was the first Indian musician to perform on American television when he appeared on Alistair Cooke's *Omnibus.* Both engagements were well received. At first, Khan was a reluctant ambassador. "I didn't want to come at all," he told the *Los Angeles Times.* "I wanted to open a college in Calcutta.... And when I came here people didn't have any idea that India had some kind of classical music.... But I played and I liked the audiences, and I think they liked me." Celebrated for his intensity, Khan's lines "are vocalistic; they sing and sigh," wrote *New York Times* music critic Jon Pareles, reviewing a 1997 performance, adding, "even in its most exuberant moments, the music kept a reflective undertone." Another critic, quoted in the *Los Angeles Times,* called Khan's playing "so exquisitely pure, so serene, so painfully human or more than human, and so beautiful."

Khan's universal popularity bloomed in the mid 1960s when the Beatles discovered Indian music and brought it to the masses. In 1971, Khan joined his brother-in-law, famed sitarist Ravi Shankar who had also studied with Khan's father, onstage during George Harrison's Concert for Bangladesh at Madison Square Garden. Though immensely popular, Khan later scorned the event as superficial, calling it "a monkey show."

In 1956, to pass along his knowledge of music, Khan founded the Ali Akbar College of Music in Calcutta, India. In 1965, he began teaching in America and was overwhelmed by the positive response from very talented Western students. Khan opened the Ali Akbar College of Music (AACM) in Marin County, California, in 1967 where he trained more than 10,000 Americans on the sarod and the tradition of Indian music. He later opened an extension of his music college in Basel, Switzerland. "I teach what I learned from my father," Khan told the *Los Angeles Times.* "The same system, with the same traditional purity. The same kind of devotion, the same love for music has to be built up. And that can only happen when it comes from the heart. Otherwise music doesn't last. It doesn't stay. It's like a medicine that doesn't work."

In 1997, Khan celebrated his seventy-fifth birthday, AACM's thirtieth anniversary, and performed at the United Nations in New York and at the Kennedy Center in Washington, D.C. at celebrations of India's fiftieth year of independence. Also that year, he received the National Endowment for the Arts' National Heritage Fellowship—the nation's highest arts honor—presented by then-first lady Hillary Clinton at a White House ceremony. "These skills passed down from generations are irreplaceable," Clinton said, according to the *Marin Independent Journal*. "This reminds us that diversity is our strength and the arts are what bind us together."

Khan's honorary degrees include a degree of Doctor of Literature, Rabindra Bharati University, Calcutta, India, in 1973; degree of Doctor of Literature, University of Dacca, Bangladesh, in 1974; degree of Doctor of Letters, University of Delhi, India, in 1984; doctorate degree, Viswa Bharati University in Shantiniketan, India, in 1998; and a degree of Doctor of Musical Arts, Honoris Causa, New England Conservatory of Music in Boston in 2000.

In the family tradition, Khan's son Alam began performing sarod publicly in 1998, and the two often perform together. In 1994, Khan founded the Baba Allauddin Institute to archive and preserve the vast collection of his father's written and recorded works. In 2001, at age 78, Khan still taught six classes a week for nine months out of the year. He also continued to tour the world extensively. "Every day I'm finding some new energy," he told the *Los Angeles Times*, "better ideas. The music gets younger as the body gets older. And one life is not enough to understand it all. My father used to say you have to be born ten times to get the music."

Selected discography

The Artistic Sound of Sarod, Chhanda Dhara, 1985.
Journey, Triloka, 1990.
Signature Series, Vol. 1, AMMP, 1990.
Signature Series, Vol. 2, AMMP, 1990.

Ustad Ali Akbar Khan Plays Alap, A Sarod Solo, Alam Madia, 1992.
Garden of Dreams, Triloka, 1993.
The Emperor of Sarod Live, Chhanda Dhara, 1994.
Signature Series, Vol. 3, Alam Madina, 1994.
Signature Series, Vol. 4, AMMP, 1994.
Rag Manj Khammaj & Rag Misra Mand, AMMP, 1994.
Live in San Francisco, AMMP, 1995.
In Berkeley (live), AMMP, 1995.
Jewels of Maihar, AMMP, 1995.
Live in Calcutta, Vol. 1, AMMP, 1995.
Live in Calcutta, Vol. 2, AMMP, 1995.
In Concert at St. John's (live), AMMP, 1995.
Live in Delhi, AMMP, 1995.
In Eugene, Oregon (live), AMMP, 1995.
Traditional Music of India, Prestige, 1995.
Then and Now: The Music of the Masters Continues, Alam Madina, 1995.
Morning Visions, AMMP, 1995.
Passing on the Tradition (live), AMMP, 1997.
Legacy: 16th-18th Century Music from India, AMMP, 1997.

Sources

Periodicals

Indian Express, February 25, 2001.
Los Angeles Times, February 28, 1999.
Marin Independent Journal (Marin County, CA), September 24, 1997.
News-Gazette (Urbana, IL), February 19, 2001.
New York Times, November 18, 1997; December 24, 1997; August 15, 2000.
Washington Post, August 18, 1997; September 21, 1997.

Online

"Ali Akbar Khan," *All Music Guide,* http://www.allmusic.com (May 31, 2001).
Ali Akbar Khan/AMMP Official Website, http://www.ammp .com (May 31, 2001).

—Brenna Sanchez

The Kingsmen

Rock group

Photograph by Frank Driggs. Hulton/Archive. Reproduced by permission.

Rising to prominence during the early 1960s, the Kingsmen found success with their hit single "Louie Louie," which continued as their trademark song throughout their career. The group experienced many personnel changes over the years, but their performances and recordings reigned as quintessential party music for more than three decades. From the release of their debut, *Kingsmen in Person,* and into the early twenty-first century, the Kingsmen have sold a total of 20 million records.

The Kingsmen formed in 1959 in Portland, Oregon, when the original group members—Lynn Easton on drums, Jack Ely on lead vocals and guitar, Don Gallucci on piano, Mike Mitchell on lead guitar, and Bob Nordby on bass—were just teenagers. Their initial performances took place primarily at school parties, dances, and fashion shows. Their live performances in the Portland area quickly grew in frequency and audience size, and soon they were one of the most popular bands in the area. Early Kingsmen performances featured several cover songs. At the time, many Northwest bands played the Wailers' 1961 version of Richard Berry's "Louie Louie," and the Kingsmen were no exception. Singer/guitarist Jack Ely took it upon himself to teach the song to the rest of the group, only it wasn't exactly the way Berry wrote it or the Wailers had recorded it. They altered the basic rhythm, giving it their own style. Later, it would set the standard for how the song was played.

Reigned with "Louie Louie"

In 1963, the Kingsmen decided to try to become the entertainment on a cruise ship bound for Australia. In order to apply for the job, they had to submit a demo tape. They booked a session at Northwest Recorders in Portland for $36, and they recorded "Louie Louie" and an original instrumental song called "Haunted Castle." Although the cruise line did not give them the job, the group played the tape for some friends at KISN, a Portland radio station. As a result, they were able to get their version of "Louie Louie" on local radio.

At the same time they recorded their demo tape, another Northwest band called Paul Revere and the Raiders had also recorded a version of "Louie Louie." The battle over radio airplay did not last long as the Kingsmen's version quickly became more popular. As a result, Jerry Dennon, a record producer from Seattle, Washington, heard the song. He decided to press a few hundred copies of the single on his regional record label, Jerdon.

That same year, the recording made its way to Boston, where radio stations began to play it frequently. The exposure led Dennon to sign an agreement with Wand Records in New York for national distribution of the single, and it reached number two on the *Billboard* charts. As the popularity began to wane, a controversy surfaced. Parents began to question the lyrics in "Louie Louie." The record was banned in Indiana and other areas, and the Federal Bureau of Investigation (FBI) conducted an official investigation into the lyrics. By the time the ban was lifted, the song and the band had achieved even greater exposure and success.

Before the end of 1963, the Kingsmen recorded a concert at The Chase nightclub in Milwaukee, Oregon. Wand took the recording and turned it into their debut album *Kingsmen in Person*. "Louie Louie" appeared on the album as well, but not in a true live version. Wand decided to have the group record the song in the studio and later add taped crowd noise to give the impression of a live concert.

Success Created Internal Struggle

By 1964, "Money" became the second single for the Kingsmen, although it did not reach the same heights of success as their first. Wand continued to reissue "Louie Louie" in 1964, 1965, and 1966. In 1964, Wand released *Kingsmen, Vol. 2*, and the band became the number one touring band in the United States. The rapid rise to success resulted in the breakup of the original lineup.

Easton and Mitchell continued performing and recording as one rendition of the Kingsmen while Ely attempted to form his own version of the group. In retaliation, Easton copyrighted the Kingsmen name, making it impossible for the other rendition to continue. Over the next two years, the Kingsmen toured and recorded such songs as "Little Latin Lupe Lu" and "The Jolly Green Giant," but they never regained their initial success.

J.D. Considine later wrote in *Rolling Stone*, "Not only was Jack Ely, the voice of 'Louie Louie,' forced out after that first hit, but apart from the Top Five novelty 'The Jolly Green Giant,' most of the Kingsmen's later output consisted of desperate attempts at recapturing the 'Louie Louie' magic."

In 1965, the Kingsmen set 56 consecutive attendance records in as many venues, which included colleges, ballrooms, arenas, state fairs, and dances. They also released *Kingsmen, Vol. 3* and *Kingsmen on Campus* that same year and appeared on the soundtrack for the film *How to Stuff a Wild Bikini*. After the release of *Up and Away* in 1966, Easton left the band, and two years later, the band decided to discontinue performing.

In 1978, the Kingsmen discovered a reason to make a comeback. The movie *Animal House* was released in theaters and featured John Belushi performing his own adaptation of "Louie Louie" in the Kingsmen style. The Kingsmen's version was also played over the film's credits. The song's popularity quickly came rushing back. "*Animal House* not only was a phenomenally successful movie, but it also spawned the revival of the popularity of music from our era," singer Barry Curtis wrote on the band's website. "Kingsmen material, especially 'Louie Louie,' figured prominently in this movement."

Fought to Win Royalty Rights

Two years later, the Kingsmen regrouped and began touring again. In the early 1990s, Jack Ely regained some of his credit for the band's early work when he headlined the thirtieth anniversary Louie Louie tour. In 1993, the Kingsmen filed a lawsuit to claim rights to the band's 105 master recordings and rights to receive royalties on their music. The suit was against G.M.L. Records, the company that had purchased the catalog in 1984. The Kingsmen won the lawsuit, allowing them to receive royalties and maintain ownership of their recordings beginning in 1993.

In 1998, a federal appeals court upheld the lower court's ruling, and the United States Supreme Court refused to hear the case. The three-judge panel of the United States Ninth Circuit Court of Appeals wrote in its unanimous opinion: "The parties do not dispute that the Kingsmen never received a single penny of the considerable royalties that 'Louie Louie' has produced over the past 30 years."

From the formation of the Kingsmen in 1959 to the early twenty-first century, the group had 20 different members. Only guitarist Mike Mitchell remained throughout the band's career. Three of the members: Mitchell, Dick Peterson, and Barry Curtis have been together since 1963. In the 1990s, the band also included drummer Steve Peterson and Todd McPherson. The Kingsmen's version of "Louie Louie" appeared in several other movies, such as *Quadrophenia*, *Coupe de Ville*, *Spaced Invaders*, *Naked Gun*, *Past Away*, *Dave*, *Jennifer 8*, and *Mr. Holland's Opus*. Despite the lineup transformations and legal battles, the Kingsmen's music, and especially "Louie Louie," managed to help them earn a reputation as one of America's biggest party bands of the 1960s.

Selected discography

Kingsmen in Person, Wand, 1963.
Kingsmen, Vol. 2, Wand, 1964.
(Contributor) *How to Stuff a Wild Bikini* (soundtrack), Wand, 1965.
Kingsmen, Vol. 3, Wand, 1965.
Kingsmen on Campus, Wand, 1965.
Up and Away, Wand, 1966.
The Best of the Kingsmen, Rhino, 1985.
Live and Unreleased, Jerden, 1992.
Since We've Been Gone, Sundazed, 1994.
Very Best of the Kingsmen, Varese, 1998.

Sources

Books

Graff, Gary, and Daniel Durchholz, editors, *MusicHound Rock: The Essential Album Guide*, Visible Ink Press, 1999.

Periodicals

Guitar Player, August 1987.
Library Journal, August 1993.
Rolling Stone, August 8, 1991.

Online

"A Brief History of the Kingsmen," The Kingsmen, http://www.oz.net/~craigb/history (June 3, 2001).
Kingsmen Official Website, http://www.louielouie.org (June 3, 2001).
"Kingsmen Win Rights to 'Louie Louie'," *RollingStone.com*, http://www.rollingstone.com (June 3, 2001).
"The Kingsmen," Classic Bands, http://www.classicbands.com/kingsmen (June 3, 2001).
"The Kingsmen," Get Music, http://www.getmusic.com (June 3, 2001).
"The Kingsmen," History of Rock, http://www.history-of-rock.com/kingsmen (June 3, 2001).
"The Kingsmen," Xentel, http://www.xentel.com/xentel/kingsmen (June 3, 2001).
"The Kingsmen Biography," *RollingStone.com*, http://www.rollingstone.com (June 3, 2001).

—Sonya Shelton

Moe Koffman

Flutist, saxophonist, clarinetist

The much-loved and celebrated Canadian jazz flutist, clarinet player, and saxophonist Moe Koffman had a five-decade career during which he recorded 30 albums and performed for internationally influential audiences such as Princess Margaret, Her Majesty Queen Elizabeth II, and the chancellor of West Germany. He was a featured soloist with the Toronto Symphony Orchestra, as well as in the bands of jazz legends such as bebop trumpeter Dizzy Gillespie and big band leader Jimmy Dorsey. From 1968-2000, Koffman also played in Canada's most renowned big band, Rob McConnell & the Boss Band. Unique in his ability to play across musical genres, he was a first-call musician for television soundtracks and commercials, and was known for his cool-toned bop music, as well as his inventive jazz interpretations of classical and pop. "It's mind-boggling what Moe has done in his career. He's a brilliant cross-musician who set standards that everybody has had to aim for," keyboardist and longtime collaborator, Doug Riley, told *Billboard*.

Cited as "one of Canada's jazz institutions" in his *New York Times* obituary, Koffman, who died from cancer at the age of 72, left behind a musical legacy. This inheritance includes the 1970s albums which sold more than 50,000 units—*Moe Koffman Plays Bach and Vivaldi's Four Seasons*—as well as the 1958 international hit, "Swingin' Shepherd Blues," a composition which has been recorded by more than 100 artists, including jazz great Ella Fitzgerald. Among his long list of accomplishments, in 1993 Koffman received the Order of Canada, an award presented by the Governor

General, in recognition of his great work and enormous contributions to the arts industry. A few years later, in 1997, the outstanding musician was inducted into the Canadian Music Hall of Fame. On the day he died, Koffman was named—along with pianist Oscar Peterson—as one of the first inductees into the Canadian Jazz and Blues Hall of Fame.

On December 28, 1928, Koffman was born to Polish parents in Toronto, Ontario. His musical schooling began at the early age of nine, when he took up the violin—an instrument that he claimed he was not good at playing. He started playing the alto saxophone at 13, and later studied clarinet and flute, laying the groundwork for the wide scope of musicianship he would demonstrate in the years to come. By the age of 15, he was attending the Royal Conservatory of Music in Toronto, and playing gigs with local dance bands on the weekends.

In the 1940s, the young Koffman became enchanted with a radical new style of jazz called bebop, which employed complicated harmonies and intense rhythms. Bebop founders Charlie Parker, Dizzy Gillespie, and Duke Ellington's alto saxophonist, Johnny Hodges, were his inspirations. "My first real true love was bebop. I just dug into it with a love and a passion," Koffman told *Billboard*'s Larry LeBlanc. As a determined teenager, he often brought his saxophone around to various clubs, in search of visiting American jazz players. Once, he even talked his way backstage at Toronto's Massey Hall in order to perform for saxophonist Illinois Jacquet. Koffman was asked to play a Charlie Parker tune—a request he was happy to oblige.

In 1948, at a mere 20 years of age, Koffman was named Best Alto Saxophonist in the Canadian Broadcasting Corporation's (CBC) Jazz Unlimited poll. As a result of this and other acknowledgements he received, Koffman was offered a record contract with Main Stem Records in Buffalo, New York. His first recordings, under the name Moe Koffman and the Main Stemmers, were two bebop 78-RPMs: "Bop Lop" and "Rocking with the Bop."

During the early 1950s, Koffman worked in the United States as a featured soloist in big bands fronted by some of the most influential jazz musicians of the time, including Sonny Durham, Art Mooney, Jimmy Dorsey, and Charlie Barnet. In 1955, Koffman returned to Toronto, where he made his first appearance at the music venue House of Hambourg. He quickly became known as a skilled studio musician with the ability to play across many genres. At the time, he split his career between performing in clubs with the Moe Koffman Quartet and appearing on top Canadian television series, such as *CrossCanada Hit Parade* and *Front Page Challenge*. In 1956, Koffman assumed the position of music director for George's Spaghetti

House, Toronto's premier jazz club. His dedication helped many new musicians get their first break at the venue until its closure in 1998.

The time between 1957 and 1958 was a magic period during which Koffman got his band a deal with Jubilee Records in New York, and released the international hit composition, "Swingin' Shepherd Blues" on his first album, *Cool and Hot Sax.* Koffman brought his group's 1957 demo tape and a tape player all around the city, until Jubilee's former producer, Morty Palitz, said he would record the group in a Toronto studio. Koffman's signature piece, which later received a Broadcasting Music, Incorporated (BMI) award for more than one million performances logged, was originally entitled "Blues A La Canadiana," but was retitled—for the sake of greater appeal—at the RCA Victor Studio in Toronto, during a recording session. The year 1958 saw "Swingin' Shepherd Blues" reach number 23 on *Bill-board's* singles charts in the United States and the United Kingdom.

Despite Koffman's initial hit, his subsequent recordings did not enjoy comparable success. He spent the next four decades recording for various labels, such as GRT Records of Canada and Duke Street, but supported himself mainly by doing concert tours and studio work. In the mid 1960s, he made more than six appearances as a soloist on the popular National Broadcasting Company's (NBC) *Tonight Show,* and in 1967, Koffman played with pianist Duke Ellington on Decca's *North of the Border* album, which featured compositions by well-known Canadian musicians. The following year, Koffman began his 32-year stint as a player in Canada's top big band, fronted by Rob McConnell, who had previously been the trombonist for Koffman's group. In 1969, CBC's news show, *As It Happens,* adopted Koffman's "Curried Soul" as its theme song—a tune which many Canadians still associate with him.

During an extremely productive time, from 1971-79, Koffman recorded nine albums for GRT. Only the 1975 album, *Live at George's,* was straight-ahead jazz, the others being contemporary jazz and pop style interpretations of classical music. Although the first two recordings, *Moe Koffman Plays Bach* and *Vivaldi's Four Seasons,* went gold in Canada, Koffman's reputation as a premier jazz musician was negatively impacted by his overlapping success with classical albums.

Koffman's name as a top jazz musician was restored in the 1980s when he began recording for the independent, Toronto-based label, Duke Street. Among the albums released were *One Moe Time, Moe-mentum, Oop-Pop-A-Da*—with an appearance by Dizzy Gillespie—and *Moe Koffman Quintet Plays.* "The pendulum of opinion [against Koffman] swung the other way, because these recordings were magnificent, straight-ahead jazz albums," CBC Radio Two's *After Hours* host, Ross Porter, told Larry LeBlanc in *Billboard.* In 1981 he was given the Harold H. Moon Award for outstanding contribution to Canadian music.

Throughout the 1990s, Koffman was the musical contractor for Andrew Lloyd Webber's Toronto runs of the musical shows *Phantom of the Opera, Joseph and the Amazing Technicolor Dreamcoat, Showboat,* and *Sunset Boulevard.* Webber's compositions inspired Koffman to produce a 1991 album, *Music for the Night;* it was a blend of jazz, symphony, and pop style versions of nine Webber favorites. The album featured performances by some of Toronto's best rhythm section players including Doug Riley, who had collaborated with Koffman on the previous *Bach* and *Vivaldi* albums. As the decade unfolded, awards and honors rained down upon Koffman. In 1991, the same year he was nominated for a Juno Award, he received a Toronto Arts Award. Then, in 1993, Koffman won the Society of Composers, Authors and Music Publishers of Canada

(SOCAN) Award for Songwriters, as well as being voted Flutist of the Year at the Annual Canadian Jazz Reports Awards ceremony. In 1993, he was also named an Officer of the Order of Canada, one of the nation's greatest honors.

Koffman's thirtieth and last album, *Moe Koffman Project,* released by Universal in the spring of 2000, is representative of the stylistic blends and musical risks that Koffman's work has become known for. The bluesy album was an ambitious collaboration for which Koffman employed a group of talented young musicians, one of whom is Riley's son, Ben, a drummer whom Koffman had known since birth. The older Riley also worked on the project, and was quoted in the *Canadian Press,* "He [Koffman] was fantastic to work with; he was extremely demanding and a perfectionist, but encouraged total creative freedom from the people that he worked with…. It was like he was a kid again. It was almost as if he knew somehow inside that this was going to be it." Indeed, shortly after finishing recording sessions for *Moe Koffman Project,* the musician was diagnosed with cancer. Despite the physical struggle he was undergoing, Koffman continued to make public appearances. His last was at the Toronto Jazz Festival in June of 2000. Koffman died from non-Hodgkin's lymphoma on March 28, 2001, leaving behind his wife, Gisele, his three sons, a stepdaughter, and a few grandchildren.

Selected discography

Hot and Cool Sax (includes "Swingin' Shepherd Blues"), Jubilee, 1957.
The Shepherd Swings Again, Jubilee, 1958.
1967, Just A Memory (Canada), 1967.
Moe Koffman Plays Bach, GRT, 1971.
Vivaldi's Four Seasons, GRT, 1972.
Master Session, GRT, 1973.
One Moe Time, Duke Street, 1986.
Moe-Mentum, Duke Street, 1987.
Oop-Pop-A-Da, Duke Street, 1988.
Featuring Dizzy Gillespie, Soundwings, 1988.
Music for the Night, 1991.
(As sideman with Rob McConnell & the Boss Brass) *Play the Jazz Classics,* Concord, 1997.
Moe Koffman Project, Emarcy/Universal, 2000.

Sources

Periodicals

Billboard, February 24, 2001, p. 4.
New York Times, April 3, 2001, p. D1.

Online

"Canada's Swingin' Shepherd of Jazz," Canada Newswire, http://www.newswire.ca (July 9, 2001).
"Friends Fondly Recall Moe Koffman," Jam!Music Canada Music News, http://www.canoe.ca (July 9, 2001).

—Valerie Linet

Lorie Line

Pianist

Photograph by Steve C. Wilson. AP/World Wide Photos. Reproduced by permission.

In the style of Liberace, pop keyboardist Lorie Line has made a name for herself and her keyboard theatrics. She succeeds onstage and in personal appearances primarily through glamour poses in designer gowns, stage makeup, and non-stop, dynamic piano performance. Line sometimes dresses in coordinated costumes of her own creation and delivers a dazzling performance with vocals by her daughter Kendall. Her husband Tim Line acts as emcee. Skilled in a full range of musical styles—from rock 'n' roll, show tunes, movie themes, holiday carols, and ballads to the classics, gospel, and her own compositions—she has earned the title of "piano diva" and "America's favorite female pianist." Line achieved popular success during the 1990s with *Heart and Soul* and *Sharing the Season, Vol. III,* which peaked in the top 15 on the New Age charts.

The Lines, owners of Time Line Productions Inc., reserve their talents and resources to record only one artist—Lorie. Born c. 1958 in Reno, Nevada, Line was the child of conservative fundamentalists who permitted no instrumental music in church, but allowed their daughter to play Christmas carols at home. The granddaughter of a pianist at Hudson's department store in Toledo, Ohio, Line was a piano prodigy at age five and enrolled for keyboard instruction the next year. In addition to playing by ear, she began teaching classmates at age nine. By her late teens, Line had won two national classical piano performance awards.

The first college graduate in her family, Line completed a fine arts degree in piano performance from the University of Nevada in 1986. She and her husband, a salesman for Josten's school rings, moved to Minneapolis, Minnesota, immediately after their marriage in 1988. In an eighth-floor auditorium, she began her career playing in the Nicollet Mall at Dayton's department store. Mobbed by local fans, whom she later named her "Linebackers," she quickly gave up her job as marketing director for a construction company and began moonlighting in bars and restaurants to become a career pianist of soulful, stylish numbers.

Line's career moved faster than most toward the top. A year after her debut playing for shoppers, Tim Line cashed in the family savings to record and distribute his wife's first CD, *Out of Line,* from the studio and office in the basement of their home. In 1995, two albums, *Heart & Soul* and *Sharing the Season, Vol. III* moved into the top 15 on the New Age charts. Line reflected on their can-do attitude to Lindsay Ackerman of Advance Newspapers: "While I waited for the major record companies to come through in the early days, over time we became a major label ourselves." The Lines' synergy has powered the business of arranging, producing, packaging, and marketing new albums and managing Line's fan club appearances and multi-city tours, which put her on the road one out of every four days of the year.

For the Record . . .

Born c. 1958 in Reno, NV; married Tim Line, 1988; children: Kendall and Jackson. *Education*: Fine arts degree, University of Nevada, 1986.

Established recording and publishing firm, Lorie Line Music, 1988; released debut album, *Out of Line*, 1989; *Heart and Soul* and *Sharing the Season, Vol. III* scored in the top 15 on New Age charts, 1995; starred in a public television special, 1996; published illustrated autobiography, *Just Me*, 2000; toured the Midwest, 2001.

Addresses: *Record company*—Lorie Line Music/Time Line, 222 Minnetonka Ave. So., Wayzata, MN 55391.

Line has enjoyed multimillion-dollar success from the sale of 20 New Age albums, sell-out tours, and holiday recitals featuring audience participation with handbells. Her sales have topped two million albums and placed her at the pinnacle of *Billboard's* New Age listing. Lauded in *Billboard*, the *Chicago Tribune, Corporate Report, Executive Female, Nation's Business, The Robb Report, Inc.*, and the *Wall Street Journal*, as well as in newspapers throughout the Midwest, she is a regular on radio broadcasts and media interviews. A greater honor came in August of 1996 with the Public Broadcasting System (PBS) television special *Lorie Line Live!*

A level-headed entrepreneur, Line pursues numerous music venues, including 13 books of sheet music. From her performance at a wedding of "Threads of Love," an original piece honoring the sewing skills of the bride, Line produced a recording by the same title. Her website offers fans downloadable music for her renditions of "Amazing Grace" and "Old Cat and the Kitty," an original piece. Line's chutzpah has boosted Lorie Line Music to America's second largest independent label. In 1999, Line also took a stand favoring downloading music from the Internet. Of her company's pro-electronic decision to go with J. River's Music Exchange, she explained, "We've always been innovators and sell music to our fans through non-traditional channels," she told PR Newswire. "With electronic commerce being so promising, yet overwhelming, it's important for us to offer our audience a safe and simple process to first hear my music, then be able to purchase it."

Line's schedule demands 90 concerts a year performing a range of styles, including such works as the English folk song "Ash Grove" and "Star of the County Down," the Appalachian classics "The River Is Wide" and "Shenandoah," Don McLean's "Starry, Starry Night," the rock classic "Norwegian Wood," Edward McDowell's piano vignette "To a Wild Rose," a medley from the film *Dances with Wolves*, "Close Every Door" from *Joseph and the Amazing Technicolor Dreamcoat*, "Music of the Night" from *Phantom of the Opera*, "I'd Give My Life for You" from *Miss Saigon*, and "Castle on a Cloud" from *Les Miserables*, which she recorded with vocals by her daughter Kendall. Line's *Silver Album* of Christmas favorites also featured Kendall singing "Away in a Manger." Favorites with fans are Line's gospel and hymn tunes, including "Sweet Hour of Prayer," "Jesus Loves Me," "In the Garden," and "He Leadeth Me," as well as the Moody Blues hit "Nights in White Satin."

In 2000, in addition to issuing an illustrated autobiography, *Just Me*, Line performed a two-hour concert at the University of North Dakota, backed by a vocalist, dance troupe, and her 14-member Pop Chamber Orchestra wearing handmade costumes. A year later, she orchestrated a Midwest bus tour of Iowa, Illinois, Ohio, Indiana, Minnesota, Wisconsin, Missouri, the Dakotas, and Nebraska. She frequently yielded center stage to other performers in her entourage, some of whom she had featured on her recording *The Heritage Collection*.

Away from the press and fans, Line's breaks take her to a private studio in Minneapolis for a daily series of pilates and keyboard practice and music composing. From her husband and their staff, she collects business updates at her office, Lorie Line Music, in Wayzata, Minnesota. Of the stress of business and performance, she commented to Mike Bockoven of the *Grand Island Independent*, "When I step on the bus, I say to myself, 'Whew, it's done.' I'm a real fanatic about being prepared. So when I finally get out on the road, the hard part is done. All that I have to do now is perform."

Selected discography

Out of Line, Time Line Productions, 1989.
Sharing the Season, Time Line Productions, 1991.
Story Line, Time Line Productions, 1991.
Sharing the Season, Vol. I, Time Line Productions, 1991.
Sharing the Season, Vol. II, Time Line Productions, 1991.
Lorie Line—Beyond a Dream, Time Line Productions, 1992.
Lorie Line—Walking With You, Time Line Productions, 1994.
Sharing the Season, Vol. III, Time Line Productions, 1995.
Heart and Soul, Time Line Productions, 1995.
Beyond a Dream, Time Line Productions, 1995.
Lorie Line Live!, Time Line Productions, 1996.
Lorie Line—Open House, Time Line Productions, 1997.
Lorie Line—Music from the Heart, Time Line Productions, 1997.
Lorie Line—Heritage Collection, Vol. I, Time Line Productions, 1998.

Lorie Line—Just Me, Time Line Productions, 1999.
Lorie Line Holiday Collection, Time Line Productions, 1999.
Lorie Line—The Silver Album, Time Line Productions, 2000.

Sources

Books

Line, Lorie, and Anita Ruth, editor, *Just Me,* Time Line Productions, 2000.

Periodicals

Advance Newspapers (Grand Rapids, MI), April 17, 2001.
Arizona Daily Star, December 29, 2000.
Brainerd Dispatch (Minnesota), March 8, 2001.
Cedar Rapids Gazette, November 18, 2000.
Des Moines Register, November 24, 1997.
Grand Island Independent, April 20, 2001; April 17, 2001; April 27, 2001.

Grand Rapids Press, April 29, 2000.
Milwaukee Journal Sentinel, December 17, 1999.
Minneapolis Star Tribune, December 10, 2000.
Minneapolis-St. Paul Magazine, November 1998.
Minnesota Monthly, January 2001.
PR Newswire, February 26, 1999.
State Journal-Register (Springfield, IL), April 25, 2001.
Star Newspapers, April 12, 2001.
St. Louis Post-Dispatch, November 8, 1999.
Toledo Blade, January 2, 2000.
Wall Street Journal, December 19, 1994.

Online

"Lorie Line," Smooth and Soul, http://www.smooth-jazz.de/Artists1/Line.html (September 14, 2001).
"Lorie Line Discography," Music by Mail, http://www.websterrecords.com/artists/line.html (September 14, 2001).
Lorie Line Official Website, http://www.lorieline.com (September 14, 2001).

—*Mary Ellen Snodgrass*

Israel "Cachao" López

Composer, bassist

In many respects, the career of Israel "Cachao" López embodies the story of Latin music in the twentieth century. Formally trained to perform European-influenced *danzón* pieces popular in Cuba in the 1930s, the prodigy soon contributed to the development of the Afro-Cuban style of *mambo*, co-writing the first song with his brother under that title in 1938. López performed with the Orquesta Arcaño y sus Maravillas during the 1940s and 1950s when Cuba reigned as the musical—not to mention Mafia—playground of North America. After fleeing Cuba in 1962, López performed in a number of Latin bands, settling down in Las Vegas for a time. Feeling the need to live among his fellow expatriates, López relocated to Miami's Cuban community where he was reduced to playing at weddings to make a living. With the revival of interest in Latin music in the 1990s, however, López made a triumphant return to the public eye. With an acclaimed documentary, Grammy Award, and both critical and commercial success, López has continued to be an innovator, mentor, and above all else, superlative musician.

The youngest child in a musical family, López earned the nickname "Cachao" from a family surname, although the term as a variant of the word *cachondeo,* meaning jokester, also seemed to fit his personality. The López family produced a number of musical talents—sometimes said to number over 50 bassists in the immediate family alone—and both of López's parents, in addition to his older brother and sister, played the bass. During his childhood, the family drew audiences to its home in Havana during daily rehearsal sessions; López supplemented this experience with formal training in piano and composition. At the age of 12, López became a member of the Havana Philharmonic Orchestra, although this was not his first professional experience. For a number of years, López had been providing background music for silent films in the movie theaters of Havana with the Bola de Nieve Ensemble.

Helped Develop New Latin Sound

With the demise of silent movies, López played more often with dance orchestras to make a living, joining the lineup of the Orquesta Arcaño y sus Maravillas in 1937. Popular in Cuba in the first decades of the twentieth century, the *orquesta típica* most often played *danzón* pieces with the emphasis on violin, brass, and timpani drums. By the time of López's arrival on the scene, however, the *danzón* had gradually moved away from it roots in European military-style marching music and adopted a more Africanized sound with syncopated percussion. Around the time that López joined the Orquesta Arcaño y sus Maravillas, the orchestra had taken this development a step further, integrating the *danzón* with the pulsating *conga*. The resulting style, with its heavy rhythmic beat, proved enduringly popular with dance audiences. Capitalizing on its popularity, López and his brother Orestes wrote an estimated 3,000 *danzónes,* one of which, 1938's *Mambo,* used a slower rhythm than typically used in a *danzón.* Over time, the new style would develop into its own distinct musical style, taking its name from the López brothers' composition. In the 1950s, mambo reigned supreme as the preeminent Latin musical style, so popular that it became almost synonymous with Latin music itself.

Descargas Recordings and Exile

Staying with the Orquesta Arcaño y sus Maravillas as a bassist, composer, and arranger until 1949, López joined a number of Cuban musical reviews and theater orchestras in the 1950s. He also played with the José Fajardo Orchestra in the mid 1950s, where he played mambo pieces along with songs in the newly popular cha-cha-cha style. By now acknowledged as one of Cuba's leading musicians, López began his first series of recordings in the late 1950s with a group of colleagues who assembled for informal jam sessions in the early morning hours after their professional appearances were done. Known as *descargas,* or discharges, the gatherings allowed the musicians to experiment with several different styles of music, from mambo to jazz. The first result of these *descarga* sessions was released in 1957, with several additional albums issued throughout the early 1960s. The releases gained

an international audience, and López was in great demand for dates around the world. Leaving for a stint with the Ernesto Duarte Orchestra in Spain in 1962, however, would turn out to be the beginning of López's exile from Cuba.

With the Cuban Revolution of 1959, Fidel Castro instituted a socialist government that abhorred the capitalist—and specifically, American—influences that had controlled much of the country's resources. Before long, the image of Havana as the hangout of American organized crime figures and pleasure-seeking vacationers was replaced by calls for a permanent socialist revolution under anti-capitalist slogans often directed at the United States. Obviously, the hotels, theaters, and nightclubs where López had played to Cuba's elite and international tourists would no longer be in business. With the government's control of all of Cuba's media outlets, it was also questionable whether artistic freedom under the new government would be guaranteed. Like many other members of Cuba's artistic community, López decided not to return to Castro's rule.

Fortunately, López's international reputation meant that he was able to secure work with a number of leading Latin music groups in the 1960s, including the Charlie Palmieri Band and the Tito Rodriguez Orchestra. López also rejoined the José Fajardo Orchestra, which had reestablished itself in the United States after the Cuban Revolution. Spending most of the 1960s in New York City, López began a long-running series of engagements in Las Vegas in 1970, working with the Latin Fire Company. Over the next decade, López played at several of the city's most famous reviews, doing shows at the MGM, Sahara, and Tropicana hotels. In 1978, however, López decided to leave Las Vegas. Feeling alienated in the community, he longed to be around other Cuban émigrés. Yet his move to Miami was a difficult one for his career, and for the next few years, López's professional engagements often including playing at wedding parties.

Latin Music Revival

López's journey back to popular recognition began with an encounter with Cuban-born actor Andy Garcia in 1989. Garcia had been a fan of López's since buying one of his records as a child. After meeting his musical idol, Garcia assembled a tribute concert that took place in Miami in July of 1992. Garcia also put together a documentary of López's career, including footage of the tribute concert, that appeared under the title *Cachao: Como Su Ritmo No Hay Dos* (or *Cachao: Like His Rhythm There Is No Other*). Not only was the documentary critically acclaimed, it also helped usher in a new interest in Latin music throughout America and Europe. Together with Emilio Estefan, Jr.—husband of Gloria Estefan and founder of the Miami Sound

Machine of the 1970s and 1980s—Garcia capitalized on the renewed interest in López by producing his first original album in several years. The result, *Master Sessions Volume I,* was another critical success. Including some traditional Cuban songs along with three *descargas,* the *Master Sessions* album earned the Grammy Award for Best Tropical Latin Performance for 1994. A follow-up album, *Master Sessions Volume II,* appeared in 1995, and López's music was heard in the films *The Birdcage, Dance With Me,* and *The Associate* as well.

As an octogenarian, López continues to be an active composer and arranger. In 2000, his new work, "Mambo Mass," debuted at Los Angeles' St. Vincent de Paul Catholic Church. Using the ritual of the Catholic Mass as its structure, the piece integrated elements of mambo, opera, and classical music. López also continues to be a celebrated concert performer with his latest band, a 15-member orchestra with Garcia making guest appearances on the bongo drums. After one such appearance, the *Los Angeles Times* commented that "The ever-youthful López never ceases to surprise" with his energetic playing and obvious love of music. López also returned to the recording studio for another original album in 2000, which resulted in the release of *Cuba Linda,* "a crisp, invigorating set," according to a *Los Angeles Times* reviewer. López's legacy also includes the rising star of his nephew, Orlando "Cachaito" López, son of his brother Orestes. Remaining in Cuba with his family during the Castro years, Cachaito's bass playing had given him a reputation almost as formidable as his uncle's. With the gradual opening of Cuba once again to the outside world, international audiences have come to appreciate another generation of the bass-playing López family.

Selected discography

Cuban Jam Sessions in Miniature, Panart, 1957.
El Gran Cachao, Kubaney, 1958.
Jam Session with Feeling, Maype, 1958.
El Ritmo de Cachao, Kubaney, 1958.
Cuban Music in Jam Session, Bonita 1959.
Descargas, Maype, 1961.
El Indio, Arhoolie, 1962.

Dos, Sony, 1976.
Descarga 77, Salsoul, 1977.
Teacher of Teachers, Tania, 1986.
Descargas Cubanas, May, 1992.
Descargas y Mambos, May, 1994.
Cachao y Su Descarga, Big World, 1994.
Descarga, May, 1994.
Latin Jazz Descarga, PTO, 1994.
Master Sessions, Vol. 1, Crescent, 1994.
15 Hits, Hacienda, 1995.
Master Sessions, Vol. 2, Crescent Moon, 1995.
La Leyenda, Vol. 1, Kubaney, 1995.
La Leyenda, Vol. 2, Kubaney, 1995.
Lumbre, Hacienda, 1995.
Descargando, International, 1997.
Descarga Cubana, Astro, 1997.
Cuban Jam Session, Vol. 2, Astro, 1999.
Descarga Cubana, International, 2000.
Superdanzones, Egrem, 2000.
Cuban Descarga, Cubacam, 2000.
Cuba Linda, EMI, 2000.
Descargando con Cachao, Orfeon, 2000.
Tres Leyendas, Orfeon, 2001.

Sources

Books

Broughton, Simon, et al., editors, *World Music: The Rough Guide Volume 2,* The Rough Guides Ltd., 1999.

Periodicals

Billboard, May 21, 1994, p. LM-6; August 6, 1994, p. 30.
Entertainment Weekly, August 12, 1994, p. 54.
Film Quarterly, Summer 2000.
Hispanic, November 1994, p. 12.
Los Angeles Times, May 6, 2000; September 11, 2000; February 12, 2001.
People, December 4, 1995, p. 26.
Times, April 18, 2001.

Online

EMI Latin, http://www.emilatin.com/english/artist.asp?artistI D=907785 (June 22, 2001).
Picadillo, http://www.picadillo.com/figueroa/cachao.html (June 22, 2001).

—Timothy Borden

Love

Rock group

In 1966, Love was the toast of the Los Angeles, California, rock community. After playing a series of clubs on the prestigious Sunset Strip, an energetic live show won them a contract with Elektra Records, and their self-titled LP garnered favorable reviews. "Love were a legend—the quintessence of Hollywood," Steve Burgess wrote in the *Marshall Cavendish History of Popular Music*, "simultaneously seedy and transcendental, pure but scandalous." Critics quickly stamped "genius" on eccentric frontman Arthur Lee and noted Love's significance as one of the first interracial rock bands. In 1967 Love completed their masterwork, *Forever Changes*, an album that synthesized folk rock, a touch of baroque, and a large dose of the psychedelic.

By 1968, however, the group was seemingly in the grips of drug addiction. Love secluded themselves in Bela Lugosi's mansion overlooking Los Angeles, and rumors of the group's bizarre lifestyle and steady intake of drugs ran rampant. "The move from acid to heroin probably gave Love an additional slackboost," noted Mickey Stephens of Pop Matters online. "By 1967, they had the money to support big, soul-sucking habits, and they sure used it." The band also gained a reputation as standoffish and unfriendly, the antitheses of the feeling the group's name implied, leading some to refer to them as "Hate." Lee's tightfisted control of the band and disintegrating mental state led to friction within the band, and by 1968, Love began to implode. In 1969 Lee re-formed the group but without the same cohesion.

Lee, whose given name is Arthur Potter Taylor, was born in Memphis, Tennessee. At age five, he moved to California, and when his mother remarried, Lee adopted his stepfather's last name. A lonely child, he found solace in music, enjoying the popular crooners of the day like Nat King Cole. He also developed something of a reputation in his neighborhood as a "tough guy." His street-smart childhood experiences contrasted sharply to Bryan MacLean's privileged childhood in Hollywood. MacLean's first crush was Liza Minnelli, and he was well versed in both show tunes and classical music. When the two men met at Ben Frank's coffeeshop on the Sunset Strip, Lee invited MacLean to hear his band, the Grass Roots, at the Brave New World.

In addition to Lee, the Grass Roots was formed by members of two other groups, American Four and the LAGs. A friend of Lee's, Johnny Echols, once a neighbor of saxophonist Ornette Coleman, played in both bands. They played R&B, but their musical taste would take a sharp turn after seeing the Byrds perform in Los Angeles in 1965. Formed with these new sounds in mind, the Grass Roots concocted their own style of folk rock mixed with a heavy dose of hard rock and blues. After seeing the band perform, MacLean joined Echols and Lee. In late 1965, the group changed its name to Love, a name that apparently no one liked, to avoid confusion with a commercially successful band also named the Grass Roots.

Love's Labored Triumph

Love carved out a reputation on the rough and tumble Los Angeles club circuit in 1965 and 1966. They played Ciro's on the Sunset Strip, Bido Lito's in Hollywood, and finally the infamous Whiskey A Go-Go. Their combination of garage rock, folk rock, and the psychedelic gave them a unique edge, separating them from the plethora of other Los Angeles bands. Lee mesmerized audiences. He donned fringed jackets, small sunglasses, Edwardian shirts, and army boots, helping to set the soon-to-be-trendy Los Angeles look. The band transformed Bacharach/David's "My Little Red Book" into an angry rock assault, while MacLean's punk rendition of "Hey Joe" proved a highlight of early shows. The band also expressed a softer side on songs like "You I'll Be Following," which leaned closer to the sound of the Byrds. "From the start," wrote David Sokol of *MusicHound Folk,* "Love fashioned itself as a dynamic, hard-edged band with a soft touch." These live shows attracted Jac Holzman, who was looking to expand Elektra Records to the West Coast. He signed Love in late 1965.

By January of 1966, the band had added bassist Ken Forssi and drummer Alban "Snoopy" Pfisterer to fill out what would become Love's classic lineup. The band entered Sound Set Recorders studio to record their

Members include **Sherwood Akuna** (joined group, 1974), bass; **Joe Blocker** (joined group, 1974),drums; **John Donnellan** (joined group, 1968), guitar; **John Echols** (left group, 1968), guitar; **Frank Fayad** (joined group, 1968), bass; **Ken Forssi** (left group, 1968), bass; **Arthur Lee**, guitar, vocals; **Bryan MacLean** (left group, 1968), guitar, vocals; **Alban Pfisterer** (left group, 1967), drums; **Jay Sterling** (joined group, 1974), guitar; **Michael Stuart** (left group, 1968), saxophone; **George Suranovitch** (joined group, 1968), drums; **Drachen Theaker** (joined group, 1969), drums; **Melvan Whittington** (joined group, 1974), guitar.

Formed group in Los Angeles, CA, 1965; played shows on the Los Angeles club circuit; signed to Elektra Records, 1965; recorded self-titled debut, 1966; expanded to a seven-piece unit for sophomore effort, *Da Capo*, recorded *Forever Changes*, 1967; original lineup disbanded, 1968; band re-formed, under Arthur Lee's leadership, released *Four Sail* and *Out There*, 1969; toured Europe, released *False Start*, 1970; group disbanded, 1974.

Addresses: *Record company*—Rhino Records, 10635 Santa Monica Boulevard, Suite 200, Los Angeles, CA 90025, (310) 474-4778, website: http://www.rhino.com.

eclectic debut, drawing on many of the songs they had been playing in live shows. The album cover, a photograph taken on the grounds of their old estate in Laurel Canyon, featured a surly and street-smart band. "Hey Joe" reached number 52 on the American charts, and by the time the group's self-titled album was released in May of 1966, Love was the hottest band on the Los Angeles underground circuit. Love also had attitude to spare, which proved off-putting to some, but the band didn't really care. If their behavior occasionally got out of control, as with an ugly incident involving mistreating a member of the press, the band believed their deeds to be innocent enough at the time. Although *Love* sold 150,000 copies, Lee was unhappy with Pfisterer's drumming. He hired a new drummer, Michael Stuart, and moved Pfisterer to the harpsichord.

Although some people Love's attitude as prematurely arrogant, the recording of "7 and 7 Is" proved the band wasn't a one-hit wonder. This single stood out as one of the premier psychedelic songs of the era, and the warped lyrics gave notice that the band had begun to experiment with drugs. The record rose to number 33 on the American charts, Love's only top 50 hit, and was called one of the greatest rock singles of the 1960s by *Mojo* magazine. "7 and 7 Is" also laid the groundwork for Love's second album, *Da Capo,* recorded in September and October of 1966. Under producer Paul Rothchild, the band softened its harder edge and moved toward a psychedelic baroque sound. Critics point to songs like "Stephen Knows Who" and "Orange Skies" when noting that the first side of *Da Capo* ranks with the best music the band ever made. The album's quality suffered, however, with the inclusion of a rambling jam called "Revelation." "Side two consisted of one continuous opus…," wrote Burgess, "an adventurous, if unsuccessful, experiment that made side two as self-indulgent as side one was concise."

Paradise Lost and Regained

Love was poised for even greater success following their sophomore triumph in the studio, but Lee's aloofness and the band's drug use began to create complications. Lee would later accuse Elektra of spending more time promoting their labelmates, the Doors, than Love, but many outsiders perceived the band as unambitious and unwilling to pay the dues required to achieve fame. Lee seldom went out of his way to work with people who could help his career, and he often refused to leave his hotel when playing out of town. "Lee eventually refused to travel more than a few miles to a gig," Burgess noted. Some speculated that the band's lack of ambition came from their plunge into heroin use following the recording of *Da Capo.* Love further sabotaged their career in the summer of 1967 by turning down a chance to play the Monterey Pop Festival.

The same summer, six months after recording *Da Capo,* the band entered the studio again to record *Forever Changes.* In retrospect, it seems a small miracle that the album was made at all. The band was too disorganized to record. Lee's drug use was out of control, and MacLean did not show up for practices. Neil Young, signed as co-producer, only managed to arrange one song, "The Daily Planet." Engineer/producer Bruce Botnick proceeded to book session musicians for studio recording. "The group was in such sad shape, apparently," wrote Richie Unterberger in *All Music Guide*, "that Elektra planned to record their third album with session men backing Lee (on his compositions) or MacLean (on his compositions)." As Love sat in the studio and watched other musicians play "Andmoreagain" and "The Daily Planet," some members were so upset that they reportedly began to cry. The shock woke the band up. They pulled themselves together and finished the album.

Forever Changes became Love's masterwork. "It wasn't a hit," wrote Unterberger, "but *Forever Changes* continues to regularly appear on critics' lists of the top ten rock albums of all time, and it had an enormously far-reaching … influence that went way beyond chart listings." The arrangements began with acoustic guitar and added a wash of strings and horns. The poetic lyrics explored paranoia and violence, themes seemingly at odds with the happy mood of the mid 1960s. MacLean penned two songs, the opening track, "Alone Again Or," and "The Red Telephone." *Forever Changes*' atmospheric combination of folk rock and psychedelia has been described as both beautiful and gentle. Commercially, however, the album did poorly in the United States, topping out at number 152 on the album charts. It fared better in Britain, though, reaching number 24.

Love did not seem bothered by the lack of public response. Critics loved the album and that was good enough. But all was not well within the group. "Things appeared to be getting out of hand at the communal chateau," wrote Burgess, "and gossip about groupies, drugs and gay liaisons between members of the band were rife." When the band entered the studio again, they seemed to have lost all sense of direction, running up a large bill and recording little of quality. Only "Laughing Stock" and "Your Mind and We Belong Together," released in 1968, were culled from the sessions. Echols' heroin habit had become so advanced that he sometimes showed up without his guitar. MacLean, frightened by these developments, felt that it was time to get out. Echols, Forssi, and Stuart soon followed, leaving Lee's band in shambles. In the summer of 1968, a demoralized Lee overdosed on heroin and almost died.

Problems Ran Deep

When Lee got back on his feet, he quickly put together a second version of Love with drummer George Suranovich, bassist Frank Fayad, and guitarist Jay Donnellan. They recorded 30 tracks that would eventually be issued on two albums, ten on *Four Sail* in 1969, and the remainder on the double-album *Out There* in 1969. The music leaned toward heavy rock, and many critics found the albums disappointing. Lee recorded with his friend Jimi Hendrix in 1970, but only one track, "The Everlasting First," was issued on the album *False Start*. The band's lineup continued to change, and two more albums were recorded between 1972 and 1974 before Love disbanded (*Black Beauty* went unreleased). "The problems ran deeper," wrote Unterberger, "than unsympathetic accompaniment: Lee's songwriting muse had largely deserted him as well, and nothing on the post-*Forever Changes* albums competes with the early Elektra records." An attempt at a reunion in 1978 that included Lee and MacLean quickly fell apart.

Though several members joined and recorded with other bands, these explorations failed to recreate the success of their work with Love. Time also proved unkind to several members. On January 5, 1998, bassist Forssi died from brain cancer, while MacLean died on December 25, 1998 of a heart attack. Lee toured with Baby Lemonade in 1996 but a subsequent arrest on a firearms charge landed the singer in jail with a 12-year sentence.

Despite these misfortunes, the music that Love made over 30 years ago continues to influence the current music scene. "[I]n later years," wrote Jam! online, "the group—and particularly frontman Arthur Lee—has become a frequently mentioned influence on the current generation of rockers." Rick Gregory of Audities online noted, "To this day, *Forever Changes* sounds as if not a speck of dust has touched it." The psychedelic music of Love influenced the Paisley Underground movement in the 1980s and has reverberated in English bands like Swervedriver and Jasmine Minks. The deluxe reissue of *Forever Changes* by Rhino in 2001, complete with bonus tracks, assures that a new generation will be introduced to the lush pop/rock of Love.

Selected discography

Love, Elektra, 1966.
Da Capo, Elektra, 1967.
Forever Changes, Elektra, 1967; reissued, Rhino, 2001.
Four Sail, Elektra, 1969.
Out Here, Blue Thumb, 1969.
False Start, Blue Thumb, 1970.
Reel To Real, RSO, 1974.
Love Live, Rhino, 1982.
The Best of Love: Golden Archive Series, Rhino, 1986.
Out There, Big Beat, 1994.
Love Story 1966—1972, Rhino/Elektra, 1995.
Once More Again, Distortions, 1996.

Sources

Books

Brown, Ashley, editor, *Marshall Cavendish History of Popular Music,* Marshall Cavendish, 1990.
Santelli, Robert, *Sixties Rock: A Listener's Guide,* Contemporary Books, 1985.
Walters, Neal, and Brian Mansfield, editors, *MusicHound Folk: The Essential Album Guide,* Visible Ink Press, 1998.

Online

"Love," *All Music Guide,* http://www.allmusic.com (June 6, 2001).
"Love: Forever Changes," Audities, http://www.audities.com/audities (June 11, 2001).
"Love: Forever Changes," Pop Matters, http://www.popmatters.com (June 11, 2001).
"1960's Band Love Getting Reissued," Jam! http://www.canoe.ca/JamMusicArtistsL/love.html (June 11, 2001).

—Ronnie D. Lankford, Jr.

Matthew Good Band

Rock group

Matthew Good has all the makings of a classic, troubled rock star. He eschews award shows, insults sponsors of his performances, and has even gone out of his way to destroy a record deal. But his fellow Canadians revel in it, spending thousands of dollars to hear his dark lyrics and witness his acerbic live shows. Good's group, the Matthew Good Band, has achieved both popular and critical success, earning accolades that include two Canadian Juno Awards (the Grammy Award equivalent) in 2000.

Born in Burnaby, British Columbia, Canada, Good began his career as a folk singer, a far cry from the guitar assault that Good now features on his records. Backed by a cellist, violinist, and pianist, Good independently released two cassettes—1993's *Broken* and 1994's *Euphony* on his own Black Spinning Disks—before the Pixies and Afghan Whigs inspired Good to move in a different musical direction. He left his group behind, moved to Vancouver, British Columbia, and hired a rock band. "I got caught up in the whole (folk music) circle, and I hated it," Good told *Billboard*. "It's terrible to get on a stage and play to people, thinking, 'I have nothing in common with any of these people.' (The original lineup of the band) went into the studio and recorded eight songs and we were going to record another eight songs, but those songs were scrapped when the band broke up."

Good and his new lineup proved to be successful rather quickly. The group's 1995 independent album, *Last of the Ghetto Astronauts*, quickly sold 20,000 copies. Monitoring Good's sales, the New Age/jazz/

adult contemporary label Private Music in Los Angeles signed the group to a two-album deal in December of 1996. The partnership did not last long. On the first day of pre-production with producer Warne Livesey at Greenhouse Studios in Burnaby for what would become the band's sophomore album, *Underdogs*, Good was told by BMG Entertainment North America that it was merging Private Music into Windham Hill/High Street Records. "We hadn't rolled the tape for 20 minutes (in the session) when I got a call from (an executive at) Private Music saying everybody in the company had been let go," Frank Weipert of Teamworks Production Management in Vancouver told *Billboard*. "I was told the company was closing its doors in 48 hours. Obviously, we had to put a halt to production."

The new label, primarily known for its New Age/smooth jazz collections, considered Good's hard-edged rock group to be too heavy for its roster. In March of 1997, Windham Hill/High Street released the Matthew Good Band from its deal. The following May, the group released the *Raygun* EP to maintain its fan base. Good and his bandmates decided to forge ahead with the record with Livesey, who agreed to work as producer even though the band did not have label financing. The unmixed tracks, however, attracted the attention of PolyGram Group Canada Chairman John Reid. He told *Billboard* magazine that he was determined to sign the group: "What appeals to me about it is that Matthew is young, he's a star, he writes great songs, and there's a great team that's been put together that has created a career for the group." An affiliate label, A&M/Island/Motown of Canada, inked a contract with Good to release *Underdogs*.

The record, released in 1997, became one of Canada's most popular albums that year. It spawned three top five singles—"Everything is Automatic," "Indestructible," and "Apparitions"—and several award nominations. When the tour behind *Underdogs* wrapped up, Good immediately returned to Greenhouse Studios to record *Beautiful Midnight*, the songs for which he wrote two months after *Underdogs* was released. "There was 40 to 50 songs, so the band and I weeded out the ones we didn't like," Good said in record company press materials for *Beautiful Midnight*. "From there, we hit the road for *Underdogs* and kept working on the new stuff. *Beautiful Midnight* is very different from *Underdogs*, mostly because we wanted to make a record that had a lot more 'sonic' qualities."

In March of 2000, Good was the target of massive media criticism for failing to attend the Juno Awards, the Canadian version of the Grammys. The group won two Junos for Best Group and Best Rock Album. Canadian and American media offered a variety of alibis for Good ranging from a radio station concert in Burlington, Vermont, to a backyard barbecue in California. His reasoning, however, was consistent. Good

Members include **Ian Browne**, drums, percussion; **Dave Genn**, guitars, keyboards, background vocals; **Matthew Good** (born on June 29, 1971, in Burnaby, British Columbia, Canada), lead vocals, guitar; **Geoff Lloyd** (left group, 1999), bass; **Rich Priske** (joined group, 1999), bass.

Formed in Vancouver, British Columbia, Canada, 1995; self-released debut, *Last of the Ghetto Astronauts*, 1995; signed to A&M Records, 1997; released EP *Raygun*, 1997; released *Underdogs*, 1998; released *Beautiful Midnight* on Universal Canada, 1999, and on Atlantic Records, United States, 2001.

Awards: Pacific Music Award (now West Coast Music Awards), Best Rock/Pop Album with Independent Distribution for *Last of the Ghetto Astronauts*, 1997; Pacific Music Award, Male Vocalist of the Year (Good), 1998; Juno Awards, Best Group, Best Rock Album for *Beautiful Midnight*, 2000; Pacific Music Awards, Best Rock Release for *Beautiful Midnight*, Live Performer of the Year, Best Songwriter of the Year (Good), 2001.

Addresses: *Record company*—Atlantic Records, 1290 Avenue of the Americas, New York, NY 10104; Universal Music, 1345 Denison Street, Markham, Ontario, Canada, L3R 5V2, website: http://www.umusic.com. *Website*—Matthew Good Band Official Website: http://www.matthewgoodband.com.

defended his decision in many magazines and newspapers including the *Ottawa Sun* the following May. "Me, I'm just not one for that whole thing. I don't need a statue to validate what I do for a living. My mom thinks it's really great, so she's got them."

Beautiful Midnight, produced and mixed by Livesey (who had worked with Talk Talk and Midnight Oil), debuted at number one on the Canadian *Soundscan* chart in September of 2000. Three songs, "Hello Time Bomb," "Loaded," and "Strange Days," were top five Canadian rock-radio singles. Fans attached themselves to the brooding, hopeless tone of his lyrics. As a tongue-in-cheek response to his depressing songs, Good sent an advance copy of *Beautiful Midnight* to a psychologist. Good took the doctor's thoughts and turned them into a band biography that was sent to the

media and radio with the album. One song on the album, "Like a Boy and His Machine Gun," inspired by the 1998 Springfield, Oregon, school shootings, prompted a critic to call Good's music "the equivalent of an action film—urgent and dangerous," according to the *National Post*.

Despite the success, Good has maintained his reputation as "the bad boy of Canadian rock." His quotations have been publicized just as much as his music. On July 5, 2000, *Calgary Sun* reporter David Veitch noted a few of Good's most colorful quotes following a 30-minute interview he held with the controversial rocker. According to Good, most Canadian rock bands are boring onstage. "They just stand there. You're in front of 40,000 f***ing people, man. Set something on fire!" Good also told Veitch that Our Lady Peace is a "put-together band" whose greatest creative influence is producer Arnold Lanni. "Don't tout (OLP) as the greatest thing since sliced f***ing bread when the four of them couldn't sit around and make f***ing butter together."

Beautiful Midnight gave the Matthew Good Band the opportunity to share its music worldwide. Signed to Mercury Records in Germany, the band headed to the country with fellow rockers I Mother Earth and Jimmie's Chicken Shack for a four-date tour. The version of *Beautiful Midnight* that was released in the United States in 2001 is a modified edition of the Canadian issue. Three songs, remixed by Chris Lord-Alge, were removed and replaced with three tracks from the band's second album. Steve Marshall of the *Daily Herald* wrote that the Matthew Good Band has "the tools to make just as big an impact [in the United States]" as they have in Canada.

Selected discography

Last of the Ghetto Astronauts, A&M (Canada), 1995.
Underdogs, A&M (Canada), 1998.
Beautiful Midnight, Universal Canada; 1999; Atlantic (United States), 2001.

Sources

Periodicals

Billboard, October 11, 1997; September 11, 1999; January 27, 2001.
Calgary Sun, July 5, 2000.
Daily Herald (Arlington Heights, IL), May 11, 2001.
Daily News, October 22, 1999.
National Post, November 26, 1999.
Ottawa Sun, May 10, 2000.

Online

RollingStone.com, http://www.rollingstone.com/artists/defa ult.asp?oid=4446 (September 17, 2001).

Additional information was provided by Universal Records Canada and Atlantic Records publicity materials, 2001.

—Christina Fuoco

Joey McIntyre

Singer

As the youngest member of New Kids on the Block, Joey McIntyre provided the falsetto vocals to some of the Boston-area group's biggest hits—"Please Don't Go Girl," "You Got It (The Right Stuff)" and "I'll be Loving You (Forever)." Often thought of as simply the "cute" one in the teen supergroup, McIntyre has emerged as a viable solo artist since the breakup of New Kids on the Block in 1994.

Raised in an upper middle class neighborhood near Boston, Massachusetts, McIntyre is the youngest of nine children born to a community theater actress. In elementary school, he followed in his mother's footsteps, joining the cast of a local production of *Oliver!* Shortly thereafter, Maurice Starr, who founded the R&B group New Edition, recruited the then 12-year-old McIntyre to join his new project, New Kids on the Block. Although the act's first album, *New Kids on the Block*, failed to produce any hits, their label, Columbia Records, saw future success and offered the group the opportunity to record a sophomore effort. That record, *Hangin' Tough,* and the top ten singles "Hangin' Tough," "You Got It (The Right Stuff)," "Cover Girl," "I'll Be Loving You (Forever)," and "Please Don't Go Girl," pushed New Kids on the Block into the superstar status category during 1988-89.

New Kids on the Block released *Step by Step, Face the Music,* and *Merry, Merry Christmas* before disbanding in 1994. According to McIntyre's Q Records biography, the next five years were an adjustment for the singer as he had spent most of his teenage years with New Kids on the Block touring, doing interviews, and making television and personal appearances. When that came to a halt, McIntyre, without management, was not sure where to go next. "The best part of that fame was when it was all about performing, just us and the crowd...," he told *Billboard* in 1999. "The worst was when we started to lose that, when all of the outside stuff began to affect us. We're only human; there was no way it couldn't impact us at such a young age."

First, McIntyre decided to return to acting. He landed a starring role in the film version of *The Fantasticks*, working with a cast that included Oscar-winner Joel Grey, in 1995. It seemed to be the perfect project for McIntyre, who had always admired the big band work of Frank Sinatra and Nat King Cole. However, McIntyre found little success with acting. It was fellow New Kid Donnie Wahlberg who persuaded McIntyre to begin writing pop tunes. Wahlberg and McIntyre's former bandmate, Danny Wood, also joined the project.

When McIntyre finished work on his new songs for an album, he approached the New Kids' former label, Columbia, about releasing it. The label turned him down. Because McIntyre did not have a record deal, he offered the songs on his website. The reaction was rabid, so he pressed 2,000 CDs, one of which he gave to his local pop station, KISS-108 (WXKS-FM) in

Boston. It included the gospel-tinged ballad "Stay the Same," which became a hit. Other radio stations heard about the tune and requested copies of the CD.

After the project was proven a success, Columbia Records contacted McIntyre and signed him to its affiliate, C2 Records. He took the songs he had and turned them into a full-length album, *Stay the Same*. It was a musical diversion from his years with New Kids on the Block. Instead of relying heavily on samples and synthesized sounds, he decided to use live musicians as his backup. McIntyre also branched into the genres of blues, rock, and dance on the album.

Stay the Same proved a popular success. The single "Stay the Same" peaked at number ten on the *Billboard* Hot 100 singles chart in April of 1999, while the album went on to sell more than 500,000 copies. During a subsequent tour, McIntyre stayed away from shows that would pair him with New Kids' siblings such as 'N Sync and the Backstreet Boys. Groups hired as support acts for teen groups are generally limited to just a microphone and recorded background music. Not wanting to venture into that arrangement, McIntyre and his band headed out on a series of small headlining club dates that would add further credibility to his reputation as a serious musician. "My predicament is this," he told Jim Sullivan of the *Boston Globe* in 2001. "My music is pop, but to me it's much more in depth than the regular pop stuff. I don't want to open for 'N Sync; I'd rather open for Smash Mouth or Sugar Ray. I need exposure to a crowd that normally wouldn't buy my record." McIntyre made frequent appearances on MTV and parlayed those visits into a job hosting the Las Vegas version of the channel's *Say What Karaoke*.

While New Kids on the Block sang of teen crushes, McIntyre's collection touched on lust but focused on spirituality and the belief in one's self. He told Hip

Online in 1999 that his beliefs helped him get through the tough times that followed New Kids on the Block's breakup. "The more you just concentrate and focus on what you want to do and believe in yourself, the more you know it's gonna happen for you. It's all a real crap shoot. I mean, six months ago, I couldn't get arrested, but the human spirit is very powerful. You just gotta hang in there and let the good things start happening."

When McIntyre and C2 parted ways, he inked a deal with the fledgling Q Records, owned and operated by the cable television network QVC. For his sophomore effort, *Meet Joe Mac*, McIntyre called in heavy hitters as collaborators—Mark Plati, whose credits include work with David Bowie; Walter Afanasieff, who worked with pop diva Mariah Carey; and guest vocalist Fred Schneider of The B-52's, who appears on "National Anthem of Love." *Meet Joe Mac*, like *Stay the Same*, features organic instrumentation ranging from acoustic and electric guitars to symphonic strings. The mood on the album is at times much lighter than *Stay the Same*. McIntyre raps on the funky "NYC Girls" and pokes fun at love on "National Anthem of Love."

The release of *Meet Joe Mac* was met with critical acclaim. Sarah Rodman of the *Boston Herald* described McIntyre's voice as "both gritty and velvety, and his delivery, like his songwriting, has become more emotional without veering too often into melodrama. Even his ballads soar without gloppiness, particularly the lovely 'Easier.'" In a review of the single "Rain," *Billboard* said that "Top 40 programmers have grown testy about revisiting the format's past, so McIntyre might meet resistance, but it's their loss. 'Rain' could mark the dawn of a new day for this entertainer."

A keen sense of humor helps McIntyre push above the pack of child-turned-adult stars who try to ignore their past. "A lot of people refer to me as Joey, which is fine," he told Sullivan. "Most of the time I say Joe but 'Joe McIntyre' sounds like the representative from the third district. The 'y' adds a little flair."

Selected discography

Solo

Stay the Same (includes "Stay the Same"), C2/Columbia, 1999.
Meet Joe Mac (includes "Rain"), Q, 2001.

With New Kids on the Block

New Kids on the Block, Columbia, 1986.
Hangin' Tough, Columbia, 1988.
Step by Step, Columbia, 1990.
Face the Music, Columbia, 1994.
Merry, Merry Christmas, Sony, 1995.
New Kids on the Block Greatest Hits, Sony/Columbia, 1999.

Sources

Books

Graff, Gary, Josh Freedom du Lac and Jim McFarlin, editors, *MusicHound R&B: The Essential Album Guide,* Visible Ink Press, 1998.

Periodicals

Billboard, January 23, 1999; February 27, 1999; April 28, 2001.
Boston Globe, May 29, 2001.
Boston Herald, September 4, 1999; July 2, 2000; June 10, 2001.
Entertainment Weekly, March 19, 1999.
Time, March 29, 1999.
TV Guide, March 17-23, 2001.

Online

"Joey McIntyre Biography," Hip Online, http://www.hiponline.com/artist/music/m/mcintyre_joey/index.html (September 17, 2001).

Additional information was provided by Columbia Records publicity materials, 1999, and Q Records publicity materials, 2001.

—Christina Fuoco

Sarah McLachlan

Singer, songwriter, guitarist

Sarah McLachlan knows where the best music comes from: "Sonically," she told *Cover* magazine's KK Kozik, "moving water is perhaps my all-time favorite sound." Water has both its aural and thematic relevance for McLachlan. "Being around any kind of water is one of the most important things in my life," she averred. "I find it soothing and it's a very female thing, too. The ocean is like the womb and I'm fascinated, drawn in." Indeed, McLachlan herself has a fluid quality; her voice is noted for its liquidity, and her lyrics and production values, for their tempest and storm.

McLachlan comes by her turbulent personality honestly. Born in Halifax, Nova Scotia, McLachlan led a relatively sequestered life while growing up. David Thigpen of *Time* reported that McLachlan was "a shy, awkward child who never fell in with the crowd." He described her as a teenager who "would kill time on long, frozen winter nights writing songs." *Billboard*'s Timothy White provided a more complex portrayal of McLachlan's youthful existence. Her mother, Dorice, sacrificed her "own academic aspirations" in order to support her husband, Jack, an American marine biologist, and then acquainted "her little girl with the isolation that regret places in the path of personal fulfillment." But for White, the results were worth celebrating. "McLachlan was able to fuse her mother's depth of pathos and her father's detached analysis into a calm grasp of our culture's callous objectification of women," he concluded.

From the start of her career at age 19, McLachlan was compared to other female songwriters such as Joni Mitchell, Kate Bush, Sinead O'Connor, and Tori Amos, comparisons one might ascribe to what Elysa Gardner of *Rolling Stone* called a voice of "astonishing strength and clarity [that] may drift at any given time from a siren-like middle range to a ghostly soprano." She has remarkable range and tends toward lyrics which explore relationships between women and men.

During her childhood, McLachlan sought out the serenading voices and sentiments of folk-rock singers Joan Baez, Cat Stevens, and Simon and Garfunkel. She had 12 years of training on guitar, six on piano, and five years of voice lessons, all of which surely contributed to what White referred to as "the wit, literate grace, and unfussy intricacy of her material." As a teenager, McLachlan worked at restaurant counters and as a dishwasher in Halifax.

Critics generally agree that with McLachlan's third album, *Fumbling Towards Ecstasy*, released in 1994, she revealed a new maturity as a singer, songwriter, and woman. Her first album, *Touch*, released in 1988, suggested a waif-like quality to Gardner. But her second album, *Solace*, in 1991, revealed a sturdier woman, one less "ethereal," one "trying to come down to earth a bit." McLachlan said of *Solace*, "There's a lot more of myself in my writing [there]—more the way I

For the Record . . .

Born on January 28, 1968, in Halifax, Nova Scotia, Canada; daughter of Jack (a marine biologist) and Dorice McLachlan; married Ashwin Sood (a drummer), February 1997.

Trained in classical guitar, piano, and voice; discovered by Nettwerk Records while performing with a New Wave band in Halifax; signed a contract with Nettwerk at age 19; moved to Vancouver; released debut album, *Touch*, Nettwerk, 1988; contributed "Hold On" to *No Alternative* compilation, 1993; featured on American Public Radio's "E-Town," 1994; released *Surfacing*, 1997; released live album *Mirrorball*, 1999.

Awards: Grammy Awards, Best Female Pop Vocal Performance for "Building a Mystery" and Best Pop Instrumental Performance for "Last Dance," 1998; Elizabeth Cady Stanton Visionary Award from New York Governor George E. Pataki, 1998; Juno Awards, Album of the Year for *Surfacing* and Female Vocalist of the Year, Single of the Year, and Songwriter of the Year for "Building a Mystery," 1998; Society of Composers, Authors, and Music Publishers of Canada (SOCAN) Award for Most Performed Pop Songs for "Adia" and "Sweet Surrender," 1998; *Billboard* Award, Adult Contemporary Track for "Angel," 1999; Grammy Award, Best Female Pop Vocal Performance for "I Will Remember You," 1999; Grammy Award, Best Song Written for a Motion Picture for "When She Loved Me" from *Toy Story 2*, 2000; Juno Award for International Achievement, 2000.

Addresses: *Record company*—Arista Records, 6 West 57th St., New York, NY 10019. *Website*—Sarah McLachlan Official Website: http://www.sarahmc lachlan.com.

think, more the way I talk." *Fumbling Towards Ecstasy* reveals a woman with a more broad sensibility; her self-awareness and her melancholy meet a political consciousness.

McLachlan has referred to the relevance here of her increased self-respect and gender appreciation. She told *Billboard*, "It took me six years to learn how not to edit myself, to remain open in my music so that I touched greater levels of darkness as well as some positive areas of escape." When Kozik noted the "femininity" of *Fumbling*, McLachlan succinctly replied, "I love women. I'm fascinated by them.... I'm definitely starting to realize more of my responsibility as a woman."

While the bulk of critical response to McLachlan's music has been admiring, some criticism contained a disparaging tone. Dave Jennings of *Melody Maker* was dismayed by the excess of "vulnerability" he found in *Solace*, which while couched in nature imagery did not add up to "New Age consciousness, but really ... just old-school singer-songwriter preciousness." Similarly, *Spin*'s Joy Press found the lyrics of *Fumbling* "mature with a capital M, to the point of sophomoric pseudo-profundity." Press' criticism ventured into the realm of gender. Sardonically, she concluded that McLachlan "obviously places herself in the category of the self-defined, strong, female song-writer," and that ultimately *Fumbling* provided only "an easy-listening portrait of a woman—a perfectly graceful, confident, and smart woman—but it's not the portrait of an artist."

Other critics, however, found in that album both an artist and a portrait of that artist. Thigpen attempted to remove the debate from the gender-biased charge of confessionalism: "Far from indulging in simple emotional bloodletting," he wrote, "McLachlan creates exquisitely poised songs that resist anger or pathos."

In *Fumbling*, Kozik appreciated McLachlan's newfound "desire and capacity to understand more than just herself," a departure from the concerns of *Touch* and *Solace*. McLachlan agreed. A trip to Southeast Asia in 1993, for which she represented her Canadian peer group, afforded her both disillusionment and wisdom. She admitted that she sang less about victimization and self-pity as a result of that mission, one that focused on AIDS, prostitution, and poverty, and where McLachlan saw rooms full of photographs of "thousands and thousands ... of victims, men, women, and children looking at the camera and they all died immediately thereafter.... There are all these souls trapped in this building ... such intense oppression.... I all of a sudden got so horrified with humanity and so disillusioned. How can people be so cruel.... Do we learn nothing from history? But the aftermath of that is, 'I feel so blessed.'"

Though McLachlan does not address the Cambodian situation directly in her songs, its impact can be felt. Critics imply that the garnered knowledge enriched her lyrics and music, even while both remained devoted to interpersonal relationships. Thigpen identified McLachlan's audience as "the desperately troubled," to whom she offers the suggestion "that the answers to life's emotional earthquakes can come through perseverance and compassion." Terry McBride, the president of Nettwerk Records, remarked, "There's more soul in her singing on this album. [This] record finally makes you believe that she means what she says."

Though still inspired to look outward, McLachlan insisted that her strengths as a singer and songwriter are nurtured in solitude. With Rainer Maria Rilke's self-searching philosophies at the core, in 1994 McLachlan was focused on how to reach the most of her artistic potential. With expressed gratitude toward her producer and sometime-collaborator, Pierre Marchand, and all the talking and thinking he required of her, she still remarked, "I find that to open up myself as much as I have to to get at what I need, I need to be by myself." Like the true romantic she is, McLachlan conjured images of herself walking the moors of Nova Scotia, out in the country where "everything just seemed so huge and so much bigger than I'd ever known it to be before and I got really … high about how overwhelmingly beautiful everything was."

Fumbling lingered on the music charts for well over one year and attained multiplatinum sales. The album's hit single, "Possession," reached number 14. Likewise "Good Enough" reached number 16. McLachlan released an alternate version of *Fumbling*, called *The Freedom Sessions*, in 1995.

In 1997 she released *Surfacing*, which made its debut at number two. The album scored two hit singles, two Grammys, four Juno (Canadian) Awards, and earned multiplatinum sales certification. McLachlan used the momentum from the success of *Surfacing* to inaugurate the first Lilith Fair music festival and tour in the summer of 1997 to honor the advances of women in music. Lilith Fair met with success and earned a reprise in 1998 and again in 1999. Also in 1999, McLachlan released a live album, *Mirrorball*, which made its debut at number three, igniting the largest sales surge of her career. The album was recorded during McLachlan's tour in support of *Surfacing* in 1998.

In February of 1997 McLachlan announced that she had eloped with drummer Ashwin Sood in Negril, Jamaica. The couple set up residence in Canada in the Dunbar District of Vancouver, British Columbia. McLachlan, who won a Grammy Award for her 2000 song, "When She Loved Me" from *Toy Story 2*, was featured among the all-star lineup of "Music Without Borders," which aired on Canadian television and radio stations on September 29, 2001, to benefit the victims of the September 11th terrorist attack on the United States.

Selected discography

Touch, Nettwerk, 1988.
Solace, Arista, 1991.
(Contributor) *No Alternative*, Arista, 1993.
Fumbling Towards Ecstasy, Arista, 1994.
The Freedom Sessions (multimedia CD-ROM), Nettwerk, 1994; BMG/Arista, 1995.
Rarities, B-Sides, and Other Stuff, Nettwerk, 1996.
Surfacing (includes "Building a Mystery" and "Sweet Surrender"), BMG/Arista, 1997.
Mirrorball, BMG/Arista, 1999.

Sources

Periodicals

Billboard, January 8, 1994; March 19, 1994.
Cover, March 1994.
Melody Maker, June 13, 1992.
Rolling Stone, February 6, 1992; June 16, 1994.
Spin, March 1994.
Stereo Review, August 1989.
Time, March 21, 1994.

Online

"Sarah McLachlan," *All Music Guide*, http://www.allmusic. com (September 26, 2001).
Sarah McLachlan Official Website, http://www.sarahmclach lan.com (September 26, 2001).
"Star! to Air 'Music Without Borders,'" Star!, http://www.star-tv.com/news/index.asp?thisArticle=252 (September 26, 2001).

Additional information was obtained from Arista publicity materials, 1994.

—*Diane Moroff*

Men
at Work

Rock group

Hailing from the Land Down Under, Men at Work began their reggae-inspired rock 'n' roll career in Melbourne, Australia, in the late 1970s. Within a year after their debut release, their success spread to the United States and around world when *Business As Usual* topped the charts in several countries. In 1986 the members went their separate ways, and some pursued solo careers. They reformed ten years later, touring South America and selected cities in the United States. Band members Greg Ham, John Rees, Jerry Speiser, and Ron Strykert are all originally from Australia. Singer Colin Hay, originally from Scotland, moved to Australia at the age of 14. Each member individually began his music career in the pubs and clubs of Melbourne. Ham, Speiser, Strykert, and Hay had informally jammed together at the Grace Darling Hotel in Melbourne and decided to form Men at Work.

The quartet played at the Cricketers Arms Hotel in Melbourne for a couple of months. Then, they recruited bassist John Rees. "It was great to find musicians who were so into what they were doing," Rees told Kurt Loder in *Rolling Stone*. "It was exciting music. There was something happening." Men at Work played every Thursday night at the hotel for over a year to ever-growing audiences. By 1980 the word about Men at

© Neal Preston/Corbis. Reproduced by permission.

Work's performances had spread around town, and they could sell out almost any venue in Melbourne without ever having been played on the radio.

The following year, the band got the attention of CBS Records Australia, which signed them to a record contract. The label introduced them to Los Angeles-based producer Peter Mclan, who was in Australia recording an album with New Zealand pop singer Sharon O'Neill. Mclan produced Men at Work's debut album *Business As Usual*, which included the songs "Who Can It Be Now?," "Be Good Johnny," and "Down Under." Both the album and the first single "Who Can It Be Now?" quickly reached number one on the Australian charts.

"We were around at the right time for Australian music," Ham told David Fricke in *Rolling Stone* in 1982. "If we'd been doing this six or seven years ago, we might never have surfaced out of Melbourne." It turned out that Men at Work's timing was right for many more countries than just Australia. In the United States, MTV had begun to expose bands that radio had ignored, which helped lead Men at Work to success even beyond their American record company's expectations.

At first, CBS Records in the United States did not want to release *Business As Usual* despite the album's Australian success. Men at Work's Australian label

representative wouldn't take "no" for an answer from his American counterparts, and complained to Dick Asher, then president of CBS Records' domestic division. At Asher's request, Al Teller, then head of Columbia Records in New York (a division of CBS), agreed to release the band's debut without listening to it first. The record executives at Columbia were stunned when Men at Work became a runaway success in the United States.

In 1982 the band traveled to the United States to open for Fleetwood Mac on that group's tour. Soon after, "Who Can It Be Now?" made its way to the top of the American charts. Both the single and *Business As Usual* stayed at number one on *Billboard*'s charts for 15 weeks. "The MTV connection cannot be over-stressed," Kurt Loder wrote in *Rolling Stone*. "Men at Work weren't simply another group with a record out, they were an audio-visual package—essentially a new commodity in what was quickly becoming a whole new music-marketing ball game." During two straight weeks in 1983, *Business As Usual* and "Down Under" were the number one album and single, respectively, in both the United States and Britain. At that time, the only other artists to have achieved that landmark were The Beatles, Rod Stewart, and Simon and Garfunkel.

That same year, Men at Work won a Grammy Award for Best New Artist. They immediately returned to the studio to record their follow-up effort, *Cargo*, which was also produced by Mclan. *Cargo* included the singles "Dr. Heckyll and Mr. Jive," "Overkill," and "It's a Mistake." After the release, the band toured twice in the United States and Canada and performed in the United Kingdom and other parts of Europe, Australia, and Japan. In the summer of 1983, the group played at the US Festival in front of 300,000 people. The concert, which took place in California, was broadcast live all over the United States and via satellite to Russia. The speed of their success and the growing audiences at their concerts only fueled Men at Work's ambition. "We have very strong ideas about our destiny," Hay told David Fricke in *Rolling Stone*. "We really believe in what we have to offer. If you put an audience in front of us, we'll win them."

In 1984 Men at Work took a break. Rees and Speiser left the band, and the remaining members decided not to replace them. Hay used his time off to produce an album for a friend's band, and Ham performed in an R&B band with his girlfriend. Hay, Ham, and Stryker regrouped in 1985 to release *Two Hearts*. The album reached gold sales status in the United States but did not produce a hit single. Ralph Novak wrote in his *People* review, "With the departure of bassist John Rees and drummer Jerry Speiser, Men at Work has succumbed to a kind of manpower shortage that doesn't help the Australian group's first album in two years."

The group followed up *Two Hearts* with a tour that included the United States, Australia, Japan, Europe, and the Caribbean. Their total record sales at the time had reached more than 12 million albums. With their greatest success behind them, the band members decided to call it quits. Hay and Ham pursued their respective solo careers. Hay released five solo albums between 1986 and 2000. Every once in a while, Ham would appear at some of Hay's shows, and the two members would showcase a couple of Men at Work songs.

Men at Work released several compilation albums during the late 1990s and in 2000, including 1995's *Puttin' in Overtime*, 1996's *Contraband—The Best of Men at Work*, and *Super Hits* in 2000. In 1996, Hay and Ham reunited for a tour of South America and a few shows in the United States, a teaming they repeated in 1997. The following year, they released a live album called *Brazil*, which they recorded live in São Paulo. The album also included a new studio recording called "The Longest Night."

Though their rise to the top was fast, Men at Work continued to labor over their music, whether it was recording and touring together or on their own projects. Their success opened the door for many other Australian bands to make their mark during the 1980s. Their persistence led them from being a pub band in Melbourne to a worldwide sensation.

Selected discography

Business As Usual (includes "Who Can It Be Now?," "Be Good Johnny," and "Down Under"), Columbia, 1981.

Cargo (includes "Dr. Heckyll and Mr. Jive," "Overkill," and "It's a Mistake"), Columbia, 1983.
Two Hearts, Columbia, 1985.
Puttin' in Overtime, Columbia, 1995.
Contraband-Best of Men at Work, Columbia, 1996.
Brazil, Columbia, 1998.
Super Hits, Columbia, 2000.

Sources

Books

Graff, Gary, and Daniel Durchholz, *MusicHound Rock: The Essential Album Guide*, Visible Ink Press, 1999.
Rees, Dafydd, and Luke Crampton, *Rock Movers & Shakers*, Billboard Books, 1991.

Periodicals

Esquire, July 1983.
Mademoiselle, October 1983.
Newsweek, August 1, 1983.
People, May 23, 1983; July 1, 1985.
Rolling Stone, July 22, 1982; November 25, 1982; June 23, 1983.
Stereo Review, September 1985.

Online

"Men at Work," Music Star Pages, http://www.musicstarpages.com/men_at_work/ (June 16, 2001).
TPA Agency, http://www.tpa.net.au/artists/menatwork/bio.htm (June 16, 2001).
"20 Years of Business As Usual," Men at Work—We Come From a Land Down Under, http://www.menatwork.com.au (June 16, 2001).

—*Sonya Shelton*

Luis Miguel

Singer

Photograph by Jose Luis Magana. AP/World Wide Photos. Reproduced by permission.

An adolescent singing sensation and teenage Grammy Award-winner, Luis Miguel went on to record a series of successful albums that made him the preeminent Spanish-language singer of the millennium. His traditional *bolero* albums of the 1990s not only defined him as the standard-bearer of contemporary Latin music, but helped him to set both sales and concert records as well. A romantic crooner with matinee-idol looks, Miguel also branched out into film roles and sent the tabloid press into overdrive with his relationship with pop star Mariah Carey. Setting his own standards for Latin music, however, Miguel bucked the trend toward crossover success with his music, consistently refusing to record his songs in English. "I am doing a good thing by giving more Spanish to the world," he explained to *Billboard*. "Spanish can express 'I love you' in so many ways. Onstage, I need to believe what I am saying and to feel that the audience is really feeling what I am singing."

Luis Miguel Gallego Basteri was born on April 19, 1970, in San Juan, Puerto Rico, to parents of Italian and Spanish heritage; during most of his career, however, the singer was based in Mexico. His musical training began early, as his father was a guitarist, and when he was 12 years old, Miguel recorded his first album as a vocalist. The young singer came to international prominence with a duet recorded with Scottish pop star Sheena Easton in 1984. The track, "Me Gustas Tal Como Eres" ("I Love You Just the Way You Are"), won the singers the Grammy Award for Best Mexican-American Performance. That same year, Miguel also collected prizes at music festivals in Chile and Italy. While still in his teens, the singing sensation recorded six Spanish-language albums, highlighted by 1987's *Soy Como Quiero Ser (I Am as I Want to Be)* and the following year's *Un Hombre Busca una Mujer (A Man Looking for a Woman),* both of which earned gold and platinum sales awards throughout Latin America.

Miguel made the transition into adulthood with the 1990 album *20 Años (20 Years),* which reflected his age at the time of its release. A collection characterized by romantic, mid-tempo ballads, the album's glossy production values and impeccable arrangements called to mind Miguel's English-language contemporary Luther Vandross, who was then dominating the American record charts with a similar sound. *20 Años* set the tone for Miguel's achievements for the next decade. Commercially successful, the release set a slew of sales records throughout Latin America. Six of its singles entered the charts in Mexico simultaneously, and the album sold more than 600,000 copies in its first week. After its release, Miguel was recognized as the leading male vocalist in Latin America.

Miguel turned to more traditional material for three of his albums during the 1990s, releasing a series of acclaimed albums in the *bolero* style. A genre characterized by romantic and sentimental themes delivered in a passionate, yet generally languid style, *bolero* perfectly suited Miguel's own distinctive vocal delivery. The first of his *bolero* albums, 1991's *Romance*, not only earned dozens of sales awards throughout Latin America, it received a gold record in the United States as well. The follow-up, 1994's *Segundo Romance (Second Romance)*, was equally popular. As *Hispanic* applauded, "Miguel's voice is pleading and seductive. *Segundo Romance* is another irresistible winner from the talented vocalist." The album went on to set another record for Miguel, entering the *Billboard* album chart in the top 30 upon its debut. It was the highest position for a new Spanish-language release up to that time, and a sign of Miguel's international appeal beyond the Latin American market. A third album, *Romances*, completed the singer's *bolero* cycle in 1997.

With Miguel's phenomenal success came criticism. While he invoked passionate responses from his mostly female concert crowds, his precise singing style and musicianship earned him a reputation from some reviewers as a predictable, old-fashioned crooner. A 1994 *Billboard* review of a Miami concert concluded, "So while the present burns brightly for Luis Miguel—and deservedly so—his future might become a bit dimmer if the only thing he has to offer fans is an occasional dollop of nostalgic romance." A 1998 concert review in the *Los Angeles Times* offered a similar sentiment, commenting that "Miguel treads a dangerous pop-rock path that can easily sidetrack into corniness. The performances were highly energetic, but the songs per se didn't offer much more than a few catchy choruses and disco-like synth effects." Even his de-

tractors admitted, however, that Miguel's albums had set the standard for quality in Latin music with their crisp arrangements and superb vocals.

In addition to the criticism of his music as staid and florid, Miguel also faced pressure to join the trend toward recording in English that swept the Latin music scene in the late 1990s. After Ricky Martin and Marc Anthony achieved major success in the United States with English-language releases, many eagerly awaited Miguel's first release aimed at the American market. Despite pleas from his record company to follow the crossover wave, however, Miguel insisted on sticking with his own musical vision. "I love my language, and I am proud of Spanish," he told *Billboard* in 1999. "Now is not the right time for me to sing in English—maybe in the future, who knows?" Instead, Miguel pushed his artistic boundaries by acting in the movie *Fiebre de Amor,* appearing on the soundtrack as well.

In addition to the *bolero* albums, Miguel continued to record a series of successful romantic-themed releases in the 1990s, including *Aries* in 1993 and *Nada Es Iqual (Nothing Is the Same)* in 1996. Like his previous works, the albums cemented Miguel's commercial status while receiving mixed critical receptions. A 1996 *Los Angeles Times* review admitted that "there is no better singer in Latin pop," upon the release of *Nada Es Igual,* but nonetheless insisted that "such corny, one-dimensional visions of love are hard to swallow." It seemed impossible for Miguel to please both his fans and the critics, but for the moment, he seemed content to set new sales records.

Another romantic album, *Amarte Es un Placer (Loving You Is a Pleasure)* was released in 1999. Miguel had also produced the album, which featured his trademark smooth vocals combined with top-notch production efforts. While some critics were disappointed in the effort—with the *Los Angeles Times* commenting that "this guaranteed blockbuster continues Latin pop's disheartening search for the glossiest production imaginable"—the album won Miguel another set of Grammy Awards. At the first-annual Latin Grammy Awards ceremony in September of 2000, the singer took home awards for Album of the Year, Best Pop Album, and Best Male Pop Vocal Performance.

By the end of the 1990s, Miguel had earned dozens of sales awards for his albums—with an estimated 35 million sold by 2000—while achieving numerous concert records as well. In addition to his success in Latin America, Miguel also gained a sizable audience in Spain and the United States. In the latter country, the tabloid press took an avid interest in Miguel's relationship with pop superstar Mariah Carey, eagerly reporting the details of his gift-giving habits to the acclaimed diva after their meeting in late 1998. While the couple guarded their privacy, Carey told *USA Today* that "It's really interesting for me to be in a place where there are thousands of girls running up to him, speaking in Spanish, and I'm not the focus of attention…. It's nice to be with someone who's secure with who they are."

Miguel attracted criticism for his refusal to appear at the Grammy Awards in 2001, which some industry observers attributed to arrogance. The charge was particularly damaging to the singer's reputation, considering that the separate Latin Grammy Awards had just been established specifically to increase awareness of Spanish-language music among a broader audience in the United States. "By pulling out at the last minute, he not only made his point but also compromised the image of Latin music to TV viewers worldwide," carped *Billboard*'s Leila Cobo. "Frankly, if Luis Miguel finds the Grammys so contemptible, he simply should not submit his music for consideration (as some labels have done). In this way, not only would he show some integrity, but he also would open the field to other competitors and the show to other performers."

With the Grammy controversy just the latest in a series of tempests, Miguel brushed aside the critics and continued to be embraced by audiences around the world. Taking an active role as producer and songwriter in addition to offering his own singular voice, Miguel has fashioned his own place as Latin America's most popular male singer. Deferring crossover ambitions to concentrate on his Spanish-language releases, Miguel also continued to define Latin pop on the contemporary music scene.

Selected discography

Soy Como Quiero Ser, WEA Latina, 1987.
Un Hombre Busca Una Mujer, WEA Latina, 1988.
14 Grandes Exitos, Capitol, 1989.
20 Años, WEA Latina, 1990.
Romance, WEA Latina, 1991.

America: Live, WEA Latina, 1992.
El Idolo de Mexico, Capitol, 1992.
Aries, WEA Latina, 1993.
Los Idolos de Mexico, Capitol, 1993.
Segundo Romance, WEA Latina, 1994.
(Contributor) *Duets II,* Capitol, 1994.
El Concierto, WEA Latina, 1995.
Nada Es Igual, WEA Latina, 1996.
Romances, WEA Latina, 1997.
Fiebre de Amor, EMI, 1998.
Amarte Es Un Placer, WEA International, 1999.
Vivo, WEA International, 2000.

Sources

Books

Broughton, Simon, et al., editors, *World Music: The Rough Guide Volume 2,* The Rough Guides Ltd., 1999.

Periodicals

Billboard, September 24, 1994, p. 10; October 22, 1994, p. 42; October 2, 1999, p. 24; September 23, 2000, p. 87; May 10, 2001, p. 54.
Hispanic, January/February 1995, p. 126.
Los Angeles Times, August 31, 1996, p. 6; February 28, 1998, p. 6; September 17, 1999, p. 6; February 5, 2000, p. F-1; September 14, 2000, p. A-26.
USA Today, November 2, 1999.

Online

Hispanico, http://www.hispanico.com/article.php?sid=14 (July 2, 2001).
Latinoise, http://www.latinoise.com/news/pop/luis%20miguel/luismiguelvivodvdeng.htm (July 2, 2001).
2000 Latin.com, http://www.2000latin.com/luismi/bio/bioluismi.htm (July 2, 2001).

—*Timothy Borden*

moe.

Rock group

Like Phish, Blues Traveler, and Widespread Panic, the jam-oriented rock group known as moe. originally came to prominence on the road, building a loyal following of fans through live performances and grassroots efforts. In fact, it is not unusual for moe. to play more than 200 shows per year. The quintet also established a strong online presence. Through their official website, they became one of the first bands to employ live webcasting of concerts and to e-mail newsletters to fans. moe. also succeeded in capturing the energy of their live set in the studio. After issuing material on their own Fatboy Records during the early 1990s, moe. secured a major-label deal with Sony/550 Music in 1996. Subsequently, the group returned to releasing albums independently, first in 2000 with *L,* a double live CD, and in 2001 with an acclaimed studio set entitled *Dither.*

The music of moe. incorporates a variety of styles, including classic rock 'n' roll, progressive rock, blues-rock, bluegrass, country-rock, calypso, and funk. Such eclecticism, in turn, resulted in critical comparisons to everyone from the Allman Brothers and the Grateful Dead to Frank Zappa, Tom Petty, Primus, Camper Van Beethoven, and the Red Hot Chili Peppers. "Everybody takes their influences and the people that they have listened to in the past and tries to put them together in a unique way," explained guitarist and vocalist Chuck Garvey to Mike Matray of *Down Beat* magazine. "Each of us likes a lot of different styles of music, and trying to put them all together in our own format is what's fun for us. It's also the challenge because we are all battling to get those influences represented in the music that we are doing."

Because their sets rely so heavily on improvisation, the band also shares common elements with the jazz idiom. "There are a lot of relationships between our music and jazz," added guitarist and vocalist Al Schnier, who serves as the other half of moe.'s frontline guitar duo. "Certainly the musical styles are different. But as for the nature of the show, there really isn't a whole lot that is different. There is going to be a head and a turnaround and a bunch of improvisation in between. It's just that we happen to be a rock band and not a jazz band. I've felt that way from the beginning."

Comprised of bassist and vocalist Rob Derhak, drummer Vinnie Amico, and percussionist and acoustic guitarist Jim Loughlin in addition to Schnier and Garvey, moe. formed in 1991 in Buffalo, New York. They derived the group's name from an old Louis Jordan song called "Five Guys Named Moe." This title was also the name of the band's first incarnation, minus Loughlin, which included a saxophone player as the fifth member. Over the years, the group has been based in Albany and in New York City, and by the later 1990s, the individual members lived in various towns throughout the Northeast.

Moe.'s ability to meld various musical elements and improvise as a cohesive unit onstage, willingness to create unity between the band and the audience, unpredictability from one show to the next, and relentless touring schedules spanning cities and towns across the United States enabled the band to acquire an ever-growing audience. Affectionately calling themselves "moe.rons," these fans often follow the group for several dates in a row. "The music is the statement," offered Garvey for the moe. official website. "If you come to three different shows, you're going to have a different experience each time, and each one will emphasize distinct portions of our music. And a lot of how that manifests itself depends on the band-audience interaction. Our shows are organic events, and there is a very real social aspect to performing that influences what and how we play on any given night."

Despite their reputation as a live "jam band," moe. achieved the same chemistry on record. Their debut recording, an independent demo titled *Fatboy,* surfaced in 1992 and was reissued on the band's own independent label, Fatboy Records, in 1999. moe. then returned with their first "proper" release, *Headseed,* in 1993. The ten-track album, also on Fatboy, remains a fan favorite for its spacey guitars, signature bass drive, improvised jamming, and overall funky energy. It contains the quintessential moe. song "Tim Ed," as well as versions of "Timmy Tucker," "Recreational Chemistry," and "Yodelittle." The album sold surprisingly well—over 20,000 units—considering that moe. was not linked with a distribution company. The group followed this

For the Record . . .

Members include **Vinnie Amico**, drums; **Rob Derhak**, bass, vocals; **Chuck Garvey**, guitar, vocals; **Jim Loughlin**, percussion, acoustic guitar; **Al Schnier**, guitar, vocals.

Formed group in Buffalo, NY, 1991; released *Headseed* on own Fatboy Records, 1993; released *Loaf,* 1995; signed with Sony/550 Music, released major-label debut *No Doy,* 1996; released *Tin Cans and Car Tires,* 1998; returned to releasing music independently with the live album *L* in 2000 and *Dither* in 2001.

Addresses: *Mail*—P.O. Box 2716, Kennebunkport, ME 04046, (212) 592-3542. *Management*—Top Artists Productions, Jon Topper and Dan Getz. *Booking*—Monterey Peninsula Artists, (831) 655-6900, e-mail: booking@moe.org. *Publicity*—Coppertop Inc., Jim Walsh, (607) 275-8217, e-mail: Coppertop@moe.org. *E-mail*—Al@moe.org, Chuck@more.org, Rob@moe.org, Vinnie@moe.org. *Website*—moe. Official Website: http://www.moe.org.

effort with a limited-edition live album from a show at Wetlands Preserve, New York City, called *Loaf.* Released on Fatboy in 1995, the now out of print set sold around 5,000 copies.

In the wake of moe.'s rising popularity, Sony signed the band to a deal with its 550 Music imprint. The nine-song *No Doy,* moe.'s major-label debut, arrived in 1996. Selling in excess of 65,000 copies, it was produced by John Porter, whose credits include work for Roxy Music, the Smiths, Taj Mahal, and Keb' Mo'. With this album, moe. continued to showcase their songwriting and instrumental skills and retain their live energy with songs such as the album opener "She Sends Me," the clever, stripped-down "Moth," and the anthemic "Rebubula."

By now, critics were speculating that moe. would surely become "big" someday. *Rolling Stone,* for instance, in 1997 named moe. one of the top ten "underground" bands of the year. However, the members of moe. themselves felt that *No Doy,* while a solid record, ultimately stifled their sound with glossy production. Thus, when they began work on their second studio album for Sony/550 Music, moe. enlisted the help of producer John Alagia, regarded for his work with the

Dave Matthews Band, as well as technical whiz/engineer John Siket, whose credits include work for the acclaimed indie band Yo La Tengo and fellow jam-rockers Phish. While technically masterful, compact, and filled with vocal harmonizing and guitar interplay, the resulting album, 1998's *Tin Cans and Car Tires* still retained moe.'s onstage flow.

In April of 1999, moe. ended their alliance with Sony and returned to their own label. They released a double live album, simply titled *L,* in the year 2000 on Fatboy. The following year saw the release of their most accessible album to date, *Dither.* Here, the band opted to explore the more personal aspects of making music—including utilizing a studio environment to its fullest—rather than trying to rework or capture the live performance. "In the studio, you have the opportunity to actually work with the instrumentation, the different sounds and explore something in a different perspective and direction, instead of stretching something out in that linear fashion," Schnier told Matray.

"It's something that we really wanted to do," Garvey explained further. "We're hoping that the fans will appreciate the fact that this is another part of the creative process that we get to indulge ourselves in, and hopefully everyone else is along for the ride." Produced by the band as well as Siket, *Dither* indeed won over fans and critics alike. The band soared with songs such as the road-weary "Can't Seem to Find," as well as a rendition of the 1980s hit "Big Country."

Selected discography

Fatboy (independent demo), 1992; reissued, Fatboy, 1999.
Headseed, Fatboy, 1993.
Loaf (live album), Fatboy, 1995.
No Doy, 550 Music, 1996.
Tin Cans and Car Tires, 550 Music, 1998.
L (double live album), Fatboy, 2000.
Dither, Fatboy, 2001.

Sources

Periodicals

Down Beat, May 2001.

Online

All Music Guide, http://www.allmusic.com (June 15, 2001).
moe. Official Website, http://www.moe.org (June 15, 2001).
RollingStone.com, http://www.rollingstone.com (June 15, 2001).

—*Laura Hightower*

Montgomery Gentry

Country group

Though seemingly negative descriptions of the country group Montgomery Gentry, "outlaws" and "redneck country rock" aptly depict the duo's hard-edged, raucous sound and attitude. Eddie Montgomery and Troy Gentry have been credited with trying to revive the traditional country sound that had taken a backseat to the pop-influenced country tunes of artists like Faith Hill, Tim McGraw, and Shania Twain. The duo introduced its rootsy country rock with the albums *Tattoos and Scars* in 1999 and *Carrying On* in 2001.

Music has long been in the blood of the Montgomery and Gentry families. Eddie Montgomery and his brother, fellow country star John Michael Montgomery, were raised by their musician parents, Carol (Snookie) Dean Hasty and Harold Edward Montgomery. The love of music was so strong that it even had a place within the Montgomery home. In Sony Music Nashville press materials, Eddie Montgomery joked about musical equipment being substituted for furniture. "When you came in the house, you sat down on a guitar amp for a chair. My dad was a guitar player, my momma was a drummer, and the bartenders were our babysitters." At the age of five, Montgomery began performing occasionally with his parents' band, Harold Montgomery and the Kentucky River Express. By his teen years, he was a full-time player in the band, replacing his mother on the drums.

Meanwhile, Troy Gentry was living a similar lifestyle. His mother, Patricia Ann, sang with the family's church choir and his father, Lloyd Gentry, Jr., was a music fan who frequently listened to records by the likes of George Jones, Conway Twitty, and Merle Haggard. Gentry realized that he wanted to be a performer as early as junior high. "I did my first performance at a talent contest in school and that sensation of everyone patting you on the back and appreciating what you could do made me want more," Gentry said in his Sony Music Nashville biography. "In high school, I heard Randy Travis for the first time and that's when I knew this was what I wanted to do for a living. So from there on out, I did everything I could to get myself out in front of people and be heard."

While the Montgomery brothers were in their late teens, they split from the family's group to start their own band called Early Tymz, and subsequently Young Country, with Gentry. John Michael Montgomery broke out on his own and Gentry did the same. Gentry's efforts paid off in 1994 when he won the Jim Beam National Talent Contest and earned the opening act slot for Patty Loveless and Tracy Byrd's tours. Working as a solo artist was difficult, so he re-teamed with Eddie Montgomery. "We had worked together so well for so long and knew each other so well that I knew it couldn't be anything but right," Gentry said in his Sony Music Nashville biography.

The duo dubbed its sound "hillbilly honky tonk." Montgomery Gentry entered the studio to record a demo, which their former manager, the now-deceased Estill Sowards, took to Sony Music Nashville President Allen Butler. Impressed with what he heard, Butler asked Montgomery Gentry to play a showcase in Nashville for executives. The performance earned the duo a record deal. For its first album, *Tattoos and Scars*, Montgomery Gentry worked with producer Joe Scaife. A perfectionist, Scaife studied several live performances so he could accurately capture Montgomery Gentry's sound on CD. During the recording process, one of the band's heroes, Charlie Daniels, stopped by the studio to record the song "All Night Long," which the singer had written for them.

In early 1999, radio latched on to Montgomery Gentry's first single, "Hillbilly Shoes," so quickly that Columbia pushed up the single's release date from March 22nd to February 22nd. "I couldn't be any more excited about these guys," Bruce Logan, program director at WSSL Greenville, South Carolina, told *Billboard* magazine reporter Deborah Evans Price in 1999. "I think the format is in desperate need of some fun and some attitude music that guys are going to like and women are going to like because it's fun."

The full-length album, *Tattoos and Scars*, followed. *Billboard,* in retrospect, dubbed the record "an un-

apologetic exercise in redneck country rock, boasting attitude galore." To push the record, Montgomery Gentry repeatedly visited radio stations for acoustic performances and interviews. The plan worked. *Tattoos and Scars* debuted at number one on *Billboard*'s Top Country Albums chart, which according to the magazine, was the first debut album to land inside the top ten since LeAnn Rimes' *Blue* in August of 1996. On SoundScan, *Tattoos and Scars* earned the highest first-week sales for a debut country act in that company's history.

The duo toured clubs to build a nationwide following for the band and *Tattoos and Scars*. They earned a reputation for keeping traditional country music alive in the wake of more pop-influenced tunes that were filling radio airwaves. Dubbing itself "pure whup-a** country," Montgomery Gentry was given the nickname "outlaws." "If people wanna put us in that category as being outlaws, it's okay with us," Gentry said in Sony Music Nashville press materials. "You're talking about Waylon [Jennings] and Willie [Nelson], Johnny Cash, Kris Kristofferson, Hank [Williams] Jr., Hank [Williams] Sr., Charlie Daniels Band, the Allman Brothers, [Lynyrd] Skynyrd. I couldn't be in any better company than those guys." In a year-end review, a *Radio and Records* poll named Montgomery Gentry the top duo of 1999. It was the first time in seven years that someone other than Brooks & Dunn won the prize.

The duo continued their Tattoos and Scars tour through the year 2000 but took a quick break in the summer to participate in the annual bike week motorcycle gathering in Sturgis, South Dakota. Their concert also featured a performance by the Marshall Tucker Band at the nearby Buffalo Chips campground. Montgomery Gentry returned to the festival in the summer of 2001, this time webcasting the event via its website. "Sturgis is a big party, no holds barred," Montgomery told *Billboard*. "You're in the middle of South Dakota and there are hundreds of thousands of bikes.... You have all these different people mixing it up. Some of the stuff you see, maybe you don't need to, but you definitely see stuff you're not going to see any place else." In August, the group shot a video for the song "All Night Long" with the tune's songwriter, Charlie Daniels, at the Kentucky State Fair in Louisville.

As soon as Montgomery Gentry left the road, they returned to the studio to record their sophomore effort *Carrying On*, produced once again by Scaife. On May 1, 2001, Montgomery Gentry released *Carrying On,* an album that carried on the duo's reputation for rowdy "redneck country rock." There was a promotional blitz behind the record. CMT, Country Music Television, gave away a Ford F-150 pickup truck and a Harley-Davidson motorcycle around the release of *Carrying On*. In the summer of 2001, Montgomery Gentry performed as part of Brooks & Dunn's Neon Circus and Wild West Show tour. To warm up for the summer jaunt, the duo hit smaller venues with Jim Beam as its sponsor. The outlaws scored a hit single with "She Couldn't Change Me." Apparently, Nashville couldn't change Montgomery Gentry either.

Selected discography

Tattoos and Scars (includes "Hillbilly Shoes," "Lonely and Gone," "All Night Long"), Sony Nashville, 1999.
Carrying On (includes "She Couldn't Change Me"), Sony Nashville, 2001.

Sources

Periodicals

Billboard, March 6, 1999; April 24, 1999; July 7, 2000; August 21, 2000; March 31, 2001; May 12, 2001.
Entertainment Weekly, May 4, 2001.
People, June 7, 1999.

Online

Billboard.com, http://www.billboard.com (July 25, 2001).
"Montgomery Gentry," Sony Nashville, http://www.sonynashville.com/montgomerygentry/bio/bio.html (July 25, 2001).

Additional information was provided by Sony Music Nashville publicity materials, 2001.

—*Christina Fuoco*

James Moody

Saxophonist, flutist

James Moody, American saxophonist famed for his 1949 version of "I'm in the Mood for Love," is an original master of bebop—the first style of modern jazz developed in the late 1940s. Early in his outstanding musical career, Moody worked with bebop founders and legends such as saxophonist Charlie Parker, pianist Thelonious Monk, drummer Kenny Clarke, and trumpeter Dizzy Gillespie to forge a radical style of music marked by complicated improvisation and vast harmonic territory for jazz soloists. Moody himself has proven to be a fluent soloist on the tenor and alto saxophone, as well as the flute. Decades after the creation of bebop, Moody's musical style and vision continue to evolve. "Over the years, Moody has become so free—not in a random fashion, but a scientific freedom—that he can do anything he wants with the saxophone…. He has true knowledge. He is in complete control," saxophonist Jimmy Heath told *Down Beat*'s Ted Panken. Moody has been honored by receiving induction into the International Jazz Hall of Fame, and he was presented with the Jazz Masters Fellowship Award from the National Endowment for the Arts in 1998.

Born on March 26, 1925, in Savannah, Georgia, and raised in Newark, New Jersey, James Moody—named after his absent, trumpet-playing father—discovered his love of music at a young age. "When I was a kid [my mother] had a washing machine outside of the house that would go 'arookata-arookata.' She said I used to stand by and dance to the washing machine," Moody explained to *Saxophone Journal*. Although he was born partially deaf, at the age of 16, Moody began playing an old, silver alto saxophone given to him by an uncle. A few years later, he heard tenor saxophonists Don Byas and Buddy Tate perform with the Count Basie Band at the Adams Theater in Newark where he became enchanted by the more full-bodied sound of the tenor. The music of two other great tenor saxophonists, Lester Young and Coleman Hawkins, electrified Moody and helped convince him to dedicate his life to playing the saxophone.

Found Friend and Mentor in Gillespie

While serving in an African American unit of the United States Air Force from 1943-46, Moody met Gillespie, the influential trumpeter in whom he would find a lifelong friend and mentor. At the time, Moody was playing in the unauthorized 'Negro Air Force Band,' led by trumpeter Dave Burns, whom Moody would soon play with in Gillespie's big band and later in Moody's own band of the mid 1950s. Moody and Burns were blown away when they heard Gillespie perform at a military base in Greensboro, North Carolina. The two young men talked to the trumpeter and told him of their upcoming discharge from the Air Force. Gillespie invited them to audition for his band in New York. A few months after failing his first audition, Moody joined

For the Record . . .

Born on March 26, 1925, in Savannah, GA. *Education*: Studied composition with Dizzy Gillespie, composition and theory with Tom McIntosh, and theory with Michael Longo.

Began playing alto saxophone at age 16; joined U.S. Air Force Band, 1943; joined Dizzy Gillespie's orchestra, 1946; recorded debut album as a leader, *James Moody and His Bebop Men,* 1948; moved to Europe, recorded "I'm in the Mood for Love," 1949; returned to U.S., formed James Moody Septet, 1951; recorded Argo debut as flutist, *Flute 'n the Blues,* 1956; joined the Dizzy Gillespie Quintet, 1963-70; played in Las Vegas Hilton Orchestra, 1970s; released *Sweet and Lovely,* 1986; released *Something Special,* 1989; toured with Gillespie and the United Nations Orchestra, early 1990s; released *Young at Heart,* 1996; appeared in film *Midnight in the Garden of Good and Evil,* 1997; released Warner Bros. album, *Moody Plays Mancini,* 1997.

Awards: Jazz Masters Fellowship Award, National Endowment for the Arts, 1998.

Member: International Jazz Hall of Fame.

Addresses: *Management*—c/o Ina Dittke, 770 NE 69th Street, Miami, FL 33138, phone: (305) 762-4309, fax: (305) 762-4308, e-mail: bprmusic@compuserve.com. *Website*—James Moody Official Website: http://www.jamesmoody.com. *E-mail*—mood4love@home. com.

Gillespie's all-star bebop big band in 1946. By joining Gillespie's group, Moody established an association that would offer him international exposure and the chance to create his own brilliant improvisational style.

The 21-year-old Moody was overwhelmed and impressed by the orchestra's awe-inspiring range of talent, which included the supreme vibraphonist Milt Jackson, Clarke on drums, bassist Ray Brown, Monk on piano, Dave Burns on trumpet, and arguably one of the twentieth century's greatest creative artists, trumpeter Miles Davis. It was during his first recording with the band that Moody established himself as a superb soloist. He made a startling impact on Gillespie's 1946 version of "Emanon," in which he opened his now-famous 16-bar solo with a surprising, trumpet-like burst of notes. "Moody's 'Emanon' solo was very exciting to all the saxophone players around Philadelphia. It was very different than any blues solo that you had heard. He had the bebop sound," Heath told Panken. One year later, Moody recorded with Jackson for Dial Records, and in 1948, he made his recording debut as a leader using players from Gillespie's band on *James Moody and His Bebop Men* for Blue Note.

Recorded Classic "I'm in the Mood for Love"

In 1949, Moody moved to Paris, where he lived with his uncle, to recover from a bout with alcoholism. He frequently played at the Club St. Germain and toured France, Scandinavia, and Switzerland, recording with both European and visiting American stars such as Davis and Clarke. He also got married and had a daughter, all the while recording over 90 sides for a variety of labels, melodically reinventing ballads, blues and bop tunes.

On October 12, 1949, while in Sweden on a two-week nightclub engagement, Moody recorded "I'm in the Mood for Love," the risky, improvisational masterpiece for which he is now renowned. A group called James Moody and His Swedish Crowns recorded Moody's adventurous interpretation of this pop song by Jimmy McHugh for Metronome in Stockholm. As fate would have it, legendary Swedish saxophonist Lars Gullin came by the studio to hear Moody in action. On a whim, Moody asked Gullin if he could borrow the beat up alto saxophone that he had brought along with him. It was the first time Moody played the alto professionally. Pianist Gosta Theselius, who arranged the music, jotted down the harmonies to "I'm in the Mood for Love" while in the bathroom. When he came out, the song was done in one fantastic take. The beginning of Moody's solo has become classic, but in fact, the musician, accustomed to playing the tenor, hesitated while he tried to find the right notes on his new instrument. The song changed Moody's life and launched a fresh career for him back in the United States where the song unexpectedly became a huge juke box hit when it was initially released by Prestige Records. In 1954, the tune had a resurgence in popularity when the singer King Pleasure released a new version called "Moody's Mood For Love" using lyrics by vocalist Eddie Jefferson, which referred to Moody by name. The song has since become a standard, with famous singers like Aretha Franklin covering it.

Due to the racism he had experienced during his service in the Air Force, Moody had not considered returning from Europe to the United States. In 1951, however, he did so in order to capitalize on his record's success as a professionally established alto and tenor player. Shortly after his arrival, he formed a septet that integrated R&B with jazz and employed bop vocalist Eddie Jefferson as the band's singer. In 1956, Moody's septet recorded *Flute 'n the Blues,* the band's label debut with Argo Records and Moody's first as a flutist. "I never really studied the flute, although I had help from many beautiful people. So I just got a flute and started 'spittin' into it not knowing what I was doing. The fingerings, some of them, seemed similar to saxophone, and I just blew like that and that's how I started," Moody told *Saxophone Journal. Flute 'n the Blues* is an album on which Moody plays all three of his instruments, conveying the same deep feeling with his flute that he does on the saxophone. The record features "Boo's Tune," one of two pieces recorded by Moody to be covered by the Ray Charles band.

Rebirth of Music and Spirit in Chicago

The 1950s saw Moody play a series of three-tenor shows with saxophonists Gene Ammons and Sonny Stitt, as well as work with R&B and soul singers Dinah Washington and Brook Benton. Despite producing a number of exceptional recordings for Argo, Moody grew dissatisfied with the incessant touring and constant pressures of road life. In 1958, Moody's career took a bad turn when a fire destroyed his band's instruments, uniforms, and arrangements. A series of events led Moody to seek treatment for alcoholism at a mental institution called Overbrook Hospital in Cedar Grove, New Jersey. He was determined not to allow his addiction to mean the end of his life and career. After a six-month recovery period, his mother picked him up from Overbrook and saw him off at the Newark train station. He was on his way to Chicago, embarking on a journey that symbolized rebirth after months of suffering. In Chicago, he recorded the inspirational, bluesy album entitled *Last Train from Overbrook* on which he demonstrates his growth and agility as a flutist.

In 1963, after more than a decade, Moody rejoined Gillespie, replacing Leo Wright as reedman-flutist in Gillespie's quintet until 1970. According to Panken, Moody's thorough study of Coltrane's harmonic system "brought his playing to new levels of complexity and abstraction." Wanting a steady job that would afford him time with his new wife and young daughter, Moody left the one-nighters behind and moved to Las Vegas in 1973. He had a seven-year stint in the Las Vegas Hilton Orchestra performing shows for rock 'n' roll mega-star Elvis Presley, popular television personality Bill Cosby, and glitzy pianist Liberace.

Moody got divorced and moved back to the East Coast in the 1980s. His career received a boost during this decade when he put together his own band again and received a 1985 Grammy Award nomination for Best

Jazz Instrumental Performance for his playing on the Manhattan Transfer's *Vocalese* album. The record launched Moody back into the jazz scene as a recording artist, and the next year, he released his RCA/Novus debut titled *Something Special.* This recording was followed by *Moving Forward,* which features Moody's energetic vocals on the tune "What Do You Do" and showcases his creative flute playing on the song "Giant Steps." His 1989 album, *Sweet and Lovely,* is dedicated to his wife Linda, whom he married in April of the same year. Gillespie was the best man, and he performed the solo on "Con Alma" to which the bride and groom walked down the aisle.

Honored for Work

Moody teamed with Gillespie again during the 1990s. They received a Grammy Award nomination for their version of Gillespie's "Get the Booty," which showcases outstanding scatting. The two men also toured Europe and the United States with the United Nations Orchestra. The 1995 Telarc release *Moody's Party* is a live recording of his historic seventieth birthday celebration at New York's Blue Note. In April of 1996, the prolific artist released his first Warner Bros. album called *Young at Heart,* a recording that pays tribute to songs associated with Frank Sinatra. While touring extensively, Moody managed to find the time to appear as Mr. Glover in the 1997 film *Midnight in the Garden of Good and Evil.* During the latter part of the decade, he received a variety of honors, including his first honorary degree from Florida Memorial College, his induction into the International Jazz Hall of Fame, the 1998 Jazz Masters Fellowship Award from the National Endowment for the Arts, and the release of his Warner Bros. album *Moody Plays Mancini.*

In the spring of 2000, Moody celebrated his seventy-fifth birthday with another remarkable party, this time at Avery Fisher Hall in New York City with the help of the Lincoln Center Jazz Orchestra and notable Gillespie disciples. The audience was packed, and guests Slide Hampton, Jon Hendricks, Annie Ross, Jon Faddis, Kenny Barron, Janis Siegel, and Bill Cosby honored Moody. In conjunction with his birthday, Moody received proclamations from the cities of New York and Newark and was honored by the Congressional Black Caucus. On July 22, 2000, Moody received an honorary doctorate from Boston's Berklee College of Music, awarded in Perugia, Italy.

Despite all of his accomplishments, Moody is humble, always seeking new knowledge about chords and scales, forever pushing the limits of jazz music. As he told *Saxophone Journal,* "I've had a saxophone for over 50 years, and still can't play it."

Selected discography

Compilations; as leader; with others

Return from Overbrook (reissue of *Flute 'n the Blues* and *Last Train from Overbrook*), Chess, 1996.
James Moody and the Swedish All-Stars Greatest Hits (remastered reissue of *James Moody's Greatest Hits* and *More of James Moody's Greatest Hits*), Prestige, 1999.

As leader; with others

Young at Heart, Warner Bros., 1996.
Moody Plays Mancini, Warner Bros., 1997.

As sideman; with Dizzy Gillespie

Dizzy Gillespie and His Big Band, GNP/Crescendo, 1948; reissued, 1993.
Something Old, Something New, Verve, 1963; reissued, 1998.

Sources

Books

Holtje, Steve, and Nancy Ann Lee, editors, *MusicHound Jazz: The Essential Album Guide,* Visible Ink Press, 1998.
Kernfeld, Barry, editor, *New Grove Dictionary of Jazz: Volume Two,* Macmillan Press, 1988.

Periodicals

Down Beat, June 2001.
New York Times, April 2, 2000.
Saxophone Journal, January 1998.

Online

James Moody Official Website, http://www.jamesmoody.com (June 29, 2001).

—*Valerie Linet*

M.O.P.

Rap group

Photograph by Anders Jones. Loud Records. Reproduced by permission.

Hip-hop saw many styles come and go during the 1990s, from the Mafioso posturing of Jay-Z to the pop music samplings of Puff Daddy and the Nation-of-Islam-meets-kung-fu mysticism of the Wu-Tang Clan. Through it all, though, Brooklyn, New York's M.O.P. (Mash Out Posse) earned respect by refusing to change their growling hard-core approach to fit the dominant style. They have recorded alongside artists as diverse as Busta Rhymes, Big Pun, and Jay-Z. "Never, never change," they told Djeneba Doukoure of *Murder Dog* magazine previous to the release of their fourth album, *Warriorz,* in 2000. "So if you're looking for a new album, different type style—no, never. Same M.O.P. Only thing, we might get more mature, but it's the same sound."

From their first album, *To the Death,* released in 1994, through *Warriorz,* that sound has been characterized by what *Muzik* magazine called "roared nastiness." The title of their first single was "How About Some Hardcore?," and the more recent "Ante Up (Robbin Hoodz Theory)," graphically (and comically) describes robbing flashy thugs of their gold and jewels. M.O.P.'s songs are about murder, drug dealing, and criminal life. For rappers Lil' Fame and Billy Danze, maintaining a consistent style amounts to staying true to the streets they grew up on: "We're the voice of the streets," Fame told Soren Baker of the *Los Angeles Times,* "and we're not letting that title go anywhere." While this commitment to their own style has earned them permanent credibility in the rap community, their refusal to bow to trends or compromise their message has cost them mainstream success.

M.O.P., short for Mash Out Posse, was the name of Fame and Danze's high school gang. Mash Out, they told *XXL* magazine, means "the level before getting killed and just a few levels after getting your a** kicked—mashed out." The two grew up in Brooklyn's notorious Brownsville neighborhood, a ghetto that was home to the young Mike Tyson and also to Christopher Wallace, The Notorious B.I.G. "He used to sell crack down the block from me, but he was a good dude" says Fame. Like Biggie Smalls, who once wrote "If I wasn't in the rap game/I'd probably have a … knee deep in the crack game," Fame and Danze divided their teenage years between drug dealing, robbery, and rap. "We did this s*it before we had a record deal," Danze told *Vibe.* "We'd be in the hallway selling crack, rhymin' about a shoot-out we just had, rhymin' about robbin'…."

The lifestyle caught up with Danze, however, and led to a prison sentence in the late 1980s. Fame continued rapping on his own, and at age 16, he was discovered by producer and Brownsville native Laze E Laze, who put him on his Brownsville/Ocean Hill compilation disc, *The Hill That's Real.* In spite of a weak reception, Fame continued doing live shows, and when Danze returned from upstate New York in 1993, Fame convinced Laze they should record together. Fame and Danze called

Members include **William "Billy" Danze** (born 1976); **Lil' Fame** (born Jamel Grinnage in 1976).

Debut single, "How About Some Hardcore?," released on *House Party 3* film soundtrack, 1993; released debut album, *To the Death*, on Select Records, 1994; released *Firing Squad* on Relativity Records, 1996; released *First Family 4 Life*, 1998; released *Warriorz* on Loud Records, 2000.

Addresses: *Record company*—Loud Records, 79 Fifth Avenue, New York, NY 10003, phone: (212) 337-5300, fax: (212) 337-5374, website: www.loudrecords.com.

themselves M.O.P. and recorded a cut called "How About Some Hardcore?" which appeared on the *House Party 3* film soundtrack. The street anthem, produced by DR Period, immediately became an East Coast radio favorite, and M.O.P's first album, *To the Death*, appeared on Select Records in 1994. The album did not sell well, but the single grabbed the attention of Gang Starr's legendary producer, DJ Premier. "You could tell that pain and anger in them for real," Premier told Shaheem Reid in the *Source*. "You could feel the hardcore in 'em. I was like, 'I gotta be a part of that.' Their music motivates me."

In Premier, M.O.P. found a producer with a style as uncompromising as their own and the ability to push M.O.P.'s own vision even further. He assumed executive production duties for the duo's next album, *Firing Squad*, which was released in 1996 on the more prestigious Relativity label. The album was an enormous critical success. The *Source* wrote that "Brownsville's Mash Out Posse put a serious dent on the rhyme game and established themselves as two of the livest ... to ever bless the mic...." *Vibe* wrote that "*Firing Squad* stacks the deck and takes home the jackpot by employing DJ Premier for the bulk of the production.... M.O.P. perform like few others do—as though their lives depend on it."

But once again, critical success did not amount to commercial success. The 1997 EP "Handle Ur Bizness" and 1998's *First Family 4 Life* fared similarly. M.O.P. had now been recording for five years, but sales of their work still did not bring the duo closer to hitting the gold sales mark. "Whenever we do a [track on an anthology], M.O.P. told *Murder Dog* magazine,

"they'll mention everyone else on there, but they'll leave out M.O.P. It'll say 'Featuring Mobb Deep,' or 'Featuring Busta Rhymes.' And then it'll say, 'And many more.' They don't even put our name."

In the year 2000, however, their luck seemed to change. Relativity Records was bought out by Loud, home of such hard-core phenomena as the Wu-Tang Clan, Big Pun, and Mobb Deep. "One of the reasons why we wanted to take on Relativity was to get M.O.P.," Loud CEO Steve Rifkind told the *Source*. Loud had, in fact, lost a bidding war over M.O.P. to Relativity Records in 1995. Loud pulled out all the stops for M.O.P.'s fourth release, *Warriorz*, hiring superstar producers Premier, Pete Rock, and Buckwild, sending the duo out on tour with Busta Rhymes and granting endless interviews. But while hopes were understandably high in M.O.P.'s First Family clique, the rappers themselves remained more cautious. "Every time we drop an album," Fame told Reid, "every label is like, 'This time it's going to be different'.... As long as I have this 20 dollars in my pocket, I'm good." As they told Doukoure, "We never asked for much, we never wanted millions of dollars. We just wanted to live in a clean comfortable house with water, heat, toilets, and to be able to put food on the table.... As long as we got that we cool...."

As expected, *Warriorz* received an excellent reception from the critics, who praised the elegance of its production and its deepening lyrical complexity. The real surprise was the fate of the first two singles—"Ante Up" and "Cold as Ice"—which received substantial airplay. This was especially surprising given that "Ante Up" was produced by Period, who had produced the group's first single in 1994, and "Cold as Ice" was produced by Fame himself, who until this album had no production credits.

Selected discography

(Contributor) *House Party 3* (soundtrack), Select, 1993.
To the Death, Select, 1994.
Firing Squad, Relativity, 1996.
Handle Ur Bizness (EP), Relativity, 1997.
First Family 4 Life, Relativity, 1998.
Warriorz, Loud, 2000.

Appears on

Big Pun, "New York Giants," *Yeeeah Baby*, Columbia, 2000.
Busta Rhymes, "Ready for War," *Anarchy*, Elektra, 2000.

Sources

Periodicals

Los Angeles Times, October 8, 2000.
Murder Dog, Vol. 7 No. 6, 2000.

Muzik, September 1998.
Rap Pages, November 1996.
Source, November 1996; September 2000, pp. 175-76; November 2000.
Vibe, November 1996; October 2000.
XXL, October 2000, p. 76; November 2000.

Online

"M.O.P.," *RollingStone.com*, http://www.rollingstone.com (August 28, 2001).

—David Levine

Ultra Naté

Singer

What started as a single dance floor hit turned into a full-fledged career for dance music diva Ultra Naté. The breakthrough success of her first single, "It's Over Now," led to her first album, *Blue Notes in the Basement.* She moved into the international spotlight with her second album, *One Woman's Insanity,* and remained there, bolstered by her second international smash hit, the club anthem "Free," and a subsequent full-length release, *Situation: Critical.* Limited somewhat by the dance music genre, which does not expect full-length albums from its stars, Naté created latitude by producing pop, disco, and jazz-influenced house music. She was able to break out in Europe where she regularly made the international charts. American audiences have been less receptive, though Naté has had top 40 success in the United States.

Ultra Naté—her real name—was born in 1968 in Baltimore, Maryland. She grew up in Boston and Baltimore listening to music by Culture Club, Dead or Alive, Chaka Khan, Marvin Gaye, the O'Jays, Diana Ross, and the *Saturday Night Fever* soundtrack. She was studying medicine in college, training to be a psychotherapist, when she discovered Baltimore's nightclub scene. She then met the production group the Basement Boys, producers for Sade and Crystal Waters, who used her to sing backing vocals in their basement studio. Before she met them, Naté had done most of her singing in church, but she went on to sing backing vocals on Monie Love's debut album.

The Basement Boys encouraged Naté to try singing solo. She occasionally recorded her own material in their studio, but it was with the Basement Boys that she wrote the song "It's Over Now" after clubbing one night. They recorded it as a single and it became a smash hit, an international underground club anthem. Naté's demo ended up in the hands of a former Warner Bros. employee who in turn passed it on to the label. Naté signed with Warner Bros. in 1989. "I really thought 'It's Over Now' was going to be it," she said in her record company biography. "I never thought that one song would evolve into an album. But it did." The album that resulted from "It's Over Now" was Naté's debut solo release, *Blue Notes in the Basement,* which was issued on the Warner Bros. label in 1991. Three tracks from the album, "Scandal," "Is It Love," and "Deeper Love," became hits.

Naté entered the international spotlight with 1993's *One Woman's Insanity,* her second release for Warner Bros. On the album, she sang a duet with 1980s British pop star Boy George, who wrote the song "I Specialize in Loneliness" for her. Dance music fans went wild over the singles "How Long," with Nellee Hooper and the Basement Boys, "Incredibly You," produced by D-Influence, as well as the Soulshock, Cutfather, and Karlin track, "Show Me." *Entertainment Weekly* critic Tracey Pepper noted that the R&B, disco, and jazz influences on Naté's work gave the album the scope to make its house music rhythms "cool enough for underground clubs yet radio-friendly." Warner Bros. heard this crossover potential, too, and tried to market Naté as a soul singer in the United States. Though American audiences failed to make the connection, "Show Me" did become a number one dance hit in the United States.

Naté considers her title as a "dance music artist" a mixed blessing. While she is known for her danceable, up-tempo songs, "anybody who's listened to my albums has a better perspective on what I do," she told *LA Weekly* writer Ernest Hardy. The downside of the title is that most dance music artists are packaged as one-hit wonders. They release a single or two that is a smash club hit and rarely ever produce an album. The upside to this, Naté told Hardy, is that it gives her "the freedom to experiment with different styles under the dance umbrella." Dance music is also where her fans are, as Warner Bros. discovered. She also has a huge fan contingent in the gay community. "A lot of people I've worked with over the years are from the gay community," she told Hardy, "so they had a big influence on my sensibilities. I love that they're not afraid to be themselves."

If for no other reason, Naté stood out from other dance music artists because she did not simply release the here today, gone tomorrow singles and remixes clubland is used to. She proved capable of producing albums with the success of multiple singles from each of her releases. As she is one of the few dance music artists who can make albums, Naté often has to fight while putting an album together to ensure that it is

For the Record . . .

Born in 1968 in Baltimore, MD.

Discovered by the Basement Boys, released breakout single, "It's Over Now," signed to Warner Bros. record label, 1989; released debut album, *Blue Notes in the Basement,* 1991; released *One Woman's Insanity,* 1993; released *Situation: Critical* on Strictly Rhythm record label, 1998; released *Stranger Than Fiction,* 2001.

Addresses: *Record company*—Strictly Rhythm, 920 Broadway, 14th Floor, New York, NY 10010, website: http://www.strictly.com. *Website*—Ultra Naté Official Website: http://www.ultranate.com.

treated as a whole by the marketing minds at a record company. "It's hard to have your vision understood or respected," she told Hardy.

In 1997, Naté moved to the independent dance music label Strictly Rhythm to release "Free." The million-selling single became an international hit and club anthem, becoming a top ten single throughout much of Europe and reaching number one on Spain and Italy's national charts. In the United States, "Free" rose to the top of the *Billboard* Club Play and Maxi-Singles sales charts and found top 40 radio play. The success of "Free" was a validation for Naté: "Who knew that 'Free' would explode in such a major way," she said in an interview with UBL ArtistDirect Network online. "I certainly didn't. But it definitely made me feel like all my hard work was not for nothing."

Naté's third album evolved from the success of "Free." *Situation: Critical,* released in 1998, was Naté's first album for Strictly Rhythm and her first without the Basement Boys. The split was amicable, she told UBL ArtistDirect, and was brought about by Naté's need to "spread my wings and fly." That she did, writing all of the lyrics on the album. Naté moved away from songs about love and the pain of it to light social commentary. "Found a Cure," "Release the Pressure," and the title track epitomize the album's focus, according to the artist, and were the result of Naté asking herself some challenging questions about life. "Merging euphoric pop melodies and innovative hooks with genre-stretching, beat-intense rhythms," the UBL critic wrote, "*Situation: Critical* finds Naté entering a new phase of

musical development, in terms of artistic control, song-writing style, and vocal verve."

Naté learned the meaning of creative flexibility while making her 2001 release, *Stranger Than Fiction.* The credits on the album include collaborations with more than one dozen artists, including rocker Lenny Kravitz, N'Dea Davenport from the Brand New Heavies, and the legendary Nona Hendryx. The group formula served to further break Naté out of the dance music mold. Hardy said that *Stranger Than Fiction* "transcends genre without completely abandoning it…. [I]t's an album as suited for the dance floor as it is for late-night, top-down cruising."

Naté continues to look forward to her next musical ventures. "There is so much ground for me to cover as an artist," she said in the UBL ArtistDirect interview. "Everyday, there's a new idea or a new sound to try out. I feel like my best music is still ahead of me, and that's an exciting feeling."

Selected discography

Blue Notes in the Basement, Warner Bros., 1991.
One Woman's Insanity, Warner Bros., 1993.
Situation: Critical, Strictly Rhythm, 1998.
Stranger Than Fiction, Strictly Rhythm, 2001.

Sources

Books

Larkin, Colin, *Encyclopedia of Popular Music,* Muze UK Ltd., 1998.

Periodicals

DMA (Dance Music Authority), May 2001, p. 24.
Entertainment Weekly, October 29, 1993, p. 64.
Interview, October 1991, p. 30.
LA Weekly, June 1-7, 2001, p. 49.

Online

"Ultra Naté," *All Music Guide,* http://www.allmusic.com (May 31, 2001).
"Ultra Naté," UBL ArtistDirect Network, http://ubl.artistdirect.com (May 31, 2001).

Additional information was provided by Strictly Rhythm publicity materials, 2001.

—*Brenna Sanchez*

The Presidents of the United States of America

Rock group

The Presidents of the United States of America emerged from the Seattle, Washington, music scene during the 1990s with a new musical perspective. At the time, the city's rock music landscape reflected the angst of grunge. The Presidents arrived with refreshingly light-hearted humor and fun-filled music. Unlike most bands, they did not have high aspirations of rock stardom. They even wrote a song for their self-titled debut called "We Are Not Going to Make It." After releasing two platinum albums, the group announced their breakup in 1997. They reunited three years later with a new album and a new record label.

Chris Ballew and Dave Dederer went to junior and senior high school together in Seattle and teamed up to make music in 1985. Ballew moved to Boston, Massachusetts, after high school, where he played in a band with Mark Sandman from the band Morphine. Ballew had been experimenting with the sound of a four-string acoustic guitar played through a bass guitar amplifier. Sandman expanded on the idea and suggested Ballew play a two-string guitar as a bass or a basitar. Ballew loved it and adopted it.

When Ballew returned to Seattle, he and Dederer began playing together. Dederer complemented Ballew's

Steve Granitz/WireImage.com. Reproduced by permission.

basitar with a three-string guitbass, giving both musicians a sense of creative freedom. "If a song is good played on an instrument with two strings, it probably is a good song," Dederer told *Guitar World*. "Also there's no body of two-string guitar work that you have to live up to. You don't have to worry about being as good as Tal Farrow or Eric Clapton or Stevie Ray Vaughan. You're just you."

In 1991, Ballew and Dederer met drummer Jason Finn. At the time, all three members were playing with different groups, although Ballew and Dederer continued to write together on the side. Ballew was in Supergroup, Dederer was in Beck, and Finn was in Love Battery. Finn began asking to join the duo to form a new group, and after two years, they agreed. The trio just needed to decide on a name. Ballew came up with the band's name at a local party. He was improvising with two other musicians and would shout out different names between songs. When he yelled, "The Presidents of the United States of America," everyone at the party started laughing, and he knew he had found the right one.

Elected to Major Label Contract

The trio played clubs around the Seattle area and recorded a ten-song demo tape in 1994. The Presidents sold 500 copies of the demo in just five or six shows. In March, the band released the songs as a self-titled CD on the Pop Llama label. They continued to play around the Seattle area, and in November of 1994, played at a Democratic rally for President Bill Clinton. The following year, they signed a record contract with Columbia Records after a bidding war between several labels. Columbia re-released their self-titled debut nationwide in July of 1995.

Despite the success of the band, the Presidents still did not take themselves seriously enough to succumb to rock stardom. "I don't think we're that big of a deal," Finn told Sara Scribner in *Rolling Stone*. "We're just a good time. I just hope people don't hate us." *The Presidents of the United States of America* included such hits as "Lump," "Peaches," and "Kitty." By early 1996, the album had moved into *Billboard*'s Top 10 albums chart and reached multiplatinum sales.

On Presidents' Day in 1996, the Presidents performed a concert at Mount Rushmore, which was broadcast live on MTV. That same year, they received a Grammy Award nomination for Best Alternative Music Performance. They toured the United States, Europe, Japan, and Australia. They headed back into the studio after the tour and recorded their second effort, aptly titled *II*, which was released on November 5, 1996. The CD included the single "Mach 5."

Although they did not receive the same response to *II* as they did to their debut, the Presidents remained undaunted. "We've achieved so much more than I'd ever imagined that it's irrelevant," Ballew told Keiran Grant in the *Toronto Sun*. "I wrote songs my whole life without anything akin to traditional success, but was very fulfilled. Even if *II* sinks and we get dropped, I'll still be a musician." Hardly a failure, their sophomore release sold more than one million copies.

Resigned from Office

In 1997, the Presidents recorded a cover version of the Buggles' hit "Video Killed the Radio Star," which appeared on the soundtrack for the film *The Wedding Singer*. That same year, Ballew had his first child, and the Presidents began to slow their pace. On December 17, 1997, the Presidents of the United States of America announced their breakup. They were ending their partnership amicably, and said the reason was that Ballew wanted to spend more time with his family. "I wasn't feeling the magic anymore," Ballew told the *Seattle Times*. "I wanted a different life where I didn't have to go out on the road to make music anymore."

On January 31, 1998, the Presidents of the United States of America performed a final concert at the Paramount Theater in Seattle to say farewell to their fans. The band donated the proceeds from the show to The Chicken Soup Brigade, a Seattle nonprofit organization that provided food, work, and transportation to people living with HIV/AIDS. In March, the band released *Pure Frosting*, which included live recordings, B-sides and outtakes.

Each of the three members continued to record and periodically perform with various groups. In 1999, the trio teamed with Seattle rap artist Sir Mix-A-Lot on a project called SUbSET. Recognizing that their chemistry and creative energies had not waned, the Presidents decided to reunite for another recording. "We just have some kind of magic when we play together," Dederer commented in the band's MusicBlitz press materials. "I can't describe it, can't define it, and I don't think any of us can take credit for it—it's just plain dumb luck to find that kind of synchronicity, and it shouldn't be trifled with."

Returned as the Presidents

In 2000, the trio released a single called "Jupiter," which was only available on the Internet under the alias the Quitters. The band formally resurfaced under the abbreviated name the Presidents and struck a deal with the Internet-based music company MusicBlitz.com. The company formed a partnership with the band in which both parties would assume the risks and the profits of their next record. In the summer of 2000, MusicBlitz.com released *Freaked Out and Small* over the Internet, then released it in stores on September 12th of that year.

By the time *Freaked Out and Small* was released, the band had won back the rights from Columbia to return to the name the Presidents of the United States of America. Although the group did not have an aggressive tour schedule planned, they had decided to continue playing and recording music together. In a 1996 interview with *Guitar World*, Ballew nearly predicted the band's future and summed up their stance: "We're a little band, we make our music, and we can do that no matter what," he said. "Everything else could disappear tomorrow, and we'd still be a band, still making songs. It might even be a blessing to go back to making our little records and playing once or twice a month in Seattle."

Selected discography

The Presidents of the United States of America (includes "Lump," "Peaches," and "Kitty"), Pop Llama, 1994; reissued, Columbia, 1995.
II (includes "Mach 5"), Columbia, 1996.
Pure Frosting, Columbia, 1998.
(Contributor) *The Wedding Singer* (soundtrack), Warner Bros., 1998.
Freaked Out and Small, MusicBlitz, 2000.

Sources

Books

Graff, Gary, and Daniel Durchholz, editors, *MusicHound Rock: The Essential Album Guide*, Visible Ink Press, 1999.

Periodicals

Guitar World, May 1996.
Pandemonium, July 1995.
Seattle Times, January 8, 1996; January 11, 1996.
The Stranger, October 5, 2001.
Toronto Sun, November 11, 1996.

Online

"Freaked Out and Small, The Presidents Are Back," MusicBlitz.com, http://www.musicblitz.com (June 9, 2001).
"Pop Trio Presidents of the U.S.A. Breaking Up," Yahoo! News, http://www.yahoo.com (June 9, 2001).
"Presidents of the United States of America," MTV News Gallery, http://www.mtv.com/news (June 9, 2001).
"Presidents of the USA Go Out With a Bang," Addict.com, http://www.addict.com (June 9, 2001).
"Presidents of USA Reunite," Jam! Showbiz, http://www.canoe.ca/jam (June 9, 2001).
"The Presidents of the United States of America," MCA Records, http://www.mca.com (June 9, 2001).
The Presidents of the United States of America (*Rolling Stone* article), http://homepage.eurobell.co.uk/comriker/articles (June 9, 2001).
"The Presidents of the United States of America Biography," RollingStone.com, http://www.rollingstone.com (June 9, 2001).

—*Sonya Shelton*

Kelly Price

Photograph by Michael Caulfield. AP/World Wide Photos. Reproduced by permission.

Called the Aretha Franklin of her generation, R&B singer Kelly Price proved both her staying power and her status as a young diva with the release of her second solo album, *Mirror Mirror,* in 2000. Known for her big, powerful, and emotional voice, Price worked for years as a backup singer for such artists as Mariah Carey, the Isley Brothers, Aretha Franklin, and Mary J. Blige. As a solo artist, her soulful voice has brought her number one hits on the R&B charts. As Chuck Taylor of *Billboard* wrote of the successful singer, "[a]nyone who doesn't yet love … Kelly Price simply doesn't know her."

Price and her two sisters were raised by their mother in Far Rockaway, New York. The family was a musical one, and Price had an early immersion in gospel music. Her grandfather was the pastor of a Pentecostal church, and her mother the music director. Price started singing in the church when she was just six years old and quickly earned the nickname "Little Mahalia," after gospel star Mahalia Jackson. Price was drawn to R&B at an early age as well, but had to listen to it in secret because it wasn't allowed in her strict religious household. When Price was 18 years old, she joined a gospel choir that performed around New York City. The choir was chosen to sing backup for pop singer George Michael when he performed in the city, and Price's professional musical career was launched.

Following her performance with the choir, Price was invited to tour with Carey and sing backup for her. The singer accepted, and she traveled with the well-known performer for four years. Price then sang on a demo for rapper Sean "Puffy" Combs, which landed her a position as a backup singer with his Bad Boy label. While at the label, Price recorded with artists such as Notorious B.I.G., Mase, Brandy, Monica, and Franklin. A big break came for the singer when she recorded Diana Ross-like vocals for Biggie Small's single, "Mo Money, Mo Problems" in 1997. The recording represented the first time that Price stepped out from behind a lead singer to let her own voice be heard. The experience inspired her to pursue a solo career.

Finding a label to launch that career was not easy for Price, however. Several recording deals fell through before she found a home at T-Neck Records/Island Black Music. Price is a full-figured woman, and her image seemed to hold her back. She told Rahel Musleah of the *New York Times,* "Studios want artists to look like models…. A lot of people felt I didn't fit that visual concept. They asked me to lose weight." Price refused to give in but found an ally in Hiram Hicks, president of Island Black Records. He told Musleah, "I was looking for someone to represent the girl next door, someone who was natural. I knew her raw talent would shine through." The label released Price's debut album, *Soul of a Woman,* in 1998.

Not only did *Soul of a Woman* showcase Price's voice, it reflected her prowess as a songwriter and producer.

She wrote or co-wrote all but one song on the album and produced roughly half of the tracks. In recording the release, Price worked with some of the biggest names in R&B, including Stevie J., R. Kelly, J Dub, and Sean Smith. She also worked with Kelly and Ronald Isley, who controlled T-Neck Records. Isley told Anita M. Samuels of *Billboard,* "Every few years, someone like her comes along…. When I heard her, I knew how special she was. She had that 'voice.' … It was a gift to have her." Singles from the album included "Secret Love," a song about finally confessing to loving someone, and "Friend of Mine," about a best friend stealing a lover. "Friend of Mine" was Price's first real hit, going to number one on *Billboard*'s Hot R&B Singles & Tracks chart and breaking into the top 20 on American pop charts. The success of the single drove sales higher for the album, which went platinum. The album climbed as high as number two on *Billboard*'s Top R&B Albums chart.

Soul of a Woman also received critical praise. Richard Harrington of the *Washington Post* called the album a "spectacular entrance" for Price, whom he called a "great soul diva." A *Jet* reviewer called the singer "sweet, strong, giving, and magnificently talented," and Taylor called her a "budding chanteuse with a voice of steel."

After the success of *Soul of a Woman,* Price had another hit—and a Grammy nomination—with "Heartbreak Hotel," a 1999 collaboration with Whitney Houston and Faith Evans. The song went to number one on

Billboard's Hot R&B Singles & Tracks chart and number three on the Hot 100 chart. That same year, Price recorded "The Gods Love Nubia" for Elton John and Tim Rice's stage musical, *Aida.* Broadening her efforts, Price also founded her own label, Big Mama Records (through Elektra), and began cultivating artists like young R&B singer Sasha Allen. Price also co-wrote and recorded songs with R. Kelly and Gerald Levert and began writing for and producing other R&B stars. But the multi-talented Price did not stop there. She also developed two different clothing lines for plus-sized women—the dressy Kelly Price Collection and the sportier Big Mama Wear.

The year 1999 proved to be a difficult one for Price, however. She began having conflicts with her label and filed suit against T-Neck Records, distributor Island Records, Ronald Isley, and the Isley Brothers Music Corp. for breach of contract and interference with other recording opportunities. The singer left her label and signed on with Def Soul Records, the R&B division of Def Jam Records. On a more personal level, Price was also struggling with the illness of her mother and mother-in-law, both of whom were diagnosed with breast cancer in 1998. While Price's mother's cancer was treatable and went into remission, her mother-in-law died; the loss hit both Price and her manger-husband Jeffrey Rolle hard, and Price suffered from a depression that caused her to lose nearly 100 pounds. One positive thing did come from Price's pain: with other Def Soul artists Kandice Love, LovHer, Case, Playa, Dru Hill, and Montell Jordan, Price recorded the single "Love Sets You Free," which originally appeared on the soundtrack of *The Hurricane.* The proceeds from the release of the 2000 single went to breast cancer research.

Price rebounded from her personal losses in 2000 with the release of her second solo album *Mirror Mirror.* The recording, like *Soul of a Woman,* includes songs that are almost exclusively about love relationships, some autobiographical in nature, and other songs the stories of other people's experiences. As Vivien Goldman described in an *Interview* review, the singer-songwriter "takes a cold microscope to our squirming emotions." Many of the songs explore troubled marriages and unfaithful lovers, like "Married Man." Price told *Jet* that her songs are "true stories but not always my story." "I set out to make music that was universal," she told Taylor in *Billboard.*

Like Price's debut release, *Mirror Mirror* also received critical praise. Amy Linden of *People* noted that Price's "womanly, from-the-gut voice" makes the album "an engaging and emotional collection," and Lynn Norment of *Ebony* applauded the release for its "tremendous vocals and poignant lyrics." Taylor called Price "one of the brightest young talents" in *Billboard,* while Kimberly Davis focused on Price's growth and nuance in *Ebony.* Davis wrote that with the second album, "Price reveals a woman of many layers, each adding up to a renewed confidence in life and love." The singer herself agreed, noting to Davis, "I'm more mine this time around."

Not all of the songs on the album received the same level of praise, though. Robert Christgau wrote in *Rolling Stone* that "the album's standouts include most of the tracks [Price] didn't compose." One song that most critics agreed was a standout was Price's version of Shirley Murdock's "As We Lay." The sexy track was a treat for Price, who had admired Murdock since she was a child. Murdock showed her respect for the younger singer by playing Price's mother in the video for the song.

A singer, songwriter, and producer, Price has already held many roles in the R&B world. With the success of her two solo albums, the strength and depth of her voice, and her continuing work behind the scenes with other recording artists, Price has only begun what promises to be a long and diverse career. As Taylor wrote in a *Billboard* review of *Mirror Mirror*, "Price is the real thing, an artist with a true gift."

Selected discography

Soul of a Woman (includes "Friend of Mine" and "Secret Love"), T-Neck/Island, 1998.
(Contributor) *Aida,* Rocket/Island, 1999.

Mirror Mirror (includes "Love Sets You Free," "You Should Have Told Me," and "Mirror Mirror"), Def Jam/Universal, 2000.

Sources

Periodicals

Billboard, May 30, 1998, p. 29; January 9, 1999, p. 15; February 27, 1999, p. 72; March 19, 1999, p. 24; June 26, 1999, p. 27; July 24, 1999, p. 32; January 29, 2000, p. 40; May 13, 2000, p. 32; August 19, 2000, p. 21; December 23, 2000, p. 20.
Ebony, August 2000, p. 18; October 2000, p. 106.
Jet, December 7, 1998, p. 64; July 17, 2000, p. 63.
Interview, July 2000, p. 42.
New York Times, September 12, 1999, p. 3.
People, July 10, 2000, p. 46.
Rolling Stone, August 3, 2000, pp. 55-56.
USA Today, July 11, 2000, p. D5; July 9, 2001, p. D4.
Washington Post, November 8, 1998, p. G5.

Online

"Kelly Price," *All Music Guide,* http://www.allmusic.com (July 10, 2001).
"Kelly Price," Listen.com, http://www.listen.com (July 10, 2001).

—*Christine Kelley*

Rockapella

Vocal group

Appearing on a children's television show, recording nationally broadcast coffee commercials, and releasing a number of records through its own label before signing a record contract, Rockapella has taken an unusual road to success. Then again, Rockapella is an unusual group. Making music solely with the voices of its five members, the group has consistently amazed and delighted audiences with songs ranging from doo-wop to updated Christmas carols. Wildly popular in Japan and with a fan base that stretches from six-year-olds to their grandparents in North America, Rockapella has survived numerous personnel changes and musical trends to become one of the most recognized a cappella groups since the days of the barbershop quartet.

Rockapella had its origins in the High Jinks, a male chorus that performed around campus at Brown University in Providence, Rhode Island. Like many college a cappella groups, the High Jinks specialized in traditional songs along with humorous parodies and some original material. In the mid 1980s, two former singers with the High Jinks, Sean Altman and Elliott Kerman, decided to form an a cappella group when they found themselves in New York City after their graduation from Brown. They recruited some other recent alumni to the

Photograph by Doug Kanter. AP/World Wide Photos.

new group, but getting the group off the ground was a difficult process as several members came and went during Rockapella's first few years. Altman also sang with his rock band, Blind Dates, while Kerman sang in jazz clubs; some of the other members fit their Rockapella duties into their graduate school schedules or full-time professional careers. As Altman recalled in an interview with the Contemporary A Cappella Society online, "In the early years of the group, we had members who were, for example, 75% computer programmer/25% Rockapella member.... Each of us has worked jobs outside the group at times, in order to pay the rent."

In 1985 and 1986, most of Rockapella's performances took place on the New York City streets where they often sang outside of an ice cream shop collecting quarters. According to band legend, they usually spent the proceeds on dinner at a local Chinese restaurant, paying for the meal entirely with change they had collected on the street. By 1987, however, Rockapella found more lucrative work at weddings, bar mitzvahs, and corporate retreats throughout the New York City region, typically performing about 20 times a month. The band also began to change its repertoire, adding more a cappella arrangements of pop songs along with more traditional fare. In 1988, Rockapella got its first

big break when it appeared on the *Regis Philbin Show,* at that time broadcast only in New York City. After the show went national as *Live with Regis and Kathie Lee,* the group made another appearance after co-host Kathie Lee Gifford enjoyed the band's performance at a dinner party. The appearance marked the beginning of Rockapella's national exposure.

Rockapella's second big break came in 1990 while the band was still playing most of its dates around New York City's music and comedy clubs. A demo tape of the group's rendition of the calypso standard "Zombie Jamboree" secured the band a place on a Public Broadcasting System (PBS) special produced by film director Spike Lee called *Spike Lee and Company: Do It A Cappella.* Rockapella's track was included in the soundtrack album from the special as well. Following up the success of the special, the band was invited to participate in another PBS project, a new show called *Where in the World Is Carmen Sandiego?*, a television adaptation of a computer game testing geographical knowledge. While the project confirmed Rockapella's success—meaning that its members could now give up their day jobs—it also led to another turnover amongst the band's ranks. One member decided to continue with his law studies instead of staying on with the band. High tenor Scott Leonard, who had worked for two years in a rock band at Disneyland's Tokyo theme park, joined Rockapella as his replacement. Leonard also assumed many of the group's songwriting duties, a crucial role in its *Carmen Sandiego* responsibilities.

By the end of 1990, Rockapella had settled on a permanent lineup. Along with Leonard and founding members Altman and Kerman, Barry Carl had become the band's bass vocalist in 1989. After completing his degree in music at the Juilliard School, Carl had sung for four years with the New York City Opera. In 1995, after appearing with the group on a number of *Carmen Sandiego* episodes, Berklee School of Music graduate Jeff Thacher joined Rockapella as the group's "vocal percussionist," creating rhythms and beats with his voice. Altman amicably left the group in 1997 to pursue a solo career, and the group recruited tenor Kevin Wright as his replacement.

As a popular children's show on PBS from 1991 to 1996, *Where in the World Is Carmen Sandiego?* brought Rockapella into an estimated ten million living rooms around the United States each day. The show featured Rockapella singing musical clues to geography questions, with the members also performing in various skits. By the end of its five-year run, Rockapella was one of the best-known groups among the preteen set. *Carmen Sandiego* also attracted one of the highest percentages of adult viewers for a children's show as well. Reflecting on the experience in 1997, Thacher told the Celebrity Cafe online, "When you're working in the music industry, you've got to take what you can get.... But the cool thing is that all the kids that watched it are now in college, or just out of college, and now are fans. And the moms of those kids still love us, too. So we've got this built-in audience that we're trying to reach and let know that we're still out there." Using the forum of a kids' television show had another side, however, and some of the band's members worried about being taken seriously by the general public. "If someone had told me it was going to make us stars with a lot of twelve-year-olds," Altman admitted to the *Brown Alumni Monthly,* "I would have thought about [taking the job] more seriously."

Rockapella also recorded backing tracks for two national ad campaigns—a television commercial for Folger's Coffee and a radio ad for the Almond Joy candy bar—that increased its exposure in the United States. Given the demanding schedule of *Carmen Sandiego* and the band's concert dates, however, it was not until 1995 that Rockapella released its first full-length album, *Primer,* which it distributed itself. The band also released albums of cover songs in Japan, where its popularity surpassed that in the United States. In 1999, Rockapella signed a deal with independent label J-Bird Records that resulted in *Don't Tell Me You Do.* Featuring original songs—most written by Leonard—the album ranged from R&B to doo-wop to gospel and dance-oriented tunes. "We feel this album is our best foot forward, the one we would like to be our benchmark in for the U.S. market, because it will be the first experience many of us have," Carl explained to the *Philadelphia Inquirer.* "What we're looking for is mainstream acceptance, so that a cappella is not something over in the corner somewhere."

The group's second album on J-Bird, *Rockapella 2,* appeared in 2000. Comprised mostly of original material, *Rockapella 2* also featured a cover version of the Squeeze hit "Tempted" as well as two versions of its Folger's commercial as bonus tracks. "This record, I'd say, is heavier on upbeat, happy, fun songs, but there are good ballads," Kerman told the *Daily Bruin.* "Our music is generally played on AC—adult contemporary—radio, but we've been crossing over to top 40 and hot AC, which is sort of more urban AC." Clearly, the band's fan base had grown from its *Carmen Sandiego* days and Rockapella was succeeding in its goal of making a cappella music a mainstream genre.

Rockapella also released a Christmas album in 2000 and followed it up with a concert album and accompanying PBS television special in 2001. In addition to its recording, television, and commercial projects, Rockapella remained a regular on the concert circuit, especially on college campuses. Describing the band's popularity, Kerman told the *Daily Bruin*: "I think anybody would enjoy the show. [Rockapella] is entertaining and that's the bottom line. We're an entertaining group that loves good music, so we do good songs." While the band has not yet matched the success that fellow artist Bobby McFerrin achieved in the 1980s with his hit "Don't Worry, Be Happy," it is well on its way to being recognized as the leading band in the a cappella field.

Selected discography

(Contributor) *Spike Lee and Company: Do It A Cappella,* Elektra, 1990.
(Contributor) *Zappa's Universe,* Verve, 1991.
(Contributor) *Where in the World Is Carmen Sandiego?,* Zoom Express/BMG Kidz, 1992.
(Contributor) *Carmen Sandiego: Out of This World,* Zoom Express/BMG Kidz, 1993.
Primer, self-released, 1995.
Lucky Seven, self-released, 1996.
Rockapella, self-released, 1997.
Don't Tell Me You Do, J-Bird, 1999.
Rockapella 2, J-Bird, 2000.
Rockapella Christmas, J-Bird, 2000.
In Concert, J-Bird, 2001.

Sources

Periodicals

Brown Alumni Monthly (Brown University, RH), May 1996.
Daily Bruin (University of California-Los Angeles, CA), May 3, 2000.
Entertainment Weekly, January 10, 1992, p. 78.
Philadelphia Inquirer, November 21, 1997.

Online

Celebrity Cafe, http://www.thecelebritycafe.com/interviews/rockapella.html (July 3, 2001).
Consumable.com, http://www.westnet.com/consumable/2000/04.12/revrocka.html (July 3, 2001).
Contemporary A Cappella Society, http://www.casa.org/publications/interview_rockapella.shtml (July 4, 2001).
J-Bird Records, http://www.jbirdrecords.com (July 3, 2001).
Rockapella Official Website, http://www.rockapella.com (July 3, 2001).

—*Timothy Borden*

The Romantics

Rock group

Decked out in matching red leather suits, the Romantics arrived on the music scene in 1980 with the song "What I Like About You," which could still be heard on television commercials 20 years later. The four members of the group all hailed from Detroit, Michigan, where they were influenced by a combination of British punk and the rock and R&B sounds of Detroit.

Bassist Rich Cole, drummer Jimmy Marinos, singer Wally Palmar, and guitarist Mike Skill formed the Romantics on Valentine's Day in 1977. They had a mutual desire to create a sound that mixed accessible pop with the energy of punk. They came up with the idea of wearing matching suits from the Detroit-based Motown groups. During their first year together, they released a single with their first two songs—"Little White Lies" and "I Can't Tell You Anything."

While the Romantics were performing a show in Toronto, Ontario, Canada, Greg Shaw, an executive from Bomp Records, saw them play. The Romantics released an EP on Bomp Records, which included the song "Tell It to Carrie." Quark Records re-released the tracks from the EP in 1980 on a compilation called *Midwest Pop Explosion*. The band continued to play live and was the opening act for the Ramones in the late 1970s. In 1979, they signed a record contract with Nemperor Records and recorded their debut album in three weeks.

The Romantics arrived in stores in 1980 and included the hit song "What I Like About You" and "When I Look in Your Eyes." Although "What I Like About You" became one of their best-known hits, it only peaked at number 49 on *Billboard*'s Hot 100 chart. Their punk-influenced pop sound caused them to be categorized as part of the New Wave genre of the 1980s. The Romantics followed their debut with tours, which included opening slots for bands such as Cheap Trick. They became a desirable booking for concerts as their red leather suits offered a strong visual image that complemented their high-energy music.

The group went from their tour directly into the studio to record their next effort, *National Breakout*, which included songs like "Tomboy" and "Stone Pony." After the release, The Romantics went right back out on tour, which included performances in Europe and Australia. When they returned, Skill left the band and was replaced by Coz Canler on guitar in 1981.

Later that year, the Romantics released their third album, *Strictly Personal*. The members of the band struggled with criticism of their appearance rather than a focus on their music. "On the second album [*National Breakout*], radio was a lot different back then; people still looked at us as odd fashion," singer Wally Palmar recalled to Gary Graff in the *Detroit Free Press*. "When the third album [*Strictly Personal*] came out, once again, it was the way we looked. Radio didn't want to see four guys dressed alike…. We wanted to have a together look. It was something we grew up with—the bands from Motown—I really admired the way they looked."

In 1982, the Romantics went through another personnel change. Cole left the band, and Skill returned to take Cole's place on bass. The following year, the band returned with another release and a different look. With *In Heat*, the Romantics appeared wearing similar snakeskin suits rather than their trademark red leather. *In Heat* burned up the charts in 1983 with the top ten singles "Talking in Your Sleep" and "One in a Million." The album soon reached platinum sales, and MTV started playing the video from 1980's "What I Like About You."

With their fourth album, the Romantics had reached commercial success. "I'm trying to make a living," Marinos told Graff. "I'm not so much obsessed with expressing myself as an artist as to be accepted and respected by coming up with something that's useful, that people can relate to. Just hearing the sales figures, the radio reports, that's telling me everything I've wanted to do is working." But for Marinos, everything did not work exactly as planned. The band blamed "success" for creating problems between the members and the group's management. Before long, Marinos left the band. He was replaced by drummer Dave Petratos.

The Romantics tried not to let the difficulties slow them down. In 1985, they released *Rhythm Romance*. Tim

For the Record . . .

Members include **Clem Burke** (joined group, 1990), drums; **Coz Canler** (joined group, 1981), guitar; **Rich Cole** (left group, 1982), bass; **Jimmy Marinos** (left group, 1983; rejoined group, 1996-97), drums; **Wally Palmar**, vocals; **Dave Petratos** (joined group, 1983; left group, 1987), drums; **Mike Skill** (left group as guitarist, 1981; returned as bassist, 1982), bass.

Formed group on Valentine's Day in Detroit, MI, 1977; released debut EP on Bomb Records, 1977; signed with Nemperor Records, 1979; released five albums, 1980-85; filed lawsuit against management, 1987; settled lawsuit and regained control of music catalog and publishing rights, 1995; re-formed and returned to the studio, 2000.

Awards: Motor City Music Award, Outstanding Pop/Rock Artists, 1994; Detroit Music Award, Distinguished Achievement, 1999.

Addresses: *Website*—The Romantics Official Website: http://www.romanticsdetroit.com.

Holmes wrote in his *Rolling Stone* review, "*Rhythm Romance* demonstrates the contemporaneity of popcraft as established by its '60s progenitors: that the gush of bubblegum puppy love is as good as life ever gets and that, for a rockin' Romantic, there's no better way to say, 'I love you,' than with two guitars, bass, and drums. And hooks."

Rhythm Romance did not match the commercial success of its predecessor, *In Heat*, and The Romantics continued to battle with management. They filed a lawsuit against their managers, which made it virtually impossible to continue recording and performing. Their royalty payments were delayed, and the group began to struggle financially.

By 1990, the Romantics began to resurface with *What I Like About You (And Other Romantic Hits)*. Petratos had left the band and was replaced by Blondie's drummer Clem Burke for live performances. When Burke had other obligations, the Romantics brought in Johnny "Bee" Badanjek, who had played with the Detroit Wheels, to perform at Rob Tyner's (of the MC5) memorial service. Following that performance, both Badanjek and Burke would alternate as the band's drummer.

The Romantics contributed three original songs to the 1994 European release of *Made in Detroit* on Westbound Records. The album also featured other Detroit musicians, such as George Clinton. That same year, the Motor City Music Awards honored the Romantics with an award for Outstanding Pop/Rock Recording Artists. Then in 1995, the weight of their legal issues was lifted. They settled their seven-year lawsuit against their former managers. As a result, they regained control of their music catalog and their publishing rights.

Marinos returned to the band the following year to record and tour. A live recording from the *King Biscuit Flower Hour* was also released in 1996. In 1997, Marinos left the Romantics once again, and Burke continued his previous role. Other compilations of the group's previous music continued to surface with *Super Hits* in 1998, *Live* in 2000, and *Hits You Remember Live* in 2001. In 1999, the band received the Distinguished Achievement Award at the Detroit Music Awards.

By 2001, the Romantics had recorded their first full-length album since 1985. It included contributions from Burke, Badanjek, and Marinos. "We're looking back on the new album, trying to find out some musical history about Detroit even prior to the '60s," Palmar told John Berger in the *Honolulu Star Bulletin*. "There was a heavy Detroit blues scene before that, with guys like John Lee Hooker, Muddy Waters, and Howlin' Wolf coming through Detroit in the '40s and '50s." The Romantics hoped to have the album titled and released by the end of 2001.

Despite the hardships of lawsuits, personnel changes, and creative struggles over the years, the Romantics continued their optimism to produce their own brand of music. When "What I Like About You" was used in television commercials for HBO, Budweiser, and Burger King 20 years after its release, the band received the recognition that their music still had an audience.

Selected discography

The Romantics (includes "What I Like About You" and "When I Look in Your Eyes"), Nemperor, 1980.
National Breakout (includes "Tomboy" and "Stone Pony"), Nemperor, 1980.
Strictly Personal, Nemperor, 1981.
In Heat (includes "Talking in Your Sleep" and "One in a Million"), Nemperor, 1983.
Rhythm Romance, Nemperor, 1985.
What I Like About You (And Other Romantic Hits), Epic, 1990.

Made in Detroit (European release), Westbound, 1994.
King Biscuit Flower Hour, King Biscuit Flower Hour, 1996.
Super Hits, Sony, 1998.
Live, Sony, 2000.
Hits You Remember Live, Madacy, 2001.

Sources

Books

Graff, Gary, and Daniel Durchholz, editors, *MusicHound Rock: The Essential Album Guide*, Visible Ink Press, 1999.

Periodicals

Detroit Free Press, November 25, 1983.
Honolulu Star-Bulletin, March 16, 2001.
Rolling Stone, October 24, 1985.

Online

"The Romantics," Ear Candy Magazine, http://members.nbci.com/XMCM/earcandy_mag/romntx.htm (June 16, 2001).

"The Romantics," Yesterdayland, http://www.yesterdayland.com (June 16, 2001).

"The Romantics-National Breakout," A Different Kind of Greatness, http://www.adkg.com/reviews/music/romantics-nationalbreakout.html (June 16, 2001).

The Romantics Official Website, http://www.romanticsdetroit.com (June 16, 2001).

"What I Like About You," Song of the Week, http://www.postalnuts.com/newwave/99-06-05/romantics.html (June 16, 2001).

—*Sonya Shelton*

Shihad

Rock group

With a population of only 3.7 million and a location that puts it about 1,000 miles away from its nearest neighboring country, New Zealand has nonetheless made the most of its unique demographic and geographic identity. Despite its potential handicaps, a vibrant music scene has developed, allowing several acts to go on to major international success. While Split Enz, Crowded House, and opera singer Kiri Te Kanawa are usually cited as the country's main musical successes, Wellington's Shihad emerged as another New Zealand act to gain a spot on the international stage. Although the band faced its own challenges on the road to international success—getting dropped by its record company among them—its concerts in the United States and Europe and genre-expanding, eclectic repertoire earned them the distinction of being New Zealand's hottest musical export in many years.

The origins of Shihad go back to a band formed by high school classmates Jon Toogood and Tom Larkin in Wellington, New Zealand's capital, around 1985. Typical of many fledgling garage bands, their first band underwent many changes as various band members joined and then left the group. By 1988, however, the lineup crystallized with Toogood on vocals and guitar and Larkin on drums, with Phil Knight joining them on guitar. A permanent bassist was harder to recruit; eventually, Karl Kippenberger took up the position and the band's permanent lineup was set. With a play list that emphasized basic rock tunes, Shihad in its first incarnation took much of its musical direction from Australia's AC/DC, the most commercially successful act ever to come out of the Australiasia region.

Took Step Toward Professional Career

In 1990, while all of Shihad's members were still in their teens, the band took its first step toward a professional music career by enlisting Gerald Dwyer, a former singer for another New Zealand band called Flesh-D-Vice, as Shihad's manager. The group scored two major successes that year, signing up as the opening act for local shows by American group Faith No More and the legendary speed-metal rockers Motorhead from Britain. The band also toured nationally throughout New Zealand. It was not until the following year, however, that Shihad entered the recording studio. The result, the 1991 EP *Devolve,* made the top 20 in New Zealand. The band further increased its visibility with dates as the opening act for AC/DC. Not only were the appearances a personal triumph for the band's members, they also exposed the band's work to audiences that numbered in the tens of thousands.

Despite the success of *Devolve* and its series of concert dates, Shihad's first full-length album would not appear until 1993. The previous year, Toogood and Larkin had spent most of their creative energies on a side project, SML, a collaboration with fellow Wellington musician Nigel Regan. Regan's own band, Head Like a Hole, was more funk-oriented than Shihad, and the influence rubbed off on Toogood and Larkin. The SML project resulted in one CD, 1995's *Is That It?,* but when Shihad regrouped to record its own debut, the results were somewhat different than its fans might have expected. Larkin's work with Killing Joke—a British goth band that had gone through several incarnations since its start as a heavy metal band in 1978—also influenced the refocused Shihad, which finally recorded *Churn* in 1993.

International Tours

Added to the band's basic rock direction was an industrial emphasis that gave *Churn* a more distinctive sound than the guitar-based heavy metal the group was previously known for. The album was an immediate top ten hit, powered by the single "I Only Said," which went into the top three in New Zealand and seemed to fulfill the band's early promise. Shihad immediately went on the road to promote its work in New Zealand and abroad, touring once again with Faith No More, this time in Europe, as well as undertaking a series of concerts with Head Like a Hole. The band achieved another breakthrough with record deals that secured the release of its albums outside of Australasia. Its signing with Noise International in 1994 meant that it would now have better access to Great Britain, Europe, and Japan for its second album, *Killjoy.* In 1995, Shihad also secured a distribution deal through Noise International for the American market.

Labeled "the country's most exciting international rock prospect" by *Billboard* in 1995, the band hoped that

Killjoy would be its breakthrough success. While the album earned praise from the magazine as "a rhythmic, near-industrial approach that avoids the usual heavy metal guitar indulgences," it failed to make a significant impression outside of Australia and New Zealand. The band toured America for three months, playing numerous dates around Los Angeles and New York, but its records sales remained minimal in the United States. In its home territory, on the other hand, the album was another hit. The band reached another milestone in 1996 when it became the first metal band to play on the telecast of the New Zealand Music and Entertainment Awards, the official awards ceremony of the New Zealand music industry. The appearance was a stamp of approval for the band, which won four awards that night: Best Group, Best Album for *Killjoy,* Top International Recording Artist, and Best Male Vocalist for Toogood. The band capped its success with another series of tours in Australia and New Zealand, opening on a number of occasions for AC/DC. Unfortunately, the band also had to endure the sudden death of its manager, Gerald Dwyer, in January of 1996.

Although its first two albums were critically and commercially well received in Australasia, Shihad turned to a pared down, less experimental sound for its third album, *Shihad,* released in 1998. As Toogood commented in an interview on Warner Music Australia's website, "On *Killjoy* we were into using the studio as a place where you can make fantasy reality. Then on the *Shihad* album it was more about making reality fantastic." With a third hit album in its home territory, the band picked up another set of New Zealand Music and Entertainment Awards for Best Group, Best Male Vocalist, and Best Video. Yet the release of *Shihad* marked a period of frustration for the band, including troubles with its record company. After a record company merger, the band was unceremoniously dropped from its label. Shihad was the only band left behind in the deal, possibly because of its many international contracts with other labels to release its music outside of Australia and New Zealand.

Returned to Form with Fourth Album

Dealing with record company politics was frustrating, but the band tried to look on the bright side. Cut loose from a contract in New Zealand, the band could rediscover its own sound again. "Because we were going through the whole record company thing, we actually didn't have any money for quite a long time," Kippenberger explained in an interview on the Warner Music Australia website, "so we didn't buy any music! In some ways that was quite good, even though we are quite interested in what's happening in the now." Fortunately, the band did not have to wait long before being offered a new contract with another record company. Released on Warner Music Australia in September of 1999 in New Zealand, where it immediately hit number one on the album chart, *The General Electric* was an all-embracing, post-punk album with some pop influences. "We're unashamedly rock," Toogood said in a press release on the Warner Music Australia website. "There's been a long period, post-Nirvana, where bands have gone, 'We're onstage, but hey we know it's a big joke and we know that rock is stupid.' But I love being onstage and I love having my guitar cranking at a million decibels. It actually fires my spirit up. Why be ashamed of that?"

Once again, however, there was great disparity between Shihad's domestic and international levels of success. As *Q* magazine commented in a back-handed compliment for *The General Electric,* "If they were American, Shihad would be massive." Back at home, the band picked up another New Zealand Music and Entertainment Award in March of 2001, this time for International Achievement during the previous year. The presenter was none other than the country's Prime Minister, Helen Clark, who had championed support for artists and musicians in New Zealand as part of her campaign platform. In fact, the federal government had already invested in Shihad as part of its New Zealand On Air program, which subsidized the country's musicians in international touring, video production, and international marketing efforts.

While Shihad's status as a government-assisted, alternative metal band might seem ironic, one record company executive explained the move as a pragmatic one: "It shows a belief that music export is a viable industry," explained Sony Music's managing director in a *Billboard* review of the New Zealand music industry in October of 2000. For its part, Shihad remained more concerned with giving explosive concerts and producing another great album than with the politics of export strategies. "It's just walking onstage and sounding like God and just doing it!" Toogood exclaimed in an interview for Warner Music Australia for *The General Electric*. "Rock!"

Selected discography

Churn, Wildside, 1993.
Killjoy, Noise International/Modern, 1995.
Shihad, Universal, 1996.
The General Electric, Warner Music Australia, 1999.

Sources

Periodicals

Billboard, May 6, 1995, p. 47; May 9, 1998, p. 59; November 6, 1999, p. 57; April 8, 2000, p. 50; September 30, 2000, p. 53; March 31, 2001, p. 43.
Music Business International, October 2000, p. 49.
Q, September 2000.

Online

New Zealand Music, http://www.nzmusic.com (June 30, 2001).
Shihad Official Website, http://www.shihad.com (June 30, 2001).
Warner Music Australia, http://www.warnermusic.com.au (June 30, 2001).

—*Timothy Borden*

Jessica Simpson

Singer

Jessica Simpson is an accomplished singer whose impressive vocal ability, commitment to faith, and accessible image have transformed her from talented religious teen to certifiable pop star within a few short years. Armed with two successful records and a solid following, the young songstress secured a much-coveted position within the crowded arena of teen chart toppers in 2001. Additionally, her strong moral convictions and positive attitude have made her a notable role model to teen girls. Boasting a reported five-octave range and vocally likened to Mariah Carey, Simpson is considered a rising star within the music industry.

Simpson was born on July 10, 1980, in Richardson Texas, an affluent suburb north of Dallas. Her father was both a psychologist and a youth minister, and from an early age, the young Southerner was instilled with a strong sense of faith. Simpson's first singing experiences were in church, participating in musicals and singing in the choir. By the age of eleven, she had already begun performing publicly on the gospel circuit. "I did dance classes, went on to dance competitions—that's what I did as a little kid. I was definitely into the whole performance thing." Despite her obvious abilities, the budding singer suffered a large disappointment at the beginning of her career that could have threatened it but instead reinforced her direction.

In 1992, The Disney Channel's *New Mickey Mouse Club* was holding open-call nationwide auditions, seeking just the right "mouseketeers." Simpson appeared at a regional audition in Dallas and was selected out of more than 30,000 other contestants as a finalist for a cast position. Ultimately, however, she was denied access into this exclusive club. Simpson was admittedly intimidated by her competition, which included more seasoned youngsters such as Britney Spears, Christina Aguilera, and young heartthrob Justin Timberlake, now of 'N Sync. The Texas preteen failed to display the confidence she needed to be on television. "They said I couldn't work in front of a camera. But that's when I knew that I had the potential and really wanted it," she explained to *Tiger Beat* in 1999.

Although disappointed, Simpson was encouraged by her close-knit religious family to diligently pursue her dream to become a singer and not to give up. According to the teen crooner, "I would have definitely quit after *The Mickey Mouse Club* if it wasn't for my family, because I was so depressed and it hurt," she explained to the *Dallas Texas Weekly*. "You know as a 12 year old, it really hurts to be that close to something and not get it."

Simpson's persistence soon paid off. In 1993 at age 13, Simpson was discovered while singing at church camp and was quickly thereafter signed to fledgling gospel label Proclaim Records. She had been spotted belting out an a capella version of "Amazing Grace" by the camp's guest speaker who was in the process of launching the label. The youngster invested a great deal of effort working on the record, acquiring songs and developing her voice. Unfortunately, by the time her first album *Jessica* was completed, the label folded, leaving Simpson with an unreleased record and yet another disappointment.

The teenager's grandmother bankrolled *Jessica*, and Simpson and her minister father hit the Christian music circuit. Joe Simpson would speak to the kids and Jessica would be the featured musical performer. Afterward, Jessica would sell her self-released album to moved listeners. Simpson became popular on the circuit and proceeded to open for such well-known spiritual performers as CeCe Winans, Kirk Franklin, and God's Property.

Despite the fact that she was successful on the faith-based circuit, Simpson, who holds strong religious and moral convictions, longed for a larger audience. "I trust that every step I take is under God's control," she explained in the *Dallas Texas Weekly*. "I knew that I would get a bigger audience by doing the secular, and I have more of an opportunity to be a positive role model." In order to help their daughter make this transition, the Simpson family hired entertainment attorney Tim Medlebaum, who proceeded to set up nine record label meetings for the budding singer. Simpson did the nine showcases in two days. Her magic star-launching moment, however, occurred after meeting legendary Sony Music executive Tommy Motolla (who coincidentally is the ex-husband of Mariah Carey). Simpson sang for Motolla and was signed on the spot. The music business legend, who was aware of Jessica's background, was surprisingly accepting. "I was determined that I be able to stay who I am if I signed to a non-Christian music label," Simpson explained to *Billboard* magazine, "and when I met with Tommy Mottola, he was genuinely impressed with my beliefs and was completely supportive."

Sweet Kisses, Simpson's major-label debut, arrived in stores in 1999. The album contained catchy ballads and pop tunes all emphasized by the singer's expressive vocal ability. According to *Billboard*, "the lovely Simpson … has the soulful pipes to go the platinum distance." *Sweet Kisses* lended the song "Did You Ever Love Somebody" to the soundtrack for the popular teen television show *Dawson's Creek*. It was also promoted heavily by Columbia Records. The album climbed up the charts to eventually reach platinum status. Simpson, well on her way to becoming a major star, toured both before and after the record's release, opening for well-known artists such as Latin pop star Ricky Martin and boy band 98 Degrees.

Simpson shortly found herself a major player in the teen pop arena, sharing chart space and magazine covers with other female hit makers including Britney Spears, Christina Aguilera, and Mandy Moore. The Texas-born vocalist was able to distinguish herself by both exercising her talent and presenting a sexy, though wholesome image. Simpson maintains a very public stance on abstinence and works hard to be a role model for teen girls. This was evidenced when she turned down the lead in the film *Coyote Ugly* in 2000 after finding out a particular sex-inclusive scene conflicted with her values. As she explained in the January 2001 issue of *YM* magazine, "I talk about how I am going to stay a virgin until I'm married, and then my fans would see this movie and be like, 'She's totally contradicting herself.'"

In 2001, Simpson released her sophomore effort entitled *Irresistible,* a more sophisticated record which showcased the singer's vocal ability as well as a solid group of songs contributed by notable outside writers. The June 16, 2001, edition of *Billboard* described *Irresistible* as "a great step forward for youth pop and sure footing for this glamorous talent." Undoubtedly her audience felt the same way. *Irresistible* landed in the *Billboard* top ten within a month of its release. Continued success is surely ahead for Simpson as a notable star in the pop world.

Selected discography

Singles

"I Wanna Love You Forever," Sony, 1999.
"Where Are You," Sony, 2000.
"I Think I'm in Love with You" (Australian import), Sony/Columbia, 2000.

Albums

Sweet Kisses, Sony, 1999.
(Contributor) *Songs from Dawson's Creek Vol. 1* (soundtrack), Sony, 1999.
(Contributor) *Songs from Dawson's Creek Vol. 2* (soundtrack), Sony, 2000.
(Contributor) *Here on Earth* (soundtrack), Sony, 2000.
Irresistible, Sony, 2001.

Sources

Periodicals

Billboard, December 4, 1999.
CosmoGirl, December 1999/January 2000; March 2001.
Dallas Texas Weekly, September 9, 1999.
Entertainment Weekly, September 24, 1999.
Fort Worth Star Telegram, August 22, 1999.
Jump, October 1999.
Lansing State Journal (Lansing, MI), April 15,1999.
McGregor Mirror and Crawford Sun, August 26,1999.
News Journal (Daytona Beach, FL), September 8, 1999.
Popstar!, September/October 1999.
*Post Star (*Glen Falls, NY), October 16, 1999.
Request, December 1999.
Rolling Stone, August 31, 2000.
16 Magazine, December 1999.
Teen, July 2000.
Teen People, October 2000.
Teen Vogue, Fall 2000.
TigerBeat, December 1999; June 2001.
TV Guide, May 13, 2000.
Twist, June 2000.
Wichita Eagle (Wichita, KS), May 30, 1999.
WWD, August 12, 1999.
YM, January 2001.

Online

Billboard, http://www.billboard.com (June 20, 2001).
"Jessica Simpson," http://www.jessica_simpson.org/about.html (June 2, 2001).
Jessica Simpson Official Website, http://www.jessicasimpson.com (June 2, 2001).
Ultimate Band List, http://www.ubl.com (June 1, 2001).

Additional information was provided by Columbia Records publicity materials, 2001.

—*Nicole Elyse*

Sisqó

Singer

AP/Wide World Photos. Reproduced by permission.

As the dynamic frontman to the multiplatinum-selling R&B group Dru Hill and as a solo artist, Sisqó has sold more than seven million albums. Dru Hill's first two albums, *Dru Hill* and *Enter the Dru*, produced the hit singles "Tell Me," "In My Bed," "How Deep Is Your Love," "These Are The Times," "Five Steps," and "We're Not Making Love." But Sisqó is best known for the summer 2000 party jam "Thong Song," a naughty ode to the scant women's undergarment. With "Thong Song," from his multiplatinum solo debut *Unleash the Dragon,* Sisqó's career took off in many different directions. He appeared in television commercials for Pepsi and McDonald's and on the big screen in the comedy film *Get Over It.* He signed a book deal and began work on a television sitcom pilot. He planned to launch a clothing collection called Dragon and reportedly signed a five-film deal with Miramax. The decision to broaden his horizons may have been sound for the outlandishly dressed, platinum-coiffed singer.

Sisqó was born Mark Andrews to Alonzo, an electrician, and Carolyn Andrews, a Social Security claims clerk. The only son and youngest of three, Sisqó grew up in a middle class Baltimore, Maryland, neighborhood with his parents, but spent summers at his grandmother's house in a tough, drug-ridden Baltimore ghetto where "thugs were respected," he told *TV Guide.* During summers with his grandmother, Sisqó learned the ways of the street and was jailed three times. Sitting in a jail cell at age 16, Sisqó said to himself, "I'm not a thug. I'm just tryin' to be a thug," he said in an interview with *TV Guide.* After being in jail, Sisqó decided to change his image and his life.

To make himself look less threatening, Sisqó bleached his hair blond. Though he has admitted to having experimented with drugs while growing up, he went the straight route. "The key is making everybody feel like they can invite you into their house," Sisqó said in an interview with *Rolling Stone.* "I don't think you gonna ever catch me in no trouble." Sisqó also became a father at age 17 and remained an involved parent, although he and his daughter's mother never married. "I provided for my child since day one," he told *People.* The child made a cameo appearance in the "Thong Song" video.

Started with Dru Hill

Nicknamed as a child for his wavy hair, which caused others to feel that he "looked Puerto Rican," according to *Jet*, Sisqó got his act together. He formed the R&B group Dru Hill in 1995 with high school friends James "Woody" Green, Larry "Jazz" Anthony Jr., and Tamir "Nokio" Ruffin. The group was named for their Baltimore neighborhood, Druid Hill Park. Alonzo Andrews was less than supportive of his son's musical aspirations, though he later became his son's biggest fan. He encouraged the teen to get a "real job," which Sisqó did, working brief stints at a pizza parlor, a movie

Born Mark Andrews c. 1976 in Baltimore, MD; son of Alonzo (an electrician) and Carolyn Andrews (a Social Security claims clerk); children: Shaione.

Formed Dru Hill with high school friends James "Woody" Green, Larry "Jazz" Anthony Jr., and Tamir "Nokio" Ruffin, 1995; signed with Island Records, released debut album, *Dru Hill,* 1996; released *Enter the Dru,* 1998; made solo debut with single "Thong Song" and album *Unleash the Dragon,* 2000; appeared on MTV show, *Sisqó's Shakedown,* and toured with 'N Sync, 2000; appeared in film *Get Over It,* 2001; released *Return of Dragon* on his own Dragon Records (a Def Soul imprint), 2001.

Awards: Two Radio Music Awards, six *Billboard* Awards, *Source* Award, World Music Award, 2000.

Addresses: *Record company*—Def Soul, 825 Eighth Ave., New York, NY 10019, website: http://www.defsoul.com. *Website*—Sisqó Official Website: http://www.sisqo.com.

theater, and a candy store called the Fudgery, where employees perform for customers. Sisqó gladly gave up his pursuit of a "real job" when his mother told him to follow his heart. Dru Hill performed at school fashion shows and improved enough to attract the attention of a manager at a talent show when Sisqó was still a high school junior. Things moved quickly. Dru Hill signed with Island Records and released its first record, *Dru Hill,* in 1996. The group went from teen talent shows to multiplatinum selling records in no time. Between *Dru Hill* and the group's second release, *Enter the Dru,* the group scored six hit singles. Though Dru Hill sold millions of records, the group consistently went home empty handed from awards ceremonies, which frustrated Sisqó.

In 1999, Dru Hill collaborated on the title song of the *Wild Wild West* soundtrack with rapper and actor Will Smith, who would become a huge influence on Sisqó. During shooting of the "Wild Wild West" video, Woody left Dru Hill to sing gospel music. Angry at first, Sisqó quickly realized that after four years together, each of the members needed to follow his own path in music. As a result, the members of Dru Hill decided to split, each to record his own solo record, though the four-

some had plans to reconvene later to record another Dru Hill album.

Decided Direction of Solo Work

Sisqó, with Smith's advice, made a decision about the direction of his solo work. The two agreed that anything Sisqó released would have to be classy. "No hardcore anything," they agreed, Sisqó told *TV Guide.* That agreement was okay, Sisqó said, until Smith heard "Thong Song," the first single from Sisqó's 1999 debut album, *Unleash the Dragon,* released on Sisqó's own Def Jam/Def Soul imprint, Dragon Records. The single, about barely there bikini bottoms and lingerie, and the video, which features women in thongs, hardly bore the touch of class the two had agreed Sisqó should have. What the risqué hit did have, though, was a sense of humor which both Smith and millions of male and female fans of all ages caught. "Thong Song" became a party anthem during the spring and summer of 2000 and *Unleash the Dragon* went on to sell more than five million copies.

Fans also caught on to Sisqó's dynamic personality, which he claimed to have gotten from his mother. Sisqó also said that his personality made up for other characteristics he may have been lacking. "My personality is so bright, it'll make up for anything I don't have, like height," the five-foot-five-inch singer said in an interview with *Jet.* Critics likened Sisqó to Stevie Wonder and Michael Jackson, the artist's childhood idol. *Entertainment Weekly* called *Unleash the Dragon* "oversung," "over-produced," and too dependent on "bump-and-grind" tempos, but *Los Angeles Times* critic Connie Johnson wrote that Sisqó's "youthful fervor" and "imagination" made the album interesting.

For his debut effort, Sisqó took home the awards he missed out on with Dru Hill. He earned two Radio Music Awards, six *Billboard* Awards, a *Source* Award, an MTV Video Music Award, and a World Music Award, and was nominated for four Grammy Awards and two American Music Awards. *Unleash the Dragon* also produced "Incomplete," a ballad that reached number one on both the pop and R&B sales charts. It is unknown whether Sisqó sought advice from Smith about his style; the "Thong Song" singer became known for his tattoos, body piercings, shiny silver, cropped hairstyle, and colorful fashions covered in rhinestones, as well as his signature dragon emblem.

Moved from Music to Television

The unexpected popularity of "Thong Song" led to Sisqó's emergence as "one of pop music's hottest new voices," according to *TV Guide.* The "Thong Song" video became a top-requested video on *Total Request Live,* a viewer-voted video countdown on MTV. Sisqó's appeal to MTV fans was so overwhelming, the cable network gave the singer his own dance competition show, *Sisqó's Shakedown,* which was the highest-rated show on MTV during the summer and fall of 2000.

Despite Sisqó's success being linked to overt sexuality in his music, he hoped to move away from that connection on his second album, *Return of Dragon.* He realized that he was unlikely to outdo the success of "Thong Song," he told *Teen People,* and he did not want to try. Instead, he wanted to attract attention with "songs of substance and mass appeal." He did a lot to attract attention at first, he admitted, with the outlandish hair and clothes, but he wanted people to look at *Return of Dragon* and "focus solely on my talent." Some critics found that difficult. *Rolling Stone* critic Barry Walters wrote *Return of Dragon* offered "more of the crass sex and playa games" found on *Unleash,* and called it a "messy album … melodically underdeveloped, vocally undercooked, and lyrically just plain lazy." *People* critic Ericka Souter was kinder: "Sisqó is still kicking, as he artfully fuses and R&B style with up-tempo rap rhythms," though she admitted the album's first single, "Off the Corner," could not "quite muster that 'Thong Song' magic." *Los Angeles Times* critic Marc Weingarten went a step further: "there's nothing even remotely as good as 'Thong Song' here," he wrote.

Return of Dragon was not all Sisqó was working on in 2001. Major record labels had signed his two protegee groups, Lovher and the Associates. His clothing line, Dragon, was set to launch soon after. "I want my name to go down in history as one of the talents," he told *People.* "I want to be a big hero."

Selected discography

Solo

Unleash the Dragon, Def Jam, 1999.
(Contributor) *Nutty Professor II: The Klumps* (soundtrack), Polygram, 2000.
Return of Dragon, Dragon, 2001.

With Dru Hill

Dru Hill, Island, 1996.
Enter the Dru, Island Black Music, 1998.
(Contributor) *Rush Hour* (soundtrack), Def Jam, 1998.
(Contributor) *Wild Wild West* (soundtrack), Interscope, 1999.

Sources

Periodicals

Billboard, October 9, 1999, p. 34; November 27, 1999, p. 26.
Entertainment Weekly, January 14, 2000, p. 78; March 2, 2001, p. 69.
Jet, August 7, 2000, p. 60.
Los Angeles Times, January 30, 2000, p. 1; June 17, 2001, p. 1.
Newsweek, May 1, 2000, p. 64.
People, April 27, 1998, p. 41; June 12, 2000, p. 147; December 25, 2000/January 1, 2001, p. 136; June 25, 2001, p. 44.
Teen People, May 2001, p. 89.
TV Guide, August 26-September 1, 2000, p. 40.
Rolling Stone, March 30, 2000, p. 28; July 5, 2001, p. 145.
USA Today, August 10, 2000; June 15, 2001, p. E11.

Online

All Music Guide, http://www.allmusic.com (May 31, 2001).

Additional information was provided by Island/Def Jam publicity materials, 2001.

—*Brenna Sanchez*

Sister Hazel

Rock group

In the summer of 1997, Sister Hazel's song "All for You" ruled the adult top 40 airwaves and topped the *Billboard* charts. These were major accomplishments given that the track was the first single released from the band's major-label debut, *Somewhere More Familiar*. Even more impressive was the fact that the song had at first been ignored by the modern and progressive rock stations that were the band's primary audience. Instead, much to its record company's surprise, Sister Hazel was embraced by a more mainstream audience, one that gave the group its first hit song and eventually a platinum-selling album. The crossover success was no surprise to the band's lead singer and co-founder Ken Block, however. As he told *Billboard* in September of 1997, "There really is something for everybody…. But the element that really defines us is that there are a lot of hooks that allow people to take a closer look; they see that there's something cerebral in there. It bridges the gap between the poets and the partyers."

Most of the members of Sister Hazel grew up in musical surroundings. Block's father, who had earned a college degree in music, played piano and wrote music. The Block family always had musicians around their Gainesville, Florida, home. This was especially true of weekend gatherings, as Ken Block recalled on the band's website: "We always had these parties in Gainesville or in our place at St. Augustine Beach where people would bring all kinds of instruments to play, strum, beat on, pluck or blow and everyone sang—or at least tried to sing…. I learned a lot about harmonies, different styles of music and wildly enter-

taining storytelling." Block also played music outside the family circle, including some coffeeshop appearances with his acoustic guitar when he was 12 years old. In high school Block joined his first band, which played heavy metal music. He later performed with a succession of similar rock bands in the Gainesville area.

By 1994, however, Block returned to a more acoustic orientation that better reflected the spirit of his self-penned songs. Looking for musicians with a similar, eclectic outlook, Block began writing songs and performing around Gainesville with guitarist Andrew Copeland, where they soon attracted the attention of architecture student and part-time bass player Jeff Beres. Ryan Newell, originally from Fairfax, Virginia, joined the lineup as a guitarist after performing with another Gainesville band called Waterdog. Newell had been playing the guitar since the age of eight, and after winning a grade school talent contest, decided that performing music was his goal. Newell nevertheless took a more practical route by studying at the University of Florida in Gainesville, where he majored in accounting.

Borrowed Name from Missionary Group

As for the band's unusual name, Block drew on a childhood memory of the operator of the Sister Hazel Rescue Mission, a Gainesville organization dedicated to missionary and outreach work in the area. Because Sister Hazel's philanthropic spirit was embodied in some of Block and Copeland's first songs, the name seemed a fitting one for the group. As Block commented in a September 1997 *Billboard* interview, "One of our basic philosophies is that we want people to think, feel, be moved, and at the end of the day or at the end of the show, we like them to leave feeling a little better than they did when they came in." In later years, after the group became successful, Sister Hazel herself met with the band and gave her blessing to carry on using the name.

Within a year of forming, the band released a self-titled album on the independent label Soul Trax, after which the band added drummer Mark Trojanowski to its permanent roster. Trojanowski had studied music at North Texas State University and later performed with the Guy Lombardo Orchestra before moving to Orlando and playing with several jazz and pop groups. After hearing the *Sister Hazel* album and learning that the band needed a drummer, he auditioned and was asked to join the band in July of 1995. Considering Sister Hazel's hectic touring schedule—limited only by the fact that Newell was still a student, completing his degree in 1996—Trojanowski's arrival was a crucial one to the band's success.

Part of a growing Southeastern music scene centered around college campuses, Sister Hazel joined bands

For the Record . . .

Members include **Jeff Beres** (born on February 23, 1971), bass guitar; **Ken Block** (born on November 23, 1966), acoustic guitar, lead vocals; **Andrew Copeland** (born on March 21, 1968), acoustic guitar; **Ryan Newell** (born on December 8, 1972), rhythm and slide guitar; **Mark Trojanowski** (born on January 26, 1970), drums.

Formed group in Gainesville, FL, 1993; released debut album, *Sister Hazel,* on independent label, 1994; released second album and major-label debut, *Somewhere More Familiar,* 1997; released *Fortress,* 2000.

Addresses: *Record company*—Universal Records, 1755 Broadway, 8th Floor, New York, NY 10019, website: http://www.universalrecords.com. *Website*—Sister Hazel Official Website: http://www.sisterhazel.com.

such as Hootie and the Blowfish and Matchbox 20 with a reputation for energetic live performances. Following Newell's graduation, the band hit the road in earnest, playing about 200 concert dates that year alone, mostly throughout the Southeastern United States. As Newell recalled in an April 2001 interview with the band's hometown newspaper, the *Gainesville Sun,* "Back in the early stages, we had to entertain a bunch of drunks. We were doing the bar circuit." Looking on the bright side, however, Newell added, "Sometimes a crowd of frat guys aren't going to purely get off on the music, so we had to really learn how to talk to an audience. Those things, we definitely look at as positive."

Breakthrough Track "All for You"

As on its first album, Sister Hazel's second release retained some of the rough edges that came from its days as a bar band. Recorded and mixed in about two weeks, *Somewhere More Familiar* featured a mix of blues, bluegrass, folk, and rock, a combination that some compared to the Southern rock of Lynyrd Skynyrd and the Black Crowes. Given the band's loyal following in the Southeast, *Somewhere More Familiar* sold well after its initial release around Gainesville in September of 1996. The release also garnered positive reviews. *Q* magazine noted that "Sister Hazel write excellent songs and play them with a controlled verve and panache," comparing the band to the Eagles, Doobie Brothers, and Jackson Browne. After signing a

contract with Universal Records later that year, the band seemed poised for even greater success.

Although the record company ordered a remix of the album to give it some professional polish, the January 1997 Universal-released *Somewhere More Familiar* was essentially the same album the band had released months earlier. Leading its promotional efforts was the single "All for You," a mid-tempo, acoustic-flavored love song with rich vocal harmonies reminiscent of the band Blues Traveler. Unfortunately, Universal's marketing of the band missed the target, at least at first. When the single was shipped to modern rock stations in January, it failed to make it on most play lists. The song got a much warmer reception at adult contemporary and top 40 stations, however, and it built momentum throughout the summer until it reached the number one spot on the *Billboard* Adult Top 40 chart. For 1997, "All for You" ranked sixth on the year-end Adult Top 40 chart and number 36 on the final tally of the magazine's Hot 100 Singles chart. Powered by the hit single, *Somewhere More Familiar* placed among the top 200 best-selling albums of the year.

Delayed Follow-Up

In the wake of its hit album, Sister Hazel continued to tour relentlessly and contributed its efforts to a number of charitable causes, including the American Cancer Society and Children's Miracle Network. Considering the hundreds of concerts they performed, perhaps the band's members were stretched a bit too thin; going into the recording studio to record its third album, the band's initial sessions left its members feeling that they had failed to produce a worthy follow-up to *Somewhere More Familiar.* Retreating to write some more songs, the band regrouped for another recording session that finally resulted in *Fortress,* released in 2000. The album was similar in spirit to *Somewhere More Familiar.* "It's a formula done right...," a *Rolling Stone* reviewer commented. "It thoroughly recaptures its predecessor's wailing guitar jams, vocalist Ken Block's Southern-grunge affectations and his narratives lionizing wayward women and their hard-living men." *Fortress* even featured a leadoff hit single similar to "All for You," the rollicking "Change Your Mind," which gained extensive airplay on adult top 40 radio stations. Its other tracks ranged from the Southern rock track "Surreal" to the anthemic ballad "Your Winter," featured in the teen-oriented movie *10 Things I Hate About You.*

Sister Hazel also continued to live up to its reputation as crowd-pleasing concert performers with more tour dates in support of *Fortress.* "We're always on the same page, and that's something you can't really practice," Newell said in a 2001 interview in *Guitar Player.* "I guess it's one of those things you grow into, gig after gig, year after year."

Selected discography

Sister Hazel, Soul Trax, 1994.
Somewhere More Familiar, Universal, 1997.
(Contributor) *Legacy: A Tribute to Fleetwood Mac's* Rumours,
   WEA/Atlantic/Lava, 1998.
(Contributor) *10 Things I Hate About You* (soundtrack),
   Hollywood, 1999.
Fortress, Universal, 2000.

Sources

Periodicals

Billboard, July 12, 1997, p. 13; September 9, 1997, p. 76;
   December 27, 1997-January 3, 1998, pp. YE-28, YE-82.
Gainesville Sun (Gainesville, FL), April 18, 2001.
Guitar Player, March 2001, p. 69.
Q, May 1998.

Online

RollingStone.com, http://www.rollingstone.com (June 18,
   2001).
Sister Hazel Official Website, http://www.sisterhazel.com
   (June 18, 2001).

—Timothy Borden

Solas

Celtic folk group

After playing only a few live shows, it seemed likely to fans that Solas would surpass the popularity of other contemporary Irish folk groups. The extensive background of the players, with stints in Cherish the Ladies and the Sharon Shannon Band, guaranteed that the group's first efforts would be memorable. "Each member is a virtuoso in his own right," wrote Seth Rogovoy of the *Berkshire Eagle.* "Together, Solas is to Irish music what some of Miles Davis's groups were to jazz in the 1960s and '70s." Their approach explores traditional music while also adding innovative instruments and vocal combinations. Whether performing a ballad or an Irish jig, the group delivered a synthesis of old and new, creating a hybrid all their own. After five albums, several tours, and a number of lineup changes, the group continues to impress critics and fans. "Solas has established itself as one of the top Irish-folk groups on either side of the Atlantic," noted Geoffrey Himes in *MusicHound Folk.*

The success of Solas lay in the experienced backgrounds of the individual players. Seamus Egan was born in the United States but moved with his family to Ireland when he was only three years old. He became proficient on the tin whistle, guitar, flute, and banjo, and by the time he was 16 years old, he had won the All-Ireland Junior Championship on flute, tin whistle, banjo, and mandolin, and recorded his solo debut, *Traditional Music of Ireland,* for Shanachie Records. He met guitarist and vocalist John Doyle during a stint with the Chanting House. Born in Dublin, Ireland, Doyle had composed music for the Irish film *Uncle Robert's*

Footsteps and was also in demand as a session player. Fiddler Winifred Horan, a native of New York, had studied at Boston's New England Conservatory and recorded with Cherish the Ladies. In 1996, both she and Doyle became intricately involved in Egan's third solo album, *When Juniper Sleeps.*

A band slowly began to take shape. A native of the United States, John Williams was active on the lively Chicago Celtic music scene. He became the first American to win the All-Ireland senior concertina championship and recorded his self-titled debut on Green Linnet Records in 1995. His concertina and button accordion skills proved a perfect fit for the other three players. Still, no one had planned to form a group. The last piece of this Celtic puzzle was Karan Casey. Casey, born in Waterford, Ireland, had studied at the Royal Irish Academy of Music in the 1980s and later at Brooklyn's Long Island University. After a brief stint in Atlantic Bridge, she was asked by Egan and Horan to play a show with the others. "I don't think we had any particular expectations when we first got together," Egan told the International Music Network (IMN) online. "We just enjoyed playing with one another, and we were frankly surprised by the reactions to our first gigs."

The band played their first show at Georgetown University in Washington, D.C., and their second at the annual Smithsonian Festival of American Folklife. The group had no plans to tour or to record, but their early shows in Manhattan's Irish bars created a buzz. Soon, the band had a record deal with Shanachie and began to appear on programs like National Public Radio's (NPR) *Morning Edition* and on *Prairie Home Companion.* Recorded in 1996, their self-titled debut was produced under Johnny Cunningham of the folk group Silly Wizard. The album included both jigs and songs and garnered good reviews. "Solas … recently put out their debut album, which marries traditional sensibilities with a decidedly youthful touch," wrote Steve Winick of *Dirty Linen.* On 1997's *Sunny Spells and Scattered Showers,* they were joined by guest percussionist John Anthony, expanding their sound while remaining firmly planted in Celtic music.

In 1997 accordion and concertina player Mick McAuley replaced Williams. The band continued a busy touring schedule and appeared on NBC's *Weekend Today* and Ireland's *The Late, Late Show.* Solas recorded their third release, *The Words that Remain,* in 1998. Like the previous albums, it included a number of Irish folk tunes. The band, however, had also begun to experiment. They recorded versions of Woody Guthrie's "Pastures of Plenty" and Peggy Seeger's "Song of Choice." Guest performances by banjoist Béla Fleck and singer Iris DeMent added new textures while giving the album more of an American tilt. "We didn't have any inkling that there was this level of an American connection to it," explained Egan to IMN, "at least not consciously. We choose material not because of its origins but because of its appeal to us musically." The band also released *Live* the same year, a 90-minute performance that captures the excitement of Solas' live shows.

Casey left the band to record her second solo album, *The Winds Begin to Sing*, in 1999 and was replaced by Deirdre Scanlan. A native of Nenagh, Tipperary, Ireland, Scanlan had gained attention from her 1999 solo release, *Speak Softly.* When she joined the band for *The Hour Before Dawn* in 2000, Solas found themselves exploring new musical territory. The cover photograph, featuring a woman sitting in the sand against the backdrop of a peaceful sunrise, is as evocative as the album's music. "As the title suggests," noted Evan Cater of *All Music Guide*, "*The Hour Before Dawn* is a mellower album than any of Solas' three previous efforts." The album also includes a version of the Sarah McLachlan hit, "I Will Remember You," a song co-written by Egan. The band supported the album by completing a tour of the Untied States in 2000-01.

The year 2000 continued to bring changes for Solas. A key founding member of the band, John Doyle, left three months after the recording of *The Hour Before Dawn* and was replaced by guitarist Dónal Clancy, son of Liam Clancy of the Clancy Brothers. "Group situations are always a delicate balancing act between egos and what's good for the group," Egan told Rogovoy. "One of the things that helps us is that we all do have other outlets for what we're doing creatively."

The group has shown a willingness to experiment while still maintaining its roots in traditional Irish music. The band's instrumental dexterity plus its mixture of male and female vocalists have given the group a broad range and flexibility. Solas has carved out a special niche on the Irish/American scene, invigorating traditional music with fresh ideas and pioneering new directions for Celtic music. "As long as there are groups such as Solas," wrote Don Heckman in the *Los Angeles Times,* "Celtic music will continue to draw new, young audiences."

Selected discography

Solas, Shanachie, 1996.
Sunny Spells and Scattered Showers, Shanachie, 1997.
The Words that Remain, Shanachie, 1998.
Live, Shanachie, 1998.
The Hour Before Dawn, Shanachie, 2000.

Sources

Books

Walters, Neal, and Brian Mansfield, editors, *MusicHound Folk: The Essential Album Guide,* Visible Ink Press, 1998.

Periodicals

Berkshire Eagle, March 7, 1997.
Los Angeles Times, March 17, 2001, p. 8.

Online

"Hour Before Dawn," *All Music Guide*, http://www.allmusic.com (June 6, 2001).
"Solas," *Dirty Linen*, http://dirtylinen.com (June 29, 2001).
"Solas," IMN, http://www.imnworld.com/solas.html (June 6, 2001).

—*Ronnie D. Lankford, Jr.*

The Spongetones

Rock group

In 2000, almost 40 years after the beginning of the British Invasion and the first wave of Beatlemania, power pop rockers the Spongetones released *Odd Fellows*. The album, influenced by the Dave Clark Five, the Hollies, and the early Beatles, came after a five-year hiatus for the group. *Odd Fellows* was the sixth full-length release for the band, and even after 20 years of performing and recording, the Spongetones have remained faithful to the cheerful, innocent sounds of British pop of the past.

Based in Charlotte, North Carolina, the Spongetones grew out of a Beatles cover act that performed at a local bar in the early 1980s. The Spongetones are Jamie Hoover, lead vocalist and guitarist; Steve Stoeckel, vocalist and bassist; Rob Thorne, drummer; and Pat Walters, vocalist and guitarist. Walters left the band in the mid 1980s but had returned by 1991. Although the band started out by covering older songs, the musicians quickly adopted the sound as their own and incorporated it into their original material. Throughout their career, the Spongetones have not only been known for their pop recordings, but also for their high-energy stage shows.

The fledgling group signed with Ripete Records in 1982 and quickly released its debut album, *Beat Music.* The Spongetones' sound is often called Merseybeat, a term used to describe music from the early British Invasion. The term borrows the name of the Mersey River that runs through Liverpool, England. It is the sound of bands like Gerry and the Pacemakers and the Searchers, as well as the Beatles between 1963-64.

The Spongetones temper the melody-driven sound—exemplified by the Beatles' song "Love Me Do"—with influences like the Who and even late 1980s psychedelic bands like XTC.

Even as their music draws comparisons to other bands and clearly evokes a certain style of pop, the Spongetones manage to keep their material fresh and original. Although Chris Woodstra of *All Music Guide* called their efforts "derivative," he also noted that the songs were ultimately "enjoyable." In another review, Woodstra called the Spongetones' albums "effortlessly catchy." Parke Puterbaugh, writing in *Rolling Stone,* went even further in asserting the originality of the music. He noted that *Beat Music* was not "the rote, dogmatic obeisance of mere revivalism," but rather was "aglow with a forward-thrusting musical abandon." Kevin Matthews of Pop Matters online also commented on the push and pull of a band devoted to a certain revivalist sound also struggling to produce original, innovative material of their own. He wrote that the Spongetones have "an uncanny ability to evoke the sound and style of their major musical influence (the Beatles circa 1964), not as a cynical act of self-promotion but a sincere labor of love." The band is able to pull off this tightrope walk "without embarrassment and without artifice," according to Matthews.

After modest success with *Beat Music,* the Spongetones released a six-song EP for Ripete called *Torn Apart.* The 1984 effort was the first time the band worked with producer Don Dixon, who was known for his ability to bring out a raw, crunchy sound from the music. Other guests on the album were producer Mitch Easter and the band R.E.M., who assisted with hand claps on the track "Shock Therapy." The release received some favorable critical attention; Kurt Loder wrote in *Rolling Stone* that the EP offered "proof that [the group] can really write," and noted that the "well crafted" songs "deserve to be heard here and now," not just taken as throwbacks to an earlier era.

In 1987, the Spongetones formed their own independent label called Triapore Records. As a sort of experiment, the band worked again with producer Dixon and recorded what stands out as the album most unlike their other releases. The Black Vinyl Records biography calls *Where-Ever Land* "[h]ighly experimental and inventive," both harder rocking and more psychedelic than earlier releases. Rick Gregory wrote for Audities online that he found *Where-Ever Land* "overblown," but Joe Brown of the *Washington Post* praised the release overall. He wrote that the album's "crisp, immediate presence … promises good things." Brown did have some criticism for the Spongetones, however. He noted that they needed work on "their occasionally haphazard lyrics."

The band seems to have heeded this advice as their next release was praised by critics for its strong songwriting. After signing with Black Vinyl Records, the Spongetones released *Oh Yeah!* in 1991. The album marks a return to the Beatles' Merseybeat sound with good effect. Woodstra called the album "infectious," and Gregory praised its "playful sense of fun." Black Vinyl released two other albums for the Spongetones, 1994's *Beat & Torn,* which was a re-release of both *Beat Music* and *Torn Apart*, and the 1995 recording *Textual Drone Thing.* The latter represented a break with the pure power pop of *Oh Yeah!* and *Beat Music,* and Gregory commented that it was "more rootsy." Woodstra wrote in *All Music Guide* that *Textual Drone Thing* was also more "subtle" than the Spongetones' other albums.

After five years of silence following *Textual Drone Thing,* the Spongetones signed with a new label, Gadfly Records. Gadfly released *Odd Fellows* in 2000. A continuation of the band's devotion to the early Beatles' sound, the album includes "On the Wings of a Nightingale," written by Paul McCartney. Both the song and the album received positive critical attention. Rick Anderson applauded the effort in *All Music Guide,* praising both the "juicy-fruit chord progressions" and the hard-rocking edge of the album: "The Spongetones deliver their pop confections with the weight and momentum of a Detroit muscle car." Illustrating that the Merseybeat genre still has valuable pop material to be mined by talented musicians, the Spongetones continue to deliver, as Claudio Sossi noted at the Power Pop website, "sound, solid, and exhilarating music."

Selected discography

Beat Music, Ripete, 1982.
Torn Apart (EP), Ripete, 1984.
Where-Ever Land, Triapore, 1987.
Oh Yeah!, Black Vinyl, 1991.
Beat & Torn (includes material from *Beat Music* and *Torn Apart*), Black Vinyl, 1994.
Textural Drone Thing, Black Vinyl, 1995.
Odd Fellows, Gadfly, 2000.

Sources

Periodicals

Billboard, March 24, 2001, p. 55.
Rolling Stone, September 15, 1983, p. 61; May 10, 1984, p. 56.
Washington Post, April 22, 1988, p. N23.

Online

"The Spongetones," *All Music Guide,* http://www.allmusic.com (July 10, 2001).
"The Spongetones," Audities, http://www.audities.com (July 10, 2001).
"The Spongetones," Black Vinyl, http://www.blackvinyl.com (July 10, 2001).
"The Spongetones," Gadfly Records, http://www.gadflyrecords.com (July 10, 2001).
"The Spongetones," Listen.com, http://www.listen.com (July 10, 2001).
"The Spongetones," Pop Matters, http://www.popmatters.com (July 10, 2001).
"The Spongetones," Power Pop, http://www.powerpop.org (July 10, 2001).

—Christine Kelley

Spoon

Rock group

Considering all the setbacks experienced by Spoon, it seems surprising that the independent rock band out of Austin, Texas, endured long enough to see the release of their third and most self-assured album to date, 2001's *Girls Can Tell.* Plagued by an unstable lineup since forming in the early 1990s, the group also fell victim to record label executives who failed to follow through on promises, a record-buying public that appeared uninterested in, or perhaps unaware of, the group's music, and the initial media stigma of sounding much like two of their primary influences—the Pixies and Wire.

While Spoon's previous albums in general fared well among the critics, *Girls Can Tell* finally established the group as forward-looking purveyors of post-punk music. Some stylistic elements of the Pixies remained, but Spoon also derived equal inspiration from Elvis Costello, Joe Jackson, and the classic sounds of the Beatles and Led Zeppelin. Moreover, the group succeeded in giving the familiar a fresh, modern feel. Spoon frontman and principal songwriter Britt Daniel—who believes that a great guitar riff does not always need to be complicated—opted for simpler lines and experimented with instruments other than guitar. "I'll often write a riff on guitar, but after I've demoed the song, I'll realize the guitar isn't the right instrument for the part," Daniel, who, in addition to guitar, performed on xylophone, harpsichord, and thumb piano for *Girls Can Tell,* explained to *Guitar Player* contributor Judah Gold. "A song can really take off in different directions when you switch instruments and perform guitar parts

on something else. In some cases, the song will actually work better without the guitar."

Daniel likewise wanted to take more chances in developing lyrics—now more thoughtful, sincere, and mature—for Spoon's music. "I just started listening to records and started thinking, 'You know what? I'm never honest with anything in my lyrics,'" he recalled to Michael Bertin for an interview in the *Austin Chronicle.* "And I love all of these records where people speak very directly, like Bruce Springsteen, or Jonathan Richman, or Ray Davies.... They show they care and have emotions. When I started realizing that, I decided that we should go for that more—songs like 'Fitted Shirt,' 'Anything You Want.' There are still some vague ones on this album, but there are some where you know what I'm talking about."

However, Daniel was not always so confident about his band's abilities and the future of Spoon as several bad breaks resulted in a mistrust of the music industry. Born in the coastal town of Galveston, Texas, Daniel spent his formative years in Temple, located about an hour's drive north of Austin. Despite living in a community where most youngsters listened to either heavy metal or country, Daniel, thanks to the MTV program *120 Minutes,* discovered the Pixies, Julian Cope, and That Petrol Emotion as a teenager. Throughout his childhood, Daniel received doses of classic rock 'n' roll on a daily basis. Daniel's father, a neurologist, loved the Beatles and the Rolling Stones and even collected guitars, though he never really became a practitioner of the instrument himself. But Daniel decided to pick up the instrument in his late teens, reportedly teaching himself to play after his first girlfriend broke up with him when she went away to college.

Spoon Took Form

After graduating from high school, Daniel arrived in Austin in 1989 to attend the University of Texas. He started his first band there in 1990 dubbed Skellington, which rose to local recognition and recorded a handful of cassettes before dissolving in 1992. Daniel earned a radio/television/film degree from the university while learning more about bands such as Wire and the Velvet Underground through working as a disc jockey at the student-run radio station KVRX. Meanwhile, a mutual friend from the station introduced Daniel to a skilled drummer named Jim Eno, a Rhode Island native from North Carolina who had moved from Houston to Austin in 1992 to design microchips for Cadence Designs Systems. With Eno, Daniel played briefly in a country/roots trio called Alien Beats, and later, when Daniel began to write songs, the guitarist reunited musically with Eno for a second time.

Taking a more rock-oriented approach, the pair next enlisted guitarist Greg Wilson and a female bass

For the Record . . .

Members include **Britt Daniel** (born in Galveston, TX; son of a neurologist; *Education*: Degree in radio/television film, University of Texas), vocals, guitar; **Jim Eno** (born in Rhode Island), drums; **Andy McGuire** (left group, 1996), bass guitar; **Greg Wilson** (left group, 1996), guitar. Touring members include **Eric Friend** (joined group, 2001), keyboards; **Roman Kuebler** (joined group, 2001), bass guitar.

Formed group in Austin, TX, 1993; released the *Nefarious* EP, 1994; signed with Matador Records, 1995; released debut album *Telephono*, 1996; released *Soft Effects* EP on Matador, signed with Elektra Records, 1997; released *A Series of Sneaks,* dropped by Elektra, 1998; signed with Merge Records, released *Girls Can Tell,* 2001.

Addresses: *Record company*—Merge Records, P.O. Box 1235, Chapel Hill, NC 27514, phone: (919) 929-0711, fax: (919) 929-4291, website: http://www.mergerecords.com. *Business*—Spoon, P.O. Box 684651, Austin, TX 78768, e-mail: detektor@ hotmail-.com. *Website*—Spoon Official Website: http://www.spoontheband.com.

guitarist named Andy McGuire, then hurriedly adopted the Spoon moniker, the title of a song by the German band Can, to participate in a 1993 competition sponsored by KVRX. Unfortunately, Spoon lost the "battle of the bands" to a group called Mr. Happy and afterwards did not receive an invitation to perform at the 1994 South By Southwest conference. Thus, in protest, the trio staged a show at a nearby punk club, the Pink Flamingo, where Matador Records co-owner Gerard Cosloy happened to be in attendance. Thereafter, word of Spoon, who had recently released their *Nefarious* EP on Fluffer Records, spread to other labels interested in the rising commercial appeal of alternative rock. Spoon received offers from Geffen, Interscope, and Warner Bros., but ultimately signed a deal in 1995 to record their first full-length set for Matador.

The punkish, driving *Telephono,* preceded by the seven-inch single "All the Negatives Have Been Destroyed," hit stores in 1996, but already the band's future appeared uncertain. Long before the release of *Telephono,* Wilson exited the group, then McGuire, viewing Spoon's music as not heavy enough, either left or was fired from the band. Next came a legal battle, in which McGuire's legal representatives claimed the bassist was entitled to a third of Spoon's advance from Matador, as well as album royalties. In the end, McGuire won her case based on an original agreement with her bandmates.

Surprisingly, Spoon's personnel problems failed to disrupt the pursuits of Daniel and Eno. For a time, Austin-based musician and *Telephono* producer John Croslin filled in as bassist and toured with the band extensively in support of the album. Eventually, Josh Zorbo took over the slot. Still, the album sold a mere 3,000 copies despite shows with established label-mates Pavement and Guided By Voices and a swell of local enthusiasm. Though the music press generally awarded the band favorable reviews, many critics pegged Spoon as a clone of the Pixies. "I thought we were hot sh*t," Daniel told *Magnet* magazine's Matthew Fritch. "Playing shows in Austin, it was fun and people liked us…. Then *Telephono* came out and we started touring, and absolutely no one would come see us. All these people had told us that, to some degree, we were going to be successful. And we weren't. In fact, I felt like people really didn't like us, and I wasn't sure what we were doing was good. I wasn't sure whether I liked the record, either."

Signed Deal with Elektra

In the late summer of 1996, Spoon's period of bad luck seemed to end when they met Ron Laffitte, the general manager at the West Coast offices of Elektra Records. Now an A&R person with Capitol Records, Laffitte genuinely enjoyed Spoon's music and believed that Elektra, whose roster then included Ween, Luna, and Stereolab, among others, would provide the perfect environment for a band such as Spoon. Throughout much of 1997, the same year which yielded Spoon's *Soft Effects* EP on Matador, the band worked on a second album, again with Coslin, entitled *A Series of Sneaks.* Upon its completion, enthusiastic Elektra executives signed Spoon to a new record deal.

Recorded in several studios in Austin and released in 1998, *A Series of Sneaks,* a departure from the tense *Telephono,* contained elements of British post-punk and minimalist rock. At the time, Daniel later noted, he was listening to and learning from records by Wire, Gang of Four, and Public Image Ltd. This time around, Spoon garnered high praises from reviewers. *Magnet* named *A Series of Sneaks* one of the best albums of the 1990s, while Raoul Hernandez in the *Austin Chronicle* judged it as "unquestionably one of the most dangerous weapons in Austin's musical arsenal last year, if not *the* most lethal."

Resilient Despite Challenges

Unfortunately, the album went largely ignored by radio and record buyers. Just four months after the release of *A Series of Sneaks,* Laffitte, their greatest ally at Elektra, was fired from the label. Soon thereafter, Elektra decided to drop Spoon, despite the fact that the company's president, Sylvia Rhone, had reassured the group that support for promotions and touring would continue. (Incidentally, later in 1999, Spoon released a single on the Saddle Creek label called "The Agony of Laffitte," featuring the B-side song "Laffitte Don't Fail Me Now.") Thus, by roughly August of 1998, Spoon found themselves again left on their own and embarked on a tour with Creeper Lagoon. Without the proper backing, though, practically no one showed up to see Spoon perform. Nonetheless, the group returned to Austin to commence work on a new set of songs, and by March of 2000, the basic tracks for the album *Girls Can Tell* were already in order.

Spoon then shopped the album around to various labels before Merge Records, based in Chapel Hill, North Carolina, and run by Superchunk's Mac McCaughan, made the group an offer. "This record is the first one I really like enough to say, 'Okay, we did something that, if we're no longer a band next year, I'm always going to be, 'I really like this one. I think it's really good,'" Daniel said to Bertin about *Girls Can Tell,* which saw release in February of 2001. "It's something that, at least for me, will stand the test of time." Critics likewise agreed and considered *Girls Can Tell* Spoon's greatest achievement to date. As *Texas Monthly* contributor Jason Cohen, speaking of the band's ups and downs and musical growth, concluded, "What doesn't kill Spoon makes it stronger."

Selected discography

Nefarious (EP), Fluffer, 1994.
Telephono, Matador, 1996.
Soft Effects (EP), Matador, 1997.
A Series of Sneaks, Elektra, 1998.
Girls Can Tell, Merge, 2001.

Sources

Periodicals

Austin Chronicle, March 16, 2001.
Billboard, February 10, 2001.
Boston Globe, April 12, 2001.
Guitar Player, August 2001.
Magnet, June/July 2001.
Texas Monthly, February 2001.
Village Voice, January 19-25, 2000; May 15, 2001.

Online

Matador Records, http://www.matador.recs.com (August 26, 2001).
Merge Records, http://www.mergerecords.com (August 26, 2001).
Spoon Official Website, http://www.spoontheband.com (August 26, 2001).

—Laura Hightower

Spyro Gyra

Jazz group

Hailing from Buffalo, New York, Spyro Gyra brought its own instrumental jazz hybrid to the forefront, combining jazz, R&B, Latin, and Brazilian music. Over the years, many critics and radio stations would try to classify their style and fit them into a category, none of which met the group's satisfaction. Their trademark hit "Morning Dance" was released in 1979. By 2001, Spyro Gyra had released 23 albums in 25 years with no signs of slowing down.

The group's formation started in 1974 when bandleader and saxophone player Jay Beckenstein and keyboardist Jeremy Wall began jamming together. Beckenstein and Wall had first met in high school and discovered a common interest in music. They reconnected after college when they were both playing in clubs around Buffalo with other blues and R&B bands. Their instrumental sessions evolved over the next year, eventually including guitarist Chet Catallo, bassist David Wolford, drummer Eli Konikoff, and percussionist Gerardo Velez. Another keyboardist named Tom Schuman joined the band later and played along with Wall.

The evolving group performed every week at a club named Jack Daniel's in Buffalo. Since they didn't have a name yet, the club's marquee simply said, "Tuesday Night—Jazz Jam." One night, the club's owner asked Beckenstein if they had decided on a name yet. Jokingly, Beckenstein said the name was "spirogyra," a type of algae that he had remembered from biology class (also known as "pond scum"). The club owner took him seriously, and the next week, the name was on the sign, incorrectly spelled as "Spyro Gyra."

In 1976, Beckenstein and a local drummer named Richard Calandra decided to form their own production company. They would use the proceeds from the company to help fund Spyro Gyra's recordings. When they had enough money, Beckenstein decided to capitalize on the fan base that they had built in their live performances by pressing 500 records himself. He sold all of them out of the trunk of his car. "When I listen to that recording, I hear seeds of the music that made us popular," Beckenstein told Jonathan Widran in *Down Beat*. "It was pretty innovative at the time, I guess, a strange but accessible blend of jazz, R&B, and even Caribbean music. It's funny how people didn't know what to make of it then, and now it's so ubiquitous."

As Spyro Gyra's popularity continued to build in the Buffalo area, they met Lenny Silver, who owned a local record store chain and the Amherst record label. Silver offered the group a distribution deal, and their first album, *Spyro Gyra,* sold 70,000 copies. After the release, Silver transferred his deal with the band to MCA Records. Before they recorded their first major label release, Wall decided to leave the band. Although he took on the role of assistant producer for Spyro Gyra and wrote songs for nearly all of their albums, his departure became the first of what would become a revolving door of Spyro Gyra members. With Wall out of the group, Tom Schuman took over as the sole keyboardist.

Spyro Gyra released their first album with MCA, *Morning Dance*, in 1979. The single "Morning Dance" rocketed to the number one spot on *Billboard*'s Adult Contemporary charts. The album ended up selling more than one million copies. Up to that point, the members of Spyro Gyra had looked at the group as more of a side project. But with the success of *Morning Dance*, they all committed to the project full-time. They released *Catching the Sun* and *Carnaval* in 1980, and moved the group's base of operations to the suburbs of New York City.

After the release of *Freetime* in 1981, Spyro Gyra's brand of music became known as "smooth jazz." Because they had broken the barriers of musical genres, music critics and radio stations found it difficult to fit them into a specific category, and even the "smooth jazz" definition didn't work for the band members themselves. "Radio represents 10 percent of what we do, and we're fortunate that they have found 10 percent of our music good for their format," Beckenstein told David Todoran at the Whatzup.com website. "But the band has such a high-energy side to it, and contemporary jazz radio is more about the relaxing kind of vibe. We are delighted that they play us, but we certainly don't define ourselves by it."

For the Record . . .

Members include **Scott Ambush** (born in Frederick, MD; son of Webster and Jeanette Ambush), bass; **Jay Beckenstein** (born on May 14, 1951, in Brooklyn, NY; married Jennifer Johnson, 1984; children: Claire, Alexandra, Isabel), saxophone; **Julio Fernandez** (born on August 29, 1954, in Havana, Cuba), guitar; **Joel Rosenblatt**, drums; **Tom Schuman** (born on January 31, 1958, in Buffalo, NY; son of Wally and Marion Schuman), keyboards. Former members include **Monolo Badrena**, percussion; **Oscar Cartaya**, bass; **Chet Catallo**, guitar; **Eli Konikoff**, drums; **Richie Morales**, drums; **Dave Samuels**, vibraphone/marimba; **Kim Stone**, bass; **Gerardo Velez**, percussion; **Jeremy Wall**, keyboards; **David Wolford**, bass.

Formed group, 1974; financed first recording, distributed by Amherst, 1976; distribution transferred to MCA Records, released *Morning Dance* album and "Morning Dance" single, 1979; released eleven albums on Amherst/MCA, 1980-89; transferred to GRP Records, 1990; released six albums on GRP, 1990-97; released *Got the Magic* on Windham Hill Records, 1999; released *In Modern Times* on Heads Up International, 2001.

Addresses: *Record company*—Heads Up International, 23309 Commerce Park Road, Cleveland, OH 44122; website: http://www.headsup.com. *Management*—Cross Eyed Bear Productions, P.O. Box 239, Tallman, NY 10930. *Website*—Spyro Gyra Official Website: http://www.spyrogyra.com.

In 1983, vibraphonist/marimba player Dave Samuels officially joined the band. Samuels had previously contributed to several of the band's albums, but hadn't become a full-fledged member. Spyro Gyra released *Access All Areas* and *City Kids* that same year. In 1984, Julio Fernandez joined the group on guitar. Around this time, Spyro Gyra centered on Beckenstein with other musicians working for short periods of time.

At the end of 1987, Beckenstein decided to try to form more of a permanent lineup. Bassist Oscar Cartaya auditioned at that time and joined the band. "I was fortunate to come in at a time when Jay Beckenstein wanted to create more of a group identity instead of taking musicians on the road, and then recording with studio players," Cartaya told Chris Jisi in *Guitar Player*. But Spyro Gyra's personnel changes hadn't stopped yet. After the release of 1988's *Rites of Summer* and 1989's *Point of View*, Joel Rosenblatt joined the group on drums.

In 1990, the GRP record label took over MCA's jazz artists, and as a result, Spyro Gyra had changed labels. Their next effort, *Fast Forward*, was released on GRP. After the release of *Three Wishes* in 1992, Spyro Gyra recruited Scott Ambush on bass. The following year, Dave Samuels decided to leave the band, although he periodically contributed to subsequent studio recordings. In 1997, Spyro Gyra celebrated their twentieth album release in 20 years with *20/20*. Despite the ever-changing lineup, Beckenstein remained committed to the project over the years, as did their audiences.

Spyro Gyra changed labels once again in 1999 with the release of *Got the Magic* on Windham Hill Records. The following year, Beckenstein released his first solo CD called *Eye Contact*. However, the recording of a solo project didn't interfere with his dedication to the success of Spyro Gyra. "Though I occasionally have recorded on records other than Spyro Gyra and have done other productions, Spyro Gyra has been my main focus and has fulfilled most of my musical dreams," Beckenstein wrote on the group's official website.

The following year, Spyro Gyra celebrated their twenty-fifth anniversary with the album *In Modern Times* on Heads Up International. After 23 albums in a quarter of a century, Spyro Gyra had no intentions of slowing their pace. "The bottom line is after 25 years, we're just not going away," Beckenstein said in the group's record company press release. "With each recording, I feel like I'm playing with a whole new band. I think that *In Modern Times* is one of our strongest albums to date. We've remained open to new ideas while keeping our identity."

By 2001, Spyro Gyra's members included Beckenstein, bassist Scott Ambush, guitarist Julio Fernandez, drummer Joel Rosenblatt, and keyboardist Tom Schuman. With what appeared to be a solid lineup in place, Spyro Gyra continued to play their own brand of hybrid instrumental music without any barriers. "What could be better than this?" Beckenstein asked Jonathan Widran for an article in *Jazziz* magazine, available at the group's website. "We still get to play music that are hearts are involved in, untainted by the world around us."

Selected discography

Spyro Gyra, Amherst, 1976.
Morning Dance, MCA, 1979.

Catching the Sun, Amherst, 1980.
Carnaval, MCA, 1980.
Freetime, MCA, 1981.
Incognito, Amherst, 1981.
Access All Areas, Amherst, 1983.
City Kids, Amherst, 1983.
Alternating Currents, Amherst, 1985.
Breakout, Amherst, 1986.
Stories Without Words, MCA, 1987.
Rites of Summer, MCA, 1988.
Point of View, MCA, 1989.
Fast Forward, GRP, 1990.
Three Wishes, GRP, 1992.
Dreams Beyond Control, GRP, 1993.
Love & Other Obsessions, GRP, 1995.
Heart of the Night, GRP, 1996.
20/20, GRP, 1997.
Road Scholars, GRP, 1997.
Got the Magic, Windham Hill, 1999.
In Modern Times, Heads Up International, 2001.

Jay Beckenstein

Eye Contact, Windham Hill Jazz, 2000.

Sources

Periodicals

Down Beat, September 1986; January 1988; September 1990; September 1997.
Guitar Player, September 1990.

Online

"Downtown Revival," Whatzup.com, http://www.whatzup.com (June 17, 2001).
"Interview with Jay Beckenstein," Contemporary Jazz.com, http://www.contemporaryjazz.com (June 17, 2001).
"Spyro Gyra," *All Music Guide,* http://www.allmusic.com (June 17, 2001).
"Spyro Gyra Make Their Magic on the Road in 2000," EMOL, http://www.emol.org (June 17, 2001).
Spyro Gyra Official Website, http://www.spyrogyra.com (June 17, 2001).

—Sonya Shelton

Stereo MC's

Pop group

Longtime friends with a cosmic bond (the same birthday), Nick "The Head" Hallam and Rob Birch are considered British hip-hop pioneers. Their group, the Stereo MC's, married rock, pop, and rap, introducing a "synthesis of hip-hop beats and milky acid-jazz-infused dance groves," according to *MusicHound Rock*. After releasing three albums, the Stereo MC's earned the worldwide fame they sought, scoring hits in the United States with the singles "Elevate My Mind" and "Connected" during the 1990s.

Hallam and Birch met as children at the age of six in Nottingham, England. Sharing a mutual love of music, the duo formed the rock band Dogman and Head. In 1985, when they were 17 years old, Hallam and Birch moved to London to tap into the city's vibrant music scene. Upon arriving in London, the duo changed their focus from rock to rap and soul. They recorded new songs for their label, Gee Street Records, which was formed with Jon Baker and DJ Richie Rich. The Gee Street Studio followed after a real estate developer gave Baker and Rich £7,000 each to move out of their flats. The label and the studio were named after a London-area street.

The Stereo MC's' first single, "Move It," and its follow-up "What is Soul?" were released in 1987. The following year, the duo hired Italian-British DJ Cesare to work with the group and their side project, Ultimatum. "Move It" received wider distribution in March of 1988 when Gee Street signed a distribution deal with Island Records. Island also put into stores Ultimatum's first remix, "Black is Black," by the Jungle Brothers.

Ultimatum headed out on the road opening for Jesus Jones. In 1989, the Stereo MC's released their debut album, *33-45-78*, which was recorded for $21,000. In the United States, the album was issued as a five-track EP dubbed *Stereo MC's*. The album was a considered a musical landmark in the United Kingdom where the amalgamation of rock and rap was rare. Unhappy with the group's direction, Cesare left Ultimatum and Stereo MC's to become a renowned producer. Hallam and Birch found a new partner in the Jungle Brothers' Afrika Baby Bam, with whom they recorded the Stereo MC's *Supernatural*, named *Supernatural American Mix* in the United States. Bam was considered a full member, co-writing, co-producing and appearing on the album, which was released in 1990.

For its live performances, the trio recruited percussionist Owen If, whose previous entertainment experience included serving as a special effects trainee at Pinewood Studios for the films *Batman* and *Full Metal Jacket*, as well as background vocal work for Cath Coffey. The band headed out on tours with the rock group Living Colour and Manchester Britpop group the Happy Mondays. Meanwhile, the Stereo MC's scored their first hit, 1991's "Lost in Music," which was based on Ultimatum's remix of the Jungle Brothers' "Doin' Your Own Dang." In 1991, the song "Elevate My Mind" became the first American top 40 hit for the Stereo MC's.

The group's follow-up album, *Connected,* was much anticipated upon its release in September of 1992. The record spawned the American top 20 hit of the same name, as well as the British favorite "Step It Up." *Connected* went platinum in 18 countries and earned the band a place as the opening group for U2 on its Zooropa tour. The success of *Connected* led the band to its first major awards, Best Group and Best Album prizes at the 1994 BRIT Awards. Claiming burn-out and hinting at allegations of exploitation on the part of its record label, the group stepped out of the spotlight and into the studio. Birch later told British Broadcasting Corporation (BBC) Radio Online that promotion and traveling wore on the group. Plus, touring occupied all of the group's time, making it difficult to write new material. Hallam and Birch briefly took the Stereo MC's out of retirement in 1998, however, to record the song "Flash" for the soundtrack to the film *The Avengers* starring Uma Thurman and Ralph Fiennes.

The duo remained in music during their time off from the Stereo MC's. They resurrected their Ultimatum identity and found success as remixers, working on pieces by Aswad ("Warrior Re-Charge"), Madonna ("Frozen"), Definition of Sound ("Wear Your Love Like Heaven"), Disposable Heroes of Hiphoprisy ("Television: The Drug of the Nation"), Dream Warriors ("Follow Me Not"), Electronic ("Idiot Country Two"), and U2 ("Mysterious Ways"). In March of 2000, more than six years after releasing *Connected*, the duo released the

Members include **Andrea Bedassie** (born on November 7, 1957; joined group, c. 1988); **Rob Birch** (born Robert Charles Birch on June 11, 1961, in Ruddington, Nottinghamshire, England), vocals, songwriter, producer; **DJ Cesare** (joined group, c. 1988), DJ; **Cath Coffey** (born Catherine Muthomi Coffey in Kenya; joined group, c. 1988), backing vocals; **Verona Davis** (born on February 18, 1952, in London, England; joined group, c. 1988), backing vocals; **Nick "The Head" Hallam** (born on June 11, 1962, in Nottingham, England), synthesizers, music orchestration; **Owen If** (born Ian Frederick Rossiter on March 20, 1959, in Newport, Wales; joined group, c. 1988), percussion.

Formed group in East London, England, c. 1987; started Gee Street Records with John Baker and DJ Richie Rich, late 1980s; released debut album, *33-45-78*, on Gee Street/Island Records, 1989; released album *Supernatural*, 1990; released single "Elevate My Mind," 1991; released *Connected*, 1992; released *Deep, Down and Dirty* on Island/Def Jam Records, 2001.

Awards: BRIT Awards, Best Group and Best Album for *Connected*, 1994.

Addresses: *Record company*—Island Def Jam Music Group, Worldwide Plaza, 825 Eighth Avenue, New York, NY 10019, website: http://www.islandrecords.com. *Website*—Stereo MC's Official Website: http://www.stereomcs.com.

mix album *DJ Kicks*, one in a series of records issued by the Berlin-based Studio K7. *Billboard* magazine's Gary Smith described the release as "a selection of tunes ranging from the classic early hip-hop of the Ultra-magnetic MCs' 'Poppa Large' and Kool G Rap's 'Road to Riches' to the contemporary Afro-funk of Blueman Presents Funky Lowlife's 'Funk Connection.'" The duo's music has also found new life in television and radio commercials.

In early 2000, Hallam and Birch decided that it was time to record a new Stereo MC's record. They worked diligently in their studio, located in a building that formerly housed an illegal nightclub. After nine months, the Stereo MC's produced *Deep, Down and Dirty*, a 13-track album released on May 28, 2001, in Europe and in June in the United States on Universal/Island Records. In advance of the release of *Deep, Down and Dirty*, the Stereo MC's returned to the stage in early 2001. The band had undergone a few changes, however. Hallam, Birch, If, and Coffey made up the core of the Stereo MC's, while two new backup singers entered the mix. Hallam told BBC Radio Online that it was nerve-wracking to tour once again. "I guess we are pretty freaked out by doing shows again. We wanted to do a few and get back into the vibe, but it's great. I think we always really loved playing live."

The critics were not as thrilled about the Stereo MC's' return as fans. Jeremy Wilks, a writer for the European news organization ITN, panned the record, calling the music dated: "The Stereo MC's end up looking, and sounding, as washed out as Rob himself." However, Wilks did backpedal a bit: "This record should not be avoided, but it does lack a certain magnetism and energy." Christine Weydig of *Interview* magazine gave it a back-handed compliment: "Despite a few awkward rhymes … these pioneers of electronica still spin an inspired web of funk, hip-hop, rock and soul." In early 2001, the Stereo MC's prepared for a massive United States tour to celebrate the release of *Deep, Down and Dirty*, but most of the jaunt was postponed so the group could return to Europe to play festivals.

Selected discography

33-45-78, Gee Street, 1989.
Supernatural (includes "Elevate My Mind"), Gee Street, 1990.
Connected (includes "Connected"), Gee Street/Island, 1993.
(Contributors) *The Avengers* (soundtrack), Columbia, 1998.
DJ Kicks, Studio K7, 2000.
Deep, Down and Dirty, Island/Def Jam, 2001.

Sources

Books

Graff, Gary, and Daniel Durchholz, editors, *MusicHound Rock: The Essential Album Guide*, Visible Ink Press, 1999.

Periodicals

Billboard, December 4, 1999.
Interview, June 2001.

Online

BBC Radio Online, http://www.bbc.co.uk/radio1/alt/alt_features/stereo_mcs_interview_apr2001.shtml (July 25, 2001).

IMusic/ARTISTdirect, http://imusic.artistdirect.com/showcas
e/urban/stereomcs.html (July 25, 2001).

ITN, http://www.itn.co.uk/news/20010523/entertainment/04s
tereomcs.shtml (July 25, 2001).

New Musical Express, http://www.nme.com/NME/External/
News/News_Story/0,1004,3005,00.html (July 25, 2001).

Sonicnet.com, http://www.sonicnet.com/artists/biography/16
904.jhtml (July 25, 2001).

Additional information was provided by Island Def Jam Music
Group publicity materials, 2001.

—Christina Fuoco

The String Cheese Incident

Rock group

By the late 1990s, Colorado's the String Cheese Incident stood as one of the most popular acts on the rock-oriented "jam" band circuit. Similar to other accomplished bands on the scene who flourished in the wake of the Grateful Dead, such as Phish and Widespread Panic, the String Cheese Incident developed a widespread following the old-fashioned way: through constant touring and maintaining close ties with fans. However, the String Cheese Incident took this grassroots ethic a step further. Since the group's inception, the String Cheese Incident has remained wholly independent. In addition to founding the SCI Fidelity record label to release their own material, the band built a multi-faceted company to handle all its needs. The venture, which grosses around $3.5 million annually, includes a management arm, a gear and merchandising company, a ticketing service, and even a travel agency to serve devoted fans who follow the String Cheese Incident from city to city to attend headlining concerts (known as String Cheese "Incidents") and summer festivals, both in the United States and overseas.

A large part of the String Cheese Incident's appeal rests in their musical versatility and penchant for performing lengthy, hallucinogenic jams. Defying easy categorization, the String Cheese Incident blends elements of rock, bluegrass, country, soul, funk, Latin, reggae, calypso, jazz, fusion, and everything in between, both live and in the studio. The band easily adapts to improvising with artists from a variety of different styles. Over the years, the String Cheese Incident has performed with the likes of Béla Fleck, multireedist Paul McCandles, as well as percussionist Baba Olantunji and pop star Femi Kuti in Africa. "Improvisation isn't just about kick-a** chops," said mandolinist and violinist Michael Kang to Down Beat contributor Isaac Josephson. "It's also about getting into a space together where you're creating good, cohesive music as a group, and that's what we try to accomplish on a nightly basis."

Along with giving solid performances regardless of what direction the music takes, the String Cheese Incident also strives to create a positive, fun atmosphere for concert goers. "We're a West Coast band, and our lives were lived around our recreation—around having a good time," Kang concluded. "We used to ski every single day. That's part of our identity, and we'd like to pass that on to everyone who comes into contact with us."

The String Cheese Incident formed in the Colorado town of Crested Butte in 1993. Originally, the group consisted of four musically inclined ski bums: Kang, acoustic guitarist Bill Nershi, bassist Keith Moseley, and drummer/percussionist Michael Travis, who admittedly had little professional experience before meeting his bandmates. "I was strictly hand percussion—congas and bongos—at the beginning," he told Josephson. "I took a village drumming course while in school in Santa Cruz [California], moved to Colorado and started playing with a couple of bands. Then I started playing with Kang and those guys, and we played so well together that I thought I might be able to make something out of this."

According to the other members of the String Cheese Incident as well, the quartet indeed felt a unique and immediate chemistry between them. Before long, the four were choosing to jam together over hitting the ski slopes. Intending to find a wider audience, the String Cheese Incident relocated to the larger city of Boulder, Colorado, where they met and enlisted pianist/organist Kyle Hollingsworth, the only trained jazz musician in the String Cheese Incident and a longtime devotee to keyboardist Herbie Hancock, in 1996.

As a result of regular performances at smaller venues, the String Cheese Incident was arguably Colorado's favorite jam band, and relentless touring thereafter brought the group to national attention. In late 1996 on their own label, SCI Fidelity Records, the group released its first studio album, Born on the Wrong Planet. The set captured the band's live sound, showcased a more acoustic, bluegrass side, and featured versions of fan favorites such as "Texas," "Black Clouds," "Johnny Cash," and "Jellyfish." A live album, A String Cheese Incident, followed in 1997.

In 1998, the String Cheese Incident released a second studio effort. Round the Wheel contained versions of

For the Record . . .

Members include **Kyle Hollingsworth** (born on March 2, 1968, in Maryland; joined group, 1996), piano, organ, accordion; **Michael Kang** (born on May 13, 1971, in South Korea), electric and acoustic mandolin, violin; **Keith Moseley** (born on February 5, 1965, in Oklahoma), five-string electric bass, four-string acoustic bass; **Bill Nershi** (born on September 16, 1961, in New York), six-string acoustic guitar; **Michael Travis** (born on April 20, 1965, in Southern California), drums, congas, djembe, percussion.

Formed group in Crested Butte, CO, 1993; after relocating to Boulder, CO, released first studio album, *Born on the Wrong Planet,* 1996; released *Round the Wheel,* 1998; released *Outside Inside,* 2001.

Addresses: *Record company*—SCI Fidelity Records, 2405 Broadway, Boulder, CO 80304, phone: (303) 544-1818, fax: (303) 544-1919. *Management and booking*—Madison House, Inc., 2405 Broadway, Boulder, CO 80304, phone: (303) 544-9900. *Website*—The String Cheese Incident Official Website: http://www.stringcheeseincident.com.

such songs as "Come as You Are" and "On the Road," as well as the title track. More eclectic than their debut, the set displayed the band's ability to jump from one genre to the next with ease, as evidenced by the Latin-infused "MLT," the bluegrass tune "Good Times Around the Bend," and the jazz-inspired "Galactic." Another live album, *Carnival '99,* surfaced the following year. The double-disc set culled music from 13 different performances and showcased the String Cheese Incident's diverse abilities and willingness to experiment as they moved from electrified bluegrass and progressive rock to fusion to funk. However, some critics complained about a lack of focus, a tendency to play away from their strengths, and too much of a reliance on cover songs.

For their next project, the String Cheese Incident broke from their traditional sound. Even their prior studio albums, *Born on the Wrong Planet* and *Round the Wheel,* were largely a reflection of their live energy, instrumental skills, and improvisational abilities. With *Outside Inside,* released in May of 2001, the band wanted to reach people outside of the String Cheese community. "You know, we're poised in a position of growth with the band, to where we can really reach a lot of people," explained Moseley to *St. Louis Post-Dispatch* contributor Alan Sculley. "That was kind of in our minds as we were doing the project, and this is the first time that we might actually get a little bit of radio airplay, or the first time we might sell perhaps 100,000 copies of the album."

Therefore, the band focused its energies more toward solid songwriting and arranging. "We tried to kind of trim things down to the essence of the song without all the extras," Moseley further noted. "That was the idea, to let the songs really shine through on the album and on their own. We wanted to make it an album of really standout songs." *Outside Inside,* produced by Los Lobos' Steve Berlin, proved the String Cheese Incident's most cohesive and accessible album. Nevertheless, the band retained their sense of adventure by drawing from an array of influences: R&B, soul, reggae, country, Latin ("Latinissmo"), and Cajun ("Up the Canyon").

In support of the album, the String Cheese Incident spent the summer on tour, headlining several dates and making appearances at festivals and with groups such as Widespread Panic. "We're coming up on 1,200 shows in the last seven years," Moseley said to Dan Julian of the *University Wire* before a concert at Michigan State University. "Things are starting to get a little blurred."

Selected discography

Born on the Wrong Planet, SCI Fidelity, 1996.
A String Cheese Incident (live), SCI Fidelity, 1997.
Round the Wheel, SCI Fidelity, 1998.
Carnival '99 (live), SCI Fidelity, 1999.
Outside Inside, SCI Fidelity, 2001.

Sources

Periodicals

Down Beat, June 2001.
St. Louis Post-Dispatch, April 19, 2001, p. 23; April 22, 2001, p. F6.
University Wire, April 23, 2001; May 7, 2001.

Online

String Cheese Incident Official Website, http://www.string cheeseincident.com (June 23, 2001).

—*Laura Hightower*

Tamia

Singer

Canadian-born singer Tamia was anointed a rising star by record producer Quincy Jones when she was just 18 years old. She appeared on his album *Q's Jook Joint* in 1994, and then spent several years recording with other stars. In 2000, though, the R&B artist finally came into her own with the release of *A Nu Day*. The album moves from sweeping torch ballads to more hard-hitting, hip-hop influenced songs and showcases the singer's vocal talents. It marks Tamia's growth as an artist and confirms her tenacity in the world of R&B.

Tamia Washington was born on May 9, 1975, in Windsor, Ontario, Canada. She was introduced to the pleasures of singing very early. She began performing in her church choir when she was just six years old, and by the time she was ten, she was taking acting and vocal lessons. Tamia sang in several choirs and appeared in theater productions such as *Godspell* and *Little Shop of Horrors* throughout her teen years. Tamia noted in her Elektra biography, "Church is always the best place for a young person to start. Everyone is so supportive when you're singing for God. You can make a few mistakes and it's still all right." Another early influence was the Motown sound; Windsor is directly across the Detroit River from Detroit, Michigan, and Tamia's mother exposed her to this music, singing it around the house.

Tamia's first real recognition came in 1993 when she was honored with the prestigious Canadian Youth TV (YTV) Vocal Achievement Award. This was followed in 1994 when Tamia was awarded the Steve Ross Music Scholarship at the American Academy of Achievement's Annual Salute to Excellence in Las Vegas, Nevada. While she did study at the Walkerville Collegiate Institute, 1994 also marked the beginning of Tamia's professional career as a singer. That year, her manager Brenda Richie invited Tamia to sing at a party for famed R&B singer/songwriter Luther Vandross. At the party, Tamia caught the eye of legendary producer Quincy Jones. Jones had founded Qwest Records, and was known for promoting the careers of R&B artists. When he asked Tamia to record a song for his new album, she knew that it was her big break.

Tamia went into the studio with Jones and recorded "You Put a Move on My Heart," which was the first single released from the album *Q's Jook Joint* in 1995. The record included performances by other stars such as Barry White and Queen Latifah. Tamia herself was a little awestruck by the opportunity. She told *Jet* magazine, "I'm very, very flattered. As a new artist, I feel that it's so much to handle. Even being on an album with such people as Ray Charles and Stevie Wonder is an honor, and then to be on the first single out—it's amazing to me." The single made it to the top ten on the R&B charts and was nominated for a Grammy Award in 1996. Another song from the album—Tamia's duet with Babyface called "Slow Jams"—was also nominated. Tamia went on to record a song for the soundtrack to the 1995 film *Set It Off;* "Missing You" was a collaboration with Brandy, Gladys Knight, and Chaka Khan. That song also garnered a nomination at the 1996 Grammy Awards, making Tamia a three-time nominee all before she had recorded her own album.

Tamia finally produced her debut album for Qwest Records in 1998. Titled simply *Tamia,* the album is a collection of collaborations between the singer and such established producers as Jermaine Dupri, Keith Crouch, and Stevie J. Jones was the executive producer on the recording and was again a big influence on Tamia. The album received mixed reviews; generally Tamia was credited for what Leo Stanley of *All Music Guide* called her "seductive voice," but he noted that the album contained "mediocre songs" that even Tamia's lovely voice couldn't save. The album was not a huge commercial success despite Tamia's earlier popular recordings and Grammy nominations. The singer herself seemed disappointed with the long-awaited debut and told an *Essence* interviewer, "I wasn't real happy about what happened with [*Tamia*].

Other people were in charge of my music, my image ... which left little space for me."

After a less-than-stellar debut, Tamia appeared on a few additional albums. She recorded "Spend My Life With You" with Eric Benet—collecting another Grammy Award nomination—and contributed to the soundtrack of *Speed 2: Cruise Control.* The singer won a small role in that film, and took time out from her music career to appear in a series of advertisements for clothing designer Tommy Hilfiger. During the years between her albums, Tamia was also developing a relationship with professional basketball superstar Grant Hill. After dating for three years, Tamia married the National Basketball Association (NBA) All-Star on July 24, 1999, in Battle Creek, Michigan. At the time Hill was a Detroit Piston, but he later signed with the Orlando Magic and the two relocated to Orlando, Florida. Tamia became a United States citizen in September of 2000 but retains a dual citizenship.

A year of changes for Tamia, 1999 found her leaving Qwest Records to sign with Elektra (also owned by Warner). At the new label she worked on developing another album, one that would allow her more control over her music. The result was *A Nu Day,* released in 2000. She told Rashaun Hall of *Billboard,* "With this album, I wanted to show my growth.... I also chose material that was a lot more difficult vocally and saying something." Tamia worked with producers such as Dallas Austin, Shep Crawford, and Missy "Misdemeanor" Elliot in developing the album. Elliot produced one hip-hop infused hit, "Can't Go For That," based on the Hall and Oates hit from the 1980s, "I Can't Go For That (No Can Do)." The two women so enjoyed working together that Elliot produced three more songs on the album. But the recording did not stick strictly to edgier tunes; Crawford produced the torch ballad "Stranger In My House," which fully exercises Tamia's vocal range.

A Nu Day was an attempt to refashion Tamia as Elektra's premiere female R&B star and to change her image from the squeaky-clean teenager that debuted on *Q's Jook Joint.* Chuck Taylor commented in *Billboard* that she is "sexy, sultry, and all grown up" on the album. Michael Paoletta, also writing in *Billboard,* commented that Tamia is "truly one of tomorrow's divas." Not all the critics praise the singer as a diva, though. *Entertainment Weekly's* Craig Seymour called the album "hammy" and "self-conscious," and Chuck Arnold commented in *People* that Tamia "[s]till hasn't found her voice." Lynn Norment strongly disagreed with these critics in her review of the album for *Ebony*: "Tamia's vocals soar, purr, pout and confess the feelings of a self-assured woman."

While critics disagree about the quality of Tamia's second album, *A Nu Day* produced a few R&B hits and enjoyed solid sales. Elektra seems satisfied with its new star as well. Michelle Murray, senior director of marketing for the label, commented to Rashaun Hall of *Billboard,* "Other labels have their Mariahs and their Whitneys.... We believe in Tamia fully, and we see her not as a one- or two-album artist but as a long term career artist with us. Our goal is to take her to every level." Tamia certainly seems ready to go.

Selected discography

(Contributor) *Q's Jook Joint,* Qwest, 1995.
(Contributor) *Set It Off* (soundtrack), Elektra/Asylum, 1996.
(Contributor) *Speed 2: Cruise Control* (soundtrack), Virgin, 1997.
Tamia (includes "Imagination" and "So Into You"), Qwest/Warner, 1998.
A Nu Day (includes "Can't Go For That" and "Stranger In My House"), Elektra/Asylum, 2000.

Sources

Periodicals

Billboard, August 12, 2000, p. 21; September 30, 2000, p. 42; October 7, 2000, p. 16; October 21, 2000, p. 25; November 11, 2000, p. 30.
Ebony, November 2000, p. 34D.
Entertainment Weekly, October 27, 2000, p. 120.
Essence, September 2000, p. 95.
Jet, November 13, 1995, p. 56; September 18, 2000, p. 32; October 16, 2000, p. 51; October 30, 2000, p. 14.
New York Times, December 21, 2000, p. E1.
People, November 13, 2000, p. 47.

Online

"Tamia," *All Music Guide,* http://www.allmusic.com (July 1, 2001).
"Tamia," Elektra Records, http://www.elektra.com (July 1, 2001).

—Christine Kelley

Third Day

Rock group

Christian rock group Third Day proved that it deserves the attention of fans and critics after sweeping the Dove Awards in 2001. The group garnered five awards, including wins for Artist of the Year and Group of the Year. The band released the praise and worship album *Offerings: A Worship Album* in 2000, and the same year contributed to a collaborative effort, *City on a Hill: Songs of Worship and Praise.* Consistently ranked among the top ten Contemporary Christian artists, Third Day combines an uncompromising evangelism with a dedication to Southern-influenced rock.

The founding members of Third Day—guitarist Mark Lee and singer/guitarist Mac Powell—have been performing together since high school. The two played in a garage band called Nuclear Hoedown in their hometown of Marietta, Georgia, but Powell soon quit the band because he didn't feel it was what God wanted him to do. Lee contacted Powell after a few weeks to convince him to help create a Christian band, and the two began writing songs that reflected their commitment to Christianity. Joined by a keyboardist, the fledgling group called themselves Third Day to honor the third day after Jesus' death, the day of his resurrection. The group was originally acoustic and per-

Photograph by James Blond. AP/World Wide Photos. Reproduced by permission.

Members include **Tai Anderson** (born on June 11, 1976), bass; **Brad Avery** (born on August 20, 1971; joined group, 1995), guitar; **David Carr** (born on November 15, 1974), drums; **Mark Lee** (born on May 29, 1973), guitar; **Mac Powell** (born on December 25, 1972), vocals, guitar.

Formed group in Marietta, GA, 1992; signed with gray dot records, released debut album, *Third Day*, 1995; signed with Reunion Records, re-released debut, 1996; released *Conspiracy No. 5,* 1997; signed with Essential Records, 1999; released *Time,* 1999; released *Offerings: A Worship Album,* 2000.

Awards: Dove Awards, Artist of the Year, Group of the Year, Rock Recorded Song of the Year for "Sky Falls Down," Praise & Worship Album of the Year for *Offerings: A Worship Album,* Special Event Album of the Year (with others) for *City on a Hill: Songs of Worship and Praise,* all 2001.

Addresses: *Record company*—Essential Records, 741 Cool Springs Blvd., Franklin, TN 37067, website: http://www.essentialrecords.com. *Booking*—Creative Artists Agency, phone: (615) 383-8787, fax: (615) 383-4937. *Management*—Creative Trust Management, phone: (615) 297-5010, fax: (615) 297-5020. *Website*—Third Day Official Website: http://www.thirdday.com.

formed at Sunday schools and for youth groups. In 1992, a pastor introduced Lee and Powell to bassist Tai Anderson and drummer David Carr. The four met lead guitarist Brad Avery in 1995, and the roster was set. The five members were all in their early- to mid-twenties and dedicated to producing Christian rock.

Third Day worked early on to build regional support, playing shows on the Southern live performance circuit. They became known for their high-energy performances and developed a loyal fan base. Dan Raines, head of Creative Trust, the group's management firm, told Deborah Evans Price of *Billboard,* "Before they even had a deal, they had been out there working, playing every dive you can imagine, building an audience at the grass-roots level." The early work paid off, and in 1995, the group signed with local independent label gray dot records and released its first album, titled simply *Third Day*. The band's release was the first for the small label, and demand for the album quickly outstripped gray dot's ability to supply. Third Day then signed on with Arista's Reunion label, quickly recorded two additional songs, and re-released the debut album.

The major label release of the group's debut produced a mainstream hit, "Nothing At All," which made the top 30 on pop charts. A video for another song from the album, "Consuming Fire," won the *Billboard* Music Video Award in the Contemporary Christian category in 1996. The record also won prime touring spots for the band. They opened for groups such as the Prayer Chain, the Waiting, and Code of Ethics. The group also played at AtlantaFest, a Christian music festival in their home state.

Third Day's sound continues to evolve, but core influences include U2 and Lynyrd Skynyrd. The group's early recording was described by Susan Hogan-Albach in the Minneapolis *Star Tribune* as "Southern folk rock, tinged with pop, blues, bluegrass and country offset by Powell's throaty vocals." The band was compared to Hootie and the Blowfish, the Gin Blossoms, and frequently to Pearl Jam. With their second album, Third Day played up grunge rock influences. Hogan-Albach noted that *Conspiracy No. 5*, released in 1997 by Reunion, was characterized by "metal-driven aggression … rife with chunky percussions and electric guitars."

Even as the band grew and changed its sound, Third Day remained committed to the original focus of the project: Christian evangelism. The group's songs consistently convey a message of faith, and Third Day never gives in to the temptation to write secular lyrics in the hopes of achieving crossover success. Carr told Jim Varsallone of the *Tampa Tribune,* "We've won awards and had top songs … but that's not our focus…. The focus is on Christ." The group's focus is maintained even on the road; Third Day travels with John Poitevent, a pastor who prays with the men before and after shows, leads them in Bible study, and counsels the musicians and crew while on tour.

The 1999 release *Time* was hailed by critics as Third Day's best album to date. This recording, too, explores new directions for the band musically. Paul Verna noted in *Billboard* that the band embraces "an earthier, looser sound that delves more deeply into its Southern roots." Powell also expressed Third Day's positive feelings about the recording, telling Jim Minge of the *Omaha World Herald* that the album was the best the band had yet produced, and noted, "we're a bit better musically and lyrically, too."

The year 2000 held other milestones for the band. Third Day's new label, Essential Records, specializes in marketing Contemporary Christian acts, and the band was invited to collaborate on a special album called *City on a Hill: Songs of Worship and Praise.* Third Day recorded the title track, and members of the band collaborated with other Christian rockers on several additional songs. Other leading artists on the album include Sixpence None the Richer, Caedmon's Call, FFH, and Jars of Clay. Third Day also released their own praise and worship album in 2000 called *Offerings: A Worship Album.* The album marked a change in the way the band worked; it contains several songs recorded live on tour, as well as additional studio recordings. Included on the album are "Thief," the story of the two other men crucified with Jesus, and "King of Kings," about the impossibility of knowing God. Third Day released a "worship kit" to complement the album; containing lyrics, chords, and transparencies, the kit is intended to help youth groups and ministers use the album as part of worship.

Offerings proved to be another hit with critics as well as with audiences. The album went gold after just a few months and collected not only a Dove Award for Praise & Worship Album of the Year in 2001, but also a Grammy Award nomination. Deborah Evans Price of *Billboard* had nothing but the highest praise for *Offerings,* saying that the album "teems with passion and spiritual commitment." Price further noted that the release includes "beautiful praise and worship songs as well as tunes that stretch the boundaries of worship music in a wonderful way."

As rising stars in one of the fastest growing segments of popular music in the United States, Third Day is poised for even greater success. While playing AtlantaFest in 1996 was a breakthrough for the band, headlining the four-day festival in 2001 marked an even greater level of success for Third Day. That success, Anderson told John Blake of the *Atlanta Journal and Constitution,* has brought new challenges: "It's an interesting place to be.... It's easier to sit back and kind of pick out the problems of Christian music as an underdog. Now that we're successful, we are Christian music, and it's up to us to raise the bar."

Selected discography

Third Day (includes "Nothing At All" and "Consuming Fire"), gray dot, 1995; reissued, Reunion, 1996.
Conspiracy No. 5, Reunion/Silver, 1997.
Time, Essential, 1999.
(Contributor) *City on a Hill: Songs of Worship and Praise,* Essential, 2000.
Offerings: A Worship Album, Essential, 2000.

Sources

Periodicals

Atlanta Journal and Constitution, June 22, 2001, p. 3P.
Billboard, March 29, 1997, p. 9-10; September 11, 1999, p. 47; August 12, 2000, p. 40; September 30, 2000, p. 26; May 5, 2001, p. 108.
Omaha World Herald, March 19, 2000, p. 3.
Star Tribune (Minneapolis, MN), October 11, 1997, p. 7B.
Tampa Tribune, November 7, 1998, p. 6.
Toronto Star, July 4, 1998, p. L10.
USA Today, August 22, 2000, p. D5; April 30, 2001, p. D1.

Online

Dove Awards, http://www.doveawards.com (July 27, 2001).
"Third Day," *All Music Guide,* http://www.allmusic.com (July 10, 2001).
"Third Day," Essential Records, http://www.essentialrecords.com (July 10, 2001).
"Third Day," gray dot records, http://www.graydot.com (July 10, 2001).
"Third Day," Listen.com, http://www.listen.com (July 10, 2001).
Third Day Official Website, http://www.thirdday.com (July 10, 2001).

—*Christine Kelley*

George Thorogood

Singer, guitarist

Photograph by Ken Settle. Reproduced by permission.

If rock 'n' roll were a dinner menu, singer/guitarist George Thorogood would be the meat and potatoes. Though more than 25 years have passed since he formed George Thorogood and the Destroyers, which has sold more than 15 million albums since its inception in 1973, Thorogood has maintained his full-force, straightforward blues/rock style. He has released several hit songs over his lengthy career, including rock classics "I Drink Alone," "Who Do You Love," and his signature song, "Bad to the Bone."

Before becoming a rock musician, Thorogood pursued a career as a baseball player. He played on a semi-professional team, which he continued for a while after he reached rock stardom. In 1970, he saw blues performer John Hammond in concert in New York and decided to change his direction. Early in his musical career, Thorogood would take time off for the baseball season, even when he was in the middle of recording an album. For decades, Thorogood's favorite baseball team was the New York Mets. "I've always been a New York Mets fan," Thorogood told *Sport* magazine. "They crawled their way to mediocrity, and that was me. It was a team I could relate to."

Throughout his career, Thorogood has kept his level of success at a steady pace. He has relied heavily on his influences, which include John Lee Hooker, Elmore James, Chuck Berry, Willie Dixon, Muddy Waters, Howlin' Wolf, and Bo Diddley. He wrote and recorded his own music, but much of his catalog includes cover versions of songs by his heroes. "I'm a Chevy Nova in a world of Rolls Royces," Thorogood told Dave Veitch in the *Calgary Sun*. "It's all that I can do. Don't overrate me. I'm not that versatile." In fact, it is his dependable style that brought audiences back as fans knew what to expect from Thorogood.

George Thorogood and the Destroyers formed in 1973 in Wilmington, Delaware. The original group included bassist Michael Lenn, second guitarist Ron Smith, and drummer Jeff Simon. With the lineup in place, the band moved to Boston where they played in local blues clubs. In 1974, the group recorded a demo, which was later released as *Better than the Rest* on MCA Records. The following year, they met John Forward, who helped them land a record contract with Rounder Records.

Before the group released its debut album, Lenn was replaced by bassist Billy Blough. In 1977, *George Thorogood and the Destroyers* arrived in record stores. The album included cover versions of Hooker's "One Bourbon, One Scotch, One Beer" and James' "Madison Blues." A criticism Thorogood received again and again during his career was that he recorded more cover versions than original songs. "Instead of rote copying, he reshapes parts in the spirit of the masters," Jas Obrecht wrote in *Guitar Player*. "By playing them

For the Record . . .

Born in Baton Rouge, LA.

Discovered interest in music while playing semi-professional baseball, 1970; formed George Thorogood and the Destroyers, 1973; signed with Rounder Records, c. 1975; released debut, *George Thorogood and the Destroyers*, 1977; released two additional albums on Rounder, 1978-80; signed with EMI Records, 1981; embarked on 50/50 tour, 1981; released *Bad to the Bone* on EMI, 1982; released eight albums, 1982-96; signed with CMC International, released three albums, 1997-99; *Anthology* released on EMI, 2000.

Addresses: *Record company*—Capitol/EMI Records, 1750 N. Vine St., Hollywood, CA 90028, website: http://www.hollwoodandvine.com. *Website*—George Thorogood and the Destroyers Official Website: http://www.gthorogood.com.

with obvious affection, he can make others' styles and songs sound like his own."

Although Rounder Records was a small label, the group sold more than 100,000 copies of its self-titled debut. Until that time, it was the top-selling record the label had ever released. This wasn't for long, though. In 1978, George Thorogood and the Destroyers released *Move It On Over*. The title track, a cover of Hank Williams' song, was the first single, and it received plenty of airplay. The album also included the tunes "The Sky Is Crying" and "Who Do You Love." By the end of the year, the album had reached the top 40. It eventually went gold, selling more than 500,000 copies.

Before the release of their next album, the Destroyers went through additional personnel changes. Saxophone player Hank Carter joined the band, and Smith left the group. In 1980, the group released *More George Thorogood and the Destroyers*. The popularity of Thorogood and his group had grown so much that they signed a major label record deal with EMI in 1981. Following a tour with the Rolling Stones, the Destroyers embarked on the now-famous 50/50 tour, one that took the group to 50 states in 50 days without a break. "It was a ludicrous venture," Joel Selvin wrote in the band's EMI biography, "but it made a statement.... This wasn't show business. To George and the band, this was life." During that time, George Thorogood and the Destroyers refused to take time off even when they had it. They would frequently show up at local clubs on their nights off and play under the name Sidewalk Frank.

In 1982, the group released its first album on EMI, *Bad to the Bone*. The first single was the title track, and the video received frequent airplay on MTV. The album eventually went gold and stayed on *Billboard*'s album charts for almost a year. Thorogood told the Knight-Ridder/Tribune News Service that he wrote "Bad to the Bone" as a teenage fantasy: "I was an average kid with average grades. How boring can you get? So I wrote this song that fantasized how I would like to be. I wanted to be cool, I wanted to be bad."

Before the release of *Maverick* in 1985, Steve Chrismar joined George Thorogood and the Destroyers as second guitarist. *Maverick* included the songs "I Drink Alone" and "Willie and the Hand Jive." The following year, the group released its first live album, *Live*, as well as *Nadine*. *Born to Be Bad*, which included the title track and "You Talk Too Much," was released in 1988. David Hiltbrand wrote in his *People* review of the album, "Handle this album with heavy gloves. It's raucous, after-midnight party music filled with screaming guitars, a driving beat, and Thorogood's tequila-gargled voice."

In the early 1990s, George Thorogood and the Destroyers released *Boogie People* and *Get a Haircut*, the latter reaching number two on the *Billboard* charts. By the end of the decade, Thorogood was still rockin' in venues and on releases. In 1997, the Destroyers released *Rockin' My Life Away*. As he toured in support of the album, Thorogood noticed a growing lack of outlets for people to have fun. "Sometimes you go to see a comedian, and you walk out feeling worse than you did when you walked into the place," Thorogood told Frisco Floyd Van Gogh of CitySites online. "So I say, let's get these people up and dancing on their feet, get 'em laughing and dancing for about 90 minutes or two hours. Let 'em know that there is still a good time to be had."

In 1999, Thorogood released *Half a Boy, Half a Man* and *Live in 1999*. The following year, EMI compiled 30 Destroyers songs in a double-CD titled *Anthology*. Although his roots were still planted firmly in blues, Thorogood's style was undeniably straight-ahead rock 'n' roll. "It's weird. When I was 20, I wanted to be a bluesman," Thorogood told Ed Symkus in the *Boston Herald*. "Now I'm 50, and I want to be a rock 'n' roll star. You figure it out."

Through the glitter, glam, and over-the-top styles that exemplified many rock bands during the 1970s, '80s, and '90s, Thorogood's guitar rock still found an audience. "Maybe we have survived because we don't fit in," Thorogood told Knight-Ridder. "A lot has changed since 1977. Radio is not the same as it was.... But honestly, the more things change, the more they stay the same. There are just a lot more guitars now than before." George Thorogood and the Destroyers toured in 2001 and planned to record a new album.

Selected discography

George Thorogood and the Destroyers (includes "One Bourbon, One Scotch, One Beer" and "Madison Blues"), Rounder, 1977.

Move It On Over (includes "Move It On Over," "The Sky Is Crying," and "Who Do You Love"), Rounder, 1978.

Better than the Rest, MCA, 1979.

More George Thorogood and the Destroyers, Rounder, 1980.

Bad to the Bone, Capitol/EMI, 1982.

Maverick (includes "Willie and the Hand Jive" and "I Drink Alone"), Capitol/EMI, 1985.

Nadine, MCA, 1986.

Live, Capitol/EMI, 1986.

Born to Be Bad (includes "Born to Be Bad" and "You Talk Too Much"), Capitol/EMI, 1988.

Boogie People (includes "If You Don't Start Drinkin' [I'm Gonna Leave]"), Capitol/EMI, 1991.

Baddest of George Thorogood, Capitol/EMI, 1992.

Get a Haircut, Capitol/EMI, 1993.

Let's Work Together Live, Capitol/EMI, 1995.

Rockin' My Life Away, CMC, 1997.

Half a Boy, Half a Man, CMC, 1999.

Live in 1999, CMC, 1999.

Anthology, Capitol/EMI, 2000.

Extended Versions, BMG, 2000.

Sources

Periodicals

Boston Herald, May 21, 2001.
Calgary Sun, November 17, 1999.
Edmonton Sun, November 15, 1999.
Guitar Player, June 1981, pp. 18-22.
Knight-Ridder/Tribune News Service, November 5, 1993, p. 110.
Ottawa Sun, December 8, 1999.
People, February 29, 1988, p. 42; April 1, 1991, p. 20.
Rolling Stone, December 10, 1981, p. 77; June 20, 1985, p. 70.
Sport, June 1999, p. 24.

Online

Capitol Records, http://www.hollywoodandvine.com (June 17, 2001).
"George Thorogood," *RollingStone.com*, http://www.rollingstone.com (June 17, 2001).
George Thorogood and the Destroyers Official Website, http://www.gthorogood.com (June 17, 2001).
"Interview with George Thorogood," CitySites, http://www.citysites.com/thorogood (June 17, 2001).
"Thoroughly Bad to the Bone: George Thorogood Still Rocks," Seacoast Online, http://www.seacoastonline.com (June 17, 2001).

—*Sonya Shelton*

Tyrese

Singer

Tyrese has touched the full entertainment spectrum, having modeled, released albums, acted in films and commercials, and hosted a television show, all before the age of 22. Despite his multiple interests and talents, singing is most important to the Los Angeles, California, native. "Singing was and still is my first love, and it opened the doors for me in all of the other show business-related things that I do," he said in an RCA Records biography. Tyrese's musical endeavors have led to popular success and recognition. Following the release of his self-titled debut album in 1998, Tyrese won an American Music Award for Favorite New Artist-Soul/R&B in 2000. He released his sophomore effort, *2000 Watts*, to favorable reviews in 2001.

Tyrese Gibson grew up with his mother, Priscilla Murray, and three siblings in the impoverished Watts neighborhood of Los Angeles. His father, Tyrone Gibson, left the family when Tyrese was six years old. Instead of succumbing to the ills of crime-infested streets, Tyrese decided to battle his way out of his neighborhood to improve the standard of living for himself and his family. "It wasn't easy and I had to watch my back all of the time, but I always believed in myself, and that I could make it out of there," he said in his RCA biography. The Gibson household was often filled with the sounds of Stevie Wonder, Jodeci, Donny Hathaway, and Marvin Gaye. Those vocalists and groups inspired Tyrese to sing, something that at first he considered a hobby.

In 1995, however, that hobby turned into a career. Tyrese answered an advertisement that was posted at his high school, Los Angeles' Locke High School, stating that an advertising firm was looking for an African American male, age 16 to 18, for a Coca-Cola commercial. Unable to get a ride to the audition, Tyrese was forced to take the bus, which caused him to be two-and-a-half hours late for his appointment. Luckily, the director was held up in the same traffic. Despite the delay, the budding entertainer got the part.

Tyrese's brief appearance as a headphone-clad singer in the commercial led to a bidding war among 20 major record labels. He eventually signed to RCA and released his self-titled debut in 1998. *Tyrese* spawned the hits "Sweet Lady" and "Lately" and hit the platinum sales mark in 1999. In addition to earning an American Music Award for Favorite New Artist-Soul/R&B and a Grammy Award nomination for Best Male R&B Performance as a singer, Tyrese was tapped for acting roles and modeling jobs for big-name outfitters Guess? and Tommy Hilfiger. During a promotional appearance on MTV for *Tyrese*, he met the producers of *MTV Jams,* who hired him as the show's host along with DJ Skribble. As host, Tyrese was responsible for interviewing guests, introducing videos, and entertaining the small audiences chosen to appear on the show. To celebrate the success of his singing, modeling, and television careers, Tyrese bought his mother a lakefront home east of Los Angeles as a Mother's Day gift in 1998.

Tyrese's career possibilities continued to broaden. He made special appearances on the television shows *Martin, Moesha,* and *Hangin' with Mr. Cooper,* as well as the MTV movie *Love Song.* In 1999, Tyrese auditioned for the part of the lead character Jody in director John Singleton's then-forthcoming film *Baby Boy,* a movie originally set to star Tupac Shakur. When the rapper was killed in 1996 in Las Vegas, Nevada, Singleton temporarily shelved the project. Singleton told the Associated Press that Tyrese was a natural for the lead in the film. "He hadn't had them (the scripts) in advance and he just started doing the character. I was so excited. I saw the character right there. Here I am writing about the streets of Los Angeles and he just read it off the page. He just got it." To prepare for the film, Tyrese left the music business for six months to study full time with an acting coach.

After beating out rapper Eve and rap/soul trio 702 to win the American Music Award for Favorite New Artist Soul/R&B, Tyrese returned to the studio to record what would become his sophomore album, *2000 Watts.* Although Tyrese co-wrote most of the songs, he recruited top-notch producers and writers to help him hone his skills, including Damon Thomas (whose credits include work with Babyface and Dru Hill), Harvey Mason Jr., Babyface himself, Diane Warren, Rodney Jerkins, and Jermaine Dupri. "When you want the best songs, you get the best producers to work with you," Tyrese said in an RCA biography. In recording the album, it was Tyrese's goal to strive for longevity. He did not want a flash-in-the-pan, one-hit album. "There's something about R&B oldies that you can play 'em today and they still sound good and make you feel good. That's what I'm trying to get back in touch with on this album, and I just hope people are going to enjoy it not just for the moment, but for many years from now," he said in the biography.

On *2000 Watts,* Tyrese offers seductive lyrics ("I Like Them Girls"), dance grooves ("Off The Heazy" and "I Ain't the One") and a smooth ballad that the singer wrote in response to a woman who broke up with him after he admittedly cheated on her ("I'm Sorry"). *Billboard* said that the album "knocks the sophomore-jinx concept on its ear" with a collection "chock-full of strong, radio-friendly tracks." The album reached number four on the magazine's R&B charts. The same year, Tyrese formed the 2000 Watts Foundation, an organization he created to allow inner city children to better themselves. A portion of the proceeds from the album *2000 Watts* are designated to fund the building of a state-of-the-art community center in Watts, Tyrese's former Los Angeles neighborhood.

The year 2001 proved to be a busy one for Tyrese. In addition to the release of *2000 Watts* on May 22, 2001, the soundtrack to the film *Baby Boy,* released the same year, included the single "Just a Baby Boy," which featured Tyrese, rapper Snoop Dogg, and newcomer Mr. Tan. The record marked the first hip-hop/R&B soundtrack released by Universal Records. In July of 2001, Tyrese appeared as a contestant on a celebrity version of ABC's *Who Wants to be a Millionaire* television game show.

To Tyrese, his career has been a blessing. "Reaching this point in my career is something I'm really grateful about," he said in his record company biography. "I also know that I couldn't be where I am without the help, support and love of my family, friends, fans, and most of all, God."

Selected discography

Tyrese, RCA, 1998.
2000 Watts, RCA, 2001.
(Contributor) *Baby Boy* (soundtrack), UNI/Varese, 2001.

Sources

Periodicals

Boston Herald, June 29, 2001.
Essence, July 2001.
Jet, June 25, 2001.
Knight-Ridder/Tribune News Service, June 27, 2001.
Naples Daily News, June 29, 2001.
New York Post, July 1, 2001.
Pacific News (San Francisco, CA), May 26, 1999.

People, November 13, 2000; June 30, 2001; July 2, 2001.
Us, July 16, 2001.

Online

Associated Press, http://elections.excite.com/news/ap/0106
27/12/wkd-tyrese (July 25, 2001).
Billboard, http://www.billboard.com (July 25, 2001).
VH1, http://www.vh1.com/thewire/content/reviews/1444280.
jhtml (July 25, 2001).
Vibe, http://www.vibe.com/new/vibewire/20010501/news02.
html (July 25, 2001).

Additional information was provided by publicity materials
from RCA Records, 2001.

—*Christina Fuoco*

U2

Rock group

In 1984, U2 lead singer Bono told Jim Miller in *Newsweek,* "The message, if there is a message in our music, is the hope that it communicates." Nearly ten years later, after being called everything from "pompous and self-righteous social crusaders" to "sincere and involved political activists," U2 decided it was time to step out of the identities the world had superimposed on them. Bono Vox, who by this time had become simply Bono, told Robert Hilburn of the *Los Angeles Times,* "We felt we were being made a cartoon of 'the good guys of rock and so forth' so we decided to make some cartoons of our own and send them out as disinformation." U2 forged ahead to reach rock icon status with multiplatinum albums including *Rattle and Hum, War, The Joshua Tree, Achtung Baby,* and the group's 2000 release, *All That You Can't Leave Behind.*

U2 started off humbly enough as a Dublin, Ireland, school boy band formed in response to an ad placed on the Mount Temple High School notice board by Larry Mullen, Jr. in 1976. Of the several students that came to his house to audition for the rock band, Mullen noted that, although some could play, technical merit wasn't the decisive factor. Mullen told Jay Cocks of *Time* that the original band consisted of one fellow who

Photograph by Paul Warner. AP/World Wide Photos. Reproduced by permission.

"meant to play the guitar, but he couldn't play very well, so he started to sing. He couldn't do that either. But, he was such a charismatic character that he was in the band as soon as he arrived." That fellow was Paul Hewson, who later adopted the name Bono Vox (Latin for "good voice," which Hewson appropriated from a billboard advertisement for a hearing aid retailer). David "The Edge" Evans, a guitarist who *could* play, Adam Clayton, a bassist who "just looked great and used all the right words, like gig," Mullen on drums, and second guitarist Dick "Dik" Evans, The Edge's older brother, made up the rest of the band.

U2 began their musical odyssey as Feedback. After playing mainly cover tunes for a few shows in small local venues, Dik Evans left the band to form the Virgin Prunes, and the band changed its name to the Hype. Clayton, acting as band manager, sought advice from all the music industry sources he knew, including Steve Rapid, a singer for the local band the Radiators, who suggested that they change their name. Clayton wanted something ambiguous; Rapid suggested U2 because there was a U2 spy plane, a U2 submarine, a U2 battery made by Eveready, as well as the obvious "you, too" and "you two."

U2 Got Serious

In March of 1978, U2 entered a talent competition sponsored by Guinness at the Limerick Civic Week. They won £500 and the opportunity to audition for CBS Ireland, after which they secured supporting spots on tours with the Stranglers and the Greedy Bastards. In September, they recorded additional demos at Dublin's Windmill Lane Studios with Chas de Whalley, which subsequently lead to their signing by CBS Ireland. After building a considerable following in Ireland, they released their first EP, *U2:3,* which featured the tracks "Out Of Control," "Stories," and "Boy-Girl." It was available only in Ireland, where it topped the charts and where U2 found themselves playing sold-out shows. It was in December of the next year that U2 played their first United Kingdom dates—to a cool reception.

In Ireland, their single "Another Day" peaked on the charts at number one. U2 was to remain popular in Ireland, while struggling for years to get a foothold in both England and the United States. Although signed to an English record company, Island Records, fairly early in their struggle, U2 found success first in the United States with a 1981 tour—their second in the U.S.—that pushed *Boy* into the charts. England was a miss with "11 o'clock Tick Tock" and with *Boy*, until "Fire" finally hit the charts (followed by *Boy* as a latecomer). In mid 1982 the band retired to the studio to record new music. It was that October, during a concert in Belfast, that they introduced "Sunday, Bloody Sunday" to their fans. That song carried a message of peace in Northern Ireland that would later become the focal point of the band, seemingly fusing their lyrics and politics. Beginning in February of 1983, U2 played a 27-date sold-out tour in the United Kingdom.

In November of 1983, as U2 was constantly meeting the demand for concerts and chart-topping hits in both the United States and the United Kingdom, they released *Under a Blood Red Sky*—their first live album—to again meet the demand for new work. It became the most successful live album of the time.

Their next studio album, 1984's *The Unforgettable Fire,* reached number one in the United Kingdom. The band headlined at Madison Square Garden in 1985, and *Rolling Stone* touted them as "The Band of the Eighties." In between the philanthropy that was to become an ever-increasing indentifying aspect of the band—participating in "Do They Know It's Christmas" for Ethiopian famine relief, singing for Artists Against Apartheid, raising funds for Irish unemployed, and doing gigs for Amnesty International—they released the EP *Wide Awake in America* and resumed world touring in 1986.

Although it seemed that U2 were the social crusaders of their generation, Bono assured *Time*'s Cocks that he "would hate to think everybody was into U2 for 'deep' and 'meaningful' reasons. We're a noisy rock 'n' roll band. If we got on stage, and instead of going 'Yeow!' the audience all went 'Ummmm' or started saying the rosary, it would be awful." Regardless of how Bono saw it, the band's social consciousness is one of the main reasons, according to Christopher Connelly of *Rolling Stone,* U2 "has become one of the handful of artists in rock (and) roll history … that people are eager to identify themselves with."

Finally Won Critical Acclaim

In 1987 U2 embarked on a 110-date world tour. Their new album, *The Joshua Tree,* entered the United Kingdom charts at number one and the album went platinum in 48 hours, making it, at the time, the fastest-selling album in United Kingdom history. In mid April, *The Joshua Tree* reached the top of the American charts where it remained for nine weeks. Shortly thereafter, the band appeared on the cover of *Time* with the headline: "U2: Rock's Hottest Ticket." The Edge released a soundtrack for the political kidnapping film *Captive.* In November, Eamon Dunphy's book *Unforgettable Fire: The Story of U2* was released. It became a bestseller in the United Kingdom although the band retracted their support of the volume after they could not get parts of the text changed that they maintained were inaccurate.

In 1988 U2 received the award for Best International Group at the British Record Industry Awards, which was followed by their first Grammy Awards for Best Rock Performance by a Group and Album of the Year for *The Joshua Tree.* That same year, the Iovine-produced double album *Rattle and Hum,* featuring live recordings from the previous two years as well as

studio tracks, was released and topped the charts in both the United States and the United Kingdom. U2 also released the live documentary film *Rattle and Hum,* directed by Philip Joanou. As if these achievements hadn't raised their profile high enough, the band also appeared on the live television show *Smile Jamaica* for Jamaican Hurricane relief, where they were joined onstage by Keith Richards and Ziggy Marley.

The year 1989 brought the group the British Record Industry Award for Best International Group for the second year in a row. Grammy Awards for Best Rock Performance for "Desire," Best Performance Music Video for "Where The Streets Have No Name," and an MTV Music Video Award for their collaboration with B. B. King on "When Love Comes to Town," followed. The rest of the year, the band spent working tirelessly, touring Australia, New Zealand, Japan, and then finally returning home to Dublin, where the tour culminated with a New Year's Eve show that was broadcast live on the radio. The British Broadcasting Corporation (BBC) and Radio Telefís Éireann (RTE), Ireland's National Public Service Broadcasting Organization, collaborated to transmit the show throughout Europe and the former U.S.S.R. to a listening audience estimated at more than 500 million.

Although they had not released an album since 1988, U2 discovered new diversions in 1990. In February, the Royal Shakespeare Company produced *A Clockwork Orange 2004,* which featured music by The Edge. In June, Mullen wrote the official Eire World Cup Soccer team's song. But as always, busy as they were, U2 found time for good works. This time they contributed to an anthology of Cole Porter songs that was released as *Red Hot + Blue* and benefitted AIDS education. They also traveled to Berlin to film a video featured in a television special airing on International AIDS Day.

In November of 1991, U2's next, long-awaited album finally surfaced, but without the media blitz that seemed to accompany all the other year-end major releases. U2 had decided that the album would sell itself to their fans just fine without the fanfare. They were right, as initial shipments of *Achtung Baby* totalled upwards of 1.4 million units.

Zoo TV Tour and Beyond

In February of 1992, U2 began their Zoo TV tour. They took the radio transmission concept inaugurated on New Year's Eve 1989 one step further by incorporating a satellite dish into the show. A short European tour followed, during which a contest winner had the show beamed live by satellite to his home in Nottinghamshire from Stockholm, courtesy of MTV. The tour concluded with a Greenpeace concert in Manchester in which barrels of contaminated United Kingdom sand were delivered back to a nuclear power plant site where U2 and others were protesting the opening of a second plant. In August, they went back on the tour circuit, taking Zoo TV to the stadiums of the United States with their outside broadcast tour. When the tour ended in mid November in Mexico City, U2 had played to an estimated 2.5 million people.

During a break in the Zoo TV tour, U2 took the time to record an EP. That EP eventually became the ten-song *Zooropa* album, winner of the Grammy Award for Alternative Album of the Year in 1993. On May 9th the Zoo TV tour, which had since mutated into the Zooropa '93 tour, started an ambitious schedule of visiting 18 countries in four months and closing the trip back in Dublin in August.

The group released the techno-oriented *Pop* in March of 1997, which featured the singles "Staring at the Sun" and "Discotheque." Though some fans and critics found the album to be a stylistic puzzle of sorts, *Time* magazine's Christopher John Farley called the album "passionate, futuristic and completely engaging." The group embarked on the massive PopMart arena tour in support of the album in May. Staging for the tour included the world's largest video screen, a 35-foot mirrorball lemon, a 12-foot wide stuffed olive, and a 100-foot high golden arch. About the tour, Bono told Chris Willman of *Entertainment Weekly*, "We thought ... let's have some fun with our bigness. You know, we can't be hung for that. Because humor is the evidence of freedom, isn't it?"

Following the success of *Pop*, U2 released *All That You Can't Leave Behind* in 2000, an album that returned to the "generous spirit that flowed through their best '80s records," according to Stephen Thomas Erlewine of *All Music Guide*. The album spawned the single "Beautiful Day," for which the band won Grammy Awards for Best Rock Performance by a Duo or Group with Vocal, Song of the Year, and Record of Year. David Browne of *Entertainment Weekly* called the album "unwaveringly assured" and said that the group "no longer seems wary of their tendency toward the anthemic and grandiose, and they shouldn't be; it still sets them apart for nearly everyone else...." *Maclean's* called *All That You Can't Leave Behind* U2's "strongest album in years." The group again headed out in support of their newest release, this time on the worldwide Elevation tour.

Continued Social Activism

In addition to their musical pursuits, social activism remains important to U2. The group has championed the causes of eliminating Third World debt and gun control. U2 often uses concert performances to address the audience about these issues. "We're treading a very fine line between artists and wanting to lecture Americans about issues that are important. It's

basically turning a mirror on the audience," The Edge told *Rolling Stone*'s Jenny Eliscu. Bono has appeared in front of the United States Congress to urge the country's participation in erasing the debt of Third World nations, and he met with Pope John Paul II to lobby support for the issue. As the *Daily Telegraph* stated in 2000, "[O]ne senses that for him (Bono) and his colleagues in U2, rock stardom is a complicated business in which the freedom that success has brought them is counterbalanced by responsibility."

When asked what they're all about, bassist Adam Clayton explained it best in an interview with Robert Hilburn of the *Los Angeles Times* when he said, "I feel we made a decision then (going into the 90s) that if we are going to be the righteous men of rock 'n' roll, we are going to be very miserable. I think we realized that issues are more complicated than we once thought, and we don't want to be continually earnest about what we do. We are not a religious cult ... we are not a political theory. We are a rock 'n' roll band."

Selected discography

U2:3 (EP; includes "Out of Control," "Stories," and "Boy-Girl"), CBS Ireland, 1979.
Boy (includes "A Day Without Me" and "I Will Follow"), Island, 1980.
October (includes "Fire" and "Gloria"), Island, 1981.
War (includes "New Year's Day" and "Two Hearts Beat as One"), Island, 1983.
Under A Blood Red Sky (live), Island, 1983.
Unforgettable Fire (includes "Pride (In the Name of Love)"), Island, 1984.
Wide Awake in America (EP; includes live version of "Bad," "Three Sunrises," and "Love Comes Tumbling"), Island, 1985.
The Joshua Tree (includes "With or Without You," "I Still Haven't Found What I'm Looking For," and "Where the Streets Have No Name"), Island, 1987.
Rattle and Hum (includes "Desire," "Angel of Harlem," "When Love Comes to Town," and "All I Want Is You"), Island, 1988.
Achtung Baby (includes "The Fly," "Mysterious Ways," "One," "Even Better Than the Real Thing," and "Wild Horses"), Island, 1991.
Zooropa (includes "Numb" and "Lemon"), Island, 1993.
Pop (includes "Discotheque" and "Staring at the Sun), Island, 1997.
(Compilation) *Best of 1980-1990*, Island, 1998.
All That You Can't Leave Behind (includes "Beautiful Day," "Wild Honey," and "Stuck in a Moment"), Interscope, 2000.

Sources

Books

Dickey, Lorraine, *The Ultimate Encyclopedia of Rock,* Carlton Books, 1993.
Dolgins, Adam, *Rock Names,* Citadel Press, 1993.

Rees, Dafydd, and Luke Crampton, *Rock Movers & Shakers,* Billboard Books/ABC CLIO, 1991.

Robbins, Ira A., *Trouser Press Record Guide,* fourth edition, Collier Books, 1991.

Periodicals

Billboard, November 16, 1991.

Daily Telegraph, October 28, 2000.

Entertainment Weekly, May 9, 1997; November 3, 2000.

Hollywood Reporter, March 2, 1994.

Los Angeles Times, March 1, 1992; March 22, 1992; June 4, 1993; September 12, 1993.

Maclean's, November 2, 1987; November 20, 2000.

Melody Maker, May 30, 1992; December 5, 1992.

Musician, March 1992; September 1992.

Newsweek, December 31, 1984.

People, April 1, 1985.

Rolling Stone, October 11, 1984; March 14, 1985; May 7, 1987; September 8, 1988.

Spin, August 1993.

Time, April 27, 1987; March 10, 1997.

Village Voice, December 10, 1991; December 22, 1992.

Online

"Robbie Williams, U2, Coldplay Dominate Brit Awards," MTV News, http://www.mtv.com/news/articles/1440978/20010226/u2.jhtml?paid=1022 (September 20, 2001).

"U2," *All Music Guide*, http://www.allmusic.com (September 20, 2001).

"U2," *RollingStone.com*, http://www.rollingstone.com (August 15, 2001).

Additional information was obtained from the Wasserman Group, Island Records, and MTV, 1994.

—Charlie Katagiri

VAST

Rock group

Jon Crosby, the brainchild behind alternative rock group VAST, has earned a reputation as a musicial chameleon. He has the rare talent of being able to work within the confines of just about any musical genre—alternative music, world music, and goth have all played a heavy hand in molding Crosby's musical journey. While still in his teens, Crosby introduced San Francisco, California, to VAST (Visual Audio Sensory Theater), which takes all of those influences and blends them into a unique rock sound.

Growing up in rural Humboldt County, California, in a town of 7,000 people, Crosby wasn't exposed to MTV or frequent live musical performances. In fact, his only concert experiences as a youngster were shows by Richard Marx and Stevie Ray Vaughan. Instead, it was the film *Amadeus* that sparked his desire to become a musician. A girl, however, quickly changed his focus. "I met this girl named Michelle and I decided I wanted to learn how to play the Beatles' 'Michelle.' It had just enough diminished chords—similar to classical music—for me to get into rock. And I became a huge Beatles fan," he said in his official website biography. Growing up in a small town gave Crosby the push he needed. After all, he said, "there was nothing else to do other than play guitar." His hometown showed little support for the young guitar prodigy, considering intro-verted Crosby an outcast.

Crosby's musical tastes evolved as he grew older. Alternative music struck a chord with him, specifically U2, Depeche Mode, and the Cure. While in his pre-teens, Crosby and his mother moved to San Francisco where he joined a guitar workshop. As a student, he recorded a demo tape and sent it to the president of Shrapnel Records. Soon thereafter, at just 13 years old, he was profiled in *Guitar Player* magazine. Crosby was offered a record deal with Shrapnel, but he turned it down because he felt he was too young. In order to fulfill his dream of becoming a musician, Crosby traded public school for home schooling. Studies were not as important to Crosby as music, though. While his friends were listening to punk and ska, Crosby formed an electronic music act, VAST, an acronym for Visual Audio Sensory Theater, when he was 16. He made the rounds of Bay Area clubs and in the mid 1990s inked a lucrative deal with Elektra Records.

Crosby soon entered the studio where he played nearly every instrument on the group's debut album. During the recording process, Crosby filled VAST's sound to the fullest. The self-titled, goth-influenced debut features an 18-piece orchestra, samples from the Bulgarian Female Choir and the Benedictine Monks of the Abbey of Saint-Mauer. Adding indie rock credibility, drummer James Lo of the group Chavez made a guest appearance. Released in April of 1998, *Visual Audio Sensory Theater* is an amalgamation of electronica, classical, world music, goth, and metal. Lyrically, it is dark and bleak with several spiritual and religious references. For example, in the song "I'm Dying," Crosby says, "Not a day goes by when I don't realize I'm dying." In an interview with *Rolling Stone*'s David Derby, he said, "I think a musician not singing about God or spirituality is like a married couple not having sex. Every band and musician that I've been into has sung about it so I don't know what makes me any different." The album piqued the attention of new fan Lars Ulrich, drummer for the heavy metal group Metallica. In VAST's official website biography, he called the record "one of the best debut albums I've heard in a long, long time. It hits you on so many levels. It's been a record I've been listening to over and over."

To promote the record, Crosby started touring with a collection of musicians: bassist Thomas Froggatt, drummer Steve Clark, and guitarist Rowan Robertson, who was later replaced by Justin Cotta. Although he comes across as serious in interviews and bleak in his lyrics, Crosby's live performances show his lighter side. He takes the time to joke around onstage to let the audience know that he is not as pretentious as he might come across. The single "Touched" hit *Bill-board*'s Modern Rock Tracks chart and was a modest success on alternative radio.

In late 1999 and early 2000, Crosby worked on the new record at various studios—Palindrome in Venice, California; Mat Hatter, Sunset Sound, the Hook North and Oceanway in Hollywood; and Western Outdoor in Mumbai, India—with Froggatt and Clark. While he co-produced just four songs on *Visual Audio Sensory Theater*, Crosby produced the new record himself. "I had a vision for the sound and feel of this record. I wanted to do something fresh, but without leaning on electronics," he said in VAST's official website biography. He dabbled with hammers, harpsichord, flute, trombone, and organ on the record.

Lyrically, *Music for the People* was much different than Crosby's debut. In his website biography, he described the album as more introspective but about other people. "It's about longing for freedom, escape—and people." Musically it was a departure as well. Whereas the group's first record was classically based, *Music for the People* was heavy on guitars and rock-inspired music, but Crosby's classical roots still came through. "Andrew Mackay, one of the biggest classical arrangers in England, had worked with the New Bombay Recording Orchestra and we felt that they would be a good choice for the album. So we traveled to Mumbai, India, to record their parts. It was an amazing learning experience," he said in his official website biography.

Released in September of 2000, *Music for the People* spawned the anthemic single "Free," a song that celebrates liberation. Crosby moves away from the heavy electronics that filled his previous work, but the tune "The Last One Alive" could have appeared on *Visual Audio Sensory Theater*, with the lyrics "You won't find me/'Cause I'll be on top of a mountain/ P*ssing on your grave." This record carries wide-ranging influences including U2, one of Crosby's early musical influences.

Crosby once again headed out on tour, this time in support of *Music for the People*. He and pop-rock outfit American Hi-Fi went out on an extensive tour of clubs. In 2001, Crosby took a break from touring to work on his third album. For Crosby, his musical journey has been an educational one. "I've learned a lot about myself. When you perform, you see what connects to the audience, but you also see what connects for yourself. It helps you to get a better sense of who you are," he said in his biography at the group's official website.

Selected discography

Visual Audio Sensory Theater, Elektra, 1998.
Music for the People, Elektra, 2000.

Sources

Periodicals

Billboard, January 23, 1999; October 7, 2000.

Online

MTV, http://www.mtv.com/bands/vast/260463/album.jthml (July 25, 2001).
MuchMusic, http://www.muchmusic.com/transcripts/vast00. htm (July 25, 2001).
Rolling Stone, http://www.rollingstone.com/artists/bio.asp ?oid-4585&cf=4584 (July 25, 2001).
"VAST," Excite Music, http://music.excite.com/artist/biogra phy/˜39167 (July 25, 2001).

Additional information was provided by Elektra Records publicity materials, 1998 and 2000.

—*Christina Fuoco*

George Walker

Composer, pianist

An accomplished and prolific classical music composer, George Walker has achieved many "firsts" in his career, mostly related to his race. He was the first African American to perform at New York City's Town Hall and with the Philadelphia Orchestra, the first African American instrumentalist to be signed by a major management company, the first African American graduate of the Curtis Institute of Music, and the first African American composer to receive the Pulitzer Prize in Music. "I believe that music is above race," Walker is quoted as saying in his American Classical Music Hall of Fame biography. "I am steeped in the universal tradition of my art. It is important to stress one's individuality beyond race, but I must do it as a black person who is aspiring to be a product of a civilized society."

Walker's published catalog exceeds 80 works and includes instrumental and vocal solos, chamber music, orchestral works, and choral music. Many of his compositions were commissioned by the New York Philharmonic, Cleveland Orchestra, Eastman School of Music, Fromm Foundation, Kennedy Center for the Performing Arts, National Endowment for the Arts, and the Boys Choir of Harlem. Nearly every major orchestra in the United States has performed his work, as well

Photograph by Mike Derer. AP/World Wide Photos. Reproduced by permission.

Born George Theophilus Walker on June 27, 1922, in Washington, D.C.; children: Gregory and Ian. *Education*: Bachelor of Music degree, Oberlin College, 1941; Artist Diploma, Curtis Institute, 1945; Artist Diploma, American Academy, Fontainbleau, France, 1947; Doctor of Musical Arts degree, Eastman School of Music, 1956.

Made debut at New York's Town Hall, 1945; signed with National Concert Artists management company, 1950; began career as composer, 1954; taught music at Smith College, 1961-68; chairman of Music Department at Rutgers University, 1969-92; premiere of *In Praise of Folly*, performed by New York Philharmonic and broadcast on the Public Broadcasting System (PBS), 1981; has published more than 80 works for orchestra, chamber orchestra, piano, strings, voice, organ, woodwinds, and chorus; has performed with orchestras and in solo recitals throughout the U.S. and Europe.

Awards: Pulitzer Prize in Music for *Lilacs*, 1996; Composers Award from Lancaster Symphony, 1998; Letter of Distinction from the American Music Center, 1998; Dorothy Maynor Outstanding Arts Citizen Award from the Harlem School of Arts, 2000; inducted into the American Classical Music Hall of Fame, 2000.

Member: American Society of Composers, Authors, and Publishers (ASCAP).

Addresses: *Record company*—Summit Records, P.O. Box 26850, Tempe, AZ 85285-6850.

1996, Curtis Institute of Music in 1996, and Montclair State University in 1996.

Raised with Classical Influences

Walker developed his interest in music from a young age. It helped that he was born into a musical family. He learned a strong sense of dedication to his goals from his father, George Walker, who taught himself to play the piano. The elder Walker was an immigrant from Jamaica who moved to the United States with $35 and a desire to become a physician. He put himself through medical school at Temple University. At the time, the American Medical Association (AMA) did not accept African American doctors as members, so the elder Walker formed his own medical associations to create dialogue and shared research among colleagues. Walker's mother, Rosa King Walker, played the piano and gave her son his first lessons when he was five years old. Walker's sister, Francis, eventually became the professor emerita for pianoforte at the Oberlin Conservatory of Music. "We had nothing but classical music growing up," Walker recalled to Mavis Clark in the *Oberlin Alumni Magazine* (*OAM*).

When Walker was just 14 years old, he played in his first public recital at Howard University's Andrew Rankin Memorial Chapel. Soon after, he graduated from Dunbar High School and received a four-year scholarship to Oberlin College. While at Oberlin, Walker studied piano with David Moyer and organ with Arthur Poister. In 1939, Walker became the organist for the Graduate School of Theology of Oberlin College. Two years later at the age of 18, he earned his Bachelor of Music degree with the highest honors.

From there, Walker attended the Curtis Institute of Music where he studied piano with Rudolph Serkin, composition with Rosario Scalero, and chamber music with William Primrose and Gregor Piatigorsky. In 1945, he received his Artist Diplomas in Piano and Composition and was the first African American graduate of the Curtis Institute. Later that year, Walker performed his debut recital at the Town Hall in New York City, the first African American instrumentalist to perform there. A *New York Times* reviewer, as quoted in Walker's American Classical Music Hall of Fame biography, described the composer as "an authentic talent of marked individuality and fine musical insight … a rare combination of elegance and sincerity, an understanding, a technical competence, and a sensitiveness rarely heard at debut recitals."

Just two weeks after his debut recital, Walker won the Philadelphia Youth Auditions. He performed with Eugene Ormandy and the Philadelphia Orchestra in a performance of the Rachmaninoff Third Piano Concerto. His performances as a pianist continued from there. He played Brahms' Second Piano Concerto with

as several orchestras in Europe. Over the years, his pieces have been recorded on several record labels, including Columbia, CRI, Desto, Mercury, Orion, Summit, and Albany Records.

Several fellowship programs recognized Walker's talent. He received a Fulbright, MacDowell Colony, two Guggenheim, and two Rockefeller Foundation Fellowships. He also earned several National Endowment for the Arts grants and two Koussevitzky Awards. Walker has been awarded a number of honorary doctorate degrees, including those from Lafayette College in 1982, Oberlin College in 1983, Bloomfield College in the Baltimore Symphony under the direction of Reginald Stewart. In 1946, Walker composed *Lyric for Strings*, which became one of his most well-known and frequently performed early works. He dedicated the piece to his grandmother.

In 1947, Walker earned an Artist's Diploma at the American Academy in Fontainbleau, France, where he had studied with Robert Casadesus. He continued to perform in solo recitals and with leading symphony orchestras and signed with the National Concert Artists management company in 1950. Four years later, he toured seven European countries, including Sweden, Denmark, Holland, Germany, Switzerland, Italy, and England.

Left Performing for Creating and Teaching

While on tour, Walker suffered several ulcer attacks which contributed to a change in his creative direction. "I became ill in the course of my first European tour … and I came back to the United States, realizing that I would be severely handicapped in attempting to pursue to appear when I wasn't physically at my best," Walker told Jim Lehrer on the Public Broadcasting System's (PBS) *NewsHour* television program. In addition to his health concerns, Walker's performances were not frequent enough to further his career. So, his father suggested that he consider supplementing his music career by teaching. "I never got the opportunities that would have allowed me to concertize like a white pianist," Walker told Ralph Blumenthal in the *New York Times*. "I never felt bitter. I strongly felt if I continued to press for what I hoped to achieve, I would achieve it."

Walker taught music at Dillard University for one year before enrolling at the Eastman School of Music where he studied with José Echániz. In 1956, he received an Artist Diploma in Piano and a Doctor of Musical Arts degree at the Eastman School of Music. He was the first African American student to receive that degree from the school. In another first, Walker was the first composer to receive the John Hay Whitney Fellowship in 1957. He also received a Fulbright Fellowship around the same time. He spent the next two years in Paris, France, where he studied with Nadia Boulanger. Then, he embarked on another, less extensive tour of Europe which included performances in France, Holland, and Italy. When he returned to the United States, Walker received a faculty appointment to the Dalcroze School of Music, The New School for Social Research, where he introduced a course in aesthetics. The following year, he joined the faculty at Smith College, where he taught until 1968. After leaving Smith College, Walker taught for a year at the University of Colorado as a visiting professor.

Although he had taken his father's advice about teaching, Walker continued to pursue his own musical career at the same time. In 1963, after a performance at Wigmore Hall in London, Walker received an honorary membership in London's Frederic Chopin Society. However, he had received few commissions and his works were not performed frequently. In 1968, Walker participated in a symposium in Atlanta, Georgia, on African American composers. "It was the first time that black composers had ever gotten together and the first time to hear our music performed well, to have discussions about common problems, and to simply meet each other," Walker told *Ebony*. The symposium inspired Walker even more, and he began to infuse his own work with references to African American music and the African American experience, particularly with old spirituals and folk songs.

The following year, Walker took the position of chairman of the Music Department at Rutgers University, which he held until his retirement in 1992. In addition to that position, he was on the faculty at the Peabody Institute of Johns Hopkins University from 1975-78 and was the recipient of the first Minority Chair established by the University of Delaware from 1975-76.

Recognized in Classical Style

In the 1980s, Walker began to receive more exposure and commissions in the classical music community. In 1981, *In Praise of Folly* was premiered by the New York Philharmonic. The performance was televised throughout the United States on PBS' *Great Performances* program. *Four Spirituals for Orchestra* (previously titled *Folksongs*) was premiered in May of 1992 by the Baltimore Symphony Orchestra under the direction of David Zinman. In April of the following year, the Detroit Symphony Orchestra premiered Walker's *Sinfonia No. 2* under the direction of Neeme Jaervi. The Serge Koussevitzky Music Foundation at the Library of Congress commissioned the piece.

In 1995, the Boston Symphony Orchestra commissioned Walker to compose a tribute to renowned African American tenor Roland Hayes. For the text, Walker used four stanzas of Walt Whitman's poem "When Lilacs Last in the Dooryard Bloom'd," which was a reflection on the assassination of President Abraham Lincoln. On February 1, 1996, the Boston Symphony premiered *Lilacs* under the direction of maestro Seiji Ozawa. Faye Robinson performed with the orchestra as the soprano soloist.

Two months later, Walker earned the Pulitzer Prize in Music for *Lilacs*. Walker's son Ian had submitted the piece to the Pulitzer Prize Committee for consideration. Walker was the first African American composer to receive the honor. "It's always nice to be known as the first doing anything," Walker told *USA Today*, as quoted in *Jet* magazine, "but what's more important is the recognition that this work has quality."

After receiving the Pulitzer Prize, Walker continued to receive more awards and recognition. In 1998, he earned the Composers Award from the Lancaster Symphony and the Letter of Distinction from the American Music Center. In May of 1999, he was inducted into membership in the Academy of Arts and Letters in New York City. The following year, he was inducted into the American Classical Music Hall of Fame and received the Dorothy Maynor Outstanding Arts Citizen Award for 2000 from the Harlem School of Arts.

Walker also continued to receive commissions for more compositions. In October of 1997, the New Jersey Symphony Orchestra premiered Walker's 1987 composition *Pageant and Proclamation*, which it had commissioned for its seventy-fifth anniversary in celebration of the orchestra's move into the New Jersey Performing Arts Center. The Columbus Pro Musica commissioned *Tangents for Chamber Orchestra*, which premiered in January of 2000. In the late 1990s and into 2000, Walker's work and performances were also released on several CDs, including *Recital, Portrait, Chamber Music,* and *Lilacs.*

Despite his occasional commissions and performances, Walker announced his retirement in the 1990s and enjoyed it from his home in Montclair, New Jersey. Though not fully recognized until later in his life, his extensive body of work and influence on American classical music reverberated into the twenty-first century.

Selected compositions

Lyric for Strings, 1946; revised, 1990.
Concerto for Trombone and Orchestra, 1957.
Address for Orchestra, 1959; revised, 1991.
Antifonys, 1968.
Variations for Orchestra, 1972.
Concerto for Piano and Orchestra, 1975.
Mass, 1977.
Dialogus, 1976; revised, 1996.
In Praise of Folly, 1981.
Cantata, 1982.
Cello Concerto, 1982.
An Eastman Overture, 1983.
Serenata, 1983.
Sinfonia No. 1, 1984.
Sinfonia No. 2, 1984; revised, 1996.

Pageant and Proclamation, 1987.
Four Spirituals for Orchestra, 1990.
Poeme, 1991.
Orpheus, 1994.
Lilacs, 1995.
Tangents for Chamber Orchestra, 1999.

Selected discography

Concerto for Trombone and Orchestra, BIS, 1957.
Antifonys, Albany, 1968.
Variations for Orchestra, Mastersound, 1972.
Cantata, Albany, 1982.
An Eastman Overture, Albany, 1983.
George Walker: Portrait, Albany, 1995.
George Walker: Chamber Music, Albany, 1996.
George Walker: Recital, Albany, 1996.
Walker: Serenata/Poeme/Orpheus/Folk Songs, Albany, 1998.
George Walker: Lilacs, Summit, 2000.

Sources

Periodicals

American Record Guide, July-August 1995; September-October 1997; November-December 1997.
Ebony, March 1985.
Jet, April 3, 1989; April 29, 1996.
New York Times, April 11, 1996.
Oberlin Alumni Magazine (OAM), Summer 1996.

Online

"ASCAP Composer George Walker Wins Pulitzer," ASCAP Playback, http://www.ascap.com/playback/1996/april/walker.html (June 16, 2001).
"Composer George Walker," NewsHour, http://www.newshour.com (June 16, 2001).
"George Walker," African American Art Song Alliance, http://www.uni.edu/taylord/walker.bio.html (June 16, 2001).
"George Walker," American Classical Music Hall of Fame, http://www.classicalhall.com (June 16, 2001).
"George Walker," http://www.geocities.com/Vienna/1617/ (June 16, 2001).
"George Walker Biography," MMB Music, http://www.mmbmusic.com (June 16, 2001).

—*Sonya Shelton*

The Warren Brothers

Country group

Photograph by Kim D. Johnson. AP/World Wide Photos. Reproduced by permission.

The Warren Brothers are siblings who turned their love for music into a viable career. In an interview on the Warren Brothers official website, Brad remembered, "We've been playing together in bands since I was in ninth grade and he [sibling Brett Warren] was in seventh, so there's never been a time when we weren't in bands together." The siblings' interest in music led to popular success and critical acclaim with the release of *Beautiful Day in the Cold Cruel World* in 1998 and *King of Nothing* in 2000.

Brad and Brett Warren started developing musically while still young, learning country guitar from their father and singing from their church-going mother. Brad picked up the guitar when he was eleven years old and practiced playing with Brett, then nine years old. Before they had turned 20, the brothers were working musicians playing the beach clubs in their hometown of Tampa, Florida. Brett elaborated in *AMZ* magazine, "For the past 11 years we've been nothing but full-time musicians, and [we] would play the Waffle House for chicken and eggs!" They would play not only for their supper but anywhere they could, continually developing their stage presence and repertoire. Brett continued, "We did three shows a day, 300 shows a year for a five-year period." During that stint the brothers honed an energetic, confident live act that would prove to be a key to their later success.

The brothers lived a life of all work, all play, while performing in Tampa beach clubs. Their daily schedule was likely the envy of friends; they played a different club every night, slept late, and then spent the waning hours of the day on the beach before beginning again, all while making good money. The Warren Brothers became the most popular act on the beach scene with their original material and covers of both country and rock standards. It seemed an ideal existence, but one that couldn't be maintained indefinitely, as Brett alluded to in an interview posted on CountryStars.com. "We looked at each other and said, 'We gotta get out of here. We could do this forever. We need to go to Nashville.'" Both brothers realized that the only way to truly develop as musicians and test their material was to move to the center of country music.

As part of their move to Nashville in 1995, the brothers took with them the advantages of proven songwriting skills, a strong work ethic, and natural charisma onstage. They also had the advantages of being physically attractive and having a radiant, scruffy, hipster coolness. Realizing that the intense competition in Nashville was preventing them from getting regular opportunities to perform, though, they strategically decided to settle in suburban Murfreesboro. The brothers then established themselves as the bar band at the Bunganut Pig. "We worked our butts off to get people to see us. We tried to be great every night," Brett told CountryStars.com. Their exciting live show earned them a rowdy, loyal, and appreciative audience.

One of the first to notice the Warren Brothers was prominent Nashville songwriter Tom Douglas. He not only collaborated with them but also gave a demo tape to RCA's Renee Bell. Bell drove out to Murfreesboro to hear the Warren Brother's live show and was amazed to see the packed crowd singing along to the brothers' original songs. Other Nashville notables soon followed. In *AMZ*, Brett related what Harlan Howard, the famous country songwriter, said after seeing them perform: "What I love about you guys is that you represent what country music used to be and needs to be again. Namely, people singing, dancing, drinking and good-looking girls everywhere!" Howard then paid them an even higher compliment—he offered to collaborate with the brothers and subsequently wrote songs with them.

The Warren Brothers were quickly signed by BNA Records, an RCA imprint. The duo had earned Nashville's respect just as they had planned. Nonetheless, the brothers were determined not to be absorbed into the Nashville machine but to make music on their own terms. Foregoing the traditional Nashville formula matching new acts with established songwriters and session musicians, the brothers insisted on recording their own original songs, playing their own instruments, and producing their recordings with a most un-Nashville rock rawness in their sound. The Warren Brothers' sound is unlike anything else in country music but is still undeniably country. In CountryStars.com, Brett elaborates, "If I had to describe it, I would say our music is rooted in the pure harmonies of the Everly Brothers, the storytelling magic of Johnny Cash and Roger Miller and the heartlands soul of John Mellencamp and Tom Petty." From this unusual blend comes a sound that is distinctly Warren Brothers but has definitive roots in the Nashville tradition.

As the brothers' star rose in Nashville, country superstars Tim McGraw and Faith Hill invited the duo on tour after the release of their debut recording, *Beautiful Day in the Cold Cruel World* in 1998. The brothers' live shows were incredibly well-received. Renee Revett of KXKC in New Iberia, Louisiana, as quoted in *Billboard*, said, "They came down to do a show at the Cajun Heartland State Fair, and I've never seen this happen—here's an act that does original music that did the opening thing and had a tremendous crowd that would not leave. They had to do encores. They were doing original music and kept the crowd spellbound."

The reviews of *Beautiful Day in the Cold Cruel World* were positive, hailing the band as a fresh, new voice in country music and predicting crossover potential. The Warren Brothers' sophomore release, *King of Nothing*, in 2000, showed the duo's more mature side. On the release, the brothers explore a lighthearted, philosophical take on life, love, and betrayal. A *Billboard* review noted the "guitar-based vignettes sometimes reminiscent of the country rock stylings of Don Henley and the Eagles. Throughout Brett's singing is soulful, Brad's playing is enthusiastic and appropriately loose and the siblings' harmonies are fresh and effective. The songs are thoughtful and incisive, with a straightforward lyrical approach." Again referring to the *King of Nothing*, Brad told *AMZ*, "I think this album is closer to how we are live, which is a raw, rockin' country band! And I think the rebellion we have against the system makes us more country like Johnny Cash and Waylon Jennings in the old days...."

If success can be defined as living the life that best suits an individual, the Warren Brothers have it made. They write songs about being open to life, have formed their own ideas about music and songwriting, and are still living with the joy and freedom of a beach club band.

Selected discography

Beautiful Day in the Cold Cruel World, BNA, 1998.
King of Nothing, BNA, 2000.

Sources

Periodicals

AMZ, February 1999.
Billboard, September, 26, 1998, p. 32; August, 5, 2000, p. 39.
Country Weekly, September 19, 2000, pg. 39-40.
Kansas City Star, January 24, 2001.
Music Crow, October 2000.
USA Today, September 26, 2000.

Online

"Warren Brothers," Countrystars.com, http://www.country
stars.com (July 15, 2001).

"Warren Brothers," GetMusic, http://www.getmusic.com (July
15, 2001).

Warren Brothers Official Website, http://www.warrenbro
thers.com (July 15, 2001).

—*Madeline Crowley*

Bill Wells

Composer, pianist, bassist

British musician Bill Wells leads one of the finest modern-day free jazz ensembles in Scotland and has collaborated with everyone from the Pastels to Lol Coxhill. Yet the Scottish jazz community, and even some members of Wells' former octet, tend to shun his work. This is because Wells, who resists playing by prescribed rules, does not merely imitate the traditional forms of his genre. Instead, he blurs his compositions—written in the spirit of 1960s-era soundtracks and film scores—with pop rhythms and elements of monolithic rock, embracing a sort of fusionist sound.

In spite of the reservations of many jazz purists, though, Wells does command a certain notoriety. In particular, the modern-day hipster crowd and underground music community in Glasgow, Scotland, have embraced Wells. His creations are "inspired, inspiring, wild, dangerous and tender. Just about everything you look for in music," wrote the Pastels' Stephen McRobbie for a story in *Scotland On Sunday.* "Of course," Wells asserted, who has also recorded with and arranged music for Belle and Sebastian, "I'm not actually sure if what I do counts as jazz. I think some people on the Scottish jazz scene might feel insulted if I'm included."

Some members of the music press also showed support. Stevie Chick in England's *Melody Maker* dubbed Wells the "British answer to Sun Ra," while others likened his talent to that of Pat Metheny and film scorer John Barry. These varied comparisons, however, illustrate why Wells has not gained a wider audience. Similarly to so many other non-mainstream artists,

Wells, in spite of his reputation as a superior writer and a creative musician, does not fit easily into any musical niche. Consequently, the industry—including some of his contemporaries—often sees him as an outsider.

Struggling to gain acceptance is nothing new to Wells, whose body of work only began to see the light of day during the 1990s, nearly 20 years after his first public performance. Unlike most contemporary jazz musicians, Wells never had the opportunity to study music in a formal setting. Instead, from his home in Falkirk, he learned how to compose and play on his own. Admittedly a painstaking journey, Wells began by reading about music and then studying the basics. But traditional fundamentals did not come easily to the aspiring musician. As a result, Wells would later insist that he never takes for granted that he can play or write music.

Throughout the course of his early studies, Wells drew inspiration from an array of unlikely sources, including the Beach Boys' *Surf's Up,* John Barry's theme from *Vendetta,* and Miles Davis' *Live-Evil.* "I don't know anyone who liked this kind of music when I first started," Wells stated in an interview with David Keenan for the *Wire.* "In the long run, though, it was probably a good thing. I really had to work things out for myself. I mean, I just could not understand music—the whole idea of keys made no sense to me—but through that I really developed a style that was fairly unique, simply because I wasn't relating to what anyone was doing around me."

Besides composing, Wells also wanted to learn how to play music. Determined to master an instrument, Wells, who learned both piano and bass, put his own compositions aside to hit the club circuit in Glasgow. At the time, he believed he needed to pay his dues before striking out on his own and joined a Shadows-influenced pub outfit called Contrast. Though frustrating career-wise, Wells admits that the process proved a learning experience. "I actually thought I should learn the ropes so that's why I did the club thing in the late '70s," Wells said, as quoted by Keenan. "We were just backing all this crap cabaret, but looking back on it now it was a pretty amazing experience. You were put in situations where you'd have to be a complete virtuoso. You'd get people come on stage and say, 'Right, I'm gonna do "MacArthur Park," but I'm gonna do Donna Summer's disco version.' And you only had guitar, bass and drums! Some of that stuff sounded absolutely amazing—completely by accident, of course."

After a while, Wells, gravitating more and more toward jazz, left the pub scene to pursue his own interests. Eventually, Wells completed some arrangements that he thought were both intriguing and promising. He naively thought that other players on the scene, like Bobby Wishart, would also find them interesting. Unfortunately, no one wanted to use Wells' compositions, and the hopeful writer soon realized that the only way

For the Record . . .

Born in Falkirk, Scotland.

Began playing in pubs in Glasgow, Scotland, 1970s; formed the Bill Wells Octet, 1990s; released debut album *Live 93-94* on his own Loathsome Reels label, 1996; released the trio album *Incorrect Practice,* 2000.

Addresses: *Record company*—Geographic Records.

to find an audience for his music was to put together his own band. Thus, Wells recruited players from the notoriously conservative Scottish jazz community to form early versions of the Bill Wells Octet. However, most of the musicians resisted Wells' avant-jazz leanings, while Wells, in turn, resisted the players' need to give his music a slick sound. The first few times the group ran through a piece, the unpolished, free feel was exactly what Wells had anticipated. "That was mainly because they were still getting to grips with it," recalled Wells to Keenan. "Once they got it right it just didn't sound so good."

In addition, Wells' preferred composing method also worried the members of his group. According to Wells, most of his music comes to him in his dreams, which he precisely transcribes when he wakes the next morning. During one fruitful period, according to Wells, music was coming to him at night three to four times a week. "There was a Beach Boys one, where I was in this bus and we were going to a Beach Boys convention, and there were all kind of Californian types with fair hair, and we stopped the bus to pick up some folk, and the whole of the bus just broke out into this amazing vocal coda. Just these awesome harmonies. That was a difficult one to transcribe," recalled Wells. "Then there was the one where I was chasing a cat along a piano. It had these weirdly elongated legs, really cartoony looking. As it ran off, it played this melody on the piano. The next day I presented it to the Octet as 'The Elongated Cat Theme,' and I drew a picture of the cat and asked them to solo on it. Two of them walked out, on the grounds that I was completely off my head."

Amid the comings and goings of personnel, Wells managed to compile a CD of live tracks. Released in 1996 on his own Loathsome Reels label, *Live 93-94* turned Wells into a local celebrity. Although many members of the Octet dismissed the set as too lo-fi, others in Glasgow's music community applauded his efforts. McRobbie—at the time just getting into the Impulse label's reissue series of recordings from the 1960s—was especially impressed by Wells' spirit. Finally, it appeared that Wells had found a place where his lack of conformity and non-traditional practices were actually celebrated rather than condemned.

Aside from promoting Wells, McRobbie also invited the musician to participate on the recording of the Pastels' 1997 album *Illumination.* In 1998, he joined Sushi K. Dade's outfit Future Pilot AKA, alongside Richard Youngs and the Pastels' Katrina Mitchell, for the well-received *The Bill Wells Octet Vs. Future Pilot AKA.* Since then, Wells has remained the contributing musician of choice for underground and indie groups in Glasgow. "I had been involved in this awful jazz scene for so long," Wells explained to Keenan. "It was like taking a step back and suddenly seeing the whole picture. I immediately felt more comfortable. These musicians just seemed to cut straight to the heart of whether something was good or not without bothering about any of the superficial aspects like flashy technique or whatever."

In 2000, Wells released a trio set entitled *Incorrect Practice,* recorded with Stevie Jackson of Belle and Sebastian on guitar and harmonica, Octet associate Robert Henderson on trumpet, and Wells on piano and sampler. *Incorrect Practice,* featuring the tracks "Four Cows" and "Bad Plumbing," continued to build upon Wells' reputation. Free and dreamily atmospheric, the recording, concluded Playlouder reviewer Alix Buscovic, leaves the listener "constantly discovering there's more depth than was first apparent."

Selected discography

(With The Bill Wells Octet) *Live 93-94,* Loathsome Reels, 1996.
(With Future Pilot AKA) *The Bill Wells Octet Vs. Future Pilot AKA,* Domino, 1998.
(With The Bill Wells Trio) *Incorrect Practice,* Geographic, 2000.

Sources

Periodicals

Melody Maker, November 28, 1998; December 12, 1998.
Scotland On Sunday, June 23, 1996.
Wire, December 2000.

Online

Playlouder, http://www.playlouder.com (February 15, 2001).
RTÉ ACE: Arts Culture and Entertainment, http://rte.ie/ace (February 15, 2001).

—Laura Hightower

Iannis Xenakis

Composer

AP/World Wide Photos. Reproduced by permission.

From a privileged, yet unsettled childhood to an early career derailed by war, Iannis Xenakis first came to prominence as an architectural draftsman before devoting himself fully to his work as a composer. Combining mathematical probability theory with composition, Xenakis became the originator of stochastic music, in which large-scale compositions were built from discrete individual units linked in precise mathematical sequences. Although few could claim to understand his complex, mathematically derived music theories, the avant-garde composer's prodigious output, technological innovation, and acclaim in the world of modern classical music gave him fame that few other contemporary composers could match. Upon hearing of his death on February 4, 2001, presidents and prime ministers from around the world paid tribute to Xenakis.

Xenakis was born on May 29, 1922, in Braila, a city in southwestern Romania near the Black Sea and the border with the Ukraine. An important shipping point on the Danube River, Braila's elite commercial class was dominated by Greek immigrants and their descendants who controlled much of the shipping trade along the river. Growing up in the Greek community in Braila, Xenakis was the son of privilege, although he would later claim that his status as an outsider would always remain central to his identity. Xenakis' mother died when he was five years old, and he was sent off to a boarding school on the island of Spetsai in Greece to complete his secondary education at the age of ten. Xenakis continued his education at the Athens Polytechnic Institute, aiming for a career as an engineer. Shortly after he was admitted to the school, however, history intervened.

With the invasion of Greece by Italy in 1940 and its subsequent occupation by Nazi Germany to secure the region for the Axis powers, Xenakis' education took a back seat to the immediate demands of the war. The young engineer joined the Greek Resistance and fought against the occupiers for four years in conjunction with British forces. In the last year of the war, however, Xenakis suffered a near-fatal injury that cost him the sight in one of his eyes. Left for dead by his compatriots, Xenakis nevertheless recovered and survived the war, which formally ended in 1945. As in many other war-torn countries, however, a civil war soon broke out in Greece, one which dragged on for another four years. As Communist Party supporters battled the ruling Greek monarchy, Xenakis was captured and sentenced to death by the government. After the death sentence was handed down, the former Resistance fighter fled the country and in 1947 made his way to Paris. Although Greece returned to a semblance of stability with the suppression of the Communists in 1949 and the adoption of a new constitution in 1951, Xenakis' death sentence was not officially revoked by the Greek government until 1974.

Worked with Le Corbusier

Xenakis turned his attention to studying musical composition after his arrival in Paris and soon met some of the most famous composers of the day, including Olivier Messiaen (1908-1992) and Darius Milhaud (1892-1974). It was Messiaen who advised Xenakis to abandon his formal training in composition in favor of continuing on with his own musical experiments. It was several years, however, before Xenakis premiered his first composition, *Metastasis for Orchestra*. Completed in 1954 and debuted at the Donaueschingen Festival in 1955, the work was a dramatically new offering in the world of modern classical music. Based on a musical adaptation of the mathematical theory of probability, which the composer labeled "stochastic principles," Xenakis took small musical units and structured them into a compositional whole using mathematical sequences. As he explained in his book *Formalized Music: Thought and Mathematics in Composition*, "All sound is an integration of grains, of elementary sonic particles, of sonic quanta. Each of these elementary grains has a threefold nature: duration, frequency, and intensity. All sound, even all continuous sonic variation, is conceived as an assemblage of the large number of elementary grains adequately disposed in time."

In terms of theory and the resulting composition, Xenakis' work as a stochastic composer was truly avant-garde. At a time when composers were more interested in breaking down each portion of the composition into discrete elements, *Metastasis* offered music on a much grander scale. Characteristic of his early works, the piece was a demanding one for musicians with its complex rhythms and explosions of sound. *Metastasis* was followed by other orchestral pieces, including *Pithoprakta* for string orchestra in 1956, *Achorripsis* in 1957, and *Syrmos* in 1959. During the 1950s, however, Xenakis' international acclaim came not from his compositions, but from his work as an engineer and draftsman for the famed Swiss-born architect Charles Edouard Jeanneret (1887-1965), better known by his pseudonym, Le Corbusier.

As Le Corbusier's assistant, Xenakis worked on several influential projects that helped define modern architecture in the postwar world, including housing developments in France and government buildings in India. His most famous work with Le Corbusier, however, was the Philips Pavilion at the 1958 World's Fair in Brussels, Belgium. Designed as a set of parabolas, the building's dramatic set of curved shapes symbolized undulating waves of sound, a fitting structure for the pavilion's sponsor, a leading recording and electronics company. As striking as the building's exterior were the presentations inside. In addition to multimedia works, Xenakis' *Concerto PH,* which used the amplified sounds of burning charcoal, surprised and delighted visitors. Representing the intersection of cutting-edge architecture, music, and technology, the Philips Pavilion was one of the modernist highlights of the late 1950s.

Electronic Music Compositions

By 1960, Xenakis had gained sufficient acclaim to abandon his engineering work and pursue composing full-time. Increasingly, he turned to composing music performed by electronic instruments, starting with the 1958 work *Diamorphosis*. Xenakis also composed pioneering works with computer programs that generated pieces based on mathematical programs. In 1966, a year after becoming a French citizen, Xenakis founded a research institution in Paris to encourage the further study of mathematics and music. The composer also taught at the Indiana University School of Music, one of the leading music programs in the world, from 1967 to 1972. The university published his work *Formalized Music: Thought and Mathematics in Composition* in 1971, a sign of Xenakis' high standing among music theorists.

Xenakis achieved another breakthrough with his development of a graphic computer interface (UPIC) that allowed users to draw shapes and have them interpreted into musical forms by a computer. In his own work, however, Xenakis gradually veered away from electronic composing. "The stochastic way of composing is something that is innate now," he told the *Village Voice* in 1996, "I don't need to use the computers anymore." As he further explained to Morton Feldman in an interview at the 1986 Festival Nieuwe Muziek in the Netherlands at the ZeelandNet website, "Whenever I listen to music, I don't want to consider any ideology whatsoever beforehand. I just want to listen and understand what happens…. When you write music, you should have the same naive approach to music as the listener often has." In the place of mathematically generated music, Xenakis derived inspiration from this approach and incorporated traditional Greek dramas and myths to deliver more emotional and expressive works, including *Oresteia* in 1966 and *Medea* in 1967.

Resurgence in Interest

Xenakis had not completely abandoned his theoretical pursuits, however. In 1985, he founded the Center for the Composition of Music Iannis Xenakis (CCMIX) with the support of the French Ministry of Culture. Housed near Paris, where Xenakis made his home with his wife, Francoise, and their daughter, the Center devoted itself to encouraging innovative compositions and performances in addition to disseminating information on Xenakis' UPIC system. During the following decade, Xenakis enjoyed a resurgence of interest in his compositions, with a growing number of music festivals performing his challenging works. During the 1990s, Xenakis received several distinguished music prizes, capping off his career with the 1999 Polar Music Prize, which endowed the composer with a cash award of $125,000.

In failing health for several years, Xenakis died in Paris on February 4, 2001. Tributes poured in, with French President Jacques Chirac lamenting, "France loses one of its most brilliant artists today," according to the *Los Angeles Times.* For his part, Xenakis was convinced that his musical innovations would long outlive him. "Sometimes I think composers talk too much. There is only music, that's it!" he exclaimed to Feldman, adding, "Music is used as acoustical energy. The problem of composition is how to use that energy." While the theories he expounded during his career were complex, the simplicity of his argument embodied the essence of his innovation in modern classical music.

Selected discography

As composer

Medea, Erato, 1969.
Mycenae-Alpha, Nonesuch, 1990.
Pleiades/Ishii: Concertante Op. 79, Denon, 1990.
Jonchaies, Col Legno, 1991.
Thallein, Neuma, 1995.
La Legende d'Eer, Montaigne, 1995.
Kraanerg, Asphodel, 1997.
Psappha/Okho/Persephassa, Stradivarius, 1998.
Media/Nuits/Knephas, Hyperion, 1998.
Works for Piano 4, Mode, 1999.
Electronic Music, Electronic, 2000.
Pleiades, Harmonia Mundi, 2000.
Ensemble Music, Vol. 1, Mode, 2000.
Ensemble Music, Vol. 2, Mode, 2000.
Ensemble Music, Vol. 3, Mode, 2000.
Chamber Music: 1955-1990, Montaigne, 2000.
Palimpset/Epei/Dikhthas/Akanthos, Wergo, 2000.

Sources

Books

Richardson, Dan, and Tim Burford, *Romania: The Rough Guide,* The Rough Guides Ltd., 1995.
Xenakis, Iannis, *Formalized Music: Thought and Mathematics in Composition,* Indiana University Press, 1971.

Periodicals

American Record Guide, March/April 1995, p. 31; September/October 1998, p. 254.
Billboard, March 6, 1999, p. 50.
Canadian Press, February 4, 2001.
Los Angeles Times, February 5, 2001.
The Times, February 5, 2001.
Village Voice, November 12, 1996, p. 50.

Online

Canadian Broadcasting Corporation Infoculture, http://www.infoculture.cbc.ca/archives/musop/musop_02231999_polar.html (July 2, 2001).
Center for Composition of Music—Iannis Xenakis, http://www.ccmix.com (July 2, 2001).
Leonardo Online, International Society for the Arts, Sciences and Technology, http://www-mitpress.mit.edu/e-journals/Leonardo/isast/spec.projects/Xenakisbibhtml (July 2, 2001).

—*Timothy Borden*

Hans Zimmer

Composer

Corbis Corporation. Reproduced by permission.

The film scores of composer Hans Zimmer are as varied as the films they provide music for. One score may cause the viewer to laugh harder, another may make the heart pound faster, and yet another might make a moviegoer cry harder. "I'm this loose cannon—all over the place," Zimmer told Edwin Black in Film Score Monthly online. "I can do action movies and romantic comedies…. The bottom line is I'm trying to serve the film just like the director is trying to serve the film." After nearly 20 years as a composer, Zimmer has provided musical scores for more than 80 films.

Hans Florian Zimmer was born on September 12, 1957, in Frankfurt, Germany. His interest in music began at a very early age. He began playing piano at the age of three, but his interest in lessons waned after just two weeks. When he was six years old, he decided that he wanted to become a composer. "My dad died when I was six," Zimmer told CNN Worldbeat. "That's when I decided I was going to become really serious about music, because it was my refuge. It was my way of calming the demons in me or at the same time sometimes letting them roar, letting them rip, letting the monster out and seeing that it wasn't so scary being able to look it in the eye."

When Zimmer was 14 years old, he moved to England. Throughout his childhood, he was expelled from several different schools because he preferred to study music instead of his schoolwork. When he finally finished school, he began his music career by writing jingles for commercials and playing in rock bands. In 1979, Zimmer, along with Trevor Horn and Geoff Downes, put together a band called the Buggles. The group recorded the album *The Age of Plastic*, which included the hit song "Video Killed the Radio Star." The video for the single became the first ever to be shown on MTV.

Despite the group's success, Zimmer did not enjoy the recording process with the Buggles, and he was not happy having to write only one style of music. "I used to be in a band, but that got to be boring," Zimmer later recalled to David Kohner Zuckerman in *Brtnwd* magazine. "Now I have bigger bands for shorter periods of time."

After leaving the Buggles, Zimmer went to work for composer Stanley Myers, who began to teach him more about scoring films. "Stanley took me in," Zimmer told Cinemusic online. "From the first day that I was his assistant, he just let me write things…. I thought it was great that there was that system in place whereby someone who really knew a lot would give you room and support, and bring you up and give you a chance." Zimmer and Myers set up the Lillie Yard Studio in London. They collaborated on several film scores, including *Moonlighting, The Lightship, The Castaway,* and *My Beautiful Launderette.*

In 1986, Zimmer worked by himself on the score for *Vardo*. The following year, he teamed with David Byrne and Ryuichi Sakamoto to produce the soundtrack for *The Last Emperor*. By the mid 1980s, his career as a film composer was well on its way, but it was in 1988 that it truly took off. Zimmer had composed the score for a small budget film called *A World Apart*, which was about South Africa. The wife of producer Barry Levinson played the soundtrack for her husband about the time that he was getting ready to hire someone to score *Rain Man*. Levinson was so impressed with Zimmer's work that he hired him to score his film as well. Zimmer won an Academy Award nomination for his work on *Rain Man*. He moved to Los Angeles following the success of the film.

In 1989 Zimmer won a Grammy Award nomination for his work on *Driving Miss Daisy*. He also received industry and audience recognition for the score for *Thelma & Louise* in 1991. In 1994, Zimmer produced his most successful score up to that point when he worked on *The Lion King*. The soundtrack became the most successful in the history of Walt Disney Records with 12 million copies sold worldwide. The following year, Zimmer won a Golden Globe for Best Original Score, a Chicago Film Critics Award for Best Score, an American Music Award for Best Album of the Year, two Grammy Awards, an Academy Award, and a Tony Award nomination for Best Original Score for *The Lion King on Broadway*.

Zimmer saw his success with *The Lion King* as a fork in the road of his career. "*Lion King* made me reassess my situation in this town," Zimmer told Black. "You can go two ways. I admit that standing on the stage and getting an Oscar [Academy Award] is the most seductive moment one can have in one's life. It is truly overwhelming. Then you go, 'Wow, if I just carry on writing nice music like this, I can have this moment again….' That's why I did the exact opposite, scoring for truly offensive projects like *The Fan*. Just to shake myself out of the desire for that Oscar experience. Otherwise, I would just stagnate."

Although he chose to take the path less glittered, Zimmer did continue to receive recognition for his work. In 1996, he won a Grammy Award for his score for *Crimson Tide*, and he received another Academy Award nomination for *The Preacher's Wife*. That same year, the performing rights organization BMI presented him with its prestigious Lifetime Achievement Award before Zimmer was even 40 years old. He received another Academy Award nomination in 1998 for the score to *As Good As It Gets*.

In the late 1990s, Zimmer accepted a position as head of the music division with the DreamWorks SKG studio. While there, he supervised the music for all of their film and television projects and wrote the score for the animated feature *The Prince of Egypt*, which earned him both a Golden Globe nomination and an Academy Award nomination. He also wrote the score for *The Road to El Dorado*, another DreamWorks animated feature. In 2000, Zimmer worked with DreamWorks and director Ridley Scott on the hit film *Gladiator*. He also wrote the score for *Mission: Impossible 2*, released that same year. On October 10, 2000, Zimmer performed a rare live concert with the Flemish Radio Orchestra in Ghent, Belgium, to celebrate the opening of the 27th Flanders International Film Festival. The following year, his scores appeared on two more hit movies, *Hannibal* and *Pearl Harbor*.

In addition to his work as a composer, Zimmer formed a business with his partner Jay Rifkin called Media Ventures in 1989. The company serves as a conglomerate of composers who can produce and record nearly anything related to media music. The business also gives Zimmer a way to help talented new composers in the same way that Myers helped him when he was just starting out. In the end, though, Zimmer's heart is firmly planted in film scoring. "If something happened where I couldn't write music anymore, it would kill me," he told CNN Worldbeat. "It's not just a job, it's not just a hobby; it's why I get up in the morning."

Over the years, Zimmer has earned a reputation for maximizing the use of electronics and technological inventions in his music. As such, he has been able to produce sounds and textures that had not previously been heard in film music. Despite all of the recognition he has received for his work, Zimmer remains one of his own harshest critics. Of all the scores he has written, he has been proud of very few. Those that make his list of personal favorites include *A World Apart, Driving Miss Daisy, Drop Zone, True Romance, The Fan, Crimson Tide, Prince of Egypt*, and *Two Deaths*, a small film he did for the British Broadcasting Corporation (BBC) in the United Kingdom.

Selected discography

As film scorer

Rain Man, Capitol, 1989.
Thelma & Louise, MCA, 1991.
A League of Their Own, Columbia, 1992.
K2—Music Inspired by the Film, Varese, 1992.
True Romance, Morgan Creek, 1993.
Cool Runnings, Sony, 1993.
The Fan, TVT Records, 1996.
The Preacher's Wife, BMG/Arista, 1996.
As Good As it Gets, Sony, 1998.
Prince of Egypt, UNI/DreamWorks, 1998.
Millennium: Tribal Wisdom, Narada, 1999.
Thin Red Line, RCA Victor, 1999.
Gladiator—Music from the Motion Picture, Decca, 2000.
Mission: Impossible 2, Hollywood Records, 2000.

The Wings of a Film, Decca, 2001.
Hannibal, Decca, 2001.
Pearl Harbor, Warner Bros., 2001.

Sources

Periodicals

Brntwd (Santa Monica, CA), May-June 2000.
Entertainment Weekly, June 24, 1994.

Online

"Fearless Visionary: Hans Zimmer," Cinemusic, http://www.cinemusic.com (June 23, 2001).
"Hans Zimmer," Film Score Monthly, http://www. filmscore-monthly.com (June 23, 2001).
"Hans Zimmer," Ilio, http://www.ilio.com/artists/zimmer (June 23, 2001).
"Hans Zimmer," Ovation: The Arts Network, http://www.ovationtv.com/rhythm/hzimmer (June 23, 2001).
"Hans Zimmer (Composer)," Sony Pictures Classics, http://www.spe.sony.com (June 23, 2001).
"Hans Zimmer: The Man Behind *The Lion King* Soundtrack and More," CNN Worldbeat, http://cnn.com.tr/2000/ (June 23, 2001).
"Hans Zimmer: They Shoot, He Scores," American Society of Composer, Authors, and Publishers (ASCAP), http://www.ascap.com/playback (June 23, 2001).
"Pearl Harbor," Cinemusic, http://www.cinemusic.com (June 23, 2001).
"Walt Disney Records: Biography of Hans Zimmer," Walt Disney Records, http://disney.go.com/disneyrecords (June 23, 2001).

—Sonya Shelton

Cumulative Subject Index

Volume numbers appear in **bold**

A cappella
Brightman, Sarah **20**
Bulgarian State Female Vocal Choir, The **10**
Golden Gate Quartet **25**
Nylons, The **6**
Rockapella **34**
Sweet Honey In The Rock **26**
  Earlier sketch in CM **1**
Take 6 **6**
Zap Mama **14**

Accordion
Buckwheat Zydeco **34**
  Earlier sketch in CM **6**
Chenier, C. J. **15**
Chenier, Clifton **6**
Queen Ida **9**
Richard, Zachary **9**
Rockin' Dopsie **10**
Simien, Terrance **12**
Sonnier, Jo-El **10**
Yankovic, "Weird Al" **7**

Ambient/Rave/Techno
Aphex Twin **14**
Basement Jaxx **29**
Chemical Brothers **20**
Clark, Anne **32**
Deep Forest **18**
808 State **31**
Front Line Assembly **20**
Gus Gus **26**
Holmes, David **31**
KMFDM **18**
Kraftwerk **9**
Lords of Acid **20**
Man or Astroman? **21**
Mouse On Mars **32**
Neu! **32**
Oakenfold, Paul **32**
Orb, The **18**
Propellerheads **26**
Shadow, DJ **19**
Sheep on Drugs **27**
Tobin, Amon **32**
2 Unlimited **18**
Underworld **26**
Van Helden, Armand **32**

Bandoneon
Piazzolla, Astor **18**
Saluzzi, Dino **23**

Banjo
Boggs, Dock **25**
Bromberg, David **18**
Clark, Roy **1**
Crowe, J.D. **5**
Fleck, Bela **8**
  Also see New Grass Revival, The
Hartford, John **1**
McCoury, Del **15**
Piazzolla, Astor **18**
Scruggs, Earl **3**

Seeger, Pete **4**
  Also see Weavers, The
Skaggs, Ricky **5**
Stanley, Ralph **5**
Watson, Doc **2**

Bass
Brown, Ray **21**
Carter, Ron **14**
Chambers, Paul **18**
Clarke, Stanley **3**
Collins, Bootsy **8**
Dixon, Willie **10**
Fell, Simon H. **32**
Fender, Leo **10**
Haden, Charlie **12**
Hinton, Milt **33**
Holland, Dave **27**
Kaye, Carol **22**
Kowald, Peter **32**
Laswell, Bill **14**
López, Israel "Cachao" **34**
  Earlier sketch in CM **14**
Love, Laura **20**
Mann, Aimee **22**
McBride, Christian **17**
McCartney, Paul **32**
  Earlier sketch in CM **4**
  Also see Beatles, The
Mingus, Charles **9**
Ndegéocello, Me'Shell **18**
Parker, William **31**
Sting **19**
  Earlier sketch in CM **2**
Sweet, Matthew **9**
Was, Don **21**
  Also see Was (Not Was)
Watt, Mike **22**
Wells, Bill **34**
Whitaker, Rodney **20**

Big Band/Swing
Andrews Sisters, The **9**
Arnaz, Desi **8**
Asleep at the Wheel **29**
  Earlier sketch in CM **5**
Atomic Fireballs, The **27**
Bailey, Pearl **5**
Basie, Count **2**
Beiderbecke, Bix **16**
Bennett, Tony **16**
  Earlier sketch in CM **2**
Berrigan, Bunny **2**
Blakey, Art **11**
Brown, Lawrence **23**
Calloway, Cab **6**
Carter, Benny **3**
Chenille Sisters, The **16**
Cherry Poppin' Daddies **24**
Clooney, Rosemary **9**
Como, Perry **14**
Cornell, Don **30**
Cugat, Xavier **23**
DeFranco, Buddy **31**
Dorsey Brothers, The **8**

Eckstine, Billy **1**
Eldridge, Roy **9**
Ellington, Duke **2**
Ferguson, Maynard **7**
Fitzgerald, Ella **1**
Fountain, Pete **7**
Getz, Stan **12**
Gillespie, Dizzy **6**
Goodman, Benny **4**
Henderson, Fletcher **16**
Herman, Woody **12**
Hines, Earl "Fatha" **12**
Jacquet, Illinois **17**
James, Harry **11**
Jones, Spike **5**
Jordan, Louis **11**
Krupa, Gene **13**
Lavay Smith and Her Red Hot
  Skillet Lickers **32**
Lee, Peggy **8**
Madness **27**
McGuire Sisters, The **27**
McKinney's Cotton Pickers **16**
Miller, Glenn **6**
Norvo, Red **12**
O'Farrill, Chico **31**
Parker, Charlie **5**
Prima, Louis **18**
Puente, Tito **14**
Ray Condo and His Ricochets **26**
Rich, Buddy **13**
Rodney, Red **14**
Roomful of Blues **7**
Royal Crown Revue **33**
Scott, Jimmy **14**
Setzer, Brian **32**
Severinsen, Doc **1**
Shaw, Artie **8**
Sinatra, Frank **23**
  Earlier sketch in CM **1**
Squirrel Nut Zippers **20**
Stafford, Jo **24**
Strayhorn, Billy **13**
Teagarden, Jack **10**
Torme, Mel **4**
Vaughan, Sarah **2**
Welk, Lawrence **13**
Whiteman, Paul **17**

Bluegrass
Auldridge, Mike **4**
Bluegrass Patriots **22**
Clements, Vassar **18**
Country Gentlemen, The **7**
Crowe, J.D. **5**
Flatt, Lester **3**
Fleck, Bela **8**
  Also see New Grass Revival, The
Gill, Vince **34**
  Earlier sketch in CM **7**
Grisman, David **17**
Hartford, John **1**
Krauss, Alison **10**
Louvin Brothers, The **12**

Martin, Jimmy **5**
  Also see Osborne Brothers, The
McCoury, Del **15**
McReynolds, Jim and Jesse **12**
Monroe, Bill **1**
Nashville Bluegrass Band **14**
New Grass Revival, The **4**
Northern Lights **19**
O'Connor, Mark **1**
Osborne Brothers, The **8**
Parsons, Gram **7**
  Also see Byrds, The
Reverend Horton Heat **19**
Scruggs, Earl **3**
Seldom Scene, The **4**
Skaggs, Ricky **5**
Stanley Brothers, The **17**
Stanley, Ralph **5**
Stuart, Marty **9**
Watson, Doc **2**
Welch, Gillian **33**
Wiseman, Mac **19**

Blues

Allison, Luther **21**
Ayler, Albert **19**
Bailey, Pearl **5**
Baker, Ginger **16**
  Also see Cream
Ball, Marcia **15**
Barnes, Roosevelt "Booba" **23**
Benoit, Tab **31**
Berry, Chuck **33**
  Earlier sketch in CM **1**
Bill Wyman & the Rhythm Kings **26**
Bland, Bobby "Blue" **12**
Block, Rory **18**
Blood, Sweat and Tears **7**
Blues Brothers, The **3**
Boggs, Dock **25**
Broonzy, Big Bill **13**
Brown, Clarence "Gatemouth" **11**
Brown, Ruth **13**
Burdon, Eric **14**
  Also see War
  Also see Animals
Burnside, R. L **34**
Cale, J. J. **16**
Charles, Ray **24**
  Earlier sketch in CM **1**
Clapton, Eric **11**
  Earlier sketch in CM **1**
  Also see Cream
  Also see Yardbirds, The
Collins, Albert **4**
Cray, Robert **8**
Davis, Reverend Gary **18**
Diddley, Bo **3**
Dixon, Willie **10**
Dr. John **7**
Dupree, Champion Jack **12**
Earl, Ronnie **5**
  Also see Roomful of Blues
Estes, John **25**
Everlast **27**
Fabulous Thunderbirds, The **1**
Fuller, Blind Boy **20**
Fulson, Lowell **20**
Gatton, Danny **16**
Guy, Buddy **4**
Handy, W. C. **7**
Hart, Alvin Youngblood **27**
Hart, Beth **29**
Hawkins, Screamin' Jay **29**
  Earlier sketch in CM **8**
Healey, Jeff **4**
Holiday, Billie **6**

Hooker, John Lee **26**
  Earlier sketch in CM **1**
Hopkins, Lightnin' **13**
House, Son **11**
Howlin' Wolf **6**
Indigenous **31**
James, Elmore **8**
James, Etta **6**
Jefferson, Blind Lemon **18**
Johnson, Blind Willie **26**
Johnson, Lonnie **17**
Johnson, Robert **6**
Jon Spencer Blues Explosion **18**
Joplin, Janis **3**
King, Albert **2**
King, B. B. **24**
  Earlier sketch in CM **1**
King, Freddy **17**
Lang, Jonny **27**
Lavay Smith and Her Red Hot
  Skillet Lickers **32**
Leadbelly **6**
Led Zeppelin **1**
Lewis, Furry **26**
Little Feat **4**
Little Walter **14**
Lockwood, Robert, Jr. **10**
Mayall, John **7**
McClennan, Tommy **25**
McClinton, Delbert **14**
McDowell, Mississippi Fred **16**
McLean, Dave **24**
McTell, Blind Willie **17**
Memphis Jug Band **25**
Memphis Minnie **25**
Montgomery, Little Brother **26**
Muldaur, Maria **18**
Owens, Jack **30**
Patton, Charley **11**
Plant, Robert **2**
  Also see Led Zeppelin
Professor Longhair **6**
Raitt, Bonnie **23**
  Earlier sketch in CM **3**
Redding, Otis **5**
Reed, Jimmy **15**
Rich, Charlie **3**
Robertson, Robbie **2**
Robillard, Duke **2**
Roomful of Blues **7**
Rush, Otis **12**
Sanborn, David **28**
  Earlier sketch in CM **1**
Santamaria, Mongo **28**
Shaffer, Paul **13**
Shines, Johnny **14**
Smith, Bessie **3**
Snow, Phoebe **4**
Spann, Otis **18**
Sunnyland Slim **16**
Sykes, Roosevelt **20**
Taj Mahal **6**
Tampa Red **25**
Taylor, Koko **10**
Thornton, Big Mama **18**
Toure, Ali Farka **18**
Turner, Big Joe **13**
Ulmer, James Blood **13**
Van Zandt, Townes **13**
Vaughan, Jimmie **24**
Vaughan, Stevie Ray **1**
Waits, Tom **27**
  Earlier sketch in CM **12**
  Earlier sketch in CM **1**
Walker, Joe Louis **28**
Walker, T-Bone **5**
Wallace, Sippie **6**

Washington, Dinah **5**
Waters, Ethel **11**
Waters, Muddy **24**
  Earlier sketch in CM **4**
Wells, Junior **17**
Weston, Randy **15**
Whitfield, Mark **18**
Whitley, Chris **16**
Whittaker, Hudson **20**
Williams, Joe **11**
Williamson, Sonny Boy **9**
Wilson, Gerald **19**
Winter, Johnny **5**
Witherspoon, Jimmy **19**
ZZ Top **2**

Cajun/Zydeco

Ball, Marcia **15**
Brown, Clarence "Gatemouth" **11**
Buckwheat Zydeco **34**
  Earlier sketch in CM **6**
Chenier, C. J. **15**
Chenier, Clifton **6**
Doucet, Michael **8**
Landreth, Sonny **16**
Queen Ida **9**
Richard, Zachary **9**
Rockin' Dopsie **10**
Simien, Terrance **12**
Sonnier, Jo-El **10**
Sturr, Jimmy **33**

Cello

Casals, Pablo **9**
Chang, Han-Na **33**
Darling, David **34**
DuPré, Jacqueline **26**
Harrell, Lynn **3**
Holland, Dave **27**
Ma, Yo Yo **24**
  Earlier sketch in CM **2**
Rasputina **26**
Rostropovich, Mstislav **17**
Starker, Janos **32**

Children's Music

Bartels, Joanie **13**
Cappelli, Frank **14**
Chapin, Tom **11**
Chenille Sisters, The **16**
Harley, Bill **7**
Lehrer, Tom **7**
Nagler, Eric **8**
Penner, Fred **10**
Raffi **8**
Riders in the Sky **33**
Rosenshontz **9**
Sharon, Lois & Bram **6**

Christian Music

Anointed **21**
Ashton, Susan **17**
Audio Adrenaline **22**
Avalon **26**
Becker, Margaret **31**
Boltz, Ray **33**
Champion, Eric **21**
Chapman, Steven Curtis **15**
dc Talk **18**
Delirious? **33**
Duncan, Bryan **19**
Eskelin, Ian **19**
4Him **23**
Grant, Amy **7**
Jars of Clay **20**
Joy Electric **26**

Keaggy, Phil **26**
King's X **7**
MxPx **33**
Newsboys, The **24**
Paris, Twila **16**
Patti, Sandi **7**
Petra **3**
P.O.D. **33**
Point of Grace **21**
Rice, Chris **25**
Sixpence None the Richer **26**
Smith, Michael W. **11**
St. James, Rebecca **26**
Stryper **2**
Taylor, Steve **26**
Third Day **34**
Velasquez, Jaci **32**
Waters, Ethel **11**
Winans, BeBe and CeCe **32**

Clarinet
Adams, John **8**
Bechet, Sidney **17**
Braxton, Anthony **12**
Brötzmann, Peter **26**
Byron, Don **22**
Carter, John **34**
DeFranco, Buddy **31**
Fountain, Pete **7**
Goodman, Benny **4**
Herman, Woody **12**
Koffman, Moe **34**
Russell, Pee Wee **25**
Scott, Tony **32**
Shaw, Artie **8**
Stoltzman, Richard **24**
Sturr, Jimmy **33**
Vandermark, Ken **28**

Classical
Abbado, Claudio **32**
Ameling, Elly **24**
Anderson, June **27**
Anderson, Marian **8**
Argerich, Martha **27**
Arrau, Claudio **1**
Ashkenazy, Vladimir **32**
Austral, Florence **26**
Baker, Janet **14**
Barber, Samuel **34**
Barenboim, Daniel **30**
Beecham, Thomas **27**
Beltrán, Tito **28**
Berio, Luciano **32**
Bernstein, Leonard **2**
Bonney, Barbara **33**
Boulez, Pierre **26**
Boyd, Liona **7**
Bream, Julian **9**
Britten, Benjamin **15**
Bronfman, Yefim **6**
Canadian Brass, The **4**
Carter, Elliott **30**
Carter, Ron **14**
Casals, Pablo **9**
Chang, Han-Na **33**
Chang, Sarah **7**
Chanticleer **33**
Chung, Kyung Wha **34**
Church, Charlotte **28**
Clayderman, Richard **1**
Cliburn, Van **13**
Copland, Aaron **2**
Corigliano, John **34**
Davis, Anthony **17**
Davis, Chip **4**
Davis, Colin **27**

DuPré, Jacqueline **26**
Dvorak, Antonin **25**
Emerson String Quartet **33**
Fiedler, Arthur **6**
Fleming, Renee **24**
Galway, James **3**
Gardiner, John Eliot **26**
Gingold, Josef **6**
Glennie, Evelyn **33**
Gould, Glenn **9**
Gould, Morton **16**
Hahn, Hilary **30**
Hamelin, Marc-André **33**
Hampson, Thomas **12**
Harrell, Lynn **3**
Hayes, Roland **13**
Heifetz, Jascha **31**
Hendricks, Barbara **10**
Herrmann, Bernard **14**
Hinderas, Natalie **12**
Horne, Marilyn **9**
Horowitz, Vladimir **1**
Hovhaness, Alan **34**
Isbin, Sharon **33**
Ives, Charles **29**
Jarrett, Keith **1**
Kennedy, Nigel **8**
Kissin, Evgeny **6**
Kremer, Gidon **30**
Kronos Quartet **5**
Kunzel, Erich **17**
Lemper, Ute **14**
Levine, James **8**
Liberace **9**
Ma, Yo Yo **24**
    Earlier sketch in CM **2**
Marsalis, Wynton **6**
Mascagni, Pietro **25**
Masur, Kurt **11**
McNair, Sylvia **15**
McPartland, Marian **15**
Mehta, Zubin **11**
Menuhin, Yehudi **11**
Midori **7**
Mutter, Anne-Sophie **23**
Nancarrow, Conlon **32**
Nyman, Michael **15**
Oregon **30**
Ott, David **2**
Parkening, Christopher **7**
Pavarotti, Luciano **20**
    Earlier sketch in CM **1**
Penderecki, Krzysztof **30**
Perahia, Murray **10**
Perlman, Itzhak **2**
Phillips, Harvey **3**
Pires, Maria João **26**
Quasthoff, Thomas **26**
Rampal, Jean-Pierre **6**
Rangell, Andrew **24**
Rieu, André **26**
Rostropovich, Mstislav **17**
Rota, Nino **13**
Rubinstein, Arthur **11**
Salerno-Sonnenberg, Nadja **3**
Salonen, Esa-Pekka **16**
Schickele, Peter **5**
Schuman, William **10**
Segovia, Andres **6**
Shankar, Ravi **9**
Shaw, Robert **32**
Solti, Georg **13**
Starker, Janos **32**
Stern, Isaac **7**
Stoltzman, Richard **24**
Sutherland, Joan **13**
Takemitsu, Toru **6**

Tan Dun **33**
Temirkanov, Yuri **26**
Thibaudet, Jean-Yves **24**
Tilson Thomas, Michael **24**
Toscanini, Arturo **14**
Turnage, Mark-Anthony **31**
Upshaw, Dawn **9**
Vanessa-Mae **26**
Van Hove, Fred **30**
Vienna Choir Boys **23**
Volodos, Arcadi **28**
von Karajan, Herbert **1**
von Otter, Anne Sofie **30**
Walker, George **34**
Weill, Kurt **12**
Wilson, Ransom **5**
Xenakis, Iannis **34**
Yamashita, Kazuhito **4**
York, Andrew **15**
Zukerman, Pinchas **4**

Composers
Adams, John **8**
Adamson, Barry **28**
Adderley, Nat **29**
Adès, Thomas **30**
Allen, Geri **10**
Alpert, Herb **11**
Anderson, Fred **32**
Anderson, Wessell **23**
Anka, Paul **2**
Arlen, Harold **27**
Atkins, Chet **26**
    Earlier sketch in CM **5**
Axelrod, David **34**
Bacharach, Burt **20**
    Earlier sketch in CM **1**
Badalamenti, Angelo **17**
Barber, Samuel **34**
Barry, John **29**
Beiderbecke, Bix **16**
Benson, George **9**
Berio, Luciano **32**
Berlin, Irving **8**
Bernstein, Leonard **2**
Blackman, Cindy **15**
Blegvad, Peter **28**
Bley, Carla **8**
Bley, Paul **14**
Boulez, Pierre **26**
Branca, Glenn **29**
Braxton, Anthony **12**
Brickman, Jim **22**
Britten, Benjamin **15**
Brown, Carlinhos **32**
Brubeck, Dave **8**
Burrell, Kenny **11**
Byrne, David **8**
    Also see Talking Heads
Byron, Don **22**
Cage, John **8**
Cale, John **9**
Carter, Elliott **30**
Carter, John **34**
Casals, Pablo **9**
Clarke, Stanley **3**
Coleman, Ornette **5**
Connors, Norman **30**
Cooder, Ry **2**
Cooney, Rory **6**
Copeland, Stewart **14**
    Also see Police, The
Copland, Aaron **2**
Corigliano, John **34**
Crouch, Andraé **9**
Curtis, King **17**
Davis, Anthony **17**

Davis, Chip **4**
Davis, Miles **1**
de Grassi, Alex **6**
Dorsey, Thomas A. **11**
Dvorak, Antonin **25**
Elfman, Danny **9**
Ellington, Duke **2**
Eno, Brian **8**
Enya **32**
  Earlier sketch in CM **6**
Eskelin, Ellery **31**
Esquivel, Juan **17**
Evans, Bill **17**
Evans, Gil **17**
Fahey, John **17**
Fell, Simon H. **32**
Foster, David **13**
Frisell, Bill **15**
Frith, Fred **19**
Fröhlich, Frank **32**
Galás, Diamanda **16**
Garner, Erroll **25**
Gillespie, Dizzy **6**
Glass, Philip **1**
Golson, Benny **21**
Gould, Glenn **9**
Gould, Morton **16**
Green, Benny **17**
Grusin, Dave **7**
Guaraldi, Vince **3**
Hamlisch, Marvin **1**
Hammer, Jan **21**
Hancock, Herbie **25**
  Earlier sketch in CM **8**
Handy, W. C. **7**
Hargrove, Roy **15**
Harris, Barry **32**
Harris, Eddie **15**
Hartke, Stephen **5**
Hemphill, Julius **34**
Henderson, Fletcher **16**
Herrmann, Bernard **14**
Hovhaness, Alan **34**
Hunter, Alberta **7**
Ibrahim, Abdullah **24**
Isham, Mark **14**
Ives, Charles **29**
Jacquet, Illinois **17**
Jamal, Ahmad **32**
Jarre, Jean-Michel **2**
Jarrett, Keith **1**
Johnson, James P. **16**
Johnson, J.J. **33**
Jones, Hank **15**
Jones, Howard **26**
Jones, Quincy **20**
  Earlier sketch in CM **2**
Joplin, Scott **10**
Jordan, Stanley **1**
Kander, John **33**
Kang, Eyvind **28**
Kenny G **14**
Kenton, Stan **21**
Kern, Jerome **13**
Kitaro **1**
Kottke, Leo **13**
Kropinski, Uwe **31**
Lacy, Steve **23**
Lateef, Yusef **16**
Lee, Peggy **8**
Legg, Adrian **17**
Lewis, John **29**
Lewis, Ramsey **14**
Lincoln, Abbey **9**
Lloyd, Charles **22**
Lloyd Webber, Andrew **6**
Loesser, Frank **19**

López, Israel "Cachao" **34**
  Earlier sketch in CM **14**
Mancini, Henry **20**
  Earlier sketch in CM **1**
Mandel, Johnny **28**
Marsalis, Branford **10**
Marsalis, Ellis **13**
Marsalis, Wynton **20**
  Earlier sketch in CM **6**
Martino, Pat **17**
Mascagni, Pietro **25**
Masekela, Hugh **7**
McBride, Christian **17**
McPartland, Marian **15**
Menken, Alan **10**
Metheny, Pat **26**
  Earlier sketch in CM **2**
Miles, Ron **22**
Mingus, Charles **9**
Minott, Sugar **31**
Moby **27**
  Earlier sketch in CM **17**
Monk, Meredith **1**
Monk, Thelonious **6**
Montenegro, Hugo **18**
Morricone, Ennio **15**
Morton, Jelly Roll **7**
Mulligan, Gerry **16**
Nancarrow, Conlon **32**
Nascimento, Milton **6**
Newman, Randy **4**
Nyman, Michael **15**
Oldfield, Mike **18**
Orff, Carl **21**
O'Rourke, Jim **31**
Osby, Greg **21**
Ott, David **2**
Palmieri, Eddie **15**
Parker, Charlie **5**
Parks, Van Dyke **17**
Partch, Harry **29**
Penderecki, Krzysztof **30**
Perez, Danilo **25**
Peterson, Oscar **11**
Piazzolla, Astor **18**
Ponty, Jean-Luc **8**
Porter, Cole **10**
Post, Mike **21**
Previn, André **15**
Puente, Tito **14**
Pullen, Don **16**
Reich, Steve **8**
Reinhardt, Django **7**
Riley, Terry **32**
Ritenour, Lee **7**
Rivers, Sam **29**
Roach, Max **12**
Rollins, Sonny **7**
Rota, Nino **13**
Sakamoto, Ryuichi **19**
Salonen, Esa-Pekka **16**
Sanders, Pharoah **28**
  Earlier sketch in CM **16**
Satie, Erik **25**
Satriani, Joe **4**
Schickele, Peter **5**
Schifrin, Lalo **29**
Schuman, William **10**
Schütze, Paul **32**
Sebesky, Don **33**
Shankar, Ravi **9**
Shaw, Artie **8**
Shearing, George **28**
Shorter, Wayne **4**
Silver, Horace **19**
Smith, Tommy **28**
Solal, Martial **4**

Sondheim, Stephen **8**
Sousa, John Philip **10**
Stern, Leni **29**
Story, Liz **2**
Strauss, Richard **25**
Stravinsky, Igor **21**
Strayhorn, Billy **13**
Styne, Jule **21**
Summers, Andy **3**
  Also see Police, The
Sun Ra **27**
  Earlier sketch in CM **5**
Sylvian, David **27**
Takemitsu, Toru **6**
Talbot, John Michael **6**
Tan Dun **33**
Tatum, Art **17**
Taylor, Billy **13**
Taylor, Cecil **9**
Tesh, John **20**
Thielemans, Toots **13**
Threadgill, Henry **9**
Tilson Thomas, Michael **24**
Tobin, Amon **32**
Towner, Ralph **22**
Tristano, Lennie **30**
Turnage, Mark-Anthony **31**
Tyner, McCoy **7**
Vangelis **21**
Van Hove, Fred **30**
Vollenweider, Andreas **30**
von Trapp, Elisabeth **29**
Wakeman, Rick **27**
  Also see Yes
Walker, George **34**
Wallace, Bennie **31**
Was, Don **21**
  Also see Was (Not Was)
Washington, Grover, Jr. **5**
Weill, Kurt **12**
Wells, Bill **34**
Weston, Randy **15**
Whelan, Bill **20**
Whiteman, Paul **17**
Wildhorn, Frank **31**
Williams, John **28**
  Earlier sketch in CM **9**
Wilson, Cassandra **26**
  Earlier sketch in CM **12**
Winston, George **9**
Winter, Paul **10**
Wolf, Peter **31**
Worrell, Bernie **11**
Xenakis, Iannis **34**
Yanni **11**
Yeston, Maury **22**
York, Andrew **15**
Young, La Monte **16**
Zappa, Frank **17**
  Earlier sketch in CM **1**
Zimmer, Hans **34**
Zimmerman, Udo **5**
Zorn, John **15**

Conductors
Abbado, Claudio **32**
Adès, Thomas **30**
Ashkenazy, Vladimir **32**
Bacharach, Burt **20**
  Earlier sketch CM **1**
Barenboim, Daniel **30**
Beecham, Thomas **27**
Bernstein, Leonard **2**
Boulez, Pierre **26**
Britten, Benjamin **15**
Casals, Pablo **9**
Copland, Aaron **2**

Davies, Dennis Russell **24**
Davis, Colin **27**
Domingo, Placido **20**
  Earlier sketch in CM **1**
Evans, Gil **17**
Fiedler, Arthur **6**
Gardiner, John Eliot **26**
Gould, Morton **16**
Herrmann, Bernard **14**
Ibrahim, Abdullah **24**
Jarrett, Keith **1**
Jones, Hank **15**
Kunzel, Erich **17**
Levine, James **8**
Mancini, Henry **20**
  Earlier sketch in CM **1**
Mandel, Johnny **28**
Marriner, Neville **7**
Mascagni, Pietro **25**
Masur, Kurt **11**
Mehta, Zubin **11**
Menuhin, Yehudi **11**
Nero, Peter **19**
Previn, André **15**
Rampal, Jean-Pierre **6**
Rieu, André **26**
Rostropovich, Mstislav **17**
Salonen, Esa-Pekka **16**
Schickele, Peter **5**
Schifrin, Lalo **29**
Shaw, Robert **32**
Solti, Georg **13**
Strauss, Richard **25**
Temirkanov, Yuri **26**
Tilson Thomas, Michael **24**
Toscanini, Arturo **14**
Valdes, Chuco **25**
von Karajan, Herbert **1**
Welk, Lawrence **13**
Williams, John **28**
  Earlier sketch in CM **9**
Zukerman, Pinchas **4**

Contemporary Dance Music
Abdul, Paula **3**
Air **33**
Aphex Twin **14**
Badly Drawn Boy **33**
Bee Gees, The **3**
Beenie Man **33**
B-52's, The **4**
Brown, Bobby **4**
Brown, James **2**
C + C Music Factory **16**
Carroll, Dina **31**
Cherry, Neneh **4**
Clinton, George **7**
Craig, Carl **19**
Daft Punk **33**
Deee-lite **9**
De La Soul **7**
Depeche Mode **5**
Earth, Wind and Fire **12**
English Beat, The **9**
En Vogue **10**
Erasure **11**
Eurythmics **31**
  Earlier sketch in CM **6**
Exposé **4**
Fox, Samantha **3**
Fun Lovin' Criminals **20**
Gang of Four **8**
Hammer, M.C. **5**
Harry, Deborah **4**
  Also see Blondie
Holmes, David **31**
Ice-T **7**

Idol, Billy **3**
Jackson, Janet **16**
  Earlier sketch in CM **3**
Jackson, Michael **17**
  Earlier sketch in CM **1**
  Also see Jacksons, The
James, Rick **2**
Jones, Grace **9**
Leftfield **29**
Madonna **16**
  Earlier sketch in CM **4**
Massive Attack **17**
Moby **27**
  Earlier sketch in CM **17**
M People **27**
  Earlier sketch in CM **15**
Naté, Ultra **34**
New Order **11**
Orbital **20**
Peniston, CeCe **15**
Pet Shop Boys **5**
Pizzicato Five **18**
Portishead **22**
Prince **14**
  Earlier sketch in CM **1**
Queen Latifah **24**
  Earlier sketch in CM **6**
Rodgers, Nile **8**
Salt-N-Pepa **6**
Shadow, DJ **19**
Shamen, The **23**
Sherwood, Adrian **31**
Simmons, Russell **7**
Size, Roni **31**
Soul II Soul **17**
Spacemen 3 **31**
Stereo MC's **34**
Sugar Ray **22**
Summer, Donna **12**
Technotronic **5**
TLC **15**
Tricky **18**
2 Unlimited **18**
Van Helden, Armand **32**
Vasquez, Junior **16**
Village People, The **7**
Was (Not Was) **6**
Waters, Crystal **15**
Young M.C. **4**

Contemporary Instrumental/New Age
Ackerman, Will **3**
Arkenstone, David **20**
Clinton, George **7**
Collins, Bootsy **8**
Cook, Jesse **33**
Darling, David **34**
Davis, Chip **4**
De Gaia, Banco **27**
de Grassi, Alex **6**
Enigma **32**
  Earlier sketch in CM **14**
Enya **32**
  Earlier sketch in CM **6**
Esquivel, Juan **17**
Hedges, Michael **3**
Isham, Mark **14**
Jarre, Jean-Michel **2**
Kitaro **1**
Kronos Quartet **5**
Legg, Adrian **17**
Liebert, Ottmar **33**
Line, Lorie **34**
Merzbow **31**
Mogwai **27**
Riley, Terry **32**
Roth, Gabrielle **26**

Schroer, Oliver **29**
Sete, Bola **26**
Story, Liz **2**
Summers, Andy **3**
  Also see Police, The
Tangerine Dream **12**
Tesh, John **20**
Vollenweider, Andreas **30**
Winston, George **9**
Winter, Paul **10**
Yanni **11**

Cornet
Adderley, Nat **29**
Armstrong, Louis **4**
Beiderbecke, Bix **16**
Cherry, Don **10**
Davison, Wild Bill **34**
Handy, W. C. **7**
Oliver, King **15**
Vaché, Jr., Warren **22**

Country
Acuff, Roy **2**
Adkins, Trace **31**
Akins, Rhett **22**
Alabama **21**
  Earlier sketch in CM **1**
Anderson, Bill **32**
Anderson, John **5**
Andrews, Jessica **34**
Arnold, Eddy **10**
Asleep at the Wheel **29**
  Earlier sketch in CM **5**
Atkins, Chet **26**
  Earlier sketch in CM **5**
Auldridge, Mike **4**
Autry, Gene **25**
  Earlier sketch in CM **12**
Barnett, Mandy **26**
Bellamy Brothers, The **13**
Berg, Matraca **16**
Berry, John **17**
Black, Clint **5**
BlackHawk **21**
Blue Rodeo **18**
Boggs, Dock **25**
Bogguss, Suzy **11**
Bonamy, James **21**
Bond, Johnny **28**
Boone, Pat **13**
Boy Howdy **21**
Brandt, Paul **22**
Brannon, Kippi **20**
Brooks, Garth **25**
  Earlier sketch in CM **8**
Brooks & Dunn **25**
  Earlier sketch in CM **12**
Brown, Junior **15**
Brown, Marty **14**
Brown, Tony **14**
Buckner, Richard **31**
Buffett, Jimmy **4**
Byrds, The **8**
Cale, J. J. **16**
Calexico **33**
Campbell, Glen **2**
Carter, Carlene **8**
Carter, Deana **25**
Carter Family, The **3**
Cash, Johnny **17**
  Earlier sketch in CM **1**
Cash, June Carter **6**
Cash, Rosanne **2**
Chapin Carpenter, Mary **25**
  Earlier sketch in CM **6**
Chapman, Gary **33**

Chesney, Kenny **20**
Chesnutt, Mark **13**
Clark, Guy **17**
Clark, Roy **1**
Clark, Terri **19**
Clements, Vassar **18**
Cline, Patsy **5**
Coe, David Allan **4**
Collie, Mark **15**
Commander Cody and His Lost
  Planet Airmen **30**
Confederate Railroad **23**
Cooder, Ry **2**
Cowboy Junkies, The **4**
Crawford, Randy **25**
Crowe, J. D. **5**
Crowell, Rodney **8**
Cyrus, Billy Ray **11**
Daniels, Charlie **6**
Davis, Linda **21**
Davis, Skeeter **15**
Dean, Billy **19**
DeMent, Iris **13**
Denver, John **22**
  Earlier sketch in CM **1**
Desert Rose Band, The **4**
Diamond Rio **11**
Dickens, Little Jimmy **7**
Diffie, Joe **27**
  Earlier sketch in CM **10**
Dixie Chicks **26**
Dylan, Bob **21**
  Earlier sketch in CM **3**
Earle, Steve **16**
Estes, John **25**
Evans, Sara **27**
Flatt, Lester **3**
Flores, Rosie **16**
Ford, Tennessee Ernie **3**
Foster, Radney **16**
Fricke, Janie **33**
Frizzell, Lefty **10**
Gayle, Crystal **1**
Germano, Lisa **18**
Giant Sand **30**
Gill, Vince **34**
  Earlier sketch in CM **7**
Gilley, Mickey **7**
Gilman, Billy **34**
Gilmore, Jimmie Dale **11**
Gordy, Jr., Emory **17**
Greenwood, Lee **12**
Griffith, Nanci **3**
Haggard, Merle **2**
Hall, Tom T. **26**
Handsome Family, The **30**
Harris, Emmylou **4**
Hartford, John **1**
Hay, George D. **3**
Herndon, Ty **20**
Hiatt, John **8**
Highway 101 **4**
Hill, Faith **18**
Hinojosa, Tish **13**
Howard, Harlan **15**
Jackson, Alan **25**
  Earlier sketch in CM **7**
Jennings, Waylon **4**
Jones, George **4**
Judds, The **2**
Keith, Toby **17**
Kentucky Headhunters, The **5**
Kershaw, Sammy **15**
Ketchum, Hal **14**
King, Pee Wee **30**
Kinleys, The **32**
Kristofferson, Kris **4**

Lamb, Barbara **19**
Lambchop **29**
Lane, Fred **28**
lang, kd **25**
  Earlier sketch in CM **4**
Lauderdale, Jim **29**
Lawrence, Tracy **11**
LeDoux, Chris **12**
Lee, Brenda **5**
Little Feat **4**
Little Texas **14**
Lonestar **27**
Louvin Brothers, The **12**
Loveless, Patty **21**
  Earlier sketch in CM **5**
Lovett, Lyle **28**
Lynn, Loretta **2**
Lynne, Shelby **29**
  Earlier sketch in CM **5**
Mandrell, Barbara **4**
Mattea, Kathy **5**
Mavericks, The **15**
McBride, Martina **14**
McCann, Lila **26**
McClinton, Delbert **14**
McCoy, Neal **15**
McCready, Mindy **22**
McEntire, Reba **11**
McGraw, Tim **17**
Messina, Jo Dee **26**
Miller, Buddy **31**
Miller, Roger **4**
Milsap, Ronnie **2**
Moffatt, Katy **18**
Monroe, Bill **1**
Montgomery, John Michael **14**
Montgomery Gentry **34**
Morgan, Lorrie **10**
Murphey, Michael Martin **9**
Murray, Anne **4**
Nelson, Willie **11**
  Earlier sketch in CM **1**
Newton-John, Olivia **8**
Nitty Gritty Dirt Band, The **6**
Oak Ridge Boys, The **7**
O'Connor, Mark **1**
Oldham, Will **32**
Old 97's **33**
Oslin, K. T. **3**
Overstreet, Paul **33**
Owens, Buck **2**
Parnell, Lee Roy **15**
Parsons, Gram **7**
  Also see Byrds, The
Parton, Dolly **24**
  Earlier sketch in CM **2**
Pearl, Minnie **3**
Peterson, Michael **31**
Pierce, Webb **15**
Price, Ray **11**
Pride, Charley **4**
Rabbitt, Eddie **24**
  Earlier sketch in CM **5**
Raitt, Bonnie **23**
  Earlier sketch in CM **3**
Ray Condo and His Ricochets **26**
Raye, Collin **16**
Reeves, Jim **10**
Restless Heart **12**
Rich, Charlie **3**
Richey, Kim **20**
Ricochet **23**
Riders in the Sky **33**
Rimes, LeAnn **19**
Robbins, Marty **9**
Rodgers, Jimmie **3**
Rogers, Kenny **1**

Rogers, Roy **24**
  Earlier sketch in CM **9**
Sahm, Doug **30**
  Also see Texas Tornados, The
Sawyer Brown **27**
  Earlier sketch in CM **13**
Scruggs, Earl **3**
Scud Mountain Boys **21**
Seals, Dan **9**
Shenandoah **17**
Skaggs, Ricky **5**
Snow, Hank **29**
Sonnier, Jo-El **10**
Statler Brothers, The **8**
Stevens, Ray **7**
Stone, Doug **10**
Strait, George **5**
Stuart, Marty **9**
Sweethearts of the Rodeo **12**
Texas Tornados, The **8**
Tillis, Mel **7**
Tillis, Pam **25**
  Earlier sketch in CM **8**
Tippin, Aaron **12**
Travis, Merle **14**
Travis, Randy **9**
Tritt, Travis **7**
Tubb, Ernest **4**
Tucker, Tanya **3**
Twain, Shania **17**
Twitty, Conway **6**
Van Shelton, Ricky **5**
Van Zandt, Townes **13**
Wagoner, Porter **13**
Walker, Clay **20**
Walker, Jerry Jeff **13**
Wariner, Steve **18**
Warren Brothers, The **34**
Watson, Doc **2**
Welch, Gillian **33**
Wells, Kitty **6**
West, Dottie **8**
White, Lari **15**
Whitley, Keith **7**
Wilkinsons, The **30**
Williams, Don **4**
Williams, Hank, Jr. **1**
Williams, Hank, Sr. **4**
Williams, Lucinda **24**
  Earlier sketch in CM **10**
Willis, Kelly **12**
Wills, Bob **6**
Wills, Mark **27**
Womack, Lee Ann **33**
Wynette, Tammy **24**
  Earlier sketch in CM **2**
Wynonna **11**
  Also see Judds, The
Yearwood, Trisha **25**
  Earlier sketch in CM **10**
Yoakam, Dwight **21**
  Earlier sketch in CM **1**
Young, Faron **7**

Dobro
Auldridge, Mike **4**
  Also see Country Gentlemen, The
  Also see Seldom Scene, The
Knopfler, Mark **25**
  Earlier sketch in CM **3**
  Also see Dire Straits
Whitley, Chris **16**

Drums
  Also see **Percussion**
Aronoff, Kenny **21**
Colaiuta, Vinnie **23**

Haynes, Roy **33**
Hussain, Zakir **32**
Oxley, Tony **32**
Parker, Leon **27**
Qureshi, Ustad Alla Rakha **29**
Scharin, Doug **32**
Schütze, Paul **32**
Sommer, Günter "Baby" **31**
Starr, Ringo **24**
  Earlier sketch in CM **10**
  Also see Beatles, The
Turner, Roger **32**

Dulcimer
Ritchie, Jean **4**

Fiddle
  Also see **Violin**
Carthy, Eliza **31**
Ivers, Eileen **30**
MacIsaac, Ashley **21**

Film Scores
Anka, Paul **2**
Arlen, Harold **27**
Bacharach, Burt **20**
  Earlier sketch in CM **1**
Badalamenti, Angelo **17**
Barry, John **29**
Bergman, Alan and Marilyn **30**
Berlin, Irving **8**
Bernstein, Leonard **2**
Blanchard, Terence **13**
Britten, Benjamin **15**
Byrne, David **8**
  Also see Talking Heads
Cahn, Sammy **11**
Cliff, Jimmy **8**
Copeland, Stewart **14**
  Also see Police, The
Copland, Aaron **2**
Crouch, Andraé **9**
Dibango, Manu **14**
Dolby, Thomas **10**
Donovan **9**
Eddy, Duane **9**
Elfman, Danny **9**
Ellington, Duke **2**
Ferguson, Maynard **7**
Froom, Mitchell **15**
Gabriel, Peter **16**
  Earlier sketch in CM **2**
  Also see Genesis
Galás, Diamanda **16**
Gershwin, George and Ira **11**
Gould, Glenn **9**
Grusin, Dave **7**
Guaraldi, Vince **3**
Hamlisch, Marvin **1**
Hancock, Herbie **25**
  Earlier sketch in CM **8**
Harrison, George **2**
Hayes, Isaac **10**
Hedges, Michael **3**
Herrmann, Bernard **14**
Isham, Mark **14**
Jones, Quincy **20**
  Earlier sketch in CM **2**
Kander, John **33**
Knopfler, Mark **25**
  Earlier sketch in CM **3**
  Also see Dire Straits
Lennon, John **9**
  Also see Beatles, The
Lerner and Loewe **13**
Loesser, Frank **19**

Mancini, Henry **20**
  Earlier sketch in CM **1**
Marsalis, Branford **10**
Mayfield, Curtis **8**
McCartney, Paul **32**
  Earlier sketch in CM **4**
  Also see Beatles, The
Menken, Alan **10**
Mercer, Johnny **13**
Metheny, Pat **26**
  Earlier sketch in CM **2**
Montenegro, Hugo **18**
Morricone, Ennio **15**
Nascimento, Milton **6**
Newman, Randy **27**
  Earlier sketch in CM **4**
Nilsson **10**
Nyman, Michael **15**
Parks, Van Dyke **17**
Peterson, Oscar **11**
Porter, Cole **10**
Previn, André **15**
Reznor, Trent **13**
  Also see Nine Inch Nails
Richie, Lionel **2**
Robertson, Robbie **2**
Rollins, Sonny **7**
Rota, Nino **13**
Sager, Carole Bayer **5**
Sakamoto, Ryuichi **18**
Schickele, Peter **5**
Schütze, Paul **32**
Shankar, Ravi **9**
Taj Mahal **6**
Tan Dun **33**
Waits, Tom **27**
  Earlier sketch in CM **12**
  Earlier sketch in CM **1**
Weill, Kurt **12**
Williams, John **28**
  Earlier sketch in CM **9**
Williams, Paul **26**
  Earlier sketch in CM **5**
Willner, Hal **10**
Young, Neil **15**
Zimmer, Hans **34**

Flugelhorn
Bowie, Lester **29**
Mangione, Chuck **23**
Sandoval, Arturo **15**

Flute
Galway, James **3**
Jethro Tull **8**
Koffman, Moe **34**
Lateef, Yusef **16**
Mangione, Chuck **23**
Mann, Herbie **16**
Moody, James **34**
Najee **21**
Nakai, R. Carlos **24**
Rampal, Jean-Pierre **6**
Ulmer, James Blood **13**
Valentin, Dave **33**
Wilson, Ransom **5**

Folk/Traditional
Altan **18**
America **16**
Anonymous 4 **23**
Arnaz, Desi **8**
Axton, Hoyt **28**
Baca, Susana **32**
Baez, Joan **1**
Battlefield Band, The **31**

Belafonte, Harry **8**
Belle and Sebastian **28**
Black, Mary **15**
Blades, Ruben **2**
Bloom, Luka **14**
Blue Rodeo **18**
Boggs, Dock **25**
Brady, Paul **8**
Bragg, Billy **7**
Brave Combo **31**
Bromberg, David **18**
Brown, Carlinhos **32**
Buckley, Tim **14**
Buffalo Springfield **24**
Bulgarian State Female Vocal Choir, The **10**
Byrds, The **8**
Campbell, Sarah Elizabeth **23**
Caravan **24**
Carter Family, The **3**
Carthy, Eliza **31**
Carthy, Martin **34**
  Also see Steeleye Span
Ceili Rain **34**
Chandra, Sheila **16**
Chapin, Harry **6**
Chapman, Tracy **20**
  Earlier sketch in CM **4**
Chenille Sisters, The **16**
Cherry, Don **10**
Chesnutt, Vic **28**
Chieftains, The **7**
Childs, Toni **2**
Clannad **23**
Clegg, Johnny **8**
Cockburn, Bruce **8**
Cohen, Leonard **3**
Collins, Judy **4**
Colvin, Shawn **11**
Cotten, Elizabeth **16**
Crosby, David **3**
  Also see Byrds, The
Cruz, Celia **22**
  Earlier sketch in CM **10**
Curtis, Catie **31**
de Lucia, Paco **1**
DeMent, Iris **13**
Donovan **9**
Drake, Nick **17**
Driftwood, Jimmy **25**
Dr. John **7**
Dylan, Bob **21**
  Earlier sketch in CM **3**
Elliot, Cass **5**
Elliott, Ramblin' Jack **32**
Enya **32**
  Earlier sketch in CM **6**
Estefan, Gloria **15**
  Earlier sketch in CM **2**
Fahey, John **17**
Fairport Convention **22**
Feliciano, José **10**
Frogs, The **31**
Gabriel, Juan **31**
Gaines, Jeffrey **34**
Galway, James **3**
Germano, Lisa **18**
Gibson, Bob **23**
Gilberto, João **33**
Gilmore, Jimmie Dale **11**
Gipsy Kings, The **8**
Gorka, John **18**
Gray, David **30**
Griffin, Patty **24**
Griffith, Nanci **3**
Grisman, David **17**
Gurtu, Trilok **29**
Guthrie, Arlo **6**

Guthrie, Woody **2**
Hakmoun, Hassan **15**
Hardin, Tim **18**
Harding, John Wesley **6**
Harper, Roy **30**
Hartford, John **1**
Havens, Richie **11**
Haza, Ofra **29**
Henry, Joe **18**
Hinojosa, Tish **13**
Hussain, Zakir **32**
Ian, Janis **24**
  Earlier sketch in CM **5**
Ian and Sylvia **18**
Iglesias, Julio **20**
  Earlier sketch in CM **2**
Incredible String Band **23**
Indigenous **31**
Indigo Girls **20**
  Earlier sketch in CM **3**
Ivers, Eileen **30**
Ives, Burl **12**
Khaled **33**
Khan, Ali Akbar **34**
Khan, Nusrat Fateh Ali **13**
Kingston Trio, The **9**
Klezmatics, The **18**
Kottke, Leo **13**
Kuti, Fela **7**
Kuti, Femi **29**
Ladysmith Black Mambazo **1**
Lamond, Mary Jane **33**
Larkin, Patty **9**
Lavin, Christine **6**
Leadbelly **6**
Les Négresses Vertes **30**
Lightfoot, Gordon **3**
López, Israel "Cachao" **34**
  Earlier sketch in CM **14**
Los Lobos **2**
MacNeil, Rita **29**
Makeba, Miriam **8**
Mamas and the Papas **21**
Masekela, Hugh **7**
McKennitt, Loreena **24**
McLean, Don **7**
Melanie **12**
Mitchell, Joni **17**
  Earlier sketch in CM **2**
Moffatt, Katy **18**
Morrison, Van **24**
  Earlier sketch in CM **3**
Morrissey, Bill **12**
Nascimento, Milton **6**
N'Dour, Youssou **6**
Near, Holly **1**
Ochs, Phil **7**
O'Connor, Sinead **31**
  Earlier sketch in CM **3**
Odetta **7**
Parsons, Gram **7**
  Also see Byrds, The
Paxton, Tom **5**
Pentangle **18**
Peter, Paul & Mary **4**
Pogues, The **6**
Prine, John **7**
Proclaimers, The **13**
Qureshi, Ustad Alla Rakha **29**
Rankins, The **24**
Redpath, Jean **1**
Ritchie, Jean, **4**
Roches, The **18**
Rodgers, Jimmie **3**
Rusby, Kate **29**
Russell, Tom **26**
Sainte-Marie, Buffy **11**

Santana, Carlos **19**
  Earlier sketch in CM **1**
Seeger, Peggy **25**
Seeger, Pete **4**
  Also see Weavers, The
Selena **16**
Shankar, Ravi **9**
Shenandoah, Joanne **33**
Simon, Paul **16**
  Earlier sketch in CM **1**
  Also see Simon and Garfunkel
Simonal, Wilson **33**
Simon and Garfunkel **24**
Snow, Pheobe **4**
Solas **34**
Steeleye Span **19**
Story, The **13**
Sweet Honey in the Rock **26**
  Earlier sketch in CM **1**
Taj Mahal **6**
Taylor, Kate **30**
Thompson, Richard **7**
Tikaram, Tanita **9**
Toure, Ali Farka **18**
Van Ronk, Dave **12**
Van Zandt, Townes **13**
Vega, Suzanne **3**
von Trapp, Elisabeth **29**
Wainwright III, Loudon **11**
Walker, Jerry Jeff **13**
Waterboys, The **27**
Watson, Doc **2**
Weavers, The **8**
Welch, Gillian **33**
Whitman, Slim **19**

Funk
Avery, Teodross **23**
Bambaataa, Afrika **13**
Brand New Heavies, The **14**
Brown, James **2**
Burdon, Eric **14**
  Also see Animals
  Also see War
Citizen King **27**
Clinton, George **7**
Collins, Bootsy **8**
Fishbone **7**
Front 242 **19**
Gang of Four **8**
Gray, Macy **32**
Jackson, Janet **16**
  Earlier sketch in CM **3**
Jamiroquai **21**
Joy Electric **26**
Khan, Chaka **19**
  Earlier sketch in CM **9**
Mayfield, Curtis **8**
Meters, The **14**
Ohio Players **16**
Parker, Maceo **7**
Prince **14**
  Earlier sketch in CM **1**
Red Hot Chili Peppers, The **29**
  Earlier sketch in CM **7**
Sly and the Family Stone **24**
Stone, Sly **8**
  Also see Sly and the Family Stone
Toussaint, Allen **11**
Worrell, Bernie **11**
Wu-Tang Clan **19**

Fusion
Anderson, Ray **7**
Avery, Teodross **23**
Beck, Jeff **4**
  Also see Yardbirds, The

Clarke, Stanley **3**
Coleman, Ornette **5**
Corea, Chick **6**
Davis, Miles **1**
Fishbone **7**
Hancock, Herbie **25**
  Earlier sketch in CM **8**
Harris, Eddie **15**
Johnson, Eric **19**
Lewis, Ramsey **14**
Mahavishnu Orchestra **19**
McLaughlin, John **12**
Metheny, Pat **26**
  Earlier sketch in CM **2**
O'Connor, Mark **1**
Ponty, Jean-Luc **8**
Reid, Vernon **2**
Ritenour, Lee **7**
Shorter, Wayne **5**
Summers, Andy **3**
  Also see Police, The
Washington, Grover, Jr. **5**

Gospel
Anderson, Marian **8**
Armstrong, Vanessa Bell **24**
Baylor, Helen **20**
Boone, Pat **13**
Brown, James **2**
Caesar, Shirley **17**
Carter Family, The **3**
Charles, Ray **24**
  Earlier sketch in CM **1**
Cleveland, James **1**
Cooke, Sam **1**
  Also see Soul Stirrers, The
Crouch, Andraé **9**
Dorsey, Thomas A. **11**
Five Blind Boys of Alabama **12**
Ford, Tennessee Ernie **3**
4Him **23**
Franklin, Aretha **17**
  Earlier sketch in CM **2**
Franklin, Kirk **22**
Golden Gate Quartet **25**
Greater Vision **26**
Green, Al **9**
Hawkins, Tramaine **17**
Houston, Cissy **26**
  Earlier sketch in CM **6**
Jackson, Mahalia **8**
Johnson, Blind Willie **26**
Kee, John P. **15**
Knight, Gladys **1**
Little Richard **1**
Louvin Brothers, The **12**
Mighty Clouds of Joy, The **17**
Oakland Interfaith Gospel Choir **26**
Oak Ridge Boys, The **7**
Paris, Twila **16**
Pickett, Wilson **10**
Presley, Elvis **1**
Redding, Otis **5**
Reese, Della **13**
Robbins, Marty **9**
Smith, Michael W. **11**
Soul Stirrers, The **11**
Sounds of Blackness **13**
Staples, Mavis **13**
Staples, Pops **11**
Sweet Honey In The Rock **26**
  Earlier sketch in CM **1**
Take 6 **6**
Waters, Ethel **11**
Watson, Doc **2**
Williams, Deniece **1**
Williams, Marion **15**

Winans, BeBe and CeCe **32**
Winans, The **12**
Womack, Bobby **5**

Guitar

Abercrombie, John **25**
Ackerman, Will **3**
Adamson, Barry **28**
Adé, King Sunny **18**
Adkins, Trace **31**
Allen, Daevid **28**
Allison, Luther **21**
Alvin, Dave **17**
Atkins, Chet **26**
  Earlier sketch in CM **5**
Autry, Gene **25**
  Earlier sketch in CM **12**
Axton, Hoyt **28**
Badly Drawn Boy **33**
Barnes, Roosevelt "Booba" **23**
Beck **18**
Beck, Jeff **4**
  Also see Yardbirds, The
Belew, Adrian **5**
Benoit, Tab **31**
Benson, George **9**
Berry, Chuck **33**
  Earlier sketch in CM **1**
Berry, John **17**
Bishop, Jeb **28**
Blegvad, Peter **28**
Block, Rory **18**
Bloom, Luka **14**
Bond, Johnny **28**
Boyd, Liona **7**
Bream, Julian **9**
Bromberg, David **18**
Brooks, Garth **25**
  Earlier sketch in CM **8**
Brooks, Meredith **30**
Brötzmann, Caspar **27**
Brown, Junior **15**
Brown, Norman **29**
Buckethead **34**
Buckingham, Lindsey **8**
  Also see Fleetwood Mac
Buckner, Richard **31**
Burnside, R. L **34**
  Earlier sketch in CM **1**
Burrell, Kenny **11**
Campbell, Glen **2**
Carter, Deana **25**
Cat Power **30**
Chadbourne, Eugene **30**
Chapin-Carpenter, Mary **25**
  Earlier sketch in CM **6**
Chaquico, Craig **23**
Chesney, Kenny **20**
Chesnutt, Mark **13**
Chesnutt, Vic **28**
Christian, Charlie **11**
Clapton, Eric **11**
  Earlier sketch in CM **1**
  Also see Cream
  Also see Yardbirds, The
Clark, Roy **1**
Cockburn, Bruce **8**
Collie, Mark **15**
Collins, Albert **19**
  Earlier sketch in CM **4**
Cooder, Ry **2**
Cook, Jesse **33**
Cotten, Elizabeth **16**
Cray, Robert **8**
Cropper, Steve **12**
Curtis, Catie **31**
Dahl, Jeff **28**

Dale, Dick **13**
Daniels, Charlie **6**
Dave, Edmunds **28**
Davis, Reverend Gary **18**
de Grassi, Alex **6**
Del Rubio Triplets **21**
de Lucia, Paco **1**
Denver, John **22**
  Earlier sketch in CM **1**
Dickens, Little Jimmy **7**
Diddley, Bo **3**
DiFranco, Ani **17**
Di Meola, Al **12**
Drake, Nick **17**
Earl, Ronnie **5**
  Also see Roomful of Blues
Eddy, Duane **9**
Elliott, Ramblin' Jack **32**
Ellis, Herb **18**
Emmanuel, Tommy **21**
Etheridge, Melissa **16**
  Earlier sketch in CM **4**
Fahey, John **17**
Fankhauser, Merrell **24**
Feliciano, José **10**
Fell, Simon H. **32**
Fender, Leo **10**
Flatt, Lester **3**
Flores, Rosie **16**
Ford, Lita **9**
Frampton, Peter **3**
Fripp, Robert **9**
Frisell, Bill **15**
Frith, Fred **19**
Fröhlich, Frank **32**
Fuller, Blind Boy **20**
Fulson, Lowell **20**
Gaillard, Slim **31**
Garcia, Jerry **4**
  Also see Grateful Dead, The
Gatton, Danny **16**
Gibson, Bob **23**
Gil, Gilberto **26**
Gilberto, João **33**
Gill, Vince **34**
  Earlier sketch in CM **7**
Gorka, John **18**
Green, Grant **14**
Guy, Buddy **4**
Hackett, Bobby **21**
Haley, Bill **6**
Hall, Tom T. **26**
Hammill, Peter **30**
Hardin, Tim **18**
Harper, Ben **17**
Harrison, George **2**
Hart, Alvin Youngblood **27**
Hatfield, Juliana **12**
  Also see Lemonheads, The
Havens, Richie **11**
Healey, Jeff **4**
Hedges, Michael **3**
Hendrix, Jimi **2**
Hepcat, Harry **23**
Hitchcock, Robyn **9**
Holly, Buddy **1**
Hooker, John Lee **26**
  Earlier sketch in CM **1**
Hopkins, Lightnin' **13**
Howlin' Wolf **6**
Hunter, Charlie **24**
Isaak, Chris **33**
  Earlier sketch in CM **6**
Isbin, Sharon **33**
Ives, Burl **12**
Jackson, Alan **25**
  Earlier sketch in CM **7**

James, Elmore **8**
James, Skip **24**
Jean, Wyclef **22**
Jefferson, Blind Lemon **18**
Jewel **25**
Jobim, Antonio Carlos **19**
Johnson, Blind Willie **26**
Johnson, Eric **19**
Johnson, Lonnie **17**
Johnson, Robert **6**
Jordan, Stanley **1**
Keaggy, Phil **26**
Keene, Tommy **31**
Keith, Toby **17**
Kelly, Jeff **31**
King, Albert **2**
King, B.B. **24**
  Earlier sketch in CM **1**
King, Freddy **17**
Klugh, Earl **10**
Knopfler, Mark **25**
  Earlier sketch in CM **3**
  Also see Dire Straits
Kottke, Leo **13**
Kropinski, Uwe **31**
Landreth, Sonny **16**
Lang, Jonny **27**
Larkin, Patty **9**
Leadbelly **6**
Legg, Adrian **17**
Lennon, John **9**
  Also see Beatles, The
Liebert, Ottmar **33**
Lindley, David **2**
Lockwood, Robert, Jr. **10**
Loeb, Lisa **19**
Lofgren, Nils **25**
Lovett, Lyle **28**
  Earlier sketch in CM **5**
Malmsteen, Yngwie **24**
Malone, Russell **27**
Martino, Pat **17**
Matthews, Eric **22**
Mayfield, Curtis **8**
McCartney, Paul **32**
  Earlier sketch in CM **4**
  Also see Beatles, The
McCaughey, Scott **31**
McClinton, Delbert **14**
McCoury, Del **15**
McDowell, Mississippi Fred **16**
McLachlan, Sarah **34**
  Earlier sketch in CM **12**
McLaughlin, John **12**
McLean, Dave **24**
McLennan, Grant **21**
McTell, Blind Willie **17**
Metheny, Pat **26**
  Earlier sketch in CM **2**
Miller, Buddy **31**
Mitchell, Joni **17**
  Earlier sketch in CM **2**
Mo', Keb' **21**
Montgomery, Wes **3**
Morrissey, Bill **12**
Muldaur, Maria **18**
Nugent, Ted **2**
Oldfield, Mike **18**
Oldham, Will **32**
O'Rourke, Jim **31**
Owens, Buck **2**
Owens, Jack **30**
Page, Jimmy **4**
  Also see Led Zeppelin
  Also see Yardbirds, The
Parkening, Christopher **7**
Parnell, Lee Roy **15**

Pass, Joe **15**
Patton, Charley **11**
Perkins, Carl **9**
Peterson, Michael **31**
Petty, Tom **9**
  Also see Tom Petty and the Heartbreakers
Phair, Liz **14**
Phillips, Sam **12**
Powell, Baden **23**
Prince **14**
  Earlier sketch in CM **1**
Prophet, Chuck **32**
Quaye, Finley **30**
Raitt, Bonnie **23**
  Earlier sketch in CM **3**
Redbone, Leon **19**
Reed, Jimmy **15**
Reichel, Hans **29**
Reid, Vernon **2**
  Also see Living Colour
Reinhardt, Django **7**
Ribot, Marc **30**
Richards, Keith **11**
  Also see Rolling Stones, The
Richman, Jonathan **12**
Ritenour, Lee **7**
Robbins, Marty **9**
Robertson, Robbie **2**
Robillard, Duke **2**
Rodgers, Nile **8**
Rush, Otis **12**
Sahm, Doug **30**
  Also see Texas Tornados, The
Salem, Kevin **32**
Sambora, Richie **24**
  Also see Bon Jovi
Santana, Carlos **19**
  Earlier sketch in CM **1**
Satriani, Joe **4**
Scofield, John **7**
Scruggs, Randy **28**
Segovia, Andres **6**
Sete, Bola **26**
Setzer, Brian **32**
Sexsmith, Ron **27**
Sharrock, Sonny **15**
Shepherd, Kenny Wayne **22**
Shines, Johnny **14**
Simon, Paul **16**
  Earlier sketch in CM **1**
  Also see Simon and Garfunkel
Skaggs, Ricky **5**
Smith, Elliott **28**
Smog **28**
Springsteen, Bruce **25**
  Earlier sketch in CM **6**
Stern, Leni **29**
Stern, Mike **29**
Stills, Stephen **5**
  Also see Buffalo Springfield
  Also see Crosby, Stills and Nash
Stuart, Marty **9**
Summers, Andy **3**
  Also see Police, The
Tampa Red **25**
Terrell **32**
Thielemans, Toots **13**
Thompson, Richard **7**
Thorogood, George **34**
Tippin, Aaron **12**
Toure, Ali Farka **18**
Towner, Ralph **22**
Townshend, Pete **1**
Travis, Merle **14**
Trynin, Jen **21**
Tubb, Ernest **4**
Ulmer, James Blood **13**

Vai, Steve **5**
Van Ronk, Dave **12**
Van Zandt, Steven **29**
Vaughan, Jimmie **24**
  Also see Fabulous Thunderbirds, The
Vaughan, Stevie Ray **1**
Wachtel, Waddy **26**
Wagoner, Porter **13**
Waits, Tom **27**
  Earlier sketch in CM **12**
  Earlier sketch in CM **1**
Walker, Jerry Jeff **13**
Walker, Joe Louis **28**
Walker, T-Bone **5**
Walsh, Joe **5**
  Also see Eagles, The
Wariner, Steve **18**
Waters, Muddy **24**
  Earlier sketch in CM **4**
Watson, Doc **2**
Weller, Paul **14**
White, Lari **15**
Whitfield, Mark **18**
Whitley, Chris **16**
Whittaker, Hudson **20**
Wilson, Brian **24**
  Also see Beach Boys, The
Winston, George **9**
Winter, Johnny **5**
Wiseman, Mac **19**
Wray, Link **17**
Yamashita, Kazuhito **4**
Yoakam, Dwight **21**
  Earlier sketch in CM **1**
York, Andrew **15**
Young, Neil **15**
  Earlier sketch in CM **2**
Zappa, Frank **17**

Harmonica
Barnes, Roosevelt "Booba" **23**
Dylan, Bob **3**
Guthrie, Woody **2**
Horton, Walter **19**
Lewis, Huey **9**
Little Walter **14**
McClinton, Delbert **14**
Musselwhite, Charlie **13**
Reed, Jimmy **15**
Thielemans, Toots **13**
Waters, Muddy **24**
  Earlier sketch in CM **4**
Wells, Junior **17**
Williamson, Sonny Boy **9**
Wonder, Stevie **17**
  Earlier sketch in CM **2**
Young, Neil **15**
  Earlier sketch in CM **2**

Heavy Metal
AC/DC **4**
Aerosmith **22**
  Earlier sketch in CM **1**
Alice in Chains **10**
Anthrax **11**
Black Sabbath **9**
Blue Oyster Cult **16**
Cinderella **16**
Circle Jerks **17**
Danzig **7**
Deep Purple **11**
Def Leppard **3**
Dokken **16**
Faith No More **7**
Fear Factory **27**
Fishbone **7**
Flying Luttenbachers, The **28**

Ford, Lita **9**
Guns n' Roses **2**
Iron Maiden **10**
Judas Priest **10**
Kilgore **24**
King's X **7**
Kiss **25**
  Earlier sketch in CM **5**
Led Zeppelin **1**
L7 **12**
Machine Head **32**
Megadeth **9**
Melvins **21**
Metallica **33**
  Earlier sketch in CM **7**
Mötley Crüe **1**
Motörhead **10**
Neurosis **28**
Nugent, Ted **2**
Osbourne, Ozzy **3**
Pantera **13**
Petra **3**
Queensryche **8**
Reid, Vernon **2**
  Also see Living Colour
Reznor, Trent **13**
  Also see Nine Inch Nails
Roth, David Lee **1**
  Also see Van Halen
Sepultura **12**
Skinny Puppy **17**
Slayer **10**
Soulfly **33**
Soundgarden **6**
Spinal Tap **8**
Staind **31**
Stryper **2**
Suicidal Tendencies **15**
Tool **21**
Type O Negative **27**
Warrant **17**
Wendy O. Williams and The Plasmatics **26**
White Zombie **17**
Whitesnake **5**

Humor
Borge, Victor **19**
Coasters, The **5**
Dr. Demento **23**
Jones, Spike **5**
Lehrer, Tom **7**
Nixon, Mojo **32**
Pearl, Minnie **3**
Russell, Mark **6**
Sandler, Adam **19**
Schickele, Peter **5**
Shaffer, Paul **13**
Spinal Tap **8**
Stevens, Ray **7**
Yankovic, "Weird Al" **7**

Inventors
Fender, Leo **10**
Harris, Eddie **15**
Partch, Harry **29**
Paul, Les **2**
Reichel, Hans **29**
Teagarden, Jack **10**
Theremin, Leon **19**

Jazz
Abercrombie, John **25**
Adderley, Cannonball **15**
Adderley, Nat **29**
Allen, Geri **10**
Allison, Mose **17**

Anderson, Fred **32**
Anderson, Ray **7**
Armstrong, Louis **4**
Art Ensemble of Chicago **23**
Avery, Teodross **23**
Axelrod, David **34**
Bailey, Mildred **13**
Bailey, Pearl **5**
Baker, Anita **9**
Baker, Chet **13**
Baker, Ginger **16**
  Also see Cream
Barbieri, Gato **22**
Basie, Count **2**
Bauer, Johannes **32**
Bechet, Sidney **17**
Beiderbecke, Bix **16**
Belle, Regina **6**
Bennett, Tony **16**
  Earlier sketch in CM **2**
Benson, George **9**
Berigan, Bunny **2**
Blackman, Cindy **15**
Blakey, Art **11**
Blanchard, Terence **13**
Bley, Carla **8**
Bley, Paul **14**
Blood, Sweat and Tears **7**
Bowie, Lester **29**
Brand New Heavies, The **14**
Braxton, Anthony **12**
Brecker, Michael **29**
Bridgewater, Dee Dee **18**
Brötzmann, Peter **26**
Brown, Clifford **24**
Brown, Lawrence **23**
Brown, Norman **29**
Brown, Ray **21**
Brown, Ruth **13**
Brubeck, Dave **8**
Burrell, Kenny **11**
Burton, Gary **10**
Caine, Uri **31**
Calloway, Cab **6**
Canadian Brass, The **4**
Carter, Benny **3**
  Also see McKinney's Cotton Pickers
Carter, Betty **6**
Carter, James **18**
Carter, John **34**
Carter, Regina **22**
Carter, Ron **14**
Chambers, Paul **18**
Chanticleer **33**
Charles, Ray **24**
  Earlier sketch in CM **1**
Cherry, Don **10**
Christian, Charlie **11**
Clarke, Stanley **3**
Clements, Vassar **18**
Clooney, Rosemary **9**
Cole, Holly **18**
Cole, Nat King **3**
Coleman, Ornette **5**
Coltrane, John **4**
Connick, Jr., Harry **4**
Connors, Norman **30**
Corea, Chick **6**
Crawford, Randy **25**
Davis, Anthony **17**
Davis, Miles **1**
Davison, Wild Bill **34**
DeFranco, Buddy **31**
DeJohnette, Jack **7**
Dietrich, Marlene **25**
Di Meola, Al **12**
Dirty Dozen **23**

Douglas, Dave **29**
Eckstine, Billy **1**
Edison, Harry "Sweets" **29**
Eldridge, Roy **9**
  Also see McKinney's Cotton Pickers
Elling, Kurt **31**
Ellington, Duke **2**
Ellis, Herb **18**
Eskelin, Ellery **31**
Evans, Bill **17**
Evans, Gil **17**
Fell, Simon H. **32**
Ferguson, Maynard **7**
Ferrell, Rachelle **17**
Fitzgerald, Ella **1**
Five Iron Frenzy **26**
Flanagan, Tommy **16**
Fleck, Bela **8**
  Also see New Grass Revival, The
Flying Luttenbachers, The **28**
Fountain, Pete **7**
Frisell, Bill **15**
Fröhlich, Frank **32**
Gaillard, Slim **31**
Galway, James **3**
Garbarek, Jan **30**
Garner, Erroll **25**
Garrett, Kenny **28**
Getz, Stan **12**
Gillespie, Dizzy **6**
Goodman, Benny **4**
Gordon, Dexter **10**
Grappelli, Stephane **10**
Green, Benny **17**
Green, Grant **14**
Guaraldi, Vince **3**
Hackett, Bobby **21**
Haden, Charlie **12**
Hampton, Lionel **6**
Hancock, Herbie **25**
  Earlier sketch in CM **8**
Hardcastle, Paul **20**
Hargrove, Roy **15**
Harrell, Tom **28**
Harris, Barry **32**
Harris, Eddie **15**
Harris, Teddy **22**
Hawkins, Coleman **11**
Hawkins, Erskine **19**
Haynes, Roy **33**
Hedges, Michael **3**
Hemphill, Julius **34**
Henderson, Fletcher **16**
Henderson, Joe **14**
Herman, Woody **12**
Hibbler, Al **34**
Hines, Earl "Fatha" **12**
Hinton, Milt **33**
Hirt, Al **5**
Holiday, Billie **6**
Holland, Dave **27**
Horn, Shirley **7**
Horne, Lena **11**
Humes, Helen **19**
Hunter, Alberta **4**
Hunter, Charlie **24**
Ibrahim, Abdullah **24**
Incognito **16**
Isham, Mark **14**
Jackson, Milt **15**
Jacquet, Illinois **17**
Jamal, Ahmad **32**
James, Boney **21**
James, Harry **11**
Jarreau, Al **1**
Jarrett, Keith **1**
Jensen, Ingrid **22**

Jobim, Antonio Carlos **19**
Johnson, James P. **16**
Johnson, J.J. **33**
Johnson, Lonnie **17**
Jones, Elvin **9**
Jones, Hank **15**
Jones, Philly Joe **16**
Jones, Quincy **20**
  Earlier sketch in CM **2**
Jones, Thad **19**
Jordan, Marc **30**
Jordan, Stanley **1**
Kang, Eyvind **28**
Kennedy, Nigel **8**
Kenny G **14**
Kent, Stacey **28**
Kenton, Stan **21**
Kirk, Rahsaan Roland **6**
Kitt, Eartha **9**
Klugh, Earl **10**
Koffman, Moe **34**
Konitz, Lee **30**
Kowald, Peter **32**
Krall, Diana **27**
Kronos Quartet **5**
Kropinski, Uwe **31**
Krupa, Gene **13**
Laine, Cleo **10**
Lambert, Hendricks and Ross **28**
Lateef, Yusef **16**
Lee, Peggy **8**
Lewis, John **29**
Lewis, Ramsey **14**
Lincoln, Abbey **9**
Lloyd, Charles **22**
London, Julie **32**
López, Israel "Cachao" **34**
  Earlier sketch in CM **14**
Los Hombres Calientes **29**
Lovano, Joe **13**
Mahavishnu Orchestra **19**
Mahogany, Kevin **26**
Malone, Russell **27**
Mancini, Henry **20**
  Earlier sketch in CM **1**
Mangione, Chuck **23**
Manhattan Transfer, The **8**
Mann, Herbie **16**
Marsalis, Branford **10**
Marsalis, Ellis **13**
Marsalis, Wynton **20**
  Earlier sketch in CM **6**
Martino, Pat **17**
Masekela, Hugh **7**
McBride, Christian **17**
McCorkle, Susannah **27**
McFerrin, Bobby **3**
McKinney's Cotton Pickers **16**
McLaughlin, John **12**
McPartland, Marian **15**
McRae, Carmen **9**
Medeski, Martin & Wood **32**
Metheny, Pat **26**
  Earlier sketch in CM **2**
Mingus, Charles **9**
Monheit, Jane **33**
Monk, Thelonious **6**
Montgomery, Wes **3**
Moody, James **34**
Morgan, Frank **9**
Morton, Jelly Roll **7**
Mulligan, Gerry **16**
Murray, Dave **28**
Najee **21**
Nascimento, Milton **6**
Navarro, Fats **25**
Northwoods Improvisers **31**

Norvo, Red 12
O'Day, Anita 21
O'Farrill, Chico 31
Oliver, King 15
Oregon 30
O'Rourke, Jim 31
Oxley, Tony 32
Palmer, Jeff 20
Palmieri, Eddie 15
Parker, Charlie 5
Parker, Evan 28
Parker, Leon 27
Parker, Maceo 7
Parker, William 31
Pass, Joe 15
Paul, Les 2
Payton, Nicholas 27
Pepper, Art 18
Perez, Danilo 25
Peterson, Oscar 11
Ponty, Jean-Luc 8
Powell, Bud 15
Previn, André 15
Professor Longhair 6
Puente, Tito 14
Pullen, Don 16
Ralph Sharon Quartet 26
Rampal, Jean-Pierre 6
Redman, Dewey 32
Redman, Joshua 25
    Earlier sketch in CM 12
Reeves, Dianne 16
Reid, Vernon 2
    Also see Living Colour
Reinhardt, Django 7
Ribot, Marc 30
Rich, Buddy 13
Rivers, Sam 29
Roach, Max 12
Roberts, Marcus 6
Robillard, Duke 2
Rodney, Red 14
Rollins, Sonny 7
Roney, Wallace 33
Russell, Pee Wee 25
Saluzzi, Dino 23
Sanborn, David 28
    Earlier sketch in CM 1
Sanders, Pharoah 28
    Earlier sketch in CM 16
Sandoval, Arturo 15
Santamaria, Mongo 28
Santana, Carlos 19
    Earlier sketch in CM 1
Schuur, Diane 6
Scofield, John 7
Scott, Jimmy 14
Scott, Tony 32
Scott-Heron, Gil 13
Sebesky, Don 33
Severinsen, Doc 1
Sharrock, Sonny 15
Shaw, Artie 8
Shaw, Woody 27
Shearing, George 28
Shorter, Wayne 5
Silver, Horace 19
Simone, Nina 11
Smith, Jimmy 30
Smith, Jocelyn B. 30
Smith, Tommy 28
Solal, Martial 4
Sommer, Günter "Baby" 31
Spyro Gyra 34
Stern, Leni 29
Stern, Mike 29
Strayhorn, Billy 13

Summers, Andy 3
    Also see Police, The
Sun Ra 27
    Earlier sketch in CM 5
Take 6 6
Tate, Buddy 33
Tatum, Art 17
Taylor, Billy 13
Taylor, Cecil 9
Teagarden, Jack 10
Terry, Clark 24
Thielemans, Toots 13
Thornton, Teri 28
Threadgill, Henry 9
Torme, Mel 4
Tristano, Lennie 30
Tucker, Sophie 12
Turner, Big Joe 13
Turner, Roger 32
Turtle Island String Quartet 9
Tyner, McCoy 7
Ulmer, James Blood 13
US3 18
Valdes, Chuco 25
Valentin, Dave 33
Vandermark, Ken 28
Van Hove, Fred 30
Vaughan, Sarah 2
Walker, T-Bone 5
Wallace, Bennie 31
Washington, Dinah 5
Washington, Grover, Jr. 5
Weather Report 19
Webb, Chick 14
Wells, Bill 34
Weston, Randy 15
Whitaker, Rodney 20
Whiteman, Paul 17
Whitfield, Mark 18
Whittaker, Rodney 19
Willem Breuker Kollektief 28
Williams, Joe 11
Wilson, Cassandra 26
    Earlier sketch in CM 12
Wilson, Nancy 28
    Earlier sketch in CM 14
Winter, Paul 10
Witherspoon, Jimmy 19
Young, La Monte 16
Young, Lester 14
Zorn, John 15

Juju
Adé, King Sunny 18

Keyboards, Electric
Air 33
Aphex Twin 14
Badly Drawn Boy 33
Bley, Paul 14
Brown, Tony 14
Chemical Brothers 20
Corea, Chick 6
Davis, Chip 4
Dolby, Thomas 10
Eno, Brian 8
Foster, David 13
Froom, Mitchell 15
Hammer, Jan 21
Hancock, Herbie 25
    Earlier sketch in CM 8
Hardcastle, Paul 20
Jackson, Joe 22
    Earlier sketch in CM 4
Jarre, Jean-Michel 2
Jones, Booker T. 8
    Also see Booker T. & the M.G.'s

Kitaro 1
Man or Astroman? 21
Merzbow 31
Orbital 20
Palmer, Jeff 20
Riley, Terry 32
Sakamoto, Ryuichi 19
Shaffer, Paul 13
Smog 28
Sun Ra 27
    Earlier sketch in CM 5
Thievery Corporation 31
To Rococo Rot 31
Wakeman, Rick 27
    Also see Yes
Waller, Fats 7
Winwood, Steve 2
    Also see Spencer Davis Group
    Also see Traffic
Wolf, Peter 31
Wonder, Stevie 17
    Earlier sketch in CM 2
Worrell, Bernie 11
Yanni 11

Liturgical Music
Cooney, Rory 6
Talbot, John Michael 6

Mandolin
Bromberg, David 18
Grisman, David 17
Hartford, John 1
Lindley, David 2
Monroe, Bill 1
Skaggs, Ricky 5
Stuart, Marty 9

Musicals
Allen, Debbie 8
Allen, Peter 11
Andrews, Julie 33
    Earlier sketch in CM 4
Andrews Sisters, The 9
Bacharach, Burt 20
    Earlier sketch in CM 1
Bailey, Pearl 5
Baker, Josephine 10
Berlin, Irving 8
Brightman, Sarah 20
Brown, Ruth 13
Buckley, Betty 16
    Earlier sketch in CM 1
Burnett, Carol 6
Carter, Nell 7
Channing, Carol 6
Chevalier, Maurice 6
Crawford, Michael 4
Crosby, Bing 6
Curry, Tim 3
Davis, Sammy, Jr. 4
Day, Doris 24
Eder, Linda 30
Garland, Judy 6
Gershwin, George and Ira 11
Hamlisch, Marvin 1
Horne, Lena 11
Johnson, James P. 16
Jolson, Al 10
Kander, John 33
Kern, Jerome 13
Laine, Cleo 10
Lerner and Loewe 13
Lloyd Webber, Andrew 6
LuPone, Patti 8
Martin, Mary 27

Masekela, Hugh **7**
Menken, Alan **10**
Mercer, Johnny **13**
Merman, Ethel **27**
Moore, Melba **7**
Patinkin, Mandy **20**
  Earlier sketch in CM **3**
Peters, Bernadette **27**
Porter, Cole **10**
Robeson, Paul **8**
Rodgers, Richard **9**
Sager, Carole Bayer **5**
Shaffer, Paul **13**
Sondheim, Stephen **8**
Styne, Jule **21**
Warfield, William **33**
Waters, Ethel **11**
Weill, Kurt **12**
Whiting, Margaret **28**
Wildhorn, Frank **31**
Yeston, Maury **22**

Oboe
Lateef, Yusef **16**

Opera
Adams, John **8**
Ameling, Elly **24**
Anderson, June **27**
Anderson, Marian **8**
Austral, Florence **26**
Baker, Janet **14**
Bartoli, Cecilia **12**
Battle, Kathleen **6**
Beltrán, Tito **28**
Blegen, Judith **23**
Bocelli, Andrea **22**
Bonney, Barbara **33**
Bumbry, Grace **13**
Caballe, Monserrat **23**
Callas, Maria **11**
Carreras, José **34**
  Earlier sketch in CM **8**
Caruso, Enrico **10**
Chanticleer **33**
Church, Charlotte **28**
Copeland, Stewart **14**
  Also see Police, The
Cotrubas, Ileana **1**
Davis, Anthony **17**
Domingo, Placido **20**
  Earlier sketch in CM **1**
Fleming, Renee **24**
Freni, Mirella **14**
Gershwin, George and Ira **11**
Graves, Denyce **16**
Hampson, Thomas **12**
Hendricks, Barbara **10**
Heppner, Ben **23**
Herrmann, Bernard **14**
Horne, Marilyn **9**
McNair, Sylvia **15**
Nilsson, Birgit **31**
Norman, Jessye **7**
Pavarotti, Luciano **20**
  Earlier sketch in CM **1**
Price, Leontyne **6**
Quasthoff, Thomas **26**
Sills, Beverly **5**
Solti, Georg **13**
Sutherland, Joan **13**
Tan Dun **33**
Te Kanawa, Kiri **2**
Terfel, Bryn **31**
Toscanini, Arturo **14**
Upshaw, Dawn **9**
von Karajan, Herbert **1**

von Otter, Anne Sofie **30**
Weill, Kurt **12**
Zimmerman, Udo **5**

Percussion
Aronoff, Kenny **21**
Baker, Ginger **16**
  Also see Cream
Blackman, Cindy **15**
Blakey, Art **11**
Brown, Carlinhos **32**
Burton, Gary **10**
Collins, Phil **20**
  Earlier sketch in CM **2**
  Also see Genesis
Connors, Norman **30**
Copeland, Stewart **14**
  Also see Police, The
DeJohnette, Jack **7**
Glennie, Evelyn **33**
Gurtu, Trilok **29**
Hampton, Lionel **6**
Henley, Don **3**
Hussain, Zakir **32**
Jones, Elvin **9**
Jones, Philly Joe **16**
Jones, Spike **5**
Krupa, Gene **13**
Mo', Keb' **21**
N'Dour, Youssou **6**
Otis, Johnny **16**
Oxley, Tony **32**
Palmieri, Eddie **15**
Parker, Leon **27**
Puente, Tito **14**
Quaye, Finley **30**
Qureshi, Ustad Alla Rakha **29**
Rich, Buddy **13**
Roach, Max **12**
Santamaria, Mongo **28**
Scharin, Doug **32**
Schütze, Paul **32**
Sheila E. **3**
Sommer, Günter "Baby" **31**
Starr, Ringo **24**
  Earlier sketch in CM **10**
  Also see Beatles, The
Turner, Roger **32**
Walden, Narada Michael **14**
Webb, Chick **14**

Piano
Adamson, Barry **28**
Adès, Thomas **30**
Allen, Geri **10**
Allison, Mose **17**
Amos, Tori **12**
Apple, Fiona **28**
Argerich, Martha **27**
Arrau, Claudio **1**
Ashkenazy, Vladimir **32**
Axton, Hoyt **28**
Bacharach, Burt **20**
  Earlier sketch in CM **1**
Ball, Marcia **15**
Barenboim, Daniel **30**
Basie, Count **2**
Berlin, Irving **8**
Blake, Eubie **19**
Bley, Carla **8**
Bley, Paul **14**
Borge, Victor **19**
Brendel, Alfred **23**
Brickman, Jim **22**
Britten, Benjamin **15**
Bronfman, Yefim **6**
Brubeck, Dave **8**

Buckwheat Zydeco **34**
  Earlier sketch in CM **6**
Bush, Kate **4**
Caine, Uri **31**
Carpenter, Richard **24**
  Also see Carpenters
Charles, Ray **24**
  Earlier sketch in CM **1**
Clayderman, Richard **1**
Cleveland, James **1**
Cliburn, Van **13**
Cole, Nat King **3**
Collins, Judy **4**
Collins, Phil **20**
  Earlier sketch in CM **2**
  Also see Genesis
Connick, Jr., Harry **4**
Crouch, Andraé **9**
Davies, Dennis Russell **24**
DeJohnette, Jack **7**
Domino, Fats **2**
Dr. John **7**
Dupree, Champion Jack **12**
Ellington, Duke **2**
Esquivel, Juan **17**
Evans, Bill **17**
Evans, Gil **17**
Feinstein, Michael **6**
Ferrell, Rachelle **17**
Flack, Roberta **5**
Flanagan, Tommy **16**
Frey, Glenn **3**
Gaillard, Slim **31**
Galás, Diamanda **16**
Garner, Erroll **25**
Glass, Philip **1**
Gould, Glenn **9**
Green, Benny **17**
Grusin, Dave **7**
Guaraldi, Vince **3**
Hamelin, Marc-André **33**
Hamlisch, Marvin **1**
Hammill, Peter **30**
Hancock, Herbie **25**
  Earlier sketch in CM **8**
Harris, Barry **32**
Harris, Teddy **22**
Helfgott, David **19**
Henderson, Fletcher **16**
Hinderas, Natalie **12**
Hines, Earl "Fatha" **12**
Horn, Shirley **7**
Hornsby, Bruce **25**
  Earlier sketch in CM **3**
Horowitz, Vladimir **1**
Ibrahim, Abdullah **24**
Jackson, Joe **22**
  Earlier sketch in CM **4**
Jamal, Ahmad **32**
James, Skip **24**
Jarrett, Keith **1**
Joel, Billy **12**
  Earlier sketch in CM **2**
John, Elton **20**
  Earlier sketch in CM **3**
Johnson, James P. **16**
Jones, Hank **15**
Jones, Howard **26**
Joplin, Scott **10**
Kenton, Stan **21**
Kissin, Evgeny **6**
Krall, Diana **27**
Kreviazuk, Chantal **33**
Levine, James **8**
Lewis, Jerry Lee **2**
Lewis, John **29**
Lewis, Ramsey **14**

Liberace **9**
Line, Lorie **34**
Little Richard **1**
Manilow, Barry **2**
Marsalis, Ellis **13**
Matthews, Eric **22**
McPartland, Marian **15**
McRae, Carmen **9**
Milsap, Ronnie **2**
Mingus, Charles **9**
Monk, Thelonious **6**
Montgomery, Little Brother **26**
Morton, Jelly Roll **7**
Nero, Peter **19**
Newman, Randy **27**
  Earlier sketch in CM **4**
Nile, Willie **31**
Palmieri, Eddie **15**
Perahia, Murray **10**
Perez, Danilo **25**
Peterson, Oscar **11**
Pires, Maria João **26**
Post, Mike **21**
Powell, Bud **15**
Pratt, Awadagin **19**
Previn, André **15**
Professor Longhair **6**
Puente, Tito **14**
Pullen, Don **16**
Quaye, Finley **30**
Rangell, Andrew **24**
Rich, Charlie **3**
Riley, Terry **32**
Roberts, Marcus **6**
Rubinstein, Arthur **11**
Russell, Mark **6**
Schickele, Peter **5**
Schifrin, Lalo **29**
Sedaka, Neil **4**
Shaffer, Paul **13**
Shipp, Matthew **31**
Solal, Martial **4**
Solti, Georg **13**
Spann, Otis **18**
Story, Liz **2**
Strayhorn, Billy **13**
Sunnyland Slim **16**
Sykes, Roosevelt **20**
Tatum, Art **17**
Taylor, Billy **13**
Taylor, Cecil **9**
Thibaudet, Jean-Yves **24**
Thornton, Teri **28**
Tilson Thomas, Michael **24**
Tristano, Lennie **30**
Tyner, McCoy **7**
Valdes, Chuco **25**
Vangelis **21**
Van Hove, Fred **30**
Volodos, Arcadi **28**
Waits, Tom **27**
  Earlier sketch in CM **12**
  Earlier sketch in CM **1**
Walker, George **34**
Waller, Fats **7**
Wells, Bill **34**
Weston, Randy **15**
Wilson, Brian **24**
  Also see Beach Boys, The
Wilson, Cassandra **26**
  Earlier sketch in CM **12**
Winston, George **9**
Winwood, Steve **2**
  Also see Spencer Davis Group
  Also see Traffic
Wolf, Peter **31**

Wonder, Stevie **17**
  Earlier sketch in CM **2**
Young, La Monte **16**

Piccolo
Galway, James **3**

Pop
A-ha **22**
Abba **12**
Abdul, Paula **3**
Adam Ant **13**
Adams, Bryan **20**
  Earlier sketch in CM **2**
Adams, Oleta **17**
Aguilera, Christina **30**
Air **33**
Air Supply **22**
All-4-One **17**
All Saints **25**
Almond, Marc **29**
Alpert, Herb **11**
America **16**
Ames, Ed **31**
Amos, Tori **12**
Anderson, Laurie **25**
  Earlier sketch in CM **1**
Andrews, Julie **33**
  Earlier sketch in CM **4**
Andrews Sisters, The **9**
Anthony, Marc **33**
  Earlier sketch in CM **19**
Aqua **34**
  Earlier sketch in CM **2**
Arden, Jann **21**
Arena, Tina **21**
Armatrading, Joan **4**
Arnold, Eddy **10**
Artifacts **23**
Ash **34**
Astley, Rick **5**
Atari Teenage Riot **27**
Atkins, Chet **26**
  Earlier sketch in CM **5**
Atomic Fireballs, The **27**
Austin, Sherrié **34**
Avalon, Frankie **5**
Bacharach, Burt **20**
  Earlier sketch in CM **1**
Backstreet Boys **21**
Badly Drawn Boy **33**
Badu, Erykah **26**
Baha Men **32**
Bailey, Pearl **5**
Baker, Arthur **23**
Bananarama **22**
Bangles **22**
Basia **5**
Bauhaus **27**
Beach Boys, The **1**
Beat Happening **28**
Beatles, The **2**
Beaver Brown Band, The **3**
Bee Gees, The **3**
Belly **16**
Bennett, Tony **16**
  Earlier sketch in CM **2**
Benson, George **9**
Benton, Brook **7**
Beta Band, The **27**
Better Than Ezra **19**
B-52's, The **4**
Blegvad, Peter **28**
Blige, Mary J. **15**
Blink 182 **27**
Blondie **27**
  Earlier sketch in CM **14**

Bloodhound Gang, The **31**
Blood, Sweat and Tears **7**
Blue Rodeo **18**
Bluetones, The **29**
BoDeans, The **20**
  Earlier sketch in CM **3**
Bolton, Michael **4**
Boltz, Ray **33**
Booker T. & the M.G.'s **24**
Boone, Pat **13**
Boo Radleys, The **21**
Boston **11**
Bowie, David **23**
  Earlier sketch in CM **1**
Boyz II Men **15**
Bragg, Billy **7**
Branca, Glenn **29**
Branigan, Laura **2**
Braxton, Toni **17**
Brickell, Edie **3**
Brooks, Garth **25**
  Earlier sketch in CM **8**
Brown, Bobby **4**
Brown, Carlinhos **32**
Brown, Foxy **25**
Browne, Jackson **3**
Bryson, Peabo **11**
Buckingham, Lindsey **8**
  Also see Fleetwood Mac
Buckley, Tim **14**
Buffett, Jimmy **4**
Burdon, Eric **14**
  Also see Animals
  Also see War
Burroughs, William S. **26**
B*Witched **33**
Cabaret Voltaire **18**
Campbell, Glen **2**
Campbell, Tevin **13**
Captain Beefheart and the Magic Band **26**
  Earlier sketch in CM **10**
Cardigans **19**
Carey, Mariah **20**
  Earlier sketch in CM **6**
Carlisle, Belinda **8**
Carmichael, Hoagy **27**
Carnes, Kim **4**
Carpenter, Richard **24**
  Also see Carpenters
Carpenters **13**
Carr, Vikki **28**
Carroll, Dina **31**
Case, Peter **13**
Catatonia **29**
Chandra, Sheila **16**
Chanticleer **33**
Chapin, Harry **6**
Chapin-Carpenter, Mary **25**
  Earlier sketch in CM **6**
Chapman, Tracy **20**
  Earlier sketch in CM **4**
Charlatans, The **13**
Charles, Ray **24**
  Earlier sketch in CM **1**
Checker, Chubby **7**
Cher **1**
  Also see Sonny and Cher
Cherry, Neneh **4**
Cherry Poppin' Daddies **24**
Cheung, Jacky **33**
Chicago **3**
Chilton, Alex **10**
Chordettes, The **34**
Cibo Matto **28**

Clapton, Eric **11**
  Earlier sketch in CM **1**
  Also see Cream
  Also see Yardbirds, The
Clayderman, Richard **1**
Clooney, Rosemary **9**
Coasters, The **5**
Cocker, Joe **4**
Cocteau Twins, The **12**
Coldplay **32**
Cole, Lloyd **9**
Cole, Natalie **21**
Cole, Nat King **3**
  Earlier sketch in CM **1**
Cole, Paula **20**
Collins, Judy **4**
Collins, Phil **20**
  Earlier sketch in CM **2**
  Also see Genesis
Color Me Badd **23**
Colvin, Shawn **11**
Commodores, The **23**
Como, Perry **14**
Connick, Jr., Harry **4**
Connor, Chris **30**
Cooke, Sam **1**
  Also see Soul Stirrers, The
Cope, Julian **16**
Cornell, Don **30**
Cornershop **24**
Corrs, The **32**
Costello, Elvis **12**
  Earlier sketch in CM **2**
Cranberries, The **14**
Crash Test Dummies **14**
Crenshaw, Marshall **5**
Croce, Jim **3**
Crosby, David **3**
  Also see Byrds, The
Crow, Sheryl **18**
Crowded House **12**
Cure, The **20**
  Earlier sketch in CM **3**
Daft Punk **33**
Dalton, Nic **31**
Daltrey, Roger **3**
  Also see Who, The
Damone, Vic **33**
D'Arby, Terence Trent **3**
Darin, Bobby **4**
Dave, Edmunds **28**
Dave Clark Five, The **12**
Davies, Ray **5**
Davis, Sammy, Jr. **4**
Davis, Skeeter **15**
Day, Doris **24**
Dayne, Taylor **4**
DeBarge, El **14**
DeFrancesco, Joey **29**
Del Amitri **18**
Delirious? **33**
Dells, The **30**
Del Rubio Triplets **21**
Denver, John **1**
Depeche Mode **5**
Des'ree **24**
  Earlier sketch in CM **15**
Destiny's Child **33**
Devo **13**
Diamond, Neil **1**
Dietrich, Marlene **25**
Dion **4**
Dion, Celine **25**
  Earlier sketch in CM **12**
Divine Comedy, The **32**
Doc Pomus **14**
Donnas, The **33**

Donovan **9**
Doobie Brothers, The **3**
Doors, The **4**
Droge, Pete **24**
Dubstar **22**
Duran Duran **4**
Dury, Ian **30**
Dylan, Bob **21**
  Earlier sketch in CM **3**
Eagles, The **3**
  Earlier sketch in CM **8**
Earth, Wind and Fire **12**
Easton, Sheena **2**
Eder, Linda **30**
Edmonds, Kenneth "Babyface" **12**
eels **29**
Elastica **29**
Electric Light Orchestra **7**
Elfman, Danny **9**
Elliot, Cass **5**
  Also see Mamas and the Papas
Enigma **32**
  Earlier sketch in CM **14**
En Vogue **10**
Estefan, Gloria **15**
  Earlier sketch in CM **2**
Eurythmics **31**
  Earlier sketch in CM **6**
Everly Brothers, The **2**
Everything But The Girl **15**
Exposé **4**
Fabian **5**
Fabian, Lara **34**
Farnham, John **32**
Fatboy Slim **22**
Feliciano, José **10**
Ferguson, Maynard **7**
Ferry, Bryan **1**
Fiedler, Arthur **6**
Fine Young Cannibals **22**
Finn, Neil **34**
  Also see Crowded House
Fisher, Eddie **12**
Fitzgerald, Ella **1**
Flack, Roberta **5**
Fleetwood Mac **5**
Fogelberg, Dan **4**
Fordham, Julia **15**
Foster, David **13**
Four Tops, The **11**
Fox, Samantha **3**
Frampton, Peter **3**
Francis, Connie **10**
Frankie Goes To Hollywood **31**
Franklin, Aretha **17**
  Earlier sketch in CM **2**
Frey, Glenn **3**
  Also see Eagles, The
Gaines, Jeffrey **34**
Garbage **25**
Garfunkel, Art **4**
  Also see Simon and Garfunkel
Gaye, Marvin **4**
Gayle, Crystal **1**
Geldof, Bob **9**
Genesis **4**
Gershwin, George and Ira **11**
Gibson, Deborah **24**
  Earlier sketch in CM **1**
  See Gibson, Debbie
Gift, Roland **3**
Gil, Gilberto **26**
Gin Blossoms **18**
Ginsberg, Allen **26**
Go-Go's, The **24**
Gong **24**
Goodman, Benny **4**

Gordy, Berry, Jr. **6**
Grant, Amy **7**
Grant, Gogi **28**
Gray, David **30**
Gray, Macy **32**
Grebenshikov, Boris **3**
Green, Al **9**
Guthrie, Arlo **6**
Hall & Oates **6**
Hammer, M.C. **5**
Hancock, Herbie **25**
  Earlier sketch in CM **8**
Hanson **20**
Harding, John Wesley **6**
Harrison, George **2**
  Also see Beatles, The
Harry, Deborah **4**
  Also see Blondie
Hawkins, Sophie B. **21**
Haza, Ofra **29**
Healey, Jeff **4**
Henley, Don **3**
  Also see Eagles, The
Herman's Hermits **5**
Hill, Lauryn **25**
  Also see Fugees, The
Hitchcock, Robyn **9**
Holland-Dozier-Holland **5**
Hootie and the Blowfish **18**
Horn, Trevor **33**
Horne, Lena **11**
Hornsby, Bruce **25**
  Earlier sketch in CM **3**
Houston, Cissy **26**
  Earlier sketch in CM **6**
Houston, Whitney **25**
  Earlier sketch in CM **8**
Human League, The **17**
Humperdinck, Engelbert **19**
Ian, Janis **24**
  Earlier sketch in CM **5**
Idlewild **30**
Idol, Billy **3**
Iglesias, Julio **20**
  Earlier sketch in CM **2**
Imbruglia, Natalie **27**
Incubus **23**
Indigo Girls **20**
  Earlier sketch in CM **3**
Ingram, James **11**
Ink Spots, The **23**
Isaak, Chris **33**
  Earlier sketch in CM **6**
Isley Brothers, The **8**
Jackson, Janet **16**
  Earlier sketch in CM **3**
Jackson, Joe **22**
  Earlier sketch in CM **4**
Jackson, Michael **17**
  Earlier sketch in CM **1**
  Also see Jacksons, The
Jacksons, The **7**
James **12**
James, Harry **11**
James, Joni **30**
James, Rick **2**
Jan & Dean **32**
Jarreau, Al **1**
Jayhawks, The **15**
Jazz Butcher, The **30**
Jefferson Airplane **5**
Jesus Jones **23**
Jewel **25**
Jimmy Jam and Terry Lewis **11**
Jodeci **13**
Joe **33**

Joel, Billy **12**
  Earlier sketch in CM **2**
Johansen, David **7**
John, Elton **20**
  Earlier sketch in CM **3**
Johnston, Freedy **20**
Jolson, Al **10**
Jones, Howard **26**
Jones, Quincy **20**
  Earlier sketch in CM **2**
Jones, Rickie Lee **4**
Jones, Tom **11**
Joplin, Janis **3**
Joy Electric **26**
Kaye, Carol **22**
Keaggy, Phil **26**
Khaled **33**
Khan, Chaka **19**
  Earlier sketch in CM **9**
King, Ben E. **7**
King, Carole **6**
Kingsmen, The **34**
Kiss **25**
  Earlier sketch in CM **5**
Kitt, Eartha **9**
Knight, Gladys **1**
Knopfler, Mark **25**
  Earlier sketch in CM **3**
  Also see Dire Straits
Kool & the Gang **13**
Kraftwerk **9**
Kreviazuk, Chantal **33**
Kristofferson, Kris **4**
LaBelle, Patti **8**
Lambert, Hendricks and Ross **28**
Lamond, Mary Jane **33**
Lane, Fred **28**
lang, kd **25**
  Earlier sketch in CM **4**
Lauper, Cyndi **11**
Lee, Brenda **5**
Leftfield **29**
Leiber and Stoller **14**
Lemper, Ute **14**
Len **32**
Lennon, John **9**
  Also see Beatles, The
Lennon, Julian **26**
  Earlier sketch in CM **2**
Lennox, Annie **18**
  Also see Eurythmics
Lettermen, The **30**
Lewis, Huey **9**
Liberace **9**
Lightfoot, Gordon **3**
Lightning Seeds **21**
Lisa Lisa **23**
Loeb, Lisa **19**
Logan, Jack **27**
Loggins, Kenny **20**
  Earlier sketch in CM **3**
London, Julie **32**
Lopez, Jennifer **27**
Loud Family, The **31**
Lovett, Lyle **28**
  Earlier sketch in CM **5**
Lowe, Nick **25**
  Earlier sketch in CM **6**
Lulu **32**
Lush **13**
Lynne, Jeff **5**
MacColl, Kirsty **12**
MacNeil, Rita **29**
Madness **27**
Madonna **16**
  Earlier sketch in CM **4**
Magnetic Fields, The **28**

Mamas and the Papas **21**
Mancini, Henry **20**
  Earlier sketch in CM **1**
Manhattan Transfer, The **8**
Manilow, Barry **2**
Mann, Barry **30**
Marley, Bob **3**
Marley, Ziggy **3**
Marsalis, Branford **10**
Marshall, Amanda **27**
Martin, Dean **1**
Martin, George **6**
Martin, Mary **27**
Martin, Ricky **26**
Marx, Richard **21**
  Earlier sketch in CM **3**
Mathis, Johnny **2**
Mazzy Star **17**
McCartney, Paul **32**
  Earlier sketch in CM **4**
  Also see Beatles, The
McFerrin, Bobby **3**
McGuire Sisters, The **27**
McIntyre, Joey **34**
  Also see New Kids on the Block
McLachlan, Sarah **34**
  Earlier sketch in CM **12**
McLean, Don **7**
McLennan, Grant **21**
Medley, Bill **3**
Melanie **12**
Merchant, Natalie **25**
Mercury Rev **28**
Merman, Ethel **27**
Michael, George **9**
Midler, Bette **8**
Mighty Mighty Bosstones **20**
Miguel, Luis **34**
Mike & the Mechanics **17**
Miller, Mitch **11**
Miller, Roger **4**
Milli Vanilli **4**
Mills Brothers, The **14**
Minnelli, Liza **19**
Minogue, Kylie **32**
Minton, Phil **29**
Mitchell, Joni **17**
  Earlier sketch in CM **2**
Mojave 3 **26**
Money, Eddie **16**
Monheit, Jane **33**
Monica **26**
Monkees, The **7**
Montand, Yves **12**
Moore, Chante **21**
Morcheeba **25**
Morgan, Jane **30**
Morissette, Alanis **19**
Morrison, Jim **3**
Morrison, Van **24**
  Earlier sketch in CM **3**
Morrissey **10**
Mouskouri, Nana **12**
Moyet, Alison **12**
Murray, Anne **4**
Mya **32**
My Bloody Valentine **29**
Myles, Alannah **4**
Naté, Ultra **34**
Negativland **30**
Neville, Aaron **5**
  Also see Neville Brothers, The
Neville Brothers, The **4**
New Kids on the Block **3**
Newman, Randy **27**
  Earlier sketch in CM **4**
Newton, Wayne **2**

Newton-John, Olivia **8**
Nicks, Stevie **25**
  Earlier sketch in CM **2**
  Also see Fleetwood Mac
Nilsson **10**
98 Degrees **32**
Nitty Gritty Dirt Band **6**
Nixon, Mojo **32**
No Doubt **20**
'N Sync **25**
Nyro, Laura **12**
Oak Ridge Boys, The **7**
Ocasek, Ric **5**
  Also see Cars, The
Ocean, Billy **4**
O'Connor, Sinead **31**
  Earlier sketch in CM **3**
Odds **20**
Oldfield, Mike **18**
Orbit, William **30**
Orchestral Manoeuvres in the Dark **21**
Orlando, Tony **15**
Orton, Beth **26**
Osborne, Joan **19**
Osmond, Donny **3**
Page, Jimmy **4**
  Also see Led Zeppelin
  Also see Yardbirds, The
Page, Patti **11**
Papas Fritas **29**
Parks, Van Dyke **17**
Parsons, Alan **12**
Parton, Dolly **2**
Paul, Prince **29**
Peebles, Ann **30**
Pendergrass, Teddy **3**
Peniston, CeCe **15**
Penn, Michael **4**
Pernice Brothers **33**
Peter, Paul & Mary **4**
Pet Shop Boys **5**
Phillips, Sam **12**
Piaf, Edith **8**
Pizzicato Five **18**
Plant, Robert **2**
  Also see Led Zeppelin
Pointer Sisters, The **9**
Porter, Cole **10**
Prefab Sprout **15**
Presley, Elvis **1**
Priest, Maxi **20**
Prince **14**
  Earlier sketch in CM **1**
Proclaimers, The **13**
Prodigy **22**
Propellerheads **26**
Pulp **18**
Queen **6**
Quickspace **30**
Rabbitt, Eddie **24**
  Earlier sketch in CM **5**
Raitt, Bonnie **23**
  Earlier sketch in CM **3**
Rea, Chris **12**
Redding, Otis **5**
Reddy, Helen **9**
Reeves, Martha **4**
  Also see Martha and the Vandellas
R.E.M. **25**
  Earlier sketch in CM **5**
Republica **20**
Richard, Cliff **14**
Richie, Lionel **2**
Riders in the Sky **33**
Riley, Teddy **14**
Robbins, Marty **9**
Robinson, Smokey **1**

Rockapella **34**
Rogers, Kenny **1**
Rolling Stones **23**
  Earlier sketch in CM **3**
Ronstadt, Linda **2**
Roots, The **27**
Ross, Diana **1**
  Also see Supremes, The
Roth, David Lee **1**
  Also see Van Halen
Roxette **23**
Royal Crown Revue **33**
Ruffin, David **6**
RuPaul **20**
Sade **2**
Sager, Carole Bayer **5**
Sainte-Marie, Buffy **11**
Saint Etienne **28**
Sanborn, David **28**
  Earlier sketch in CM **1**
Santamaria, Mongo **28**
Savage Garden **32**
Seal **14**
Seals, Dan **9**
Seals & Crofts **3**
Secada, Jon **13**
Sedaka, Neil **4**
Selena **16**
Setzer, Brian **32**
Shaffer, Paul **13**
Shakira **33**
Shamen, The **23**
Shearing, George **28**
Sheep on Drugs **27**
Sheik, Duncan **32**
Sheila E. **3**
Shirelles, The **11**
Shonen Knife **13**
Siberry, Jane **6**
Simon, Carly **22**
  Earlier sketch in CM **4**
Simon, Paul **16**
  Earlier sketch in CM **1**
  Also see Simon and Garfunkel
Simpson, Jessica **34**
Sinatra, Frank **23**
  Earlier sketch in CM **1**
Sisqó **34**
Sixpence None the Richer **26**
Smith, Elliott **28**
Smith, Keely **29**
Smiths, The **3**
Snow, Pheobe **4**
Sobule, Jill **20**
Sonny and Cher **24**
Soul Coughing **21**
Sparks **18**
Spears, Britney **28**
Spector, Phil **4**
Spector, Ronnie **28**
Spice Girls **22**
Springfield, Dusty **20**
Springfield, Rick **9**
Spring Heel Jack **30**
Springsteen, Bruce **25**
  Earlier sketch in CM **6**
Squeeze **5**
Stafford, Jo **24**
Stansfield, Lisa **9**
Starr, Kay **27**
Starr, Ringo **24**
  Earlier sketch in CM **10**
  Also see Beatles, The
Steely Dan **29**
  Earlier sketch in CM **5**
Stereolab **18**
Stereo MC's **34**

Stevens, Cat **3**
Stewart, Rod **20**
  Earlier sketch in CM **2**
  Also see Faces, The
Stills, Stephen **5**
  Also see Buffalo Springfield
  Also see Crosby, Stills and Nash
Sting **19**
  Earlier sketch in CM **2**
  Also see Police, The
Stockwood, Kim **26**
Story, The **13**
Straw, Syd **18**
Streisand, Barbra **2**
Sturr, Jimmy **33**
Suede **20**
Summer, Donna **12**
Sundays, The **20**
Sunset Valley **31**
Superchunk **29**
Super Furry Animals **28**
Supremes, The **6**
Surfaris, The **23**
Sweat, Keith **13**
Sweet, Matthew **9**
Swell **31**
SWV **14**
Sylvian, David **27**
Talking Heads **1**
Talk Talk **19**
Taylor, James **25**
  Earlier sketch in CM **2**
Taylor, Steve **26**
Tears for Fears **6**
Teenage Fanclub **13**
Temptations, The **3**
10,000 Maniacs **3**
Texas **27**
The The **15**
They Might Be Giants **7**
Thievery Corporation **31**
Thomas, Irma **16**
Three Dog Night **5**
Tiffany **4**
Tikaram, Tanita **9**
Timbuk 3 **3**
TLC **15**
Toad the Wet Sprocket **13**
Tony! Toni! Toné! **12**
Torme, Mel **4**
Townshend, Pete **1**
  Also see Who, The
Trevi, Gloria **29**
Turner, Tina **29**
  Earlier sketch in CM **1**
  Also see Turner, Ike and Tina
Turtles, The **29**
Vale, Jerry **30**
Valli, Frankie **10**
Vandross, Luther **2**
Vanessa-Mae **26**
Vega, Suzanne **3**
Velasquez, Jaci **32**
Velocity Girl **23**
Veloso, Caetano **28**
Velvet Crush **28**
Vinton, Bobby **12**
Vitamin C **33**
Wainwright, Rufus **29**
Walsh, Joe **5**
Warnes, Jennifer **3**
Warwick, Dionne **2**
Was (Not Was) **6**
Washington, Dinah **5**
Waters, Crystal **15**
Watley, Jody **26**
  Earlier sketch in CM **9**

Webb, Jimmy **12**
Weller, Paul **14**
Westlife **33**
Who, The **3**
Williams, Andy **2**
Williams, Dar **21**
Williams, Deniece **1**
Williams, Joe **11**
Williams, Lucinda **24**
  Earlier sketch in CM **10**
Williams, Paul **26**
  Earlier sketch in CM **5**
Williams, Robbie **25**
Williams, Vanessa **10**
Williams, Victoria **17**
Wilson, Brian **24**
  Also see Beach Boys, The
Wilson, Jackie **3**
Wilson, Nancy **28**
  Earlier sketch in CM **14**
Wilson Phillips **5**
Winwood, Steve **2**
  Also see Spencer Davis Group
  Also see Traffic
Womack, Bobby **5**
Womack, Lee Ann **33**
Wonder, Stevie **17**
  Earlier sketch in CM **2**
Yankovic, "Weird Al" **7**
Young, Neil **15**
Young M.C. **4**

Producers

Ackerman, Will **3**
Afanasieff, Walter **26**
Albini, Steve **15**
Alpert, Herb **11**
Austin, Dallas **16**
Axelrod, David **34**
Baker, Anita **9**
Bass, Ralph **24**
Benitez, Jellybean **15**
Brown, Junior **15**
Brown, Tony **14**
Browne, Jackson **3**
Burnett, T Bone **13**
Cale, John **9**
Child, Desmond **30**
Clark, Dick **25**
  Earlier sketch in CM **2**
Clarke, Stanley **3**
Clinton, George **7**
Cohen, Lyor **29**
Collins, Phil **2**
  Also see Genesis
Combs, Sean "Puffy" **25**
  Earlier sketch in CM **16**
Connors, Norman **30**
Costello, Elvis **12**
  Earlier sketch in CM **2**
Cropper, Steve **12**
Crowell, Rodney **8**
Dalton, Nic **31**
Dave, Edmunds **28**
Dixon, Willie **10**
Dolby, Thomas **10**
Dr. Dre **15**
  Also see N.W.A.
Dupri, Jermaine **25**
  Earlier sketch in CM **2**
Dust Brothers **32**
Edmonds, Kenneth "Babyface" **12**
Elliott, Missy **30**
Enigma **32**
  Earlier sketch in CM **14**
Eno, Brian **8**

Ertegun, Ahmet **10**
Ertegun, Nesuhi **24**
Foster, David **13**
Fripp, Robert **9**
Froom, Mitchell **15**
Gabler, Milton **25**
Gabriel, Juan **31**
Garnier, Laurent **29**
Gordy, Jr., Emory **17**
Gray, F. Gary **19**
Grusin, Dave **7**
Hardcastle, Paul **20**
Horn, Trevor **33**
Jackson, Millie **14**
Jimmy Jam and Terry Lewis **11**
Jones, Booker T. **8**
    Also see Booker T. & the M.G.'s
Jones, Quincy **20**
    Earlier sketch in CM **2**
Jordan, Montell **26**
Krasnow, Bob **15**
Lanois, Daniel **8**
Laswell, Bill **14**
Leiber and Stoller **14**
Lillywhite, Steve **13**
Lynne, Jeff **5**
Mandel, Johnny **28**
Marley, Rita **10**
Martin, George **6**
Master P **22**
Mayfield, Curtis **8**
McKnight, Brian **22**
McLaren, Malcolm **23**
Miller, Mitch **11**
Most, Mickie **29**
Oakenfold, Paul **32**
Orbit, William **30**
O'Rourke, Jim **31**
Osby, Greg **21**
Parks, Van Dyke **17**
Parsons, Alan **12**
Paul, Prince **29**
Post, Mike **21**
Prince **14**
    Earlier sketch in CM **1**
Queen Latifah **24**
    Earlier sketch in CM **6**
Riley, Teddy **14**
Robertson, Robbie **2**
Rodgers, Nile **8**
Rubin, Rick **9**
Rundgren, Todd **11**
Salem, Kevin **32**
Scruggs, Randy **28**
Sherwood, Adrian **31**
Shocklee, Hank **15**
Simmons, Russell **7**
Size, Roni **31**
Skaggs, Ricky **5**
Spector, Phil **4**
Sure!, Al B. **13**
Sweat, Keith **13**
Too $hort **16**
Toussaint, Allen **11**
Tricky **18**
Vandross, Luther **2**
Van Helden, Armand **32**
Van Zandt, Steven **29**
Vasquez, Junior **16**
Vig, Butch **17**
Wachtel, Waddy **26**
Walden, Narada Michael **14**
Was, Don **21**
Watt, Mike **22**
Wexler, Jerry **15**
Whelan, Bill **20**
Wildhorn, Frank **31**

Willner, Hal **10**
Wilson, Brian **24**
    Also see Beach Boys, The
Winbush, Angela **15**
Wolf, Peter **31**
Woods-Wright, Tomica **22**

Promoters
Clark, Dick **25**
    Earlier sketch in CM **2**
Cohen, Lyor **29**
Geldof, Bob **9**
Graham, Bill **10**
Hay, George D. **3**
Simmons, Russell **7**

Ragtime
Johnson, James P. **16**
Joplin, Scott **10**

Rap
Arrested Development **14**
Austin, Dallas **16**
Bambaataa, Afrika **13**
Basehead **11**
Beastie Boys **25**
    Earlier sketch in CM **8**
Biz Markie **10**
Black Sheep **15**
Bone Thugs-N-Harmony **18**
Busta Rhymes **18**
Campbell, Luther **10**
Cherry, Neneh **4**
Combs, Sean "Puffy" **25**
    Earlier sketch in CM **16**
Common **23**
Coolio **19**
Cypress Hill **11**
Da Brat **30**
Das EFX **14**
De La Soul **7**
Del the Funky Homosapien **30**
Digable Planets **15**
Digital Underground **9**
DJ Jazzy Jeff and the Fresh Prince **5**
DMX **25**
Dr. Dre **15**
    Also see N.W.A.
Dupri, Jermaine **25**
Eazy-E **13**
    Also see N.W.A.
Elliott, Missy **30**
Eminem **28**
EPMD **10**
Eric B. and Rakim **9**
Evans, Faith **25**
Eve **34**
Franti, Michael **16**
Fugees, The **17**
Gang Starr **13**
Geto Boys, The **11**
Ghostface Killah **33**
Goodie Mob **24**
Grandmaster Flash **14**
Gravediggaz **23**
Hammer, M.C. **5**
Heavy D **10**
House of Pain **14**
Ice Cube **10**
Ice-T **7**
Insane Clown Posse **22**
Jackson, Millie **14**
Jay-Z **28**
Jeru the Damaja **33**
Kane, Big Daddy **7**
Kid 'n Play **5**

Kid Rock **27**
Knight, Suge **15**
Kool Moe Dee **9**
Kris Kross **11**
KRS-One **8**
Last Poets **21**
Lil' Kim **30**
L.L. Cool J. **5**
Love, G. **24**
Mase **27**
Master P **22**
MC Breed **17**
MC Eiht **27**
MC Lyte **8**
MC 900 Ft. Jesus **16**
MC Serch **10**
Method Man **31**
Monch, Pharoahe **29**
M.O.P. **34**
Mystikal **29**
Nas **19**
Naughty by Nature **11**
Notorious B.I.G. **20**
N.W.A. **6**
OutKast **33**
Pharcyde, The **17**
P.M. Dawn **11**
Public Enemy **4**
Queen Latifah **24**
    Earlier sketch in CM **6**
Rage Against the Machine **18**
Riley, Teddy **14**
Rubin, Rick **9**
Run D.M.C. **25**
    Earlier sketch in CM **4**
Salt-N-Pepa **6**
Scott-Heron, Gil **13**
Shaggy **19**
Shanté **10**
Shocklee, Hank **15**
Simmons, Russell **7**
Sir Mix-A-Lot **14**
Slick Rick **27**
Smith, Will **26**
Snoop Doggy Dogg **17**
Snow **23**
Spearhead **19**
Special Ed **16**
Sure!, Al B. **13**
TLC **15**
Tone-Loc **3**
Too $hort **16**
Tribe Called Quest, A **8**
Trick Daddy **28**
Tricky **18**
2Pac **17**
Usher **23**
US3 **18**
Vanilla Ice **6**
Warren G **33**
Williams, "Slim" and "Baby" **31**
Wu-Tang Clan **19**
Xzibit **31**
Young M.C. **4**
Yo Yo **9**

Record Company Executives
Ackerman, Will **3**
Alpert, Herb **11**
Blackwell, Chris **26**
Brown, Tony **14**
Busby, Jheryl **9**
Chess, Leonard **24**
Cohen, Lyor **29**
Combs, Sean "Puffy" **25**
    Earlier sketch in CM **16**
Davis, Chip **4**

Davis, Clive **14**
Ertegun, Ahmet **10**
Foster, David **13**
Gabriel, Peter **16**
  Earlier sketch in CM **2**
  Also see Genesis
Geffen, David **8**
Gordy, Berry, Jr. **6**
Hammond, John **6**
Harley, Bill **7**
Harrell, Andre **16**
Jimmy Jam and Terry Lewis **11**
Knight, Suge **15**
Koppelman, Charles **14**
Krasnow, Bob **15**
LiPuma, Tommy **18**
Madonna **16**
  Earlier sketch in CM **4**
Marley, Rita **10**
Martin, George **6**
Master P **22**
Mayfield, Curtis **8**
Mercer, Johnny **13**
Miller, Mitch **11**
Mingus, Charles **9**
Near, Holly **1**
Ostin, Mo **17**
Penner, Fred **10**
Phillips, Sam **5**
Reznor, Trent **13**
  Also see Nine Inch Nails
Rhone, Sylvia **13**
Robinson, Smokey **1**
Rubin, Rick **9**
Simmons, Russell **7**
Size, Roni **31**
Spector, Phil **4**
Teller, Al **15**
Too $hort **16**
Wexler, Jerry **15**
Williams, "Slim" and "Baby" **31**
Woods-Wright, Tomica **22**

Reggae
Aswad **34**
Bad Brains **16**
Beenie Man **33**
Big Mountain **23**
Black Uhuru **12**
Brown, Carlinhos **32**
Brown, Dennis **29**
Burning Spear **15**
Cliff, Jimmy **8**
Dube, Lucky **17**
Inner Circle **15**
Israel Vibration **21**
Kitchener, Lord **29**
Marley, Bob **3**
Marley, Rita **10**
Marley, Ziggy **3**
Minott, Sugar **31**
Mystic Revealers **16**
Quaye, Finley **30**
Sherwood, Adrian **31**
Skatalites, The **18**
Sly and Robbie **13**
Steel Pulse **14**
Third World **13**
Tosh, Peter **3**
UB40 **4**
Wailer, Bunny **11**
Wailing Souls **32**

Rhythm and Blues/Soul
Aaliyah **21**
Abdul, Paula **3**
Adams, Johnny **33**

Adams, Oleta **17**
Alexander, Arthur **14**
All-4-One **17**
Austin, Dallas **16**
Badu, Erykah **26**
Baker, Anita **9**
Baker, LaVern **25**
Ball, Marcia **15**
Ballard, Hank **17**
Basehead **11**
Becker, Margaret **31**
Belle, Regina **6**
Benét, Eric **27**
Berry, Chuck **33**
  Earlier sketch in CM **1**
Blackstreet **23**
Bland, Bobby "Blue" **12**
Blessid Union of Souls **20**
Blige, Mary J. **15**
Blues Brothers, The **3**
Bolton, Michael **4**
Booker T. & the M.G.'s **24**
Boyz II Men **15**
Brandy **19**
Braxton, Toni **17**
Brown, James **16**
  Earlier sketch in CM **2**
Brown, Ruth **13**
Brownstone **21**
Bryson, Peabo **11**
Burdon, Eric **14**
  Also see Animals
  Also see War
Busby, Jheryl **9**
Campbell, Tevin **13**
C + C Music Factory **16**
Carey, Mariah **20**
  Earlier sketch in CM **6**
Carr, James **23**
Charles, Ray **24**
  Earlier sketch in CM **1**
Cole, Natalie **21**
  Earlier sketch in CM **1**
Color Me Badd **23**
Commodores, The **23**
Cooke, Sam **1**
  Also see Soul Stirrers, The
Crawford, Randy **25**
Cropper, Steve **12**
Curtis, King **17**
D'Angelo **20**
D'Arby, Terence Trent **3**
DeBarge, El **14**
Des'ree **24**
  Earlier sketch in CM **15**
Destiny's Child **33**
Dibango, Manu **14**
Diddley, Bo **3**
Domino, Fats **2**
Dr. John **7**
Dru Hill **25**
Earth, Wind and Fire **12**
Edmonds, Kenneth "Babyface" **12**
En Vogue **10**
Evora, Cesaria **19**
Fabulous Thunderbirds, The **1**
Four Tops, The **11**
Fox, Samantha **3**
Franklin, Aretha **17**
  Earlier sketch in CM **2**
Gaye, Marvin **4**
Gill, Johnny **20**
Ginuwine **34**
Gordy, Berry, Jr. **6**
Gray, Macy **32**
Green, Al **9**
Guthrie, Gwen **26**

Hall & Oates **6**
Hawkins, Screamin' Jay **29**
  Earlier sketch in CM **8**
Hayes, Isaac **10**
Hill, Lauryn **25**
  Also see Fugees, The
Holland-Dozier-Holland **5**
Houston, Whitney **25**
  Earlier sketch in CM **8**
Howland, Don **24**
Hurt, Mississippi John **24**
Incognito **16**
Ingram, James **11**
Isley Brothers, The **8**
Jackson, Freddie **3**
Jackson, Janet **3**
Jackson, Michael **17**
  Earlier sketch in CM **1**
  Also see Jacksons, The
Jackson, Millie **14**
Jacksons, The **7**
James, Etta **6**
Jimmy Jam and Terry Lewis **11**
Jodeci **13**
Joe **33**
John, Willie **25**
Jones, Booker T. **8**
  Also see Booker T. & the M.G.'s
Jones, Grace **9**
Jones, Quincy **20**
  Earlier sketch CM **2**
Jordan, Louis **11**
Jordan, Montell **26**
K-Ci & JoJo **34**
Kelly, R. **19**
Khan, Chaka **19**
  Earlier sketch CM **9**
King, B. B. **24**
  Earlier sketch in CM **1**
King, Ben E. **7**
Knight, Gladys **1**
Kool & the Gang **13**
LaBelle, Patti **8**
Los Lobos **2**
Love, G. **24**
Martha and the Vandellas **25**
Maxwell **22**
Mayfield, Curtis **8**
McKnight, Brian **22**
McPhatter, Clyde **25**
Medley, Bill **3**
Meters, The **14**
Milli Vanilli **4**
Mills, Stephanie **21**
Mint Condition **29**
Mo', Keb' **21**
Monica **26**
Monifah **24**
Moonglows, The **33**
Moore, Chante **21**
Moore, Melba **7**
Morrison, Van **24**
  Earlier sketch in CM **3**
Mya **32**
Ndegéocello, Me'Shell **18**
Neville, Aaron **5**
  Also see Neville Brothers, The
Neville Brothers, The **4**
Ocean, Billy **4**
Ohio Players **16**
O'Jays, The **13**
Otis, Johnny **16**
Pendergrass, Teddy **3**
Peniston, CeCe **15**
Perry, Phil **24**
Pickett, Wilson **10**
Platters, The **25**

Pointer Sisters, The **9**
Price, Kelly **34**
Price, Lloyd **25**
Priest, Maxi **20**
Prince **14**
  Earlier sketch in CM **1**
Rainey, Ma **22**
Rawls, Lou **19**
Redding, Otis **5**
Reese, Della **13**
Reeves, Martha **4**
Richie, Lionel **2**
Riley, Teddy **14**
Robinson, Smokey **1**
Ross, Diana **1**
  Also see Supremes, The
Ruffin, David **6**
  Also see Temptations, The
Sam and Dave **8**
Scaggs, Boz **12**
Secada, Jon **13**
Shai **23**
Shanice **14**
Shirelles, The **11**
Shocklee, Hank **15**
Silk **26**
Sisqó **34**
Sledge, Percy **15**
Sly & the Family Stone **24**
Soul II Soul **17**
Spinners, The **21**
Stansfield, Lisa **9**
Staples, Mavis **13**
Staples, Pops **11**
Stewart, Rod **20**
  Earlier sketch in CM **2**
  Also see Faces, The
Stone, Sly **8**
Subdudes, The **18**
Supremes, The **6**
  Also see Ross, Diana
Sure!, Al B. **13**
Sweat, Keith **13**
SWV **14**
Tamia **34**
Temptations, The **3**
Third World **13**
Thomas, Irma **16**
Thornton, Big Mama **18**
TLC **15**
Tony! Toni! Toné! **12**
Toussaint, Allen **11**
Turner, Ike and Tina **24**
Turner, Tina **29**
  Earlier sketch in CM **1**
  Also see Turner, Ike and Tina
Tyrese **34**
Vandross, Luther **24**
  Earlier sketch in CM **2**
Walker, Junior **30**
Was (Not Was) **6**
Waters, Crystal **15**
Watley, Jody **26**
  Earlier sketch in CM **9**
Wexler, Jerry **15**
White, Karyn **21**
Williams, Deniece **1**
Williams, Vanessa **10**
Wilson, Jackie **3**
Wilson, Nancy **28**
  Earlier sketch in CM **14**
Winans, The **12**
Winbush, Angela **15**
Womack, Bobby **5**
Wonder, Stevie **17**
  Earlier sketch in CM **2**
Zhane **22**

Rock
AC/DC **4**
Adam Ant **13**
Adams, Bryan **20**
  Earlier sketch in CM **2**
Aerosmith **22**
  Earlier sketch in CM **3**
Afghan Whigs **17**
Alarm **2**
Albini, Steve **15**
Alexander, Arthur **14**
Alice in Chains **10**
Alien Sex Fiend **23**
Alkaline Trio **34**
Allen, Daevid **28**
Allman Brothers, The **6**
Alvin, Dave **17**
America **16**
American Music Club **15**
Animals **22**
Anthrax **11**
Apple, Fiona **28**
Apples in Stereo **30**
Aquabats **22**
Arab Strap **33**
Archers of Loaf **21**
Art of Noise **22**
Ash **34**
Asian Dub Foundation **30**
At The Drive-In **32**
Audio Adrenaline **22**
Aztec Camera **22**
Babes in Toyland **16**
Bad Brains **16**
Bad Company **22**
Badfinger **23**
Bad Religion **28**
Baker, Ginger **16**
  Also see Cream
Ballard, Hank **17**
Band, The **9**
Bardo Pond **28**
Barenaked Ladies **18**
Barlow, Lou **20**
  Also see Sebadoh
Basehead **11**
Basement Jaxx **29**
Beach Boys, The **1**
Beastie Boys, The **25**
  Earlier sketch in CM **8**
Beat Farmers, The **23**
Beatles, The **2**
Beaver Brown Band, The **3**
Beck **18**
Beck, Jeff **4**
  Also see Yardbirds, The
Belew, Adrian **5**
Belle and Sebastian **28**
Belly **16**
Benatar, Pat **8**
Ben Folds Five **20**
Berry, Chuck **33**
  Earlier sketch in CM **1**
Bettie Serveert **17**
Bevis Frond **23**
Biafra, Jello **18**
  Also see Dead Kennedys
Big Audio Dynamite **18**
Big Head Todd and the Monsters **20**
Bill Wyman & the Rhythm Kings **26**
Bishop, Jeb **28**
Björk **16**
  Also see Sugarcubes, The
Black, Frank **14**
Black Crowes, The **7**
Black Flag **22**
Blackman, Cindy **15**

Black Sabbath **9**
Blind Melon **21**
Blink 182 **27**
Blonde Redhead **28**
Blondie **27**
  Earlier sketch in CM **14**
Bloodhound Gang, The **31**
Blood, Sweat and Tears **7**
Blue Oyster Cult **16**
Blue Rodeo **18**
Blues Traveler **15**
Blur **17**
BoDeans, The **20**
  Earlier sketch in CM **3**
Bonham, Tracy **34**
Bon Jovi **34**
  Earlier sketch in CM **10**
Bonzo Dog Doo-Dah Band **30**
Boredoms, The **28**
Boss Hog **29**
Boston **11**
Bowie, David **23**
  Earlier sketch in CM **1**
Brad **21**
Bragg, Billy **7**
Breeders **19**
Brickell, Edie **3**
Brooks, Meredith **30**
Brötzmann, Caspar **27**
Browne, Jackson **3**
Buckethead **34**
Buckingham, Lindsey **8**
Buckley, Tim **14**
Buffalo Springfield **24**
Buffalo Tom **18**
Built to Spill **27**
Burdon, Eric **14**
  Also see Animals
  Also see War
Burnett, T Bone **13**
Bush **18**
Butthole Surfers **16**
Buzzcocks, The **9**
Byrds, The **8**
Byrne, David **8**
  Also see Talking Heads
Cake **27**
Cale, J. J. **16**
  Earlier sketch in CM **9**
Calexico **33**
Calvert, Robert **30**
Camel **21**
Can **28**
Candlebox **32**
Captain Beefheart and the Magic Band **26**
  Earlier sketch in CM **10**
Caravan **24**
Cardigans **19**
Cars, The **20**
Carter USM **31**
Catherine Wheel **18**
Cat Power **30**
Caustic Resin **31**
Cave, Nick **10**
Ceili Rain **34**
Chadbourne, Eugene **30**
Chainsaw Kittens, The **33**
Charlatans, The **13**
Charm Farm **20**
Cheap Trick **12**
Cher **1**
  Also see Sonny and Cher
Chicago **3**
Childish, Billy **28**
Christian Death **28**
Chumbawamba **21**
Church, The **14**

Cinderella **16**
Circle Jerks, The **17**
Citizen King **27**
Clapton, Eric **11**
  Earlier sketch in CM **1**
  Also see Cream
  Also see Yardbirds, The
Clark, Anne **32**
Clash, The **4**
Clemons, Clarence **7**
Clinton, George **7**
Coasters, The **5**
Cobra Verde **28**
Cochrane, Tom **22**
Cocker, Joe **4**
Cold **34**
Cold Chisel **34**
Collective Soul **16**
Collins, Phil **2**
  Also see Genesis
Commander Cody and His Lost
  Planet Airmen **30**
Compulsion **23**
Concrete Blonde **32**
Congo Norvell **22**
Cooder, Ry **2**
  Also see Captain Beefheart and His Magic
  Band
Cooke, Sam **1**
  Also see Soul Stirrers, The
Cooper, Alice **8**
Cope, Julian **16**
Costello, Elvis **12**
  Earlier sketch in CM **2**
Cougar, John(ny)
  See Mellencamp, John
Counting Crows **18**
Coverdale, David **34**
  See Deep Purple
  Also see Whitesnake
Cows, The **32**
Cracker **12**
Cramps, The **16**
Cranberries, The **14**
Crash Test Dummies **14**
Cream **9**
Creed **28**
Creedence Clearwater Revival **16**
Crenshaw, Marshall **5**
Crosby, David **3**
  Also see Byrds, The
  Also see Crosby, Stills, and Nash
Crosby, Stills, and Nash **24**
Crow, Sheryl **18**
Crowded House **12**
Cult, The **16**
Cure, The **20**
  Earlier sketch in CM **3**
Curry, Tim **3**
Curve **13**
Dahl, Jeff **28**
Dale, Dick **13**
Daltrey, Roger **3**
  Also see Who, The
Damned, The **34**
Damon and Naomi **25**
Dandy Warhols, The
Daniels, Charlie **6**
Danzig **7**
D'Arby, Terence Trent **3**
Dark Star **29**
Dave, Edmunds **28**
Dave Clark Five, The **12**
Dave Matthews Band **18**
Davies, Ray **5**
dc Talk **18**
Dead Can Dance **16**

Dead Kennedys **29**
Dead Milkmen **22**
Death in Vegas **28**
de Burgh, Chris **22**
Deep Purple **11**
Def Leppard **3**
Deftones **22**
Del Amitri **18**
Delgados, The **31**
Depeche Mode **5**
Devo **13**
D Generation **26**
Diddley, Bo **3**
DiFranco, Ani **17**
Dinosaur Jr. **10**
Dire Straits **22**
Dirty Three **31**
D.O.A. **28**
Doc Pomus **14**
Dog's Eye View **21**
Dokken **16**
Donnas, The **33**
Doobie Brothers, The **3**
Doors, The **4**
Down By Law **34**
Dreamtheater **23**
Drivin' N' Cryin' **31**
Dropkick Murphys **26**
Duran Duran **4**
Durutti Column, The **30**
Dylan, Bob **3**
Eagles, The **3**
Echo and the Bunnymen **32**
Echobelly **21**
Eddy, Duane **9**
Einstürzende Neubauten **13**
Electric Light Orchestra **7**
Elf Power **30**
Elliot, Cass **5**
Emerson, Lake & Palmer/Powell **5**
Eminem **28**
Emmet Swimming **24**
English Beat, The **9**
Eno, Brian **8**
Erickson, Roky **16**
Escovedo, Alejandro **18**
Etheridge, Melissa **16**
  Earlier sketch in CM **4**
Eurythmics **31**
  Earlier sketch in CM **6**
Eve 6 **31**
Everclear **18**
Ex, The **28**
Extreme **10**
Faces, The **22**
Fairport Convention **22**
Faithfull, Marianne **14**
Faith No More **7**
Fall, The **12**
Fastbacks, The **29**
Fastball **32**
Faust **32**
Fear Factory **27**
Felt **32**
Ferry, Bryan **1**
Filter **28**
fIREHOSE **11**
Fishbone **7**
Five Iron Frenzy **26**
Fixx, The **33**
Flaming Lips **22**
Fleetwood Mac **5**
Flores, Rosie **16**
Flying Luttenbachers, The **28**
Flying Saucer Attack **29**
Fogelberg, Dan **4**

Fogerty, John **2**
  Also see Creedence Clearwater Revival
Folk Implosion, The **28**
Foo Fighters **20**
Ford, Lita **9**
Foreigner **21**
Fountains of Wayne **26**
Four Seasons, The **24**
Fox, Samantha **3**
Frampton, Peter **3**
Frankie Lymon and The Teenagers **24**
Franti, Michael **16**
Frey, Glenn **3**
  Also see Eagles, The
Frogs, The **31**
Front 242 **19**
Froom, Mitchell **15**
Fuel **27**
Fugazi **13**
Fu Manchu **22**
Gabriel, Peter **16**
  Earlier sketch in CM **2**
  Also see Genesis
Gaines, Jeffrey **34**
Galaxie 500 **33**
Gang of Four **8**
Garcia, Jerry **4**
  Also see Grateful Dead, The
Gatton, Danny **16**
Gene Loves Jezebel **27**
Genesis **4**
Geraldine Fibbers **21**
Ghost **24**
Giant Sand **30**
Gift, Roland **3**
Gin Blossoms **18**
Girls Against Boys **31**
Glitter, Gary **19**
Go-Betweens, The **28**
God Is My Co-Pilot **29**
Godsmack **30**
Golden Palominos **32**
Gomez **33**
Goo Goo Dolls, The **16**
Gorky's Zygotic Mynci **30**
Graham, Bill **10**
Grant Lee Buffalo **16**
Grapes of Wrath, The **33**
Grateful Dead **5**
Grebenshikov, Boris **3**
Green Day **16**
Griffin, Patty **24**
Guess Who **23**
Guided By Voices **18**
Guns n' Roses **2**
Gus Gus **26**
Guster **29**
Gwar **13**
Hagar, Sammy **21**
Hagen, Nina **25**
Hall & Oates **6**
Hammill, Peter **30**
Harper, Ben **17**
Harper, Roy **30**
Harrison, George **2**
  Also see Beatles, The
Harry, Deborah **4**
  Also see Blondie
Hart, Beth **29**
Harvey, Polly Jean **11**
Hassman, Nikki **26**
Hatfield, Juliana **12**
  Also see Lemonheads, The
Hawkins, Screamin' Jay **29**
  Earlier sketch in CM **8**
Healey, Jeff **4**
Heart **1**

Helmet **15**
Hendrix, Jimi **2**
Henley, Don **3**
  Also see Eagles, The
Henry, Joe **18**
Hiatt, John **8**
Hodgson, Roger **26**
  Also see Supertramp
Hole **14**
Holland-Dozier-Holland **5**
Hoodoo Gurus **33**
Hooters **20**
Hootie and the Blowfish **18**
Houston, Penelope **28**
Idol, Billy **3**
Imperial Teen **26**
Indigenous **31**
INXS **21**
  Earlier sketch in CM **2**
Iron Maiden **10**
Isaak, Chris **33**
  Earlier sketch in CM **6**
Jackson, Joe **22**
  Earlier sketch in CM **4**
Jackyl **24**
Jagger, Mick **7**
  Also see Rolling Stones, The
Jam, The **27**
Jane's Addiction **6**
Jars of Clay **20**
Jawbox **31**
Jayhawks, The **15**
Jefferson Airplane **5**
Jesus and Mary Chain, The **10**
Jesus Lizard **19**
Jethro Tull **8**
Jett, Joan **3**
Jimmie's Chicken Shack **22**
Joel, Billy **12**
  Earlier sketch in CM **2**
Johansen, David **7**
John, Elton **20**
  Earlier sketch in CM **3**
Jon Spencer Blues Explosion **18**
Joplin, Janis **3**
Journey **21**
Joy Division **19**
Judas Priest **10**
Kansas **32**
Keene, Tommy **31**
Kelly, Jeff **31**
Kennedy, Nigel **8**
Kidjo, Anjelique **17**
Kid Rock **27**
Killing Joke **30**
King Crimson **17**
King Missile **22**
Kingsmen, The **34**
Kinks, The **15**
Kiss **25**
  Earlier sketch in CM **5**
KMFDM **18**
Knopfler, Mark **25**
  Earlier sketch in CM **3**
  Also see Dire Straits
Korn **20**
Kravitz, Lenny **26**
  Earlier sketch in CM **5**
La Ley **33**
Lambchop **29**
Landreth, Sonny **16**
Lanternjack, The **31**
Led Zeppelin **1**
Lee, Ben **26**
Leiber and Stoller **14**
Lemonheads, The **12**

Lennon, John **9**
  Also see Beatles, The
Lennon, Julian **26**
  Earlier sketch in CM **2**
Les Négresses Vertes **30**
Less Than Jake **22**
Letters to Cleo **22**
Limp Bizkit **27**
Lindley, David **2**
Linkous, Mark **26**
Lit **27**
Little Feat **4**
Little Texas **14**
Live **14**
Living Colour **7**
Lofgren, Nils **25**
Logan, Jack **27**
Loggins, Kenny **20**
  Earlier sketch in CM **3**
Los Lobos **2**
Loud Family, The **31**
Love **34**
Love and Rockets **15**
Love Spit Love **21**
Lowe, Nick **25**
  Earlier sketch in CM **6**
L7 **12**
Luna **18**
Luscious Jackson **27**
  Earlier sketch in CM **19**
Lush **13**
Lydon, John **9**
  Also see Sex Pistols, The
Lynne, Jeff **5**
Lynyrd Skynyrd **9**
Machine Head **32**
MacIsaac, Ashley **21**
Madder Rose **17**
Malone, Michelle **30**
Manic Street Preachers **27**
Mansun **30**
Marcy Playground **31**
Marilyn Manson **18**
Martin, George **6**
Marx, Richard **3**
Matchbox 20 **27**
Matthew Good Band **34**
McCartney, Paul **32**
  Earlier sketch in CM **4**
  Also see Beatles, The
McCaughey, Scott **31**
McClinton, Delbert **14**
MC5, The **9**
McKee, Maria **11**
McLachlan, Sarah **34**
  Earlier sketch in CM **12**
McMurtry, James **10**
Meat Loaf **12**
Meat Puppets, The **13**
Megadeth **9**
Mekons, The **15**
Mellencamp, John **20**
  Earlier sketch in CM **2**
Men at Work **34**
Metallica **33**
  Earlier sketch in CM **7**
Midnight Oil **11**
Mighty Mighty Bosstones **20**
Mike & the Mechanics **17**
Miller, Steve **2**
Ministry **10**
Minty **32**
Minutemen, The **31**
Misfits, The **32**
Moby Grape **12**
Modest Mouse **30**
moe. **34**

Mogwai **27**
Mojave 3 **26**
Monch, Pharoahe **29**
Money, Eddie **16**
Monks of Doom **28**
Moody Blues, The **18**
Moonglows, The **33**
Morphine **29**
  Earlier sketch in CM **16**
Morrison, Jim **3**
  Also see Doors, The
Morrison, Van **24**
  Earlier sketch in CM **3**
Mötley Crüe **1**
Motörhead **10**
Mott the Hoople **31**
Mould, Bob **10**
Mountain **30**
M People **27**
  Earlier sketch in CM **15**
Mr. T Experience, The **29**
Mudhoney **16**
Muldaur, Maria **18**
Mullins, Shawn **33**
Murphy, Peter **22**
MxPx **33**
Myles, Alannah **4**
Naked, Bif **33**
Nelson, Rick **2**
Neu! **32**
Neurosis **28**
Neutral Milk Hotel **31**
Newman, Randy **4**
Newsboys, The **24**
New York Dolls **20**
Nicks, Stevie **25**
  Earlier sketch in CM **2**
  Also see Fleetwood Mac
Nile, Willie **31**
Nine Inch Nails **29**
Nirvana **8**
NOFX **28**
Nova, Heather **30**
NRBQ **12**
Nugent, Ted **2**
Oasis **16**
Ocasek, Ric **5**
  Also see Cars, The
O'Connor, Sinead **31**
  Earlier sketch in CM **3**
Offspring **19**
Oldham, Will **32**
Olivia Tremor Control **28**
Ono, Yoko **11**
Orbison, Roy **2**
Orgy **27**
O'Rourke, James **31**
Osbourne, Ozzy **3**
Our Lady Peace **22**
OutKast **33**
Page, Jimmy **4**
  Also see Led Zeppelin
  Also see Yardbirds, The
Palmer, Robert **2**
Pantera **13**
Papa Roach **30**
Parker, Graham **10**
Parker, Maceo **7**
Parsons, Alan **12**
Parsons, Gram **7**
  Also see Byrds, The
Paul Revere & The Raiders **30**
Pavement **14**
Pearl Jam **32**
  Earlier sketch in CM **12**
Pearls Before Swine **24**
Pennywise **27**

Pere Ubu **17**
Perkins, Carl **9**
Petty, Tom **9**
  Also see Tom Petty and the Heartbreakers
Phillips, Sam **5**
Phish **25**
  Earlier sketch in CM **13**
Pigface **19**
Pink Floyd **2**
Pixies, The **21**
Placebo **27**
Plant, Robert **2**
  Also see Led Zeppelin
P.O.D. **33**
Pogues, The **6**
Poi Dog Pondering **17**
Poison **11**
Police, The **20**
Pop, Iggy **23**
  Earlier sketch in CM **1**
Porno for Pyros **31**
Powderfinger **33**
Presidents of the United States of
  America, The **34**
Presley, Elvis **1**
Pretenders, The **8**
Pretty Things, The **26**
Primal Scream **14**
Primus **11**
Prince **14**
  Earlier sketch in CM **1**
Prine, John **7**
Proclaimers, The **13**
Promise Ring, The **28**
Prong **23**
Prophet, Chuck **32**
Pulp **18**
Quasi **24**
Queen **6**
Queens of the Stone Age **31**
Queensryche **8**
Quicksilver Messenger Service **23**
Radiohead **24**
Rage Against the Machine **18**
Raitt, Bonnie **23**
  Earlier sketch in CM **3**
Rammstein **25**
Ramones, The **9**
Rancid **29**
Rasputina **26**
Redd Kross **20**
Red Hot Chili Peppers **29**
  Earlier sketch in CM **7**
Reed, Lou **16**
  Earlier sketch in CM **1**
  Also see Velvet Underground, The
Reef **24**
Reid, Vernon **2**
  Also see Living Colour
R.E.M. **25**
  Earlier sketch in CM **5**
REO Speedwagon **23**
Replacements, The **7**
Residents, The **14**
Reverend Horton Heat **19**
Reznor, Trent **13**
  Also see Nine Inch Nails
Richards, Keith **11**
  Also see Rolling Stones, The
Richman, Jonathan **12**
Riley, Terry **32**
Robertson, Robbie **2**
Rolling Stones, The **23**
  Earlier sketch in CM **3**
Rollins, Henry **11**
Romantics, The **34**

Roth, David Lee **1**
  Also see Van Halen
Royal Trux **29**
Rube Waddell **29**
Rubin, Rick **9**
Rundgren, Todd **11**
Rush **8**
Rusted Root **26**
Ryder, Mitch **11**
Salem, Kevin **32**
Sambora, Richie **24**
  Also see Bon Jovi
Santana, Carlos **19**
  Earlier sketch in CM **1**
Satriani, Joe **4**
Scaggs, Boz **12**
Scharin, Doug **32**
Scorpions, The **12**
Screaming Trees **19**
Scud Mountain Boys **21**
Seal **14**
Sebadoh **26**
Seger, Bob **15**
Semisonic **32**
Sepultura **12**
Sex Pistols, The **5**
Shadows, The **22**
Shaffer, Paul **13**
Shannon, Del **10**
Shihad **34**
Shipp, Matthew **31**
Shocked, Michelle **4**
Shonen Knife **13**
Shudder to Think **20**
Sigur Rós **31**
Silver Apples **23**
Silverchair **20**
Simon, Carly **22**
  Earlier sketch in CM **4**
Simon, Paul **16**
  Earlier sketch in CM **1**
  Also see Simon and Garfunkel
Simon and Garfunkel **24**
Simple Minds **21**
Siouxsie and the Banshees **8**
Sister Hazel **34**
Skinny Puppy **17**
Skunk Anansie **27**
Slayer **10**
Sleater-Kinney **20**
Slick, Grace **33**
  Also see Jefferson Airplane
Slipknot **30**
Sloan **28**
Smashing Pumpkins **13**
Smash Mouth **27**
Smith, Patti **17**
  Earlier sketch in CM **1**
Smithereens, The **14**
Smiths, The **3**
Smog **28**
Social Distortion **27**
  Earlier sketch in CM **19**
Sonic Youth **26**
  Earlier sketch in CM **9**
Son Volt **21**
Soul Asylum **10**
Soulfly **33**
Soundgarden **6**
Spacehog **29**
Spacemen 3 **31**
Sparks **18**
Specials, The **21**
Spector, Phil **4**
Spencer Davis Group **19**
Spinal Tap **8**
Spin Doctors **14**

Spirit **22**
Sponge **18**
Spongetones, The **34**
Spoon **34**
Springsteen, Bruce **25**
  Earlier sketch in CM **6**
Squeeze **5**
Staind **31**
Starr, Ringo **24**
  Earlier sketch in CM **10**
  Also see Beatles, The
Steeleye Span **19**
Steely Dan **29**
  Earlier sketch in CM **5**
Steppenwolf **20**
Stereophonics **29**
Stern, Mike **29**
Stevens, Cat **3**
Stewart, Rod **20**
  Earlier sketch in CM **2**
  Also see Faces, The
Stills, Stephen **5**
  Also see Buffalo Springfield
  Also see Crosby, Stills and Nash
Sting **19**
  Earlier sketch in CM **2**
  Also see Police, The
Stone, Sly **8**
  Also see Sly & the Family Stone
Stone Roses, The **16**
Stone Temple Pilots **14**
Stranglers, The **31**
Straw, Syd **18**
Stray Cats, The **11**
String Cheese Incident, The **34**
Stryper **2**
Sublime **19**
Sugarcubes, The **10**
Suicidal Tendencies **15**
Summers, Andy **3**
  Also see Police, The
Sunny Day Real Estate **28**
Superchunk **29**
Superdrag **23**
Supergrass **30**
Supertramp **25**
Surfin' Pluto **24**
Swervedriver **31**
Taylor, Mick
  Also see Beatles, The
Taylor, Steve **26**
Tears for Fears **6**
Teenage Fanclub **13**
Television **17**
10,000 Maniacs **3**
Terrell **32**
Tesla **15**
Texas Tornados, The **8**
The The **15**
They Might Be Giants **7**
Thin Lizzy **13**
Third Day **34**
Third Eye Blind **25**
Thompson, Richard **7**
Thorogood, George **34**
Three Dog Night **5**
311 **20**
Throwing Muses **15**
Tijuana No! **32**
Timbuk 3 **3**
To Rococo Rot **31**
Toad the Wet Sprocket **13**
Tom Petty and the Heartbreakers **26**
Tonic **32**
Tool **21**
Tortoise **32**

Townshend, Pete **1**
  Also see Who, The
Traffic **19**
Tragically Hip, The **18**
Train **33**
Travis **29**
Treadmill Trackstar **21**
T. Rex **11**
Trynin, Jen **21**
Tsunami **21**
Turner, Tina **29**
  Earlier sketch in CM **1**
  Also see Turner, Ike and Tina
Tuxedomoon **21**
23 Skidoo **31**
Type O Negative **27**
  Earlier sketch in CM **2**
Ulmer, James Blood **13**
Underworld **26**
Unitt, Victor
  Also see Beatles, The
Urge Overkill **17**
Uriah Heep **19**
U2 **34**
  Earlier sketch in CM **12**
Vai, Steve **5**
Valens, Ritchie **23**
Valli, Frankie **10**
Vandermark, Ken **28**
Van Halen **25**
  Earlier sketch in CM **8**
Van Zandt, Steven **29**
VAST **34**
Vaughan, Jimmie **24**
Vaughan, Stevie Ray **1**
Velvet Underground, The **7**
Ventures **19**
Vertical Horizon **33**
Veruca Salt **20**
Verve, The **18**
Verve Pipe, The **20**
Vincent, Gene **19**
Violent Femmes **12**
Waits, Tom **27**
  Earlier sketch in CM **12**
  Earlier sketch in CM **1**
Wakeman, Rick **27**
  Also see Yes
Wallflowers, The **20**
Walsh, Joe **5**
  Also see Eagles, The
Wannadies, The **29**
War **14**
Warrant **17**
Waterboys, The **27**
Wedding Present, The **28**
Ween **30**
Weezer **20**
Weller, Paul **14**
Wendy O. Williams and The Plasmatics **26**
Westerberg, Paul **26**
Whitesnake **5**
White Zombie **17**
Whitley, Chris **16**
Who, The **3**
Wilson, Brian **24**
  Also see Beach Boys, The
Winter, Johnny **5**
Winwood, Steve **2**
  Also see Spencer Davis Group
  Also see Traffic
Wire **29**
Wolf, Peter **25**
Workhorse Movement, The **30**
Wray, Link **17**
Wyatt, Robert **24**
Wynn, Steve **31**

X **11**
X-Ray Spex **31**
XTC **26**
  Earlier sketch in CM **10**
Yardbirds, The **10**
Yes **8**
Yo La Tengo **24**
Young, Neil **15**
  Earlier sketch in CM **2**
Zappa, Frank **17**
  Earlier sketch in CM **1**
Zevon, Warren **9**
Zombies, The **23**
ZZ Top **2**

Rock and Roll Pioneers
Ballard, Hank **17**
Berry, Chuck **33**
  Earlier sketch in CM **1**
Clark, Dick **25**
  Earlier sketch in CM **2**
Darin, Bobby **4**
Diddley, Bo **3**
Dion **4**
Domino, Fats **2**
Eddy, Duane **9**
Everly Brothers, The **2**
Francis, Connie **10**
Glitter, Gary **19**
Haley, Bill **6**
Hawkins, Screamin' Jay **29**
  Earlier sketch in CM **8**
Holly, Buddy **1**
James, Etta **6**
Jordan, Louis **11**
Lewis, Jerry Lee **2**
Little Richard **1**
Nelson, Rick **2**
Orbison, Roy **2**
Otis, Johnny **16**
Paul, Les **2**
Perkins, Carl **9**
Phillips, Sam **5**
Presley, Elvis **1**
Professor Longhair **6**
Sedaka, Neil **4**
Shannon, Del **10**
Shirelles, The **11**
Spector, Phil **4**
Twitty, Conway **6**
Valli, Frankie **10**
Wilson, Jackie **3**
Wray, Link **17**

Saxophone
Adderley, Cannonball **15**
Anderson, Fred **32**
Anderson, Wessell **23**
Ayler, Albert **19**
Barbieri, Gato **22**
Bechet, Sidney **17**
Braxton, Anthony **12**
Brecker, Michael **29**
Brötzmann, Peter **26**
Carter, Benny **3**
  Also see McKinney's Cotton Pickers
Carter, James **18**
Chenier, C. J. **15**
Clemons, Clarence **7**
Coleman, Ornette **5**
Coltrane, John **4**
Curtis, King **17**
Desmond, Paul **23**
Dibango, Manu **14**
Eskelin, Ellery **31**
Garbarek, Jan **30**
Garrett, Kenny **28**

Getz, Stan **12**
Golson, Benny **21**
Gordon, Dexter **10**
Harris, Eddie **15**
Hawkins, Coleman **11**
Hemphill, Julius **34**
Henderson, Joe **14**
Herman, Woody **12**
Hodges, Johnny **24**
Jacquet, Illinois **17**
James, Boney **21**
Kenny G **14**
Kirk, Rahsaan Roland **6**
Koffman, Moe **34**
Konitz, Lee **30**
Koz, Dave **19**
Kuti, Femi **29**
Lacy, Steve **23**
Lateef, Yusef **16**
Lloyd, Charles **22**
López, Israel "Cachao" **34**
  Earlier sketch in CM **14**
Lovano, Joe **13**
Marsalis, Branford **10**
Moody, James **34**
Morgan, Frank **9**
Mulligan, Gerry **16**
Murray, Dave **28**
Najee **21**
Osby, Greg **21**
Parker, Charlie **5**
Parker, Evan **28**
Parker, Maceo **7**
Pepper, Art **18**
Redman, Dewey **32**
Redman, Joshua **25**
  Earlier sketch in CM **12**
Rollins, Sonny **7**
Russell, Pee Wee **25**
Sanborn, David **28**
  Earlier sketch in CM **1**
Sanders, Pharoah **28**
  Earlier sketch in CM **16**
Scott, Tony **32**
Shorter, Wayne **5**
Smith, Tommy **28**
Tate, Buddy **33**
Threadgill, Henry **9**
Vandermark, Ken **28**
Walker, Junior **30**
Wallace, Bennie **31**
Washington, Grover, Jr. **5**
Winter, Paul **10**
Young, La Monte **16**
Young, Lester **14**
Zorn, John **15**

Sintir
Hakmoun, Hassan **15**

Songwriters
Acuff, Roy **2**
Adams, Bryan **20**
  Earlier sketch in CM **2**
Adams, Yolanda **23**
Adkins, Trace **31**
Afanasieff, Walter **26**
Aikens, Rhett **22**
Albini, Steve **15**
Alexander, Arthur **14**
Allen, Peter **11**
Allison, Mose **17**
Almond, Marc **29**
Alpert, Herb **11**
Alvin, Dave **17**
Amos, Tori **12**
Anderson, Bill **32**

Anderson, John **5**
Anka, Paul **2**
Anthony, Marc **33**
  Earlier sketch in CM **19**
Anu, Christine **34**
Apple, Fiona **28**
Armatrading, Joan **4**
Atkins, Chet **26**
  Earlier sketch in CM **5**
Austin, Sherrié **34**
Autry, Gene **25**
  Earlier sketch in CM **12**
Axelrod, David **34**
Bacharach, Burt **20**
  Earlier sketch in CM **1**
Badly Drawn Boy **33**
Badu, Erykah **26**
Baez, Joan **1**
Baker, Anita **9**
Barlow, Lou **20**
Basie, Count **2**
Becker, Margaret **31**
Belew, Adrian **5**
Benét, Eric **27**
Benton, Brook **7**
Berg, Matraca **16**
Bergman, Alan and Marilyn **30**
Berlin, Irving **8**
Berry, Chuck **33**
  Earlier sketch in CM **1**
Björk **16**
  Also see Sugarcubes, The
Black, Clint **5**
Black, Frank **14**
Blades, Ruben **2**
Blegvad, Peter **28**
Blige, Mary J. **15**
Bloom, Luka **14**
Bond, Johnny **28**
Brady, Paul **8**
Bragg, Billy **7**
Brandt, Paul **22**
Brickell, Edie **3**
Brokop, Lisa **22**
Brooks, Garth **25**
  Earlier sketch in CM **8**
Brooks, Meredith **30**
Brown, Bobby **4**
Brown, James **16**
  Earlier sketch in CM **2**
Brown, Junior **15**
Brown, Marty **14**
Browne, Jackson **3**
Buckingham, Lindsey **8**
  Also see Fleetwood Mac
Buckley, Jeff **22**
Buckley, Tim **14**
Buckner, Richard **31**
Buffett, Jimmy **4**
Burdon, Eric **14**
  Also see Animals
  Also see War
Burnett, T Bone **13**
Burning Spear **15**
Burroughs, William S. **26**
Bush, Kate **4**
Byrne, David **8**
  Also see Talking Heads
Cahn, Sammy **11**
Cale, J. J. **16**
Calloway, Cab **6**
Calvert, Robert **30**
Campbell, Sarah Elizabeth **23**
Captain Beefheart **10**
Cardwell, Joi **22**
Carlisle, Bob **22**
Carmichael, Hoagy **27**

Carter, Carlene **8**
Carter, Deana **25**
Carthy, Martin **34**
  Also see Steeleye Span
Cash, Johnny **17**
  Earlier sketch in CM **1**
Cash, Rosanne **2**
Cat Power **30**
Chandra, Sheila **16**
Chapin, Harry **6**
Chapin-Carpenter, Mary **25**
  Earlier sketch in CM **6**
Chapman, Gary **33**
Chapman, Steven Curtis **15**
Chapman, Tracy **4**
Chaquico, Craig **23**
  Also see Jefferson Starship
Charles, Ray **24**
  Earlier sketch in CM **1**
Chenier, C. J. **15**
Chesnutt, Vic **28**
Child, Desmond **30**
Childish, Billy **28**
Childs, Toni **2**
Chilton, Alex **10**
Clapton, Eric **11**
  Earlier sketch in CM **1**
  Also see Cream
  Also see Yardbirds, The
Clark, Anne **32**
Clark, Guy **17**
Clements, Vassar **18**
Cleveland, James **1**
Clinton, George **7**
Cochrane, Tom **23**
Cockburn, Bruce **8**
Cohen, Leonard **3**
Cole, Lloyd **9**
Cole, Nat King **3**
Collie, Mark **15**
Collins, Albert **4**
Collins, Judy **4**
Collins, Phil **2**
  Also see Genesis
Cooder, Ry **2**
Cooke, Sam **1**
  Also see Soul Stirrers, The
Cooper, Alice **8**
Cope, Julian **16**
Costello, Elvis **12**
  Earlier sketch in CM **2**
Cotten, Elizabeth **16**
Coverdale, David **34**
  See Deep Purple
  Also see Whitesnake
Crenshaw, Marshall **5**
Croce, Jim **3**
Cropper, Steve **12**
Crosby, David **3**
  Also see Byrds, The
Crow, Sheryl **18**
Crowe, J. D. **5**
Crowell, Rodney **8**
Curtis, Catie **31**
Dahl, Jeff **28**
Dalton, Nic **31**
Daniels, Charlie **6**
Davies, Ray **5**
  Also see Kinks, the
DeBarge, El **14**
de Burgh, Chris **22**
DeMent, Iris **13**
Denver, John **22**
  Earlier sketch in CM **1**
Des'ree **24**
  Earlier sketch in CM **15**
Diamond, Neil **1**

Diddley, Bo **3**
Diffie, Joe **27**
  Earlier sketch in CM **10**
DiFranco, Ani **17**
Dion **4**
Dixon, Willie **10**
DMX **25**
Doc Pomus **14**
Domino, Fats **2**
Donovan **9**
Dorsey, Thomas A. **11**
Doucet, Michael **8**
Drake, Nick **17**
Dube, Lucky **17**
Dulli, Greg **17**
  Also see Afghan Whigs, The
Dury, Ian **30**
Dylan, Bob **21**
  Earlier sketch in CM **3**
Earle, Steve **16**
Edmonds, Kenneth "Babyface" **12**
Elfman, Danny **9**
Ellington, Duke **2**
Elliott, Ramblin' Jack **32**
Emmanuel, Tommy **21**
English, Michael **23**
Enigma **32**
  Earlier sketch in CM **14**
Enya **32**
  Earlier sketch in CM **6**
Erickson, Roky **16**
Ertegun, Ahmet **10**
Escovedo, Alejandro **18**
Estefan, Gloria **15**
  Earlier sketch in CM **2**
Etheridge, Melissa **16**
  Earlier sketch in CM **4**
Evans, Sara **27**
Everlast **27**
Fabian, Lara **34**
Faithfull, Marianne **14**
Ferry, Bryan **1**
Finn, Neil **34**
  Also see Crowded House
Flack, Roberta **5**
Flatt, Lester **3**
Fogelberg, Dan **4**
Fogerty, John **2**
  Also see Creedence Clearwater Revival
Fordham, Julia **15**
Foster, David **13**
Frampton, Peter **3**
Franti, Michael **16**
Frey, Glenn **3**
  Also see Eagles, The
Fripp, Robert **9**
Frizzell, Lefty **10**
Gabriel, Juan **31**
Gabriel, Peter **16**
  Earlier sketch in CM **2**
  Also see Genesis
Gaines, Jeffrey **34**
Garcia, Jerry **4**
  Also see Grateful Dead, The
Gaye, Marvin **4**
Geldof, Bob **9**
Gershwin, George and Ira **11**
Gibson, Bob **23**
Gibson, Deborah **24**
  Earlier sketch in CM **1**
  Also see Gibson, Debbie
Gift, Roland **3**
Gill, Vince **34**
  Earlier sketch in CM **7**
Gilley, Mickey **7**
Goffin-King **24**
Gold, Julie **22**

Goodman, Benny **4**
Gordy, Berry, Jr. **6**
Gorka, John **18**
Grant, Amy **7**
Gray, David **30**
Gray, Macy **32**
Green, Al **9**
Greenwood, Lee **12**
Griffin, Patty **24**
Griffith, Nanci **3**
Guthrie, Arlo **6**
Guthrie, Gwen **26**
Guthrie, Woodie **2**
Guy, Buddy **4**
Hagen, Nina **25**
Haggard, Merle **2**
Hall, Tom T. **26**
  Earlier sketch in CM **4**
Hamlisch, Marvin **1**
Hammer, M.C. **5**
Hammill, Peter **30**
Hancock, Herbie **25**
  Earlier sketch in CM **8**
Hardin, Tim **18**
Harding, John Wesley **6**
Harley, Bill **7**
Harper, Ben **17**
Harper, Roy **30**
Harris, Emmylou **4**
Harrison, George **2**
  Also see Beatles, The
Harry, Deborah **4**
  Also see Blondie
Hart, Beth **29**
Hartford, John **1**
Hatfield, Juliana **12**
  Also see Lemonheads, The
Hawkins, Screamin' Jay **29**
  Earlier sketch in CM **8**
Hayes, Isaac **10**
Healey, Jeff **4**
Hedges, Michael **3**
Hendrix, Jimi **2**
Henley, Don **3**
  Also see Eagles, The
Henry, Joe **18**
Hiatt, John **8**
Hill, Lauryn **25**
  Also see Fugees, The
Hinojosa, Tish **13**
Hitchcock, Robyn **9**
Holly, Buddy **1**
Hornsby, Bruce **25**
  Earlier sketch in CM **3**
Houston, Penelope **28**
Howard, Harlan **15**
Ian, Janis **24**
  Earlier sketch in CM **5**
Ice Cube **10**
Ice-T **7**
Idol, Billy **3**
Imbruglia, Natalie **27**
Isaak, Chris **33**
  Earlier sketch in CM **6**
Jackson, Alan **25**
  Earlier sketch in CM **7**
Jackson, Janet **16**
  Earlier sketch in CM **3**
Jackson, Joe **22**
  Earlier sketch in CM **4**
Jackson, Michael **17**
  Earlier sketch in CM **1**
  Also see Jacksons, The
Jackson, Millie **14**
Jagger, Mick **7**
  Also see Rolling Stones, The
James, Rick **2**

Jarreau, Al **1**
Jennings, Waylon **4**
Jett, Joan **3**
Jewel **25**
Jimmy Jam and Terry Lewis **11**
Joel, Billy **12**
  Earlier sketch in CM **2**
Johansen, David **7**
John, Elton **20**
  Earlier sketch in CM **3**
Johnson, Lonnie **17**
Jones, George **4**
Jones, Quincy **20**
  Earlier sketch in CM **2**
Jones, Rickie Lee **4**
Joplin, Janis **3**
Jordan, Marc **30**
Jordan, Montell **26**
Kane, Big Daddy **7**
Kee, John P. **15**
Keene, Tommy **31**
Keith, Toby **17**
Kelly, Jeff **31**
Kelly, R. **19**
Ketchum, Hal **14**
Khan, Chaka **19**
  Earlier sketch in CM **9**
King, Albert **2**
King, B. B. **24**
  Earlier sketch in CM **1**
King, Ben E. **7**
King, Carole **6**
King, Freddy **17**
Knopfler, Mark **25**
  Earlier sketch in CM **3**
  Also see Dire Straits
Kottke, Leo **13**
Kravitz, Lenny **26**
  Earlier sketch in CM **5**
Kreviazuk, Chantal **33**
Kristofferson, Kris **4**
Landreth, Sonny **16**
lang, kd **25**
  Earlier sketch in CM **4**
Larkin, Patty **9**
Lauderdale, Jim **29**
Lavin, Christine **6**
LeDoux, Chris **12**
Lee, Ben **26**
Lee, Peggy **8**
Lehrer, Tom **7**
Leiber and Stoller **14**
Lennon, John **9**
  Also see Beatles, The
Lennon, Julian **26**
  Earlier sketch in CM **2**
Lewis, Huey **9**
Lightfoot, Gordon **3**
Linkous, Mark **26**
Little Richard **1**
L.L. Cool J **5**
Loeb, Lisa **23**
Logan, Jack **27**
Loggins, Kenny **20**
  Earlier sketch in CM **3**
Love, Laura **20**
Loveless, Patty **5**
Lovett, Lyle **28**
  Earlier sketch in CM **5**
Lowe, Nick **25**
  Earlier sketch in CM **6**
Lydon, John **9**
  Also see Sex Pistols, The
Lynn, Loretta **2**
Lynne, Jeff **5**
Lynne, Shelby **29**
  Earlier sketch in CM **5**

MacColl, Kirsty **12**
MacNeil, Rita **29**
Madonna **16**
  Earlier sketch in CM **4**
Malone, Michelle **30**
Manilow, Barry **2**
Mann, Aimee **22**
Mann, Barry **30**
Mann, Billy **23**
Marley, Bob **3**
Marley, Ziggy **3**
Marshall, Amanda **27**
Marx, Richard **3**
Mattea, Kathy **5**
Mayfield, Curtis **8**
MC Breed **17**
McCartney, Paul **32**
  Earlier sketch in CM **4**
  Also see Beatles, The
McCaughey, Scott **31**
McClinton, Delbert **14**
McCorkle, Susannah **27**
McCoury, Del **15**
McCulloch, Ian **23**
McLachlan, Sarah **34**
  Earlier sketch in CM **12**
McLaren, Malcolm **23**
McLean, Don **7**
McLennan, Grant **21**
McMurtry, James **10**
MC 900 Ft. Jesus **16**
McTell, Blind Willie **17**
Medley, Bill **3**
Melanie **12**
Mellencamp, John **20**
  Earlier sketch in CM **2**
  Also see John Cougar Mellencamp
Mercer, Johnny **13**
Merchant, Natalie **25**
  Also see 10,000 Maniacs
Messina, Jo Dee **26**
Michael, George **9**
Miller, Buddy **31**
Miller, Roger **4**
Miller, Steve **2**
Milsap, Ronnie **2**
Mitchell, Joni **17**
  Earlier sketch in CM **2**
Moffatt, Katy **18**
Morrison, Jim **3**
Morrison, Van **24**
  Earlier sketch in CM **3**
Morrissey **10**
Morrissey, Bill **12**
Morton, Jelly Roll **7**
Mould, Bob **10**
Moyet, Alison **12**
Mullins, Shawn **33**
Nascimento, Milton **6**
Ndegéocello, Me'Shell **18**
Near, Holly **1**
Nelson, Rick **2**
Nelson, Willie **11**
  Earlier sketch in CM **1**
Newman, Randy **27**
  Earlier sketch in CM **4**
Nicks, Stevie **25**
  Earlier sketch in CM **2**
  Also see Fleetwood Mac
Nile, Willie **31**
Nilsson **10**
Nova, Heather **30**
Nugent, Ted **2**
Nyro, Laura **12**
Ocasek, Ric **5**
  Also see Cars, The
Ocean, Billy **4**

Ochs, Phil **7**
O'Connor, Sinead **31**
  Earlier sketch in CM **3**
Odetta **7**
Oldham, Will **32**
Orbison, Roy **2**
Orton, Beth **26**
Osbourne, Ozzy **3**
Oslin, K. T. **3**
Overstreet, Paul **33**
Owens, Buck **2**
Page, Jimmy **4**
  Also see Led Zeppelin
  Also see Yardbirds, The
Palmer, Robert **2**
Paris, Twila **16**
Parker, Graham **10**
Parks, Van Dyke **17**
Parnell, Lee Roy **15**
Parsons, Gram **7**
  Also see Byrds, The
Parton, Dolly **24**
  Earlier sketch in CM **2**
Paul, Les **2**
Paxton, Tom **5**
Peebles, Ann **30**
Peniston, CeCe **15**
Penn, Michael **4**
Perkins, Carl **9**
Peterson, Michael **31**
Petty, Tom **9**
  Also see Tom Petty and the Heartbreakers
Phair, Liz **14**
Phillips, Sam **12**
Pickett, Wilson **10**
Plant, Robert **2**
  Also see Led Zeppelin
Pop, Iggy **23**
Porter, Cole **10**
Price, Kelly **34**
Price, Lloyd **25**
Prince **14**
  Earlier sketch in CM **1**
Prine, John **7**
Professor Longhair **6**
Prophet, Chuck **32**
Rabbitt, Eddie **24**
  Earlier sketch in CM **5**
Raitt, Bonnie **23**
  Earlier sketch in CM **3**
Rea, Chris **12**
Redding, Otis **5**
Reddy, Helen **9**
Reed, Lou **16**
  Earlier sketch in CM **1**
  Also see Velvet Underground, The
Reid, Vernon **2**
  Also see Living Colour
Rice, Chris **25**
Rich, Charlie **3**
Richards, Keith **11**
  Also see Rolling Stones, The
Richey, Kim **20**
Richie, Lionel **2**
Richman, Jonathan **12**
Riley, Teddy **14**
Ritchie, Jean **4**
Robbins, Marty **9**
Robertson, Robbie **2**
Robillard, Duke **2**
Robinson, Smokey **1**
Rodgers, Jimmie **3**
Rodgers, Richard **9**
Roth, David Lee **1**
  Also see Van Halen
Rusby, Kate **29**
Russell, Mark **6**

Ryder, Mitch **23**
Sade **2**
Sager, Carole Bayer **5**
Salem, Kevin **32**
Sanborn, David **28**
  Earlier sketch in CM **1**
Sangare, Oumou **22**
Satriani, Joe **4**
Scaggs, Boz **12**
Scott-Heron, Gil **13**
Scruggs, Earl **3**
Scruggs, Randy **28**
Seal **14**
Seals, Dan **9**
Secada, Jon **13**
Sedaka, Neil **4**
Seeger, Pete **4**
  Also see Weavers, The
Seger, Bob **15**
Setzer, Brian **32**
Sexsmith, Ron **27**
Shakira **33**
Shannon, Del **10**
Sheik, Duncan **32**
Sheila E. **3**
Shenandoah, Joanne **33**
Shepherd, Kenny Wayne **22**
Shocked, Michelle **4**
Siberry, Jane **6**
Simon, Carly **22**
  Earlier sketch in CM **4**
Simon, Paul **16**
  Earlier sketch in CM **1**
  Also see Simon and Garfunkel
Skaggs, Ricky **5**
Sledge, Percy **15**
Smith, Elliott **28**
Smith, Patti **17**
  Earlier sketch in CM **1**
Smith, Will **26**
Snoop Doggy Dogg **17**
Sondheim, Stephen **8**
Spector, Phil **4**
Springsteen, Bruce **25**
  Earlier sketch in CM **6**
Stanley, Ralph **5**
Starr, Ringo **24**
  Earlier sketch in CM **10**
  Also see Beatles, The
Stevens, Cat **3**
Stevens, Ray **7**
Stewart, Rod **20**
  Earlier sketch in CM **2**
  Also see Faces, The
Stills, Stephen **5**
  Also see Buffalo Springfield
  Also see Crosby, Stills and Nash
Sting **19**
  Earlier sketch in CM **2**
  Also see Police, The
St. James, Rebecca **26**
Stockwood, Kim **26**
Strait, George **5**
Straw, Syd **18**
Streisand, Barbra **2**
Stuart, Marty **9**
Styne, Jule **21**
Summer, Donna **12**
Summers, Andy **3**
  Also see Police, The
Sure!, Al B. **13**
Sweat, Keith **13**
Sweet, Matthew **9**
Taj Mahal **6**
Taupin, Bernie **22**
Taylor, James **25**
  Earlier sketch in CM **2**

Taylor, Kate **30**
Taylor, Koko **10**
Taylor, Steve **26**
Terrell **32**
Thompson, Richard **7**
Thornton, Big Mama **18**
Tikaram, Tanita **9**
Tillis, Mel **7**
Tillis, Pam **25**
  Earlier sketch in CM **8**
Tippin, Aaron **12**
Tone-Loc **3**
Torme, Mel **4**
Tosh, Peter **3**
Toussaint, Allen **11**
Townshend, Pete **1**
  Also see Who, The
Travis, Merle **14**
Travis, Randy **9**
Treadmill Trackstar **21**
Tricky **18**
Tritt, Travis **7**
Trynin, Jen **21**
Tubb, Ernest **4**
Twain, Shania **17**
Twitty, Conway **6**
2Pac **17**
Vai, Steve **5**
  Also see Whitesnake
Vandross, Luther **24**
  Earlier sketch in CM **2**
Van Ronk, Dave **12**
Van Shelton, Ricky **5**
Van Zandt, Steven **29**
Van Zandt, Townes **13**
Vega, Suzanne **3**
Wachtel, Waddy **26**
Wagoner, Porter **13**
Wainwright, Rufus **29**
Waits, Tom **27**
  Earlier sketch in CM **12**
  Earlier sketch in CM **1**
Walden, Narada Michael **14**
Walker, Jerry Jeff **13**
Walker, T-Bone **5**
Waller, Fats **7**
Walsh, Joe **5**
  Also see Eagles, The
Wariner, Steve **18**
Warren, Diane **21**
Waters, Crystal **15**
Waters, Muddy **24**
  Earlier sketch in CM **4**
Watley, Jody **26**
  Earlier sketch in CM **9**
Watt, Mike **22**
Webb, Jimmy **12**
Weill, Kurt **12**
Welch, Gillian **33**
Weller, Paul **14**
West, Dottie **8**
Westerberg, Paul **26**
White, Karyn **21**
White, Lari **15**
Whitley, Chris **16**
Whitley, Keith **7**
Wildhorn, Frank **31**
Williams, Dar **21**
Williams, Deniece **1**
Williams, Don **4**
Williams, Hank, Jr. **1**
Williams, Hank, Sr. **4**
Williams, Lucinda **24**
  Earlier sketch in CM **10**
Williams, Paul **26**
  Earlier sketch in CM **5**
Williams, Victoria **17**

Wills, Bob **6**
Wilson, Brian **24**
  Also see Beach Boys, The
Winbush, Angela **15**
Winter, Johnny **5**
Winwood, Steve **2**
  Also see Spencer Davis Group
  Also see Traffic
Womack, Bobby **5**
Wonder, Stevie **17**
  Earlier sketch in CM **2**
Wray, Link **17**
Wyatt, Robert **24**
Wynette, Tammy **24**
  Earlier sketch in CM **2**
Yearwood, Trisha **25**
  Earlier sketch in CM **10**
Yoakam, Dwight **21**
  Earlier sketch in CM **1**
Young, Neil **15**
  Earlier sketch in CM **2**
Zappa, Frank **17**
  Earlier sketch in CM **1**
Zevon, Warren **9**

Trombone
Anderson, Ray **7**
Bauer, Johannes **32**
Bishop, Jeb **28**
Brown, Lawrence **23**
Johnson, J.J. **33**
Mandel, Johnny **28**
Miller, Glenn **6**
Rudd, Roswell **28**
Teagarden, Jack **10**
Turre, Steve **22**

Trumpet
Alpert, Herb **11**
Armstrong, Louis **4**
Baker, Chet **13**
Berigan, Bunny **2**
Blanchard, Terence **13**
Bowie, Lester **29**
Brown, Clifford **24**
Cherry, Don **10**
Coleman, Ornette **5**
Davis, Miles **1**

Douglas, Dave **29**
Edison, Harry "Sweets" **29**
Eldridge, Roy **9**
  Also see McKinney's Cotton Pickers
Ferguson, Maynard **7**
Gillespie, Dizzy **6**
Hargrove, Roy **15**
Harrell, Tom **28**
Hawkins, Erskine **19**
Hirt, Al **5**
Isham, Mark **14**
James, Harry **11**
Jensen, Ingrid **22**
Jones, Quincy **20**
  Earlier sketch in CM **2**
Jones, Thad **19**
Loughnane, Lee **3**
Mandel, Johnny **28**
Marsalis, Wynton **20**
  Earlier sketch in CM **6**
Masekela, Hugh **7**
Matthews, Eric **22**
Mighty Mighty Bosstones **20**
Miles, Ron **22**
Minton, Phil **29**
Navarro, Fats **25**
Oliver, King **15**
Payton, Nicholas **27**
Rodney, Red **14**
Roney, Wallace **33**
Sandoval, Arturo **15**
Severinsen, Doc **1**
Shaw, Woody **27**
Terry, Clark **24**

Tuba
Phillips, Harvey **3**

Vibraphone
Burton, Gary **10**
Hampton, Lionel **6**
Jackson, Milt **15**
Norvo, Red **12**

Viola
Menuhin, Yehudi **11**
Zukerman, Pinchas **4**

Violin
Acuff, Roy **2**
Anderson, Laurie **25**
  Earlier sketch in CM **1**
Bell, Joshua **21**
Bonham, Tracy **34**
Bromberg, David **18**
Carter, Regina **22**
Carthy, Eliza **31**
Chang, Sarah **7**
Chung, Kyung Wha **34**
Clements, Vassar **18**
Coleman, Ornette **5**
Cugat, Xavier **23**
Daniels, Charlie **6**
Doucet, Michael **8**
Germano, Lisa **18**
Gingold, Josef **6**
Grappelli, Stephane **10**
Hahn, Hilary **30**
Hartford, John **1**
Heifetz, Jascha **31**
Kang, Eyvind **28**
Kennedy, Nigel **8**
Krauss, Alison **10**
Kremer, Gidon **30**
Lamb, Barbara **19**
Marriner, Neville **7**
Menuhin, Yehudi **11**
Midori **7**
Mutter, Anne-Sophie **23**
O'Connor, Mark **1**
Perlman, Itzhak **2**
Ponty, Jean-Luc **8**
Rieu, André **26**
Sahm, Doug **30**
  Also see Texas Tornados, The
Salerno-Sonnenberg, Nadja **3**
Schroer, Oliver **29**
Skaggs, Ricky **5**
Stern, Isaac **7**
Vanessa-Mae **26**
Whiteman, Paul **17**
Wills, Bob **6**
Zukerman, Pinchas **4**

Cumulative Musicians Index

Volume numbers appear in **bold**

A-ha **22**
Aaliyah **21**
Aaron
  See Mr. T Experience, The
Abba **12**
Abbado, Claudio **32**
Abbott, Gary
  See Kingsmen, The
Abbott, Jacqueline
  See Beautiful South
Abbott, Jude
  See Chumbawamba
Abbruzzese, Dave
  See Pearl Jam
Abdul, Paula **3**
Abercrombie, Jeff
  See Fuel
Abercrombie, John **25**
Aboitiz, Rodrigo
  See La Ley
Abong, Fred
  See Belly
Abrahams, Mick
  See Jethro Tull
Abrams, Bryan
  See Color Me Badd
Abrantes, Fernando
  See Kraftwerk
AC/DC **4**
Ace of Base **22**
Achor, James
  See Royal Crown Revue
Ackerman, Will **3**
Acland, Christopher
  See Lush
Acuff, Roy **2**
Acuna, Alejandro
  See Weather Report
Adam Ant **13**
Adamendes, Elaine
  See Throwing Muses
Adams, Bryan **20**
  Earlier sketch in CM **2**
Adams, Clifford
  See Kool & the Gang
Adams, Craig
  See Cult, The
Adams, Donn
  See NRBQ
Adams, John **8**
Adams, Johnny **33**
Adams, Mark
  See Specials, The
Adams, Oleta **17**
Adams, Terry
  See NRBQ
Adams, Tim
  See Swell
Adams, Victoria
  See Spice Girls
Adams, Yolanda **23**
Adamson, Barry **28**
Adcock, Eddie
  See Country Gentleman, The
Adderley, Cannonball **15**

Adderley, Julian
  See Adderley, Cannonball
Adderley, Nat **29**
Adé, King Sunny **18**
Adès, Thomas **30**
Adkins, Trace **31**
Adler, Steven
  See Guns n' Roses
Aerosmith **22**
  Earlier sketch in CM **3**
Ævar, Ágúst
  See Sigur Rós
Afanasieff, Walter **26**
Afghan Whigs **17**
Afonso, Marie
  See Zap Mama
AFX
  See Aphex Twin
Agius, Alfie
  See Fixx, The
Agnew, Rikk
  See Christian Death
Aguilera, Christina **30**
Agust, Daniel
  See Gus Gus
Ainge, Gary
  See Felt
Air **33**
Airport, Jak
  See X-Ray Spex
Air Supply **22**
Aitchison, Dominic
  See Mogwai
Ajile
  See Arrested Development
Akingbola, Sola
  See Jamiroquai
Akins, Rhett **22**
Akita, Masami
  See Merzbow
Akuna, Sherwood
  See Love
Alabama **21**
  Earlier sketch in CM **1**
Alan, Skip
  See Pretty Things, The
Alarm **22**
Alatorre, Eric
  See Chanticleer
Albarn, Damon
  See Blur
Alber, Matt
  See Chanticleer
Albert, Nate
  See Mighty Mighty Bosstones
Alberti, Dorona
  See KMFDM
Albini, Steve **15**
Albuquerque, Michael de
  See Electric Light Orchestra
Alder, John
  See Gong
  Also see Pretty Things, The
Alex
  See Mr. T Experience, The

Alexakis, Art
  See Everclear
Alexander, Arthur **14**
Alexander, Tim
  See Asleep at the Wheel
Alexander, Tim "Herb"
  See Primus
Ali
  See Tribe Called Quest, A
Alice in Chains **10**
Alien Sex Fiend **23**
Alkaline Trio **34**
Alkema, Jan Willem
  See Compulsion
Allcock, Martin
  See Fairport Convention
  Also see Jethro Tull
Allen, April
  See C + C Music Factory
Allen, Chad
  See Guess Who
Allen, Daevid **28**
  Also see Gong
Allen, Dave
  See Gang of Four
Allen, Debbie **8**
Allen, Duane
  See Oak Ridge Boys, The
Allen, Eric
  See Apples in Stereo
Allen, Geri **10**
Allen, Jeff
  See Mint Condition
Allen, Johnny Ray
  See Subdudes, The
Allen, Papa Dee
  See War
Allen, Peter **11**
Allen, Red
  See Osborne Brothers, The
Allen, Rick
  See Def Leppard
Allen, Ross
  See Mekons, The
Allen, Verden "Phally"
  See Mott the Hoople
Allen, Wally
  See Pretty Things, The
All-4-One **17**
Allison, Luther **21**
Allison, Mose **17**
Allison, Verne
  See Dells, The
Allman, Chris
  See Greater Vision
Allman, Duane
  See Allman Brothers, The
Allman, Gregg
  See Allman Brothers, The
Allman Brothers, The **6**
All Saints **25**
Allsup, Michael Rand
  See Three Dog Night
Almond, Marc **29**
Alpert, Herb **11**

Alphonso, Roland
  See Skatalites, The
Alsing, Pelle
  See Roxette
Alston, Andy
  See Del Amitri
Alston, Shirley
  See Shirelles, The
Altan **18**
Altenfelder, Andy
  See Willem Breuker Kollektief
Alvin, Dave **17**
  Also see X
Am, Svet
  See KMFDM
Amato, Dave
  See REO Speedwagon
Ambush, Scott
  See Spyro Gyra
Amedee, Steve
  See Subdudes, The
Ameling, Elly **24**
Ament, Jeff
  See Pearl Jam
America **16**
America, Lenny
  See Sunset Valley
American Music Club **15**
Ames, Ed **31**
Amico, Vinnie
  See moe.
Amon, Robin
  See Pearls Before Swine
Amos, Tori **12**
Anastasio, Trey
  See Phish
Anderson, Al
  See NRBQ
Anderson, Andy
  See Cure, The
Anderson, Bill **32**
Anderson, Brett
  See Suede
Anderson, Brett
  See Donnas, The
Anderson, Cleave
  See Blue Rodeo
Anderson, Emma
  See Lush
Anderson, Fred **32**
Anderson, Gladstone
  See Skatalites, The
Anderson, Ian
  See Jethro Tull
Anderson, Jhelisa
  See Shamen, The
Anderson, John **5**
Anderson, Jon
  See Yes
Anderson, June **27**
Anderson, Keith
  See Dirty Dozen Brass Band
Anderson, Laurie **25**
  Earlier sketch in CM **1**
Anderson, Marian **8**
Anderson, Pamela
  See Incognito
Anderson, Ray **7**
Anderson, Signe
  See Jefferson Airplane
Anderson, Tai
  See Third Day
Anderson, Wessell **23**
Andersson, Benny
  See Abba
Andes, Mark
  See Spirit

Andes, Matt
  See Spirit
Andes, Rachel
  See Spirit
Andrews, Barry
  See XTC
Andrews, Christopher
  See Mojave 3
Andrews, Jessica **34**
Andrews, Julie **33**
  Earlier sketch in CM **4**
Andrews, Laverne
  See Andrews Sisters, The
Andrews, Mark
  See Dru Hill
Andrews, Maxene
  See Andrews Sisters, The
Andrews, Patty
  See Andrews Sisters, The
Andrews, Revert
  See Dirty Dozen Brass Band
Andrews Sisters, The **9**
Andriano, Dan
  See Alkaline Trio
Andy
  See Ex, The
Andy, Horace
  See Massive Attack
Anger, Darol
  See Turtle Island String Quartet
Angus, Colin
  See Shamen, The
Animals, The **22**
Anka, Paul **2**
Anointed **21**
Anonymous 4 **23**
Anonymous, Rodney
  See Dead Milkmen
Anselmo, Philip
  See Pantera
Ant, Adam
  See Adam Ant
Anthony, Larry
  See Dru Hill
Anthony, Marc **33**
  Earlier sketch in CM **19**
Anthony, Michael
  See Massive Attack
Anthony, Michael
  See Van Halen
Anthrax **11**
Antin, Jesse
  See Chanticleer
Anton, Alan
  See Cowboy Junkies, The
Antoni, Mark De Gli
  See Soul Coughing
Antunes, Michael
  See Beaver Brown Band, The
Anu, Christine **34**
Anway, Susan
  See Magnetic Fields, The
Aphex Twin **14**
Appice, Vinnie
  See Black Sabbath
Apple, Fiona **28**
Apples in Stereo **30**
Appleton, Natalie
  See All Saints
Appleton, Nicole
  See All Saints
April, Johnny
  See Staind
Aqua **34**
Aquabats, The **22**
Aqua Velvets **23**
Arab Strap **33**

Araya, Tom
  See Slayer
Arbulu, Shia
  See La Ley
Archers of Loaf **21**
Arden, Jann **21**
Ardolino, Tom
  See NRBQ
Arellano, Rod
  See Aquabats, The
Arena, Tina **21**
Argent, Rod
  See Zombies, The
Argerich, Martha **27**
Arias, Raymond
  See Ceili Rain
Arkenstone, David **20**
Arlen, Harold **27**
Arm, Mark
  See Mudhoney
Armaou, Lindsay
  See B*Witched
Armatrading, Joan **4**
Armerding, Jake
  See Northern Lights
Armerding, Taylor
  See Northern Lights
Armstrong, Billie Joe
  See Green Day
Armstrong, Louis **4**
Armstrong, Robbie
  See Royal Trux
Armstrong, Tim
  See Rancid
Armstrong, Vanessa Bell **24**
Arnaz, Desi **8**
Arni, Stefan
  See Gus Gus
Arnold, Eddy **10**
Arnold, Kristine
  See Sweethearts of the Rodeo
Aronoff, Kenny **21**
Arrau, Claudio **1**
Arrested Development **14**
Art Ensemble of Chicago, The **23**
Arthurs, Paul
  See Oasis
Artifacts **23**
Art of Noise **22**
Ash **34**
Ash, Daniel
  See Bauhaus
  Also see Love and Rockets
Ashcroft, Richard
  See Verve, The
Ashford, Rosalind
  See Martha and the Vandellas
Ashkenazy, Vladimir **32**
Ashley, Bob
  See Guess Who
Ashton, John
  See Psychedelic Furs
Ashton, Nick
  See Northwoods Improvisers
Ashton, Susan **17**
Asian Dub Foundation **30**
Asleep at the Wheel **29**
  Earlier sketch in CM **5**
Astbury, Ian
  See Cult, The
Asthana, Shivika
  See Papas Fritas
Astley, Rick **5**
Aston, Jay "J"
  See Gene Loves Jezebel
Aston, Michael
  See Gene Loves Jezebel

Astro
  See UB40
Asuo, Kwesi
  See Arrested Development
Aswad **34**
Atari Teenage Riot **27**
Atkins, Chet **26**
  Earlier sketch in CM **5**
Atkins, Martin
  See Killing Joke
  Also see Pigface
Atkins, Victor "Red"
  See Los Hombres Calientes
Atkinson, Lyle
  See Brave Combo
Atkinson, Paul
  See Zombies, The
Atkinson, Sweet Pea
  See Was (Not Was)
Atomic Fireballs, The **27**
ATR
  See Boredoms, The
At The Drive-In **32**
Audio Adrenaline **22**
Auf Der Maur, Melissa
  See Hole
Augustyniak, Jerry
  See 10,000 Maniacs
Auldridge, Mike **4**
  Also see Country Gentlemen, The
  Also see Seldom Scene, The
Austin, Cuba
  See McKinney's Cotton Pickers
Austin, Dallas **16**
Austin, Sherrié **34**
Austral, Florence **26**
Autry, Gene **25**
  Earlier sketch in CM **12**
Avalon **26**
Avalon, Frankie **5**
Avery, Brad
  See Third Day
Avery, Eric
  See Jane's Addiction
Avery, Teodross **23**
Avory, Mick
  See Kinks, The
  Also see Rolling Stones, The
Axelrod, David **34**
Axton, Hoyt **28**
Ayers, Kevin
  See Gong
Aykroyd, Dan
  See Blues Brothers, The
Ayler, Albert **19**
Ayres, Ben
  See Cornershop
Azorr, Chris
  See Cherry Poppin' Daddies
Aztec Camera **22**
B, Daniel
  See Front 242
Baah, Reebop Kwaku
  See Can
  Also see Traffic
Babatunde, Don
  See Last Poets
Babes in Toyland **16**
Babjak, James
  See Smithereens, The
Babyface
  See Edmonds, Kenneth "Babyface"
Baca, Susana **32**
Bacchus, Richard
  See D Generation
Bacharach, Burt **20**
  Earlier sketch in CM **1**

Bachman, Eric
  See Archers of Loaf
Bachman, Randy
  See Guess Who
Backstreet Boys **21**
Badalamenti, Angelo **17**
Bad Brains **16**
Bad Company **22**
Badfinger **23**
Badger, Pat
  See Extreme
Bad Livers, The **19**
Badly Drawn Boy **33**
Badoux, Gwen
  See Les Négresses Vertes
Badowski, Henry
  See Damned, The
Bad Religion **28**
Badrena, Manola
  See Weather Report
Badrena, Monolo
  See Spyro Gyra
Badu, Erykah **26**
Baez, Joan **1**
Bagarozzi, Chris
  See Down By Law
Baha Men **32**
Bailey, Keith
  See Gong
Bailey, Mildred **13**
Bailey, Pearl **5**
Bailey, Phil
  See Earth, Wind and Fire
Bailey, Victor
  See Weather Report
Bain, Pete
  See Spacemen 3
Baker, Anita **9**
Baker, Arthur **23**
Baker, Bobby
  See Tragically Hip, The
Baker, Brian
  See Bad Religion
Baker, Chet **13**
Baker, Dale
  See Sixpence None the Richer
Baker, David
  See Mercury Rev
Baker, Ginger **16**
  Also see Cream
Baker, James
  See Hoodoo Gurus
Baker, Janet **14**
Baker, Jon
  See Charlatans, The
Baker, Josephine **10**
Baker, LaVern **25**
Balakrishnan, David
  See Turtle Island String Quartet
Balch, Bob
  See Fu Manchu
Balch, Michael
  See Front Line Assembly
Baldes, Kevin
  See Lit
Baldursson, Sigtryggur
  See Sugarcubes, The
Baldwin, Donny
  See Starship
Baliardo, Diego
  See Gipsy Kings, The
Baliardo, Paco
  See Gipsy Kings, The
Baliardo, Tonino
  See Gipsy Kings, The
Balin, Marty
  See Jefferson Airplane

Ball, Ian
  See Gomez
Ball, Marcia **15**
Ballance, Laura
  See Superchunk
Ballard, Florence
  See Supremes, The
Ballard, Hank **17**
Ballew, Chris
  See Presidents of the United States of
    America, The
Balsamo, Terry
  See Cold
Balsley, Phil
  See Statler Brothers, The
Baltes, Peter
  See Dokken
Balzano, Vinnie
  See Less Than Jake
Bambaataa, Afrika **13**
Bamonte, Perry
  See Cure, The
Bananarama **22**
Bancroft, Cyke
  See Bevis Frond
Band, The **9**
Bangalter, Thomas
  See Daft Punk
Bangles, The **22**
Banks, Nick
  See Pulp
Banks, Peter
  See Yes
Banks, Tony
  See Genesis
Baptiste, David Russell
  See Meters, The
Barbarossa, Dave
  See Republica
Barbata, John
  See Jefferson Starship
Barber, Don
  See Northwoods Improvisers
Barber, Keith
  See Soul Stirrers, The
Barber, Samuel **34**
Barbero, Lori
  See Babes in Toyland
Barbieri, Gato **22**
Barbot, Bill
  See Jawbox
Bardens, Peter
  See Camel
Bardo Pond **28**
Barenaked Ladies **18**
Barenboim, Daniel **30**
Bargeld, Blixa
  See Einstürzende Neubauten
Bargeron, Dave
  See Blood, Sweat and Tears
Barham, Meriel
  See Lush
Barile, Jo
  See Ventures, The
Barker, Andrew
  See 808 State
Barker, Paul
  See Ministry
Barker, Travis Landon
  See Aquabats, The
  Also see Blink 182
Barksdale, Charles
  See Dells, The
Barlow, Barriemore
  See Jethro Tull

Barlow, Bruce
  See Commander Cody and His Lost Planet Airmen
Barlow, Lou **20**
  See Dinosaur Jr.
  Also see Folk Implosion, The
  Also see Sebadoh
Barlow, Tommy
  See Aztec Camera
Barnes, Danny
  See Bad Livers, The
Barnes, Jeffrey
  See Brave Combo
Barnes, Jeremy
  See Neutral Milk Hotel
Barnes, Jimmy
  See Cold Chisel
Barnes, Micah
  See Nylons, The
Barnes, Neil
  See Leftfield
Barnes, Prentiss
  See Moonglows, The
Barnes, Roosevelt "Booba" **23**
Barnett, Mandy **26**
Barnwell, Duncan
  See Simple Minds
Barnwell, Ysaye Maria
  See Sweet Honey in the Rock
Barocas, Zach
  See Jawbox
Barr, Al
  See Dropkick Murphys
Barr, Ralph
  See Nitty Gritty Dirt Band, The
Barradas, Miggy
  See Divine Comedy, The
Barre, Martin
  See Jethro Tull
Barrere, Paul
  See Little Feat
Barret, Charlie
  See Fixx, The
Barrett, (Roger) Syd
  See Pink Floyd
Barrett, Dicky
  See Mighty Mighty Bosstones
Barrett, Mike
  See Lettermen, The
Barrett, Robert "T-Mo"
  See Goodie Mob
Barron, Christopher
  See Spin Doctors
Barrow, Geoff
  See Portishead
Barry, John **29**
Barson, Mike
  See Madness
Bartels, Joanie **13**
Bartholomew, Simon
  See Brand New Heavies, The
Bartoli, Cecilia **12**
Barton, Lou Ann
  See Fabulous Thunderbirds, The
Barton, Rick
  See Dropkick Murphys
Bartos, Karl
  See Kraftwerk
Basehead **11**
Basement Jaxx **29**
Basher, Mick
  See X
Basia **5**
Basie, Count **2**
Bass, Colin
  See Camel

Bass, Lance
  See 'N Sync
Bass, Ralph **24**
Bastida, Ceci (Cecilia)
  See Tijuana No!
Batchelor, Kevin
  See Big Mountain
  Also see Steel Pulse
Batel, Beate
  See Einstürzende Neubauten
Bates, Stuart "Pinkie"
  See Divine Comedy, The
Batiste, Lionel
  See Dirty Dozen Brass Band
Batoh, Masaki
  See Ghost
  Also see Pearls Before Swine
Battin, Skip
  See Byrds, The
Battle, Kathleen **6**
Battlefield Band, The **31**
Bauer, Johannes **32**
Bauer, Judah
  See Jon Spencer Blues Explosion
Bauhaus **27**
Baum, Kevin
  See Chanticleer
Baumann, Peter
  See Tangerine Dream
Bautista, Roland
  See Earth, Wind and Fire
Baxter, Adrian
  See Cherry Poppin' Daddies
Baxter, Jeff
  See Doobie Brothers, The
Bayer Sager, Carole
  See Sager, Carole Bayer
Baylor, Helen **20**
Baynton-Power, David
  See James
Bazilian, Eric
  See Hooters
Beach Boys, The **1**
Beale, Michael
  See Earth, Wind and Fire
Beard, Annette
  See Martha and the Vandellas
Beard, Frank
  See ZZ Top
Beasley, Paul
  See Mighty Clouds of Joy, The
Beastie Boys **25**
  Earlier sketch in CM **8**
Beat Farmers **23**
Beat Happening **28**
Beatles, The **2**
Beauford, Carter
  See Dave Matthews Band
Beautiful South **19**
Beauvoir, Jean
  See Wendy O. Williams and The Plasmatics
Beaver Brown Band, The **3**
Bechdel, John
  See Fear Factory
Bechet, Sidney **17**
Beck **18**
Beck, Jeff **4**
  Also see Yardbirds, The
Beck, William
  See Ohio Players
Beckenstein, Jay
  See Spyro Gyra
Becker, Joseph
  See Loud Family, The
Becker, Margaret **31**
Becker, Walter
  See Steely Dan

Beckford, Theophilus
  See Skatalites, The
Beckley, Gerry
  See America
Bedassie, Andrea
  See Stereo MC's
Bedford, Mark
  See Madness
Beech, Wes
  See Wendy O. Williams and The Plasmatics
Beecham, Thomas **27**
Bee Gees, The **3**
Beenie Man **33**
Beers, Garry Gary
  See INXS
Begs
  See Les Négresses Vertes
Behler, Chuck
  See Megadeth
Beiderbecke, Bix **16**
Belafonte, Harry **8**
Belanger, George
  See Christian Death
Belew, Adrian **5**
  Also see King Crimson
Belfield, Dennis
  See Three Dog Night
Belitsky, Mike
  See Pernice Brothers
Belk, Darren
  See Wedding Present, The
Bell, Andy
  See Erasure
Bell, Brian
  See Weezer
Bell, Burton C.
  See Fear Factory
Bell, Carl
  See Fuel
Bell, Chris
  See Gene Loves Jezebel
Bell, Derek
  See Chieftains, The
Bell, Eric
  See Thin Lizzy
Bell, Jayn
  See Sounds of Blackness
Bell, Joshua **21**
Bell, Melissa
  See Soul II Soul
Bell, Robert "Kool"
  See Kool & the Gang
Bell, Ronald
  See Kool & the Gang
Bell, Taj
  See Charm Farm
Bell, Trent
  See Chainsaw Kittens, The
Belladonna, Joey
  See Anthrax
Bellamy, David
  See Bellamy Brothers, The
Bellamy, Howard
  See Bellamy Brothers, The
Bellamy Brothers, The **13**
Belle, Regina **6**
Belle and Sebastian **28**
Bello, Elissa
  See Go-Go's, The
Bello, Frank
  See Anthrax
Belly **16**
Belove, David
  See Oakland Interfaith Gospel Choir
Beltrán, Tito **28**
Belushi, John
  See Blues Brothers, The

Benante, Charlie
  See Anthrax
Benatar, Pat **8**
Benckert, Vicki
  See Roxette
Bender, Ariel
  See Mott the Hoople
Benedict, Scott
  See Pere Ubu
Benét, Eric **27**
Ben Folds Five **20**
Bengry, Peter
  See Cornershop
Benitez, Jellybean **15**
Benjamin, Andre "Dre"
  See OutKast
Bennett, Brian
  See Shadows, The
Bennett, Tony **16**
  Earlier sketch in CM **2**
Bennett-Nesby, Ann
  See Sounds of Blackness
Benoit, Tab **31**
Benson, George **9**
Benson, Ray
  See Asleep at the Wheel
Benson, Renaldo "Obie"
  See Four Tops, The
Bentley, Jay
  See Circle Jerks
  Also see Bad Religion
Bentley, John
  See Squeeze
Benton, Brook **7**
Bentyne, Cheryl
  See Manhattan Transfer, The
Berenyi, Miki
  See Lush
Beres, Jeff
  See Sister Hazel
Berg, Matraca **16**
Bergeson, Ben
  See Aquabats, The
Berggren, Jenny
  See Ace of Base
Berggren, Jonas
  See Ace of Base
Berggren, Linn
  See Ace of Base
Bergman, Alan and Marilyn **30**
Bergmark, Christina
  See Wannadies, The
Berigan, Bunny **2**
Berio, Luciano **32**
Berkely, Anthony (Poetic the Grym Reaper)
  See Gravediggaz
Berlin, Irving **8**
Berlin, Liz
  See Rusted Root
Berlin, Steve
  See Los Lobos
Bernal, Steve
  See Poi Dog Pondering
Berndt, Jay
  See Kilgore
Bernstein, Leonard **2**
Berry, Bill
  See R.E.M.
Berry, Chuck **33**
  Earlier sketch in CM **1**
Berry, Jan
  See Jan & Dean
Berry, John **17**
Berry, Robert
  See Emerson, Lake & Palmer/Powell
Berryhill, Bob
  See Surfaris, The

Berryman, Guy
  See Coldplay
Bert, Bob
  See Sonic Youth
Beschta, Scott
  See Promise Ring, The
Bessant, Jack
  See Reef
Best, Nathaniel
  See O'Jays, The
Best, Pete
  See Beatles, The
Beta Band, The **27**
Betha, Mason
  See Mase
Bethea, Ken
  See Old 97's
Bettencourt, Nuno
  See Extreme
Better Than Ezra **19**
Bettie Serveert **17**
Bettini, Tom
  See Jackyl
Betts, Dicky
  See Allman Brothers, The
Bevan, Bev
  See Black Sabbath
  Also see Electric Light Orchestra
Bever, Pete
  See Workhorse Movement, The
Bevis Frond **23**
Bezozi, Alan
  See Dog's Eye View
B-52's, The **4**
Bhag-dad-a, Omar
  See Lane, Fred
Biafra, Jello **18**
  Also see Dead Kennedys
Big Audio Dynamite **18**
Biger, Guenole
  See Les Négresses Vertes
Bigham, John
  See Fishbone
Big Head Todd and the Monsters **20**
Big Mike
  See Geto Boys, The
Big Money Odis
  See Digital Underground
Big Mountain **23**
Big Paul
  See Killing Joke
Bill Wyman & the Rhythm Kings **26**
Bingham, John
  See Fishbone
Bin Hassan, Umar
  See Last Poets
Binks, Les
  See Judas Priest
Biondo, George
  See Steppenwolf
Birch, Rob
  See Stereo MC's
Birchfield, Benny
  See Osborne Brothers, The
Bird
  See Parker, Charlie
Birdsong, Cindy
  See Supremes, The
Birdstuff
  See Man or Astroman?
Birgisson, Jón Pór
  See Sigur Rós
Biscuits, Chuck
  See Circle Jerks
  Also see Danzig
  Also see D.O.A.
  Also see Social Distortion

Bishop, Jeb **28**
  Also see Flying Luttenbachers, The
Bishop, Michael
  See Gwar
Bishop, Steven
  See Powderfinger
Bitney, Dan
  See Tortoise
Bixler, Cedric
  See At The Drive-In
Biz Markie **10**
BizzyBone
  See Bone Thugs-N-Harmony
Bjelland, Kat
  See Babes in Toyland
Björk **16**
  Also see Sugarcubes, The
Bjork, Brant
  See Fu Manchu
Black, Bobby
  See Commander Cody and His Lost Planet
  Airmen
Black, Clint **5**
Black, Frank **14**
Black, Jet
  See Stranglers, The
Black, Jimmy Carl "India Ink"
  See Captain Beefheart and His Magic Band
Black, Mary **15**
Black, Vic
  See C + C Music Factory
Blackburn, Paul
  See Gomez
Black Crowes, The **7**
Black Flag **22**
Black Francis
  See Black, Frank
BlackHawk **21**
Blackman, Cindy **15**
Blackman, Nicole
  See Golden Palominos
Blackman, Tee-Wee
  See Memphis Jug Band
Blackmore, Ritchie
  See Deep Purple
Black Sabbath **9**
Black Sheep **15**
Blackstreet **23**
Black Uhuru **12**
Blackwell, Chris **26**
Blackwood, Sarah
  See Dubstar
Bladd, Stephen Jo
  See J. Geils Band
Blades, Ruben **2**
Blair, Ron
  See Tom Petty and the Heartbreakers
Blake, Eubie **19**
Blake, Norman
  See Teenage Fanclub
Blake, Tim
  See Gong
Blakely, Paul
  See Captain Beefheart and His Magic Band
Blakey, Art **11**
Blakey, Colin
  See Waterboys, The
Blanchard, Terence **13**
Bland, Bobby "Blue" **12**
Blatt, Melanie
  See All Saints
Blegen, Jutith **23**
Blegvad, Peter **28**
Blessid Union of Souls **20**
Bley, Carla **8**
  Also see Golden Palominos
Bley, Paul **14**

Blige, Mary J. **15**
Blind Melon **21**
Blink 182 **27**
Bliss, Lang
 See Ceili Rain
Bloch, Alan
 See Concrete Blonde
Bloch, Kurt
 See Fastbacks, The
Block, Ken
 See Sister Hazel
Block, Norman
 See Rasputina
Block, Rory **18**
Blocker, Joe
 See Love
Blonde Redhead **28**
Blondie **27**
 Earlier sketch in CM **14**
Blood, Dave
 See Dead Milkmen
Blood, Johnny
 See Magnetic Fields, The
Bloodhound Gang, The **31**
Blood, Sweat and Tears **7**
Bloom, Eric
 See Blue Oyster Cult
Bloom, Luka **14**
Blount, Herman "Sonny"
 See Sun Ra
Blue, Buddy
 See Beat Farmers
Bluegrass Patriots **22**
Blue Oyster Cult **16**
Blue Rodeo **18**
Blues, Elwood
 See Blues Brothers, The
Blues, "Joliet" Jake
 See Blues Brothers, The
Blues Brothers, The **3**
Blues Traveler **15**
Bluetones, The **29**
Blunstone, Colin
 See Zombies, The
Blunt, Martin
 See Charlatans, The
Blur **17**
Bob, Tim
 See Rage Against the Machine
Bobe, Andrés
 See La Ley
Bocelli, Andrea **22**
BoDeans, The **20**
 Earlier sketch in CM **3**
Boff, Richard
 See Chumbawamba
Bogaert, Jo
 See Technotronic
Bogdan, Henry
 See Helmet
Boggs, Dock **25**
Bogguss, Suzy **11**
Bogle, Bob
 See Ventures, The
Bohannon, Jim
 See Pearls Before Swine
Bohay-Nowell, Victor Dudley
 See Bonzo Dog Doo-Dah Band
Bolade Casel, Nitanju
 See Sweet Honey in the Rock
Bolan, Marc
 See T. Rex
Bold, Thomas
 See Chanticleer
Bolton, Michael **4**
Boltz, Ray **33**
Bonamy, James **21**

Bond, Johnny **28**
Bonebrake, D. J.
 See X
Bone Thugs-N-Harmony **18**
Bonham, John
 See Led Zeppelin
Bonham, Tracy **34**
Bon Jovi **34**
 Earlier sketch in CM **10**
Bon Jovi, Jon
 See Bon Jovi
Bonnar, Graham
 See Swervedriver
Bonnecaze, Cary
 See Better Than Ezra
Bonner, Leroy "Sugarfoot"
 See Ohio Players
Bonney, Barbara **33**
Bono
 See U2
Bono, Sonny
 See Sonny and Cher
Bonsall, Joe
 See Oak Ridge Boys, The
Bonzo Dog Doo-Dah Band **30**
Booher, Chris
 See Asleep at the Wheel
Booker T. & the M.G.'s **24**
Books
 See Das EFX
Boom Boom, Mahatma
 See Rube Waddell
Boon, D.
 See Minutemen, The
Boone, Pat **13**
Boo Radleys, The **21**
Booth, Tim
 See James
Boquist, Dave
 See Son Volt
Boquist, Jim
 See Son Volt
Borchardt, Jeffrey
 See Velvet Crush
Bordin, Mike
 See Faith No More
Boredoms, The **28**
Borg, Bobby
 See Warrant
Borge, Victor **19**
Borland, Wes
 See Limp Bizkit
Borowiak, Tony
 See All-4-One
Boss Hog **29**
Bostaph, Paul
 See Slayer
Bostek, James
 See Atomic Fireballs, The
Bostic-Summers, Yvette
 See Los Hombres Calientes
Boston **11**
Boston, Mark "Rockette Morton"
 See Captain Beefheart and His Magic Band
Bostrom, Derrick
 See Meat Puppets, The
Bottum, Roddy
 See Faith No More
 Also see Imperial Teen
Bouchard, Albert
 See Blue Oyster Cult
Bouchard, Joe
 See Blue Oyster Cult
Bouchikhi, Chico
 See Gipsy Kings, The
Boulez, Pierre **26**

Bowen, Jimmy
 See Country Gentlemen, The
Bowens, Sir Harry
 See Was (Not Was)
Bowery, Leigh
 See Minty
Bowery, Nicole
 See Minty
Bowie, David **23**
 Earlier sketch in CM **1**
Bowie, Lester **29**
 Also see Art Ensemble of Chicago, The
Bowman, Steve
 See Counting Crows
Box, Mick
 See Uriah Heep
Boyd, Brandon
 See Incubus
Boyd, Eadie
 See Del Rubio Triplets
Boyd, Elena
 See Del Rubio Triplets
Boyd, Liona **7**
Boyd, Milly
 See Del Rubio Triplets
Boyer, Patrick
 See Northwoods Improvisers
Boy Howdy **21**
Boyle, Doug
 See Caravan
Boyz II Men **15**
Bozulich, Carla
 See Geraldine Fibbers
Bracken, Ben
 See Northwoods Improvisers
Brad **21**
Bradbury, John
 See Specials, The
Bradbury, Randy
 See Pennywise
Bradfield, James Dean
 See Manic Street Preachers
Bradshaw, Tim
 See Dog's Eye View
Bradstreet, Rick
 See Bluegrass Patriots
Brady, Paul **8**
Bragg, Billy **7**
Brain, Matt
 See Grapes of Wrath, The
Braithwaite, Stuart
 See Mogwai
Bramah, Martin
 See Fall, The
Bramley, Clyde
 See Hoodoo Gurus
Branca, Glenn **29**
Brand New Heavies, The **14**
Brandt, Paul **22**
Brandy **19**
Branigan, Laura **2**
Brannon, Kippi **20**
Brantley, Junior
 See Roomful of Blues
Brave Combo **31**
Braxton, Anthony **12**
Braxton, Toni **17**
B-Real
 See Cypress Hill
Bream, Julian **9**
Brecker, Michael **29**
Breeders **19**
Brendel, Alfred **23**
Brennan, Ciaran
 See Clannad
Brennan, Maire
 See Clannad

Brennan, Paul
  See Odds
Brennan, Pol
  See Clannad
Brenner, Simon
  See Talk Talk
Breuker, Willem
  See Willem Breuker Kollektief
Brevette, Lloyd
  See Skatalites, The
Brickell, Edie **3**
Brickman, Jim **22**
Bridgeman, Noel
  See Waterboys, The
Bridgewater, Dee Dee **18**
Briggs, David
  See Pearls Before Swine
Briggs, James Randall
  See Aquabats, The
Briggs, Vic
  See Animals, The
Bright, Garfield
  See Shai
Bright, Ronnie
  See Coasters, The
Brightman, Sarah **20**
Briley, Alex
  See Village People, The
Brindley, Paul
  See Sundays, The
Britt, Michael
  See Lonestar
Britten, Benjamin **15**
Brittingham, Eric
  See Cinderella
Brix
  See Fall, The
Brock, Isaac
  See Modest Mouse
Brockenborough, Dennis
  See Mighty Mighty Bosstones
Brockie, Dave
  See Gwar
Brokop, Lisa **22**
Bromberg, David **18**
Bronfman, Yefim **6**
Brook, Rachel
  See Flying Saucer Attack
Brooke, Jonatha
  See Story, The
Brooker, Gary
  See Bill Wyman & the Rhythm Kings
Brooker, Nicholas "Natty"
  See Spacemen 3
Brookes, Jon
  See Charlatans, The
Brookes, Steve
  See Jam, The
Brooks, Baba
  See Skatalites, The
Brooks, DJ
  See Citizen King
Brooks, Garth **25**
  Earlier sketch in CM **8**
Brooks, Leon Eric "Kix" III
  See Brooks & Dunn
Brooks, Meredith **30**
Brooks, Stuart
  See Pretty Things, The
Brooks & Dunn **25**
  Earlier sketch in CM **12**
Broonzy, Big Bill **13**
Brotherdale, Steve
  See Joy Division
  Also see Smithereens, The
Brötzmann, Caspar **27**
Brötzmann, Peter **26**

Broudie, Ian
  See Lightning Seeds
Broussard, Jules
  See Lavay Smith and Her Red Hot Skillet Lickers
Brown, Amanda
  See Go-Betweens, The
Brown, Bobby **4**
Brown, Brooks
  See Cherry Poppin' Daddies
Brown, Bundy K.
  See Tortoise
Brown, Carlinhos **32**
Brown, Clarence "Gatemouth" **11**
Brown, Clifford **24**
Brown, Dan
  See Royal Trux
Brown, Dan K.
  See Fixx, The
Brown, Dennis **29**
Brown, Donny
  See Verve Pipe, The
Brown, Duncan
  See Stereolab
Brown, Foxy **25**
Brown, George
  See Kool & the Gang
Brown, Greg
  See Cake
Brown, Harold
  See War
Brown, Heidi
  See Treadmill Trackstar
Brown, Ian
  See Stone Roses, The
Brown, James **16**
  Earlier sketch in CM **2**
Brown, Jimmy
  See UB40
Brown, Junior **15**
Brown, Lawrence **23**
Brown, Marty **14**
Brown, Melanie
  See Spice Girls
Brown, Mick
  See Dokken
Brown, Morris
  See Pearls Before Swine
Brown, Norman
  See Mills Brothers, The
Brown, Norman **29**
Brown, Paula
  See Giant Sand
Brown, Rahem
  See Artifacts
Brown, Ray **21**
Brown, Ruth **13**
Brown, Selwyn "Bumbo"
  See Steel Pulse
Brown, Steven
  See Tuxedomoon
Brown, Tim
  See Boo Radleys, The
Brown, Tony **14**
Browne, Ian
  See Matthew Good Band
Browne, Jackson **3**
  Also see Nitty Gritty Dirt Band, The
Brownstein, Carrie
  See Sleater-Kinney
Brownstone **21**
Brubeck, Dave **8**
Bruce, Dustan
  See Chumbawamba
Bruce, Jack
  See Golden Palominos

Bruce, Jack
  See Cream
Bruce, Joseph Frank
  See Insane Clown Posse
Bruford, Bill
  See King Crimson
  Also see Yes
Bruno, Gioia
  See Exposé
Bruster, Thomas
  See Soul Stirrers, The
Bryan, David
  See Bon Jovi
Bryan, Karl
  See Skatalites, The
Bryan, Mark
  See Hootie and the Blowfish
Bryant, Elbridge
  See Temptations, The
Bryant, Jeff
  See Ricochet
Bryant, Junior
  See Ricochet
Bryson, Bill
  See Desert Rose Band, The
Bryson, David
  See Counting Crows
Bryson, Peabo **11**
Buchanan, Wallis
  See Jamiroquai
Buchholz, Francis
  See Scorpions, The
Buchignani, Paul
  See Afghan Whigs
Buck, Mike
  See Fabulous Thunderbirds, The
Buck, Peter
  See R.E.M.
Buck, Robert
  See 10,000 Maniacs
Buckethead **34**
Buckingham, Lindsey **8**
  Also see Fleetwood Mac
Buckland, John
  See Coldplay
Buckler, Rick
  See Jam, The
Buckley, Betty **16**
  Earlier sketch in CM **1**
Buckley, Jeff **22**
Buckley, Tim **14**
Buckner, David
  See Papa Roach
Buckner, Richard **31**
Buckwheat Zydeco **34**
  Earlier sketch in CM **6**
Budgie
  See Siouxsie and the Banshees
Buerstatte, Phil
  See White Zombie
Buffalo Springfield **24**
Buffalo Tom **18**
Buffett, Jimmy **4**
Built to Spill **27**
Bulgarian State Female Vocal Choir, The **10**
Bulgarian State Radio and Television Female Vocal Choir
  See Bulgarian State Female Vocal Choir, The
Bulgin, Lascelle
  See Israel Vibration
Bulloch, Martin
  See Mogwai
Bullock, Craig "DJ Homicide"
  See Sugar Ray
Bumbry, Grace **13**
Bumpus, Cornelius
  See Doobie Brothers, The

Bunford, Huw "Bunf"
  See Super Furry Animals
Bunker, Clive
  See Jethro Tull
Bunkley, John
  See Atomic Fireballs, The
Bunnell, Dewey
  See America
Bunskoeke, Herman
  See Bettie Serveert
Bunton, Emma
  See Spice Girls
Burch, Curtis
  See New Grass Revival, The
Burchill, Charlie
  See Simple Minds
Burden, Ian
  See Human League, The
Burdon, Eric 14
  Also see War
  Also see Animals, The
Burgess, Paul
  See Camel
Burgess, Tim
  See Charlatans, The
Burke, Clem
  See Romantics, The
Burke, Clem
  See Blondie
Burkum, Tyler
  See Audio Adrenaline
Burnel, J.J.
  See Stranglers, The
Burnett, Carol 6
Burnett, T Bone 13
Burnette, Billy
  See Fleetwood Mac
Burnham, Hugo
  See Gang of Four
Burning Spear 15
Burns, Barry
  See Mogwai
Burns, Bob
  See Lynyrd Skynyrd
Burns, Joey
  See Calexico
  Also see Giant Sand
Burns, Karl
  See Fall, The
Burnside, R. L 34
Burr, Clive
  See Iron Maiden
Burrell, Boz
  See Bad Company
Burrell, Kenny 11
Burrell, Raymond "Boz"
  See King Crimson
Burroughs, William S. 26
Burse, Charlie
  See Memphis Jug Band
Burse, Robert
  See Memphis Jug Band
Burton, Cliff
  See Metallica
Burton, Gary 10
Burton, Tim
  See Mighty Mighty Bosstones
Burton, Tim
  See Promise Ring, The
Busby, Jheryl 9
Buschman, Carol
  See Chordettes, The
Bush 18
Bush, Dave
  See Elastica
  Also see Fall, The

Bush, John
  See Anthrax
Bush, Kate 4
Bush, Sam
  See New Grass Revival, The
Bushwick, Bill
  See Geto Boys, The
Busta Rhymes 18
Butala, Tony
  See Lettermen, The
Butcher, Bilinda
  See My Bloody Valentine
Butler, Bernard
  See Suede
Butler, Richard
  See Love Spit Love
  Also see Psychedelic Furs
Butler, Terry "Geezer"
  See Black Sabbath
Butler, Tim
  See Love Spit Love
  Also see Psychedelic Furs
Butterfield, Paul 23
Butterfly
  See Digable Planets
Butthole Surfers 16
Buttrey, Kenneth
  See Pearls Before Swine
Buxton, Felix
  See Basement Jaxx
Buynak, John
  See Rusted Root
Buzzcocks, The 9
B*Witched 33
Byers, Roddy
  See Specials, The
Byrds, The 8
Byrne, David 8
  Also see Talking Heads
Byrne, Dermot
  See Altan
Byrne, Nicky
  See Westlife
Byrom, Larry
  See Steppenwolf
Byron, David
  See Uriah Heep
Byron, Don 22
Byron, Lord T.
  See Lords of Acid
Caballe, Monserrat 23
Cabaret Voltaire 18
Cable, Stuart
  See Stereophonics
Cachao
  See López, Israel "Cachao"
Cadogan, Kevin
  See Third Eye Blind
Caesar, Shirley 17
Cafferty, John
  See Beaver Brown Band, The
Caffey, Charlotte
  See Go-Go's, The
Cage, John 8
Cahn, Sammy 11
Cain, Jonathan
  See Journey
Caine, Uri 31
Cake 27
Calderon, Mark
  See Color Me Badd
Cale, J. J. 16
Cale, John 9
  Also see Velvet Underground, The
Calexico 33
Calhoun, Will
  See Living Colour

California, Randy
  See Spirit
Calire, Mario
  See Wallflowers, The
Callahan, Ken
  See Jayhawks, The
Callahan, Ray
  See Wendy O. Williams and The Plasmatics
Callas, Maria 11
Callis, Jo
  See Human League, The
Calloway, Cab 6
Calvert, Robert 30
Camaro, Vivian
  See Lanternjack, The
Camel 21
Camel, Abdul Ben
  See Lane, Fred
Cameron, Clayton
  See Ralph Sharon Quartet
Cameron, Dave "Tito"
  See Brave Combo
Cameron, Duncan
  See Sawyer Brown
Cameron, G. C.
  See Spinners, The
Cameron, Matt
  See Pearl Jam
  Also see Soundgarden
Cameron, Timothy
  See Silk
Camp, Greg
  See Smash Mouth
Campbell, Ali
  See UB40
Campbell, Eddie
  See Texas
Campbell, Glen 2
Campbell, Isobel
  See Belle and Sebastian
Campbell, Kerry
  See War
Campbell, Luther 10
Campbell, Martyn
  See Lightning Seeds
Campbell, Mike
  See Tom Petty and the Heartbreakers
Campbell, Phil
  See Motörhead
Campbell, Robin
  See UB40
Campbell, Sarah Elizabeth 23
Campbell, Tevin 13
Campeau, Don
  See Lettermen, The
Can 28
Canadian Brass, The 4
Canavase, Matthias
  See Les Négresses Vertes
C + C Music Factory 16
Candlebox 32
Canler, Coz
  See Romantics, The
Cantrell, Jerry
  See Alice in Chains
Canty, Brendan
  See Fugazi
Capaldi, Jim
  See Traffic
Cappelli, Frank 14
Cappos, Andy
  See Built to Spill
Captain Beefheart and the Magic Band 26
  Earlier sketch in CM 10
Caravan 24
Carbonara, Paul
  See Blondie

Cardigans **19**
Cardwell, Joi **22**
Carey, Danny
  See Tool
Carey, Mariah **20**
  Earlier sketch in CM **6**
Carey, Pat
  See Baha Men
Carey, Ron
  See Baha Men
Carl, Barry
  See Rockapella
Carlisle, Belinda **8**
  Also see Go-Go's, The
Carlisle, Bob **22**
Carlos, Bun E.
  See Cheap Trick
Carlos, Don
  See Black Uhuru
Carlson, Paulette
  See Highway 101
Carmichael, Hoagy **27**
Carnes, Kim **4**
Carpenter, Bob
  See Nitty Gritty Dirt Band, The
Carpenter, Karen
  See Carpenters, The
Carpenter, Richard **24**
  Also see Carpenters, The
Carpenter, Stephen
  See Deftones
Carpenters, The **13**
Carr, Ben
  See Mighty Mighty Bosstones
Carr, David
  See Third Day
Carr, Eric
  See Kiss
Carr, James **23**
Carr, Martin
  See Boo Radleys, The
Carr, Teddy
  See Ricochet
Carr, Vikki **28**
Carrack, Paul
  See Mike & the Mechanics
  Also see Squeeze
Carreras, José **34**
  Earlier sketch in CM **8**
Carrigan, Andy
  See Mekons, The
Carroll, Dina **31**
Carroll, Earl "Speedo"
  See Coasters, The
Carruthers, John
  See Siouxsie and the Banshees
Carruthers, William B. "Willie"
  See Spacemen 3
Cars, The **20**
Carson, Lori
  See Golden Palominos
Cartaya, Oscar
  See Spyro Gyra
Carter, A. P.
  See Carter Family, The
Carter, Anita
  See Carter Family, The
Carter, Benny **3**
  Also see McKinney's Cotton Pickers
Carter, Betty **6**
Carter, Carlene **8**
Carter, Deana **25**
Carter, Elliott **30**
Carter, Helen
  See Carter Family, The
Carter, James **18**

Carter, Janette
  See Carter Family, The
Carter, Jimmy
  See Five Blind Boys of Alabama
Carter, Joe
  See Carter Family, The
Carter, John **34**
Carter, Johnnie
  See Dells, The
Carter, June Cash **6**
  Also see Carter Family, The
Carter, Laura
  See Elf Power
Carter, Maybell
  See Carter Family, The
Carter, Nell **7**
Carter, Nick
  See Backstreet Boys
Carter, Regina **22**
Carter, Ron **14**
Carter, Sara
  See Carter Family, The
Carter Family, The **3**
Carter USM **31**
Carthy, Eliza **31**
Carthy, Martin **34**
  Also see Steeleye Span
Caruso, Enrico **10**
Cary, Justin
  See Sixpence None the Richer
Casady, Jack
  See Jefferson Airplane
Casale, Bob
  See Devo
Casale, Gerald V.
  See Devo
Casals, Pablo **9**
Case, Peter **13**
Casey, Karan
  See Solas
Casey, Ken
  See Dropkick Murphys
Cash, Johnny **17**
  Earlier sketch in CM **1**
Cash, Rosanne **2**
Cashdollar, Cindy
  See Asleep at the Wheel
Cashion, Doc "Bob"
  See Lane, Fred
Cassidy, Ed
  See Spirit
Castellano, Torry
  See Donnas, The
Catallo, Chet
  See Spyro Gyra
Catallo, Chris
  See Surfin' Pluto
Catallo, Gene
  See Surfin' Pluto
Catatonia **29**
Catching, Dave
  See Queens of the Stone Age
Cates, Ronny
  See Petra
Catherall, Joanne
  See Human League, The
Catherine Wheel **18**
Catlin, Fritz
  See 23 Skidoo
Cat Power **30**
Caustic Resin **31**
Caustic Window
  See Aphex Twin
Cauty, Jimmy
  See Orb, The
Cavacas, Chris
  See Giant Sand

Cavalera, Igor
  See Sepultura
Cavalera, Max
  See Sepultura
  Also see Soulfly
Cavanaugh, Frank
  See Filter
Cave, Nick **10**
Cavoukian, Raffi
  See Raffi
Cazares, Dino
  See Fear Factory
Cease, Jeff
  See Black Crowes, The
Ceili Rain **34**
Cervenka, Exene
  See X
Cesare, DJ
  See Stereo MC's
Cetera, Peter
  See Chicago
Chad, Dominic
  See Mansun
Chadbourne, Eugene **30**
Chainsaw Kittens, The **33**
Chamberlin, Jimmy
  See Smashing Pumpkins
Chambers, Guy
  See Waterboys, The
Chambers, Jimmy
  See Mercury Rev
Chambers, Martin
  See Pretenders, The
Chambers, Paul **18**
Chambers, Terry
  See XTC
Champion, Eric **21**
Champion, Will
  See Coldplay
Chan, Spencer
  See Aqua Velvets
Chance, Slim
  See Cramps, The
Chancellor, Justin
  See Tool
Chandler, Chas
  See Animals, The
Chandler, Knox
  See Golden Palominos
Chandra, Sheila **16**
Chandrasonic
  See Asian Dub Foundation
Chaney, Jimmy
  See Jimmie's Chicken Shack
Chang, Han-Na **33**
Chang, Sarah **7**
Channing, Carol **6**
Chanticleer **33**
Chapin, Harry **6**
Chapin, Tom **11**
Chapin Carpenter, Mary **25**
  Earlier sketch in CM **6**
Chapman, Gary **33**
Chapman, Steven Curtis **15**
Chapman, Tony
  See Rolling Stones, The
Chapman, Tracy **20**
  Earlier sketch in CM **4**
Chaquico, Craig **23**
  Also see Jefferson Starship
Charlatans, The **13**
Charles, Ray **24**
  Earlier sketch in CM **1**
Charles, Yolanda
  See Aztec Camera
Charman, Shaun
  See Wedding Present, The

Charm Farm **20**
Charmichael, Chris
  See Ceili Rain
Chasez, Joshua Scott "JC"
  See 'N Sync
Chastain, Paul
  See Velvet Crush
Chea, Alvin "Vinnie"
  See Take 6
Cheap Trick **12**
Cheatam, Aldolphus "Doc"
  See McKinney's Cotton Pickers
Checker, Chubby **7**
Che Colovita, Lemon
  See Jimmie's Chicken Shack
Cheeks, Julius
  See Soul Stirrers, The
Chemical Brothers **20**
Cheng, Chi
  See Deftones
Chenier, C. J. **15**
Chenier, Clifton **6**
Chenille Sisters, The **16**
Cher **1**
  Also see Sonny and Cher
Cherise, Cyd
  See Lane, Fred
Cherone, Gary
  See Extreme
  Also see Van Halen
Cherry, Don **10**
Cherry, Neneh **4**
Cherry Poppin' Daddies **24**
Chesney, Kenny **20**
Chesnutt, Mark **13**
Chesnutt, Vic **28**
Chess, Leonard **24**
Chesters, Eds D.
  See Bluetones, The
Cheung, Jacky **33**
Chevalier, Maurice **6**
Chevron, Phillip
  See Pogues, The
Chicago **3**
Chieftains, The **7**
Child, Desmond **30**
Childish, Billy **28**
Childress, Ross
  See Collective Soul
Childress Saxton, Shirley
  See Sweet Honey in the Rock
Childs, Euros
  See Gorky's Zygotic Mynci
Childs, Megan
  See Gorky's Zygotic Mynci
Childs, Toni **2**
Chilton, Alex **10**
Chimes, Terry
  See Clash, The
Chin
  See Quickspace
Chin, Tony
  See Big Mountain
Chipperfield, Sheila
  See Elastica
Chisholm, Melanie
  See Spice Girls
Chopmaster J
  See Digital Underground
Chordettes, The **34**
Chris
  See Apples in Stereo
Chrisman, Andy
  See 4Him
Chrisman, Paul "Woody Paul"
  See Riders in the Sky

Christ, John
  See Danzig
Christian, Charlie **11**
Christian Death **28**
Christina, Fran
  See Fabulous Thunderbirds, The
  Also see Roomful of Blues
Christo, Guy-Manuel de Homem
  See Daft Punk
Chuck D
  See Public Enemy
Chud, Dr.
  See Misfits, The
Chumbawamba **21**
Chung, Kyung Wha **34**
Chung, Mark
  See Einstürzende Neubauten
Church, Charlotte **28**
Church, Kevin
  See Country Gentlemen, The
Church, The **14**
Churilla, Scott
  See Reverend Horton Heat
Ciaran, Clan
  See Super Furry Animals
Cibo Matto **28**
Ciccone, Don
  See Four Seasons, The
Cieka, Rob
  See Boo Radleys, The
Cinderella **16**
Cinelu, Mino
  See Weather Report
Cipollina, John
  See Quicksilver Messenger Service
Circle Jerks, The **17**
Cissell, Ben
  See Audio Adrenaline
Citizen King **27**
Clancy, Dónal
  See Solas
Clannad **23**
Clapton, Eric **11**
  Earlier sketch in CM **1**
  Also see Cream
  Also see Yardbirds, The
Clark, Alan
  See Dire Straits
Clark, Anne **32**
Clark, Dave
  See Dave Clark Five, The
Clark, Dick **25**
  Earlier sketch in CM **2**
Clark, Gene
  See Byrds, The
Clark, Graham
  See Gong
Clark, Guy **17**
Clark, Keith
  See Circle Jerks, The
Clark, Mike
  See Suicidal Tendencies
Clark, Roy **1**
Clark, Steve
  See VAST
Clark, Steve
  See Def Leppard
Clark, Terri **19**
Clark, Tony
  See Blessid Union of Souls
Clarke, Bernie
  See Aztec Camera
Clarke, "Fast" Eddie
  See Motörhead
Clarke, Mark
  See Mountain

Clarke, Michael
  See Byrds, The
Clarke, Stanley **3**
Clarke, Vince
  See Depeche Mode
  Also see Erasure
Clarke, William
  See Third World
Clash, The **4**
Claveria, Mauricio
  See La Ley
Clayderman, Richard **1**
Claypool, Les
  See Primus
Clayton, Adam
  See U2
Clayton, Sam
  See Little Feat
Clayton-Thomas, David
  See Blood, Sweat and Tears
Clean, Dean
  See Dead Milkmen
Cleave, Simon
  See Wedding Present, The
Cleaves, Jessica
  See Earth, Wind and Fire
Clegg, Johnny **8**
Clements, Vassar **18**
Clemons, Clarence **7**
Cleveland, James **1**
Clewley, Harry
  See Lettermen, The
Cliburn, Van **13**
Cliff, Jimmy **8**
Clifford, Douglas Ray
  See Creedence Clearwater Revival
Cline, Nels
  See Geraldine Fibbers
Cline, Patsy **5**
Clinton, George **7**
Clivilles, Robert
  See C + C Music Factory
Clooney, Rosemary **9**
Close, Bill
  See Dropkick Murphys
Cloud, Jeff
  See Joy Electric
Clouser, Charlie
  See Nine Inch Nails
  Also see Prong
Coasters, The **5**
Cobain, Kurt
  See Nirvana
Cobham, Billy
  See Mahavishnu Orchestra
Cobra Verde **28**
Cochran, Bobby
  See Steppenwolf
Cochrane, Tom **23**
Cockburn, Bruce **8**
Cocker, Jarvis
  See Pulp
Cocker, Joe **4**
Cocking, William "Willigan"
  See Mystic Revealers
Coco the Electronic Monkey Wizard
  See Man or Astroman?
Cocteau Twins, The **12**
Codenys, Patrick
  See Front 242
Codling, Neil
  See Suede
Cody, John
  See Ray Condo and His Ricochets
Coe, Charlie
  See Paul Revere & The Raiders
Coe, David Allan **4**

Coffey, Cath
  See Stereo MC's
Coffey, Jeff
  See Butthole Surfers
Coffey, Jr., Don
  See Superdrag
Coffie, Calton
  See Inner Circle
Coghill, Jon
  See Powderfinger
Cohen, Jeremy
  See Turtle Island String Quartet
Cohen, Leonard 3
Cohen, Lyor 29
Cohen, Porky
  See Roomful of Blues
Coke, Alex
  See Willem Breuker Kollektief
Colaiuta, Vinnie 23
Colbourn, Chris
  See Buffalo Tom
Colburn, Richard
  See Belle and Sebastian
Cold 34
Cold Chisel 34
Coldplay 32
Cole, David
  See C + C Music Factory
Cole, Holly 18
Cole, Lloyd 9
Cole, Natalie 21
  Earlier sketch in CM 1
Cole, Nat King 3
Cole, Paula 20
Cole, Ralph
  See Nylons, The
Cole, Rich
  See Romantics, The
Coleman, Helen
  See Sweet Honey in the Rock
Coleman, Jaz
  See Killing Joke
Coleman, Kevin
  See Smash Mouth
Coleman, Michael
  See Seldom Scene, The
Coleman, Ornette 5
Coles, Dennis
  See Ghostface Killah
Coletta, Kim
  See Jawbox
Colin, Charlie
  See Train
Collective Soul 16
Collen, Phil
  See Def Leppard
Colletti, Dominic
  See Bevis Frond
Colley, Dana
  See Morphine
Collie, Mark 15
Colligan, Michael
  See Flying Luttenbachers, The
Collingwood, Chris
  See Fountains of Wayne
Collins, Albert 19
  Earlier sketch in CM 4
Collins, Allen
  See Lynyrd Skynyrd
Collins, Bootsy 8
  Also see Golden Palominos
Collins, Chris
  See Dream Theater
Collins, John
  See Powderfinger
Collins, Judy 4

Collins, Mark
  See Charlatans, The
Collins, Max
  See Eve 6
Collins, Mel
  See Camel
  Also see King Crimson
Collins, Phil 20
  Earlier sketch in CM 2
  Also see Genesis
Collins, Rob
  See Charlatans, The
Collins, William
  See Collins, Bootsy
Colomby, Bobby
  See Blood, Sweat and Tears
Color Me Badd 23
Colt, Johnny
  See Black Crowes, The
Colthart, Chris
  See Papas Fritas
Coltrane, John 4
Colvin, Shawn 11
Colwell, David
  See Bad Company
Coma, Franche
  See Misfits, The
Combs, Sean "Puffy" 25
  Earlier sketch in CM 16
Comess, Aaron
  See Spin Doctors
Commander Cody
  See Commander Cody and His Lost
  Planet Airmen
Commander Cody and His Lost
  Planet Airmen 30
Commodores, The 23
Common 23
Como, Perry 14
Compulsion 23
Concrete Blonde 32
Condo, Ray
  See Ray Condo and His Ricochets
Confederate Railroad 23
Congo Norvell 22
Conneff, Kevin
  See Chieftains, The
Connelly, Chris
  See KMFDM
  Also see Pigface
Conner, Gary Lee
  See Screaming Trees
Conner, Van
  See Screaming Trees
Connick, Jr., Harry 4
Connolly, Buddy
  See Ceili Rain
Connolly, Pat
  See Surfaris, The
Connor, Chris 30
Connors, Marc
  See Nylons, The
Connors, Norman 30
Conti, Neil
  See Prefab Sprout
Convertino, John
  See Calexico
  Also see Giant Sand
Conway, Billy
  See Morphine
Conway, Dave
  See My Bloody Valentine
Conway, Gerry
  See Pentangle
Cooder, Ry 2
  Also see Captain Beefheart and His Magic
  Band

Cook, David Kyle
  See Matchbox 20
Cook, Greg
  See Ricochet
Cook, Jeffrey Alan
  See Alabama
Cook, Jesse 33
Cook, Paul
  See Sex Pistols, The
Cook, Stuart
  See Creedence Clearwater Revival
Cook, Wayne
  See Steppenwolf
Cooke, Mick
  See Belle and Sebastian
Cooke, Sam 1
  Also see Soul Stirrers, The
Cool, Tre
  See Green Day
Cooley, Dave
  See Citizen King
Coolio 19
Coombes, Gary
  See Supergrass
Coomes, Sam
  See Quasi
Cooney, Rory 6
Cooper, Alice 8
Cooper, Jason
  See Cure, The
Cooper, Martin
  See Orchestral Manoeuvres in the Dark
Cooper, Michael
  See Third World
Cooper, Paul
  See Nylons, The
Cooper, Ralph
  See Air Supply
Coore, Stephen
  See Third World
Cope, Julian 16
Copeland, Andrew
  See Sister Hazel
Copeland, Stewart 14
  Also see Police, The
Copland, Aaron 2
Copley, Al
  See Roomful of Blues
Coppola, Donna
  See Papas Fritas
Corea, Chick 6
Corella, Doug
  See Verve Pipe, The
Corgan, Billy
  See Smashing Pumpkins
Corigliano, John 34
Corina, Sarah
  See Mekons, The
Cornelius, Robert
  See Poi Dog Pondering
Cornell, Chris
  See Soundgarden
Cornell, Don 30
Cornershop 24
Cornick, Glenn
  See Jethro Tull
Cornwell, Hugh
  See Stranglers, The
Corr, Andrea
  See Corrs, The
Corr, Caroline
  See Corrs, The
Corr, Jim
  See Corrs, The
Corr, Sharon
  See Corrs, The

Corrigan, Brianna
  See Beautiful South
Corrs, The **32**
Cosper, Kina
  See Brownstone
Costanzo, Marc
  See Len
Costanzo, Sharon
  See Len
Costello, Elvis **12**
  Earlier sketch in CM **2**
Coté, Billy
  See Madder Rose
Cotoia, Robert
  See Beaver Brown Band, The
Cotrubas, Ileana **1**
Cotta, Justin
  See VAST
Cotten, Elizabeth **16**
Cotton, Caré
  See Sounds of Blackness
Cotton, Jeff "Antennae Jimmy Siemens"
  See Captain Beefheart and His Magic Band
Cougar, John(ny)
  See Mellencamp, John
Coughlan, Richard
  See Caravan
Counting Crows **18**
Country Gentlemen, The **7**
Coury, Fred
  See Cinderella
Coutts, Duncan
  See Our Lady Peace
Coverdale, David **34**
  See Deep Purple
  Also see Whitesnake
Cowan, Dennis
  See Bonzo Dog Doo-Dah Band
Cowan, John
  See New Grass Revival, The
Cowboy Junkies, The **4**
Cows, The **32**
Cox, Andy
  See English Beat, The
  Also see Fine Young Cannibals
Cox, Terry
  See Pentangle
Coxon, Graham
  See Blur
Coxon, John
  See Spring Heel Jack
Coyne, Mark
  See Flaming Lips
Coyne, Wayne
  See Flaming Lips
Crack, Carl
  See Atari Teenage Riot
Cracker **12**
Cracknell, Sarah
  See Saint Etienne
Cragg, Jonny
  See Spacehog
Crahan, Shawn
  See Slipknot
Craig, Albert
  See Israel Vibration
Craig, Carl **19**
Crain, S. R.
  See Soul Stirrers, The
Cramps, The **16**
Cranberries, The **14**
Craney, Mark
  See Jethro Tull
Crash Test Dummies **14**
Crawford, Dave Max
  See Poi Dog Pondering

Crawford, Ed
  See fIREHOSE
Crawford, Michael **4**
Crawford, Randy **25**
Crawford, Steve
  See Anointed
Crawford-Greathouse, Da'dra
  See Anointed
Cray, Robert **8**
Creach, Papa John
  See Jefferson Starship
Creager, Melora
  See Rasputina
Cream **9**
Creed **28**
Creedence Clearwater Revival **16**
Creegan, Andrew
  See Barenaked Ladies
Creegan, Jim
  See Barenaked Ladies
Crenshaw, Marshall **5**
Cretu, Michael
  See Enigma
Cripps, Joe
  See Brave Combo
Criss, Peter
  See Kiss
Crissinger, Roger
  See Pearls Before Swine
Croce, Jim **3**
Crofts, Dash
  See Seals & Crofts
Cronin, Kevin
  See REO Speedwagon
Cropper, Steve **12**
  Also see Booker T. & the M.G.'s
Crosby, Bing **6**
Crosby, David **3**
  Also see Byrds, The
  Also see Crosby, Stills, and Nash
Crosby, Jon
  See VAST
Crosby, Stills, and Nash **24**
Cross, Bridget
  See Velocity Girl
Cross, David
  See King Crimson
Cross, Mike
  See Sponge
Cross, Tim
  See Sponge
Crouch, Andraé **9**
Crover, Dale
  See Melvins
Crow, Sheryl **18**
Crowded House **12**
Crowe, J. D. **5**
Crowell, Rodney **8**
Crowley, Martin
  See Bevis Frond
Cruikshank, Gregory
  See Tuxedomoon
Cruz, Celia **22**
  Earlier sketch in CM **10**
Cua, Rick
  See Ceili Rain
Cuddy, Jim
  See Blue Rodeo
Cuevas, Alberto "Beto"
  See La Ley
Cuffee, Ed
  See McKinney's Cotton Pickers
Cugat, Xavier **23**
Cullinan, Tom
  See Quickspace
Culp, Dennis
  See Five Iron Frenzy

Cult, The **16**
Culver, Joe
  See Bardo Pond
Cumming, Graham
  See Bevis Frond
Cummings, Burton
  See Guess Who
Cummings, Danny
  See Dire Straits
Cummings, David
  See Del Amitri
Cummings, John
  See Mogwai
Cumplido, J. C.
  See La Ley
Cunniff, Jill
  See Luscious Jackson
Cunningham, Abe
  See Deftones
Cunningham, Blair
  See Echo and the Bunnymen
Cunningham, Ruth
  See Anonymous 4
Cuomo, Rivers
  See Weezer
Cure, The **20**
  Earlier sketch in CM **3**
Curiel, Marcos
  See P.O.D.
Curl, Langston
  See McKinney's Cotton Pickers
Curless, Ann
  See Exposé
Curley, John
  See Afghan Whigs
Curnin, Cy
  See Fixx, The
Curran, Ciaran
  See Altan
Curran, Doug
  See Lettermen, The
Currie, Justin
  See Del Amitri
Currie, Kevin
  See Supertramp
Currie, Steve
  See T. Rex
Curry, Tim **3**
Curtis, Barry
  See Kingsmen, The
Curtis, Catie **31**
Curtis, Ian
  See Joy Division
Curtis, King **17**
Curve **13**
Custance, Mickey
  See Big Audio Dynamite
Cuthbert, Scott
  See Everclear
Cutler, Chris
  See Pere Ubu
Cypress Hill **11**
Cyrus, Billy Ray **11**
Czukay, Holger
  See Can
Da Brat **30**
Dachert, Peter
  See Tuxedomoon
Dacus, Donnie
  See Chicago
Dacus, Johnny
  See Osborne Brothers, The
Daddy G
  See Massive Attack
Daddy Mack
  See Kris Kross

Daellenbach, Charles
  See Canadian Brass, The
Daft Punk **33**
Dahl, Jeff **28**
Dahlgren, Erik
  See Wannadies, The
Dahlheimer, Patrick
  See Live
Daisley, Bob
  See Black Sabbath
Dale, Dick **13**
Daley, Paul
  See Leftfield
Daley, Richard
  See Third World
Dall, Bobby
  See Poison
Dallin, Sarah
  See Bananarama
Dalton, John
  See Kinks, The
Dalton, Nic **31**
  Also see Lemonheads, The
Daltrey, Roger **3**
  Also see Who, The
Damiani, Victor
  See Cake
Dammers, Jerry
  See Specials, The
Damned, The **34**
Damon and Naomi **25**
Damone, Vic **33**
D'Amour, Paul
  See Tool
Dando, Evan
  See Lemonheads, The
Dandy Warhols **22**
Danell, Dennis
  See Social Distortion
D'Angelo **20**
D'Angelo, Greg
  See Anthrax
Daniel, Britt
  See Spoon
Daniels, Charlie **6**
Daniels, Jack
  See Highway 101
Daniels, Jerry
  See Ink Spots
Danko, Rick
  See Band, The
Danny Boy
  See House of Pain
Danze, William "Billy"
  See M.O.P.
Danzig **7**
Danzig, Glenn
  See Danzig
  Also see Misfits, The
Dap, Bill The Kid
  See Lane, Fred
D'Arby, Terence Trent **3**
Darin, Bobby **4**
D'Arko, Joe
  See Godsmack
Dark Star **29**
Darling, David **34**
Darling, Eric
  See Weavers, The
Darriau, Matt
  See Klezmatics, The
Darvill, Benjamin
  See Crash Test Dummies
Das EFX **14**
Daugherty, Jay Dee
  See Church, The
  Also see Waterboys, The

Daulne, Marie
  See Zap Mama
Dave, Doggy
  See Lords of Acid
Dave Clark Five, The **12**
Dave Matthews Band **18**
Davenport, N'Dea
  See Brand New Heavies, The
David, Stuart
  See Belle and Sebastian
Davidson, Lenny
  See Dave Clark Five, The
Davie, Hutch
  See Pearls Before Swine
Davies, Cliff
  See Northwoods Improvisers
Davies, Dave
  See Kinks, The
Davies, Dennis Russell **24**
Davies, James
  See Jimmie's Chicken Shack
Davies, Keith
  See Down By Law
Davies, Ray **5**
  Also see Kinks, The
Davies, Richard
  See Supertramp
Davies, Saul
  See James
Davis, Anthony **17**
Davis, Brad
  See Fu Manchu
Davis, Chip **4**
Davis, Clive **14**
Davis, Colin **27**
Davis, Gregory
  See Dirty Dozen Brass Band
Davis, Jody
  See Newsboys, The
Davis, John
  See Superdrag
Davis, John
  See Folk Implosion, The
Davis, Jonathan
  See Korn
Davis, Linda **21**
Davis, Michael
  See MC5, The
Davis, Miles **1**
Davis, Miles F.
  See Northwoods Improvisers
Davis, Norman
  See Wailing Souls
Davis, Reverend Gary **18**
Davis, Sammy, Jr. **4**
Davis, Santa
  See Big Mountain
Davis, Skeeter **15**
Davis, Spencer
  See Spencer Davis Group
Davis, Steve
  See Mystic Revealers
Davis, Verona
  See Stereo MC's
Davis, Zelma
  See C + C Music Factory
Davison, Wild Bill **34**
Davol, Sam
  See Magnetic Fields, The
Dawdy, Cheryl
  See Chenille Sisters, The
Dawn, Sandra
  See Platters, The
Day, Doris **24**
Dayne, Taylor **4**
dc Talk **18**

Deacon, John
  See Queen
Dead Can Dance **16**
Dead Kennedys **29**
Dead Milkmen **22**
Deakin, Paul
  See Mavericks, The
Deal, Kelley
  See Breeders
Deal, Kim
  See Breeders
  Also see Pixies, The
de Albuquerque, Michael
  See Electric Light Orchestra
Dean, Billy **19**
Dean, Paul
  See X-Ray Spex
Death in Vegas **28**
DeBarge, El **14**
De Borg, Jerry
  See Jesus Jones
de Burgh, Chris **22**
de Coster, Jean Paul
  See 2 Unlimited
Dederer, Dave
  See Presidents of the United States of
  America, The
Dee, Mikkey
  See Dokken
  Also see Motörhead
Deebank, Maurcie
  See Felt
Deee-lite **9**
Deep Forest **18**
Deep Purple **11**
Def Leppard **3**
DeFrancesco, Joey **29**
DeFranco, Buddy **31**
DeFreitas, Pete
  See Echo and the Bunnymen
Deftones **22**
De Gaia, Banco **27**
DeGarmo, Chris
  See Queensryche
de Grassi, Alex **6**
Deibert, Adam Warren
  See Aquabats, The
Deily, Ben
  See Lemonheads, The
DeJohnette, Jack **7**
de Jonge, Henk
  See Willem Breuker Kollektief
Delaet, Nathalie
  See Lords of Acid
De La Luna, Shai
  See Lords of Acid
Del Amitri **18**
de la Rocha, Zack
  See Rage Against the Machine
De La Soul **7**
DeLeo, Dean
  See Stone Temple Pilots
DeLeo, Robert
  See Stone Temple Pilots
Delgados, The **31**
Delirious? **33**
De Lisle, Paul
  See Smash Mouth
Dells, The **30**
Del Mar, Candy
  See Cramps, The
Delonge, Tom
  See Blink 182
DeLorenzo, Victor
  See Violent Femmes
de Lourcqua, Helno Rota
  See Les Négresses Vertes

Delp, Brad
  See Boston
Del Rubio Triplets **21**
Del the Funky Homosapien **30**
de Lucia, Paco **1**
DeMent, Iris **13**
Demeski, Stanley
  See Luna
De Meyer, Jean-Luc
  See Front 242
Deming, Michael
  See Pernice Brothers
DeMone, Gitane
  See Christian Death
Demos, Greg
  See Guided By Voices
Dempsey, Michael
  See Cure, The
Denison, Duane
  See Jesus Lizard
Dennis, Garth
  See Black Uhuru
Dennis, Rudolph "Garth"
  See Wailing Souls
Denny, Sandy
  See Fairport Convention
Densmore, John
  See Doors, The
Dent, Cedric
  See Take 6
Denton, Sandy
  See Salt-N-Pepa
d'Enton, Steve
  See Quickspace
Denver, John **22**
  Earlier sketch in CM **1**
De Oliveria, Laudir
  See Chicago
Depeche Mode **5**
Depew, Don
  See Cobra Verde
de Prume, Ivan
  See White Zombie
Derakh, Amir
  See Orgy
Derhak, Rob
  See moe.
Derosier, Michael
  See Heart
Desaulniers, Stephen
  See Scud Mountain Boys
Deschamps, Kim
  See Blue Rodeo
Desert Rose Band, The **4**
Desjardins, Claude
  See Nylons, The
Desmond, Paul **23**
Des'ree **24**
  Earlier sketch in CM **15**
Destiny's Child **33**
Destri, Jimmy
  See Blondie
Dettman, John
  See Swell
Deupree, Jerome
  See Morphine
Deurloo, Hermine
  See Willem Breuker Kollektief
Deutrom, Mark
  See Melvins
Deutsch, Stu
  See Wendy O. Williams and The Plasmatics
DeVille, C. C.
  See Poison
Devito, Nick
  See Four Seasons, The

Devito, Tommy
  See Four Seasons, The
Devlin, Adam P.
  See Bluetones, The
Devo **13**
Devoto, Howard
  See Buzzcocks, The
DeWitt, Lew C.
  See Statler Brothers, The
Dexter X
  See Man or Astroman?
de Young, Joyce
  See Andrews Sisters, The
D Generation **26**
Diagram, Andy
  See James
Diamond, "Dimebag" Darrell
  See Pantera
Diamond, Mike "Mike D"
  See Beastie Boys, The
Diamond, Neil **1**
Diamond Rio **11**
Di'anno, Paul
  See Iron Maiden
Dibango, Manu **14**
Dick, Coby
  See Papa Roach
Dick, Magic
  See J. Geils Band
Dickens, Little Jimmy **7**
Dickerson, B.B.
  See War
Dickerson, Lance
  See Commander Cody and His Lost Planet
  Airmen
Dickinson, Paul Bruce
  See Iron Maiden
Dickinson, Rob
  See Catherine Wheel
Diddley, Bo **3**
Didier, Daniel
  See Promise Ring, The
Diermaier, Werner
  See Faust
Dietrich, Marlene **25**
Dif, René
  See Aqua
Diffie, Joe **27**
  Earlier sketch in CM **10**
Difford, Chris
  See Squeeze
di Fiore, Vince
  See Cake
DiFranco, Ani **17**
Digable Planets **15**
Diggle, Steve
  See Buzzcocks, The
Diggs, Robert "RZA" (Prince Rakeem)
  See Gravediggaz
  Also see Wu-Tang Clan
Digital Underground **9**
Dillon, James
  See Caustic Resin
  Also see Built to Spill
Dillon, Jerome
  See Nine Inch Nails
Dilworth, Joe
  See Stereolab
DiMambro, "Angry" John
  See Down By Law
DiMant, Leor
  See House of Pain
Di Meola, Al **12**
DiMucci, Dion
  See Dion
Dinger, Klaus
  See Neu!

DiNizo, Pat
  See Smithereens, The
Dinning, Dean
  See Toad the Wet Sprocket
Dinosaur Jr. **10**
Dio, Ronnie James
  See Black Sabbath
Dion **4**
Dion, Celine **25**
  Earlier sketch in CM **12**
Dire Straits **22**
Dirks, Michael
  See Gwar
Dirnt, Mike
  See Green Day
Dirty Dozen Brass Band **23**
Dirty Three **31**
DiSpirito, Jim
  See Rusted Root
DiStefano, Peter
  See Porno for Pyros
Dittrich, John
  See Restless Heart
Divine Comedy, The **32**
Dixie Chicks **26**
Dixon, George W.
  See Spinners, The
Dixon, Jerry
  See Warrant
Dixon, Willie **10**
DJ Domination
  See Geto Boys, The
DJ Fuse
  See Digital Underground
DJ Jazzy Jeff and the Fresh Prince **5**
D.J. Lethal
  See House of Pain
D.J. Minutemix
  See P.M. Dawn
DJ Muggs
  See Cypress Hill
DJ Premier
  See Gang Starr
DJ Ready Red
  See Geto Boys, The
DJ Terminator X
  See Public Enemy
DMC
  See Run DMC
DMX **25**
D.O.A. **28**
Doc Pomus **14**
Doe, John
  See X
Dogbowl
  See King Missile
Dog's Eye View **21**
Doherty, Denny
  See Mamas and the Papas
Dokken **16**
Dokken, Don
  See Dokken
Dolby, Monica Mimi
  See Brownstone
Dolby, Thomas **10**
Dolenz, Micky
  See Monkees, The
Doling, Mikey
  See Soulfly
Dollimore, Kris
  See Damned, The
Dombroski, Vinnie
  See Sponge
Domingo, Placido **20**
  Earlier sketch in CM **1**
Dominici, Charlie
  See Dream Theater

Domino, Fats **2**
Domino, Floyd
　See Asleep at the Wheel
Don, Rasa
　See Arrested Development
Donahue, Jerry
　See Fairport Convention
Donahue, Jonathan
　See Flaming Lips
Donahue, Jonathan
　See Mercury Rev
Donald, Tony
　See Simple Minds
Donelly, Tanya
　See Belly
　Also see Breeders
　Also see Throwing Muses
Donnas, The **33**
Donnellan, John
　See Love
Donohue, Tim
　See Cherry Poppin' Daddies
Donovan **9**
Donovan, Bazil
　See Blue Rodeo
Donovan, Jim
　See Rusted Root
Doobie Brothers, The **3**
Doodlebug
　See Digable Planets
Doors, The **4**
Dorame, Mando
　See Royal Crown Revue
Doran, Rob
　See Alkaline Trio
Dorge, Michel (Mitch)
　See Crash Test Dummies
Dorney, Tim
　See Republica
Dorough, Bob
　See Pearls Before Swine
Dorough, Howie
　See Backstreet Boys
Dorrington, Paul
　See Wedding Present, The
Dorsey, Jimmy
　See Dorsey Brothers, The
Dorsey, Thomas A. **11**
Dorsey, Tommy
　See Dorsey Brothers, The
Dorsey Brothers, The **8**
Doss, Bill
　See Olivia Tremor Control
Doth, Anita
　See 2 Unlimited
Dott, Gerald
　See Incredible String Band
Doucet, Michael **8**
Doucette, Paul John
　See Matchbox 20
Doughty, M.
　See Soul Coughing
Doughty, Neal
　See REO Speedwagon
Douglas, Dave **29**
Douglas, Jerry
　See Country Gentlemen, The
Dowd, Christopher
　See Fishbone
Dowler, Darren
　See Lettermen, The
Dowling, Dave
　See Jimmie's Chicken Shack
Down By Law **34**
Downes, Geoff
　See Yes

Downes, Oswald
　See Wailing Souls
Downey, Brian
　See Thin Lizzy
Downie, Gordon
　See Tragically Hip, The
Downing, K. K.
　See Judas Priest
Doyle, Candida
　See Pulp
Doyle, John
　See Solas
Dozier, Lamont
　See Holland-Dozier-Holland
Dragge, Fletcher
　See Pennywise
Drake, Nick **17**
Drake, Steven
　See Odds
Draper, Paul
　See Mansun
Drayton, Leslie
　See Earth, Wind and Fire
Dr. Das
　See Asian Dub Foundation
Dr. Demento **23**
Dr. Dre **15**
　Also see N.W.A.
Dreadful, Garrie
　See Damned, The
Dream Theater **23**
Dreja, Chris
　See Yardbirds, The
Dres
　See Black Sheep
Drew, Dennis
　See 10,000 Maniacs
Drews, Jonathan
　See Sunset Valley
Driftwood, Jimmy **25**
Drivin' N' Cryin' **31**
Dr. John **7**
Droge, Pete **24**
Dropkick Murphys **26**
Drozd, Stephen
　See Flaming Lips
Drucker, Eugene
　See Emerson String Quartet
Dru Hill **25**
Drumbago
　See Skatalites, The
Drumdini, Harry
　See Cramps, The
Drummond, Don
　See Skatalites, The
Drummond, Tom
　See Better Than Ezra
Dryden, Spencer
　See Jefferson Airplane
Dryer, Debroah
　See Skunk Anansie
Dubbe, Berend
　See Bettie Serveert
Dube, Lucky **17**
Dubstar **22**
Duce, Adam
　See Machine Head
Dudley, Anne
　See Art of Noise
Duffey, John
　See Country Gentlemen, The
　Also see Seldom Scene, The
Duffy, Billy
　See Cult, The
Duffy, Martin
　See Primal Scream

Dufresne, Mark
　See Confederate Railroad
Duggan, Noel
　See Clannad
Duggan, Paidraig
　See Clannad
Duke, John
　See Pearls Before Swine
Dukowski, Chuck
　See Black Flag
Dulli, Greg
　See Afghan Whigs
Dumont, Tom
　See No Doubt
Dunbar, Aynsley
　See Jefferson Starship
　Also see Journey
　Also see Whitesnake
Dunbar, Sly
　See Sly and Robbie
Duncan, Bryan **19**
Duncan, Gary
　See Quicksilver Messenger Service
Duncan, Steve
　See Desert Rose Band, The
Duncan, Stuart
　See Nashville Bluegrass Band
Dunckel, Jean-Benoit
　See Air
Dunham, Nathanel "Brad"
　See Five Iron Frenzy
Dunlap, Slim
　See Replacements, The
Dunlop, Andy
　See Travis
Dunn, Donald "Duck"
　See Booker T. & the M.G.'s
Dunn, Holly **7**
Dunn, Larry
　See Earth, Wind and Fire
Dunn, Ronnie Gene
　See Brooks & Dunn
Dunning, A.J.
　See Verve Pipe, The
DuPré, Jacqueline **26**
Dupree, Champion Jack **12**
Dupree, Jesse James
　See Jackyl
Dupri, Jermaine **25**
Dural, Stanley Jr.
　See Buckwheat Zydeco
Duran Duran **4**
Durante, Mark
　See KMFDM
Duritz, Adam
　See Counting Crows
Durrill, Johnny
　See Ventures, The
Durst, Fred
　See Limp Bizkit
Durutti Column, The **30**
Dury, Ian **30**
Dust Brothers **32**
Dutt, Hank
　See Kronos Quartet
Dutton, Garrett
　See G. Love
Dutton, Lawrence
　See Emerson String Quartet
Dvorak, Antonin **25**
Dyble, Judy
　See Fairport Convention
Dylan, Bob **21**
　Earlier sketch in CM **3**
Dylan, Jakob
　See Wallflowers, The

Dyrason, Orri Páll
  See Sigur Rós
E., Sheila
  See Sheila E.
Eacrett, Chris
  See Our Lady Peace
Eagles, The 3
Earl, Ronnie 5
  Also see Roomful of Blues
Earle, Steve 16
Early, Ian
  See Cherry Poppin' Daddies
Earth, Wind and Fire 12
Easton, Elliot
  See Cars, The
Easton, Lynn
  See Kingsmen, The
Easton, Sheena 2
Eazy-E 13
  Also see N.W.A.
Echeverria, Rob
  See Helmet
Echo and the Bunnymen 32
Echobelly 21
Echols, John
  See Love
Eckstine, Billy 1
Eddy, Chris
  See Ceili Rain
Eddy, Duane 9
Eden, Sean
  See Luna
Eder, Linda 30
Edge, Graeme
  See Moody Blues, The
Edge, The
  See U2
Edison, Harry "Sweets" 29
Edmonds, Kenneth "Babyface" 12
Edmonds, Lu
  See Damned, The
Edmonton, Jerry
  See Steppenwolf
Edmunds, Dave 28
Edson, Richard
  See Sonic Youth
Edward, Scott
  See Bluetones, The
Edwards, Dennis
  See Temptations, The
Edwards, Edgar
  See Spinners, The
Edwards, Gordon
  See Kinks, The
  Also see Pretty Things, The
Edwards, John
  See Spinners, The
Edwards, Johnny
  See Foreigner
Edwards, Leroy "Lion"
  See Mystic Revealers
Edwards, Mark
  See Aztec Camera
Edwards, Michael James
  See Jesus Jones
Edwards, Mike
  See Electric Light Orchestra
Edwards, Nokie
  See Ventures, The
Edwards, Skye
  See Morcheeba
Edwardson, Dave
  See Neurosis
eels 29
Efrem, Towns
  See Dirty Dozen Brass Band

Egan, Kian
  See Westlife
Egan, Seamus
  See Solas
Ehart, Phil
  See Kansas
Ehran
  See Lords of Acid
Eid, Tamer
  See Emmet Swimming
808 State 31
Einheit
  See Einstürzende Neubauten
Einheit, F.M.
  See KMFDM
Einstürzende Neubauten 13
Einziger, Michael
  See Incubus
Eisenstein, Michael
  See Letters to Cleo
Eisentrager, Thor
  See Cows, The
Eitzel, Mark
  See American Music Club
Ekberg, Ulf
  See Ace of Base
Eklund, Greg
  See Everclear
Elastica 29
Eldon, Thór
  See Sugarcubes, The
Eldridge, Ben
  See Seldom Scene, The
Eldridge, Roy 9
  Also see McKinney's Cotton Pickers
Electric Light Orchestra 7
Elfman, Danny 9
Elf Power 30
El-Hadi, Sulieman
  See Last Poets
El Hefe
  See NOFX
Elias, Hanin
  See Atari Teenage Riot
Elias, Manny
  See Tears for Fears
Ellefson, Dave
  See Megadeth
Elling, Kurt 31
Ellington, Duke 2
Elliot, Cass 5
  Also see Mamas and the Papas
Elliott, Dennis
  See Foreigner
Elliott, Doug
  See Odds
Elliott, Joe
  See Def Leppard
Elliott, Missy 30
Elliott, Ramblin' Jack 32
Ellis, Arti
  See Pearls Before Swine
Ellis, Bobby
  See Skatalites, The
Ellis, Herb 18
Ellis, Ingrid
  See Sweet Honey in the Rock
Ellis, John
  See Stranglers, The
Ellis, Rob
  See Swell
Ellis, Terry
  See En Vogue
Ellis, Warren
  See Dirty Three
Ellison, Rahsaan
  See Oakland Interfaith Gospel Choir

Elmore, Greg
  See Quicksilver Messenger Service
ELO
  See Electric Light Orchestra
Ely, Jack
  See Kingsmen, The
Ely, John
  See Asleep at the Wheel
Ely, Vince
  See Cure, The
  Also see Psychedelic Furs
Emerson, Bill
  See Country Gentlemen, The
Emerson, Darren
  See Underworld
Emerson, Keith
  See Emerson, Lake & Palmer/Powell
Emerson, Lake & Palmer/Powell 5
Emerson String Quartet 33
Emert, Alan
  See Brave Combo
Emery, Jill
  See Hole
Eminem 28
Emmanuel, Tommy 21
Emmet Swimming 24
Empire, Alec
  See Atari Teenage Riot
Endo, Nic
  See Atari Teenage Riot
Engemann, Bob
  See Lettermen, The
English, Michael 23
English, Richard
  See Flaming Lips
English Beat, The 9
Enigk, Jeremy
  See Sunny Day Real Estate
Enigma 32
  Earlier sketch in CM 14
Eno, Brian 8
Eno, Jim
  See Spoon
Enos, Bob
  See Roomful of Blues
Enright, Pat
  See Nashville Bluegrass Band
Entwistle, John
  See Who, The
En Vogue 10
Enya 32
  Earlier sketch in CM 6
  Also see Clannad
EPMD 10
Epstein, Howie
  See Tom Petty and the Heartbreakers
Erasure 11
Erchick, Peter
  See Olivia Tremor Control
Eric B.
  See Eric B. and Rakim
Eric B. and Rakim 9
Erickson, Roky 16
Erikson, Duke
  See Garbage
Erlandson, Eric
  See Hole
Erna, Sully
  See Godsmack
Erner, Jeff "The Shark"
  See Dropkick Murphys
Errico, Greg
  See Sly & the Family Stone
  Also see Quicksilver Messenger Service
Erskine, Peter
  See Weather Report
Ertegun, Ahmet 10

Ertegun, Nesuhi **24**
Ertel, Janet
See Chordettes, The
Erwin, Emily
See Dixie Chicks
Esch, En
See KMFDM
Also see Pigface
Escovedo, Alejandro **18**
Eshe, Montsho
See Arrested Development
Eskelin, Ellery **31**
Eskelin, Ian **19**
Esler-Smith, Frank
See Air Supply
Esperance, Tobin
See Papa Roach
Esquivel, Juan **17**
Estefan, Gloria **15**
Earlier sketch in CM **2**
Estes, Sleepy John **25**
Estms, Shep
See Lane, Fred
Estrada, Roy
See Little Feat
Also see Captain Beefheart and His Magic
Band
Etheridge, Melissa **16**
Earlier sketch in CM **4**
Eurythmics **31**
Earlier sketch in CM **6**
Evan, John
See Jethro Tull
Evans, Bill **17**
Evans, Dick "Dik"
See U2
Evans, Faith **25**
Evans, Gil **17**
Evans, Lynn
See Chordettes, The
Evans, Mark
See AC/DC
Evans, Sara **27**
Evans, Shane
See Collective Soul
Evans, Tom
See Badfinger
Eve **34**
Eve 6 **31**
Everclear **18**
Everlast **27**
Also see House of Pain
Everly, Don
See Everly Brothers, The
Everly, Phil
See Everly Brothers, The
Everly Brothers, The **2**
Everman, Jason
See Soundgarden
Everything But The Girl **15**
Evora, Cesaria **19**
Ewen, Alvin
See Steel Pulse
Ex, The **28**
Exkano, Paul
See Five Blind Boys of Alabama
Exposé **4**
Extreme **10**
Ezell, Ralph
See Shenandoah
Fabian **5**
Fabian, Lara **34**
Fabulous Thunderbirds, The **1**
Faces, The **22**
Fadden, Jimmie
See Nitty Gritty Dirt Band, The

Fagen, Donald
See Steely Dan
Fagenson, Tony
See Eve 6
Fahey, John **17**
Fahey, Siobhan
See Bananarama
Fairfoull, Bob
See Idlewild
Fairport Convention **22**
Fairs, Jim
See Pearls Before Swine
Faithfull, Marianne **14**
Faith No More **7**
Fakir, Abdul "Duke"
See Four Tops, The
Falconer, Earl
See UB40
Fall, The **12**
Fallon, David
See Chieftains, The
Fältskog, Agnetha
See Abba
Falzone, Chuck
See Flying Luttenbachers, The
Fambrough, Henry
See Spinners, The
Fame, Georgie
See Bill Wyman & the Rhythm Kings
Fame, Lil'
See M.O.P.
Fankhauser, Merrell **24**
Fanning, Bernard
See Powderfinger
Farley, J. J.
See Soul Stirrers, The
Farlow, Billy C.
See Commander Cody and His Lost Planet
Airmen
Farndon, Pete
See Pretenders, The
Farnham, John **32**
Farnsworth, Ed
See Bardo Pond
Farrar, Jay
See Son Volt
Farrar, John
See Shadows, The
Farrell, Frank
See Supertramp
Farrell, Perry
See Jane's Addiction
Also see Porno for Pyros
Farrer, Rob
See Divine Comedy, The
Farris, Dionne
See Arrested Development
Farris, Tim
See Israel Vibration
Farriss, Andrew
See INXS
Farriss, Jon
See INXS
Farriss, Tim
See INXS
Fast
See Fun Lovin' Criminals
Fastbacks, The **29**
Fastball **32**
Fatboy Slim **22**
Fat Mike
See NOFX
Fatone, Joey
See 'N Sync
Faulkner, Dave
See Hoodoo Gurus
Faust **32**

Fay, Bob
See Sebadoh
Fay, Johnny
See Tragically Hip, The
Fay, Martin
See Chieftains, The
Fayad, Frank
See Love
Fear Factory **27**
Fearless, Richard
See Death in Vegas
Fearnley, James
See Pogues, The
Feedback, Captain
See Rube Waddell
Feehily, Mark
See Westlife
Fehlmann, Thomas
See Orb, The
Fehn, Chris
See Slipknot
Feinstein, Michael **6**
Fela
See Kuti, Fela
Felber, Dean
See Hootie and the Blowfish
Felder, Don
See Eagles, The
Feldman, Eric Drew
See Pere Ubu
Also see Captain Beefheart and His Magic
Band
Feliciano, José **10**
Fell, Simon H. **32**
Felt **32**
Felumlee, Mike
See Alkaline Trio
Fender, Freddy
See Texas Tornados, The
Fender, Leo **10**
Fennell, Kevin
See Guided By Voices
Fennelly, Gere
See Redd Kross
Fent-Lister, Johnny
See Lane, Fred
Fenwick, Ray
See Spencer Davis Group
Ferguson, Doug
See Camel
Ferguson, Jay
See Sloan
Ferguson, Jay
See Spirit
Ferguson, Keith
See Fabulous Thunderbirds, The
Ferguson, Maynard **7**
Ferguson, Neil
See Chumbawamba
Ferguson, Steve
See NRBQ
Fernandes, John
See Olivia Tremor Control
Fernandez, Julio
See Spyro Gyra
Ferrell, Rachelle **17**
Ferrer, Frank
See Love Spit Love
Ferry, Bryan **1**
Ficca, Billy
See Television
Fiedler, Arthur **6**
Fielder, Jim
See Blood, Sweat and Tears
Fields, Johnny
See Five Blind Boys of Alabama

Fieldy
See Korn
Fier, Anton
See Golden Palominos
Also see Pere Ubu
Filan, Shane
See Westlife
Filter 28
Finch, Adrian
See Elf Power
Finch, Carl
See Brave Combo
Finch, Jennifer
See L7
Finck, Robin
See Nine Inch Nails
Finckel, David
See Emerson String Quartet
Finer, Jem
See Pogues, The
Finestone, Peter
See Bad Religion
Fine Young Cannibals 22
Fink, Jr., Rat
See Alien Sex Fiend
Finn, Jason
See Presidents of the United States of
America, The
Finn, Micky
See T. Rex
Finn, Neil 34
Also see Crowded House
Finn, Tim
See Crowded House
fIREHOSE 11
Fischer, Matt
See Minty
Fish, Pat
See Jazz Butcher, The
Fishbone 7
Fisher, Brandon
See Superdrag
Fisher, Eddie 12
Fisher, Jerry
See Blood, Sweat and Tears
Fisher, John "Norwood"
See Fishbone
Fisher, Morgan
See Mott the Hoople
Fisher, Phillip "Fish"
See Fishbone
Fisher, Roger
See Heart
Fishman, Jon
See Phish
Fitzgerald, Ella 1
Fitzgerald, Kevin
See Geraldine Fibbers
Five Blind Boys of Alabama 12
Five Iron Frenzy 26
Fixx, The 33
Flack, Roberta 5
Flaming Lips 22
Flanagan, Tommy 16
Flanagin, Craig
See God Is My Co-Pilot
Flannery, Sean
See Cherry Poppin' Daddies
Flansburgh, John
See They Might Be Giants
Flash, Flying Johnny
See Lanternjack, The
Flatt, Lester 3
Flavor Flav
See Public Enemy
Flea
See Red Hot Chili Peppers, The

Fleck, Bela 8
Also see New Grass Revival, The
Fleetwood, Mick
See Fleetwood Mac
Fleetwood Mac 5
Fleischmann, Robert
See Journey
Fleisig, Alexis
See Girls Against Boys
Fleming, Renee 24
Flemion, Dennis
See Frogs, The
Flemion, Jimmy
See Frogs, The
Flemons, Wade
See Earth, Wind and Fire
Flesh-N-Bone
See Bone Thugs-N-Harmony
Fletcher, Andy
See Depeche Mode
Fletcher, Guy
See Dire Straits
Flint, Keith
See Prodigy
Flores, Rosie 16
Floyd, Heather
See Point of Grace
Fluoride, Klaus
See Dead Kennedys
Flür, Wolfgang
See Kraftwerk
Flying Luttenbachers, The 28
Flying Saucer Attack 29
Flynn, Pat
See New Grass Revival, The
Flynn, Robert
See Machine Head
Fogelberg, Dan 4
Fogerty, John 2
Also see Creedence Clearwater Revival
Fogerty, Thomas
See Creedence Clearwater Revival
Folds, Ben
See Ben Folds Five
Foley
See Arrested Development
Folk Implosion, The 28
Foo Fighters 20
Foote, Dick
See Lane, Fred
Forbes, Derek
See Simple Minds
Forbes, Graham
See Incredible String Band
Ford, Frankie
See Pretty Things, The
Ford, Lita 9
Ford, Marc
See Black Crowes, The
Ford, Maya
See Donnas, The
Ford, Penny
See Soul II Soul
Ford, Robert "Peg"
See Golden Gate Quartet
Ford, Tennessee Ernie 3
Forde, Brinsley "Dan"
See Aswad
Fordham, Julia 15
Foreigner 21
Foreman, Chris
See Madness
Forrester, Alan
See Mojave 3
Forsi, Ken
See Surfaris, The

Forster, Robert
See Go-Betweens, The
Forte, Juan
See Oakland Interfaith Gospel Choir
Fortune, Jimmy
See Statler Brothers, The
Fortus, Richard
See Love Spit Love
Fossen, Steve
See Heart
Foster, David 13
Foster, Malcolm
See Pretenders, The
Foster, Paul
See Soul Stirrers, The
Foster, Radney 16
Fountain, Clarence
See Five Blind Boys of Alabama
Fountain, Pete 7
Fountains of Wayne 26
4Him 23
Four Seasons, The 24
Four Tops, The 11
Fowler, Bruce "Fossil Fowler"
See Captain Beefheart and His Magic Band
Fowler, Buren
See Drivin' N' Cryin'
Fox, Lucas
See Motörhead
Fox, Oz
See Stryper
Fox, Samantha 3
Foxton, Bruce
See Jam, The
Foxwell Baker, Iain Richard
See Jesus Jones
Foxx, Leigh
See Blondie
Frame, Roddy
See Aztec Camera
Frampton, Peter 3
Francis, Black
See Pixies, The
Francis, Connie 10
Francis, Michael
See Asleep at the Wheel
Francolini, Dave
See Dark Star
Franke, Chris
See Tangerine Dream
Frankenstein, Jeff
See Newsboys, The
Frankie Goes to Hollywood 31
Frankie Lymon and The Teenagers 24
Franklin, Adam
See Swervedriver
Franklin, Aretha 17
Earlier sketch in CM 2
Franklin, Elmo
See Mighty Clouds of Joy, The
Franklin, Farrah
See Destiny's Child
Franklin, Kirk 22
Franklin, Larry
See Asleep at the Wheel
Franklin, Melvin
See Temptations, The
Franti, Michael 16
Also see Spearhead
Frantz, Chris
See Talking Heads
Fraser, Elizabeth
See Cocteau Twins, The
Frater, Shaun
See Fairport Convention
Frazier, Stan
See Sugar Ray

Frederiksen, Lars
  See Rancid
Fredriksson, Marie
  See Roxette
Freel, David
  See Swell
Freeman, Aaron
  See Ween
Freeman, Matt
  See Rancid
Freese, Josh
  See Suicidal Tendencies
Frehley, Ace
  See Kiss
Freiberg, David
  See Quicksilver Messenger Service
  Also see Jefferson Starship
French, Frank
  See Cake
French, John "Drumbo"
  See Captain Beefheart and His Magic Band
French, Mark
  See Blue Rodeo
Freni, Mirella 14
Freshwater, John
  See Alien Sex Fiend
Frey, Glenn 3
  Also see Eagles, The
Fricke, Janie 33
Fricker, Sylvia
  See Ian and Sylvia
Fridmann, Dave
  See Mercury Rev
Friedman, Marty
  See Megadeth
Friel, Tony
  See Fall, The
Friend, Eric
  See Spoon
Fripp, Robert 9
  Also see King Crimson
Frischmann, Justine Elinor
  See Elastica
Frisell, Bill 15
Frishmann, Justine
  See Suede
Frith, Fred 19
  Also see Golden Palominos
Fritzsche, Chris
  See Chanticleer
Frizzell, Lefty 10
Froese, Edgar
  See Tangerine Dream
Froggatt, Thomas
  See VAST
Frogs, The 31
Fröhlich, Frank 32
Front 242 19
Front Line Assembly 20
Froom, Mitchell 15
Frugone, Pedro "Archi"
  See La Ley
Fruitbat
  See Carter USM
Frusciante, John
  See Red Hot Chili Peppers, The
Fuel 27
Fugazi 13
Fugees, The 17
Fulber, Rhys
  See Front Line Assembly
Fuller, Blind Boy 20
Fuller, Craig
  See Little Feat
Fuller, Jim
  See Surfaris, The
Fulson, Lowell 20

Fu Manchu 22
Funahara, O. Chosei
  See Wendy O. Williams and The Plasmatics
Funches, Johnny
  See Dells, The
Fun Lovin' Criminals 20
Fuqua, Charlie
  See Ink Spots
Fuqua, Harvey
  See Moonglows, The
Furay, Richie
  See Buffalo Springfield
Furler, Peter
  See Newsboys, The
Furlong, Eric
  See Sunset Valley
Furr, John
  See Treadmill Trackstar
Furuholmen, Magne
  See A-ha
Futter, Brian
  See Catherine Wheel
Gabay, Yuval
  See Soul Coughing
Gabler, Milton 25
Gabriel, Juan 31
Gabriel, Peter 16
  Earlier sketch in CM 2
  Also see Genesis
Gaby
  See Les Négresses Vertes
Gadler, Frank
  See NRBQ
Gaffney, Eric
  See Sebadoh
Gagliardi, Ed
  See Foreigner
Gahan, Dave
  See Depeche Mode
Gaillard, Slim 31
Gaines, Jeffrey 34
Gaines, Steve
  See Lynyrd Skynyrd
Gaines, Timothy
  See Stryper
Galás, Diamanda 16
Galaxie 500 33
Gale, Melvyn
  See Electric Light Orchestra
Galea, Darren
  See Jamiroquai
Gallagher, Liam
  See Oasis
Gallagher, Noel
  See Oasis
Gallucci, Don
  See Kingsmen, The
Gallup, Simon
  See Cure, The
Galore, Lady
  See Lords of Acid
Galway, James 3
Gambill, Roger
  See Kingston Trio, The
Gamble, Cheryl "Coko"
  See SWV
Gane, Tim
  See Stereolab
Gang of Four 8
Gang Starr 13
Gannon, Craig
  See Aztec Camera
Gano, Gordon
  See Violent Femmes
Garbage 25
Garbarek, Jan 30

Garcia, Dean
  See Curve
Garcia, Jerry 4
  Also see Grateful Dead, The
Garcia, Leddie
  See Poi Dog Pondering
Garcia, Teca
  See Tijuana No!
Gardiner, John Eliot 26
Gardner, Adam
  See Guster
Gardner, Carl
  See Coasters, The
Gardner, Suzi
  See L7
Garfunkel, Art 4
  Also see Simon and Garfunkel
Gargiulo, Lulu
  See Fastbacks, The
Garland, Judy 6
Garner, Erroll 25
Garnes, Sherman
  See Frankie Lymon and The Teenagers
Garnier, Laurent 29
Garrard, Stuart
  See Delirious?
Garrett, Amos
  See Pearls Before Swine
Garrett, Kenny 28
Garrett, Peter
  See Midnight Oil
Garrett, Scott
  See Cult, The
Garrison, Chuck
  See Superchunk
Garvey, Chuck
  See moe.
Garvey, Steve
  See Buzzcocks, The
Garza, Rob
  See Thievery Corporation
Gaskill, Jerry
  See King's X
Gaston, Asa
  See Lane, Fred
Gates, Jimmy Jr.
  See Silk
Gatton, Danny 16
Gaudio, Bob
  See Four Seasons, The
Gaudreau, Jimmy
  See Country Gentlemen, The
Gaugh, IV, "Bud" Floyd
  See Sublime
Gavurin, David
  See Sundays, The
Gay, Marc
  See Shai
Gayden, Mac
  See Pearls Before Swine
Gaye, Angus "Drummie Zeb"
  See Aswad
Gaye, Marvin 4
Gayle, Crystal 1
Gaynor, Adam
  See Matchbox 20
Gaynor, Mel
  See Simple Minds
Gayol, Rafael "Danny"
  See BoDeans
Geary, Paul
  See Extreme
Geddes, Chris
  See Belle and Sebastian
Gedge, David
  See Wedding Present, The

Gee, Rosco
  See Traffic
Gee, Rosko
  See Can
Geffen, David **8**
Geils, J.
  See J. Geils Band
Gelb, Howe
  See Giant Sand
Geldof, Bob **9**
Gendel, Keith
  See Papas Fritas
Gene Loves Jezebel **27**
Genensky, Marsha
  See Anonymous 4
Genesis **4**
Genn, Dave
  See Matthew Good Band
Gentling, Matt
  See Archers of Loaf
Gentry, Teddy Wayne
  See Alabama
Gentry, Troy
  See Montgomery Gentry
George, Lowell
  See Little Feat
George, Rocky
  See Suicidal Tendencies
George, Stephen
  See Swervedriver
Georges, Bernard
  See Throwing Muses
Georgiev, Ivan
  See Tuxedomoon
Geraldine Fibbers **21**
Gerber, Scott
  See Giant Sand
Germano, Lisa **18**
Gerrard, Lisa
  See Dead Can Dance
Gershwin, George and Ira **11**
Gessle, Per
  See Roxette
Geto Boys, The **11**
Getz, Stan **12**
Ghost **24**
Ghostface Killah **33**
  Also see Wu-Tang Clan
Giammalvo, Chris
  See Madder Rose
Gianni, Angelo
  See Treadmill Trackstar
Giant Sand **30**
Gibb, Barry
  See Bee Gees, The
Gibb, Maurice
  See Bee Gees, The
Gibb, Robin
  See Bee Gees, The
Gibbins, Mike
  See Badfinger
Gibbons, Beth
  See Portishead
Gibbons, Billy
  See ZZ Top
Gibbons, Ian
  See Kinks, The
Gibbons, John
  See Bardo Pond
Gibbons, Michael
  See Bardo Pond
Giblin, John
  See Simple Minds
Gibson, Bob **23**
Gibson, Debbie
  See Gibson, Deborah

Gibson, Deborah **24**
  Earlier sketch in CM **1**
Gibson, Wilf
  See Electric Light Orchestra
Gifford, Alex
  See Propellerheads
  Also see Electric Light Orchestra
Gifford, Katharine
  See Stereolab
Gifford, Peter
  See Midnight Oil
Gift, Roland **3**
  Also see Fine Young Cannibals
Gil, Gilberto **26**
Gilbert, Bruce
  See Wire
Gilbert, Gillian
  See New Order
Gilbert, Nick
  See Felt
Gilbert, Nicole Nicci
  See Brownstone
Gilbert, Ronnie
  See Weavers, The
Gilbert, Simon
  See Suede
Gilberto, João **33**
Giles, Michael
  See King Crimson
Gilkyson, Tony
  See X
Gill, Andy
  See Gang of Four
Gill, George
  See Wire
Gill, Janis
  See Sweethearts of the Rodeo
Gill, Johnny **20**
Gill, Ped
  See Frankie Goes To Hollywood
Gill, Pete
  See Motörhead
Gill, Vince **34**
  Earlier sketch in CM **7**
Gillan, Ian
  See Deep Purple
  Also see Black Sabbath
Gillard, Doug
  See Cobra Verde
Gillespie, Bobby
  See Jesus and Mary Chain, The
  Also see Primal Scream
Gillespie, Dizzy **6**
Gilley, Mickey **7**
Gillies, Ben
  See Silverchair
Gillingham, Charles
  See Counting Crows
Gillis, Steve
  See Filter
Gilman, Billy **34**
Gilmore, Jimmie Dale **11**
Gilmore, Mike
  See Northwoods Improvisers
Gilmour, David
  See Pink Floyd
Gilvear, Marcus
  See Gene Loves Jezebel
Gin Blossoms **18**
Gingold, Josef **6**
Ginn, Greg
  See Black Flag
Ginsberg, Allen **26**
Ginuwine **34**
Gioia
  See Exposé

Gipp, Cameron "Big Gipp"
  See Goodie Mob
Gipsy Kings, The **8**
Giraudy, Miquitte
  See Gong
Girls Against Boys **31**
Gittleman, Joe
  See Mighty Mighty Bosstones
Glabicki, Michael
  See Rusted Root
Glamorre, Matthew
  See Minty
Glascock, John
  See Jethro Tull
Glaser, Gabby
  See Luscious Jackson
Glass, Daniel
  See Royal Crown Revue
Glass, David
  See Christian Death
Glass, Eddie
  See Fu Manchu
Glass, Philip **1**
Glasscock, John
  See Jethro Tull
Glenn, Gary
  See Silk
Glennie, Evelyn **33**
Glennie, Jim
  See James
Glitter, Gary **19**
G. Love **24**
Glover, Corey
  See Living Colour
Glover, Roger
  See Deep Purple
Gnewikow, Jason
  See Promise Ring, The
Gobel, Robert
  See Kool & the Gang
Go-Betweens, The **28**
Goble, Brian Roy
  See D.O.A.
Godchaux, Donna
  See Grateful Dead, The
Godchaux, Keith
  See Grateful Dead, The
Goddess, Tony
  See Papas Fritas
Godfrey, Paul
  See Morcheeba
Godfrey, Ross
  See Morcheeba
Godin, Nicolas
  See Air
God Is My Co-Pilot **29**
Godsmack **30**
Goettel, Dwayne Rudolf
  See Skinny Puppy
Goffey, Danny
  See Supergrass
Goffin, Gerry
  See Goffin-King
Goffin-King **24**
Gogin, Toni
  See Sleater-Kinney
Go-Go's, The **24**
Goh, Rex
  See Air Supply
Gold, Julie **22**
Golden, William Lee
  See Oak Ridge Boys, The
Golden Gate Quartet **25**
Golden Palominos **32**
Golding, Lynval
  See Specials, The

Goldsmith, William
  See Foo Fighters
  Also see Sunny Day Real Estate
Goldstein, Jerry
  See War
Golson, Benny **21**
Gomez **33**
Gong **24**
Gonson, Claudia
  See Magnetic Fields, The
Good, Matthew
  See Matthew Good Band
Gooden, Ramone Pee Wee
  See Digital Underground
Goodie Mob **24**
Goodman, Benny **4**
Goodman, Jerry
  See Mahavishnu Orchestra
Goodridge, Robin
  See Bush
Googe, Debbie
  See My Bloody Valentine
Goo Goo Dolls, The **16**
Googy, Arthur
  See Misfits, The
Gordon, Dexter **10**
Gordon, Dwight
  See Mighty Clouds of Joy, The
Gordon, Jay
  See Orgy
Gordon, Jim
  See Traffic
Gordon, Kim
  See Sonic Youth
Gordon, Mike
  See Phish
Gordon, Nina
  See Veruca Salt
Gordy, Berry, Jr. **6**
Gordy, Emory, Jr. **17**
Gore, Martin
  See Depeche Mode
Gorham, Scott
  See Thin Lizzy
Gorka, John **18**
Gorky's Zygotic Mynci **30**
Gorman, Christopher
  See Belly
Gorman, Steve
  See Black Crowes, The
Gorman, Thomas
  See Belly
Gorter, Arjen
  See Willem Breuker Kollektief
Gosling, John
  See Kinks, The
Gossard, Stone
  See Brad
  Also see Pearl Jam
Goswell, Rachel
  See Mojave 3
Gotobed, Robert
  See Wire
Gott, Larry
  See James
Goudreau, Barry
  See Boston
Gould, Billy
  See Faith No More
Gould, Glenn **9**
Gould, Morton **16**
Goulding, Steve
  See Gene Loves Jezebel
Grable, Steve
  See Pearls Before Swine
Gracey, Chad
  See Live

Gradney, Ken
  See Little Feat
Graffety-Smith, Toby
  See Jamiroquai
Graffin, Greg
  See Bad Religion
Graham, Bill **10**
Graham, Glen
  See Blind Melon
Graham, Johnny
  See Earth, Wind and Fire
Graham, Larry
  See Sly & the Family Stone
Gramm, Lou
  See Foreigner
Gramolini, Gary
  See Beaver Brown Band, The
Grandmaster Flash **14**
Grant, Amy **7**
Grant, Bob
  See The Bad Livers
Grant, Colyn "Mo"
  See Baha Men
Grant, Gogi **28**
Grant, Lloyd
  See Metallica
Grant Lee Buffalo **16**
Grapes of Wrath, The **33**
Grappelli, Stephane **10**
Grateful Dead, The **5**
Gratzer, Alan
  See REO Speedwagon
Gravatt, Eric
  See Weather Report
Gravediggaz **23**
Graves, Alexander
  See Moonglows, The
Graves, Denyce **16**
Graves, Michale
  See Misfits, The
Gray, David
  See Spearhead
Gray, David **30**
Gray, Del
  See Little Texas
Gray, Ella
  See Kronos Quartet
Gray, F. Gary **19**
Gray, James
  See Blue Rodeo
Gray, James
  See Spearhead
Gray, Luther
  See Tsunami
Gray, Macy **32**
Gray, Paul
  See Damned, The
Gray, Paul
  See Slipknot
Gray, Tom
  See Country Gentlemen, The
  Also see Seldom Scene, The
Gray, Tom
  See Gomez
Gray, Walter
  See Kronos Quartet
Gray, Wardell
  See McKinney's Cotton Pickers
Greater Vision **26**
Grebenshikov, Boris **3**
Grech, Rick
  See Traffic
Greco, Paul
  See Chumbawamba
Green, Al **9**
Green, Benny **17**

Green, Carlito "Cee-lo"
  See Goodie Mob
Green, Charles
  See War
Green, David
  See Air Supply
Green, Douglas "Ranger Doug"
  See Riders in the Sky
Green, Grant **14**
Green, James
  See Dru Hill
Green, Jeremiah
  See Modest Mouse
Green, Peter
  See Fleetwood Mac
Green, Susaye
  See Supremes, The
Green, Willie
  See Neville Brothers, The
Greenall, Rupert
  See Fixx, The
Green Day **16**
Greene, Karl Anthony
  See Herman's Hermits
Greenfield, Dave
  See Stranglers, The
Greenhalgh, Tom
  See Mekons, The
Greensmith, Domenic
  See Reef
Greenspoon, Jimmy
  See Three Dog Night
Greentree, Richard
  See Beta Band, The
Greenwood, Al
  See Foreigner
Greenwood, Colin
  See Radiohead
Greenwood, Gail
  See Belly
Greenwood, Jonny
  See Radiohead
Greenwood, Lee **12**
Greer, Jim
  See Guided By Voices
Gregg, Dave
  See D.O.A.
Gregg, Paul
  See Restless Heart
Gregory, Bryan
  See Cramps, The
Gregory, Dave
  See XTC
Gregory, Keith
  See Wedding Present, The
Gregory, Troy
  See Prong
Greller, Al
  See Yo La Tengo
Grey, Charles Wallace
  See Aquabats, The
Grice, Gary "The Genius"
  See Wu-Tang Clan
Griffin, A.C. "Eddie"
  See Golden Gate Quartet
Griffin, Bob
  See BoDeans, The
Griffin, Dale "Buffin"
  See Mott the Hoople
Griffin, Kevin
  See Better Than Ezra
  Also see NRBQ
Griffin, Mark
  See MC 900 Ft. Jesus
Griffin, Patty **24**
Griffin, Rodney
  See Greater Vision

Griffith, Nanci **3**
Griffiths, Donald "Benjamin"
  See Aswad
Grigg, Chris
  See Treadmill Trackstar
Grisman, David **17**
Grohl, Dave
  See Nirvana
  Also see Foo Fighters
Grossman, Rick
  See Hoodoo Gurus
Grotberg, Karen
  See Jayhawks, The
Groucutt, Kelly
  See Electric Light Orchestra
Grove, George
  See Kingston Trio, The
Grover, Charlie
  See Sponge
Grundy, Hugh
  See Zombies, The
Grusin, Dave **7**
Guaraldi, Vince **3**
Guard, Dave
  See Kingston Trio, The
Gudmundsdottir, Björk
  See Björk
  Also see Sugarcubes, The
Güereña, Luis
  See Tijuana No!
Guerin, John
  See Byrds, The
Guess Who **23**
Guest, Christopher
  See Spinal Tap
Guided By Voices **18**
Gun, John
  See X-Ray Spex
Gunn, Trey
  See King Crimson
Guns n' Roses **2**
Gunther, Cornell
  See Coasters, The
Gunther, Ric
  See Bevis Frond
Gurewitz, Brett
  See Bad Religion
Gurtu, Trilok **29**
  Also see Oregon
Guru
  See Gang Starr
Gus Gus **26**
Guss, Randy
  See Toad the Wet Sprocket
Gustafson, Steve
  See 10,000 Maniacs
Guster **29**
Gut, Grudrun
  See Einstürzende Neubauten
Guthrie, Arlo **6**
Guthrie, Gwen **26**
Guthrie, Robin
  See Cocteau Twins, The
Guthrie, Woody **2**
Guy, Billy
  See Coasters, The
Guy, Buddy **4**
Guy, Geordie
  See Killing Joke
Guyett, Jim
  See Quicksilver Messenger Service
Gwar **13**
Hacke, Alexander
  See Einstürzende Neubauten
Hackett, Bobby **21**
Hackett, Steve
  See Genesis

Haden, Charlie **12**
Hadjopulos, Sue
  See Simple Minds
Hagar, Regan
  See Brad
Hagar, Sammy **21**
  Also see Van Halen
Hagen, Nina **25**
Hagerty, Neil
  See Royal Trux
Haggard, Merle **2**
HaHa, Jimi
  See Jimmie's Chicken Shack
Hahn, Hilary **30**
Hailey, Cedric "K-Ci"
  See Jodeci
  Also see K-Ci & JoJo
Hailey, Joel "JoJo"
  See Jodeci
  Also see K-Ci & JoJo
Hajjar, Tony
  See At The Drive-In
Hakim, Omar
  See Weather Report
Hakmoun, Hassan **15**
Hale, Simon
  See Incognito
Haley, Bill **6**
Haley, Mark
  See Kinks, The
Haley, Paige
  See Orgy
Halford, Rob
  See Judas Priest
Hall, Bruce
  See REO Speedwagon
Hall, Daryl
  See Hall & Oates
Hall, John S.
  See King Missile
Hall, Lance
  See Inner Circle
Hall, Randall
  See Lynyrd Skynyrd
Hall, Terry
  See Specials, The
Hall, Tom T. **26**
  Earlier sketch in CM **4**
Hall, Tony
  See Neville Brothers, The
Hallam, Nick "The Head"
  See Stereo MC's
Hall & Oates **6**
Halliday, Toni
  See Curve
Halligan Jr., Bob
  See Ceili Rain
Halliwell, Geri
  See Spice Girls
Halstead, Neil
  See Mojave 3
Ham, Greg
  See Men at Work
Ham, Pete
  See Badfinger
Hamelin, Marc-André **33**
Hamer, Harry
  See Chumbawamba
Hamilton, Arnold (Frukwan da Gatekeeper)
  See Gravediggaz
Hamilton, Frank
  See Weavers, The
Hamilton, Katie
  See Treadmill Trackstar
Hamilton, Mark
  See Ash

Hamilton, Milton
  See Third World
Hamilton, Page
  See Helmet
Hamilton, Tom
  See Aerosmith
Hamlisch, Marvin **1**
Hammer, Jan **21**
  Also see Mahavishnu Orchestra
Hammer, M.C. **5**
Hammerstein, Oscar
  See Rodgers, Richard
Hammett, Kirk
  See Metallica
Hammill, Peter **30**
Hammon, Ron
  See War
Hammond, John **6**
Hammond, Murry
  See Old 97's
Hammond-Hammond, Jeffrey
  See Jethro Tull
Hampson, Sharon
  See Sharon, Lois & Bram
Hampson, Thomas **12**
Hampton, Lionel **6**
Hancock, Herbie **25**
  Earlier sketch in CM **8**
Handley, Jerry
  See Captain Beefheart and His Magic Band
Handsome Family, The **30**
Handy, W. C. **7**
Hanley, Kay
  See Letters to Cleo
Hanley, Steve
  See Fall, The
Hanna, Jeff
  See Nitty Gritty Dirt Band, The
Hannan, Patrick
  See Sundays, The
Hanneman, Jeff
  See Slayer
Hannibal, Chauncey "Black"
  See Blackstreet
Hannon, Frank
  See Tesla
Hannon, Neil
  See Divine Comedy, The
Hansen, Mary
  See Stereolab
Hanson **20**
Hanson, Isaac
  See Hanson
Hanson, Paul (Prince Paul A.K.A. Dr. Strange)
  See Paul, Prince
  Also see Gravediggaz
Hanson, Taylor
  See Hanson
Hanson, Zachary
  See Hanson
Hardcastle, Paul **20**
Hardin, Eddie
  See Spencer Davis Group
Hardin, Geraldine
  See Sweet Honey in the Rock
Hardin, Tim **18**
Harding, John Wesley **6**
Hardson, Tre "Slimkid"
  See Pharcyde, The
Hargreaves, Brad
  See Third Eye Blind
Hargrove, Kornell
  See Poi Dog Pondering
Hargrove, Roy **15**
Harkelroad, Bill "Zoot Horn Rollo"
  See Captain Beefheart and His Magic Band

Harket, Morten
　See A-ha
Harley, Bill **7**
Harley, Wayne
　See Pearls Before Swine
Harmon, Bob "Buff"
　See Ceili Rain
Harmon, Eric
　See Chainsaw Kittens, The
Harms, Jesse
　See REO Speedwagon
Harper, Ben **17**
Harper, Raymond
　See Skatalites, The
Harper, Roy **30**
Harrell, Andre **16**
Harrell, Lynn **3**
Harrell, Tom **28**
Harrington, Ayodele
　See Sweet Honey in the Rock
Harrington, Carrie
　See Sounds of Blackness
Harrington, David
　See Kronos Quartet
Harris, Addie "Micki"
　See Shirelles, The
Harris, Barry **32**
Harris, Damon Otis
　See Temptations, The
Harris, Eddie **15**
Harris, Emmylou **4**
Harris, Eric
　See Olivia Tremor Control
Harris, Evelyn Maria
　See Sweet Honey in the Rock
Harris, Gerard
　See Kool & the Gang
Harris, James
　See Echobelly
Harris, Jason
　See Damned, The
Harris, Jet
　See Shadows, The
Harris, Jody
　See Golden Palominos
Harris, Joey
　See Beat Farmers
Harris, Kevin
　See Dirty Dozen Brass Band
Harris, Lee
　See Talk Talk
Harris, Mark
　See 4Him
Harris, Mary
　See Spearhead
Harris, Nigel
　See Jam, The
Harris, R. H.
　See Soul Stirrers, The
Harris, Shawntae
　See Da Brat
Harris, Steve
　See Iron Maiden
Harris, Teddy **22**
Harrison, George **2**
　Also see Beatles, The
Harrison, Jerry
　See Talking Heads
Harrison, Nigel
　See Blondie
Harrison, Richard
　See Stereolab
Harry, Deborah **4**
　Also see Blondie
Harry, Neil
　See Giant Sand
Hart, Alvin Youngblood **27**

Hart, Beth **29**
Hart, Chuck
　See Surfin' Pluto
Hart, Douglas
　See Jesus and Mary Chain, The
Hart, Emerson
　See Tonic
Hart, Hattie
　See Memphis Jug Band
Hart, Lorenz
　See Rodgers, Richard
Hart, Mark
　See Crowded House
Hart, Mark
　See Supertramp
Hart, Mickey
　See Grateful Dead, The
Hart, Robert
　See Bad Company
Hart, Tim
　See Steeleye Span
Hart, William Cullen
　See Olivia Tremor Control
Hartford, John **1**
Hartke, Stephen **5**
Hartley, Matthieu
　See Cure, The
Hartman, Bob
　See Petra
Hartman, John
　See Doobie Brothers, The
Hartnoll, Paul
　See Orbital
Hartnoll, Phil
　See Orbital
Hartridge, Jimmy
　See Swervedriver
Harvey, Bernard "Touter"
　See Inner Circle
Harvey, Philip "Daddae"
　See Soul II Soul
Harvey, Polly Jean **11**
Harvie, Iain
　See Del Amitri
Harwell, Steve
　See Smash Mouth
Harwood, Justin
　See Luna
Haseltine, Dan
　See Jars of Clay
Hashian
　See Boston
Haskell, Gordon
　See King Crimson
Haskins, Kevin
　See Bauhaus
　Also see Love and Rockets
Haslinger, Paul
　See Tangerine Dream
Hassan, Norman
　See UB40
Hasselhoff, Evil "Jared"
　See Bloodhound Gang, The
Hassman, Nikki
　See Avalon
Hastings, Jimmy
　See Caravan
Hastings, Pye
　See Caravan
Hatfield, Juliana **12**
　Also see Lemonheads, The
Hathaway, Jane
　See Lane, Fred
Hatherley, Charlotte
　See Ash
Hatori, Miho
　See Cibo Matto

Haug, Ian
　See Powderfinger
Hauser, Tim
　See Manhattan Transfer, The
Havens, Richie **11**
Hawes, Dave
　See Catherine Wheel
Hawkes, Greg
　See Cars, The
Hawkins, Coleman **11**
Hawkins, Erskine **19**
Hawkins, Lamont "U-God"
　See Wu-Tang Clan
Hawkins, Nick
　See Big Audio Dynamite
Hawkins, Richard (Dick)
　See Gene Loves Jezebel
Hawkins, Roger
　See Traffic
Hawkins, Screamin' Jay **29**
　Earlier sketch in CM **8**
Hawkins, Sophie B. **21**
Hawkins, Taylor
　See Foo Fighters
Hawkins, Tramaine **17**
Hawkins, Xian
　See Silver Apples
Hay, Colin
　See Men at Work
Hay, George D. **3**
Hayden, Victor "The Mascara Snake"
　See Captain Beefheart and His Magic Band
Haye, George "Buddy"
　See Wailing Souls
Hayes, Christian "Bic"
　See Dark Star
Hayes, Darren
　See Savage Garden
Hayes, Gordon
　See Pearls Before Swine
Hayes, Isaac **10**
Hayes, Kelley
　See Cold
Hayes, Roland **13**
Haynes, Gibby
　See Butthole Surfers
Haynes, Roy **33**
Haynes, Warren
　See Allman Brothers, The
Hays, Lee
　See Weavers, The
Hays, Tom
　See Swell
Hayward, David Justin
　See Moody Blues, The
Hayward, Lawrence
　See Felt
Hayward, Richard
　See Little Feat
Haza, Ofra **29**
Headliner
　See Arrested Development
Headon, Topper
　See Clash, The
Healey, Jeff **4**
Healy, Fran
　See Travis
Heard, Paul
　See M People
Hearn, Kevin
　See Barenaked Ladies
Heart **1**
Heath, James
　See Reverend Horton Heat
Heaton, Paul
　See Beautiful South
Heavy D **10**

Hecker, Robert
See Redd Kross
Hedford, Eric
See Dandy Warhols
Hedges, Eddie
See Blessid Union of Souls
Hedges, Michael 3
Heggie, Will
See Cocteau Twins, The
Heidorn, Mike
See Son Volt
Heifetz, Jascha 31
Heitman, Dana
See Cherry Poppin' Daddies
Helfgott, David 19
Helium, Bryan
See Elf Power
Hell, Richard
See Television
Hellauer, Susan
See Anonymous 4
Hellerman, Fred
See Weavers, The
Hellier, Steve
See Death in Vegas
Helliwell, John
See Supertramp
Helm, Levon
See Band, The
Also see Nitty Gritty Dirt Band, The
Helmet 15
Hemingway, Dave
See Beautiful South
Hemmings, Courtney
See Aswad
Hemmings, Paul
See Lightning Seeds
Hemphill, Julius 34
Henderson, Andy
See Echobelly
Henderson, Billy
See Spinners, The
Henderson, Fletcher 16
Henderson, Joe 14
Henderson, Stewart
See Delgados, The
Hendricks, Barbara 10
Hendricks, Jon
See Lambert, Hendricks and Ross
Hendrix, Jimi 2
Henley, Don 3
Also see Eagles, The
Henrit, Bob
See Kinks, The
Henry, Bill
See Northern Lights
Henry, Joe 18
Henry, Kent
See Steppenwolf
Henry, Nicholas "Drummie"
See Mystic Revealers
Hensley, Ken
See Uriah Heep
Hepcat, Harry 23
Hepner, Rich
See Captain Beefheart and His Magic Band
Heppner, Ben 23
Herdman, Bob
See Audio Adrenaline
Herman, Maureen
See Babes in Toyland
Herman, Tom
See Pere Ubu
Herman, Woody 12
Herman's Hermits 5
Hernandez, Alfredo
See Queens of the Stone Age

Hernandez, Bubba
See Brave Combo
Hernandez, Phil
See Brave Combo
Herndon, John
See Tortoise
Herndon, Mark Joel
See Alabama
Herndon, Ty 20
Heron, Mike
See Incredible String Band
Herrema, Jennifer
See Royal Trux
Herrera, Mike
See MxPx
Herrera, R. J.
See Suicidal Tendencies
Herrera, Raymond
See Fear Factory
Herrlin, Anders
See Roxette
Herrmann, Bernard 14
Herron, Cindy
See En Vogue
Hersh, Kristin
See Throwing Muses
Hester, Paul
See Crowded House
Hetfield, James
See Metallica
Hetson, Greg
See Bad Religion
Also see Circle Jerks, The
Heveroh, Ben
See Oakland Interfaith Gospel Choir
Hewitt, Bobby
See Orgy
Hewitt, Steve
See Placebo
Hewson, Paul
See U2
Hexum, Nick
See 311
Hiatt, John 8
Hibbard, Bill
See Paul Revere & The Raiders
Hibbler, Al 34
Hickey, Kenny
See Type O Negative
Hickman, Johnny
See Cracker
Hicks, Chris
See Restless Heart
Hicks, Sheree
See C + C Music Factory
Hidalgo, David
See Los Lobos
Hield, Nehemiah
See Baha Men
Hield, Omerit
See Baha Men
Higgins, Jimmy
See Altan
Higgins, Terence
See Dirty Dozen Brass Band
Highway 101 4
Hijbert, Fritz
See Kraftwerk
Hilah
See Boredoms, The
Hill, Brendan
See Blues Traveler
Hill, Brian "Beezer"
See Frogs, The
Hill, Dave
See Cobra Verde

Hill, Dusty
See ZZ Top
Hill, Faith 18
Hill, Ian
See Judas Priest
Hill, John
See Apples in Stereo
Hill, Lauryn 25
Also see Fugees, The
Hill, Scott
See Fu Manchu
Hill, Stuart
See Shudder to Think
Hillage, Steve
See Orb, The
Also see Gong
Hillier, Steve
See Dubstar
Hillman, Bones
See Midnight Oil
Hillman, Chris
See Byrds, The
Also see Desert Rose Band, The
Hilton, Eric
See Thievery Corporation
Hinderas, Natalie 12
Hinds, David
See Steel Pulse
Hines, Earl "Fatha" 12
Hines, Gary
See Sounds of Blackness
Hinojos, Paul
See At The Drive-In
Hinojosa, Tish 13
Hinton, Milt 33
Hirst, Rob
See Midnight Oil
Hirt, Al 5
Hitchcock, Robyn 9
Hitchcock, Russell
See Air Supply
Hitt, Bryan
See REO Speedwagon
Hobson, Motor
See Lane, Fred
Hodge, Alex
See Platters, The
Hodges, Johnny 24
Hodgson, Roger 26
Also see Supertramp
Hodo, David
See Village People, The
Hoed, Pat
See Down By Law
Hoenig, Michael
See Tangerine Dream
Hoerig, Keith
See Five Iron Frenzy
Hoerner, Dan
See Sunny Day Real Estate
Hoffman, Ellen
See Oakland Interfaith Gospel Choir
Hoffman, Guy
See BoDeans, The
Also see Violent Femmes
Hoffman, Kristian
See Congo Norvell
Hoffman, Sam
See Captain Beefheart and His Magic Band
Hoffs, Susanna
See Bangles, The
Hogan, Mike
See Cranberries, The
Hogan, Noel
See Cranberries, The
Hoke, Jim
See NRBQ

Holder, Gene
   See Yo La Tengo
Hole **14**
Holiday, Billie **6**
Holland, Annie
   See Elastica
Holland, Brian
   See Holland-Dozier-Holland
Holland, Bryan "Dexter"
   See Offspring
Holland, Dave
   See Judas Priest
Holland, Dave **27**
Holland, Eddie
   See Holland-Dozier-Holland
Holland, Julian "Jools"
   See Squeeze
Holland-Dozier-Holland **5**
Hollingsworth, Kyle
   See String Cheese Incident, The
Hollis, Mark
   See Talk Talk
Hollister, Dave
   See Blackstreet
Holly, Buddy **1**
Holm, Georg
   See Sigur Rós
Holmes, David **31**
Holmes, Malcolm
   See Orchestral Manoeuvres in the Dark
Holmes, Tim
   See Death in Vegas
Holmstrom, Peter
   See Dandy Warhols
Holt, David Lee
   See Mavericks, The
Holy Goat
   See Lanternjack, The
Homme, Josh
   See Screaming Trees
Homme, Joshua
   See Queens of the Stone Age
Honda, Yuka
   See Cibo Matto
Honeyman, Susie
   See Mekons, The
Honeyman-Scott, James
   See Pretenders, The
Honolulu
   See Minty
Hood, David
   See Traffic
Hoodoo Gurus **33**
Hook, Peter
   See Joy Division
   Also see New Order
Hooker, John Lee **26**
   Earlier sketch in CM **1**
Hooks, Rosie Lee
   See Sweet Honey in the Rock
Hoon, Shannon
   See Blind Melon
Hooper, Chris
   See Grapes of Wrath, The
Hooper, Nellee
   See Soul II Soul
   Also see Massive Attack
Hooper, Tom
   See Grapes of Wrath, The
Hooper, Tony
   See Ceili Rain
Hooters **20**
Hootie and the Blowfish **18**
Hoover, Jamie
   See Spongetones, The
Hope, Dave
   See Kansas

Hope, Gavin
   See Nylons, The
Hopkins, Doug
   See Gin Blossoms
Hopkins, Lightnin' **13**
Hopkins, Nicky
   See Quicksilver Messenger Service
Hoppus, Mark
   See Blink 182
Hopwood, Keith
   See Herman's Hermits
Horan, Winifred
   See Solas
Horn, Shirley **7**
Horn, Trevor **33**
   Also see Yes
Horne, Lena **11**
Horne, Marilyn **9**
Horner, Jessica
   See Less Than Jake
Hornsby, Bruce **25**
   Earlier sketch in CM **3**
Horovitz, Adam "King Ad-Rock"
   See Beastie Boys
Horowitz, Vladimir **1**
Horse
   See Indigenous
Horton, Jeff
   See Northern Lights
Horton, Jerry
   See Papa Roach
Horton, Walter **19**
Hosler, Mark
   See Negativland
Hossack, Michael
   See Doobie Brothers, The
Hotchkiss, Rob
   See Train
Houari, Rachid
   See Gong
House, Kenwyn
   See Reef
House, Son **11**
House of Pain **14**
Houston, Cissy **26**
   Earlier sketch in CM **6**
Houston, Penelope **28**
Houston, Whitney **25**
   Earlier sketch in CM **8**
Hovhaness, Alan **34**
Howard, Harlan **15**
Howe, Brian
   See Bad Company
Howe, Steve
   See Yes
Howell, Ian
   See Chanticleer
Howell, Porter
   See Little Texas
Howland, Don **24**
Howlett, Liam
   See Prodigy
Howlett, Mike
   See Gong
Howlin' Wolf **6**
H.R.
   See Bad Brains
Hubbard, Gregg "Hobie"
   See Sawyer Brown
Hubbard, Preston
   See Fabulous Thunderbirds, The
   Also see Roomful of Blues
Huber, Connie
   See Chenille Sisters, The
Hubrey, Georgia
   See Yo La Tengo

Hudson, Earl
   See Bad Brains
Hudson, Garth
   See Band, The
Hudson, Ian
   See Gene Loves Jezebel
Huey
   See Fun Lovin' Criminals
Huffman, Doug
   See Boston
Huffman, Joey
   See Drivin' N' Cryin'
Hughes, Bruce
   See Cracker
   Also see Poi Dog Pondering
Hughes, Glenn
   See Village People, The
Hughes, Glenn
   See Black Sabbath
Hughes, Leon
   See Coasters, The
Huld, Hafdis
   See Gus Gus
Human League, The **17**
Humes, Helen **19**
Humperdinck, Engelbert **19**
Humphreys, Paul
   See Orchestral Manoeuvres in the Dark
Hunnekink, Bernard
   See Willem Breuker Kollektief
Hunt, Darryl
   See Pogues, The
Hunter, Alberta **7**
Hunter, Charlie **24**
Hunter, Ian
   See Mott the Hoople
Hunter, Jason "The Rebel INS" (Inspectah Deckk)
   See Wu-Tang Clan
Hunter, Mark
   See James
Hunter, Shepherd "Ben"
   See Soundgarden
Hurding, B.P.
   See X-Ray Spex
Hurley, George
   See fIREHOSE
   Also see Minutemen, The
Hurley, Sean
   See Vertical Horizon
Hurst, Ron
   See Steppenwolf
Hurt, Mississippi John **24**
Hussain, Zakir **32**
Husted, Andy
   See MxPx
Hutchence, Michael
   See INXS
Hutchings, Ashley
   See Fairport Convention
   Also see Steeleye Span
Hutchinson, Trevor
   See Waterboys, The
Huth, Todd
   See Primus
Hütter, Ralf
   See Kraftwerk
Hutton, Danny
   See Three Dog Night
Huxley, Rick
   See Dave Clark Five, The
Hyatt, Aitch
   See Specials, The
Hyde, Karl
   See Underworld
Hyde, Michael
   See Big Mountain

Hyman, Jerry
  See Blood, Sweat and Tears
Hyman, Rob
  See Hooters
Hynd, Richard
  See Texas
Hynde, Chrissie
  See Pretenders, The
Hyslop, Kenny
  See Simple Minds
Ian, Janis **24**
  Earlier sketch in CM **5**
Ian, Scott
  See Anthrax
Ian and Sylvia **18**
Ibbotson, Jimmy
  See Nitty Gritty Dirt Band, The
Ibold, Mark
  See Pavement
Ibrahim, Abdullah **24**
Ice Cube **10**
  Also see N.W.A
Ice-T **7**
Idlewild **30**
Idol, Billy **3**
Ieuan, Dafydd "Daf"
  See Super Furry Animals
If, Owen
  See Stereo MC's
Iglesias, Enrique **27**
Iglesias, Julio **20**
  Earlier sketch in CM **2**
Iha, James
  See Smashing Pumpkins
Illsley, John
  See Dire Straits
Image, Joey
  See Misfits, The
Imbruglia, Natalie **27**
Immergluck, David
  See Monks of Doom
Imperial Teen **26**
Incognito **16**
Incredible String Band **23**
Incubus **23**
Indigenous **31**
Indigo Girls **20**
  Earlier sketch in CM **3**
Inez, Mike
  See Alice in Chains
Infante, Frank
  See Blondie
Ingber, Elliot "Winged Eel Fingerling"
  See Captain Beefheart and His Magic Band
Inge, Edward
  See McKinney's Cotton Pickers
Ingram, Jack
  See Incredible String Band
Ingram, James **11**
Ink Spots **23**
Inner Circle **15**
Innes, Andrew
  See Primal Scream
Innes, Neil
  See Bonzo Dog Doo-Dah Band
Innis, Dave
  See Restless Heart
Insane Clown Posse **22**
Interior, Lux
  See Cramps, The
INXS **21**
  Earlier sketch in CM **2**
Iommi, Tony
  See Black Sabbath
Irmler, Hans-Joachim
  See Faust
Iron Maiden **10**

Irons, Jack
  See Pearl Jam
  Also see Red Hot Chili Peppers, The
Isaak, Chris **33**
  Earlier sketch in CM **6**
Isabelle, Jeff
  See Guns n' Roses
Isacsson, Jonas
  See Roxette
Isbin, Sharon **33**
Isham, Mark **14**
Isles, Bill
  See O'Jays, The
Isley, Ernie
  See Isley Brothers, The
Isley, Marvin
  See Isley Brothers, The
Isley, O'Kelly, Jr.
  See Isley Brothers, The
Isley, Ronald
  See Isley Brothers, The
Isley, Rudolph
  See Isley Brothers, The
Isley Brothers, The **8**
Israel Vibration **21**
Iuean, Dafydd
  See Catatonia
Ivers, Eileen **30**
Ives, Burl **12**
Ives, Charles **29**
Ivey, Michael
  See Basehead
Ivins, Michael
  See Flaming Lips
J.
  See White Zombie
J, David
  See Bauhaus
  Also see Love and Rockets
Jabs, Matthias
  See Scorpions, The
Jackson, Al
  See Booker T. & the M.G.'s
Jackson, Alan **25**
  Earlier sketch in CM **7**
Jackson, Clive
  See Ray Condo and His Ricochets
Jackson, Eddie
  See Queensryche
Jackson, Freddie **3**
Jackson, Jackie
  See Jacksons, The
Jackson, Janet **16**
  Earlier sketch in CM **3**
Jackson, Jermaine
  See Jacksons, The
Jackson, Joe **22**
  Earlier sketch in CM **4**
Jackson, Karen
  See Supremes, The
Jackson, Mahalia **8**
Jackson, Marlon
  See Jacksons, The
Jackson, Michael **17**
  Earlier sketch in CM **1**
  Also see Jacksons, The
Jackson, Millie **14**
Jackson, Milt **15**
Jackson, Pervis
  See Spinners, The
Jackson, Quentin
  See McKinney's Cotton Pickers
Jackson, Randy
  See Jacksons, The
Jackson, Stevie
  See Belle and Sebastian

Jackson, Tito
  See Jacksons, The
Jackson 5, The
  See Jacksons, The
Jacksons, The **7**
Jackyl **24**
Jacobs, Christian Richard
  See Aquabats, The
Jacobs, Jeff
  See Foreigner
Jacobs, Parker
  See Aquabats, The
Jacobs, Walter
  See Little Walter
Jacox, Martin
  See Soul Stirrers, The
Jacquet, Illinois **17**
Jade 4U
  See Lords of Acid
Jaffee, Rami
  See Wallflowers, The
Jagger, Mick **7**
  Also see Rolling Stones, The
Jairo T.
  See Sepultura
Jalal
  See Last Poets
Jam, Jimmy
  See Jimmy Jam and Terry Lewis
Jam, The **27**
Jamal, Ahmad **32**
James **12**
James, Alex
  See Blur
James, Andrew "Bear"
  See Midnight Oil
James, Boney **21**
James, Brian
  See Damned, The
James, Cheryl
  See Salt-N-Pepa
James, David
  See Alien Sex Fiend
James, David
  See Spearhead
James, Doug
  See Roomful of Blues
James, Elmore **8**
James, Etta **6**
James, Gregg
  See D.O.A.
James, Harry **11**
James, Jesse
  See Jackyl
James, John
  See Newsboys, The
James, Joni **30**
James, Onieda
  See Spearhead
James, Richard
  See Aphex Twin
James, Richard
  See Gorky's Zygotic Mynci
James, Richey
  See Manic Street Preachers
James, Rick **2**
James, Ruby
  See Aztec Camera
James, Skip **24**
James, Sylvia
  See Aztec Camera
James, Will
  See Papa Roach
Jamiroquai **21**
Jamison, Le Le
  See Spearhead

Jam Master Jay
  See Run DMC
Jan & Dean **32**
Jane's Addiction **6**
Janney, Eli
  See Girls Against Boys
Janovitz, Bill
  See Buffalo Tom
Jansch, Bert
  See Pentangle
Jardine, Al
  See Beach Boys, The
Jarman, Joseph
  See Art Ensemble of Chicago, The
Jarobi
  See Tribe Called Quest, A
Jarre, Jean-Michel **2**
Jarreau, Al **1**
Jarrett, Irwin
  See Third World
Jarrett, Keith **1**
Jars of Clay **20**
Jasper, Chris
  See Isley Brothers, The
Jawbox **31**
Jaworski, Al
  See Jesus Jones
Jay, Miles
  See Village People, The
Jayhawks, The **15**
Jayson, Mackie
  See Bad Brains
Jay-Z **28**
Jazz Butcher, The **30**
Jazzie B
  See Soul II Soul
Jean, Wyclef **22**
  Also see Fugees, The
Jeanrenaud, Joan Dutcher
  See Kronos Quartet
Jeczalik, Jonathan
  See Art of Noise
Jefferson, Blind Lemon **18**
Jefferson Airplane **5**
Jefferson Starship
  See Jefferson Airplane
Jeffre, Justin
  See 98 Degrees
Jemmott, Gerald
  See Pearls Before Swine
Jenifer, Darryl
  See Bad Brains
Jenkins, Barry
  See Animals, The
Jenkins, Gary
  See Silk
Jenkins, Stephan
  See Third Eye Blind
Jennings, Greg
  See Restless Heart
Jennings, Waylon **4**
Jensen, Ingrid **22**
Jensen, Ken
  See D.O.A.
Jerry, Jah
  See Skatalites, The
Jeru the Damaja **33**
Jessee, Darren
  See Ben Folds Five
Jessie, Young
  See Coasters, The
Jesus and Mary Chain, The **10**
Jesus Jones **23**
Jesus Lizard **19**
Jethro Tull **8**
Jett, Joan **3**
Jewel **25**

"Jez"
  See Swervedriver
J. Geils Band **25**
Jimbo
  See Reverend Horton Heat
Jimbob
  See Carter USM
Jimenez, Flaco
  See Texas Tornados, The
Jiménez, Jorge
  See Tijuana No!
Jimmie's Chicken Shack **22**
Jimmy Jam and Terry Lewis **11**
Joannou, Chris
  See Silverchair
Jobim, Antonio Carlos **19**
Jobson, Edwin
  See Jethro Tull
Jodeci **13**
Joe **33**
Joel, Billy **12**
  Earlier sketch in CM **2**
Joel, Phil
  See Newsboys, The
Johansen, David **7**
  Also see New York Dolls
Johanson, Jai Johanny
  See Allman Brothers, The
Johansson, Glenn
  See Echobelly
Johansson, Lars-Olof
  See Cardigans
John, Elton **20**
  Earlier sketch in CM **3**
John, Little Willie **25**
Johns, Daniel
  See Silverchair
Johnson, Alphonso
  See Weather Report
Johnson, Billy
  See Moonglows, The
Johnson, Blind Willie **26**
Johnson, Bob
  See Steeleye Span
Johnson, Brian
  See AC/DC
Johnson, Calvin
  See Beat Happening
Johnson, Courtney
  See New Grass Revival, The
Johnson, Danny
  See Steppenwolf
Johnson, Daryl
  See Neville Brothers, The
Johnson, David
  See Can
Johnson, Eric **19**
Johnson, Eric
  See Archers of Loaf
Johnson, Eric **19**
Johnson, Ethyl
  See Swell
Johnson, Gene
  See Diamond Rio
Johnson, Gerry
  See Steel Pulse
Johnson, Holly
  See Frankie Goes To Hollywood
Johnson, James P. **16**
Johnson, Jerry
  See Big Mountain
Johnson, J.J. **33**
Johnson, Kurt
  See Flying Luttenbachers, The
Johnson, Lonnie **17**
Johnson, Matt
  See Chainsaw Kittens, The

Johnson, Matt
  See The The
Johnson, Mike
  See Dinosaur Jr.
Johnson, Patricia
  See Sweet Honey in the Rock
Johnson, Ralph
  See Earth, Wind and Fire
Johnson, Robert **6**
Johnson, Scott
  See Gin Blossoms
Johnson, Shirley Childres
  See Sweet Honey in the Rock
Johnson, Tamara "Taj"
  See SWV
Johnson, Willie
  See Golden Gate Quartet
John Spencer Blues Explosion **18**
Johnston, Bruce
  See Beach Boys, The
Johnston, Freedy **20**
Johnston, Howie
  See Ventures, The
Johnston, Mike
  See Northwoods Improvisers
Johnston, Sonnie
  See Five Iron Frenzy
Johnston, Tom
  See Doobie Brothers, The
JoJo
  See Jodeci
  Also see K-Ci & JoJo
Jolly, Bill
  See Butthole Surfers
Jolly, Herman
  See Sunset Valley
Jolson, Al **10**
Jones, Adam
  See Tool
Jones, Benny
  See Dirty Dozen Brass Band
Jones, Booker T. **8**
  Also see Booker T. & the M.G.'s
Jones, Brian
  See Rolling Stones, The
Jones, Busta
  See Gang of Four
Jones, Claude
  See McKinney's Cotton Pickers
Jones, Craig
  See Slipknot
Jones, Daniel
  See Savage Garden
Jones, Darryl
  See Rolling Stones, The
Jones, Davy
  See Monkees, The
Jones, Denise
  See Point of Grace
Jones, Elvin **9**
Jones, Geoffrey
  See Sounds of Blackness
Jones, George **4**
Jones, Grace **9**
Jones, Hank **15**
Jones, Howard **26**
Jones, Jab
  See Memphis Jug Band
Jones, Jamie
  See All-4-One
Jones, Jim
  See Pere Ubu
Jones, John Paul
  See Led Zeppelin
Jones, Kelly
  See Stereophonics

Jones, Kendall
  See Fishbone
Jones, Kenny
  See Faces, The
  Also see Who, The
Jones, Kimberly
  See Lil' Kim
Jones, Marshall
  See Ohio Players
Jones, Maxine
  See En Vogue
Jones, Mic
  See Big Audio Dynamite
  Also see Clash, The
Jones, Michael
  See Kronos Quartet
Jones, Mick
  See Clash, The
Jones, Mick
  See Foreigner
Jones, Orville
  See Ink Spots
Jones, Paul
  See Elastica
Jones, Paul
  See Catatonia
Jones, Philly Joe 16
Jones, Quincy 20
  Earlier sketch in CM 2
Jones, Randy
  See Village People, The
Jones, Richard
  See Stereophonics
Jones, Rickie Lee 4
Jones, Robert "Kuumba"
  See Ohio Players
Jones, Robin
  See Beta Band, The
Jones, Rod
  See Idlewild
Jones, Ronald
  See Flaming Lips
Jones, Russell "Ol Dirty Bastard"
  See Wu-Tang Clan
Jones, Sandra "Puma"
  See Black Uhuru
Jones, Simon
  See Verve, The
Jones, Spike 5
Jones, Stacy
  See Letters to Cleo
  Also see Veruca Salt
Jones, Steve
  See Sex Pistols, The
Jones, Teren
  See Del the Funky Homosapien
Jones, Terry
  See Point of Grace
Jones, Thad 19
Jones, Tom 11
Jones, Vincent
  See Grapes of Wrath, The
Jones, Will "Dub"
  See Coasters, The
Jon Spencer Blues Explosion 18
Jonsson, Magnus
  See Gus Gus
Joplin, Janis 3
Joplin, Scott 10
Jordan, Lonnie
  See War
Jordan, Louis 11
Jordan, Marc 30
Jordan, Montell 26
Jordan, Stanley 1
Jordison, Joey
  See Slipknot

Jorgenson, John
  See Desert Rose Band, The
Jos
  See Ex, The
Joseph, Charles
  See Dirty Dozen Brass Band
Joseph, Kirk
  See Dirty Dozen Brass Band
Joseph-I, Israel
  See Bad Brains
Josephmary
  See Compulsion
Jourgensen, Al
  See Ministry
Journey 21
Joyce, Don
  See Negativland
Joyce, Mike
  See Buzzcocks, The
  Also see Smiths, The
Joy Division 19
Joy Electric 26
Juanita
  See Les Négresses Vertes
Judas Priest 10
Judd, Naomi
  See Judds, The
Judd, Wynonna
  See Judds, The
  Also see Wynonna
Judds, The 2
Judy, Eric
  See Modest Mouse
Jugg, Roman
  See Damned, The
Juhlin, Dag
  See Poi Dog Pondering
Jukebox
  See Geto Boys, The
Julot
  See Les Négresses Vertes
Jungle DJ "Towa" Towa
  See Deee-lite
Junior, Marvin
  See Dells, The
Jupp, Tim
  See Delirious?
Jurado, Jeanette
  See Exposé
Jurgensen, Jens
  See Boss Hog
Justman, Seth
  See J. Geils Band
Jym
  See Mr. T Experience, The
Kabongo, Sabine
  See Zap Mama
Kaczor, Neil
  See Minty
Kaczynski, Ray
  See Northwoods Improvisers
Kahlil, Aisha
  See Sweet Honey in the Rock
Kain, Gylan
  See Last Poets
Kaiser, Henry
  See Golden Palominos
Kakoulli, Harry
  See Squeeze
Kale, Jim
  See Guess Who
Kalligan, Dick
  See Blood, Sweat and Tears
Kamanski, Paul
  See Beat Farmers
Kaminski, Mik
  See Electric Light Orchestra

Kamomiya, Ryo
  See Pizzicato Five
Kanal, Tony
  See No Doubt
Kanawa, Kiri Te
  See Te Kanawa, Kiri
Kand, Valor
  See Christian Death
Kander, John 33
Kane, Arthur
  See New York Dolls
Kane, Big Daddy 7
Kane, Keith
  See Vertical Horizon
Kane, Kevin
  See Grapes of Wrath, The
Kane, Nick
  See Mavericks, The
Kang, Eyvind 28
Kang, Michael
  See String Cheese Incident, The
Kannberg, Scott
  See Pavement
Kansas 32
Kantner, Paul
  See Jefferson Airplane
Kaplan, Ira
  See Yo La Tengo
Karajan, Herbert von
  See von Karajan, Herbert
Karges, Murphy
  See Sugar Ray
Karlsson, Gunnar
  See Wannadies, The
Karoli, Michael
  See Can
Kath, Terry
  See Chicago
Kato, Nash
  See Urge Overkill
Katrin
  See Ex, The
Katunich, Alex
  See Incubus
Katz, Mike
  See Battlefield Band, The
Katz, Simon
  See Jamiroquai
Katz, Steve
  See Blood, Sweat and Tears
Kaukonen, Jorma
  See Jefferson Airplane
Kavanagh, Chris
  See Big Audio Dynamite
Kavanaugh, Lydia
  See Golden Palominos
Kay, Jason
  See Jamiroquai
Kay, John
  See Steppenwolf
Kaye, Carol 22
Kaye, Tony
  See Yes
Kay Gee
  See Naughty by Nature
Kaylan, Howard
  See Turtles, The
K-Ci
  See Jodeci
  Also see K-Ci & JoJo
K-Ci & JoJo 34
Keaggy, Phil 26
Kean, Martin
  See Stereolab
Keane, Sean
  See Chieftains, The
Kee, John P. 15

Keefe, Dylan
　See Marcy Playground
Keelor, Greg
　See Blue Rodeo
Keenan, Maynard James
　See Tool
Keene, Barry
　See Spirit
Keene, Tommy **31**
Keifer, Tom
　See Cinderella
Keitaro
　See Pizzicato Five
Keith, Jeff
　See Tesla
Keith, Toby **17**
Keithley, Joey "Sh**head"
　See D.O.A.
Kelly, Betty
　See Martha and the Vandellas
Kelly, Charlotte
　See Soul II Soul
Kelly, Ed
　See Oakland Interfaith Gospel Choir
Kelly, Hugh
　See Wedding Present, The
Kelly, Jeff **31**
Kelly, Johnny
　See Type O Negative
Kelly, Kevin
　See Byrds, The
Kelly, Matt
　See Dropkick Murphys
Kelly, R. **19**
Kelly, Rashaan
　See US3
Kelly, Scott
　See Neurosis
Kelly, Sean
　See Sixpence None the Richer
Kelly, Terrance
　See Oakland Interfaith Gospel Choir
Kember, Pete
　See Spacemen 3
Kemp, Rick
　See Steeleye Span
Kendrick, David
　See Devo
Kendricks, Eddie
　See Temptations, The
Kennedy, Delious
　See All-4-One
Kennedy, Frankie
　See Altan
Kennedy, Nigel **8**
Kenner, Doris
　See Shirelles, The
Kenny, Bill
　See Ink Spots
Kenny, Clare
　See Aztec Camera
Kenny, Herb
　See Ink Spots
Kenny G **14**
Kent, Julia
　See Rasputina
Kent, Stacey **28**
Kenton, Stan **21**
Kentucky Headhunters, The **5**
Kerman, Elliott
　See Rockapella
Kern, Jerome **13**
Kerr, Jim
　See Simple Minds
Kerr, Scott
　See Five Iron Frenzy

Kerr, Stuart
　See Texas
Kershaw, Sammy **15**
Kessel, Kenny
　See Loud Family, The
Ketchum, Hal **14**
Key, Cevin
　See Skinny Puppy
Keyser, Alex
　See Echobelly
Khaled **33**
Khan, Ali Akbar **34**
Khan, Chaka **19**
　Earlier sketch in CM **9**
Khan, Nusrat Fateh Ali **13**
Khan, Praga
　See Lords of Acid
Kibble, Mark
　See Take 6
Kibby, Walter
　See Fishbone
Kick, Johnny
　See Madder Rose
Kidjo, Anjelique **17**
Kidney, Robert
　See Golden Palominos
Kid 'n Play **5**
Kid Rock **27**
Kiedis, Anthony
　See Red Hot Chili Peppers, The
Kilbey, Steve
　See Church, The
Kilbourn, Duncan
　See Psychedelic Furs
Kilgallon, Eddie
　See Ricochet
Kilgore **24**
Killian, Tim
　See Kronos Quartet
Killing Joke **30**
Kimball, Jennifer
　See Story, The
Kimball, Jim
　See Jesus Lizard
Kimble, Paul
　See Grant Lee Buffalo
Kinard, Tulani Jordan
　See Sweet Honey in the Rock
Kincaid, Jan
　See Brand New Heavies, The
Kinchen, Ricky
　See Mint Condition
Kinchla, Chan
　See Blues Traveler
Kinde, Geoff
　See Atomic Fireballs, The
King, Albert **2**
King, Andy
　See Hooters
King, B.B. **24**
　Earlier sketch in CM **1**
King, Ben E. **7**
King, Bob
　See Soul Stirrers, The
King, Carole **6**
　Also see Goffin-King
King, Ed
　See Lynyrd Skynyrd
King, Freddy **17**
King, John
　See Dust Brothers
King, Jon
　See Gang of Four
King, Kerry
　See Slayer
King, Pee Wee **30**

King, Philip
　See Lush
King, Stove
　See Mansun
King, William Jr.
　See Commodores, The
King Ad-Rock
　See Horovitz, Adam
King Crimson **17**
Kingins, Duke
　See Atomic Fireballs, The
King Missile **22**
Kingsmen, The **34**
Kingsmill, Mark
　See Hoodoo Gurus
Kingston Trio, The **9**
King's X **7**
Kinks, The **15**
Kinley, Heather
　See Kinleys, The
Kinley, Jennifer
　See Kinleys, The
Kinleys, The **32**
Kinney, Kevn
　See Drivin' N' Cryin'
Kinney, Sean
　See Alice in Chains
Kippenberger, Karl
　See Shihad
Kirchen, Bill
　See Commander Cody and His Lost Planet
　Airmen
Kirk, Rahsaan Roland **6**
Kirk, Richard H.
　See Cabaret Voltaire
Kirke, Simon
　See Bad Company
Kirkland, Mike
　See Prong
Kirkpatrick, Chris
　See 'N Sync
Kirkpatrick, Sean
　See Swell
Kirkwood, Cris
　See Meat Puppets, The
Kirkwood, Curt
　See Meat Puppets, The
Kirtley, Peter
　See Pentangle
Kirwan, Danny
　See Fleetwood Mac
Kiss **25**
　Earlier sketch in CM **5**
Kisser, Andreas
　See Sepultura
Kissin, Evgeny **6**
Kitaro **1**
Kitchener, Lord **29**
Kitsos, Nick
　See BoDeans
Kitt, Eartha **9**
Kjartansson, Siggi
　See Gus Gus
Klein, Danny
　See J. Geils Band
Klein, Jon
　See Siouxsie and the Banshees
Klein, Mark
　See Cobra Verde
Klett, Peter
　See Candlebox
Klezmatics, The **18**
Klugh, Earl **10**
Kmatsu, Bravo
　See Pizzicato Five
KMFDM **18**
Knight, Gladys **1**

Knight, Jon
   See New Kids on the Block
Knight, Jordan
   See New Kids on the Block
Knight, Larry
   See Spirit
Knight, Peter
   See Steeleye Span
Knight, Phil
   See Shihad
Knight, Steve
   See Mountain
Knight, Suge 15
Knighton, Willie "Khujo"
   See Goodie Mob
Knopfler, David
   See Dire Straits
Knopfler, Mark 25
   Earlier sketch in CM 3
   Also see Dire Straits
Know, Dr.
   See Bad Brains
Knowledge
   See Digable Planets
Knowles, Beyoncé
   See Destiny's Child
Knox, Nick
   See Cramps, The
Knox, Richard
   See Dirty Dozen Brass Band
Knudsen, Keith
   See Doobie Brothers, The
Koffman, Moe 34
Konietzko, Sascha
   See KMFDM
Konikoff, Eli
   See Spyro Gyra
Konishi, Yasuharu
   See Pizzicato Five
Konitz, Lee 30
Konto, Skip
   See Three Dog Night
Kontos, Chris
   See Machine Head
Kool & the Gang 13
Kool Moe Dee 9
Kooper, Al
   See Blood, Sweat and Tears
Koppelman, Charles 14
Koppes, Peter
   See Church, The
Korn 20
Koster, Julian
   See Neutral Milk Hotel
Kottke, Leo 13
Kotzen, Richie
   See Poison
Kowalczyk, Ed
   See Live
Kowald, Peter 32
Koz, Dave 20
Kraftwerk 9
Krakauer, David
   See Klezmatics, The
Krall, Diana 27
Kramer, Amanda
   See Golden Palominos
Kramer, Joey
   See Aerosmith
Kramer, Wayne
   See MC5, The
Krasnow, Bob 15
Krause, Bernie
   See Weavers, The
Krauss, Alison 10
Krauss, Scott
   See Pere Ubu

Kravitz, Lenny 26
   Earlier sketch in CM 5
Krawits, Michael
   See Pearls Before Swine
Krayzie Bone
   See Bone Thugs-N-Harmony
Krazy Drayz
   See Das EFX
Kremer, Gidon 30
Kretz, Eric
   See Stone Temple Pilots
Kreutzman, Bill
   See Grateful Dead, The
Kreviazuk, Chantal 33
Krieger, Robert
   See Doors, The
Kriesel, Greg "Greg K."
   See Offspring
Kris Kross 11
Kristofferson, Kris 4
Krizan, Anthony
   See Spin Doctors
Kronos Quartet 5
Kropinski, Uwe 31
Kropp, Mike
   See Northern Lights
KRS-One 8
Krukowski, Damon
   See Damon and Naomi
   Also see Galaxie 500
Krummenacher, Victor
   See Monks of Doom
Krupa, Gene 13
Krusen, Dave
   See Pearl Jam
Kruspe, Richard
   See Rammstein
Kuba
   See D.O.A.
Kuebler, Roman
   See Spoon
Kulak, Eddie
   See Aztec Camera
Kulick, Bruce
   See Kiss
Kunkel, Bruce
   See Nitty Gritty Dirt Band, The
Kunzel, Erich 17
Kurdziel, Eddie
   See Redd Kross
Kurihara, Michio
   See Ghost
Kuti, Fela 7
Kuti, Femi 29
LaBar, Jeff
   See Cinderella
LaBelle, Patti 8
LaBour, Frederick "Too Slim"
   See Riders in the Sky
LaBrie, James
   See Dream Theater
Labrum, Jerry
   See Paul Revere & The Raiders
Lachey, Drew
   See 98 Degrees
Lachey, Nick
   See 98 Degrees
Lack, Steve
   See Veruca Salt
LaCroix, Dimples
   See Lane, Fred
Lacy, Steve 23
Ladybug
   See Digable Planets
Lady Miss Kier
   See Deee-lite
Ladysmith Black Mambazo 1

Lafalce, Mark
   See Mekons, The
Lagerborg, Chris
   See Down By Law
Lagerburg, Bengt
   See Cardigans, The
Laine, Cleo 10
Laine, Denny
   See Moody Blues, The
Laing, Corky
   See Mountain
Laird, Rick
   See Mahavishnu Orchestra
Lake, Greg
   See Emerson, Lake & Palmer/Powell
   Also see King Crimson
LaKind, Bobby
   See Doobie Brothers, The
La Ley 33
Lally, Joe
   See Fugazi
LaLonde, Larry "Ler"
   See Primus
Lamb, Barbara 19
Lamb, Michael
   See Confederate Railroad
Lambchop 29
Lambert, Ben
   See Carter USM
Lambert, Dave
   See Lambert, Hendricks and Ross
Lambert, Hendricks and Ross 28
Lamble, Martin
   See Fairport Convention
Lamm, Robert
   See Chicago
Lamond, Mary Jane 33
Lampkin, Troy
   See Oakland Interfaith Gospel Choir
Lancaster, Brian
   See Surfin' Pluto
Landers, Paul
   See Rammstein
Landreth, Sonny 16
Lane, Fred 28
Lane, Jani
   See Warrant
Lane, Jay
   See Primus
Lane, Ronnie
   See Faces, The
Lanegan, Mark
   See Screaming Trees
Lang, Jonny 27
lang, k. d. 25
   Earlier sketch in CM 4
Langan, Gary
   See Art of Noise
Langdon, Antony
   See Spacehog
Langdon, Royston
   See Spacehog
Langford, Jon
   See Mekons, The
Langford, Willie
   See Golden Gate Quartet
Langley, John
   See Mekons, The
Langlois, Paul
   See Tragically Hip, The
Langosch, Paul
   See Ralph Sharon Quartet
Langston, Leslie
   See Throwing Muses
Lanier, Allen
   See Blue Oyster Cult

Lanker, Dustin
See Cherry Poppin' Daddies
Lanois, Daniel **8**
Lanternjack, The **31**
LaPread, Ronald
See Commodores, The
Larkin, Patty **9**
Larkin, Tom
See Shihad
Larkins, Tom
See Giant Sand
Larson, Chad Albert
See Aquabats, The
Larson, Nathan
See Shudder to Think
Lash, Tony
See Sunset Valley
Last Poets **21**
Laswell, Bill **14**
Also see Golden Palominos
Lataille, Rich
See Roomful of Blues
Lateef, Yusef **16**
Latimer, Andrew
See Camel
Lauderdale, Jim **29**
Laughner, Peter
See Pere Ubu
Laughren, Matt
See Cold
Lauper, Cyndi **11**
Laurence, Lynda
See Supremes, The
Lava, Larry
See Lanternjack, The
Lavay Smith and Her Red Hot Skillet Lickers **32**
Lavery, Dan
See Tonic
Lavin, Christine **6**
Lavis, Gilson
See Squeeze
Lawler, Feargal
See Cranberries, The
Lawnge
See Black Sheep
Lawrence, John
See Gorky's Zygotic Mynci
Lawrence, Tracy **11**
Lawry, John
See Petra
Laws, Roland
See Earth, Wind and Fire
Lawson, Doyle
See Country Gentlemen, The
Layzie Bone
See Bone Thugs-N-Harmony
Leadbelly **6**
Leader, Ted
See Chainsaw Kittens, The
Leadon, Bernie
See Eagles, The
Also see Nitty Gritty Dirt Band, The
Lear, Graham
See REO Speedwagon
Leary, Paul
See Butthole Surfers
Leavell, Chuck
See Allman Brothers, The
Le Bon, Simon
See Duran Duran
Leckenby, Derek "Lek"
See Herman's Hermits
Ledbetter, Huddie
See Leadbelly
LeDoux, Chris **12**
Led Zeppelin **1**

Lee, Arthur
See Love
Lee, Ben **26**
Lee, Beverly
See Shirelles, The
Lee, Brenda **5**
Lee, Buddy
See McKinney's Cotton Pickers
Lee, Buddy
See Less Than Jake
Lee, Garret
See Compulsion
Lee, Geddy
See Rush
Lee, Hunter
See Ceili Rain
Lee, Mark
See Third Day
Lee, Peggy **8**
Lee, Pete
See Gwar
Lee, Sara
See Gang of Four
Lee, Stan
See Incredible String Band
Lee, Tommy
See Mötley Crüe
Lee, Tony
See Treadmill Trackstar
Leeb, Bill
See Front Line Assembly
Leen, Bill
See Gin Blossoms
Leese, Howard
See Heart
Leftfield **29**
Legg, Adrian **17**
Legowitz, Herr
See Gus Gus
Leherer, Keith "Lucky"
See Circle Jerks
Lehrer, Tom **7**
Leiber, Jerry
See Leiber and Stoller
Leiber and Stoller **14**
LeMaistre, Malcolm
See Incredible String Band
Lemmy
See Motörhead
Lemonheads, The **12**
Lemper, Ute **14**
Le Mystère des Voix Bulgares
See Bulgarian State Female Vocal Choir, The
Len **32**
Lenear, Kevin
See Mighty Mighty Bosstones
Lenners, Rudy
See Scorpions, The
Lennon, John **9**
Also see Beatles, The
Lennon, Julian **26**
Earlier sketch in CM **2**
Lennox, Annie **18**
Also see Eurythmics
Le Noble, Martyn
See Porno for Pyros
Lenz, Paul
See Drivin' N' Cryin'
Leonard, Geno
See Filter
Leonard, Glenn
See Temptations, The
Leonard, Scott
See Rockapella
Lepisto, Veikko
See Royal Crown Revue

Lerner, Alan Jay
See Lerner and Loewe
Lerner and Loewe **13**
Lesh, Phil
See Grateful Dead, The
Leskiw, Greg
See Guess Who
Leslie, Chris
See Fairport Convention
Les Négresses Vertes **30**
Lessard, Stefan
See Dave Matthews Band
Less Than Jake **22**
Lester, Bobby
See Moonglows, The
Lethal, DJ
See Limp Bizkit
Lettermen, The **30**
Letters to Cleo **22**
Levene, Keith
See Clash, The
Levert, Eddie
See O'Jays, The
Leverton, Jim
See Caravan
Levin, Danny
See Asleep at the Wheel
Levin, Tony
See King Crimson
Levine, James **8**
Levinshefski, Drake
See Paul Revere & The Raiders
Levy, Alison Faith
See Loud Family, The
Levy, Andrew
See Brand New Heavies, The
Levy, Ron
See Roomful of Blues
Lewis, Aaron
See Staind
Lewis, Furry **26**
Lewis, Graham
See Wire
Lewis, Hambone
See Memphis Jug Band
Lewis, Heather
See Beat Happening
Lewis, Huey **9**
Lewis, Ian
See Inner Circle
Lewis, Jerry Lee **2**
Lewis, John **29**
Lewis, Kerri
See Mint Condition
Lewis, Marcia
See Soul II Soul
Lewis, Michael
See Quicksilver Messenger Service
Lewis, Mike
See Yo La Tengo
Lewis, Otis
See Fabulous Thunderbirds, The
Lewis, Peter
See Moby Grape
Lewis, Ramsey **14**
Lewis, Roger
See Dirty Dozen Brass Band
Also see Inner Circle
Lewis, Roy
See Kronos Quartet
Lewis, Samuel K.
See Five Blind Boys of Alabama
Lewis, Shaznay T.
See All Saints
Lewis, Terry
See Jimmy Jam and Terry Lewis

Lhote, Morgan
  See Stereolab
Libbea, Gene
  See Nashville Bluegrass Band
Liberace 9
Liberty, Earl
  See Circle Jerks
Licht, David
  See Klezmatics, The
Lichtenauer, Michael
  See Chanticleer
Liebert, Ottmar 33
Liebezeit, Jaki
  See Can
Liesegang, Brian
  See Filter
Lifeson, Alex
  See Rush
Lightfoot, Gordon 3
Lightning Seeds 21
Ligon, Willie Joe
  See Mighty Clouds of Joy, The
Liles, Brent
  See Social Distortion
Lilienstein, Lois
  See Sharon, Lois & Bram
Lilker, Dan
  See Anthrax
Lil' Kim 30
Lilley, John
  See Hooters
Lillywhite, Steve 13
Limp Bizkit 27
Lincoln, Abbey 9
Lindberg, Jim
  See Pennywise
Lindemann, Till
  See Rammstein
Lindes, Hal
  See Dire Straits
Lindley, David 2
Lindner, Michael
  See Aqua Velvets
Lindsay, Arto
  See Golden Palominos
Lindsay, Mark
  See Paul Revere & The Raiders
Line, Lorie 34
Linkous, Mark 26
Linna, Miriam
  See Cramps, The
Linnell, John
  See They Might Be Giants
Lippok, Robert
  See To Rococo Rot
Lippok, Ronald
  See To Rococo Rot
Lipsius, Fred
  See Blood, Sweat and Tears
Li Puma, Tommy 18
Lisa, Lisa 23
Lisher, Greg
  See Monks of Doom
Lit 27
Little, Keith
  See Country Gentlemen, The
Little, Levi
  See Blackstreet
Little Feat 4
Little Richard 1
Little Texas 14
Little Walter 14
Littrell, Brian
  See Backstreet Boys
Live 14
Livgren, Kerry
  See Kansas

Living Colour 7
Livingston, Edwin
  See Los Hombres Calientes
Llanas, Sam
  See BoDeans
L.L. Cool J. 5
Lloyd, Charles 22
Lloyd, Geoff
  See Matthew Good Band
Lloyd, Mick
  See Felt
Lloyd, Richard
  See Television
Lloyd Webber, Andrew 6
Locke, John
  See Spirit
Locking, Brian
  See Shadows, The
Lockley, Jayne
  See Wedding Present, The
Lockwood, Robert, Jr. 10
Lodge, John
  See Moody Blues, The
Loeb, Lisa 23
  Earlier sketch in CM 19
Loesser, Frank 19
Loewe, Frederick
  See Lerner and Loewe
Loewenstein, Jason
  See Sebadoh
Lofgren, Nils 25
Lo Fidelity All Stars 27
Logan, Jack 27
Loggins, Kenny 20
  Earlier sketch in CM 3
Logic, Laura
  See X-Ray Spex
Lohner, Danny
  See Nine Inch Nails
Lombardo, Dave
  See Slayer
Lonberg-Holm, Fred
  See Flying Luttenbachers, The
London, Frank
  See Klezmatics, The
London, Julie 32
Lonestar 27
Lopes, Lisa "Left Eye"
  See TLC
López, Israel "Cachao" 34
  Earlier sketch in CM 14
Lopez, Jennifer 27
Lord, Jon
  See Deep Purple
Lords of Acid 20
Lorenz, Flake
  See Rammstein
Loria, Steve
  See Spirit
Lorimer, Roddy
  See Waterboys, The
Lorson, Mary
  See Madder Rose
Los Hombres Calientes 29
Los Lobos 2
Los Reyes
  See Gipsy Kings, The
Loud Family, The 31
Loughlin, Jim
  See moe.
Loughnane, Lee
  See Chicago
Louison, Steve
  See Massive Attack
Louris, Gary
  See Jayhawks, The

Louvin, Charlie
  See Louvin Brothers, The
Louvin, Ira
  See Louvin Brothers, The
Louvin Brothers, The 12
Lovano, Joe 13
Love 34
Love, Courtney
  See Hole
Love, Gerry
  See Teenage Fanclub
Love, Laura 20
Love, Mike
  See Beach Boys, The
Love, Rollie
  See Beat Farmers
Love and Rockets 15
Loveless, Patty 21
  Earlier sketch in CM 5
Lovering, David
  See Cracker
  Also see Pixies, The
Love Spit Love 21
Lovett, Lyle 28
  Earlier sketch in CM 5
Lowe, Chris
  See Pet Shop Boys
Lowe, Nick 25
  Earlier sketch in CM 6
Lowe, Victoria
  See Tuxedomoon
Lowell, Charlie
  See Jars of Clay
Lowery, David
  See Cracker
Lozano, Conrad
  See Los Lobos
L7 12
Luc
  See Ex, The
Luca, Nick
  See Giant Sand
Lucas, Gary
  See Captain Beefheart and His Magic Band
Lucas, Kirk
  See Northwoods Improvisers
Lucas, Trevor
  See Fairport Convention
Luccketta, Troy
  See Tesla
Lucero, Nick
  See Queens of the Stone Age
Lucia, Paco de
  See de Lucia, Paco
Luciano, Felipe
  See Last Poets
Luckett, LaToya
  See Destiny's Child
Luke
  See Campbell, Luther
Lukin, Matt
  See Mudhoney
Lulu 32
Luna 18
Lunsford, Bret
  See Beat Happening
Lupo, Pat
  See Beaver Brown Band, The
LuPone, Patti 8
Luscious Jackson 27
  Earlier sketch in CM 19
Lush 13
Luster, Ahrue
  See Machine Head
Luttell, Terry
  See REO Speedwagon

Lydon, John **9**
　Also see Golden Palominos
　Also see Sex Pistols, The
Lyfe, DJ
　See Incubus
Lymon, Frankie
　See Frankie Lymon and The Teenagers
Lynch, David
　See Platters, The
Lynch, Dermot
　See Dog's Eye View
Lynch, Edele
　See B*Witched
Lynch, George
　See Dokken
Lynch, Keavy
　See B*Witched
Lynch, Laura
　See Dixie Chicks
Lynch, Stan
　See Tom Petty and the Heartbreakers
Lyngstad, Anni-Frid
　See Abba
Lynn, Lonnie Rashid
　See Common
Lynn, Loretta **2**
Lynne, Jeff **5**
　Also see Electric Light Orchestra
Lynne, Shelby **29**
　Earlier sketch in CM **5**
Lynott, Phil
　See Thin Lizzy
Lynyrd Skynyrd **9**
Lyons, Leanne "Lelee"
　See SWV
Lyons, Richard
　See Negativland
Ma, Yo-Yo **24**
　Earlier sketch in CM **2**
Mabry, Bill
　See Asleep at the Wheel
MacCaniess, Michael
　See Ceili Rain
MacColl, Kirsty **12**
MacDonald, Barbara Kooyman
　See Timbuk 3
MacDonald, Eddie
　See Alarm
MacDonald, Iain
　See Battlefield Band, The
MacDonald, Pat
　See Timbuk 3
Macfarlane, Lora
　See Sleater-Kinney
MacGowan, Shane
　See Pogues, The
Machine Head **32**
MacIsaac, Ashley **21**
MacKaye, Ian
　See Fugazi
Mack Daddy
　See Kris Kross
Mackey, Steve
　See Pulp
MacLean, Bryan
　See Love
MacNeil, Michael
　See Simple Minds
MacNeil, Rita **29**
MacPherson, Jim
　See Breeders
Macy, Robin
　See Dixie Chicks
Madan, Sonya Aurora
　See Echobelly
Madder Rose **17**

Mader, Logan
　See Machine Head
Madness **27**
Madonna **16**
　Earlier sketch in CM **4**
Mael, Ron
　See Sparks
Mael, Russell
　See Sparks
Magehee, Marty
　See 4Him
Maghostut, Malachi Favors
　See Art Ensemble of Chicago, The
Maginnis, Tom
　See Buffalo Tom
Magnetic Fields, The **28**
Magnie, John
　See Subdudes, The
Magoogan, Wesley
　See English Beat, The
Mahavishnu Orchestra **19**
Maher, John
　See Buzzcocks, The
Mahogany, Kevin **26**
Mahoney, Tim
　See 311
Maida, Raine
　See Our Lady Peace
Maillard, Carol
　See Sweet Honey in the Rock
Maimone, Tony
　See Pere Ubu
Maines, Natalie
　See Dixie Chicks
Maïtra, Shyamal
　See Gong
Majewski, Hank
　See Four Seasons, The
Makeba, Miriam **8**
Makie, Joe
　See Workhorse Movement, The
Makino, Kazu
　See Blonde Redhead
Malcolm, Hugh
　See Skatalites, The
Malcolm, Joy
　See Incognito
Male, Johnny
　See Republica
Malherbe, Didier
　See Gong
Malin, Jesse
　See D Generation
Malins, Mike
　See Goo Goo Dolls, The
Malkmus, Stephen
　See Pavement
Malley, Matt
　See Counting Crows
Mallinder, Stephen
　See Cabaret Voltaire
Malmsteen, Yngwie **24**
Malo, Raul
　See Mavericks, The
Malone, Michelle **30**
Malone, Russell **27**
Malone, Tom
　See Blood, Sweat and Tears
Malone, Tommy
　See Subdudes, The
Maloney, Pete
　See Tonic
Mamas and the Papas **21**
Mancini, Henry **20**
　Earlier sketch in CM **1**
Mandel, Johnny **28**
Mandrell, Barbara **4**

Maness, J. D.
　See Desert Rose Band, The
Mangione, Chuck **23**
Mangum, Jeff
　See Neutral Milk Hotel
Manhattan Transfer, The **8**
Manic Street Preachers **27**
Manilow, Barry **2**
Mankey, Jim
　See Concrete Blonde
Mann, Aimee **22**
Mann, Barry **30**
Mann, Billy **23**
Mann, Bob
　See Mountain
Mann, Herbie **16**
Manninger, Hank
　See Aqua Velvets
Man or Astroman? **21**
Manson, Shirley
　See Garbage
Mansun **30**
Manuel, Richard
　See Band, The
Manzarek, Ray
　See Doors, The
March, Kevin
　See Shudder to Think
Marcy Playground **31**
Marie, Buffy Sainte
　See Sainte-Marie, Buffy
Marilyn Manson **18**
Marine, Mitch
　See Brave Combo
Marini, Lou, Jr.
　See Blood, Sweat and Tears
Marinos, Jimmy
　See Romantics, The
Marker, Steve
　See Garbage
Marks, Toby
　See De Gaia, Banco
Marley, Bob **3**
Marley, Rita **10**
Marley, Ziggy **3**
Marr, Johnny
　See Smiths, The
　Also see The The
Marriner, Neville **7**
Mars, Chris
　See Replacements, The
Mars, Derron
　See Less Than Jake
Mars, Mick
　See Mötley Crüe
Marsalis, Branford **10**
Marsalis, Ellis **13**
Marsalis, Jason
　See Los Hombres Calientes
Marsalis, Wynton **20**
　Earlier sketch in CM **6**
Marsh, Ian Craig
　See Human League, The
Marsh, Randy
　See Northwoods Improvisers
Marshal, Cornel
　See Third World
Marshall, Amanda **27**
Marshall, Arik
　See Red Hot Chili Peppers
Marshall, Brian
　See Creed
Marshall, Chan
　See Cat Power
Marshall, David Alan
　See Chanticleer

Marshall, Jenell
See Dirty Dozen Brass Band
Marshall, Jeremy
See Cold
Marshall, Steve
See Gene Loves Jezebel
Martensen, Vic
See Captain Beefheart and His Magic Band
Martha and the Vandellas 25
Martin, Barbara
See Supremes, The
Martin, Bardi
See Candlebox
Martin, Barrett
See Screaming Trees
Martin, Billy
See Medeski, Martin & Wood
Martin, Carl
See Shai
Martin, Chris
See Coldplay
Martin, Christopher
See Kid 'n Play
Martin, Dean 1
Martin, Dewey
See Buffalo Springfield
Martin, George 6
Martin, Greg
See Kentucky Headhunters, The
Martin, Jim
See Faith No More
Martin, Jimmy 5
Also see Osborne Brothers, The
Martin, Johnney
See Mighty Clouds of Joy, The
Martin, Kevin
See Candlebox
Martin, Mary 27
Martin, Phonso
See Steel Pulse
Martin, Ricky 26
Martin, Ronnie
See Joy Electric
Martin, Sarah
See Belle and Sebastian
Martin, Sennie
See Kool & the Gang
Martin, Tony
See Black Sabbath
Martinez, Anthony
See Black Flag
Martinez, Christina
See Boss Hog
Martinez, Cliff
See Captain Beefheart and His Magic Band
Martinez, S. A.
See 311
Martini, Jerry
See Sly & the Family Stone
Martino, Pat 17
Martsch, Doug
See Built to Spill
Marvin, Hank B.
See Shadows, The
Marx, Richard 21
Earlier sketch in CM 3
Mascagni, Pietro 25
Mascis, J
See Dinosaur Jr.
Masdea, Jim
See Boston
Mase 27
Masekela, Hugh 7
Maseo, Baby Huey
See De La Soul
Masi, Nick
See Four Seasons, The

Mason, Dave
See Traffic
Mason, Nick
See Pink Floyd
Mason, Stephen
See Beta Band, The
Mason, Steve
See Jars of Clay
Mason, Terry
See Joy Division
Masse, Laurel
See Manhattan Transfer, The
Massey, Bobby
See O'Jays, The
Massey, Graham
See 808 State
Massi, Nick
See Four Seasons, The
Massive Attack 17
Mastelotto, Pat
See King Crimson
Master D
See Asian Dub Foundation
Master P 22
Masur, Kurt 11
Matchbox 20 27
Material
See Laswell, Bill
Mathis, Johnny 2
Mathus, Jim
See Squirrel Nut Zippers
Matlock, Glen
See Sex Pistols, The
Mattacks, Dave
See Fairport Convention
Mattea, Kathy 5
Matthew Good Band 34
Matthews, Cerys
See Catatonia
Matthews, Chris
See Shudder to Think
Matthews, Dave
See Dave Matthews Band
Matthews, Donna Lorraine
See Elastica
Matthews, Eric 22
Matthews, Ian
See Fairport Convention
Matthews, Quinn
See Butthole Surfers
Matthews, Scott
See Butthole Surfers
Matthews, Simon
See Jesus Jones
Matthews, Winston "Pipe"
See Wailing Souls
Mattock, John
See Spacemen 3
Maunick, Bluey
See Incognito
Maurer, John
See Social Distortion
Mavericks, The 15
Maxwell 22
Maxwell, Charmayne
See Brownstone
Maxwell, Tom
See Squirrel Nut Zippers
May, Brian
See Queen
May, Phil
See Pretty Things, The
Mayall, John 7
Mayfield, Curtis 8
Mayfield, Irvin
See Los Hombres Calientes

Mays, Odeen, Jr.
See Kool & the Gang
Mazelle, Kym
See Soul II Soul
Mazibuko, Abednigo
See Ladysmith Black Mambazo
Mazibuko, Albert
See Ladysmith Black Mambazo
Mazzola, Joey
See Sponge
Mazzy Star 17
MCA
See Yauch, Adam
McAloon, Martin
See Prefab Sprout
McAloon, Paddy
See Prefab Sprout
McArthur, Keith
See Spearhead
McAuley, Mick
See Solas
McBay, Clint
See Chainsaw Kittens, The
McBoutie, Rip
See Lane, Fred
McBrain, Nicko
See Iron Maiden
McBrayer, Jody
See Avalon
MC Breed 17
McBride, Christian 17
McBride, Martina 14
McCabe, Nick
See Verve, The
McCabe, Zia
See Dandy Warhols
McCall, Renee
See Sounds of Blackness
McCandless, Paul
See Oregon
McCandless, Sam
See Cold
McCann, Lila 26
McCarrick, Martin
See Siouxsie and the Banshees
McCarroll, Tony
See Oasis
McCartney, Paul 32
Earlier sketch in CM 4
Also see Beatles, The
McCarty, Jim
See Yardbirds, The
McCary, Michael S.
See Boyz II Men
McCaughan, Mac
See Superchunk
McCaughey, Scott 31
McClain, Dave
See Machine Head
McClary, Thomas
See Commodores, The
McClennan, Tommy 25
MC Clever
See Digital Underground
McClinton, Delbert 14
McCloud, Scott
See Girls Against Boys
McCluskey, Andy
See Orchestral Manoeuvres in the Dark
McColgan, Mike
See Dropkick Murphys
McCollum, Rick
See Afghan Whigs
McCombs, Doug
See Tortoise
McConnell, Page
See Phish

McCook, Jack
  See Superchunk
McCook, Tommy
  See Skatalites, The
McCorkle, Susannah 27
McCoury, Del 15
McCowin, Michael
  See Mighty Clouds of Joy, The
McCoy, Neal 15
McCracken, Chet
  See Doobie Brothers, The
McCrea, John
  See Cake
McCready, Mike
  See Pearl Jam
McCready, Mindy 22
McCullagh, John
  See Divine Comedy, The
McCulloch, Andrew
  See King Crimson
McCulloch, Ian 23
  Also see Echo and the Bunnymen
McCullough, Danny
  See Animals, The
McCuloch, Ian 23
McCurdy, Xan
  See Cake
McCusker, John
  See Battlefield Band, The
McCutcheon, Ian
  See Mojave 3
McD, Jimmy
  See Jimmie's Chicken Shack
McDaniel, Chris
  See Confederate Railroad
McDaniels, Darryl "D"
  See Run DMC
McDermott, Brian
  See Del Amitri
McDonald, Hugh
  See Bon Jovi
McDonald, Ian
  See Foreigner
  Also see King Crimson
McDonald, Jeff
  See Redd Kross
McDonald, Lloyd "Bread"
  See Wailing Souls
McDonald, Michael
  See Doobie Brothers, The
McDonald, Richie
  See Lonestar
McDonald, Steven
  See Redd Kross
McDorman, Joe
  See Statler Brothers, The
McDougall, Don
  See Guess Who
McDowell, Hugh
  See Electric Light Orchestra
McDowell, Mississippi Fred 16
McDuffie, Chris
  See Apples in Stereo
MC Eiht 27
McElhaney, Kevin
  See Chainsaw Kittens, The
McElhone, John
  See Texas
McEntire, John
  See Tortoise
McEntire, Reba 11
MC Eric
  See Technotronic
McErlaine, Ally
  See Texas
McEuen, John
  See Nitty Gritty Dirt Band, The

McFadden, Bryan
  See Westlife
McFarlane, Elaine
  See Mamas and the Papas
McFee, John
  See Doobie Brothers, The
McFerrin, Bobby 3
McFessel, Sean
  See Cake
MC5, The 9
McGearly, James
  See Christian Death
McGee, Brian
  See Simple Minds
McGee, Jerry
  See Ventures, The
McGeoch, John
  See Siouxsie and the Banshees
McGill, Lucius
  See Dells, The
McGill, Michael
  See Dells, The
McGinley, Raymond
  See Teenage Fanclub
McGinniss, Will
  See Audio Adrenaline
McGrath, Mark
  See Sugar Ray
McGraw, Tim 17
McGuigan, Paul
  See Oasis
McGuinn, Jim
  See McGuinn, Roger
McGuinn, Roger
  See Byrds, The
McGuinness
  See Lords of Acid
McGuire, Andy
  See Spoon
McGuire, Christine
  See McGuire Sisters, The
McGuire, Dorothy
  See McGuire Sisters, The
McGuire, Mike
  See Shenandoah
McGuire, Phyllis
  See McGuire Sisters, The
McGuire Sisters, The 27
M.C. Hammer
  See Hammer, M.C.
McIntosh, Robbie
  See Pretenders, The
McIntyre, Jim
  See Apples in Stereo
McIntyre, Joey 34
  Also see New Kids on the Block
McJohn, Goldy
  See Steppenwolf
McKagan, Duff
  See Guns n' Roses
McKay, Al
  See Earth, Wind and Fire
McKay, John
  See Siouxsie and the Banshees
McKean, Michael
  See Spinal Tap
McKee, Julius
  See Dirty Dozen Brass Band
McKee, Maria 11
McKeehan, Toby
  See dc Talk
McKenna, Greg
  See Letters to Cleo
McKennitt, Loreena 24
McKenzie, Christina "Licorice"
  See Incredible String Band

McKenzie, Derrick
  See Jamiroquai
McKenzie, Scott
  See Mamas and the Papas
McKernan, Ron "Pigpen"
  See Grateful Dead, The
McKinney, William
  See McKinney's Cotton Pickers
McKinney's Cotton Pickers 16
McKnight, Brian 22
McKnight, Claude V., III
  See Take 6
McLachlan, Sarah 34
  Earlier sketch in CM 12
McLagan, Ian
  See Faces, The
McLaren, Malcolm 23
McLaughlin, John 12
  Also see Mahavishnu Orchestra
McLean, A. J.
  See Backstreet Boys
McLean, Dave 24
McLean, Don 7
McLean, John
  See Beta Band, The
McLennan, Grant 21
  Also see Go-Betweens, The
McLeod, Rory
  See Roomful of Blues
McLoughlin, Jon
  See Del Amitri
MC Lyte 8
McMackin, Bryon
  See Pennywise
McMeel, Mickey
  See Three Dog Night
McMurray, Rick
  See Ash
McMurtry, James 10
McNabb, Travis
  See Better Than Ezra
McNair, Sylvia 15
McNeill, Brian
  See Battlefield Band, The
McNeilly, Mac
  See Jesus Lizard
McNew, James
  See Yo La Tengo
MC 900 Ft. Jesus 16
McPartland, Marian 15
McPhatter, Clyde 25
McPherson, Graham "Suggs"
  See Madness
McPherson, Todd
  See Kingsmen, The
McQuillar, Shawn
  See Kool & the Gang
McRae, Carmen 9
M.C. Ren
  See N.W.A.
McReynolds, Jesse
  See McReynolds, Jim and Jesse
McReynolds, Jim
  See McReynolds, Jim and Jesse
McReynolds, Jim and Jesse 12
MC Serch 10
McShane, Ronnie
  See Chieftains, The
McShee, Jacqui
  See Pentangle
McTell, Blind Willie 17
McVie, Christine
  See Fleetwood Mac
McVie, John
  See Fleetwood Mac
McWhinney, James
  See Big Mountain

McWhinney, Joaquin
  See Big Mountain
Mdletshe, Geophrey
  See Ladysmith Black Mambazo
Meade, Tyson
  See Chainsaw Kittens, The
Meat Loaf 12
Meat Puppets, The 13
Medeski, John
  See Medeski, Martin & Wood
Medeski, Martin & Wood 32
Medley, Bill 3
Medlock, James
  See Soul Stirrers, The
Meehan, Tony
  See Shadows, The
Megadeth 9
Mehldau, Brad 27
Mehta, Zubin 11
Meifert, Arnulf
  See Faust
Meine, Klaus
  See Scorpions, The
Meisner, Randy
  See Eagles, The
Mekons, The 15
Melanie 12
Melax, Einar
  See Sugarcubes, The
Melchiondo, Mickey
  See Ween
Mellencamp, John 20
  Earlier sketch in CM 2
Mellino, Iza
  See Les Négresses Vertes
Mellino, Stéfane
  See Les Négresses Vertes
Melvin, Eric
  See NOFX
Melvins 21
Memphis Jug Band 25
Memphis Minnie 25
Men at Work 34
Menck, Ric
  See Velvet Crush
Mendel, Nate
  See Foo Fighters
  Also see Sunny Day Real Estate
Mengede, Peter
  See Helmet
Menken, Alan 10
Menuhin, Yehudi 11
Menza, Nick
  See Megadeth
Mercado, Scott
  See Candlebox
Mercer, Johnny 13
Merchant, Jimmy
  See Frankie Lymon and The Teenagers
Merchant, Natalie 25
  Also see 10,000 Maniacs
Mercier, Peadar
  See Chieftains, The
Mercury, Freddie
  See Queen
Mercury Rev 28
Merman, Ethel 27
Merrick, Bryn
  See Damned, The
Merrill, Robbie
  See Godsmack
Merritt, Stephin
  See Magnetic Fields, The
Mertens, Paul
  See Poi Dog Pondering
Merzbow 31

Mesaros, Michael
  See Smithereens, The
Messecar, Dek
  See Caravan
Messina, Jim
  See Buffalo Springfield
Messina, Jo Dee 26
Metallica 33
  Earlier sketch in CM 7
Meters, The 14
Methembu, Russel
  See Ladysmith Black Mambazo
Metheny, Pat 26
  Earlier sketch in CM 2
Method Man 31
  Also see Wu-Tang Clan
Metzger, Mark
  See Chainsaw Kittens, The
Mew, Sharon
  See Elastica
Meyer, Eric
  See Charm Farm
Meyers, Augie
  See Texas Tornados, The
Mhaonaigh, Mairead Ni
  See Altan
Michael, George 9
Michaels, Bret
  See Poison
Michel, Luke
  See Emmet Swimming
Michel, Prakazrel "Pras"
  See Fugees, The
Michiles, Malcolm
  See Citizen King
Middlebrook, Ralph "Pee Wee"
  See Ohio Players
Middleton, Darren
  See Powderfinger
Middleton, Malcolm
  See Arab Strap
Middleton, Mark
  See Blackstreet
Midler, Bette 8
Midnight Oil 11
Midori 7
Mighty Clouds of Joy, The 17
Mighty Mighty Bosstones 20
Miguel, Luis 34
Mike & the Mechanics 17
Mike D
  See Diamond, Michael
Mikens, Dennis
  See Smithereens, The
Mikens, Robert
  See Kool & the Gang
Milchem, Glenn
  See Blue Rodeo
Miles, Chris
  See Northern Lights
Miles, Richard
  See Soul Stirrers, The
Miles, Ron 22
Millar, Deborah
  See Massive Attack
Miller, Buddy 31
Miller, Charles
  See War
Miller, David
  See Asleep at the Wheel
Miller, Glenn 6
Miller, Jacob "Killer"
  See Inner Circle
Miller, Jerry
  See Moby Grape
Miller, Kevin
  See Fuel

Miller, Mark
  See Sawyer Brown
Miller, Mitch 11
Miller, Rhett
  See Old 97's
Miller, Rice
  See Williamson, Sonny Boy
Miller, Robert
  See Supertramp
Miller, Roger 4
Miller, Ryan
  See Guster
Miller, Scott
  See Loud Family, The
Miller, Steve 2
Milli Vanilli 4
Mills, Bryan
  See Divine Comedy, The
Mills, Donald
  See Mills Brothers, The
Mills, Fred
  See Canadian Brass, The
Mills, Harry
  See Mills Brothers, The
Mills, Herbert
  See Mills Brothers, The
Mills, John, Jr.
  See Mills Brothers, The
Mills, John, Sr.
  See Mills Brothers, The
Mills, Mike
  See R.E.M.
Mills, Sidney
  See Steel Pulse
Mills, Stephanie 21
Mills Brothers, The 14
Milsap, Ronnie 2
Milton, Doctor
  See Alien Sex Fiend
Mingus, Charles 9
Ministry 10
Minnelli, Liza 19
Minns, Danielle
  See Minty
Minogue, Kylie 32
Minott, Sugar 31
Mint Condition 29
Minton, Phil 29
Minty 32
Minutemen, The 31
Misfits, The 32
Miskulin, Joey "The Cowpolka King"
  See Riders in the Sky
Miss Kier Kirby
  See Lady Miss Kier
Mitchell, Alex
  See Curve
Mitchell, Bruce
  See Durutti Column, The
Mitchell, Burt
  See Ceili Rain
Mitchell, John
  See Asleep at the Wheel
Mitchell, Joni 17
  Earlier sketch in CM 2
Mitchell, Keith
  See Mazzy Star
Mitchell, Mike
  See Kingsmen, The
Mitchell, Mitch
  See Guided By Voices
Mitchell, Roscoe
  See Art Ensemble of Chicago, The
Mittoo, Jackie
  See Skatalites, The
Mize, Ben
  See Counting Crows

Mizell, Jay "Jam Master Jay"
  See Run DMC
Mo', Keb' **21**
Moby **27**
  Earlier sketch in CM **17**
Moby Grape **12**
Modeliste, Joseph "Zigaboo"
  See Meters, The
Modest Mouse **30**
moe. **34**
Moerlen, Pierre
  See Gong
Moffat, Aidan
  See Arab Strap
Moffatt, Katy **18**
Moginie, Jim
  See Midnight Oil
Mogwai **27**
Mohan, John
  See Felt
Mohr, Todd
  See Big Head Todd and the Monsters
Mojave 3 **26**
Molko, Brian
  See Placebo
Molla, Chris
  See Monks of Doom
Molland, Joey
  See Badfinger
Molloy, Matt
  See Chieftains, The
Moloney, Paddy
  See Chieftains, The
Monahan, Pat
  See Train
Monahan, Thom
  See Pernice Brothers
Monarch, Michael
  See Steppenwolf
Monch, Pharoahe **29**
Money, Eddie **16**
Money B
  See Digital Underground
Monheit, Jane **33**
Monica **26**
Monifah **24**
Monk, Meredith **1**
Monk, Thelonious **6**
Monkees, The **7**
Monks of Doom **28**
Monroe, Bill **1**
Monster, Drunkness
  See Len
Montana, Country Dick
  See Beat Farmers
Montand, Yves **12**
Montenegro, Hugo **18**
Montgomery, Eddie
  See Montgomery Gentry
Montgomery, John Michael **14**
Montgomery, Ken "Dimwit"
  See D.O.A.
Montgomery, Little Brother **26**
Montgomery, Wes **3**
Montgomery Gentry **34**
Monti, Steve
  See Curve
Montoya, Craig
  See Everclear
Montrose, Ronnie **22**
Moody, James **34**
Moody Blues, The **18**
Moon, Doug
  See Captain Beefheart and His Magic Band
Moon, Keith
  See Who, The

Mooney, Malcolm
  See Can
Mooney, Tim
  See American Music Club
Moonglows, The **33**
Moore, Alan
  See Judas Priest
Moore, Angelo
  See Fishbone
Moore, Archie
  See Velocity Girl
Moore, Chante **21**
Moore, Glen
  See Oregon
Moore, Johnny "Dizzy"
  See Skatalites, The
Moore, Kevin
  See Dream Theater
Moore, LeRoi
  See Dave Matthews Band
Moore, Melba **7**
Moore, Sam
  See Sam and Dave
Moore, Sean
  See Manic Street Preachers
Moore, Thurston
  See Sonic Youth
M.O.P. **34**
Morales, Richie
  See Spyro Gyra
Morand, Grace
  See Chenille Sisters, The
Moraz, Patrick
  See Moody Blues, The
  Also see Yes
Morcheeba **25**
Moreira, Airto
  See Weather Report
Morello, Tom
  See Rage Against the Machine
Moreno, Chino
  See Deftones
Moreve, Rushton
  See Steppenwolf
Morgan, Frank **9**
Morgan, Jane **30**
Morgan, John Russell
  See Steppenwolf
Morgan, Lorrie **10**
Morissette, Alanis **19**
Morley, Pat
  See Soul Asylum
Moron, Monty Oxy
  See Damned, The
Morphine **29**
  Earlier sketch in CM **16**
Morricone, Ennio **15**
Morris, Keith
  See Circle Jerks, The
Morris, Kenny
  See Siouxsie and the Banshees
Morris, Nate
  See Boyz II Men
Morris, Roger
  See Psychedelic Furs
Morris, Stephen
  See Joy Division
  Also see New Order
  Also see Pogues, The
Morris, Wanya
  See Boyz II Men
Morrison, Bram
  See Sharon, Lois & Bram
Morrison, Claude
  See Nylons, The
Morrison, Jim **3**
  Also see Doors, The

Morrison, Lindy
  See Go-Betweens, The
Morrison, Patricia
  See Damned, The
Morrison, Sterling
  See Velvet Underground, The
Morrison, Van **24**
  Earlier sketch in CM **3**
Morriss, Mark James
  See Bluetones, The
Morriss, Reginald Ilanthriy
  See Bluetones, The
Morrissett, Paul
  See Klezmatics, The
Morrissey **10**
  Also see Smiths, The
Morrissey, Bill **12**
Morrissey, Steven Patrick
  See Morrissey
Morton, Everett
  See English Beat, The
Morton, Jelly Roll **7**
Morvan, Fab
  See Milli Vanilli
Mosbaugh, Garth
  See Nylons, The
Moseley, Keith
  See String Cheese Incident, The
Mosely, Chuck
  See Faith No More
Moser, Scott "Cactus"
  See Highway 101
Moses, Cactus
  See Ceili Rain
Mosher, Ken
  See Squirrel Nut Zippers
Mosley, Bob
  See Moby Grape
Moss, Ian
  See Cold Chisel
Moss, Jason
  See Cherry Poppin' Daddies
Moss, Jon
  See Damned, The
Most, Mickie **29**
Mothersbaugh, Bob
  See Devo
Mothersbaugh, Mark
  See Devo
Mötley Crüe **1**
Motörhead **10**
Motta, Danny
  See Roomful of Blues
Mott the Hoople **31**
Mould, Bob **10**
  Also see Golden Palominos
Moulding, Colin
  See XTC
Mounfield, Gary
  See Stone Roses, The
Mountain **30**
Mouquet, Eric
  See Deep Forest
Mouse On Mars **32**
Mouskouri, Nana **12**
Mouzon, Alphonse
  See Weather Report
Moves, DJ
  See Len
Moye, Famoudou Don
  See Art Ensemble of Chicago, The
Moyet, Alison **12**
Moyse, David
  See Air Supply
M People **27**
  Earlier sketch in CM **15**

Mr. Dalvin
　See Jodeci
Mr. T Experience, The **29**
Mudhoney **16**
Mueller, Karl
　See Soul Asylum
Muir, Jamie
　See King Crimson
Muir, Mike
　See Suicidal Tendencies
Muldaur, Maria **18**
Mulholland, Dave
　See Aztec Camera
Mullen, Larry, Jr.
　See U2
Mullen, Mary
　See Congo Norvell
Mulligan, Gerry **16**
Mullins, Shawn **33**
Munson, John
　See Semisonic
Murcia, Billy
　See New York Dolls
Murdoch, Stuart
　See Belle and Sebastian
Murdock, Roger
　See King Missile
Murph
　See Dinosaur Jr.
Murphey, Michael Martin **9**
Murphy, Brigid
　See Poi Dog Pondering
Murphy, Chris
　See Sloan
Murphy, Dan
　See Soul Asylum
Murphy, John
　See Gene Loves Jezebel
Murphy, Michael
　See REO Speedwagon
Murphy, Peter **22**
　Also see Bauhaus
Murray, Anne **4**
Murray, Dave
　See Iron Maiden
Murray, Dave **28**
Murray, Dee
　See Spencer Davis Group
Murray, Don
　See Turtles, The
Murray, Jim
　See Quicksilver Messenger Service
Musburger, Mike
　See Fastbacks, The
Mushok, Mike
　See Staind
Mushroom
　See Massive Attack
Musselwhite, Charlie **13**
Mustaine, Dave
　See Megadeth
　Also see Metallica
Mutter, Anne-Sophie **23**
Mwelase, Jabulane
　See Ladysmith Black Mambazo
MxPx **33**
Mya **32**
My Bloody Valentine **29**
Mydland, Brent
　See Grateful Dead, The
Myers, Alan
　See Devo
Myles, Alannah **4**
Mystic Revealers **16**
Mystikal **29**
Myung, John
　See Dream Theater

Na'dirah
　See Arrested Development
Naftalin, Mark
　See Quicksilver Messenger Service
Nagler, Eric **8**
Najee **21**
Nakai, R. Carlos **24**
Nakamura, Tetsuya "Tex"
　See War
Nakatami, Michie
　See Shonen Knife
Naked, Bif **29**
Nana
　See Rasputina
Nancarrow, Conlon **32**
Nanji, Mato
　See Indigenous
Napolitano, Johnette
　See Concrete Blonde
Narcizo, David
　See Throwing Muses
Nas **19**
Nascimento, Milton **6**
Nash, Graham
　See Crosby, Stills, and Nash
Nash, Leigh
　See Sixpence None the Richer
Nash, Nasher
　See Frankie Goes To Hollywood
Nashville Bluegrass Band **14**
Nasta, Ken
　See Royal Trux
Nastanovich, Bob
　See Pavement
Naté, Ultra **34**
Naughty by Nature **11**
Navarro, David
　See Jane's Addiction
　Also see Red Hot Chili Peppers
Navarro Fats **25**
Nawasadio, Sylvie
　See Zap Mama
Nazworthy, Dave
　See Down By Law
Ndegéocello, Me'Shell **18**
N'Dour, Youssou **6**
Ndugu
　See Weather Report
Near, Holly **1**
Needham, Margie
　See Chordettes, The
Neel, Johnny
　See Allman Brothers, The
Negativland **30**
Negron, Chuck
　See Three Dog Night
Negroni, Joe
　See Frankie Lymon and The Teenagers
Neil, Chris
　See Less Than Jake
Neil, Vince
　See Mötley Crüe
Nelson, Brett
　See Built to Spill
Nelson, Brian
　See Velocity Girl
Nelson, David
　See Last Poets
Nelson, Errol
　See Black Uhuru
Nelson, Gabe
　See Cake
Nelson, Nate
　See Platters, The
Nelson, Rick **2**
Nelson, Shara
　See Massive Attack

Nelson, Willie **11**
　Earlier sketch in CM **1**
Nero, Peter **19**
Nershi, Bill
　See String Cheese Incident, The
Nesbitt, John
　See McKinney's Cotton Pickers
Nesmith, Mike
　See Monkees, The
Ness, Mike
　See Social Distortion
Netson, Brett
　See Built to Spill
　Also see Caustic Resin
Neu! **32**
Neufville, Renee
　See Zhane
Neumann, Kurt
　See BoDeans
Neurosis **28**
Neutral Milk Hotel **31**
Nevarez, Alfred
　See All-4-One
Neville, Aaron **5**
　Also see Neville Brothers, The
Neville, Art
　See Meters, The
　Also see Neville Brothers, The
Neville, Charles
　See Neville Brothers, The
Neville, Cyril
　See Meters, The
　Also see Neville Brothers, The
Neville Brothers, The **4**
Nevin, Brian
　See Big Head Todd and the Monsters
Newell, Ryan
　See Sister Hazel
New Grass Revival, The **4**
New Kids on the Block **3**
Newman, Colin
　See Wire
Newman, Randy **27**
　Earlier sketch in CM **4**
Newmann, Kurt
　See BoDeans, The
New Order **11**
New Rhythm and Blues Quartet
　See NRBQ
Newsboys, The **24**
Newsham, Sean
　See Quickspace
Newson, Arlene
　See Poi Dog Pondering
Newsted, Jason
　See Metallica
Newton, Colin
　See Idlewild
Newton, Paul
　See Uriah Heep
Newton, Wayne **2**
Newton-Davis, Billy
　See Nylons, The
Newton-John, Olivia **8**
New York Dolls **20**
Nibbs, Lloyd
　See Skatalites, The
Nichol, Al
　See Turtles, The
Nicholas, James Dean "J.D."
　See Commodores, The
Nicholls, Geoff
　See Black Sabbath
Nicholls, Chad
　See Lettermen, The
Nichols, Eddie
　See Royal Crown Revue

Nichols, Gates
  See Confederate Railroad
Nichols, Todd
  See Toad the Wet Sprocket
Nickerson, Charlie
  See Memphis Jug Band
Nicks, Stevie **25**
  Earlier sketch in CM **2**
  Also see Fleetwood Mac
Nico
  See Velvet Underground, The
Nicol, Simon
  See Fairport Convention
Nicolette
  See Massive Attack
Nielsen, Rick
  See Cheap Trick
Nielsen, Tim
  See Drivin' N' Cryin'
Nijholt, Nico
  See Willem Breuker Kollektief
Nikleva, Steven
  See Ray Condo and His Ricochets
Nile, Willie **31**
Nilija, Robert
  See Last Poets
Nilsson **10**
Nilsson, Birgit **31**
Nilsson, Harry
  See Nilsson
Nine Inch Nails **29**
98 Degrees **32**
Nirvana **8**
Nisbett, Steve "Grizzly"
  See Steel Pulse
Nishino, Kohji
  See Ghost
Nitty Gritty Dirt Band, The **6**
Nixon, Mojo **32**
Nobacon, Danbert "The Cat"
  See Chumbawamba
Nocentelli, Leo
  See Meters, The
No Doubt **20**
NOFX **28**
Nolan, Jerry
  See New York Dolls
Nomiya, Maki
  See Pizzicato Five
Nono
  See Les Négresses Vertes
Noone, Peter "Herman"
  See Herman's Hermits
Nordby, Bob
  See Kingsmen, The
Norica, Sugar Ray
  See Roomful of Blues
Norman, Jessye **7**
Norman, Jimmy
  See Coasters, The
Norman, Patrick
  See Rusted Root
Norreen, Claus
  See Aqua
Norris, Jean
  See Zhane
Northern Lights **19**
Northey, Craig
  See Odds
Northwoods Improvisers **31**
Norton, Butch
  See eels
Norum, John
  See Dokken
Norvell, Sally
  See Congo Norvell
Norvo, Red **12**

Notorious B.I.G. **20**
Nova, Heather **30**
Novoselic, Chris
  See Nirvana
Nowell, Bradley James
  See Sublime
NRBQ **12**
'N Sync **25**
Nugent, Ted **2**
Nunez, Joe
  See Soulfly
Nunn, Bobby
  See Coasters, The
Nutter, Alice
  See Chumbawamba
N.W.A. **6**
Nylons, The **6**
Nyman, Michael **15**
Nyolo, Sally
  See Zap Mama
Nyro, Laura **12**
Nystrøm, Lene Grawford
  See Aqua
Oakenfold, Paul **32**
Oakes, Richard
  See Suede
Oakey, Philip
  See Human League, The
Oakland Interfaith Gospel Choir **26**
Oakley, Berry
  See Allman Brothers, The
Oak Ridge Boys, The **7**
  Earlier sketch in CM **4**
Oasis **16**
Oates, John
  See Hall & Oates
Oban, George "Ras Levi"
  See Aswad
O'Brien, Brien
  See D.O.A.
O'Brien, Danny
  See Brave Combo
O'Brien, Darrin Kenneth
  See Snow
O'Brien, Derek
  See Social Distortion
O'Brien, Dwayne
  See Little Texas
O'Brien, Ed
  See Radiohead
O'Brien, Marty
  See Kilgore
O'Bryant, Alan
  See Nashville Bluegrass Band
O'Carroll, Sinead
  See B*Witched
Ocasek, Ric **5**
  Also see Cars, The
Ocean, Billy **4**
Oceans, Lucky
  See Asleep at the Wheel
Ochowiak, Michel
  See Les Négresses Vertes
Ochs, Phil **7**
O'Ciosoig, Colm
  See My Bloody Valentine
O'Connell, Chris
  See Asleep at the Wheel
O'Connor, Billy
  See Blondie
O'Connor, Daniel
  See House of Pain
O'Connor, Mark **1**
O'Connor, Sinead **31**
  Earlier sketch in CM **3**
O'Day, Anita **21**
Odds **20**

O'Dell, Homer
  See Mint Condition
Odetta **7**
Odmark, Matt
  See Jars of Clay
O'Donnell, Roger
  See Cure, The
O'Farrill, Chico **31**
Offspring, The **19**
Ofwerman, Clarence
  See Roxette
Ofwerman, Staffan
  See Roxette
Ogino, Kazuo
  See Ghost
Ogletree, Mike
  See Simple Minds
Ogre, Nivek
  See Pigface
  Also see Skinny Puppy
O'Hagan, Sean
  See Stereolab
Ohanian, David
  See Canadian Brass, The
O'Hare, Brendan
  See Mogwai
  Also see Teenage Fanclub
Ohio Players **16**
O'Jays, The **13**
Oje, Baba
  See Arrested Development
O'Keefe, Laurence
  See Dark Star
Olafsson, Bragi
  See Sugarcubes, The
Olander, Jimmy
  See Diamond Rio
Olaverra, Margot
  See Go-Go's, The
Old 97's **33**
Olde-Wolbers, Christian
  See Fear Factory
Oldfield, Mike **18**
Oldham, Jack
  See Surfaris, The
Oldham, Sean
  See Cherry Poppin' Daddies
Oldham, Will **32**
Olds, Brent
  See Poi Dog Pondering
Oliver, Joe
  See Oliver, King
Oliver, King **15**
Oliveri, Nick
  See Queens of the Stone Age
Olivia Tremor Control **28**
Olsdal, Stefan
  See Placebo
Olson, Jeff
  See Village People, The
Olson, Mark
  See Jayhawks, The
Olsson, Nigel
  See Spencer Davis Group
Oltman, Matt
  See Chanticleer
Onassis, Blackie
  See Urge Overkill
Ondras, Charlie
  See Boss Hog
Ono, Yoko **11**
Opokuwaa, Akua
  See Sweet Honey in the Rock
Orange, Walter "Clyde"
  See Commodores, The
Orb, The **18**
Orbison, Roy **2**

Orbit, William **30**
Orbital **20**
Orchestral Manoeuvres in the Dark **21**
O'Reagan, Tim
  See Jayhawks, The
Oregon **30**
Orff, Carl **21**
Organ, Chad
  See Flying Luttenbachers, The
Orgy **27**
O'Riordan, Cait
  See Pogues, The
O'Riordan, Dolores
  See Cranberries, The
Orlando, Tony **15**
Örn, Einar
  See Sugarcubes, The
Örnolfsdottir, Margret
  See Sugarcubes, The
O'Rourke, Jim **31**
Orr, Benjamin
  See Cars, The
Orr, Casey
  See Gwar
Orrall, Frank
  See Poi Dog Pondering
Ortega, Leonor "Jeff"
  See Five Iron Frenzy
Ortega, Micah
  See Five Iron Frenzy
Ortiz, Bill
  See Lavay Smith and Her Red Hot Skillet Lickers
Ortoli
  See Les Négresses Vertes
Orton, Beth **26**
Orzabal, Roland
  See Tears for Fears
Osborn, Jinny
  See Chordettes, The
Osborne, Bob
  See Osborne Brothers, The
Osborne, Buzz
  See Melvins
Osborne, Joan **19**
Osborne, Sonny
  See Osborne Brothers, The
Osborne Brothers, The **8**
Osbourne, Ozzy **3**
  Also see Black Sabbath
Osby, Greg **21**
Oskar, Lee
  See War
Oslin, K. T. **3**
Osman, Mat
  See Suede
Osmond, Donny **3**
Ostin, Mo **17**
Oswald, Hunter
  See Down By Law
Otis, Johnny **16**
O'Toole, Mark
  See Frankie Goes To Hollywood
Ott, David **2**
Ottewell, Ben
  See Gomez
Otto, John
  See Limp Bizkit
Our Lady Peace **22**
OutKast **33**
Outler, Jimmy
  See Soul Stirrers, The
Overstreet, Paul **33**
Overton, Nancy
  See Chordettes, The
Owen, Randy Yueull
  See Alabama

Owens, Buck **2**
Owens, Campbell
  See Aztec Camera
Owens, Henry
  See Golden Gate Quartet
Owens, Jack **30**
Owens, Ricky
  See Temptations, The
Oxley, Tony **32**
Oyewole, Abiodun
  See Last Poets
Pace, Amedeo
  See Blonde Redhead
Pace, Simone
  See Blonde Redhead
Page, Jimmy **4**
  Also see Led Zeppelin
  Also see Yardbirds, The
Page, Patti **11**
Page, Steven
  See Barenaked Ladies
Paice, Ian
  See Deep Purple
Pajo, Dave
  See Tortoise
Paliotta, Cherie
  See Avalon
Palmar, Wally
  See Romantics, The
Palmer, Bruce
  See Buffalo Springfield
Palmer, Carl
  See Emerson, Lake & Palmer/Powell
Palmer, Clive
  See Incredible String Band
Palmer, David
  See Jethro Tull
Palmer, Jeff
  See Sunny Day Real Estate
Palmer, Jeff **20**
Palmer, Keeti
  See Prodigy
Palmer, Phil
  See Dire Straits
Palmer, Richard
  See Supertramp
Palmer, Robert **2**
Palmer-Jones, Robert
  See King Crimson
Palmieri, Eddie **15**
Paluzzi, Jimmy
  See Sponge
Pamer, John
  See Tsunami
Pandit G
  See Asian Dub Foundation
Pankow, James
  See Chicago
Panter, Horace
  See Specials, The
Pantera **13**
Papach, Leyna
  See Geraldine Fibbers
Papa Roach **30**
Papas Fritas **29**
Pappalardi, Felix
  See Mountain
Pappas, Tom
  See Superdrag
Parazaider, Walter
  See Chicago
Paris, Twila **16**
Park, Cary
  See Boy Howdy
Park, Larry
  See Boy Howdy
Parkening, Christopher **7**

Parker, Charlie **5**
Parker, Evan **28**
Parker, Graham **10**
Parker, Jeff
  See Tortoise
Parker, Kris
  See KRS-One
Parker, Leon **27**
Parker, Maceo **7**
Parker, Tom
  See Animals, The
Parker, William **31**
Parkin, Chad
  See Aquabats, The
Parks, Van Dyke **17**
Parnell, Lee Roy **15**
Parsons, Alan **12**
Parsons, Dave
  See Bush
Parsons, Gene
  See Byrds, The
Parsons, Gram **7**
  Also see Byrds, The
Parsons, Ted
  See Prong
Parsons, Tony
  See Iron Maiden
Partch, Harry **29**
Partington, Darren
  See 808 State
Parton, Dolly **24**
  Earlier sketch in CM **2**
Partridge, Andy
  See XTC
Parvo, Carpella
  See Rasputina
Pascale, Nina
  See Quickspace
Pasemaster, Mase
  See De La Soul
Pash, Jim
  See Surfaris, The
Pasillas, Jose
  See Incubus
Pass, Joe **15**
Passons, Michael
  See Avalon
Pastorius, Jaco
  See Weather Report
Paterson, Alex
  See Orb, The
Patinkin, Mandy **20**
  Earlier sketch CM **3**
Patrick, Richard
  See Filter
Patti, Sandi **7**
Pattinson, Les
  See Echo and the Bunnymen
Patton, Antwan "Big Boi"
  See OutKast
Patton, Charley **11**
Patton, Mike
  See Faith No More
Paul, Alan
  See Manhattan Transfer, The
Paul, Les **2**
Paul, Prince **29**
  Also see Gravediggaz
Paul III, Henry
  See BlackHawk
Paul, Vinnie
  See Pantera
Paulo, Jr.
  See Sepultura
Paul Revere & The Raiders **30**
Paulus, Jean-Marie
  See Les Négresses Vertes

Pavarotti, Luciano **20**
  Earlier sketch in CM **1**
Pavement **14**
Pavia, John
  See Four Seasons, The
Paxton, Tom **5**
Payne, Bill
  See Little Feat
Payne, Dougie
  See Travis
Payne, Richard
  See Bluetones, The
Payne, Scherrie
  See Supremes, The
Payton, Denis
  See Dave Clark Five, The
Payton, Lawrence
  See Four Tops, The
Payton, Nicholas **27**
Pea, Planet
  See Len
Peacock, Olly
  See Gomez
Pearce, David
  See Flying Saucer Attack
Pearl, Minnie **3**
Pearl Jam **32**
  Earlier sketch in CM **12**
Pearls Before Swine **24**
Pearson, Dan
  See American Music Club
Peart, Neil
  See Rush
Pedersen, Chris
  See Monks of Doom
Pedersen, Herb
  See Desert Rose Band, The
Peduzzi, Larry
  See Roomful of Blues
Peebles, Ann **30**
Peek, Dan
  See America
Peeler, Ben
  See Mavericks, The
Peeples, Philip
  See Old 97's
Pegg, Dave
  See Fairport Convention
  Also see Jethro Tull
Pegrum, Nigel
  See Steeleye Span
Peligro, Darren H.
  See Dead Kennedys
Pelletier, Mike
  See Kilgore
Pence, Jeff
  See Blessid Union of Souls
Penderecki, Krzysztof **30**
Pendergrass, Teddy **3**
Pendleton, Brian
  See Pretty Things, The
Pengilly, Kirk
  See INXS
Peniston, CeCe **15**
Penn, Michael **4**
Penner, Fred **10**
Pennywise **27**
Pentangle **18**
Pentland, Patrick
  See Sloan
Pepper, Art **18**
Perahia, Murray **10**
Peretz, Jesse
  See Lemonheads, The
Pere Ubu **17**
Perez, Danilo **25**

Perez, Louie
  See Los Lobos
Perkins, Carl **9**
Perkins, John
  See XTC
Perkins, Percell
  See Five Blind Boys of Alabama
Perkins, Stephen
  See Porno for Pyros
Perkins, Steve
  See Jane's Addiction
Perko, Lynn
  See Imperial Teen
Perlman, Itzhak **2**
Perlman, Marc
  See Jayhawks, The
Pernice, Bob
  See Pernice Brothers
Pernice, Joe
  See Pernice Brothers
  Also see Scud Mountain Boys
Pernice Brothers **33**
Peron, Jean-Hervé
  See Faust
Perry, Brendan
  See Dead Can Dance
Perry, Doane
  See Jethro Tull
Perry, Joe
  See Aerosmith
Perry, John G.
  See Caravan
Perry, Phil **24**
Perry, Steve
  See Cherry Poppin' Daddies
Perry, Steve
  See Journey
Perry, Virgshawn
  See Artifacts
Persson, Nina
  See Cardigans
Peter, Paul & Mary **4**
Peters, Bernadette **27**
  Earlier sketch in CM **7**
Peters, Dan
  See Mudhoney
Peters, Joey
  See Grant Lee Buffalo
Peters, Mike
  See Alarm
Petersen, Chris
  See Front Line Assembly
Peterson, Debbi
  See Bangles, The
Peterson, Dick
  See Kingsmen, The
Peterson, Garry
  See Guess Who
Peterson, Michael **31**
Peterson, Oscar **11**
Peterson, Steve
  See Kingsmen, The
Peterson, Vicki
  See Bangles, The
Petersson, Tom
  See Cheap Trick
Petkovic, John
  See Cobra Verde
Petra **3**
Petratos, Dave
  See Romantics, The
Petri, Tony
  See Wendy O. Williams and The Plasmatics
Petrucci, John
  See Dream Theater
Pet Shop Boys **5**

Petty, Tom **9**
  Also see Tom Petty and the Heartbreakers
Pfaff, Kristen
  See Hole
Pfisterer, Alban
  See Love
Phair, Liz **14**
Phantom, Slim Jim
  See Stray Cats, The
Pharcyde, The **17**
Phelps, Doug
  See Kentucky Headhunters, The
Phelps, Ricky Lee
  See Kentucky Headhunters, The
Phife
  See Tribe Called Quest, A
Phil, Gary
  See Boston
Philbin, Greg
  See REO Speedwagon
Philips, Anthony
  See Genesis
Phillips, Chris
  See Squirrel Nut Zippers
Phillips, Chynna
  See Wilson Phillips
Phillips, Glenn
  See Toad the Wet Sprocket
Phillips, Grant Lee
  See Grant Lee Buffalo
Phillips, Harvey **3**
Phillips, John
  See Mamas and the Papas
Phillips, Mackenzie
  See Mamas and the Papas
Phillips, Mark
  See Down By Law
Phillips, Michelle
  See Mamas and the Papas
Phillips, Sam **5**
Phillips, Sam **12**
Phillips, Scott
  See Creed
Phillips, Shelley
  See Point of Grace
Phillips, Simon
  See Judas Priest
Phish **25**
  Earlier sketch in CM **13**
Phungula, Inos
  See Ladysmith Black Mambazo
Piaf, Edith **8**
Piazza, Sammy
  See Quicksilver Messenger Service
Piazzolla, Astor **18**
Picciotto, Joe
  See Fugazi
Piccolo, Greg
  See Roomful of Blues
Pickerel, Mark
  See Screaming Trees
Pickering, Michael
  See M People
Pickett, Wilson **10**
Pier, Fred
  See D.O.A.
Pierce, Charlie
  See Memphis Jug Band
Pierce, Jason
  See Spacemen 3
Pierce, Marvin "Merv"
  See Ohio Players
Pierce, Webb **15**
Pierson, Kate
  See B-52's, The
Pigface **19**

Pike, Donny
  See Lettermen, The
Pike, Gary
  See Lettermen, The
Pike, Jim
  See Lettermen, The
Pilatus, Rob
  See Milli Vanilli
Pilson, Jeff
  See Dokken
Pinch
  See Damned, The
Pincock, Dougie
  See Battlefield Band, The
Pinder, Michael
  See Moody Blues, The
Pine, Courtney
  See Soul II Soul
Pinkerton, Peyton
  See Pernice Brothers
Pink Floyd 2
Pinkus, Jeff
  See Butthole Surfers
Pinnick, Doug
  See King's X
Piper, Jeff "Freedom"
  See Workhorse Movement, The
Pires, Maria João 26
Pirner, Dave
  See Soul Asylum
Pirroni, Marco
  See Siouxsie and the Banshees
Pisarri, Bill
  See Flying Luttenbachers, The
Pixies, The 21
Pizzicato Five 18
Placebo 27
Plakas, Dee
  See L7
Plant, Robert 2
  Also see Led Zeppelin
Platters, The 25
Pleasant, Alvin
  See Carter Family, The
Ploog, Richard
  See Church, The
Plouf, Scott
  See Built to Spill
Plough, John
  See Northwoods Improvisers
P.M. Dawn 11
P.O.D. 33
Pogues, The 6
Pohom, Chris
  See D.O.A.
Poi Dog Pondering 17
Poindexter, Buster
  See Johansen, David
Pointer, Anita
  See Pointer Sisters, The
Pointer, Bonnie
  See Pointer Sisters, The
Pointer, June
  See Pointer Sisters, The
Pointer, Ruth
  See Pointer Sisters, The
Pointer Sisters, The 9
Point of Grace 21
Poison 11
Poison Ivy
  See Rorschach, Poison Ivy
Poland, Chris
  See Megadeth
Polce, Tom
  See Letters to Cleo
Polci, Gerry
  See Four Seasons, The

Police, The 20
Pollard, Jim
  See Guided By Voices
Pollard, Robert, Jr.
  See Guided By Voices
Pollard, Russ
  See Sebadoh
Pollock, Courtney Adam
  See Aquabats, The
Pollock, Emma
  See Delgados, The
Polwart, Karine
  See Battlefield Band, The
Polygon Window
  See Aphex Twin
Pomus, Doc
  See Doc Pomus
Pontiere, Ernie
  See Lettermen, The
Ponty, Jean-Luc 8
  Also see Mahavishnu Orchestra
Pop, Iggy 23
  Earlier sketch in CM 1
Pop, Jimmy
  See Bloodhound Gang, The
Popoff, A. Jay
  See Lit
Popoff, Jeremy
  See Lit
Popper, John
  See Blues Traveler
Porno for Pyros 31
Porter, Cole 10
Porter, George, Jr.
  See Meters, The
Porter, Glenn
  See Alkaline Trio
Porter, Jody
  See Fountains of Wayne
Porter, Tiran
  See Doobie Brothers, The
Portishead 22
Portman, Dr. Frank
  See Mr. T Experience, The
Portman-Smith, Nigel
  See Pentangle
Portnoy, Mike
  See Dream Theater
Portz, Chuck
  See Turtles, The
Posa, Dylan
  See Flying Luttenbachers, The
Posdnuos
  See De La Soul
Post, Louise
  See Veruca Salt
Post, Mike 21
Potter, Janna
  See Avalon
Potts, Sean
  See Chieftains, The
Povey, John
  See Pretty Things, The
Powderfinger 33
Powell, Baden 23
Powell, Billy
  See Lynyrd Skynyrd
Powell, Bud 15
Powell, Cozy
  See Emerson, Lake & Palmer/Powell
Powell, Kobie
  See US3
Powell, Mac
  See Third Day
Powell, Owen
  See Catatonia

Powell, Paul
  See Aztec Camera
Powell, William
  See O'Jays, The
Powers, Kid Congo
  See Congo Norvell
  Also see Cramps, The
Poynton, Bobby
  See Lettermen, The
Prater, Dave
  See Sam and Dave
Pratt, Awadagin 19
Pratt, Guy
  See Killing Joke
Prefab Sprout 15
Presidents of the United States of
  America, The 34
Presley, Elvis 1
Preston, Aaron
  See Chainsaw Kittens, The
Preston, Leroy
  See Asleep at the Wheel
Preston, Mark
  See Lettermen, The
Prestwich, Steven
  See Cold Chisel
Pretenders, The 8
Pretty Things, The 26
Previn, André 15
Price, Alan
  See Animals, The
Price, Kelly 34
Price, Leontyne 6
Price, Lloyd 25
Price, Louis
  See Temptations, The
Price, Mark
  See Archers of Loaf
Price, Martin
  See 808 State
Price, Ray 11
Price, Rick
  See Electric Light Orchestra
Pride, Charley 4
Priest, Gretchen
  See Ceili Rain
Priest, Maxi 20
Prima, Louis 18
Primal Scream 14
Primettes, The
  See Supremes, The
Primrose, Neil
  See Travis
Primus 11
Prince 14
  Earlier sketch in CM 1
Prince, Prairie
  See Journey
Prince, Vivian
  See Pretty Things, The
Prince Be
  See P.M. Dawn
Prine, John 7
Prior, Maddy
  See Steeleye Span
Priske, Rich
  See Matthew Good Band
Proclaimers, The 13
Prodigy 22
Professor Longhair 6
Promise Ring, The 28
Prong 23
Propatier, Joe
  See Silver Apples
Propellerheads 26
Propes, Duane
  See Little Texas

Prophet, Chuck **32**
Prosper, Marvin
　See Baha Men
Prout, Brian
　See Diamond Rio
Pryce, Guto
　See Super Furry Animals
Psychedelic Furs **23**
Ptacek, Rainer
　See Giant Sand
Pte
　See Indigenous
Public Enemy **4**
Puccini, Giacomo **25**
Puente, Tito **14**
Puff Daddy
　See Combs, Sean "Puffy"
Pullen, Don **16**
Pulp **18**
Pulsford, Nigel
　See Bush
Pusey, Clifford "Moonie"
　See Steel Pulse
Pyle, Andy
　See Kinks, The
Pyle, Artemis
　See Lynyrd Skynyrd
Pyle, Chris
　See Royal Trux
Pyle, Pip
　See Gong
Pyro, Howie
　See D Generation
Q-Ball, D.J.
　See Bloodhound Gang, The
Q-Tip
　See Tribe Called Quest, A
Quaife, Peter
　See Kinks, The
Quasi **24**
Quasthoff, Thomas **26**
Quaye, Finley **30**
Queen **6**
Queen Ida **9**
Queen Latifah **24**
　Earlier sketch in CM **6**
Queens, Hollis
　See Boss Hog
Queens of the Stone Age **31**
Queensryche **8**
Querfurth, Carl
　See Roomful of Blues
Quicksilver Messenger Service **23**
Quickspace **30**
Quinn, Mickey
　See Supergrass
Qureshi, Ustad Alla Rakha **29**
Raaymakers, Boy
　See Willem Breuker Kollektief
Rabbitt, Eddie **24**
　Earlier sketch in CM **5**
Rabin, Trevor
　See Yes
Race, Tony
　See Felt
Radalj, Rod
　See Hoodoo Gurus
Radiohead **24**
Raekwon
　See Wu-Tang Clan
Raffi **8**
Rage Against the Machine **18**
Raheem
　See Geto Boys, The
Rainey, Ma **22**
Rainey, Sid
　See Compulsion

Rainford, Simone
　See All Saints
Rainwater, Keech
　See Lonestar
Raitt, Bonnie **23**
　Earlier sketch in CM **3**
Rakim
　See Eric B. and Rakim
Raleigh, Don
　See Squirrel Nut Zippers
Ralphs, Mick
　See Bad Company
Ralphs, Mick
　See Mott the Hoople
Ralph Sharon Quartet **26**
Rammstein **25**
Ramone, C. J.
　See Ramones, The
Ramone, Dee Dee
　See Ramones, The
Ramone, Joey
　See Ramones, The
Ramone, Johnny
　See Ramones, The
Ramone, Marky
　See Ramones, The
Ramone, Ritchie
　See Ramones, The
Ramone, Tommy
　See Ramones, The
Ramones, The **9**
Rampage, Randy
　See D.O.A.
Rampal, Jean-Pierre **6**
Ramsay, Andy
　See Stereolab
Ranaldo, Lee
　See Sonic Youth
Rancid **29**
Randall, Bobby
　See Sawyer Brown
Raney, Jerry
　See Beat Farmers
Rangell, Andrew **24**
Ranglin, Ernest
　See Skatalites, The
Ranken, Andrew
　See Pogues, The
Rankin, Cookie
　See Rankins, The
Rankin, Heather
　See Rankins, The
Rankin, Jimmy
　See Rankins, The
Rankin, John Morris
　See Rankins, The
Rankin, Raylene
　See Rankins, The
Ranking, Roger
　See English Beat, The
Rankins, The **24**
Rapp, Marcelo D.
　See Soulfly
Rapp, Tom
　See Pearls Before Swine
Rarebell, Herman
　See Scorpions, The
Rasboro, Johnathen
　See Silk
Rasputina **26**
Rasted, Søren
　See Aqua
Ratcliffe, Simon
　See Basement Jaxx
Rathbone, Andie
　See Mansun
Ravel, Maurice **25**

Raven, Paul
　See Killing Joke
Raven, Paul
　See Prong
Rawls, Lou **19**
Ray, Amy
　See Indigo Girls
Ray, East Bay
　See Dead Kennedys
Raybon, Marty
　See Shenandoah
Ray Condo and His Ricochets **26**
Raye, Collin **16**
Raymonde, Simon
　See Cocteau Twins, The
Raynor, Scott
　See Blink 182
Rea, Chris **12**
Rea, Matt "Myron"
　See Workhorse Movement, The
Read, John
　See Specials, The
Reader, Joel
　See Mr. T Experience, The
Reagon, Bernice Johnson
　See Sweet Honey in the Rock
Redbone, Leon **19**
Redding, Otis **5**
Redd Kross **20**
Reddy, Helen **9**
Red Hot Chili Peppers **29**
　Earlier sketch in CM **7**
Redman, Dewey **32**
Redman, Don
　See McKinney's Cotton Pickers
Redman, Joshua **25**
　Earlier sketch in CM **12**
Redpath, Jean **1**
Redus, Richard
　See Captain Beefheart and His Magic Band
Reece, Chris
　See Social Distortion
Reed, Brett
　See Rancid
Reed, Herbert
　See Platters, The
Reed, Jimmy **15**
Reed, Lou **16**
　Earlier sketch in CM **1**
　Also see Velvet Underground, The
Reef **24**
Rees, John
　See Men at Work
Reese, Della **13**
Reese, Joey
　See Wendy O. Williams and The Plasmatics
Reeves, Dianne **16**
Reeves, Jim **10**
Reeves, Lois
　See Martha and the Vandellas
Reeves, Martha **4**
　Also see Martha and the Vandellas
Refoy, Mark
　See Spacemen 3
Regan, Julianne
　See Gene Loves Jezebel
Reich, Steve **8**
Reichel, Hans **29**
Reid, Alan
　See Battlefield Band, The
Reid, Charlie
　See Proclaimers, The
Reid, Christopher
　See Kid 'n Play
Reid, Craig
　See Proclaimers, The

Reid, Delroy "Junior"
See Black Uhuru
Reid, Don
See Statler Brothers, The
Reid, Ellen Lorraine
See Crash Test Dummies
Reid, Harold
See Statler Brothers, The
Reid, Janet
See Black Uhuru
Reid, Jim
See Jesus and Mary Chain, The
Reid, Lou
See Seldom Scene, The
Reid, Vernon 2
Also see Living Colour
Reid, William
See Jesus and Mary Chain, The
Reifman, William
See KMFDM
Reilly, Vini
See Durutti Column, The
Reinhardt, Django 7
Reininger, Blaine
See Tuxedomoon
Reiser, Dan
See Marcy Playground
Reitzell, Brian
See Redd Kross
Relf, Keith
See Yardbirds, The
R.E.M. 25
Earlier sketch in CM 5
Renaud, Hélène
See Swell
Renbourn, John
See Pentangle
Rendall, Kimble
See Hoodoo Gurus
Reno, Ronnie
See Osborne Brothers, The
REO Speedwagon 23
Replacements, The 7
Republica 20
Residents, The 14
Restless Heart 12
Revell, Adrian
See Jamiroquai
Revere, Paul
See Paul Revere & The Raiders
Reverend Horton Heat 19
Rex
See Pantera
Reyes, Andre
See Gipsy Kings, The
Reyes, Canut
See Gipsy Kings, The
Reyes, Nicolas
See Gipsy Kings, The
Reynolds, Nick
See Kingston Trio, The
Reynolds, Robert
See Mavericks, The
Reynolds, Sheldon
See Earth, Wind and Fire
Reznor, Trent 13
Also see Nine Inch Nails
Rhodes, Nick
See Duran Duran
Rhodes, Philip
See Gin Blossoms
Rhodes, Todd
See McKinney's Cotton Pickers
Rhone, Sylvia 13
Rhys, Gruff
See Super Furry Animals
Ribot, Marc 30

Rice, Chris 25
Rich, Buddy 13
Rich, Charlie 3
Rich, John
See Lonestar
Richard, Cliff 14
Richard, Zachary 9
Richards, Aled
See Catatonia
Richards, Edward
See Shamen, The
Richards, Keith 11
Also see Rolling Stones, The
Richards, Lee
See Godsmack
Richardson, Geoffrey
See Caravan
Richardson, Kevin
See Backstreet Boys
Richey, Kim 20
Richie, Lionel 2
Also see Commodores, The
Richling, Greg
See Wallflowers, The
Richman, Jonathan 12
Richrath, Gary
See REO Speedwagon
Rick, Dave
See King Missile
Ricochet 23
Riders in the Sky 33
Riebling, Scott
See Letters to Cleo
Rieckermann, Ralph
See Scorpions, The
Riedel, Oliver
See Rammstein
Rieflin, William
See Ministry
Also see Pigface
Rieger, Andrew
See Elf Power
Rieu, André 26
Riles, Kelly
See Velocity Girl
Riley, Herman
See Lavay Smith and Her Red Hot Skillet
Lickers
Riley, Kristian
See Citizen King
Riley, Teddy "Street" 14
See Blackstreet
Riley, Terry 32
Riley, Timothy Christian
See Tony! Toni! Toné!
Rimes, LeAnn 19
Rippon, Steve
See Lush
Ritchie, Brian
See Violent Femmes
Ritchie, Jean 4
Ritchie, John Simon
See Sid Vicious
Ritchie, Robert
See Kid Rock
Ritenour, Lee 7
Rivers, Sam
See Limp Bizkit
Rivers, Sam 29
Rizzo, Joe
See D Generation
Rizzo, Peter
See Gene Loves Jezebel
Roach, Max 12
Roback, David
See Mazzy Star

Robbins, Charles David
See BlackHawk
Robbins, J
See Jawbox
Robbins, Marty 9
Roberson, LaTavia
See Destiny's Child
Roberts, Brad
See Crash Test Dummies
Roberts, Brad
See Gwar
Roberts, Dan
See Crash Test Dummies
Roberts, Jason
See Asleep at the Wheel
Roberts, Ken
See Charm Farm
Roberts, Marcus 6
Roberts, Mark
See Catatonia
Roberts, Nathan
See Flaming Lips
Roberts, Paul
See Stranglers, The
Robertson, Allison
See Donnas, The
Robertson, Brian
See Motörhead
Also see Thin Lizzy
Robertson, Ed
See Barenaked Ladies
Robertson, Robbie 2
Also see Band, The
Robertson, Rowan
See VAST
Robeson, Paul 8
Robi, Paul
See Platters, The
Robie, Milton
See Memphis Jug Band
Robillard, Duke 2
Also see Roomful of Blues
Robinson, Arnold
See Nylons, The
Robinson, Chris
See Black Crowes, The
Robinson, Cynthia
See Sly & the Family Stone
Robinson, David
See Cars, The
Robinson, Dawn
See En Vogue
Robinson, Louise
See Sweet Honey in the Rock
Robinson, Prince
See McKinney's Cotton Pickers
Robinson, R. B.
See Soul Stirrers, The
Robinson, Rich
See Black Crowes, The
Robinson, Romye "Booty Brown"
See Pharcyde, The
Robinson, Smokey 1
Robinson, Tony "Gad"
See Aswad
Roche, Maggie
See Roches, The
Roche, Suzzy
See Roches, The
Roche, Terre
See Roches, The
Roches, The 18
Rock, D.
See Len
Rockapella 34
Rockenfield, Scott
See Queensryche

Rocker, Lee
   See Stray Cats, The
Rockett, Rikki
   See Poison
Rockin' Dopsie **10**
Rodford, Jim
   See Kinks, The
Rodgers, Jimmie **3**
Rodgers, Nile **8**
Rodgers, Paul
   See Bad Company
Rodgers, Richard **9**
Rodney, Red **14**
Rodriguez, Omar
   See At The Drive-In
Rodriguez, Rico
   See Skatalites, The
   Also see Specials, The
Rodriguez, Sal
   See War
Roe, Marty
   See Diamond Rio
Roeder, Jason
   See Neurosis
Roeder, Klaus
   See Kraftwerk
Roeser, Donald
   See Blue Oyster Cult
Roeser, Eddie "King"
   See Urge Overkill
Roessler, Kira
   See Black Flag
Roger, Ranking
   See English Beat, The
Rogers, Dan
   See Bluegrass Patriots
Rogers, Kenny **1**
Rogers, Norm
   See Jayhawks, The
Rogers, Norm
   See Cows, The
Rogers, Roy **24**
   Earlier sketch in CM **9**
Rogers, Willie
   See Soul Stirrers, The
Rogerson, Roger
   See Circle Jerks
Rojas, Luciano Andrés
   See La Ley
Roland, Dean
   See Collective Soul
Roland, Ed
   See Collective Soul
Rolie, Gregg
   See Journey
Rolling Stones, The **23**
   Earlier sketch in CM **3**
Rollins, Henry **11**
   Also see Black Flag
Rollins, Sonny **7**
Rollins, Winston
   See Jamiroquai
Romanelli, Chris "Junior"
   See Wendy O. Williams and The Plasmatics
Romano, Ruben
   See Fu Manchu
Romantics, The **34**
Rombola, Tony
   See Godsmack
Romich, Jr., Tom
   See Caustic Resin
Romm, Ronald
   See Canadian Brass, The
Roney, Wallace **33**
Ronson, Mick
   See Mott the Hoople
Ronstadt, Linda **2**

Roomful of Blues **7**
Root, James
   See Slipknot
Roots, The **27**
Roper, Dee Dee
   See Salt-N-Pepa
Roper, Reese
   See Five Iron Frenzy
Roper, Todd
   See Cake
Rorschach, Poison Ivy
   See Cramps, The
Rosas, Cesar
   See Los Lobos
Rose, Axl
   See Guns n' Roses
Rose, Felipe
   See Village People, The
Rose, Johanna Maria
   See Anonymous 4
Rose, Michael
   See Black Uhuru
Rosen, Gary
   See Rosenshontz
Rosen, Peter
   See War
Rosenblatt, Joel
   See Spyro Gyra
Rosenshontz **9**
Rosenthal, Jurgen
   See Scorpions, The
Rosenthal, Phil
   See Seldom Scene, The
Rosenworcel, Brian
   See Guster
Ross, Annie
   See Lambert, Hendricks and Ross
Ross, Diana **1**
   Also see Supremes, The
Ross, Malcolm
   See Aztec Camera
Rossdale, Gavin
   See Bush
Rossi, John
   See Roomful of Blues
Rossington, Gary
   See Lynyrd Skynyrd
Rossy, Jose
   See Weather Report
Rostill, John
   See Shadows, The
Rostropovich, Mstislav **17**
Roswell, Stewart "Rosco"
   See Spacemen 3
Rota, Nino **13**
Roth, C. P.
   See Blessid Union of Souls
Roth, David Lee **1**
   Also see Van Halen
Roth, Gabrielle **26**
Roth, Ulrich
   See Scorpions, The
Rothchild, Dan
   See Tonic
Rother, Michael
   See Neu!
Rotheray, Dave
   See Beautiful South
Rotsey, Martin
   See Midnight Oil
Rotten, Johnny
   See Lydon, John
   Also see Sex Pistols, The
Rourke, Andy
   See Killing Joke
Rourke, Andy
   See Smiths, The

Rowberry, Dave
   See Animals, The
Rowe, Dwain
   See Restless Heart
Rowe, Simon
   See Mojave 3
Rowland, Kelly
   See Destiny's Child
Rowlands, Bruce
   See Fairport Convention
Rowlands, Euros
   See Gorky's Zygotic Mynci
Rowlands, Tom
   See Chemical Brothers
Rowntree, Dave
   See Blur
Roxette **23**
Roy, Jimmy
   See Ray Condo and His Ricochets
Royal Crown Revue **33**
Royal Trux **29**
Rube Waddell **29**
Rubin, Mark
   See Bad Livers, The
Rubin, Rick **9**
Rubinstein, Arthur **11**
Rucker, Darius
   See Hootie and the Blowfish
Rudd, Phillip
   See AC/DC
Rudd, Roswell **28**
Rue, Caroline
   See Hole
Ruffin, David **6**
   Also see Temptations, The
Ruffin, Tamir
   See Dru Hill
Ruffy, Dave
   See Aztec Camera
   Also see Waterboys, The
Ruley, Yuri
   See MxPx
Run
   See Run DMC
Rundgren, Todd **11**
Run DMC **25**
   Earlier sketch in CM **4**
RuPaul **20**
Rusby, Kate **29**
Rush **8**
Rush, Otis **12**
Rushakoff, Harry
   See Concrete Blonde
Rushlow, Tim
   See Little Texas
Russell, Alecia
   See Sounds of Blackness
Russell, Alistair
   See Battlefield Band, The
Russell, Graham
   See Air Supply
Russell, Hal
   See Flying Luttenbachers, The
Russell, John
   See Steppenwolf
Russell, Mark **6**
Russell, Mike
   See Shudder to Think
Russell, Pee Wee **25**
Russell, Tom **26**
Russo, Jeff
   See Tonic
Rusted Root **26**
Rutherford, Mike
   See Genesis
   Also see Mike & the Mechanics

Rutherford, Paul
　See Frankie Goes To Hollywood
Rutmanis, Kevin
　See Cows, The
Rutsey, John
　See Rush
Ryan, David
　See Lemonheads, The
Ryan, Mark
　See Quicksilver Messenger Service
Ryan, Mick
　See Dave Clark Five, The
Ryan, Pat "Taco"
　See Asleep at the Wheel
Rybska, Agnieszka
　See Rasputina
Ryder, Mitch **23**
　Earlier sketch in CM **11**
Ryland, Jack
　See Three Dog Night
Rzeznik, Johnny
　See Goo Goo Dolls, The
Sabo, Dave
　See Bon Jovi
Sade **2**
Sadier, Laetitia
　See Stereolab
Saffery, Anthony
　See Cornershop
Saffron
　See Republica
Sage, Danny
　See D Generation
Sager, Carole Bayer **5**
Sahm, Doug **30**
　Also see Texas Tornados, The
Sainte-Marie, Buffy **11**
Saint Etienne **28**
Saint-Saëns, Camille **25**
Sakamoto, Ryuichi **19**
Salazar, Arion
　See Third Eye Blind
Salem, Kevin **32**
Salerno-Sonnenberg, Nadja **3**
Saliers, Emily
　See Indigo Girls
Salisbury, Peter
　See Verve, The
Salmon, Michael
　See Prefab Sprout
Saloman, Nick
　See Bevis Frond
Salonen, Esa-Pekka **16**
Salt-N-Pepa **6**
Saltzman, Jeff
　See Sunset Valley
Saluzzi, Dino **23**
Salv
　See Carter USM
Sam and Dave **8**
Sambora, Richie **24**
　Also see Bon Jovi
Sampson, Doug
　See Iron Maiden
Sams, Dean
　See Lonestar
Samuels, Dave
　See Spyro Gyra
Samuelson, Gar
　See Megadeth
Samwell-Smith, Paul
　See Yardbirds, The
Sanborn, David **28**
　Earlier sketch in CM **1**
Sanchez, Michel
　See Deep Forest

Sanctuary, Gary
　See Aztec Camera
Sanders, Pharoah **28**
　Earlier sketch in CM **16**
Sanders, Ric
　See Fairport Convention
Sanders, Steve
　See Oak Ridge Boys, The
Sandler, Adam **19**
Sandman, Mark
　See Morphine
Sandoval, Arturo **15**
Sandoval, Hope
　See Mazzy Star
Sandoval, Sonny
　See P.O.D.
Sands, Aaron
　See Jars of Clay
Sanford, Gary
　See Aztec Camera
Sangare, Oumou **22**
Sanger, David
　See Asleep at the Wheel
Santamaria, Mongo **28**
Santana, Carlos **19**
　Earlier sketch in CM **1**
Santiago, Herman
　See Frankie Lymon and The Teenagers
Santiago, Joey
　See Pixies, The
Saraceno, Blues
　See Poison
Sargent, Gray
　See Ralph Sharon Quartet
Sasaki, Mamiko
　See Pulp
Satchell, Clarence "Satch"
　See Ohio Players
Satie, Erik **25**
Satriani, Joe **4**
Savage, Paul
　See Delgados, The
Savage, Rick
　See Def Leppard
Savage, Scott
　See Jars of Clay
Savage Garden **32**
Sawyer, Phil
　See Spencer Davis Group
Sawyer Brown **27**
　Earlier sketch in CM **13**
Saxa
　See English Beat, The
Saxon, Stan
　See Dave Clark Five, The
Scaccia, Mike
　See Ministry
Scaggs, Boz **12**
Scaggs, Shawn
　See Atomic Fireballs, The
Scallions, Brett
　See Fuel
Scalzo, Tony
　See Fastball
Scanlan, Deirdre
　See Solas
Scanlon, Craig
　See Fall, The
Scanlon, Phil
　See Idlewild
Scannell, Matt
　See Vertical Horizon
Scarface
　See Geto Boys, The
Scharin, Doug **32**
Schayer, Bobby
　See Bad Religion

Scheidt, Dean Norman
　See Lane, Fred
Schelhaas, Jan
　See Camel
　Also see Caravan
Schellenbach, Kate
　See Luscious Jackson
Schemel, Patty
　See Hole
Schenker, Michael
　See Scorpions, The
Schenker, Rudolf
　See Scorpions, The
Schenkman, Eric
　See Spin Doctors
Schermie, Joe
　See Three Dog Night
Scherpenzeel, Ton
　See Camel
Schickele, Peter **5**
Schifrin, Lalo **29**
Schlesinger, Adam
　See Fountains of Wayne
Schlitt, John
　See Petra
Schloss, Zander
　See Circle Jerks, The
Schmelling, Johannes
　See Tangerine Dream
Schmid, Daniel
　See Cherry Poppin' Daddies
Schmidt, Irmin
　See Can
Schmit, Timothy B.
　See Eagles, The
Schmoovy Schmoove
　See Digital Underground
Schneider, Christoph
　See Rammstein
Schneider, Florian
　See Kraftwerk
Schneider, Fred III
　See B-52's, The
Schneider, Robert
　See Apples in Stereo
Schneider, Stefan
　See To Rococo Rot
Schnier, Al
　See moe.
Schnitzler, Conrad
　See Tangerine Dream
Schock, Gina
　See Go-Go's, The
Schoenbeck, Scott
　See Promise Ring, The
Scholten, Jim
　See Sawyer Brown
Scholz, Tom
　See Boston
Schon, Neal
　See Journey
Schönfeldt, Fredrik
　See Wannadies, The
Schönfeldt, Stefan
　See Wannadies, The
Schramm, Dave
　See Yo La Tengo
Schrody, Erik
　See House of Pain
　Also see Everlast
Schroer, Oliver **29**
Schroyder, Steve
　See Tangerine Dream
Schulman, Mark
　See Foreigner
Schulz, Guenter
　See KMFDM

Schulzberg, Robert
  See Placebo
Schulze, Klaus
  See Tangerine Dream
Schuman, Tom
  See Spyro Gyra
Schuman, William 10
Schütze, Paul 32
Schuur, Diane 6
Schwartz, Dorothy
  See Chordettes, The
Schwartz, Will
  See Imperial Teen
Schwartzberg, Alan
  See Mountain
Sclavunos, Jim
  See Congo Norvell
Scofield, John 7
Scorpions, The 12
Scott, Andrew
  See Sloan
Scott, George
  See Five Blind Boys of Alabama
Scott, Howard
  See War
Scott, Jimmy 14
Scott, Mike
  See Waterboys, The
Scott, Ronald Belford "Bon"
  See AC/DC
Scott, Sherry
  See Earth, Wind and Fire
Scott, Tony 32
Scott-Heron, Gil 13
Screaming Trees 19
Scruggs, Earl 3
Scruggs, Randy 28
Scud Mountain Boys 21
Seal 14
Seales, Jim
  See Shenandoah
Seals, Brady
  See Little Texas
Seals, Dan 9
Seals, Jim
  See Seals & Crofts
Seals & Crofts 3
Seaman, Ken
  See Bluegrass Patriots
Sears, Pete
  See Jefferson Starship
Sebadoh 26
Sebesky, Don 33
Secada, Jon 13
Secrest, Wayne
  See Confederate Railroad
Sed, Billy
  See Giant Sand
Sedaka, Neil 4
Seeger, Peggy 25
Seeger, Pete 4
  Also see Weavers, The
Seger, Bob 15
Seger, David
  See Giant Sand
Segovia, Andres 6
Seidel, Martie
  See Dixie Chicks
Selberg, Shannon
  See Cows, The
Seldom Scene, The 4
Selena 16
Selway, Phil
  See Radiohead
Semisonic 32
Sen Dog
  See Cypress Hill

Senior, Milton
  See McKinney's Cotton Pickers
Senior, Russell
  See Pulp
Sensi
  See Soul II Soul
Sepultura 12
Seraphine, Daniel
  See Chicago
Sergeant, Will
  See Echo and the Bunnymen
Sermon, Erick
  See EPMD
Sete, Bola 26
Setzer, Brian 32
  Also see Stray Cats, The
Setzer, Philip
  See Emerson String Quartet
Severin, Steven
  See Siouxsie and the Banshees
Severinsen, Doc 1
Sex Pistols, The 5
Sexsmith, Ron 27
Sexton, Chad
  See 311
Seymour, Neil
  See Crowded House
Shabalala, Ben
  See Ladysmith Black Mambazo
Shabalala, Headman
  See Ladysmith Black Mambazo
Shabalala, Jockey
  See Ladysmith Black Mambazo
Shabalala, Joseph
  See Ladysmith Black Mambazo
Shabo, Eric
  See Atomic Fireballs, The
Shade, Will
  See Memphis Jug Band
Shadow, DJ 19
Shadows, The 22
Shaffer, James
  See Korn
Shaffer, Paul 13
Shaggy 19
Shaggy 2 Dope
  See Insane Clown Possee
Shai 23
Shakespeare, Robbie
  See Sly and Robbie
Shakira 33
Shakur, Tupac
  See 2Pac
Shallenberger, James
  See Kronos Quartet
Shamen, The 23
Shane, Bob
  See Kingston Trio, The
Shanice 14
Shankar, Ravi 9
Shannon, Del 10
Shannon, Sarah
  See Velocity Girl
Shannon, Sharon
  See Waterboys, The
Shanté 10
Shapiro, Jim
  See Veruca Salt
Shapiro, Lee
  See Four Seasons, The
Shapps, Andre
  See Big Audio Dynamite
Sharon, Lois & Bram 6
Sharon, Ralph
  See Ralph Sharon Quartet
Sharp, Dave
  See Alarm

Sharp, Laura
  See Sweet Honey in the Rock
Sharpe, Matt
  See Weezer
Sharpe, Trevor
  See Minty
Sharrock, Chris
  See Lightning Seeds
Sharrock, Sonny 15
Shaw, Adrian
  See Bevis Frond
Shaw, Artie 8
Shaw, Martin
  See Jamiroquai
Shaw, Robert 32
Shaw, Woody 27
Shea, Tom
  See Scud Mountain Boys
Shearer, Harry
  See Spinal Tap
Shearing, George 28
Sheehan, Bobby
  See Blues Traveler
Sheehan, Fran
  See Boston
Sheep on Drugs 27
Sheik, Duncan 32
Sheila E. 3
Shellenberger, Allen
  See Lit
Shelley, Peter
  See Buzzcocks, The
Shelley, Steve
  See Sonic Youth
Shenandoah 17
Shenandoah, Joanne 33
Shepard, Kevin
  See Tonic
Shepherd, Brad
  See Hoodoo Gurus
Shepherd, Hunter "Ben"
  See Soundgarden
Shepherd, John
  See Northwoods Improvisers
Shepherd, Kenny Wayne 22
Sheppard, Rodney
  See Sugar Ray
Sherba, John
  See Kronos Quartet
Sherinian, Derek
  See Dream Theater
Sherman, Jack
  See Red Hot Chili Peppers, The
Sherwood, Adrian 31
Shields, Kevin
  See My Bloody Valentine
Shihad 34
Shilton, Paul
  See Quickspace
Shines, Johnny 14
Shipp, Matthew 31
Shirelles, The 11
Shirley, Danny
  See Confederate Railroad
Shively, William
  See Big Mountain
Shives, Andrew
  See Fear Factory
Shocked, Michelle 4
Shock G
  See Digital Underground
Shocklee, Hank 15
Shogren, Dave
  See Doobie Brothers, The
Shonen Knife 13
Shontz, Bill
  See Rosenshontz

Shore, Pete
  See Boss Hog
Shorter, Wayne **5**
  Also see Weather Report
Shovell
  See M People
Shuck, Ryan
  See Orgy
Shudder to Think **20**
Shuffield, Joey
  See Fastball
Siberry, Jane **6**
Sice
  See Boo Radleys, The
Sidelnyk, Steve
  See Aztec Camera
Sidney, Hilarie
  See Apples in Stereo
Siebels, Jon
  See Eve 6
Siebenberg, Bob
  See Supertramp
Siebert, Chris
  See Lavay Smith and Her Red Hot Skillet
  Lickers
Siegal, Janis
  See Manhattan Transfer, The
Signorelli, Mark
  See Swell
Sigur Rós **31**
Sikes, C. David
  See Boston
Silk **26**
Sills, Beverly **5**
Silva, Kenny Jo
  See Beaver Brown Band, The
Silver, Horace **19**
Silver, Josh
  See Type O Negative
Silver Apples **23**
Silverchair **20**
Silveria, David
  See Korn
Simeon
  See Silver Apples
Simien, Terrance **12**
Simins, Russell
  See Jon Spencer Blues Explosion
Simmons, Gene
  See Kiss
Simmons, Joe "Run"
  See Run DMC
Simmons, Patrick
  See Doobie Brothers, The
Simmons, Russell **7**
Simmons, Trinna
  See Spearhead
Simms, Nick
  See Cornershop
Simon, Carly **22**
  Earlier sketch in CM **4**
Simon, Paul **16**
  Earlier sketch in CM **1**
  Also see Simon and Garfunkel
Simonal, Wilson **33**
Simon and Garfunkel **24**
Simone, Nina **11**
Simonon, Paul
  See Clash, The
Simons, Ed
  See Chemical Brothers
Simple Minds **21**
Simpson, Denis
  See Nylons, The
Simpson, Derrick "Duckie"
  See Black Uhuru

Simpson, Gerald
  See 808 State
Simpson, Jessica **34**
Simpson, Mel
  See US3
Simpson, Mike
  See Dust Brothers
Simpson, Ray
  See Village People, The
Simpson, Rose
  See Incredible String Band
Sims, David William
  See Jesus Lizard
Sims, Matt
  See Citizen King
Sims, Neil
  See Catherine Wheel
Sin, Will
  See Shamen, The
Sinatra, Frank **23**
  Earlier sketch in CM **1**
Sinclair, David
  See Camel
  Also see Caravan
Sinclair, Gord
  See Tragically Hip, The
Sinclair, Richard
  See Camel
  Also see Caravan
Sinfield, Peter
  See King Crimson
Singer, Eric
  See Kiss
  Also see Black Sabbath
Singh, Talvin
  See Massive Attack
Singh, Tjinder
  See Cornershop
Sioux, Siouxsie
  See Siouxsie and the Banshees
Siouxsie and the Banshees **8**
Sir Mix-A-Lot **14**
Sirois, Joe
  See Mighty Mighty Bosstones
Sir Rap-A-Lot
  See Geto Boys, The
Sisqó **34**
Sister Hazel **34**
Siverton
  See Specials, The
Sixpence None the Richer **26**
Sixx, Nikki
  See Mötley Crüe
Sixx, Roger
  See Less Than Jake
Size, Roni **31**
Skaggs, Ricky **5**
  Also see Country Gentlemen, The
Skatalites, The **18**
Skeete, Beverley
  See Bill Wyman & the Rhythm Kings
Skeoch, Tommy
  See Tesla
Sketch
  See 23 Skidoo
Skiba, Matt
  See Alkaline Trio
Skill, Mike
  See Romantics, The
Skillings, Muzz
  See Living Colour
Skinny Puppy **17**
Sklamberg, Lorin
  See Klezmatics, The
Skoob
  See Das EFX

Skopelitis, Nicky
  See Golden Palominos
Skunk Anansie **27**
Slash
  See Guns n' Roses
Slater, Rodney
  See Bonzo Dog Doo-Dah Band
Slayer **10**
Sleater-Kinney **20**
Sledd, Dale
  See Osborne Brothers, The
Sledge, Percy **15**
Sledge, Robert
  See Ben Folds Five
Slesinger, Bruce "Ted"
  See Dead Kennedys
Slichter, Jake
  See Semisonic
Slick, Grace **33**
  Also see Jefferson Airplane
Slick Rick **27**
Slijngaard, Ray
  See 2 Unlimited
Slipknot **30**
Sloan **28**
Sloan, Eliot
  See Blessid Union of Souls
Slocum, Matt
  See Sixpence None the Richer
Slovak, Hillel
  See Red Hot Chili Peppers, The
Sly, Randy "Ginger"
  See Atomic Fireballs, The
Sly and Robbie **13**
Sly & the Family Stone **24**
Small, Heather
  See M People
Small, Phil
  See Cold Chisel
Smalley, Dave
  See Down By Law
Smalls, Derek
  See Spinal Tap
Smart, Terence
  See Butthole Surfers
Smart II, N.D.
  See Mountain
Smash, Chas
  See Madness
Smashing Pumpkins **13**
Smash Mouth **27**
Smear, Pat
  See Foo Fighters
Smelly
  See NOFX
Smith, Adrian
  See Iron Maiden
Smith, Allen
  See Lavay Smith and Her Red Hot Skillet
  Lickers
Smith, Bessie **3**
Smith, Brad
  See Blind Melon
Smith, Chad
  See Red Hot Chili Peppers, The
Smith, Charles
  See Kool & the Gang
Smith, Chas
  See Cobra Verde
Smith, Clifford
  See Method Man
Smith, Curt
  See Tears for Fears
Smith, Debbie
  See Curve
  Also see Echobelly
Smith, Elliott **28**

Smith, Fran
  See Hooters
Smith, Fred
  See Blondie
Smith, Fred
  See MC5, The
Smith, Fred
  See Television
Smith, Garth
  See Buzzcocks, The
Smith, James "Smitty"
  See Three Dog Night
Smith, Jimmy **30**
Smith, Jocelyn B. **30**
Smith, Joe
  See McKinney's Cotton Pickers
Smith, Keely **29**
Smith, Kevin
  See dc Talk
Smith, Lavay
  See Lavay Smith and Her Red Hot Skillet
  Lickers
Smith, "Legs" Larry
  See Bonzo Dog Doo-Dah Band
Smith, Mark E.
  See Fall, The
Smith, Martin
  See Delirious?
Smith, Michael W. **11**
Smith, Mike
  See Paul Revere & The Raiders
Smith, Mike
  See Dave Clark Five, The
Smith, Parrish
  See EPMD
Smith, Patti **17**
  Earlier sketch in CM **1**
Smith, Rick
  See Underworld
Smith, Robert
  See Spinners, The
Smith, Robert
  See Cure, The
  Also see Siouxsie and the Banshees
Smith, Shawn
  See Brad
Smith, Simon
  See Wedding Present, The
Smith, Smitty
  See Three Dog Night
Smith, Steve
  See Journey
Smith, Stewart
  See Delirious?
Smith, Tommy **28**
Smith, Tweed
  See War
Smith, Wendy
  See Prefab Sprout
Smith, Will **26**
  Also see DJ Jazzy Jeff and the Fresh Prince
Smith, Zachary
  See Loud Family, The
Smithereens, The **14**
Smiths, The **3**
Smog **28**
Smyth, Gilli
  See Gong
Smyth, Joe
  See Sawyer Brown
Sneed, Floyd Chester
  See Three Dog Night
Snoop Doggy Dogg **17**
Snouffer, Alex "Alex St. Clair"
  See Captain Beefheart and His Magic Band
Snow **23**

Snow, Don
  See Squeeze
Snow, Hank **29**
Snow, Phoebe **4**
Snyder, Richard "Midnight Hatsize Snyder"
  See Captain Beefheart and His Magic Band
Soan, Ashley
  See Del Amitri
Sobule, Jill **20**
Social Distortion **27**
  Earlier sketch in CM **19**
Solal, Martial **4**
Solas **34**
Sollenberger, Isobel
  See Bardo Pond
Soloff, Lew
  See Blood, Sweat and Tears
Solowka, Peter
  See Wedding Present, The
Solti, Georg **13**
Sommer, Günter "Baby" **31**
Sondheim, Stephen **8**
Sonefeld, Jim
  See Hootie and the Blowfish
Sonic Youth **26**
  Earlier sketch in CM **9**
Sonnenberg, Nadja Salerno
  See Salerno-Sonnenberg, Nadja
Sonni, Jack
  See Dire Straits
Sonnier, Jo-El **10**
Sonny and Cher **24**
Son Volt **21**
Sorum, Matt
  See Cult, The
Sosa, Mercedes **3**
Sosna, Rudolf
  See Faust
Soucie, Michael
  See Surfin' Pluto
Soul Asylum **10**
Soul Coughing **21**
Soulfly **33**
Soul Stirrers, The **11**
Soul II Soul **17**
Soundgarden **6**
Sounds of Blackness **13**
Sousa, John Philip **10**
Southerland, Bill
  See Kilgore
Spacehog **29**
Spacemen 3 **31**
Spampinato, Joey
  See NRBQ
Spampinato, Johnny
  See NRBQ
Spann, Otis **18**
Sparks **18**
Sparks, Brett
  See Handsome Family, The
Sparks, Chris "Cornbread"
  See Workhorse Movement, The
Sparks, Donita
  See L7
Sparks, Rennie
  See Handsome Family, The
Spear, Roger Ruskin
  See Bonzo Dog Doo-Dah Band
Spearhead **19**
Spears, Britney **28**
Special Ed **16**
Specials, The **21**
Spector, Phil **4**
Spector, Ronnie **28**
Speech
  See Arrested Development

Speiser, Jerry
  See Men at Work
Spellman, Jim
  See Velocity Girl
Spence, Alexander "Skip"
  See Jefferson Airplane
  Also see Moby Grape
Spence, Cecil
  See Israel Vibration
Spence, Skip
  See Spence, Alexander "Skip"
Spencer, Jeremy
  See Fleetwood Mac
Spencer, Jim
  See Dave Clark Five, The
Spencer, Jon
  See Boss Hog
  Also see Jon Spencer Blues Explosion
Spencer, Thad
  See Jayhawks, The
Spencer Davis Group **19**
Sperske, Aaron
  See Pernice Brothers
Spice Girls **22**
Spillane, Scott
  See Neutral Milk Hotel
Spinal Tap **8**
Spin Doctors **14**
Spindt, Don
  See Aqua Velvets
Spinners, The **21**
Spirit **22**
Spiteri, Sharleen
  See Texas
Spitz, Dan
  See Anthrax
Spitz, Dave
  See Black Sabbath
Sponge **18**
Spongetones, The **34**
Spoon **34**
Spoons, Sam
  See Bonzo Dog Doo-Dah Band
Spring, Keith
  See NRBQ
Springfield, Dusty **20**
Springfield, Rick **9**
Spring Heel Jack **30**
Springsteen, Bruce **25**
  Earlier sketch in CM **6**
Sproule, Daithi
  See Altan
Sprout, Tobin
  See Guided By Voices
Spyro Gyra **34**
Squeeze **5**
Squire, Chris
  See Yes
Squire, John
  See Stone Roses, The
Squires, Rob
  See Big Head Todd and the Monsters
Squirrel Nut Zippers **20**
Stacey, Peter "Spider"
  See Pogues, The
Stacy, Jeremy
  See Aztec Camera
Staehely, Al
  See Spirit
Staehely, J. Christian
  See Spirit
Stafford, Jimmy
  See Train
Stafford, Jo **24**
Stahl, Franz
  See Foo Fighters
Staind **31**

Staley, Layne
  See Alice in Chains
Staley, Tom
  See NRBQ
Stallings, Ron
  See Lavay Smith and Her Red Hot Skillet
  Lickers
Stanier, John
  See Helmet
Stanisic, Ched
  See Cobra Verde
Stanley, Bob
  See Saint Etienne
Stanley, Ian
  See Tears for Fears
Stanley, Paul
  See Kiss
Stanley, Ralph 5
Stansfield, Lisa 9
Stanshall, Vivian
  See Bonzo Dog Doo-Dah Band
Staples, Mavis 13
Staples, Neville
  See Specials, The
Staples, Pops 11
Stapp, Scott
  See Creed
Starcrunch
  See Man or Astroman?
Starker, Janos 32
Starkey, Kathryn La Verne
  See Starr, Kay
Starkey, Richard
  See Starr, Ringo
Starks, Tia Juana
  See Sweet Honey in the Rock
Starling, John
  See Seldom Scene, The
Starr, Kay 27
Starr, Mike
  See Alice in Chains
Starr, Ringo 24
  Earlier sketch in CM 10
  Also see Beatles, The
Starship
  See Jefferson Airplane
Statler Brothers, The 8
Stax, John
  See Pretty Things, The
Stead, David
  See Beautiful South
Steady
  See Minty
Steaks, Chuck
  See Quicksilver Messenger Service
Stebbins, Jone
  See Imperial Teen
Steel, John
  See Animals, The
Steel, Richard
  See Spacehog
Steele, Billy
  See Sounds of Blackness
Steele, David
  See English Beat, The
  Also see Fine Young Cannibals
Steele, Davy
  See Battlefield Band, The
Steele, Jeffrey
  See Boy Howdy
Steele, Michael
  See Bangles, The
Steele, Peter
  See Type O Negative
Steeleye Span 19
Steel Pulse 14

Steely Dan 29
  Earlier sketch in CM 5
Steen, Scott
  See Royal Crown Revue
Stefani, Gwen
  See No Doubt
Stefansson, Baldur
  See Gus Gus
Steier, Rick
  See Warrant
Stein, Andy
  See Commander Cody and His Lost Planet
  Airmen
Stein, Chris
  See Blondie
Stein, Hal
  See Lavay Smith and Her Red Hot Skillet
  Lickers
Stein, Laura
  See Pernice Brothers
Steinberg, Lewis
  See Booker T. & the M.G.'s
Steinberg, Sebastian
  See Soul Coughing
Steinhardt, Robby
  See Kansas
Stephenson, Van Wesley
  See BlackHawk
Steppenwolf 20
Sterban, Richard
  See Oak Ridge Boys, The
Stereolab 18
Stereo MC's 34
Stereophonics 29
Sterling, Jay
  See Love
Sterling, Lester
  See Skatalites, The
Stern, Isaac 7
Stern, Leni 29
Stern, Mike 29
Steve
  See Carter USM
Steve
  See Fun Lovin' Criminals
Stevens, Cat 3
Stevens, Ray 7
Stevens, Roger
  See Blind Melon
Stevens, Vol
  See Memphis Jug Band
Stevenson, Bill
  See Black Flag
Stevenson, Don
  See Moby Grape
Stevenson, James
  See Gene Loves Jezebel
Steward, Pat
  See Odds
Stewart, Bill
  See Lavay Smith and Her Red Hot Skillet
  Lickers
Stewart, Dave
  See Eurythmics
Stewart, Derrick "Fatlip"
  See Pharcyde, The
Stewart, Freddie
  See Sly & the Family Stone
Stewart, Ian
  See Rolling Stones, The
Stewart, Jamie
  See Cult, The
Stewart, John
  See Kingston Trio, The
Stewart, Larry
  See Restless Heart

Stewart, Rex
  See McKinney's Cotton Pickers
Stewart, Robert
  See Lavay Smith and Her Red Hot Skillet
  Lickers
Stewart, Rod 20
  Earlier sketch in CM 2
  Also see Faces, The
Stewart, Sylvester
  See Sly & the Family Stone
Stewart, Tommy
  See Godsmack
Stewart, Tyler
  See Barenaked Ladies
Stewart, Vaetta
  See Sly & the Family Stone
Stewart, William
  See Third World
Stewart, Winston "Metal"
  See Mystic Revealers
St. Hubbins, David
  See Spinal Tap
Stiff, Jimmy
  See Jackyl
Stills, Stephen 5
  See Buffalo Springfield
  Also see Crosby, Stills, and Nash
Sting 19
  Earlier sketch in CM 2
  Also see Police, The
Stinson, Bob
  See Replacements, The
Stinson, Tommy
  See Replacements, The
Stipe, Michael
  See Golden Palominos
  Also see R.E.M.
St. James, Rebecca 26
St. John, Mark
  See Kiss
St. Marie, Buffy
  See Sainte-Marie, Buffy
St. Nicholas, Nick
  See Steppenwolf
Stockman, Shawn
  See Boyz II Men
Stockwood, Kim 26
Stoeckel, Steve
  See Spongetones, The
Stoll
  See Clannad
  Also see Big Mountain
Stoller, Mike
  See Leiber and Stoller
Stoltz, Brian
  See Neville Brothers, The
Stoltzman, Richard 24
Stonadge, Gary
  See Big Audio Dynamite
Stone, Curtis
  See Highway 101
Stone, Doug 10
Stone, Kim
  See Spyro Gyra
Stone, Sly 8
Stone Roses, The 16
Stone Temple Pilots 14
Stookey, Paul
  See Peter, Paul & Mary
Story, Liz 2
Story, The 13
Stotts, Richie
  See Wendy O. Williams and The Plasmatics
Stradlin, Izzy
  See Guns n' Roses
Strain, Sammy
  See O'Jays, The

Strait, George **5**
Stranglers, The **31**
Stratton, Dennis
  See Iron Maiden
Strauss, Richard **25**
Stravinsky, Igor **21**
Straw, Syd **18**
  Also see Golden Palominos
Stray Cats, The **11**
Strayhorn, Billy **13**
Street, Richard
  See Temptations, The
Streisand, Barbra **2**
Strickland, Keith
  See B-52's, The
String Cheese Incident, The **34**
Stringer, Gary
  See Reef
Strummer, Joe
  See Clash, The
Strykert, Ron
  See Men at Work
Stryper **2**
Stuart, Mark
  See Audio Adrenaline
Stuart, Marty **9**
Stuart, Michael
  See Love
Stuart, Peter
  See Dog's Eye View
Stubbs, Levi
  See Four Tops, The
Sturr, Jimmy **33**
St. Werner, Jan
  See Mouse On Mars
Styne, Jule **21**
Styrene, Poly
  See X-Ray Spex
Sub Commander Ras I Zulu
  See Spearhead
Subdudes, The **18**
Sublime **19**
Such, Alec John
  See Bon Jovi
Suede **20**
Sugarcubes, The **10**
Sugar Ray **22**
Suicidal Tendencies **15**
Sulley, Suzanne
  See Human League, The
Sullivan, Jacqui
  See Bananarama
Sullivan, Jeff
  See Drivin' N' Cryin'
Sullivan, Kirk
  See 4Him
Summer, Donna **12**
Summer, Mark
  See Turtle Island String Quartet
Summers, Andy **3**
  Also see Police, The
Summers, Bill
  See Los Hombres Calientes
Sumner, Bernard
  See Joy Division
  Also see New Order
Sundays, The **20**
Sundholm, Norm
  See Kingsmen, The
Sun-J
  See Asian Dub Foundation
Sunny Day Real Estate **28**
Sunnyland Slim **16**
Sun Ra **27**
  Earlier sketch in CM **5**
Sunset Valley **31**
Superchunk **29**

Super DJ Dmitry
  See Deee-lite
Superdrag **23**
Super Furry Animals **28**
Supergrass **30**
Supertramp **25**
Supremes, The **6**
Suranovitch, George
  See Love
Sure!, Al B. **13**
Surfaris, The **23**
Surfin' Pluto **24**
Sutcliffe, Stu
  See Beatles, The
Sutherland, Joan **13**
Suzuki, Kenji "Damo"
  See Can
Sveinsson, Kjartan
  See Sigur Rós
Svenigsson, Magnus
  See Cardigans
Svensson, Peter
  See Cardigans
Svigals, Alicia
  See Klezmatics, The
Swanson, Dave
  See Cobra Verde
Swarbrick, Dave
  See Fairport Convention
Sweat, Keith **13**
Sweet, Matthew **9**
Sweet, Michael
  See Stryper
Sweet, Robert
  See Stryper
Sweethearts of the Rodeo **12**
Sweet Honey In The Rock **26**
  Earlier sketch in CM **1**
Swell **31**
Swervedriver **31**
Swing, DeVante
  See Jodeci
SWV **14**
Sykes, John
  See Whitesnake
Sykes, Roosevelt **20**
Sylvain, Sylvain
  See New York Dolls
Sylvian, David **27**
Tabac, Tony
  See Joy Division
Tabor, Ty
  See King's X
Tackett, Fred
  See Little Feat
Tacuma, Jamaaladeen
  Golden Palominos
Tadlock, Tom
  See Tuxedomoon
Taff
  See Killing Joke
TAFKAP (The Artist Formerly Known as Prince)
  See Prince
Taggart, Jeremy
  See Our Lady Peace
Tait, Chris
  See Fixx, The
Tait, Michael
  See dc Talk
Tajima, Takao
  See Pizzicato Five
Taj Mahal **6**
Takac, Robby
  See Goo Goo Dolls, The
Takahashi, Maki
  See Blonde Redhead

Takanami
  See Pizzicato Five
Take 6 **6**
Takeda, Clint
  See Bardo Pond
Takemitsu, Toru **6**
Takizawa, Taishi
  See Ghost
Talbot, Ivor
  See Divine Comedy, The
Talbot, Joby
  See Divine Comedy, The
Talbot, John Michael **6**
Talcum, Joe Jack
  See Dead Milkmen
Talking Heads **1**
Talk Talk **19**
Tamia **34**
Tampa Red **25**
Tan Dun **33**
Tandy, Richard
  See Electric Light Orchestra
Tangerine Dream **12**
Taree, Aerle
  See Arrested Development
Tate, Buddy **33**
Tate, Geoff
  See Queensryche
Tatum, Art **17**
Taupin, Bernie **22**
Taylor, Aaron
  See MC Eiht
Taylor, Andy
  See Duran Duran
Taylor, Billy **13**
Taylor, Cecil **9**
Taylor, Chad
  See Live
Taylor, Corey
  See Slipknot
Taylor, Courtney
  See Dandy Warhols
Taylor, Dan
  See Silver Apples
Taylor, Dave
  See Pere Ubu
Taylor, Dick
  See Rolling Stones, The
Taylor, Earl
  See Country Gentlemen, The
Taylor, Isaiah
  See Baha Men
Taylor, James **25**
  Earlier sketch in CM **2**
Taylor, James "J.T."
  See Kool & the Gang
Taylor, John
  See Duran Duran
Taylor, Johnnie
  See Soul Stirrers, The
Taylor, Kate **30**
Taylor, Koko **10**
Taylor, Leroy
  See Soul Stirrers, The
Taylor, Melvin
  See Ventures, The
Taylor, Mick
  See Rolling Stones, The
  Also see Pretty Things, The
Taylor, Philip "Philthy Animal"
  See Motörhead
Taylor, Roger
  See Duran Duran
Taylor, Roger Meadows
  See Queen
Taylor, Teresa
  See Butthole Surfers

Taylor, Steve
  See Ray Condo and His Ricochets
Taylor, Steve **26**
Taylor, Zola
  See Platters, The
Teagarden, Jack **10**
Tears for Fears **6**
Technotronic **5**
Teel, Jerry
  See Boss Hog
Teenage Fanclub **13**
Te Kanawa, Kiri **2**
Television **17**
Teller, Al **15**
Temirkanov, Yuri **26**
Tempesta, John
  See White Zombie
Temple, Johnny
  See Girls Against Boys
Temple, Michelle
  See Pere Ubu
Temptations, The **3**
Tench, Benmont
  See Tom Petty and the Heartbreakers
Tennant, Neil
  See Pet Shop Boys
10,000 Maniacs **3**
Tepper, Jeff "Morris"
  See Captain Beefheart and His Magic Band
Terfel, Bryn **31**
Terminator X
  See Public Enemy
Terrell **32**
Terrell, Jean
  See Supremes, The
Terrie
  See Ex, The
Terry, Boyd
  See Aquabats, The
Terry, Clark **24**
Tesh, John **20**
Tesla **15**
Texas **27**
Texas Tornados, The **8**
Thacher, Jeff
  See Rockapella
Thacker, Rocky
  See Shenandoah
Thain, Gary
  See Uriah Heep
Thatcher, Jon
  See Delirious?
Thayil, Kim
  See Soundgarden
Theaker, Drachen
  See Love
Theremin, Leon **19**
The The **15**
They Might Be Giants **7**
Thibaudet, Jean-Yves **24**
Thielemans, Toots **13**
Thievery Corporation **31**
Thi-Lihn Le
  Also see Golden Palominos
Thin Lizzy **13**
Third Day **34**
Third Eye Blind **25**
Third World **13**
Thirsk, Jason
  See Pennywise
Thistlethwaite, Anthony
  See Waterboys, The
Thomas, Alex
  See Earth, Wind and Fire
Thomas, David
  See Take 6

Thomas, David
  See Pere Ubu
Thomas, David Clayton
  See Clayton-Thomas, David
Thomas, Dennis "D.T."
  See Kool & the Gang
Thomas, George "Fathead"
  See McKinney's Cotton Pickers
Thomas, Irma **16**
Thomas, John
  See Captain Beefheart and His Magic Band
Thomas, Mickey
  See Jefferson Starship
Thomas, Olice
  See Five Blind Boys of Alabama
Thomas, Ray
  See Moody Blues, The
Thomas, Richard
  See Jesus and Mary Chain, The
Thomas, Rob
  See Matchbox 20
Thomas, Rozonda "Chilli"
  See TLC
Thompson, Chester
  See Weather Report
Thompson, Danny
  See Pentangle
Thompson, Dennis
  See MC5, The
Thompson, Dougie
  See Supertramp
Thompson, Lee
  See Madness
Thompson, Les
  See Nitty Gritty Dirt Band, The
Thompson, Mayo
  See Pere Ubu
Thompson, Mick
  See Slipknot
Thompson, Paul
  See Concrete Blonde
Thompson, Porl
  See Cure, The
Thompson, Richard **7**
  Also see Fairport Convention
  Also see Golden Palominos
Thompson, Rudi
  See X-Ray Spex
Thomson, Kristin
  See Tsunami
Thoranisson, Biggi
  See Gus Gus
Thorn, Christopher
  See Blind Melon
Thorn, Stan
  See Shenandoah
Thorn, Tracey
  See Everything But The Girl
  Also see Massive Attack
Thornalley, Phil
  See Cure, The
Thornbury, Lee
  See Supertramp
Thorne, Rob
  See Spongetones, The
Thornhill, Leeroy
  See Prodigy
Thornton, Big Mama **18**
Thornton, Kevin "KT"
  See Color Me Badd
Thornton, Teri **28**
Thornton, Willie Mae
  See Thornton, Big Mama
Thorogood, George **34**
Threadgill, Henry **9**
3-D
  See Massive Attack

Three Dog Night **5**
311 **20**
Throwing Muses **15**
Thünder, Lüpüs
  See Bloodhound Gang, The
Thunders, Johnny
  See New York Dolls
Tichy, John
  See Commander Cody and His Lost Planet Airmen
Tickner, George
  See Journey
Tiffany **4**
Tijuana No! **32**
Tikaram, Tanita **9**
Tilbrook, Glenn
  See Squeeze
Tiller, Jay
  See Frogs, The
Tiller, Mary
  See Anointed
Tilley, Sandra
  See Martha and the Vandellas
Tillis, Mel **7**
Tillis, Pam **25**
  Earlier sketch in CM **8**
Tilson Thomas, Michael **24**
Timberlake, Justin
  See 'N Sync
Timbuk 3 **3**
Timmins, Margo
  See Cowboy Junkies, The
Timmins, Michael
  See Cowboy Junkies, The
Timmins, Peter
  See Cowboy Junkies, The
Timmons, Jeff
  See 98 Degrees
Timms, Sally
  See Mekons, The
Tinsley, Boyd
  See Dave Matthews Band
Tippin, Aaron **12**
Tipton, Glenn
  See Judas Priest
TLC **15**
Toad the Wet Sprocket **13**
Toback, Jeremy
  See Brad
Tobias, Jesse
  See Red Hot Chili Peppers
Tobin, Amon **32**
Todd, Andy
  See Republica
Todesco, Milo
  See Down By Law
Tolhurst, Laurence
  See Cure, The
Tolland, Bryan
  See Del Amitri
Toller, Dan
  See Allman Brothers, The
Tolliver, T.C.
  See Wendy O. Williams and The Plasmatics
Tolson, Peter
  See Pretty Things, The
Toma, Andi
  See Mouse On Mars
Tom Petty and the Heartbreakers **26**
Tone-Loc **3**
Tong, Winston
  See Tuxedomoon
Tonic **32**
Tontoh, Frank
  See Aztec Camera
Tony! Toni! Toné! **12**

Tony K
  See Roomful of Blues
Tony Williams **6**
Too $hort **16**
Toogood, Jon
  See Shihad
Toohey, Dan
  See Guided By Voices
Took, Steve Peregrine
  See T. Rex
Tool **21**
Toomey, Jenny
  See Tsunami
Topham, Anthony "Top"
  See Yardbirds, The
Topper, Sharon
  See God Is My Co-Pilot
Tork, Peter
  See Monkees, The
Torme, Mel **4**
To Rococo Rot **31**
Torrence, Dean
  See Jan & Dean
Torres, Hector "Tico"
  See Bon Jovi
Torry, Richard
  See Minty
Tortoise **32**
Toscanini, Arturo **14**
Tosh, Peter **3**
Toth, Ed
  See Vertical Horizon
Toure, Ali Farka **18**
Tourish, Ciaran
  See Altan
Toussaint, Allen **11**
Towner, Ralph **22**
  Also see Oregon
Townes, Jeffery
  See DJ Jazzy Jeff and the Fresh Prince
Towns, Efrem
  See Dirty Dozen Brass Band
Townshend, Pete **1**
  Also see Who, The
Traa
  See P.O.D.
Traffic **19**
Tragically Hip, The **18**
Train **33**
Trammell, Mark
  See Greater Vision
Trautmann, Gene
  See Queens of the Stone Age
Travers, Brian
  See UB40
Travers, Mary
  See Peter, Paul & Mary
Travis **29**
Travis, Abby
  See Elastica
Travis, Merle **14**
Travis, Michael
  See String Cheese Incident, The
Travis, Randy **9**
Traynor, Kevin
  See Divine Comedy, The
Treach
  See Naughty by Nature
Treadmill Trackstar **21**
Tremonti, Mark
  See Creed
Trevi, Gloria **29**
T. Rex **11**
Tribe Called Quest, A **8**
Trick Daddy **28**
Tricky **18**
  Also see Massive Attack

Trimble, Vivian
  See Luscious Jackson
Trimm, Rex
  See Cherry Poppin' Daddies
Tripp, Art "Art Marimba"
  See Captain Beefheart and His Magic Band
Tristano, Lennie **30**
Tritsch, Christian
  See Gong
Tritt, Travis **7**
Trojanowski, Mark
  See Sister Hazel
Trotter, Kera
  See C + C Music Factory
Trucks, Butch
  See Allman Brothers, The
Trugoy the Dove
  See De La Soul
Trujillo, Robert
  See Suicidal Tendencies
Truman, Dan
  See Diamond Rio
Trynin, Jen **21**
Trytten, Lorre Lynn
  See Willem Breuker Kollektief
Tsunami **21**
Tubb, Ernest **4**
Tubridy, Michael
  See Chieftans, The
Tucker, Corin
  See Sleater-Kinney
Tucker, Jim
  See Turtles, The
Tucker, Moe
  See Velvet Underground, The
Tucker, Sophie **12**
Tucker, Tanya **3**
Tucker, William
  See Ministry
  Also see Pigface
Tufnel, Nigel
  See Spinal Tap
Tull, Bruce
  See Scud Mountain Boys
Turbin, Neil
  See Anthrax
Turgon, Bruce
  See Foreigner
Turnage, Mark-Anthony **31**
Turnbull, Alex
  See 23 Skidoo
Turnbull, Johnny
  See 23 Skidoo
Turner, Big Joe **13**
Turner, Elgin "Masta Killa"
  See Wu-Tang Clan
Turner, Erik
  See Warrant
Turner, Ike
  See Turner, Ike and Tina
Turner, Ike and Tina **24**
Turner, Joe Lynn
  See Deep Purple
Turner, Mick
  See Dirty Three
Turner, Mike
  See Our Lady Peace
Turner, Roger **32**
Turner, Sonny
  See Platters, The
Turner, Steve
  See Mudhoney
Turner, Tina **29**
  Earlier sketch in CM **1**
  Also see Turner, Ike and Tina
Turpin, Will
  See Collective Soul

Turre, Steve **22**
Turtle Island String Quartet **9**
Turtles, The **29**
Tutton, Bill
  See Geraldine Fibbers
Tutuska, George
  See Goo Goo Dolls, The
Tuxedomoon **21**
Twain, Shania **17**
Twist, Nigel
  See Alarm
Twitty, Conway **6**
23, Richard
  See Front 242
23 Skidoo **31**
2Pac **17**
  Also see Digital Underground
2 Unlimited **18**
Tyagi, Paul
  See Del Amitri
Tyler, Steve
  See Aerosmith
Tyner, McCoy **7**
Tyner, Rob
  See MC5, The
Type O Negative **27**
Tyrese **34**
Tyson, Ian
  See Ian and Sylvia
Tyson, Ron
  See Temptations, The
UB40 **4**
Ulmer, James Blood **13**
Ulrich, Lars
  See Metallica
Ulvaeus, Björn
  See Abba
Um Romao, Dom
  See Weather Report
Underwood, Scott
  See Train
Underworld **26**
Ungerman, Bill
  See Royal Crown Revue
Unitt, Victor
  See Pretty Things, The
Unruh, N. U.
  See Einstürzende Neubauten
Uosikkinen, David
  See Hooters
Upshaw, Dawn **9**
Urge Overkill **17**
Uriah Heep **19**
Urlik, Ed
  See Down By Law
Usher **23**
US3 **18**
Utley, Adrian
  See Portishead
Utsler, Joseph
  See Insane Clown Possee
U2 **34**
  Earlier sketch in CM **12**
  Earlier sketch in CM **2**
Vaché Jr., Warren **22**
Vachon, Chris
  See Roomful of Blues
Vai, Steve **5**
  Also see Whitesnake
Valdès, Chucho **25**
Vale, Jerry **30**
Valens, Ritchie **23**
Valenti, Dino
  See Quicksilver Messenger Service
Valentin, Dave **33**
Valentine, Gary
  See Blondie

Valentine, Hilton
  See Animals, The
Valentine, Kathy
  See Go-Go's, The
Valentine, Rae
  See War
Valenzuela, Jesse
  See Gin Blossoms
Valley, Jim
  See Paul Revere & The Raiders
Valli, Frankie 10
  Also see Four Seasons, The
Vallier, Monte
  See Swell
Valory, Ross
  See Journey
Vandenburg, Adrian
  See Whitesnake
Vander Ark, Brad
  See Verve Pipe, The
Vander Ark, Brian
  See Verve Pipe, The
Vandermark, Ken 28
  Also see Flying Luttenbachers, The
van Dijk, Carol
  See Bettie Serveert
Vandross, Luther 24
  Earlier sketch in CM 2
Vanessa-Mae 26
Van Gelder, Nick
  See Jamiroquai
Vangelis 21
Van Halen 25
  Earlier sketch in CM 8
Van Halen, Alex
  See Van Halen
Van Halen, Edward
  See Van Halen
Van Helden, Armand 32
Van Hook, Peter
  See Mike & the Mechanics
Van Hove, Fred 30
Vanilla Ice 6
van Lieshout, Lars
  See Tuxedomoon
Van Rensalier, Darnell
  See Shai
Van Ronk, Dave 12
Van Shelton, Ricky 5
Van Vliet, Don "Captain Beefheart"
  See Captain Beefheart and His Magic Band
Van Zandt, Steven 29
Van Zandt, Townes 13
Van Zant, Johnny
  See Lynyrd Skynyrd
Van Zant, Ronnie
  See Lynyrd Skynyrd
Vasquez, Junior 16
VAST 34
Vaughan, Jimmie 24
  Also see Fabulous Thunderbirds, The
Vaughan, Sarah 2
Vaughan, Stevie Ray 1
Vazzano, Frank
  See Cobra Verde
Vedder, Eddie
  See Pearl Jam
Vega, Bobby
  See Quicksilver Messenger Service
Vega, Suzanne 3
Velasquez, Jaci 32
Velásquez, Jorge "Norja"
  See Tijuana No!
Velez, Gerardo
  See Spyro Gyra
Velocity Girl 23
Veloso, Caetano 28

Velvet Crush 28
Velvet Underground, The 7
Ventures, The 19
Verdecchio, Andy
  See Five Iron Frenzy
Verdurmen, Rob
  See Willem Breuker Kollektief
Verlaine, Tom
  See Television
Verta-Ray, Matt
  See Madder Rose
Vertical Horizon 33
Veruca Salt 20
Verve, The 18
Verve Pipe, The 20
Vettese, Peter-John
  See Jethro Tull
Vicious, Sid
  See Sex Pistols, The
  Also see Siouxsie and the Banshees
Vickers, Robert
  See Go-Betweens, The
Vickrey, Dan
  See Counting Crows
Victor, Tommy
  See Prong
Vienna Choir Boys 23
Vig, Butch 17
  Also see Garbage
Village People, The 7
Vincent, Gene 19
Vincent, Vinnie
  See Kiss
Vinnie
  See Naughty by Nature
Vinton, Bobby 12
Violent Femmes 12
Violent J
  See Insane Clown Posse
Virtue, Michael
  See UB40
Visser, Peter
  See Bettie Serveert
Vitamin C 33
Vito, Rick
  See Fleetwood Mac
Vitous, Mirslav
  See Weather Report
Voelz, Susan
  See Poi Dog Pondering
Vogt, Jeremy
  See Tonic
Voigl, Pete
  See Swell
Volk, Phil
  See Paul Revere & The Raiders
Vollenweider, Andreas 30
Volman, Mark
  See Turtles, The
Volodos, Arcadi 28
Volz, Greg
  See Petra
Von, Eerie
  See Danzig
Von, Jon
  See Mr. T Experience, The
Von Bohlen, Davey
  See Promise Ring, The
Von Frankenstein, Doyle Wolfgang
  See Misfits, The
von Karajan, Herbert 1
von Otter, Anne Sofie 30
von Trapp, Elisabeth 29
Votel, Freddy
  See Cows, The
Vox, Bono
  See U2

Vrenna, Chris
  See Nine Inch Nails
Vudi
  See American Music Club
Vynes, Adrian "Adi"
  See Swervedriver
Waaktaar, Pal
  See A-ha
Wachtel, Waddy 26
Waddell, Larry
  See Mint Condition
Wade, Adam
  See Shudder to Think
Wade, Adam
  See Jawbox
Wade, Chrissie
  See Alien Sex Fiend
Wade, Nik
  See Alien Sex Fiend
Wadenius, George
  See Blood, Sweat and Tears
Wadephal, Ralf
  See Tangerine Dream
Wagner, Kurt
  See Lambchop
Wagoner, Faidest
  See Soul Stirrers, The
Wagoner, Porter 13
Wahlberg, Donnie
  See New Kids on the Block
Wailer, Bunny 11
Wailing Souls 32
Wainwright III, Loudon 11
Wainwright, Rufus 29
Waits, Tom 27
  Earlier sketch in CM 12
  Earlier sketch in CM 1
Wakeling, David
  See English Beat, The
Wakeman, Rick 27
  Also see Yes
Walcott, Collin
  See Oregon
Walden, Narada Michael 14
Waldman, Clem
  See Swell
Waldroup, Jason
  See Greater Vision
Wales, Ashley
  See Spring Heel Jack
Walford, Britt
  See Breeders
Walker, Clay 20
Walker, Colin
  See Electric Light Orchestra
Walker, Don
  See Cold Chisel
Walker, Ebo
  See New Grass Revival, The
Walker, George 34
Walker, Jerry Jeff 13
Walker, Joe Louis 28
Walker, Junior 30
Walker, Mark
  See Oregon
Walker, Matt
  See Filter
Walker, T-Bone 5
Wall, Jeremy
  See Spyro Gyra
Wallace, Bennie 31
Wallace, Bill
  See Guess Who
Wallace, Ian
  See King Crimson
Wallace, Richard
  See Mighty Clouds of Joy, The

Wallace, Sippie **6**
Waller, Charlie
  See Country Gentlemen, The
Waller, Dave
  See Jam, The
Waller, Fats **7**
Wallflowers, The **20**
Wallinger, Karl **11**
  Also see Waterboys, The
Wallis, Larry
  See Motörhead
Walls, Chris
  See Dave Clark Five, The
Walls, Denise "Nee-C"
  See Anointed
Walls, Greg
  See Anthrax
Walsh, Joe **5**
  Also see Eagles, The
Walsh, Marty
  See Supertramp
Walsh, Steve
  See Kansas
Walsh, Tim
  See Brave Combo
Walter, Tommy
  See eels
Walter, Weasel
  See Flying Luttenbachers, The
Walters, Pat
  See Spongetones, The
Walters, Richard
  See Slick Rick
Walters, Robert "Patch"
  See Mystic Revealers
Walton, Mark
  See Giant Sand
Wanbdi
  See Indigenous
Wannadies, The **29**
War **14**
Ward, Andy
  See Bevis Frond
  Also see Camel
Ward, Bill
  See Black Sabbath
Ward, Jim
  See At The Drive-In
Ward, Michael
  See Wallflowers, The
Ward, Scooter
  See Cold
Ware, Martyn
  See Human League, The
Wareham, Dean
  See Galaxie 500
  Also see Luna
Warfield, William **33**
Wariner, Steve **18**
Warmling, Hans
  See Stranglers, The
Warner, Les
  See Cult, The
Warnes, Jennifer **3**
Warnick, Kim
  See Fastbacks, The
Warrant **17**
Warren, Brad
  See Warren Brothers, The
Warren, Brett
  See Warren Brothers, The
Warren, Diane **21**
Warren, George W.
  See Five Blind Boys of Alabama
Warren, Mervyn
  See Take 6
Warren Brothers, The **34**

Warren G **33**
Warwick, Clint
  See Moody Blues, The
Warwick, Dionne **2**
Was, David
  See Was (Not Was)
Was, Don **21**
  Also see Was (Not Was)
Was (Not Was) **6**
Wash, Martha
  See C + C Music Factory
Washington, Chester
  See Earth, Wind and Fire
Washington, Dinah **5**
Washington, Grover, Jr. **5**
Wasserman, Greg "Noodles"
  See Offspring
Waterboys, The **27**
Waters, Crystal **15**
Waters, Ethel **11**
Waters, Muddy **24**
  Earlier sketch in CM **4**
Waters, Roger
  See Pink Floyd
Watkins, Christopher
  See Cabaret Voltaire
Watkins, Tionne "T-Boz"
  See TLC
Watley, Jody **26**
  Earlier sketch in CM **9**
Watson, Doc **2**
Watson, Guy
  See Surfaris, The
Watson, Ivory
  See Ink Spots
Watt, Ben
  See Everything But The Girl
Watt, Mike **22**
  Also see fIREHOSE
  Also see Minutemen, The
Watters, Sam
  See Color Me Badd
Watts, Bari
  See Bevis Frond
Watts, Charlie
  See Rolling Stones, The
Watts, Eugene
  See Canadian Brass, The
Watts, Lou
  See Chumbawamba
Watts, Pete "Overend"
  See Mott the Hoople
Watts, Raymond
  See KMFDM
Watts, Todd
  See Emmet Swimming
Weather Report **19**
Weaver, Louie
  See Petra
Weavers, The **8**
Webb, Chick **14**
Webb, Jimmy **12**
Webb, Paul
  See Talk Talk
Webber, Andrew Lloyd
  See Lloyd Webber, Andrew
Webber, Mark
  See Pulp
Webster, Andrew
  See Tsunami
Wedding Present, The **28**
Wedgwood, Mike
  See Caravan
Wedren, Craig
  See Shudder to Think
Ween **30**
Weezer **20**

Wegelin, Aaron
  See Elf Power
Wehner, Marty
  See Lavay Smith and Her Red Hot Skillet
  Lickers
Weider, John
  See Animals, The
Weiland, Scott
  See Stone Temple Pilots
Weill, Kurt **12**
Weir, Bob
  See Grateful Dead, The
Weiss, Janet
  See Sleater-Kinney
  Also see Quasi
Weissman, Marco
  See Waterboys, The
Welch, Bob
  See Fleetwood Mac
Welch, Brian
  See Korn
Welch, Bruce
  See Shadows, The
Welch, Gillian **33**
Welch, Justin
  See Elastica
Welch, Mcguinness
  See Lords of Acid
Welch, Sean
  See Beautiful South
Welk, Lawrence **13**
Weller, Freddy
  See Paul Revere & The Raiders
Weller, Paul **14**
  Also see Jam, The
Wells, Bill **34**
Wells, Cory
  See Three Dog Night
Wells, Junior **17**
Wells, Kitty **6**
Welnick, Vince
  See Grateful Dead, The
Welsh, Alan
  See Aztec Camera
Welty, Ron
  See Offspring
Wenberg, Erik
  See Emmet Swimming
Wendy O. Williams and The Plasmatics **26**
Wenner, Niko
  See Swell
Werner, Mike
  See Handsome Family, The
Wertz, Jenn
  See Rusted Root
West, Brian
  See Cherry Poppin' Daddies
West, Dottie **8**
West, Leslie
  See Mountain
West, Steve
  See Pavement
Westerberg, Paul **26**
  Also see Replacements, The
Westlife **33**
Westman, Danny
  See Down By Law
Weston
  See Orb, The
Weston, Randy **15**
West-Oram, Jamie
  See Fixx, The
West Virginia Creeper
  See Commander Cody and His Lost Planet
  Airmen
Wetton, John
  See King Crimson

Wexler, Jerry **15**
Weymouth, Tina
  See Talking Heads
Wez
  See Carter USM
Whalen, Katharine
  See Squirrel Nut Zippers
Whalley, Dennis
  See Captain Beefheart and His Magic Band
Wharton, Dianaruthe
  See Sweet Honey in the Rock
Wheat, Brian
  See Tesla
Wheeler, Audrey
  See C + C Music Factory
Wheeler, Caron
  See Soul II Soul
Wheeler, Harriet
  See Sundays, The
Wheeler, Robert
  See Pere Ubu
Wheeler, Tim
  See Ash
Whelan, Bill **20**
Whelan, Gavan
  See James
Whitaker, Rodney **20**
Whitaker, Yolanda
  See Yo Yo
White, Alan
  See Yes
White, Alan
  See Oasis
White, Barry **6**
White, Billy
  See Dokken
White, Chris
  See Dire Straits
White, Clarence
  See Byrds, The
White, Dave
  See Warrant
White, Dennis
  See Charm Farm
White, Freddie
  See Earth, Wind and Fire
White, Jay
  See Chanticleer
White, Jim
  See Dirty Three
White, Karyn **21**
White, Lari **15**
White, Mark
  See Spin Doctors
White, Mark
  See Mekons, The
White, Maurice
  See Earth, Wind and Fire
White, Ralph
  See Bad Livers, The
White, Richard
  See Paul Revere & The Raiders
White, Robert
  See Paul Revere & The Raiders
White, Roland
  See Nashville Bluegrass Band
White, Verdine
  See Earth, Wind and Fire
White, Will
  See Propellerheads
Whitehead, Donald
  See Earth, Wind and Fire
Whiteman, Paul **17**
Whitesnake **5**
White Zombie **17**
Whitfield, Mark **18**

Whitford, Brad
  See Aerosmith
Whiting, Margaret **28**
Whitley, Chris **16**
Whitley, Keith **7**
Whitman, Slim **19**
Whittaker, Hudson **20**
Whitten, Chris
  See Dire Straits
Whittington, Melvan
  See Love
Whitwam, Barry
  See Herman's Hermits
Who, The **3**
Wichnewski, Stephen
  See Yo La Tengo
Wickham, Steve
  See Waterboys, The
Widenhouse, Je
  See Squirrel Nut Zippers
Wiedlin, Jane
  See Go-Go's, The
Wieneke, Paul
  See Loud Family, The
Wiggins, Dwayne
  See Tony! Toni! Toné!
Wiggins, Raphael
  See Tony! Toni! Toné!
Wiggs, Josephine
  See Breeders
Wiggs, Pete
  See Saint Etienne
Wikso, Ron
  See Foreigner
Wiksten, Pär
  See Wannadies, The
Wilborn, Dave
  See McKinney's Cotton Pickers
Wilbur, James "Jim"
  See Superchunk
Wilburn, Ishmael
  See Weather Report
Wilco **27**
Wilcox, Imani
  See Pharcyde, The
Wilde, Phil
  See 2 Unlimited
Wilder, Alan
  See Depeche Mode
Wilder, Philip
  See Chanticleer
Wildhorn, Frank **31**
Wildwood, Michael
  See D Generation
Wiley, Howard
  See Lavay Smith and Her Red Hot Skillet Lickers
Wilk, Brad
  See Rage Against the Machine
Wilkeson, Leon
  See Lynyrd Skynyrd
Wilkie, Chris
  See Dubstar
Wilkinson, Amanda
  See Wilkinsons, The
Wilkinson, Geoff
  See US3
Wilkinson, Keith
  See Squeeze
Wilkinson, Kevin
  See Waterboys, The
Wilkinson, Steve
  See Wilkinsons, The
Wilkinson, Tyler
  See Wilkinsons, The
Wilkinsons, The **30**
Willem Breuker Kollektief **28**

Williams, Andy **2**
Williams, Boris
  See Cure, The
Williams, Cliff
  See AC/DC
Williams, Dana
  See Diamond Rio
Williams, Dar **21**
Williams, Deniece **1**
Williams, Don **4**
Williams, Eric
  See Blackstreet
Williams, Fred
  See C + C Music Factory
Williams, Hank, Jr. **1**
Williams, Hank, Sr. **4**
Williams, James "Diamond"
  See Ohio Players
Williams, Joe **11**
Williams, John
  See Solas
Williams, John **28**
  Earlier sketch in CM **9**
Williams, Lamar
  See Allman Brothers, The
Williams, Lucinda **24**
  Earlier sketch in CM **10**
Williams, Marion **15**
Williams, Michelle
  See Destiny's Child
Williams, Milan
  See Commodores, The
Williams, Otis
  See Temptations, The
Williams, Paul
  See Temptations, The
Williams, Paul **26**
  Earlier sketch in CM **5**
Williams, Phillard
  See Earth, Wind and Fire
Williams, Rich
  See Kansas
Williams, Robbie **25**
Williams, Robert
  See Captain Beefheart and His Magic Band
Williams, Rozz
  See Christian Death
Williams, "Slim" and "Baby" **31**
Williams, Stokley
  See Mint Condition
Williams, Terry
  See Dire Straits
Williams, Tony **6**
Williams, Tony
  See Platters, The
Williams, Vanessa **10**
Williams, Victoria **17**
Williams, Walter
  See O'Jays, The
Williams, Wendy O.
  See Wendy O. Williams and The Plasmatics
Williams, Wilbert
  See Mighty Clouds of Joy, The
Williams, William Elliot
  See Artifacts
Williams, Yasmeen
  See Sweet Honey in the Rock
Williams III, Sam
  See Down By Law
Williamson, Gloria
  See Martha and the Vandellas
Williamson, Robin
  See Incredible String Band
Williamson, Sonny Boy **9**
Willie D.
  See Geto Boys, The

Willie the New Guy
  See Bloodhound Gang, The
Willis, Clarence "Chet"
  See Ohio Players
Willis, Kelly **12**
Willis, Larry
  See Blood, Sweat and Tears
Willis, Pete
  See Def Leppard
Willis, Rick
  See Foreigner
Willis, Victor
  See Village People, The
Willner, Hal **10**
Wills, Aaron (P-Nut)
  See 311
Wills, Bob **6**
Wills, David
  See Negativland
Wills, Mark **27**
Wills, Rick
  See Bad Company
Willson-Piper, Marty
  See Church, The
Willsteed, John
  See Go-Betweens, The
Wilmot, Billy "Mystic"
  See Mystic Revealers
Wilson, Anne
  See Heart
Wilson, Brian **24**
  Also see Beach Boys, The
Wilson, Carl
  See Beach Boys, The
Wilson, Carnie
  See Wilson Phillips
Wilson, Cassandra **26**
  Earlier sketch in CM **12**
Wilson, Chris
  See Love Spit Love
Wilson, Cindy
  See B-52's, The
Wilson, Dan
  See Semisonic
Wilson, Dennis
  See Beach Boys, The
Wilson, Don
  See Ventures, The
Wilson, Eric
  See Sublime
Wilson, Gerald **19**
Wilson, Greg
  See Spoon
Wilson, Jackie **3**
Wilson, Kim
  See Fabulous Thunderbirds, The
Wilson, Mary
  See Supremes, The
Wilson, Nancy
  See Heart
Wilson, Nancy **28**
  Earlier sketch in CM **14**
Wilson, Orlandus
  See Golden Gate Quartet
Wilson, Patrick
  See Weezer
Wilson, Ransom **5**
Wilson, Ricky
  See B-52's, The
Wilson, Robin
  See Gin Blossoms
Wilson, Ron
  See Surfaris, The
Wilson, Shanice
  See Shanice
Wilson, Sid
  See Slipknot

Wilson, Wendy
  See Wilson Phillips
Wilson-James, Victoria
  See Soul II Soul
  Also see Shamen, The
Wilson Phillips **5**
Wilton, Michael
  See Queensryche
Wimpfheimer, Jimmy
  See Roomful of Blues
Winans, BeBe and CeCe **32**
Winans, Carvin
  See Winans, The
Winans, Marvin
  See Winans, The
Winans, Michael
  See Winans, The
Winans, Ronald
  See Winans, The
Winans, The **12**
Winbush, Angela **15**
Winfield, Chuck
  See Blood, Sweat and Tears
Winston, George **9**
Winter, Johnny **5**
Winter, Kurt
  See Guess Who
Winter, Paul **10**
Winthrop, Dave
  See Supertramp
Winwood, Muff
  See Spencer Davis Group
Winwood, Steve **2**
  Also see Spencer Davis Group
  Also see Traffic
Wire **29**
Wire, Nicky
  See Manic Street Preachers
Wiseman, Bobby
  See Blue Rodeo
Wiseman, Mac **19**
WishBone
  See Bone Thugs-N-Harmony
Wisniewski, Tom
  See MxPx
Withers, Pick
  See Dire Straits
Witherspoon, Jimmy **19**
Wolf, Kurt
  See Boss Hog
Wolf, Peter **31**
Wolf, Peter
  See J. Geils Band
Wolfe, Gerald
  See Greater Vision
Wolstencraft, Simon
  See Fall, The
Womack, Bobby **5**
Womack, Lee Ann **33**
Wonder, Stevie **17**
  Earlier sketch in CM **2**
Woo, John
  See Magnetic Fields, The
Wood, Chris
  See Traffic
Wood, Chris
  See Medeski, Martin & Wood
Wood, Danny
  See New Kids on the Block
Wood, Ron
  See Faces, The
  Also see Rolling Stones, The
Wood, Roy
  See Electric Light Orchestra
Woodgate, Dan
  See Madness

Woods, Adam
  See Fixx, The
Woods, Gay
  See Steeleye Span
Woods, Terry
  See Pogues, The
  Also see Steeleye Span
Woodson, Ollie
  See Temptations, The
Woods-Wright, Tomica **22**
Woodward, Alun
  See Delgados, The
Woodward, Keren
  See Bananarama
Woody, Allen
  See Allman Brothers, The
Woolfolk, Andrew
  See Earth, Wind and Fire
Woomble, Roddy
  See Idlewild
Workhorse Movement, The **30**
Worley, Chris
  See Jackyl
Worley, Jeff
  See Jackyl
Worrell, Bernie **11**
  Also see Golden Palominos
Wozniak, John
  See Marcy Playground
Wray, Link **17**
Wreede, Katrina
  See Turtle Island String Quartet
Wren, Alan
  See Stone Roses, The
Wretzky, D'Arcy
  See Smashing Pumpkins
Wright, Adrian
  See Human League, The
Wright, David "Blockhead"
  See English Beat, The
Wright, Heath
  See Ricochet
Wright, Hugh
  See Boy Howdy
Wright, Jimmy
  See Sounds of Blackness
Wright, Kevin
  See Rockapella
Wright, Norman
  See Country Gentlemen, The
Wright, Rick
  See Pink Floyd
Wright, Simon
  See AC/DC
Wright, Tim
  See Pere Ubu
Wupass, Reverend
  See Rube Waddell
Wurster, Jon
  See Superchunk
Wurzel
  See Motörhead
Wusthoff, Gunter
  See Faust
Wu-Tang Clan **19**
Wuv
  See P.O.D.
Wyatt, Robert **24**
Wyman, Bill
  See Rolling Stones, The
  Also see Bill Wyman & the Rhythm Kings
Wynette, Tammy **24**
  Earlier sketch in CM **2**
Wynn, Steve **31**
Wynne, Philippe
  See Spinners, The

Wynonna **11**
  Also see Judds, The
Wysocki, Jon
  See Staind
X **11**
Xefos, Chris
  See King Missile
Xenakis, Iannis **34**
X-Ray Spex **31**
XTC **26**
  Earlier sketch in CM **10**
Xzibit **31**
Ya Kid K
  See Technotronic
Yale, Brian
  See Matchbox 20
Yamamoto, Hiro
  See Soundgarden
Yamamoto, Seichi
  See Boredoms, The
Yamano, Atsuko
  See Shonen Knife
Yamano, Naoko
  See Shonen Knife
Yamashita, Kazuhito **4**
Yamataka, Eye
  See Boredoms, The
Yamauchi, Tetsu
  See Faces, The
Yamazaki, Iwao
  See Ghost
Yang, Naomi
  See Damon and Naomi
  Also see Galaxie 500
Yankovic, "Weird Al" **7**
Yanni **11**
Yardbirds, The **10**
Yarrow, Peter
  See Peter, Paul & Mary
Yates, Bill
  See Country Gentlemen, The
Yauch, Adam
  See Beastie Boys, The
Yearwood, Trisha **25**
  Earlier sketch in CM **10**
Yella
  See N.W.A.
Yes **8**
Yeston, Maury **22**

Yoakam, Dwight **21**
  Earlier sketch in CM **1**
Yo La Tengo **24**
Yoot, Tukka
  See US3
York, Andrew **15**
York, John
  See Byrds, The
York, Pete
  See Spencer Davis Group
Yorke, Thom E.
  See Radiohead
Yoshida, Tatsuya
  See Flying Luttenbachers, The
Yoshikawa, Toyohito
  See Boredoms, The
Yoshimi
  See Boredoms, The
Young, Adrian
  See No Doubt
Young, Angus
  See AC/DC
Young, Brian
  See Fountains of Wayne
Young, Faron **7**
Young, Fred
  See Kentucky Headhunters, The
Young, Gary
  See Pavement
Young, Grant
  See Soul Asylum
Young, Jeff
  See Megadeth
Young, La Monte **16**
Young, Lester **14**
Young, Malcolm
  See AC/DC
Young, Neil **15**
  Earlier sketch in CM **2**
  Also see Buffalo Springfield
Young, Paul
  See Mike & the Mechanics
Young, Richard
  See Kentucky Headhunters, The
Young, Robert "Throbert"
  See Primal Scream
Young M.C. **4**
Youth
  See Killing Joke

Youth, Todd
  See D Generation
Youtz, Raif
  See Built to Spill
Yow, David
  See Jesus Lizard
Yo Yo **9**
Yseult, Sean
  See White Zombie
Yule, Doug
  See Velvet Underground, The
Zander, Robin
  See Cheap Trick
Zankey, Glen
  See Bluegrass Patriots
Zap Mama **14**
Zappa, Frank **17**
  Earlier sketch in CM **1**
Zawinul, Josef
  See Weather Report
Zender, Stuart
  See Jamiroquai
Zevon, Warren **9**
Zhane **22**
Zilinskas, Annette
  See Bangles, The
Zimmer, Hans **34**
Zimmerman, Udo **5**
Ziskrout, Jay
  See Bad Religion
Zombie, Rob
  See White Zombie
Zombies, The **23**
Zoom, Billy
  See X
Zorn, John **15**
  Also see Golden Palominos
Zoyes, Dino
  See Charm Farm
Zuccaro, Steve
  See Charm Farm
Zukerman, Pinchas **4**
Zulu, Ras I
  See Spearhead
Zuniga, Alex
  See Tijuana No!
Zuniga, Miles
  See Fastball
ZZ Top **2**

DATE DUE
